# UNDERSTANDING RELIGIOUS SACRIFICE

*Controversies in the Study of Religion*

Series Editor: Russell T. McCutcheon

This anthology series brings together related scholarly essays which are of particular importance for studying a variety of methodological and theoretical issues in the academic study of religion. Each anthology is organized around original introductory essays written by the volume editor. The series' emphasis is on writers involved in theoretical controversies and debates that address traditional as well as current problems and issues in the field, issues to which students should be introduced. Each volume investigates a common problem in the study of religion from a variety of theoretical viewpoints, thereby providing a collection of extended discussions between a group of scholars grappling with a common topic.

Published titles in this series:

*The Insider/Outsider Problem in the Study of Religion: A Reader*, edited by Russell T. McCutcheon

*Feminism in the Study of Religion: A Reader*, edited by Darlene M. Juschka

# UNDERSTANDING RELIGIOUS SACRIFICE

## A Reader

Edited by

JEFFREY CARTER

LONDON • NEW YORK

**Continuum**
The Tower Building, 11 York Road, London, SE1 7NX
370 Lexington Avenue, New York, NY 10017-6503

First published 2003

**British Library Cataloguing-in-Publication Data**
A catalogue record for this book is available
from the British Library.

ISBN 0-8264-4879-8 (hardback)
0-8264-4880-1 (paperback)

Typeset by Kenneth Burnley, Wirral, Cheshire
Printed and bound in Great Britain by Bookcraft, Midsomer Norton, Bath

# CONTENTS

# Contents

# Contents

# PREFACE

My first introduction to the importance of sacrifice in the study of religion occurred while I was a graduate student at Harvard Divinity School. There, in the spring of 1989, I took a seminar with Nancy Jay entitled "Sacrifice in Comparative Perspective." As a thematic, comparative course, it particularly appealed to my interests in anthropological and theoretical issues. It was in that course that I first encountered Girard, Burkert, Valeri, Daly, and several of the other authors represented in this anthology. In that seminar, as in her own work, Nancy Jay emphasized the importance of theory and sought insights from the comparison of theoretical approaches. She conveyed a wonderful passion for her work, great care in her teaching, and a calm and encouraging voice. I was privileged to have learned from her, and now I am honored to include her among those to whom this book is dedicated.

Later at the University of Chicago, while studying the History of Religions, I was able to add to my list of thinkers who published work on the nature of religious sacrifice. It was a topic of interest, I realized, for a surprising number of figures central to the history of the discipline, figures like Tylor, Frazer, Durkheim, Freud, and Turner for example. It seemed as if almost every scholarly generation (including contemporary authors), every basic theoretical approach (psychological, sociological, anthropological, intellectualist, functionalist, phenomenological, structuralist, etc.), and perhaps every cultural area of study had grappled to some degree with sacrifice or sacrifice-like phenomena. Without thinking much about it, I filed away my list of theories of sacrifice.

Then in 1997, while teaching Ritual Studies and African Religions at Davidson College, I designed a course on sacrifice called "Violence and Religion." It examined a number of religious texts and ethnographic accounts of sacrifice as well as several of the most important theories of sacrifice I had collected in graduate school. As I pulled together reading materials for this course, it soon became clear that there was no common resource for these ideas about sacrifice. There seemed to be a need for a reader of classic and modern writings dealing with this topic.

The occasion for this book arose after conversations with Russell McCutcheon about the series "Controversies in the Study of Religion" he was editing. We discussed how a volume devoted to sacrifice could present an intriguing number of theoretical positions, provide students with a valuable resource, and serve as an excellent example of how theories compete. Given the fact that theories of sacrifice often implicate other supporting theoretical claims about the nature of religion generally, I suggested that all students concerned with understanding religion (and the application of theory that entails) would find such an anthology of interest. Knowing that no collection of writings on sacrifice already existed, I proposed to compile this volume.

Collected here are twenty-five influential selections devoted to the topic of sacrifice. They each present a different theoretical point of view and reach a different understanding about the origin of sacrifice, its meaning, or its overall significance for religion. For each selection, I have written a brief but detailed introduction, something that provides a biographical sketch of its author, an account of how the author understands religion or ritual generally, and additional information about the author's theory not contained in the selection. I have kept editorial comment about the selections, about their relative merit for example, to a minimum and chosen instead to organize what I hope will be a useful tool for those who wish to revisit the task of understanding sacrifice. This volume will permit readers to know the array of theoretical issues that task involves.

It is impossible to thank all those who have influenced my thinking on sacrifice or have somehow contributed to the arrival of this book. Nevertheless, I would like to recognize William K. Mahony, whose friendship and wise council helped, on many occasions, to lead me and this work along. Throughout my time in Chicago, Frank Reynolds gave invaluable advice and constant encouragement, all the while finding ways to ask the right question that would send me off in a new direction. I am also grateful to Jonathan Z. Smith for his keen insights into issues of method and theory in the study of religion, for our spirited conversations, and his true generosity. I want to thank David Jessop for his detailed and dedicated work as my research assistant. He accomplished the daunting task of typing the majority of the selections, and this book would not exist if not for his efforts. Andrea Rosario provided some last minute transcription as well. I wish to thank the Castle Rock Institute for providing time for me to work on this project, particularly its president Jerry Stone for his almost daily participation. I am also grateful for the understanding and support of Janet Joyce and Valerie Hall at Continuum. Their patience, despite delays, and enthusiasm have made working on this project surprisingly delightful. Finally, I must thank Sarah Reed Carter for her unfailing support over the course of this work. Her understanding, encouragement, and affection truly made this book possible.

JEFFREY CARTER
*Brevard, North Carolina*

*For my parents
and to the memory of
Nancy Jay*

# GENERAL INTRODUCTION

From the very beginning sacrificial worship expressed, however crudely, certain ideas which lie at the very root of true religion.

William Robertson Smith

Sacrifice is perhaps the most universal and intense form of ritual.

Richard D. Hecht

Most religious systems function (to a greater or lesser extent) by means of sacrificial activity.

Bruce Chilton

Any explanation of sacrifice is, in fact, a theory of religion in miniature.

Jonathan Z. Smith

Intriguing claims. These epigraphs represent merely a sample of scholarly opinion on the importance of sacrifice in the study of religion. Indeed, understanding sacrifice, much like interest in and attention to myth, has been a persistent issue throughout the history of religious studies. Since the very beginning of the field, scholars studying religion have grappled with the diversity yet apparent similarity and widespread occurrence of sacrifice-like activity. The violence and destruction often associated with sacrifice can explain a good deal of this scholarly interest, but, more fundamentally, there is the immediate issue of how to reconcile such seemingly incongruous features of sacrifice with the nature of religion in general. How, for example, can a benevolent deity demand the death of a child? Or, why do so many religious

*1*

traditions advocate killing an animal for treating disease? As scholars have compared religious phenomena from around the world in hopes of formulating a systematic understanding of religion, sacrifice has been particularly prominent, significant, and in many cases troubling. In short, it demands explanation and interpretation.

This book, for the first time, collects and organizes the most important and influential scholarly writings that attempt to explain and interpret sacrifice. It brings together competing theories and ideas focused on the nature of sacrifice, and can serve as a resource for illustrating this particular theoretical controversy in the study of religion. The readings gathered here provide a vast array of cultural details. They will suggest surprising convergences, reveal astounding assumptions, and argue for challenging claims about the meaning of religion, sacrificial behaviors, and human life in general. Working at both the level of data and theory, we find amongst these writings devoted to sacrifice unexamined assumptions and problematic perspectives. Taken together, they reveal a true controversy in the study of religion, an issue that like other debates over theory, has come to define and organize the field.

## Defining Sacrifice

Looking for examples of the word "sacrifice," we find it within popular discourse, academic writings, theological ideologies, and religious texts. We find accounts of men and women killing animals and offering certain parts to superhuman beings. We hear of fathers giving up their golf games to attend their son's football match. We read divination texts outlining an elaborate protocol of invocation and immolation prescribed to heal a sick child. We watch as a baseball player, to advance a teammate, intentionally bunts the ball and is thrown out. We listen to prayers asking ancestors to accept certain food stuffs as compensation for ethical infractions. We meet couples who forgo holiday spending to save money for the purchase a house. We observe a man, thankful for some good fortune, giving a large sum of money to his church. We learn of archeological evidence for massive killings of women and captives in Tenochtitlan. Libations of beer are poured, agricultural products burned, kings suffocated, household goods buried, fingers amputated, domestic animals bled and dismembered, children are bound and cast in a river: all these examples— and more—have been associated with the notion of "sacrifice." What, then, distinguishes sacrifice or sacrifice-like phenomena from other cultural practices? How have scholars identified sacrificial beliefs and practices? Answering these questions of definition is a necessary first step to grasping the overall importance of sacrifice for religious studies.

The Latin word *sacrificium*, derived from *sacer*, "holy," and *facere*, "to make," is the etymological basis for the English word "sacrifice." These roots imply that sacrifice is in fact a process of sanctification, a means by which to consecrate something. If so, we are then pressed to ask "Who or what is 'made holy' and how is this accomplished?" Furthermore, it relies on some notion of what it means to "be holy." At best, this etymological method of defining "sacrifice" leaves us with a rather general, somewhat vague description we could call "religious action," which is not really a definition at all, but rather a higher-order category within which sacrifice falls. It may be the case that certain features of human behavior we identify as "sacrificial" help us answer this issue of "the holy" (e.g., the violence associated with religious killing), but still sacrifice cannot be equated with "religious action" because clearly there exist other such acts (other "rituals") that we would not include in the category of "sacrifice."

The Sanskrit word for Vedic sacrifice (*yajña*) is derived from *yaj* meaning "to offer" and the German *Opfer* (sacrifice, offering) is most likely derived from the Latin *offerre*, meaning "to offer" or "to present." These roots provide another clue to how sacrifice is often defined; it refers to gift giving, to the presentation of something, and the transference of that something to another party or being. As we shall see, the place of "gift theory" amidst discussions of sacrifice is highly prominent and a great number of conclusions about the meaning of sacrifice have come from it. Here too, though, this etymological strategy only highlights a broader category encompassing sacrifice, a classification that can include what may be deemed non-sacrificial phenomena (e.g., a parent giving food to a child), and thus can only be of indirect assistance to defining the term. It is true that certain aspects of "gift giving" (e.g., the sense of obligation or other relationship it creates between the parties involved) can play an important role in defining "sacrifice," but simply identifying the two is inadequate as a definition.

Popular use of the word "sacrifice," as one might encounter it in mass media publications, revolves around the notion of renouncement or specifically the "giving up" of something valuable. While related to gift giving, in this sense, there is an emphasis on the deprivation resulting from an act of sacrifice. Something precious, beneficial, advantageous, costly, or "worth keeping" is lost. As such, this popular conception of sacrifice denotes a level of unpleasantness; almost anything unpleasant that one voluntarily endures can be considered a sacrifice. It is interesting to note that this notion of sacrifice includes an implicit rationale explaining why a person or a group of people would give up something worth keeping. It is quite simple really; the renunciation carries an expectation of a more valuable return. People give up items they value (money, food, pleasure, time, and so forth) so that more pressing concerns, ideals they consider "higher," may be realized, whether it be health, prestige, or some other enhanced quality of relationship between the parties involved. Put differently, this popular usage of "sacrifice" prompts us to consider the importance of exchange in gift giving—the giver receives something in the end—and as such recalls the Latin phrase *do ut des* ("I give so that you will give") often quoted in the context of sacrifice. Whether this is consciously calculated for sacrifice is open to debate.

Combining these clues, "making sacred," "gift-giving" and "exchange" (renouncement and return), allows us to consider additional variables involved in sacrifice, further points of attention for defining and explaining sacrifice. These concepts highlight the fact that many sacrifice-like phenomena involve three distinct participating entities, three beings, objects, personifications, or domains—two, between which the giving or exchange takes place, and a third, that which *is* given or exchanged. There will be one who initiates the exchange or giving, one that is exchanged or given, and one that receives (and reciprocates) the gift. Put differently, defining and understanding sacrifice depends, for many thinkers, on the nature of the participants of a sacrifice—their status (ontological, social, political, economic, and so forth) and prior relationship vis-à-vis each other and the broader world. Whether seen as an exchange or not, every cultural example we identify as "sacrifice" involves interaction between variously interested parties, some active and others passive, some willing and others averse, and does include, generally, a third sacrificed domain. There will always be an agent acting "sacrificially," employing some "thing" to be "sacrificed," and, often, sacrificing "to" some other "being." Throughout this book we shall encounter a number of attempts to place one or more of these parties (or the specific relationships between them) at the center of what sacrifice "means." Understanding sacrifice very commonly depends on understanding the nature of these participants.

With this model, it is possible to identify the "sacred" character of sacrifice, the essential feature that can distinguish it from ordinary giving or more common forms of exchange (e.g., linguistic communication, commercial transactions, marriage, donations, etc.). "Religious sacrifice" is any sacrifice where one or more of the central parties involved is believed to be, or to represent, an agent of the superhuman realm. Understood as supernatural, spiritual, divine, or sacred, this agent is most commonly the recipient during a sacrifice; for example, a god or ancestor receives an offering made by a human being. There are, however, examples in myth of a deity making a sacrifice, acting as the giver, the offerer; consider the Vedic hymn of *Puruṣa*. And the third variation— it is quite common to understand the "thing" sacrificed as either divine or somehow representative of the divine. As an example, recall the divine status of *soma* in Vedic sacrifice. Finally, to further complicate matters, there are examples where a single divine being can be both sacrificing and sacrificed in the same event. Some have considered the death of Jesus in the Christian tradition an example of this, a "supreme sacrifice" where the life of the giver is given.

Of all the parties involved in sacrificial activity, the "thing sacrificed," or what is sometimes referred to as "the victim," has attracted the most attention in definitions and explanations of sacrifice. Whole theories have been built upon what the sacrificial victim "stands for." For example, an animal ritually slaughtered may, according to one theory, be a "surrogate" for the subject (or community) initiating the sacrifice, or according to another, it may "represent" or be "identified with" the divine recipient of the sacrifice, and to still a third, it may somehow "embody" both the offerer and the recipient and thereby serve as an "intermediary" between the two. We can explain the prominent position of the victim in theories of sacrifice with two observations. First, the "thing" sacrificed, whether it be animal, vegetable, a certain liquid or manufactured good, is ordinarily a central and necessary element in the overall sacrificial ritual. It is the item, often selected with great care, around which the entire ritual complex revolves. It may indeed be valid to assume understanding the sacrificial victim would allow us to understand the nature of the entire sacrificial event, for not everything is equally appropriate for sacrifice. Certain substances and not others are employed in specific examples, and how that discrimination takes place ought to be significant. Secondly, many theories have focused on the victim because it lends itself to being interpreted as a symbol. Scholars of religion are particularly prone to positing the symbolic character of certain phenomena, and in this context we find this hermeneutical impulse expressed in a concept widely employed in theories of sacrifice: substitution. By invoking the logic of symbolism or of part-whole relations (where a part represents the whole), the sacrificial victim serves, according to many theorists, as a substitute for some other party, being, or notion. An animal might be cast out instead of a sick child, a finger severed rather than the death of an individual, a material symbol of "life" (e.g., blood), "fertility" (e.g., milk), or "value" (e.g., cloth) held up in the place of these concepts—each posits an added significance to the "thing" sacrificed in the service of representing some other "thing." A number of the writings collected in this book will rely on claims of the symbolic meanings tied to the materials sacrificed.

In addition to the nature of the victim (the thing sacrificed), how it is altered in the course of the sacrificial event is also a widespread concern to theorists of sacrifice. For those employing a gift or exchange theory, the means of the exchange, how the gift is made, or the technique of transferring the offering between parties, is seen as central. The most common observation here is the fact that most practices labeled sacrificial involve the destruction of some object or material understood as valuable. In the forfeiture of this good, of something that is ordinarily relinquished only reluctantly, the subject initiating the sacrifice loses the good, and from his or her perspective, it is destroyed. Varying among cultural examples, the sacrificial material may be presented at a shrine, abandoned at a certain place, cast out, burned, buried, poured, and so forth. Of all the ritual operations performed on sacrificial materials, however, there are two that have attracted the most attention when scholars have sought to explain sacrificial traditions. The first is the fact that many sacrificial rituals require that when forfeiting (or offering, giving, presenting, etc.) a particular item, it must be killed. Hence, examples of blood letting, decapitation, dismemberment, suffocation, drowning, and cremation are quite common in religious actions identified as sacrificial. This widespread occurrence of killing (or at least destroying) a "victim" has led several scholars to construct their theories of sacrifice upon the notion of violence. As several writings in this book indicate, there may be significant psychological and social consequences brought from ordaining violence in the context of religion.

Secondly, a number of theorists have emphasized the fact that quite often sacrificial rituals include an obligation that the thing sacrificed, or at least part of it, be eaten. The details, who eats what and with whom, vary between specific examples, of course, but it is true that consumption is frequently an important part of sacrifice-like religious activities. In many examples, "sharing" is the operative concept, for local interpretations sometimes stress that superhuman beings join human beings (those making the sacrifice) in a "communal meal." Here too, it is difficult to universalize this observation (without resorting to overly inventive hermeneutics regarding the nature of "what" is "eaten"), but speaking generally, as a person forfeits (gives, destroys, abandons, and so forth) material for sacrifice, it is certainly removed from his or her control, and can be understood therefore as a process of "consumption." Arguing for the significance of this sort of consumption becomes a line of thought for several of the authors collected in this book.

One final feature of sacrificial phenomena that some theorists stress when defining sacrifice is the intentionality of the event, the reasons subjects give for sacrificing. Sacrifice, according to this view, is simply religious behavior designed to "do" something, and once this motive is identified, a scholar can make a claim about the basis of sacrifice. For example, native accounts about why one might conduct a sacrifice frequently include references to: thanksgiving (offering praise for a past good), expiation (seeking conciliation for a past wrong, propitiation), and prevention (acting to avoid a future problem and insure thereby a future good). In this way, bringing forth a valuable "thing", a person sacrificing implores "may goodness continue," or "may misfortune end" or "may danger be averted." Keying on these motives, it becomes possible to describe sacrifice as a "communication" between cosmic realms, as a material expression of supplicatory impulses, or as a bargain between human and "higher" beings. Sacrifice is, accordingly, what sacrifice "does." Several of the writings collected in this book offer evidence and argument to support this approach to defining sacrifice.

In the end, definitions of sacrifice compete based on how useful they are in distinguishing phenomena as more or less "sacrifice-like." Much like the term/concept "religion," defining sacrifice is a matter of stipulating a bounded set of criteria that can be used to judge whether a certain phenomenon is or is not a "sacrifice" (or a "religion," to follow the simile). What constitutes this set, for example whether a particular feature is necessary or sufficient, or whether there are "enough" features present (to comprise a polythetic class), is open to argument. The task of defining sacrifice, this is to say, revolves around selecting and ranking the elements discussed here: the etymological points suggesting "offering" or "transference," the popular usage indicating deprivation and forfeiture, the notion of a gift or exchange, the various parties involved (the subject sacrificing, the "object" sacrificed, and a third recipient party—any of which could have a superhuman status), the nature of the "object" sacrificed, how the "object" is altered during the event, and the motive given for the event. Whether implicitly (i.e., without attention to the contested character of what constitutes a "sacrifice") or explicitly, all of the writings collected in this anthology grapple with these elements as they attempt to define, and ultimately understand, sacrifice.

## Sacrifice and Religious Studies

Sacrifice is not a casual curiosity for scholars of religion. Certainly, as the selection of writings collected here attest, there has been a persistent academic interest in sacrifice and sacrifice-like beliefs and practices. Richard Hecht goes so far as to claim sacrifice is almost "universal" and Bruce Chilton sees sacrificial activity functioning in "most religious systems." Indeed, the presence of sacrifice throughout history and across cultures, much like the notion of "myth," seems to indicate that it is something fundamental for religious human beings. With such widespread examples, it is not surprising that sacrifice would become for many scholars a key concept in their attempts to understand religion generally. As several of the writings collected here confirm, there is no shortage of opinion supporting William Robertson Smith's claim that sacrificial activity lies "at the very root of true religion," that it is somehow basic, essential, or original. Jonathan Z. Smith goes so far as to declare that all explanations of sacrifice are also theories of religion in "miniature," that attempts to understand sacrifice and to understand religion share certain assumptions, methods, and goals. Put differently, a study of attempts to understand sacrifice (the *raison d'être* for this volume) will mirror a history of attempts to understand religion. By collecting theories of sacrifice (explanations and interpretations seeking better understanding of certain phenomena), this anthology, therefore, also presents the reader with a glimpse into many theoretical issues that have marked the academic study of religion since its beginning. It is quite surprising how many of these "classic theoretical issues" in the study of religion arise when scholars grapple with sacrifice. Briefly, here are a few major examples.

The most significant theoretical issue prevalent among writings about sacrifice is the "origin of religion." Several of the authors here, for example Tylor, Spencer, Robertson Smith and others, tap the dominant intellectual trends of their time and devise evolutionary theories of religion that place sacrifice at or near the beginning of a chronological scheme. We will encounter the details of these in each chapter, but in general sacrificial ritual is said to be the original form of religious activity, to be an early expression of basic religious sentiments, or to be an example of some primary element or process of religion. Even several contemporary authors, for example Burkert, Girard, and others, argue for the "original character" of sacrifice and formulate theories of religion that posit an actual primordial event, a killing, that develops into religious phenomena generally. We have, in other words, several historical arguments about the origin and development of religion that make explicit reference to sacrifice. Many have settled on a position where religion began with a sacrifice or sacrifice-like activity and unfolded through history to produce the widespread diversity, yet degree of commonality, of phenomena known today.

For other authors collected here, sacrifice serves as a means to identify the "essence of religion." Unlike the time-dependent character of evolutionary schemes and "origin of religion" arguments, sacrifice, or what it represents, is here understood as a core or root element. Whether it be a basic human experience (e.g., a sense of powerlessness and awe), mode of thought (e.g., magical correlation), concern (e.g., desire to answer existential questions), or behavior (e.g., gathering as a group), some essential attribute related to sacrifice is identified as that which gives rise to the manifest traits of religion. The ideas of scholars like Freud, van der Leeuw, Frazer, and others can be placed in this category, even as the exact role sacrifice plays for each differs. These theories speculate that throughout the history of religions around the world, a single, elemental characteristic has ruled.

There are a number of other theories and concepts supporting these arguments for the essence and the origin of religion. As different mechanisms of manifestation (what exhibits from an essence) or development (what proceeds from a prior condition or phase), these too play some role in certain understandings of sacrifice. In this volume, the reader will encounter, for example, animism (the notion that natural phenomena have animating spirits), magic (the notion that associations based on imitation and contact exert mutual influence), totemism (the respect, by a group, of a particular plant, animal or object that represents the original ancestor or other essence of the group), the "psychic unity of mankind" (the notion that all human beings share common psychological tendencies, capacities, and needs), and diffusion (the theory that similarities between religions can be explained through a process of borrowing). While each of these concepts and theories could, in a different context, be the subject of an entire study, here it is simply important to recognize that many classic writings about sacrifice have employed them as well.

Also present among theories of sacrifice are examples from the major categories of classic approaches to understanding religion as a whole. There are sociological theories, for example those of Durkheim, Hubert, and Mauss—their claims are about the importance of collective representations. There are psychological approaches such as Freud's argument that religion and religious phenomena are derived from the dynamics of the human personality, and Beers' argument about the effects of narcissistic tendencies early in life. Functionalist claims abound, for example Burkert's thesis about channeling "intra-specific aggression," and Jay's point about insuring "male intergenerational continuity." There are structuralist theories of sacrifice here as well, for example that of de Heusch and his highlighting dialectics of raw and cooked, heat and coolness, eating and the eaten. Finally, there are a number of phenomenological, symbolic, or hermeneutical theories, explanations that argue for the representational character of religious, including sacrificial, phenomena or the efficacy of symbolic action, as for example with Valeri.

In addition to theories, several key concepts commonly employed in religious studies hold prominent positions in discussions of the meaning of sacrifice. Most common among these is the idea of the gift. As we shall see, numerous authors (e.g., Tylor, Westermarck, Evans-Pritchard, etc.) understand the dynamics of gift giving or exchange as the most significant aspect of sacrifice. Another concept from religious studies that appears among theories of sacrifice (for example in the writings of Jensen) is the notion of commemoration, the idea that certain religious behaviors can be understood as re-enactments of mythic or primordial events. Issues of gender arise in some treatments of sacrifice, for example in the work of Jay and Beers with their attention to the particular effects sacrifice has for men. Just as prominent is the issue of power, the political dimension of religion and sacrifice, the dynamics of inequality, agency, and control, as recognized for example by Lincoln, Bataille, Bloch, and others. Finally, for many scholars (such as J. Z. Smith and Turner), understanding sacrifice becomes a matter of seeing it as a particular form of ritual. A more general position on ritual makes it possible to understand the more particular features of sacrifice such as the use of animals, the presence of distinct phases, and so forth.

From sociologists, anthropologists, psychologists, historians, political theorists, even theologians, we find opinions about the nature of sacrifice that overlap with understandings of religion. We discover accounts of the intellectual, symbolic, emotional, and ideological character of sacrificial phenomena. In this anthology, there is attention to language, ethics, social structure, and human needs, as thinkers have struggled to reconcile the complexities of sacrifice with their understanding of religion.

## A Plan for the Work

There are three main sections of this book. The first is this general introduction examining the terms and theories commonly employed in discussions of sacrifice. It is written to provide a broad outline of the intellectual context in which debates on sacrifice have taken, and continue to take place. It argues that ways of understanding sacrifice correspond to ways of understanding religion, that authors employ parallel theoretical assumptions in these two endeavors. Overall, it provides a framework for examining the different writings on sacrifice that comprise the bulk of the volume.

The second section, the main section, consists of the selected writings. They are organized chronologically (by date of publication) to allow readers a view of the development of sacrifice theory in the field of Religious Studies. With occasional references to and endorsements and/or critiques of preceding authors, each subsequent selection adds to the controversy surrounding sacrifice while also providing the reader with new ethnographic material and theoretical insights. Accompanying each selection, there is a brief introductory essay on the author describing his or her intellectual assumptions and ambitions, and the specific contribution the selection makes to the volume and to sacrifice theory overall. These essays provide summary accounts of each author's intellectual background, and attempt to identify how each under-stands religion and the ways that understanding affects his or her approach to sacrifice. These essays also identify the various theories and concepts (discussed above) supporting each author's point of view.

Overall, the writings that appear here have been selected for two basic reasons. First, several (e.g., Tylor, Hubert and Mauss, and Robertson Smith) can be understood simply as "classic" works on the subject of sacrifice. These are the authors cited repeatedly whenever the concept of sacrifice is addressed in the academy. These are the essentials, those authors with whom every student of religion should be familiar. Next, the extracts have been selected because they make explicit theoretical claims about the nature of sacrifice, and in most cases about sacrifice generally. Using cross-cultural data, most of the authors included here provide a different theoretical perspective, some distinc-tive contribution to the topic of theorizing about sacrifice. A student of Religious Studies will recognize many of these authors (e.g., Victor Turner, Jonathan Z. Smith, Emile Durkheim), but may also be unaware of the contri-butions they make to the topic of sacrifice. Certainly some readers will identify omissions, recalling other outstanding writings with valuable theoretical positions that are absent from the anthology (the work of Detienne and Vernant, Lienhardt, or Lévi Strauss, for example). Regrettably, a number of logistical issues prevent this volume from being more complete. To compensate, at least partially, for this limitation, a more complete bibliography of works is also included.

The third and final section is a short postscript addressing the question of why understanding sacrifice is controversial. With reference to several of the theories developed in the second section of the book, this essay takes up a broader discussion of theory making in general. It describes some inevitable aspects of theorizing that make it inherently controversial. In this way, this postscript encourages readers to identify similar theoretical controversies informing other academic domains.

Like other books in this series, this volume serves as a focused discussion of a persistent problem in the academic study of religion. By presenting divergent viewpoints about the nature of sacrifice, it illustrates the role of theory generally. At the same time, it grounds the discussion in concrete arenas of human behavior, people manipulating themselves (their possessions, their bodies, their speech, etc.) and their environment according to shared conceptual systems. The complexities surrounding the concept of sacrifice, combined with its consistently prominent place in the history of thinking about religion, make it a particularly well-suited topic for examining the interplay between theory and practice. Taken together, the essays presented here should provide readers with a more critical view of sacrifice and its place in Religious Studies.

# 1

# EDWARD BURNETT TYLOR (b. 1832)

The British anthropologist Edward Burnett Tylor was born into a middle-class Quaker family and never went to college. After traveling to America, Mexico, and other places he became fascinated with other cultures. He later received academic recognition and became a full professor at Oxford, and R. R. Marret deemed him the "Father of Anthropology." Tylor wrote three main works, *Anahuac* (1861), *Researches into the Early History of Mankind* (1865), and his most famous, *Primitive Culture: Researches in the Development of Mythology, Philosophy, Religion, Language, Arts and Custom* (1871) in two volumes. Writing under the influence of a Victorian English emphasis on progress and in the wake of recent work on the notion of evolution by Darwin and Lyell, Tylor adopted a social evolutionary scheme in his comparisons of modern and "primitive" cultures, and suggested that similarities can be attributed to some common cause, that deterministic principles are at work in culture just as they are in nature.

In the first volume of *Primitive Culture*, Tylor defined culture as the "complex whole which includes knowledge, belief, art, morals, law, custom and any other capabilities and habits acquired by man as a member of society." He included a claim that all culture was unified from the beginning because all human beings share a "common psychic base." He explained the diversity of cultures, the examples of both "savagery" and "civilization," by claiming that the process of evolution, the ability to adapt to social change, proceeds at different rates for different peoples. Consequently, modern "primitive" cultures exhibit, he claimed, characteristics of "advanced" groups' previous forms. They can be analyzed as "windows to the past." Even modern cultures show signs of "survivals," beliefs and practices (e.g., "superstitions") that have their origin in primitive cultures.

Tylor is well known for his "minimum definition of religion," the "belief in spiritual beings." This belief he traced to the common human experience of dreams, hallucinations, and death, aberrant psychic experiences that primitive people explained, rationally, by inventing the concept of the soul, an immaterial essence of the human being. Extending this theory of the soul, early human beings attributed souls to animals, plants and even natural objects. Tylor called this animism, and considered it the earliest form of religion. From this form, more "advanced" forms of religion evolved—as "souls" became "gods," guardian spirits and nature spirits became the basis for polytheism, and later combined to develop the notion of monotheism. Tylor thought the history of religions progressed along this unilinear scheme.

Tylor approached sacrifice with an equally evolutionary frame and hypothesized that it progressed through three developmental phases. The first phase, and the origin of sacrifice, springs from ordinary gift giving, the giving of something to a superior, or in this case the giving "to a deity as if he were a man." As death releases the soul of a man, sacrifice allows the "essence" of the thing given (through its blood or breath—each symbolizing "life") to be transported to the spirit realm. Hence, in clear intellectualist fashion, Tylor understood why sacrifices to earth spirits are buried, those to water gods are drowned, and those to air spirits often burned. The second phase of sacrificial practices developed when people began to believe that the gods care for their well-being, appreciate praise, and could be asked for favors. Tylor called this the "homage" phase, and he noted it often included a banquet to honor the deity, a shared meal where the people eat the physical food and the god receives the immaterial, spiritual portion of the victim. The final development in sacrificial practices, and the "highest" for Tylor, occurred when the primary motive for sacrificing became the giving up of something valuable. Tylor described this phase as "abnegation," as a ritual act performed not for the benefit of the spirit (as in the previous phase), but for the sacrificer. He also noted that during this phase various methods of substitution came into practice—part for the whole (hair instead of the person, for example), the less valuable for the valuable (e.g., animals for humans), and images or representatives (e.g., effigies).

The present selection, taken from his *Primitive Culture*, is a lengthy account of Tylor's theory of sacrifice. While not the earliest scholarly work on sacrifice (cf. Plato, Sykes, Davison, Kurtz, etc.), it is the best starting point for this anthology because it has had enormous influence on subsequent attempts to understand sacrifice. His "gift-theory," in particular, has framed many of the writings that will appear later in the volume. His attention to the importance of the sacrificial meal, the widespread incidence of substitution, and the fact that a sense of homage and abnegation accompany many sacrifices—each of these was taken up later, reinterpreted, and employed to construct a new theory of sacrifice. Clearly, it was Edward Tylor who gave religious studies a certain trajectory when it came to sacrifice.

# From *Primitive Culture: Researches in the Development of Mythology, Philosophy, Religion, Language, Arts, and Custom*

S ACRIFICE has its apparent origin in the same early period of culture and its place in the same animistic scheme as prayer, with which through so long a range of history it has been carried on in the closest connexion. As prayer is a request made to a deity as if he were a man, so sacrifice is a gift to a deity as if he were a man. The human types of both may be studied unchanged in social life to this day. The suppliant who bows before his chief, laying a gift at his feet and making his humble petition, displays the anthropomorphic model and origin at once of sacrifice and prayer. But sacrifice, though in its early stages as intelligible as prayer is in early and late stages alike, has passed in the course of religious history into transformed conditions, not only of the rite itself but of the intention with which the worshipper performs it. And theologians, having particularly turned their attention to sacrifice as it appears in the higher religions, have been apt to gloss over with mysticism ceremonies which, when traced ethnographically up from their savage forms, seem open to simply rational interpretation. Many details of offerings have already been given incidentally here, as a means of elucidating the nature of the deities they are offered to. Moreover, a main part of the doctrine of sacrifice has been anticipated in examining the offerings to spirits of the dead, and indeed the ideal distinction between soul and deity breaks down among the lower races, when it appears how often the deities receiving sacrifice are themselves divine human souls. In now attempting to classify sacrifice in its course through the religions of the world, it seems a satisfactory plan to group the evidence as far as may be according to the manner in which the offering is given by the worshipper, and received by the deity. At the same time, the examples may be so arranged as to bring into view the principal lines along which the rite has undergone alteration. The ruder conception that the deity takes and values the offering for itself, gives place on the one hand to the idea of mere homage expressed by a gift, and on the other to the negative view that the virtue lies in the worshipper depriving himself of something prized. These ideas may be broadly distinguished as the gift-theory, the homage-theory, and the abnegation-theory. Along all three the usual ritualistic changes may be traced, from practical reality to formal ceremony. The originally valuable offering is compromised for a smaller tribute or a cheaper substitute, dwindling at last to a mere trifling token or symbol.

Reprinted from Sir Edward Tylor, *Primitive Culture: Researches in the Development of Mythology, Philosophy, Religion, Language, Arts, and Custom* (New York: Henry Holt and Co., LLC, 1874), pages 375–410. In the public domain.

The gift-theory, as standing on its own independent basis, properly takes the first place. That most childlike kind of offering, the giving of a gift with as yet no definite thought how the receiver can take and use it, may be the most primitive as it is the most rudimentary sacrifice. Moreover, in tracing the history of the ceremony from level to level of culture, the same simple unshaped intention may still largely prevail, and much of the reason why it is often found difficult to ascertain what savages and barbarians suppose to become of the food and valuables they offer to the gods, may be simply due to ancient sacrificers knowing as little about it as modern ethnologists do, and caring less. Yet rude races begin and civilized races continue to furnish with the details of their sacrificial ceremonies the key also to their meaning, the explanation of the manner in which the offering is supposed to pass into the possession of the deity.

Beginning with cases in which this transmission is performed bodily, it appears that when the deity is the personal Water, Earth, Fire, Air, or a fetish-spirit animating or inhabiting such element, he can receive and sometimes actually consume the offerings given over to this material medium. How such notions may take shape is not ill shown in the quaintly rational thought noticed in old Peru, that the Sun drinks the libations poured out before him; and in modern Madagascar, that the Angatra drinks the arrack left for him in the leaf-cup. Do not they see the liquids diminish from day to day?[1] The sacrifice to Water is exemplified by Indians caught in a storm on the North American lakes, who would appease the angry tempest-raising deity by tying the feet of a dog and throwing it overboard.[2] The following case from Guinea well shows the principle of such offerings. Once in 1693, the sea being unusually rough, the headmen complained to the king, who desired them to be easy, and he would make the sea quiet next day. Accordingly he sent his fetishman with a jar of palm oil, a bag of rice and corn, a jar of pitto, a bottle of brandy, a piece of painted calico, and several other things to present to the sea. Being come to the seaside, he made a speech to it, assuring it that his king was its friend, and loved the white men; that they were honest fellows and came to trade with him for what he wanted; and that he requested the sea not to be angry, nor hinder them to land their goods; he told it that, if it wanted palm oil, his king had sent it some; and so threw the jar with the oil into the sea, as he did, with the same compliment, the rice, corn, pitto, brandy, calico, etc.[3] Among the North American Indians the Earth also receives offerings buried in it. The distinctness of idea with which such objects may be given is well shown in a Sioux legend. The Spirit of the Earth, it seems, requires an offering from those who perform extraordinary achievements, and accordingly the prairie gapes open with an earthquake before the victorious hero of the tale; he casts a partridge into the crevice, and springs over.[4] One of the most explicit recorded instances of the offering to the Earth is the hideous sacrifice to the Earth-goddess among the Khonds of Orissa, the tearing of the flesh of the human victim from the bones, the priest burying half of it in a hole in the earth behind his back without looking round, and each householder carrying off a particle to bury in like manner in his favourite field.[5] For offerings to the Fire, we may take for an example the Yakuts, who not only give him the first spoonful of food, but instead of washing their earthen pots allow him to clean out the remains.[6] Here is a New Zealand charm called Wangaihau, i.e., feeding the Wind:

> Lift up his offering,
> To Uenga a te Rangi his offering,
> Eat, O invisible one, listen to me,
> Let that food bring you down from the sky.[7]

Beside this may be set the quaint description of the Fanti Negroes assisting at the sacrifice of men and cattle to the local fetish; the victims were considered to be carried up in a whirlwind out of the midst of the small inner ring of priests and priestesses; this whirlwind was, however, not perceptible to the senses of the surrounding worshippers.[8] These series of details collected from the lower civilization throw light on curious problems as to sacrificial ideas in the religions of the classic world; such questions as what Xerxes meant when he threw the golden goblet and the sword into the Hellespont, which he had before chained and scourged; why Hannibal cast animals into the sea as victims to Poseidon; what religious significance underlay the patriotic Roman legend of the leap of Marcus Curtius.[9]

Sacred animals in their various characters of divine beings, incarnations, representatives, agents, symbols, naturally receive meat and drink offerings, and sometimes other gifts. For examples may be mentioned the sun-birds (tonatzuli), for which the Apalaches of Florida set out crushed maize and seed;[10] the Polynesian deities coming incarnate in the bodies of birds to feed on the meat-offerings and carcases of human victims set out upon the altar-scaffolds;[11] the well-fed sacred snakes of West Africa, and local fetish animals like the alligator at Dix Cove which will come up at a whistle, and follow a man half a mile if he carries a white fowl in his hands, or the shark at Bonny that comes to the river bank every day to see if a human victim has been provided for his repast;[12] in modern India the cows reverently fed with fresh grass, Durga's meat offerings laid out on stones for the jackals, the famous alligators in their temple-tanks.[13] The definition of sacred animal from this point of view distinctly includes man. Such in Mexico was the captive youth adored as living representative of Tezcatlipoca, and to whom banquets were made during the luxurious twelvemonth which preceded his sacrifice at the festival of the deity whom he personated: such still more definitely was Cortes himself, when Montezuma supposed him to be the incarnate Quetzalcoatl come back into the land, and sent human victims accordingly to be slaughtered before him, should he seem to lust for blood.[14] Such in modern India is the woman who as representative of Radha eats and drinks the offerings at the shameless orgies of the Saktas.[15] More usually it is the priest who as minister of the deities has the lion's share of the offerings or the sole privilege of consuming them, from the Fijian priest who watches for the turtle and puddings apportioned to his god,[16] and the West African priest who carries the allowances of food sent to the local spirits of mountain, or river, or grove, which food he eats himself as the spirit's proxy,[17] to the Brahmans who receive for the divine ancestors the oblation of a worshipper who has no sacred fire to consume it, "for there is no difference between the Fire and a Brahman, such is the judgment declared by them who know the Veda."[18] It is needless to collect details of a practice so usual in the great systematic religions of the world, where priests have become professional ministers and agents of deity, as for them to partake of the sacrificial meats. It by no means follows from this usage that the priest is necessarily supposed to consume the food representative of his divinity; in the absence of express statement to such effect, the matter can only be treated as one of ceremonial ordinance. Indeed, the case shows the caution needed in interpreting religious rites, which in particular districts may have meanings attached to them quite foreign to their general intent.

The feeding of an idol, as when Ostyaks would pour daily broth into the dish at the image's mouth,[19] or when the Aztecs would pour the blood and put the heart of the slaughtered human victim into the monstrous idol's mouth,[20] seems ceremonial make-believe, but shows that in each case the deity was somehow considered to devour the meal. The conception among the lower races of deity, as in disembodied spiritual form, is even less compatible with the notion that such a being should consume solid matter. It is true that the notion does occur. In old times it appears in the legend of Bel and the Dragon, where the footprints in the strewn ashes betray the knavish priests who come by secret doors to eat up the banquet set before Bel's image.[21] In modern centuries, it may be exemplified by the negroes of Labode, who could hear the noise of their god Jimawong emptying one after another the bottles of brandy handed in at the door of his straw-roofed temple;[22] or among the Ostyaks, who, as Pallas relates, used to leave a horn of snuff for their god, with a shaving of willow bark to stop his nostrils with after the country fashion; the traveller describes their astonishment when sometimes an unbelieving Russian has emptied it in the night, leaving the simple folk to conclude that the deity must have gone out hunting to have snuffed so much.[23] But these cases turn on fraud, whereas absurdities in which low races largely agree are apt to have their origin rather in genuine error. Indeed, their dominant theories of the manner in which deities receive sacrifice are in accordance not with fraud but with facts, and must be treated as strictly rational and honest developments of the lower animism. The clearest and most general of these theories are as follows.

When the deity is considered to take actual possession of the food or other objects offered, this may be conceived to happen by abstraction of their life, savour, essence, quality, and in yet more definite conception their spirit or soul. The solid part may die, decay, be taken away or consumed or destroyed, or may simply remain untouched. Among this group of conceptions, the most materialized is that which carries out the obvious primitive world-wide doctrine that the life is the blood. Accordingly, the blood is offered to the deity, and even disembodied spirits are thought capable of consuming it, like the ghosts for whom Odysseus entering Hades poured into the trench the blood of the sacrificed ram and black ewe, and the pale shades drank and spoke;[24] or the evil spirits which the Mintira of the Malay Peninsula keep away from the wife in childbirth by placing her near the fire, for the demons are believed to drink human blood when they can find it.[25] Thus in Virginia the Indians (in pretence or reality) sacrificed children, whose blood the oki or spirit was said to suck from their left breast.[26] The Kayans of Borneo used to offer human sacrifice when a great chief took possession of a newly built house; in one late case, about 1847, a Malay slave girl was bought for the purpose and bled to death, the blood, which alone is efficacious, being sprinkled on the pillars and under the house, and the body being thrown into the river.[27] The same ideas appear among the indigenes of India, alike in North Bengal and in the Deccan, where the blood alone of the sacrificed animal is for the deities, and the votary retains the meat.[28] Thus, in West Africa, the negroes of Benin are described as offering a cock to the idol, but it receives only the blood, for they like the flesh very well themselves;[29] while in the Yoruba country, when a beast is sacrificed for a sick man, the blood is sprinkled on the wall and smeared on the patient's forehead, with the idea, it is said, of thus transferring to him the victim's life.[30] The Jewish law of sacrifice marks clearly the distinction between shedding the blood as life, and offering it as food. As the Israelites themselves might not eat with the flesh the blood which is the life, but must pour it on the earth as water, so the rule applies to sacrifice. The blood must be sprinkled before the sanctuary, put upon the horns of the altar, and there sprinkled or poured out, but not presented as a drink offering—"their drink-offerings of blood will I not offer."[31]

Spirit being considered in the lower animism as somewhat of the ethereal nature of smoke or mist, there is an obvious reasonableness in the idea that offerings reduced to this condition are fit to be consumed by, or transmitted to, spiritual beings towards whom the vapour rises in the air. This idea is well shown in the case of incense, and especially a peculiar kind of incense offered among the native tribes of America. The habit of smoking tobacco is not suggestive of religious rites among ourselves, but in its native country, where it is so widely diffused as to be perhaps the best point assignable in favour of a connexion in the culture of the northern and southern continent, its place in worship is very important. The Osages would begin an undertaking by smoking a pipe, with such a prayer as this: "Great Spirit, come down to smoke with me as a friend! Fire and Earth, smoke with me and help me to overthrow my foes!" The Sioux in Hennepin's time would look toward the sun when they smoked, and when the calumet was lighted, they presented it to him, saying: "Smoke, Sun!" The Natchez chief at sunrise smoked first to the east and then to the other quarters; and so on. It is not merely, however, that puffs from the tobacco-pipe are thus offered to deities as drops of drink or morsels of food might be. The calumet is a special gift of the Sun or the Great Spirit, tobacco is a sacred herb, and smoking is an agreeable sacrifice ascending into the air to the abode of gods and spirits.[32] Among the Caribs, the native sorcerer evoking a demon would puff tobacco-smoke into the air as an agreeable perfume to attract the spirit; while among Brazilian tribes the sorcerers smoked round upon the bystanders and on the patient to be cured.[33] How thoroughly incense and burnt-offering are of the same nature, the Zulus well show, burning incense together with the fat of the caul of the slaughtered beast, to give the spirits of the people a sweet savour.[34] As to incense more precisely of the sort we are familiar with, it was in daily use in the temples of Mexico, where among the commonest antiquarian relics are the earthen incense-pots in which "copali" (whence our word copal) and bitumen were burnt.[35] Though incense was hardly usual in the ancient religion of China, yet in modern Chinese houses and temples the "joss-stick" and censer do honour to all divine beings, from the ancestral manes to the great gods and Heaven and Earth.[36] The history of incense in the religion of Greece and Rome points the contrast between old thrift and new extravagance, where the early fumigations with herbs and chips of fragrant wood are contrasted with the later oriental perfumes, myrrh and cassia and frankincense.[37] In the temples of ancient Egypt, numberless representations of sacrificial ceremony show the burning of the incense pellets in censers before the images of the gods; and Plutarch speaks of the incense burnt thrice daily to the Sun, resin at his rising, myrrh at his meridian, kuphi at his setting.[38] The ordinance held as prominent a place among the Semitic nations. At the yearly festival of Bel in Babylon, the Chaldeans are declared by Herodotus to have burned a thousand talents of incense on the large altar in the temple where sat his golden image.[39] In the records of ancient Israel, there has come down to us the very recipe for compounding incense after the art of the apothecary. The priests carried every man his censer, and on the altar of incense, overlaid with gold, standing before the vail in the tabernacle, sweet spices were burned morn and even, a perpetual incense before the Lord.[40]

The sacrifice by fire is familiar to the religion of North American tribes. Thus the Algonquins knew the practice of casting into the fire the first morsel of the feast; and throwing fat into the flames for the spirits, they would pray to them "make us find food." Catlin has described and sketched the Mandans dancing round the fire where the first kettleful of the green-corn is being burned, an offering to the Great Spirit before the feast begins.[41] The Peruvians burnt llamas as offerings to the Creator, Sun, Moon, and Thunder, and other lesser deities. As to the operation of sacrifice, an idea of theirs comes well into view in the legend of Manco Ceapac ordering the sacrifice of the most beautiful of his sons, "cutting off his head, and sprinkling the blood over the fire, that the smoke might reach the Maker of heaven and earth."[42] In Siberia the sacrifices of the Tunguz and Buraets, in the course of which bits of meat and liver and fat are cast into the fire, carry on the same idea.[43] Chinese sacrifices to sun and moon, stars and constellations, show their purpose in most definite fashion; beasts and even silks and precious stones are burned, that their vapour may ascend to these heavenly spirits.[44] No less significant, though in a different sense, is the Siamese offering to the household deity, incense and arrack and rice steaming hot; he does not eat it all, not always any part of it, it is the fragrant steam which he loves to inhale.[45] Looking now to the records of Aryan sacrifice, views similar to these are not obscurely expressed. When the Brahman burns the offerings on the altar-fire, they are received by Agni the divine Fire, mouth of the gods, messenger of the All-knowing, to whom is chanted the Vedic strophe, "Agni! the sacrifice which thou encompassest whole, it goes unto the gods!"[46] The Homeric poems show the plain meaning of the hecatombs of old barbaric Greece, where the savour of the burnt offering went up in wreathing smoke to heaven, "Κνίσση δ' οὐρανὸν ἶκεν ἑλισσομένη περὶ καπνῷ."[47] Passed into a far other stage of history, men's minds had not lost sight of the archaic thought even in Porphyry's time, for he knows how the demons who desire to be gods rejoice in the libations and fumes of sacrifice, whereby their spiritual and bodily substance fattens, for this lives on the steam and vapours and is strengthened by the fumes of the blood and flesh.[48]

The view of commentators, that sacrifice, as a religious act of remote antiquity and world-wide prevalence, was adopted, regulated, and sanctioned in the Jewish law, is in agreement with the general ethnography of the subject. Here sacrifice appears not with the lower conception of a gift acceptable and even beneficial to deity, but with the higher significance of devout homage or expiation for sin. As is so usual in the history of religion, the offering consisted in general of food, and the consummation of the sacrifice was by fire. To the ceremonial details of the sacrificial rites of Israel, whether prescribing the burning of the carcases of oxen and sheep or of the bloodless gifts of flour mingled with oil, there is appended again and again the explanation of the intent of the rite; it is "an offering made by fire, of a sweet savour unto the Lord." The copious records of sacrifice in the Old Testament enable us to follow its expansion from the simple patriarchal forms of a pastoral tribe, to the huge and complex system organized to carry on the ancient service in a now populous and settled kingdom. Among writers on the Jewish religion, Dean Stanley has vividly portrayed the aspect of the Temple, with the flocks of sheep and droves of cattle crowding its courts, the vast apparatus of slaughter, the great altar of burnt-offering towering above the people, where the carcases were laid, the drain beneath to carry off the streams of blood. To this historian, in sympathy rather with the spirit of the prophet than the ceremony of the priest, it is a congenial task to dwell upon the great movement in later Judaism to maintain the place of ethical above ceremonial religion.[49] In those times of Hebrew history, the prophets turned with stern rebuke on those who ranked ceremonial ordinance above weightier matters of the law. "I desired mercy and not sacrifice, and the knowledge of God more than burnt offerings." "I delight not in the blood of bullocks, or of lambs, or of he goats . . . Wash you, make you clean; put away the evil of your doings from before mine eyes. Cease to do evil, learn to do well."

Continuing the enquiry into the physical operation ascribed to sacrifice, we turn to a different conception. It is an idea well vouched for in the lower culture, that the deity, while leaving apparently untouched the offering set out before him, may nevertheless partake of or abstract what in a loose way may be described as its essence. The Zulus leave the flesh of the sacrificed bullock all night, and the divine ancestral spirits come and eat, yet next morning everything remains just as it was. Describing this practice, a native Zulu thus naïvely comments on it: "But when we ask, 'What do the Amadhlozi eat? for in the morning we still see all the meat,' the old men say, 'The Amatongo lick it.' And we are unable to contradict them, but are silent, for they are older than we, and tell us all things and we listen; for we are told all things, and assent without seeing clearly whether they are true or not."[50] Such imagination was familiar to the native religion of the West Indian islands. In Columbus' time, and with particular reference to Hispaniola, Roman Pane describes the native mode of sacrifice. Upon any solemn day, when they provide much to eat, whether fish, flesh, or any other thing, they put it all into the house of the cemis, that the idol may feed on it. The next day they carry all home, after the cemi has eaten. And God so help them (says the friar), as the cemi eats of that or anything else, they being inanimate stocks or stones. A century and a half later, a similar notion still prevailed in these islands. Nothing could show it more neatly than the fancy of the Caribs that they could hear the spirits in the night moving the vessels and champing the food set out for them, yet next morning there was nothing touched; it was held that the viands thus partaken of by the spirits had become holy, so that only the old men and considerable people might taste them, and even these required a certain bodily purity.[51] Islanders of Pulo Aur, though admitting that their banished disease-spirits did not actually consume the grains of rice set out for them, nevertheless believed them to appropriate its essence.[52] In India, among the indigenes of the Garo hills, we hear of the head and blood of the sacrificed animal being placed with some rice under a bamboo arch covered with a white cloth; the god comes and takes what he wants, and after a time this special offering is dressed for the company with the rest of the animal.[53] The Khond deities live on the flavours and essences drawn from the offerings of their votaries, or from animals or grain which they cause to die or disappear.[54] When the Buraets of Siberia have sacrificed a sheep and boiled the mutton, they set it up on a scaffold for the gods while the shaman is chanting his song, and then themselves fall to.[55] And thus, in the folklore of mediaeval Europe, Domina Abundia would come with her dames into the houses at night, and eat and drink from the vessels left uncovered for their increase-giving visit, yet nothing was consumed.[56]

The extreme animistic view of sacrifice is that the soul of the offered animal or thing is abstracted by or transmitted to the deity. This notion of spirits taking souls is in a somewhat different way exemplified among the Binua of Johore, who hold that the evil River-spirits inflict diseases on man by feeding on the "semangat," or unsubstantial body (in ordinary parlance the spirit) in which his life resides,[57] while the Karen demon devours not the body but the "la," spirit or vital principle; thus when it eats a man's eyes, their material part remains, but they are blind.[58] Now an idea similar to this furnished the Polynesians with a theory of sacrifice. The priest might send commissions by the sacrificed human victim; spirits of the dead are eaten by the gods or demons; the spiritual part of the sacrifices is eaten by the spirit of the idol (i.e., the deity dwelling or embodied in the idol) before whom it is presented.[59] Of the Fijians it is observed that of the great offerings of food native belief apportions merely the soul to the gods, who are described as being enormous eaters; the substance is consumed by the worshippers. As in various other districts of the world, human sacrifice is here in fact a meat-offering; cannibalism is a part of the Fijian religion, and the gods are described as delighting in human flesh.[60] Such ideas are explicit among Indian tribes of the American lakes, who consider that offerings, whether abandoned or consumed by the worshippers, go in a spiritual form to the spirit they are devoted to. Native legends afford the clearest illustrations. The following is a passage from an Ottawa tale which recounts the adventures of Wassamo, he who was conveyed by the spirit-maiden to the lodge of her father, the Spirit of the Sand Downs, down below the waters of Lake Superior. "Son-in-law," said the Old Spirit, "I am in want of tobacco. You shall return to visit your parents, and can make known my wishes. For it is very seldom that those few who pass these Sand Hills, offer a piece of tobacco. When they do it, it immediately comes to me. Just so," he added, putting his hand out of the side of the lodge, and drawing in several pieces of tobacco, which some one at that moment happened to offer to the Spirit, for a smooth lake and prosperous voyage. "You see," he said, "every thing offered me on earth, comes immediately to the side of my lodge." Wassamo saw the women also putting their hands to the side of the lodge, and then handing round something, of which all partook. This he found to be offerings of food made by mortals on earth. The distinctly spiritual nature of this transmission is shown immediately after, for Wassamo cannot eat such

mere spirit-food, wherefore his spirit-wife puts out her hand from the lodge
and takes in a material fish out of the lake to cook for him.[61] Another Ottawa
legend, the already cited nature-myth of the Sun and Moon, is of much interest
not only for its display of this special thought, but as showing clearly the
motives with which savage animists offer sacrifices to their deities, and
consider these deities to accept them. Onowuttokwutto, the Ojibwa youth who
has followed the Moon up to the lovely heaven-prairies to be her husband, is
taken one day by her brother the Sun to see how he gets his dinner. The two
look down together through the hole in the sky upon the earth below, the Sun
points out a group of children playing beside a lodge, at the same time
throwing a tiny stone to hit a beautiful boy. The child falls, they see him
carried into the lodge, they hear the sound of the sheesheegwun (the rattle),
and the song and prayer of the medicine-man that the child's life may be
spared. To this entreaty of the medicine-man, the Sun makes answer, "Send me
up the white dog." Then the two spectators above could distinguish on the
earth the hurry and bustle of preparation for a feast, a white dog killed and
singed, and the people who were called assembling at the lodge. While these
things were passing, the Sun addressed himself to Onowuttokwutto, saying,
"There are among you in the lower world some whom you call great medicine-
men; but it is because their ears are open, and they hear my voice, when I have
struck any one, that they are able to give relief to the sick. They direct the
people to send me whatever I call for and when they have sent it, I remove my
hand from those I had made sick." When he had said this, the white dog was
parcelled out in dishes for those that were at the feast; then the medicine-man
when they were about to begin to eat, said, "We send thee this, Great Manito."
Immediately the Sun and his Ojibwa companion saw the dog, cooked and ready
to be eaten, rising to them through the air—and then and there they dined upon
it.[62] How such ideas bear on the meaning of human sacrifice, we may perhaps
judge from this prayer of the Iroquois, offering a human victim to the War-god:
"To thee, O Spirit Arieskoi, we slay this sacrifice, that thou mayst feed upon the
flesh, and be moved to give us henceforth luck and victory over our enemies!"[63]
So among the Aztec prayers, there occurs this one addressed to Tezcatlipoca-
Yautl in time of war: "Lord of battles; it is a very certain and sure thing, that a
great war is beginning to make, ordain, form, and concert itself; the War-god
opens his mouth, hungry to swallow the blood of many who shall die in this
war; it seems that the Sun and the Earth-God Tlatecutli desire to rejoice; they
desire to give meat and drink to the gods of Heaven and Hades, making them a
banquet of the flesh and blood of the men who are to die in this war." etc.[64]
There is remarkable definiteness in the Peruvian idea that the souls of human
victims are transmitted to another life in divine as in funeral sacrifice; at one
great ceremony, where children of each tribe were sacrificed to propitiate the
gods, "they strangled the children, first giving them to eat and drink, that
they might not enter the presence of the Creator discontented and hungry."[65]

Similar ideas of spiritual sacrifice appear in other regions of the world. Thus in West Africa we read of the tree-fetish enjoying the spirit of the food-offering, but leaving its substance, and an account of the religion of the Gold Coast mentions how each great wong or deity has his house, and his priest and priestess to clean the room and give him daily bread kneaded with palm-oil, "of which, as of all gifts of this kind, the wong eats the invisible soul."[66] So, in India, the Limbus of Darjeeling make small offerings of grain, vegetables, and sugar-cane, and sacrifice cows, pigs, fowls, etc., on the declared principle "the life breath to the gods, the flesh to ourselves."[67] It seems likely that such meaning may largely explain the sacrificial practices of other religions. In conjunction with these accounts, the unequivocal meaning of funeral sacrifices, whereby offerings are conveyed spiritually into the possession of spirits of the dead, may perhaps justify us in inferring that similar ideas of spiritual transmission prevail extensively among the many nations whose sacrificial rites we know in fact, but cannot trace with certainty to their original significance.

Having thus examined the manner in which the operation of sacrifice is considered to take physical effect, whether indefinitely or definitely, and having distinguished its actual transmission as either substantial, essential, or spiritual, let us now follow the question of the sacrificer's motive in presenting the sacrifice. Important and complex as this problem is, its key is so obvious that it may be almost throughout treated by mere statement of general principle. If the main proposition of animistic natural religion be granted, that the idea of the human soul is the model of the idea of deity, then the analogy of man's dealing with man ought, *inter alia*, to explain his motives in sacrifice. It does so, and very fully. The proposition may be maintained in wide generality, that the common man's present to the great man, to gain good or avert evil, to ask aid or to condone offence, needs only substitution of deity for chief, and proper adaptation of the means of conveying the gift to him, to produce a logical doctrine of sacrificial rites, in great measure explaining their purpose directly as they stand, and elsewhere suggesting what was the original meaning which has passed into changed shape in the course of ages. Instead of offering a special collection of evidence here on this proposition, it may be enough to ask attentive reference to any extensive general collection of accounts of sacrifice, such for instance as those cited for various purposes in these volumes. It will be noticed that offerings to divinities may be classed in the same way as earthly gifts. The occasional gift made to meet some present emergency, the periodical tribute brought by subject to lord, the royalty paid to secure possession or protection of acquired wealth, all these have their evident and well-marked analogues in the sacrificial systems of the world. It may impress some minds with a stronger sense of the sufficiency of this theory of sacrifice, to consider how the transition is made in the same imperceptible way from the idea of substantial value received, to that of ceremonial homage rendered, whether the recipient be man or god. We do not find it easy to analyse the impression which a gift makes on our own feelings, and to separate the actual value of the object from the sense of gratification in the giver's good-will or respect, and thus we may well scruple to define closely how uncultured men work out this very same distinction in their dealings with their deities. In a general way it may be held that the idea of practical acceptableness of the food or valuables presented to the deity, begins early to shade into the sentiment of divine gratification or propitiation by a reverent offering, though in itself of not much account to so mighty a divine personage. These two stages of the sacrificial idea may be fairly contrasted, the one among the Karens who offer to a demon arrack or grain or a portion of the game they kill, considering invocation of no avail without a gift,[68] the other among the negroes of Sierra Leone, who sacrifice an ox to "make God glad very much and do Kroomen good."[69]

Hopeless as it may be in hundreds of accounts of sacrifice to guess whether the worshipper means to benefit or merely to gratify the deity, there are also numbers of cases in which the thought in the sacrificer's mind can scarcely be more than an idea of ceremonial homage. One of the best-marked sacrificial rites of the world is that of offering by fire or otherwise morsels or libations at meals. This ranges from the religion of the North American Indian to that of the classic Greek and the ancient Chinese, and still holds its place in peasant custom in Europe.[70] Other groups of cases pass into yet more absolute formality of reverence. See the Guinea negro passing in silence by the sacred tree or cavern, and dropping a leaf or a sea-shell as an offering to the local spirit;[71] the Talein of Burma holding up the dish at his meal to offer it to the nat, before the company fall to;[72] the Hindu holding up a little of his rice in his fingers to the height of his forehead, and offering it in thought to Siva or Vishnu before he eats it.[73] The same argument applies to the cases ranging far and wide through religion, where, whatever may have been the original intent of sacrifice, it has practically passed into a feast. A banquet where the deity has but the pretence and the worshippers the reality, may seem to us a mere mockery of sacrifice. Yet how sincerely men regard it as a religious ceremony, the following anecdote of a North American Indian tribe will show. A travelling party of Potawatomis, for three days finding no game, were in great distress for want of food. On the third night, a chief, named Saugana, had a dream, wherein a person appearing to him showed him that they were suffering because they had set out without a sacrificial feast. He had started on this important journey, the dreamer said, "as a white man would," without making any religious preparation. Therefore the Great Spirit had punished them with scarcity. Now, however, twelve men were to go and kill four deer before the sun was thus high (about nine o'clock). The chief in his dream had seen these four deer lying dead, the hunters duly killed them, and the sacrificial feast was held.[74] Further illustrative examples of such sacred banquets may be chosen through the long range of culture. The Zulus propitiate the Heaven-god above with a sacrifice of black cattle, that they may have rain; the village chiefs select the oxen, one is killed, the rest are merely mentioned; the flesh of the slaughtered ox is eaten in the house in perfect silence, a token of humble submission; the bones are burnt outside the village; and after the feast they chant in musical sounds, a song without words.[75] The Serwatty Islanders sacrifice buffaloes, pigs, goats, and fowls to the idols when an individual or the community undertakes an affair or expedition of importance, and as the carcases are devoured by the devotees, this ensures a respectable attendance when the offerings are numerous.[76] Thus among rude tribes of Northern India, sacrifices of beasts are accompanied by libations of fermented liquor, and in fact sacrifice and feast are convertible words.[77] Among the Aztecs, prisoners of war furnished first an acceptable sacrifice to the deity, and then the staple of a feast for the captors and their friends;[78] while in ancient Peru whole flocks of sacrificed llamas were eaten by the people.[79] The history of Greek religion plainly records the transition from the early holocausts devoted by fire to the gods, to the great festivals where the sacrifices provided meat for the public banquets held to honour them in ceremonial homage.[80]

Beside this development from gift to homage, there arises also a doctrine that the gist of sacrifice is rather in the worshipper giving something precious to himself, than in the deity receiving benefit. This may be called the abnegation-theory, and its origin may be fairly explained by considering it as derived from the original gift-theory. Taking our own feelings again for a guide, we know how it satisfies us to have done our part in giving, even if the gift be ineffectual, and how we scruple to take it back if not received, but rather get rid of it in some other way—it is corban. Thus we may enter into the feelings of the Assinaboin Indians, who considered that the blankets and pieces of cloth and brass kettles and such valuables abandoned in the woods as a medicine-sacrifice, might be carried off by any friendly party who chanced to discover them;[81] or of the Ava Buddhists bringing to the temples offerings of boiled rice and sweetmeats and coco-nut fried in oil, and never attempting to disturb the crows and wild dogs who devoured it before their eyes;[82] of the modern Moslems sacrificing sheep, oxen, and camels in the valley of Muna on their return from Mekka, it being a meritorious act to give away a victim without eating any of it, while parties of Takruri watch around like vultures, ready to pounce upon the carcases.[83] If the offering to the deity be continued in ceremonial survival, in spite of a growing conviction that after all the deity does not need and cannot profit by it, sacrifice will be thus kept up in spite of having become practically unreasonable, and the worshipper may still continue to measure its efficacy by what it costs him. But to take this abnegation-theory as representing the primitive intention of sacrifice would be, I think, to turn history upside down. The mere fact of sacrifices to deities, from the lowest to the highest levels of culture, consisting to the extent of nine-tenths or more of gifts of food and sacred banquets, tells forcibly against the originality of the abnegation-theory. If the primary motive had been to give up valuable property, we should find the sacrifice of weapons, garments, ornaments, as prevalent in the lower culture as in fact it is unusual. Looking at the subject in a general view, to suppose men to have started by devoting to their deities what they considered practically useless to them, in order that they themselves might suffer a loss which none is to gain, is to undervalue the practical sense of savages, who are indeed apt to keep up old rites after their meaning has fallen away, but seldom introduce new ones without a rational motive. In studying the religion of the lower races, men are found dealing with their gods in as practical and straightforward a way as with their neighbours, and where plain original purpose is found, it may well be accepted as sufficient explanation. Of the way in which gift can pass into abnegation, an instructive example is forth-coming in Buddhism. It is held that sinful men are liable to be re-born in course of transmigration as wandering, burning, miserable demons (preta). Now these demons may receive offerings of food and drink from their relatives, who can further benefit them by acts of merit done in their name, as giving food to priests, unless the wretched spirits be so low in merit that this cannot profit them. Yet even in this case it is held that though the act does not benefit the spirit whom it is directed to, it does benefit the person who performs it.[84] Unequivocal examples of abnegation in sacrifice may be best found among those offerings of which the value to the offerer utterly exceeds the value they can be supposed to have to the deity. The most striking of these found among nations somewhat advanced in general culture, appear in the history of human sacrifice among Semitic nations. The king of Moab, when the battle was too sore for him, offered up his eldest son for a burnt-offering on the wall. The Phoenicians sacrificed the dearest children to propitiate the angry gods, they enhanced their value by choosing them of noble families, and there was not wanting among them even the utmost proof that the efficacy of the sacrifice lay in the sacrificer's grievous loss, for they must have for yearly sacrifice only-begotten sons of their parents (Κρόνῳ γαρ Φοίνικες καθ' ἕκαστον ἔτος ἔθυον τὰ ἀγαπητὰ καὶ μονογενῆ τῶν τέκνων). Heliogabalus brought the hideous Oriental rite into Italy, choosing for victims to his solar divinity high-born lads throughout the land. Of all such cases, the breaking of the sacred law of hos-pitality by sacrificing the guest to Jupiter hospitalis, Ζεὺς ξένιος, shows in the strongest light in Semitic regions how the value to the offerer might become the measure of acceptableness to the god.[85] In such ways, slightly within the range of the lower culture, but strongly in the religion of the higher nations, the transition from the gift-theory to the abnegation-theory seems to have come about. Our language displays it in a word, if we do but compare the sense of presentation and acceptance which "sacrificium" had in a Roman temple, with the sense of mere giving up and loss which "sacrifice" conveys in an English market.

Through the history of sacrifice, it has occurred to many nations that cost may be economized without impairing efficiency. The result is seen in ingenious devices to lighten the burden on the worshipper by substituting something less valuable than what he ought to offer, or pretends to. Even in such a matter as this, the innate correspondence in the minds of men is enough to produce in distant and independent races so much uniformity of development, that three or four headings will serve to class the chief divisions of sacrificial substitution among mankind.

To give part for the whole is a proceeding so closely conformed to ordinary tribute by subject to lord, that in great measure it comes directly under the gift-theory, and as such has already had its examples here. It is only when the part given to the gods is of contemptible value in proportion to the whole, that full sacrifice passes gradually into substitution. This is the case when in Madagascar the head of the sacrificed beast is set up on a pole, and the blood and fat are rubbed on the stones of the altar, but the sacrificers and their friends and the officiating priest devour the whole carcase;[86] when rich Guinea negroes sacrifice a sheep or goat to the fetish, and feast on it with their friends, only leaving for the deity himself part of the entrails;[87] when Tunguz, sacrificing cattle, would give a bit of liver and fat and perhaps hang up the hide in the woods as the god's share, or Mongols would set the heart of the beast before the idol till next day.[88] Thus the most ancient whole burnt-offering of the Greeks dwindled to burning for the gods only the bones and fat of the slaughtered ox, while the worshippers feasted themselves on the meat, an economic rite which takes mythic shape in the legend of the sly Prometheus giving Zeus the choice of the two parts of the sacrificed ox he had divided for gods and mortals, on the one side bones covered seemly with white fat, on the other the joints hidden under repulsive hide and entrails.[89] With a different motive, not that of parsimony, but of keeping up in survival an ancient custom, the Zarathustrian religion performed by substitution the old Aryan sacrifice by fire. The Vedic sacrifice Agnishtoma required that animals should be slain, and their flesh partly committed to the gods by fire, partly eaten by sacrificers and priests. The Parsi ceremony Izeshne, formal successor of this bloody rite, requires no animal to be killed, but it suffices to place the hair of an ox in a vessel, and show it to the fire.[90]

The offering of a part of the worshipper's own body is a most usual act, whether its intention is simply that of gift or tribute, or whether it is considered as a *pars pro toto* representing the whole man, either in danger and requiring to be ransomed, or destined to actual sacrifice for another and requiring to be redeemed. How a finger-joint may thus represent a whole body, is perfectly shown in the funeral sacrifices of the Nicobar islanders; they bury the dead man's property with him, and his wife has a finger-joint cut off (obviously a substitute for herself), and if she refuses even this, a deep notch is cut in a pillar of the house.[91] We are now concerned, however, with the finger-offering, not as a sacrifice to the dead, but as addressed to other deities. This idea is apparently

worked out in the Tongan custom of tutu-nima, the chopping off of a portion
of the little finger with a hatchet or sharp stone as a sacrifice to the gods, for
the recovery of a sick relation of higher rank; Mariner saw children of five
years old quarrelling for the honour of having it done to them.[92] In the
Mandan ceremonies of initiation into manhood, when the youth at last hung
senseless and (as they called it) lifeless by the cords made fast to splints through
his flesh, he was let down, and coming to himself crawled on hands and feet
round the medicine-lodge to where an old Indian sat with hatchet in his hand
and a buffalo skull before him; then the youth, holding up the little finger of
his left hand to the Great Spirit, offered it as a sacrifice, and it was chopped off
and sometimes the forefinger afterwards, upon the skull.[93] In India, probably as
a Dravidian rather than Aryan rite, the practice with full meaning comes into
view; as Siva cut off his finger to appease the wrath of Kali, so in the southern
provinces mothers will cut off their own fingers as sacrifices lest they lose their
children, and one hears of a golden finger being allowed instead, the substitute
of a substitute.[94] The New Zealanders hang locks of hair on branches of trees
in the burying-ground, a recognized place for offerings.[95] That hair may be a
substitute for its owner is well shown in Malabar, where we read of the demon
being expelled from the possessed patient and flogged by the exorcist to a tree;
there the sick man's hair is nailed fast, cut away, and left for a propitiation to
the demon.[96] Thus there is some ground for interpreting the consecration of the
boy's cut hair in Europe as a representative sacrifice.[97] As for the formal
shedding of blood, it may represent fatal bloodshed, as when the Jagas or
priests in Quilombo only marked with spears the children brought in, instead
of running them through;[98] or when in Greece a few drops of human blood had
come to stand instead of the earlier and more barbaric human sacrifice;[99] or
when in our own time and under our own rule a Vishnuite who has inadver-
tently killed a monkey, a garuda, or a cobra, may expiate his offence by a mock
sacrifice, in which a human victim is wounded in the thigh, pretends to die, and
goes through the farce of resuscitation, his drawn blood serving as substitute
for his life.[100] One of the most noteworthy cases of the survival of such formal
bloodshed within modern memory in Europe must be classed as not Aryan but
Turanian, belonging as it does to the folklore of Esthonia. The sacrificer had to
draw drops of blood from his forefinger, and therewith to pray this prayer,
which was taken down verbatim from one who remembered it:—"I name thee
with my blood and betroth thee with my blood, and point thee out my
buildings to be blessed, stables and cattle-pens and hen-roosts; let them be
blessed through my blood and thy might!" "Be my joy, thou Almighty,
upholder of my forefathers, my protector and guardian of my life! I beseech
thee by strength of flesh and blood; receive the food that I bring thee to thy
sustenance and the joy of my body; keep me as thy good child, and I will thank
and praise thee. By the help of the Almighty, my own God, hearken to me!
What through negligence I have done imperfectly toward thee, do thou forget!

But keep it truly in remembrance, that I have honestly paid my gifts to my parents' honour and joy and requital. Moreover falling down I thrice kiss the earth. Be with me quick in doing, and peace be with thee hitherto!"[101] These various rites of finger-cutting, hair-cutting, and blood-letting, have required mention here from the special point of view of their connexion with sacrifice. They belong to an extensive series of practices, due to various and often obscure motives, which come under the general heading of ceremonial mutilations.

When a life is given for a life, it is still possible to offer a life less valued than the life in danger. When in Peru the Inca or some great lord fell sick, he would offer to the deity one of his sons, imploring him to take this victim in his stead.[102] The Greeks found it sufficient to offer to the gods criminals or captives;[103] and the like was the practice of the heathen tribes of northern Europe, to whom indeed Christian dealers were accused of selling slaves for sacrificial purposes.[104] Among such accounts, the typical story belongs to Punic history. The Carthaginians, overcome and hard pressed in the war with Agathokles, set down the defeat to divine wrath. Now Kronos had in former times received his sacrifice of the chosen of their sons, but of late they had put him off with children bought and nourished for the purpose. In fact they had obeyed the sacrificer's natural tendency to substitution, but now in time of misfortune the reaction set in. To balance the account and condone the parsimonious fraud, a monstrous sacrifice was celebrated. Two hundred children, of the noblest of the land, were brought to the idol. "For there was among them a brazen statue of Kronos, holding out his hands sloping downward, so that the child placed on them rolled off and fell into a certain chasm full of fire."[105] The Phoenician god here called Kronos is commonly though not certainly identified with Moloch. Next, it will help us to realize how the sacrifice of an animal may atone for a human life, if we notice in South Africa how a Zulu will redeem a lost child from the finder by a bullock, or a Kimbunda will expiate the blood of a slave by the offering of an ox, whose blood will wash away the other.[106] For instances of the animal substituted for man in sacrifice the following may serve. Among the Khonds of Orissa, when Colonel Macpherson was engaged in putting down the sacrifice of human victims by the sect of the Earth-goddess, they at once began to discuss the plan of sacrificing cattle by way of substitutes. Now there is some reason to think that this same course of ceremonial change may account for the following sacrificial practice in the other Khond sect. It appears that those who worship the Light-god hold a festival in his honour, when they slaughter a buffalo in commemoration of the time when, as they say, the Earth-goddess was prevailing on men to offer human sacrifices to her, but the Light-god sent a tribe-deity who crushed the bloody-minded Earth-goddess under a mountain, and dragged a buffalo out of the jungle, saying, "Liberate the man, and sacrifice the buffalo!"[107] This legend, divested of its mythic garb, may really record a historical substitution of animal for human sacrifice. In Ceylon, the exorcist will demand the name of the demon possessing a demoniac, and the patient in frenzy answers, giving the demon's name, "I am So-and-so, I demand a human sacrifice and will not go out without!" The victim is promised, the patient comes to from the fit, and a few weeks later the sacrifice is made, but instead of a man they offer a fowl.[108] Classic examples of substitution of this sort may be found in the sacrifice of a doe for a virgin to Artemis in Laodicaea, a goat for a boy to Dionysus at Potniæ. There appears to be a Semitic connexion here, as there clearly is in the story of the Æolians of Tenedos sacrificing to Melikertes (Melkarth) instead of a new-born child a new-born calf, shoeing it with buskins and tending the mother-cow as if a human mother.[109]

One step more in the course of substitution leads the worshipper to make his sacrifice by effigy. An instructive example of the way in which this kind of substitution arises may be found in the rites of ancient Mexico. At the yearly festival of the water-gods and mountain-gods, certain actual sacrifices of human victims took place in the temples. At the same time, in the house of the people, there was celebrated an unequivocal but harmless imitation of this bloody rite. They made paste images, adored them, and in due pretence of sacrifice cut them open at the breast, took out their hearts, cut off their heads, divided and devoured their limbs.[110] In the classic religions of Greece and Rome, the desire to keep up the consecrated rites of ages more barbaric, more bloodthirsty, or more profuse, worked itself out in many a compromise of this class, such as the brazen statues offered for human victims, the cakes of dough or wax in the figure of the beasts for which they were presented as symbolic substitutes.[111] Not for economy, but to avoid taking life, Brahmanic sacrifice has been known to be brought down to offering models of the victim-animals in meal and butter.[112] The modern Chinese, whose satisfaction in this kind of make-believe is so well shown by their dispatching paper figures to serve as attendants for the dead, work out in the same fanciful way the idea of the sacrificial effigy, in propitiating the presiding deity of the year for the cure of a sick man. The rude figure of a man is drawn on or cut out of a piece of paper, pasted on a slip of bamboo, and stuck upright in a packet of mock-money. With proper exorcism, this representative is carried out into the street with the disease, the priest squirts water from his mouth over the patient, image, and mock-money, the two latter are burnt, and the company eat up the little feast laid out for the year-deity.[113] There is curious historical significance in the custom at the inundation of the Nile at Cairo of setting up a conical pillar of earth which the flood washes away as it rises. This is called the arûseh or bride, and appears to be a substitute introduced under humaner Moslem influence, for the young virgin in gay apparel who in older time was thrown into the river, a sacrifice to obtain a plentiful inundation.[114] Again, the patient's offering the model of his diseased limb is distinctly of the nature of a sacrifice, whether it be propitiatory offering before cure, or thank-offering after. On the one hand, the ex-voto models of arms and ears dedicated in ancient Egyptian temples are thought to be grateful memorials,[115] as seems to have been the case with metal models of faces, breasts, hands, etc., in Boeotian temples.[116] On the other hand, there are cases where the model and, as it were, substitute of the diseased part is given to obtain a cure; thus in early Christian times in Germany protest was made against the heathen custom of hanging up carved wooden limbs to a helpful idol for relief,[117] and in modern India the pilgrim coming for cure will deposit in the temple the image of his diseased limb, in gold or silver or copper according to his means.[118]

If now we look for the sacrificial idea within the range of modern Christendom, we shall find it in two ways not obscurely manifest. It survives in traditional folklore, and it holds a place in established religion. One of its most remarkable survivals may be seen in Bulgaria, where sacrifice of live victims is to this day one of the accepted rites of the land. They sacrifice a lamb on St George's day, telling to account for the custom a legend which combines the episodes of the offering of Isaac and the miracle of the Three Children. On the feast of the Panagia (Virgin Mary), sacrifices of lambs, kids, honey, wine, etc., are offered in order that the children of the house may enjoy good health throughout the year. A little child divines by touching one of three saints' candles to which the offering is to be dedicated; when the choice is thus made, the bystanders each drink a cup of wine, saying "Saint So-and-So, to thee is the offering." Then they cut the throat of the lamb, or smother the bees, and in the evening the whole village assembles to eat the various sacrifices, and the men end the ceremony with the usual drunken bout.[119] Within the borders of Russia, many and various sacrifices are still offered; such is the horse with head smeared with honey and mane decked with ribbons, cast into the river with two millstones to its neck to appease the water-spirit, the Vodyany, at his spiteful flood-time in early spring; and such is the portion of supper left out for the house-demon, the domovoy, who if not thus fed is apt to turn spirit-rapper, and knock the tables and benches about at night.[120] In many another district of Europe, the tenacious memory of the tiller of the soil has kept up in wondrous perfection heirlooms from pre-Christian faiths. In Franconia, people will pour on the ground a libation before drinking; entering a forest they will put offerings of bread and fruit on a stone, to avert the attacks of the demon of the woods, the "bilberry-man"; the bakers will throw white rolls into the oven flue for luck, and say, "Here, devil, they are thine!" The Carinthian peasant will fodder the wind by setting up a dish of food in a tree before his house, and the fire by casting in lard and dripping, in order that gale and conflagration may not hurt him. At least up to the end of the eighteenth century this most direct elemental sacrifice might be seen in Germany at the midsummer festival in the most perfect form; some of the porridge from the table was thrown into the fire and some into running water, some was buried in the earth, and some smeared on leaves and put on the chimney-top for the winds.[121] Relics of such ancient sacrifice may be found in Scandinavia to this day; to give but one example, the old country altars, rough earth-fast stones with cup-like hollows, are still visited by mothers whose children have been smitten with sickness by the trolls, and who smear lard into the hollows and leave rag-dolls as offerings.[122] France may be represented by the country-women's custom of beginning a meal by throwing down a spoonful of milk or bouillon; and by the record of the custom of Andrieux in Dauphiny, where at the solstice the villagers went out upon the bridge when the sun rose, and offered him an omelet.[123] The custom of burning alive the finest calf, to save a murrain-struck herd, had its last examples in Cornwall in the nineteenth century; the records of bealtuinn sacrifices in Scotland continue in the Highlands within a century ago; and Scotchmen still living remember the corner of a field being left untilled for the Goodman's Croft (i.e., the Devil's), but the principle of "cheating the devil" was already in vogue and the piece of land allotted was but a worthless scrap.[124] It is a remnant of old sacrificial rite, when the Swedes still bake at yule-tide a cake in the shape of a boar, representing the boar sacrificed of old to Freyr, and Oxford to this day commemorates the same ancestral ceremony, when the boar's head is carried in to the Christmas feast at Queen's College, with its appointed carol, "Caput apri defero, Reddens laudes Domino."[125] With a lingering recollection of the old libations, the German toper's saying still runs that heeltaps are a devil's offering.[126]

As for sacrificial rites most fully and officially existing in modern Christendom, the presentation of ex-votos is one. The ecclesiastical opposition to the continuance of these classic thank-offerings was but temporary and partial. In the fifth century it seems to have been usual to offer silver and gold eyes, feet, etc., to saints in acknowledgement of cures they had effected. At the beginning of the sixteenth century, Polydore Vergil, describing the classic custom, goes on to say: "In the same manner do we now offer up in our churches sigillaria, that is, little images of wax, and oscilla. As oft as any part of the body is hurt, as the hand, foot, breast, we presently make a vow to God, and his saints, to whom upon our recovery we make an offering of that hand or food or breast shaped in wax, which custom has so far obtained that this kind of images have passed to the other animals. Wherefore so for an ox, so for a horse, so for a sheep, we place puppets in the temples. In which thing any modestly scrupulous person may perhaps say he knows not whether we are rivalling the religion or the superstition of the ancients."[127] In modern Europe the custom prevails largely, but has perhaps somewhat subsided into low levels of society, to judge by the general use of mock silver and such-like worthless materials for the dedicated effigies. In Christian as in pre-Christian temples, clouds of incense rise as of old. Above all, though the ceremony of sacrifice did not form an original part of Christian worship, its prominent place in the ritual was obtained in early centuries. In that Christianity was recruited among nations to whom the conception of sacrifice was among the deepest of religious ideas, and the ceremony of sacrifice among the sincerest efforts of worship, there arose an observance suited to supply the vacant place. This result was obtained not by new introduction, but by transmutation. The solemn eucharistic meal of the primitive Christians in time assumed the name of the sacrifice of the mass, and was adapted to a ceremonial in which an offering of food and drink is set out by a priest on an altar in a temple, and consumed by priest and worshippers. The natural conclusion of an ethnographic survey of sacrifice, is to point to the controversy between Protestants and Catholics, for centuries past one of the keenest which have divided the Christian world, on this express question of whether sacrifice is or is not a Christian rite.

# Notes

1. Garcilaso de la Vega, "Commentarios Reales," v. 19. Ellis, "Madagascar," vol. I, p. 421.
2. Charlevoix, "Nouv. Fr.," vol. I, p. 394. See also Smith, "Virginia," in "Pinkerton," vol. XIII, p. 41.
3. Phillips in Astley's "Voyages," vol. II, p. 411; Lubbock, "Origin of Civilization," p. 216. Bosman, "Guinea," in Pinkerton, vol. XVI, p. 500. Bastian in "Ztschr. für Ethnologie," 1869, p. 315.
4. Schoolcraft, "Algic Res.," vol. II, p. 75. See also Tanner, "Narr." p. 193, and above, p. 270.
5. Macpherson, "India," p. 129.
6. Billings, "Exp. to Northern Russia," p. 125. Chinese sacrifices buried for earth spirits, see ante, vol. I, p. 107; Plath, part ii, p. 50.
7. Taylor, "New Zealand," p. 182.
8. Römer, "Guinea," p. 67.
9. Herod, vii. 35, 54. Liv. vii. 6. Grote, *Hist. of Greece*, vol. X, p. 589, see p. 715.
10. Rochefort, "Iles Antilles," p. 367.
11. Ellis, "Polyn. Res." vol. I, pp. 336, 358. Williams, "Fiji," vol. I, p. 220.
12. Bosman, "Guinea," in Pinkerton, vol. XVI, p. 494; J. L. Wilson, "W. Afr.," p. 218; Burton, "W. and W. fr. W. Afr.," p. 331.
13. Ward, "Hindoos," vol. II, p. 195, etc.
14. Clavigero, "Messico," vol. II, p. 69. J. G. Müller, p. 631.
15. Ward, vol. II, p. 194; "Mem. Anthrop. Soc.," vol. I, p. 332.
16. Williams, "Fiji," vol. I, p. 226.
17. J. L. Wilson, "W. Afr.," p. 218.
18. Manu, iii, 212. See also "Avesta," tr. Spiegel, vol. II, p. lxxvii (sacrificial cakes eaten by priest).
19. Ysbrants Ides, "Reize naar China," p. 38. Meiners, vol. I, p. 162.
20. Clavigero, vol. II, p. 46. J. G. Müller, p. 631.
21. Bel and the Dragon.
22. Römer, "Guinea," p. 47.

23. Bastian, "Mensch," part ii, p. 210.

24. Homer, *Odyss.*, XI. xii.

25. "Journ. Ind. Archip.," vol. I, p. 270.

26. Smith, "Virginia," in Pinkerton, vol. XIII, p. 41; see J. G. Müller, p. 143; Waitz, vol. III, p. 207. Comp. Meiners, vol. II, p. 89. See also Bollaert in "Mem. Anthrop. Soc.," vol. II, p. 96.

27. "Journ. Ind. Archip.," vol. III, p. 145. See also St John, "Far East," vol. I, p. 160.

28. Hodgson, "Abor. of India," p. 147; Hunter, "Rural Bengal," p. 181; Forbes Leslie, "Early Races of Scotland," vol. II, p. 458.

29. Bosman, "Guinea," letter xxi, in Pinkerton, vol. XVI, p. 531. See also Waitz, vol. II, p. 192.

30. Bastian, "Psychologie," p. 96.

31. Levit. i. etc.; Deuteron. xii. 23; Psalm xvi. 4.

32. Waitz, vol. III, p. 181. Hennepin, "Voyage," p. 302. Charlevoix, "Nouvelle France," vol. V, p. 311; VI, p. 178. Schoolcraft, "Ind. Tribes," part i, p. 49, part ii, p. 127. Catlin, vol. I, pp. 181, 229. Morgan, "Iroquois," p. 164. J. G. Müller, p. 58.

33. Rochefort, "Iles Antilles," pp. 418, 507. Lery, "Voy. en Brésil," p. 268. See also Musters in "Journ. Anthrop. Inst.," vol. I, p. 202 (Patagonians).

34. Callaway, "Religion of Amazulu," pp. 11, 141, 177. See also Casalis, "Basutos," p. 258.

35. Clavigero, "Messico," vol. II, p. 39. See also Piedrahita, part i, lib. i. c. 3 (Muyscas).

36. Plath, "Religion der alten Chinesen," part ii, p. 31. Doolittle, "Chinese."

37. Porphyr. de Abstinentia, ii. 5. Arnob. contra Gentes., vii. 26. Meiners, vol. II, p. 14.

38. Wilkinson, "Ancient Egyptians," vol. V, pp. 315, 338. Plutarch. de Is. et Osir.

39. Herodot. i. 183.

40. Exod. xxx., xxxvii. Lev. x. 1, xvi. 12, etc.

41. Smith, "Virginia," in Pinkerton, vol. XIII, p. 41. Le Jeune in "Rel. des Jés.," 1634, p. 16. Catlin, "N. A. Ind.," vol. I, p. 189.

42. "Rites and Laws of Incas," p. 16, etc., 79; see "Ollanta, an ancient Ynca Drama," tr. C. R. Markham, p. 81. Garcilaso de la Vega, lib. I. II. VI.

43. Klemm, "Cultur-Gesch." vol. III, pp. 106, 114.

44. Plath, part ii, p. 65.

45. Latham, "Descr. Eth." vol. I, p. 191.

46. "Rig-Veda," i, 1, 4.

47. Homer, Il. i. 317.

48. Porphyr. de Abstinentia, ii, 42; see 58.

49. Stanley, "Jewish Church," 2d Ser., pp. 410, 424. See Kalisch on Leviticus; Barry in Smith's *Dictionary of the Bible*, art. "sacrifice."

50. Callaway, "Religion of Amazulu," p. 11 (amadhlozi or amatongo = ancestral spirits).

51. Roman Pane, ch. xvi, in "Life of Colon," in Pinkerton, vol. XII, p. 86. Rochefort, "Iles Antilles," p. 418; see Meiners, vol. II, p. 516; J. G. Müller, p. 212.

52. "Journ. Ind. Archip.," vol. IV, p. 194.

53. Eliot in "As. Res.," vol. III, p. 30.
54. Macpherson, "India," pp. 88, 100.
55. Klemm, "Cultur-Gesch.," vol. III, p. 114.
56. Grimm, "Deutsche Myth.," p. 264.
57. "Journ. Ind. Archip.," vol. I, p. 27.
58. Mason, "Karens," l.c., p. 208.
59. Bastian, "Mensch," vol. II, p. 407. Ellis, "Polyn. Res.," vol. I, p. 358. Taylor, "New Zealand," pp. 104, 220.
60. Williams, "Fiji," vol. I, p. 231.
61. Schoolcraft, "Algic Researches," vol. II, p. 140; see p. 190.
62. Tanner's "Narrative," pp. 286, 318. See also Waitz, vol. III, p. 207.
63. J. G. Müller, p. 142; see p. 282.
64. Sahagun, lib. VI, in Kingsborough, vol. V.
65. "Rites and Laws of Yncas," tr. and ed. C. R. Markham, pp. 55, 58, 166. See ante, p. 385 (possible connexion of smoke with soul).
66. Waitz, vol. II, pp. 188, 196. Steinhauser, l.c., p. 136. See also Schlegel, "Ewe-Sprache," p. xv; Magyar, "Süd-Afrika," p. 273.
67. A. Campbell in "Tr. Eth. Soc.," vol. VII, p. 153.
68. O'Riley, in "Journ. Ind. Archip.," vol. IV, p. 592. Bastian, "Oestl. Asien," vol. II, p. 12.
69. R. Clarke, "Sierra Leone," p. 43.
70. Smith, "Virginia," in Pinkerton, vol. XIII, p. 41. Welcker, "Griech. Götterlehre," vol. II, p. 693. Legge, "Confucius," p. 179. Grohmann, Aberglauben aus Böhmen," p. 41, etc.
71. J. L. Wilson, "W. Afr.," p. 218; Bosman, "Guinea," in Pinkerton, vol. XVI, p. 400.
72. Bastian, "Oestl. Asien," vol. II, p. 387.
73. Roberts, "Oriental Illustrations," p. 545.
74. M'Coy, "Baptist Indian Missions," p. 305.
75. Callaway, "Religion of Amazulu," p. 59. See Casalis, p. 252.
76. Earl in "Journ. Ind. Archip.," vol. IV, p. 174.
77. Hodgson, "Abor. of India," p. 170, see p. 146; Hooker, "Himalayan Journals," vol. II, p. 276.
78. Prescott, "Mexico," book I, ch. III.
79. "Rites and Laws of Yncas," p. 33, etc.
80. Welcker, "Griech. Götterlehre," vol. II, p. 50; Pauly, "Real-Encyclopedie," s.v. "Sacrificia."
81. Tanner's "Nar.," p. 154; see also Waitz, vol. III, p. 167.
82. Symes, "Ava," in Pinkerton, vol. IX, p. 440; Caron, "Japan," ib. vol. VII., p. 629.
83. Burton, "Medinah," etc., vol. III, p. 302; Lane, "Mod. Eg.," vol. I, p. 132.
84. Hardy, "Manual of Buddhism," p. 59.
85. 2 Kings III. 27. Euseb. Præp. Evang. I. 10, IV. 156; Laud. Constant. XIII. Porphyr. de Abstin. II. 56, etc. Lamprid, Heliogabal. VII. Movers, "Phönizier," vol. I, p. 300, etc.
86. Ellis, "Madagascar," vol. I, p. 419.
87. Römer, "Guinea," p. 59. Bosman in Pinkerton, vol. XVI, p. 399.
88. Klemm, "Cultur-Gesch.," vol. III, p. 106; Castrén, "Finn. Myth.," p. 232.

89. Hesiod, Theog. 537. Welcker, vol. I, p. 764; vol. II, p. 51.
90. Haug, "Parsis," Bombay, 1862, p. 238.
91. Hamilton in "As. Res.," vol. II, p. 342.
92. Mariner's "Tonga Is." vol. I, p. 454; vol. II, p. 222. Cook's "3rd Voy.," vol. I, p. 403. Details from S. Africa in Bastian, "Mensch," vol. III, pp. 4, 24; Scherzer, "Voy. of Novara," vol. I, p. 212.
93. Catlin, "N. A. Ind.," vol. I, p. 172; Klemm, "Cultur-Gesch.," vol. II, p. 170. See also Venegas, "Noticia de la California," vol. I, p. 117; Garcilaso de la Vega, lib. II. c. 8 (Peru).
94. Buchanan, "Mysore," etc. in Pinkerton, vol. VIII, p. 661; Meiners, vol. II, p. 472; Bastian, l.c. See also Dubois, "India," vol. I, p. 5.
95. Polack, "New Zealand," vol. I, p. 264.
96. Bastian, "Psychologie," p. 184.
97. Theodoret, in Levit. xix.; Hanusch, "Slaw. Myth." Details in Bastian, "Mensch," vol. II, p. 229, etc.
98. Bastian, "Mensch," vol. III, p. 113 (see other details).
99. Pausan, viii. 23; ix. 8.
100. "Encyc. Brit." art. "Brahma." See "Asiat. Res.," vol. IX, p. 387.
101. Boecler, "Ehsten Aberglaübische Gebraüche," etc., p. 4.
102. Rivero and Tschudi, p. 196. See "Rites of Yncas," p. 79.
103. Bastian, p. 112, etc.; Smith's "Dic. of Gr. and Rom. Ant.," art. "Sacrificium."
104. Grimm, "Deutsche Myth.," p. 40.
105. Diodor, Sic. XX. 14.
106. Callaway, "Zulu Tales," vol. I., p. 88; Magyar, "Süd-Afrika," p. 256.
107. Macpherson, "India," pp. 108, 187.
108. De Silva in Bastian, "Psychologie," p. 181.
109. Details in Pauly, "Real-Encyclop.," s.v. "Sacrificia"; Bastian, "Mensch," vol. III, p. 114; Movers, "Phönizier," vol. I, p. 300.
110. Clavigero, "Messico," vol. II, p. 82; Torquemada, "Monarquia Indiana," x. c. 29; J. G. Müller, pp. 502, 640. See also ibid., p. 379 (Peru); "Rites and Laws of Yncas," pp. 46, 54.
111. Grote, vol. V, p. 366. Schmidt in Smith's "Dic. of Gr. And Rom. Ant.," art. "Sacrificium," Bastian, l. c.
112. Bastian, "Oestl. Asien," vol. III, p. 501.
113. Doolittle, "Chinese," vol. I, p. 152.
114. Lane, "Modern Eg.," vol. II, p. 262. Meiners, vol. II, p. 85.
115. Wilkinson, "Ancient Eg.," vol. III, p. 395; and in Rawlinson's Herodotus, vol. II, p. 137. See 1 Sam. vi. 4.
116. Grimm, "Deutsche Myth.," p. 1131.
117. Ibid.
118. Bastian, vol. III, p. 116.
119. St. Clair and Brophy, "Bulgaria," p. 43. Compare modern Circassian sacrifice of animal before cross, as substitute for child, in Bell, "Circassia," vol. II.
120. Ralston, "Songs of Russian People," pp. 123, 153, etc.
121. Wuttke, "Deutsche Volksaberglaube," p. 86. See also Grimm, "Deutsche Myth.," pp. 417, 602.

122. Hyltén-Cavallius, "Wärend och Wirdarne," part i, pp. 131, 146, 157, etc.
123. Monnier, "Traditions Populaires," pp. 187, 666.
124. R. Hunt, "Pop. Rom. of W. of England," 1st Ser., p. 237. Pennant, "Tour in Scotland," in Pinkerton, vol. III, p. 49. J. Y. Simpson, Address to Soc. Antiq. Scotland, 1861, p. 33; Brand, "Pop. Ant.," vol. III, pp. 74, 317.
125. Brand, vol. I, p. 484. Grimm, "D. M.," pp. 45, 194, 1188, see p. 250; "Deutsche Rechtsalterthümer," p. 900; Hyltén-Cavallius, part i, p. 175.
126. Grimm, "D. M.," p. 962.
127. Beausobre, vol. II, p. 667. Polydorus Vergilius, De Inventoribus Rerum (Basel, 1521), lib. v. i.

# 2

# HERBERT SPENCER (b. 1820)

Herbert Spencer, writer, inventor and one-time railroad engineer, was once lauded during his lifetime as the "greatest living philosopher of England." A practical-minded man, dedicated to scientific principles, he was instrumental in developing the theory of evolution. Seven years before the publication of Darwin's *Origin of Species* (1859), Spencer published an article entitled "The Development Hypothesis" (1852) where he described a process of "evolution through successive modifications," and then in 1857 he completed "Progress: Its Law and Cause" where he argued that nature, society and the human mind all evolve. It was Spencer, not Darwin, who coined the phrase "survival of the fittest," even as Darwin identified the biological mechanisms at work. His *Synthetic Philosophy*, a ten-volume work addressing biology, psychology, sociology, and morality, published between 1855 and 1896, is, however, Spencer's most ambitious, controversial, and fascinating work.

Two central ideas inform Spencer's thinking. The first is the concept of evolution. He defined evolution as a universal process of development that proceeds from a state of relatively "indefinite incoherent homogeneity" to a state of relatively "definite coherent heterogeneity." It is a movement from an undifferentiated simple system (an "organism") toward greater specialization, complexity, and differences. In nature, species diversify and new breeds appear, just as for the human mind, knowledge becomes more differentiated and new disciplines arise, and for societies, specialized functions lead to more complex structures within the whole system. In Spencer's writings we find the germ of what later became structural functionalism, the idea that society is comprised of an organized system of "structures" that function harmoniously to satisfy certain individual or collective needs. Spencer's insight was to recognize that the structures of society change over time just as they do in the natural world.

The second important idea Spencer developed was a claim about the human mind, a psychological theory that placed a "tendency to generalize" at the core of human thought. Given the great diversity of empirical experience, something that only increases with the progress of evolution, the mind builds abstract concepts and comprehensive ideas to encompass forms of variety. Working in the opposite direction of evolution (which leads to increased particularity), human beings work to organize their experience into generalities, to classify their world. Over time people forget the empirical referents that led to these general concepts and categories, and then frequently make mistakes when extrapolating back to particularities. Beginning with general concepts and positing the existence of specific realities is a common human endeavor, but it is also fraught with inevitable dangers. Here too Spencer's work can be seen to forecast important anthropological, sociological, and psychological concepts.

Spencer traces the origin of religion to two domains of human experience that when linked, through a process of rational thought and "generalizing," form the basis of primitive religious beliefs and practices. The first of these he describes simply as "out of the ordinary occurrences," the surprisingly good and bad events that call out for explanation, and the second, experiences of death and dreams, those times when a dead acquaintance appears in a dream, or when the soul of a dead person returns as a "ghost." It was a short step, Spencer argues, for primitive peoples to explain strange occurrences—simply put, ghosts cause them. Like the actual people who preceded them, ghosts can be influenced, and since ghosts cause both good and bad events, it makes sense for the living to act in ways they think will encourage the dead to behave positively toward their interests. Hence for Spencer the first religious practices (rituals) were simply specific behaviors thought to please departed ancestors, and equally they were originally performed at graves or other places of importance to the departed. Then, as the process of generalization unfolded, it drove an evolution of religion, of these practices addressing ghosts, from specific individual agents (ghosts) to collective agents (gods) and finally to a single all-powerful agent (the Christian God). Graveside activities evolved to activities at altars and in temples.

Knowing his general theory of ritual, it is not difficult to understand how Spencer interprets specific ritual forms. Prayers are petitions for favors. Vows are promises of good behavior. Pilgrimages are journeys to burial sites, and so forth. Sacrifice is no different. For Spencer, it is essentially an offering to the dead. Whatever the dead were thought to need in the next life would serve as a sacrificial offering, as a gift to encourage the ancestors (later, the gods) to provide good fortune. Like Tylor, Spencer offers a "gift-theory" of sacrifice. At the same time, though, he makes a contribution to this theory by highlighting what he thinks is the basic motivation for the giving. It is fear. The dead are always possible agents of destruction, powerful beings who can threaten the order of things with unexpected tragedies and other unpleasant events ("diseases" and "pestilences," for example). As such, the living must offer what the dead demand, what they need, or else risk potentially negative consequences. Put differently, Spencer argues that fundamentally religious beliefs and practices stem from a human psychological need to placate superhuman beings who inspire fear, those personalities who control the quality of human life on earth.

Sacrifice, in the form of offerings, was the earliest and most basic expression of human beings acting to fulfill this need.

The selection reproduced here comes from the first volume of Spencer's *Principles of Sociology* (the sixth volume of his overall Synthetic Philosophy). Originally published in 1877, it followed very closely behind Tylor's writing on sacrifice. The selection presents a wide variety of cultural details collected from around the world and, with its "fear theory" of sacrifice, makes intriguing, and still debatable, theoretical claims.

# From *The Principles of Sociology*

O N GRAVE-STONES, inscriptions often begin with the words "Sacred to the memory of." The sacredness thus ascribed to the tomb, extends to whatever is, or has been, closely associated with the dead. The bedroom containing the corpse is entered with the least possible noise; words are uttered in low tones; and by the subdued manner is shown a feeling which, however variable in other elements, always includes the element of awe.

This sentiment excited in us by the dead, by the place of the dead, and by the immediate belongings of the dead, while doubtless partly unlike that of the primitive man, is in essence like it. When we read of savages in general, as of the Dakotahs, that "they stand in great awe of the spirits of the dead," and that thinking men's ghosts haunt places of death, many tribes, like the Hottentots, "leave the huts they died in standing," with all their contents untouched; we are sufficiently shown that fear is a chief component of the sentiment. Shrinking from the chamber of death, often shown among ourselves, like aversion to going through a churchyard at night, arises partly from a vague dread. Common to uncivilized and civilized, this feeling colours all the ideas which the dead arouse.

Be this as it may, however, we have abundant proof that the place where the dead are, excites in savages an emotion of fear, is approached with awe, and acquires the character of sacredness. Mariner tells us that in the Tonga Islands, the cemeteries containing the great chiefs are considered sacred. We learn from Angas that when a New Zealand chief is buried in a village, the whole village becomes immediately *tapu*: no one, on pain of death, being permitted to

---

Reprinted from Herbert Spencer, *The Principles of Sociology*, vol. 1 (New York: D. Appleton and Company, 1882), pages 271–2, 300–3. In the public domain.

approach it. The Tahitians, according to Cook, never repair or live in the house of one who is dead: that, and everything belonging to him, is tabooed. Food for the departed is left by New Zealanders in "sacred calabashes"; in Aneiteum, where they "worship the spirits of their ancestors," the groves in which they leave offerings of food for them, are "sacred groves"; and by Ashantis, the town of Bantama "is regarded as sacred because it contains the fetish-house, which is a mausoleum of the kings of Ashanti."

Here the fact to be noted is that this awe excited by the dead grows into a sentiment like that excited by the places and things used for religious purposes. The kinship is forced on our attention when we read such statements as that of Cook concerning the Sandwich Islanders, that the *morai* seems to be their pantheon as well as their burial-place and his kindred statement that the *morais* or burying-grounds of the Tahitians are also places of worship.

. . . . . . . . . . . . . . . . . . . . . . . . . . . . . . . . . .

Altars imply sacrifices; and we pass naturally from the genesis of the one to the genesis of the other.

Already, I have exemplified at length the practice of leaving food for the dead; and I might, space permitting, double the number of examples. I might, too, illustrate the various motives shown us by various peoples—by the Lower Californians, among whom "the priest demands provisions for the spirit's journey"; by the Coras of Mexico, who, after a man's death, "placed some meat upon sticks about the fields, for fear he might come for the cattle he formerly owned"; by the Damaras, who, bringing provisions to the grave of a relation, request "him to eat and make merry," and in return "invoke his blessing" and aid. But it is needless to do more than remind the reader that uncivilized races in general, differing however they may do in their assigned reasons, agree in making offerings of meat and drink to the dead. A truth also before illustrated, but which, as bearing directly on the argument, it will be well to re-illustrate here, is that these offerings are repeated at intervals: in some places for a short time; in other places for a long time. Of the Nootka-Sound people we are told that "for some days after death the relatives burn salmon or venison before the tomb"; and among the Mosquito Indians, "the widow was bound to supply the grave of her husband with provisions for a year." These are extremes between which various degrees of persistence might be placed. And when, with practices of this kind, we join such practices and interpretations as those of the Karen, who thinks himself surrounded by the spirits of the departed dead, "whom he has to appease by varied and unceasing offerings"; we cannot fail to recognize the transition from funeral gifts to religious sacrifices.

The kinship becomes further manifest on observing that in both cases there are, along with offerings of the ordinary kind, festival offerings. The Karens just named as habitually making oblations, have also annual feasts for the dead, at which they ask the spirits to eat and drink. Similarly of the Bodo and Dhimals, Hodgson tells us that "at harvest home, they offer fruits and a fowl to deceased parents." Such yearly offerings, occurring in November among the natives of the Mexican Valley, who then lay animals, edibles, and flowers on the graves of their dead relatives and friends, and occurring in August among the Pueblos, who then place corn, bread, meat, etc., in the "haunts frequented by the dead," have prevailed widely: modern Chinese still exemplifying them, as they were exemplified by the ancient Peruvians and Aztecs.

Beyond the making of offerings to deceased persons for various periods after death, and beyond these annual feasts for the dead, we have the making of offerings on occasions specially suggesting them. St. John tells that "when passing a burial-ground, the Sea Dyaks throw on it something they consider acceptable to the departed"; and according to Anderson, the Hottentots throw an offering on passing a burial-place, and ask the protection of the spirit. In Samoa, where the spirits of the dead are supposed to roam the bush, "people in going far inland to work, would scatter food here and there as a peace-offering to them, and utter a word or two of prayer for protection." Development of funeral offerings into habitual sacrifices is carried a stage further in the practice of reserving for the dead a portion of each meal. Of the Fijians, Seeman tells us that "often when the natives eat or drink anything, they throw portions of it away, stating them to be for their departed ancestors." Malcome says of the Bhils that always when liquor is given them, they pour a libation on the ground before drinking any; and as their dead ancestors are their deities, the meaning of this practice is unmistakable. So, too, we learn from Smith that the Araucanians spill a little of their drink, and scatter a little of their food, before eating and drinking; and, according to Drury, the Virzimbers of Madagascar, when they sit down to meals, "take a bit of meat and throw it over their heads, saying—'There's a bit for the spirit.'" Ancient historic races had like ways.

The motive for these offerings, made first to the corpse of the dead man and afterwards at his grave—the motive for these occasional feasts and for these daily shares of meals, is everywhere the same, and is often avowed. We read in Livingstone that a Berotse having a headache said, "'My father is scolding me because I do not give him any of the food I eat.' I asked him where his father was. 'Among the Barimo,' [gods] was the reply." The Kaffirs, who are described by Gardiner as attributing every untoward event to the spirit of a deceased person, and as "slaughtering a beast to propitiate its favour," show us the same thing. So do the Amazulu. "There, then, is your food," they say: "all ye spirits of our tribe, summon one another. I am not going to say, 'So-and-so, there is your food,' for you are jealous. But thou, So-and-so, who art making this man ill, call all the spirits; come all of you to eat this food."

Alike in motive and in method, this offering of food and drink to the dead man is paralleled by the offering of food and drink to a deity. Observe the points of community. The giving of portions of meals is common to the two. Cook tells us that in the Sandwich Islands, before the priests begin a meal, they offer up a sort of prayer, and then offer some of the provisions to the deity. As with these Polynesians, so with the Homeric Greeks: "the share which is given to the gods of the wine that flows, and the flesh that smokes on the festal board" corresponds with the share cast aside by savages for the ancestral spirits. The like is true of the larger oblations on special occasions. Sacrifices made to gain favours or to ward off evils, are made here to ghosts and here to gods. When a Kaffir chief kills a bullock that he may thereby get the help in war of a dead ancestor, we are reminded that "King Agamemnon offered up a fat ox, of five years old, to the powerful son of Saturn." When among the Amazulu, after "an abundant harvest sometimes the head of the village dreams that it is said to him—'How is it, when you have been given so much food, that you do not give thanks?'" and when he thereupon sacrifices to the Amatongo (ghosts of the dead), his act differs in no respect from that of offering first-fruits to deities. And when at another time "he tells his dream, and says—'Let a sin-offering be sacrificed, lest the Itongo be angry and kill us'" we are reminded of sin-offerings made among various peoples to avert divine vengeance. There is a no less complete correspondence between the sacrifices made at fixed periods. As above shown, we find in addition to other oblations to the dead, annual oblations; and these answer to the festivals in honour of deities. Moreover, in both cases guidance by astronomical events is used. The parallel holds also in respect of the things offered: they are identical, so far as the products of different regions permit. In both cases we have oxen, goats, etc.; in both cases bread and cakes occur; in both cases the local drink is given—wine where it exists, chicha among American races, beer among various African tribes; in both cases, too, we find incense used; and in both cases flowers. In short, whatever consumable commodities are most valued, down even to tobacco. As we saw above, an African chief expected to get aid by emptying his snuff-box to the gods; and among the Kaffirs, when the spirits "are invited to eat, beer and snuff are usually added." Nor is there any difference in the mode of preparation. Both to spirits and to deities we find uncooked offerings and also burnt offerings. Yet another likeness must be named. Ghosts and gods are supposed to profit by the sacrifices in like ways and to be similarly pleased. As given in the *Iliad,* Zeus' reason for favouring Troy is that "there my altars never lacked a due banquet and libation and savour." And in the *Odyssey,* Athena is represented as coming in person to receive the roasted heifer offered to her, and as rewarding the offerer. So that food for deities and food for ancestors, similarly utilized, has similar effects. Lastly, we have the significant fact that in sundry cases the sacrifices to ghosts and gods coexist in undistinguishable forms. By the Sandwich Islanders provisions are placed before the dead and before images of the deities. Among the Egyptians "the offerings made to the dead were similar to the ordinary oblations in honour of the gods." The mummies were kept in closets, "out of which they were taken by the minor functionaries to a small altar, before which the priest officiated"; and on this altar they made "offerings of incense and libations, with cakes, flowers, and fruits."

There is, then, an unbroken connection between refreshments placed for the dead and religious offerings at large. The derivation of the last from the first, made sufficiently clear by the traceable gradations, is made still clearer by the maintenance of the same essential traits.

There are reasons for suspecting that another religious observance arises incidentally along with the foregoing observances. Little as we should look for such an origin, we meet with facts suggesting that fasting, as a religious rite, is a sequence of funeral rites. Probably the practice arises in more ways than one. Involuntary as the going without food often is with the primitive man, and causing as it then does vivid dreams, it becomes a deliberately adopted method of obtaining interviews with the spirits. Among various savage races fasting has now, as it had among the Jews of Talmudic times, this as one of its motives. In other cases it has the allied motive of bringing on that preternatural excitement regarded as inspiration. But besides fastings of these kinds there is the fasting which results from making excessive provision for the dead. This, by implication, becomes an accepted mark of reverence for the dead; and finally a religious act.

It [has been] shown how extensive is in many cases the destruction of property, of cattle, of food, at the tomb. I have cited the fact that, as a consequence, among the Dyaks burial-rites frequently reduce survivors to poverty; and that, on the Gold Coast, "a funeral is usually absolute ruin to a poor family." If, as in some extinct American societies, everything a man had except his land went into his grave with him—if on the death of a Toda "his entire herd" of oxen was sacrificed; the implication is that his widow and children had to suffer great want. When, of the Chippewayans, we are told that "no article is spared by these unhappy men when a near relative dies"—when we learn that among the Bagos a chief's widows burn all their stores of food at his funeral; we cannot but infer lack of food as a result. And so we find it to be. Bancroft tells us that "the Indians of the Rocky Mountains burn with the deceased all his effects, and even those of his nearest relatives, so that it not unfrequently happens that a family is reduced to absolute starvation"; and of the Bagos above named, Caillié says "the family of the deceased, who are ruined by this act of superstition [burning his property], are supported through the next harvest by the inhabitants of the village." Now when along with these facts, so obviously related as cause and consequence, we join the fact stated by Cruikshank, that the Gold Coast people, to their other mourning observances, add fasting; as well as the fact concerning the Dahomans which Burton gives, that "the weeping relatives must fast"; we can scarcely avoid the conclusion that what is at first a natural result of great sacrifice to the dead, becomes eventually a usage of signifying such sacrifice; and continues as a usage when no longer made needful by impoverishment. We shall see the more reason for concluding this on finding that fasting was a funeral rite among extinct peoples whose attentions to the dead were elaborate. According to Landa, the Yucatanese "fasted for the sake of the dead"; and the like happened among the Egyptians: during the mourning for a king "a solemn fast was established." Even among the Hebrews fasting was associated with mourning dresses.

This connection of practices and ideas is strengthened by the like connection consequent on daily offerings to the dead. The habit of throwing aside a portion of each meal for the spirits, must often associate in thought sacrificing with fasting. Short of food, as the improvident savage frequently is, the giving of a part of his meal to the ancestral ghosts, diminishing the little he has, entails hunger; and voluntarily borne hunger thus becomes a vividly impressed symbol of duty to the dead. How it thence passes into the notion of duty to the gods, is well shown by the Polynesian legend concerning the Maui and his brothers. Having had a great success in fishing, Maui says to them—"After I am gone, be courageous and patient; do not eat food until I return, and do not let our fish be cut up, but rather leave it until I have carried an offering to the gods for this great haul of fish. * * * I will then return, and we can cut up this fish in safety." And the story goes on to describe the catastrophe resulting from the anger of the gods, because the brothers proceeded to eat before the offerings had been made.

Naturally the fasting arising in this manner, and giving occasions for self-discipline, comes to be used for self-discipline after the original purpose is forgotten. There still clings to it, however, the notion that the approval of a supernatural power is gained; and the clinging of this notion supports the inference which we otherwise find probable.

Returning from this incidental result, introduced parenthetically, and resuming our study of the way in which the offerings at burials develop into religious offerings, we come next to observances scarcely separable from those described above, but which yet may be conveniently grouped by themselves. I refer to propitiations in which human beings are sacrificed to the dead, and in which those who do not sacrifice themselves, sacrifice parts of themselves.

We have seen that for the immolation of human victims at funerals, there are two motives: one of them being the supply of food for the dead; and the other being the supply of attendants for service in the future life. We will glance at the two in this order. Remembering how prevalent cannibalism is among primitive men, and remembering that a man's other-self is supposed still to like the food he liked before death, we shall see that among cannibals the offering of human flesh to the dead as a propitiation is inevitable. Those ferocious anthropophagi the Fijians, who have victims buried with them, and whose apotheosized chiefs join other gods to whom "human flesh is still the most valued offering," show us the entire series of sequences—cannibalism during life, cannibal ghosts, cannibal deities, and human sacrifices made as religious rites. So, too, was it with the ancient Mexicans. The man-eating habits of their ruling race, were accompanied by slayings of slaves, etc., at burials, as well as by slayings of prisoners before their gods; and though the immolations at graves were not, during their later times, avowedly food-offerings, yet we may suspect that they were so in earlier times, on seeing how literally a victim immolated to the god was made a food-offering—the heart being torn out, put into the mouth of the idol, and its lips anointed with the blood. When, too, Piedrahita tells us of the Chibchas that they offered men to the Spaniards as food; and when Acosta, remarking that the Chibchas were not themselves cannibals, asks "can they have believed that the Spaniards, as sons of the Sun (as they were styled by them), must take delight in the barbarous holocausts they offered to that star?" we may suspect that their immolations at funerals, like their immolations to the Sun, were the remains of an extinct cannibalism. Having before us such facts as that some Khonds believe the god eats the human being killed for him; that the Tahitians thought their gods fed on the spirits of the dead, and therefore provided them with such spirits by frequent slaughterings; and that the Tongans made offerings of children to their gods, who were deified chiefs; we cannot doubt that human sacrifices at graves had originally the purpose of supplying human flesh, along with other food, for the soul of the deceased; and that the sacrificing of human beings as a religious rite was a sequence. The like holds of slaying men as attendants. Already we have seen how common, in uncivilized and semi-civilized societies, is the killing of prisoners, and slaves, and wives, and friends, to follow the departed; and in some cases there is a repetition of the observance. Among the Mexicans additional slaves were slain on the fifth day after the burial, on the twentieth, on the fortieth, on the sixtieth, and on the eightieth days. In Dahomy there are frequent beheadings that the victims, going to the other world to serve the dead king, may carry messages from his living descendant. Human sacrifices thus repeated to propitiate the ghosts of the dead, evidently pass without break into the periodic human sacrifices that have commonly been elements in primitive religions.

[There are], from peoples in all parts of the world, examples of blood-offerings to the dead. Meaningless as such offerings otherwise are, they have meaning as made by primitive cannibals. That any men, in common with most ferocious brutes, should delight in drinking blood—especially the blood of their own species—is almost incredible to us. But on reading that in Australia, human flesh "is eaten raw" by "the blood-revengers"; that the Fijian chief Tanoa,.cut off a cousin's arm, drank the blood, cooked the arm, and ate it in presence of the owner; that the cannibal Vateans will exhume, cook, and eat, bodies that have been buried even more than three days; that among the Haidahs of the Pacific States, the taamish, or inspired medicine-man, "springs on the first person he meets, bites out and swallows one or more mouthfuls of the man's living flesh wherever he can fix his teeth, then rushes to another and another"; and that among the neighbouring Nootkas the medicine-man, instead of doing this, "is satisfied with what his teeth can tear from the corpses in the burial-places"; we see that horrors beyond our imaginations of possibility are committed by primitive men, and, among them, the drinking of warm human blood. We may infer, indeed, that the vampyre legends of European folk-lore, probably grew out of such facts concerning primitive cannibals: the original vampyre being the supposed other-self of a ferocious savage, still seeking to satisfy his blood-sucking propensities. And we shall not doubt that those blood-offerings to the dead were originally, as Burton says they are now in Dahomy, "drink for the deceased." Indeed, as there is no greater difference between drinking animal blood and drinking human blood than there is between eating animal-flesh and eating human flesh, hesitation disappears on reading that, even now, the Samoyedes delight in the warm blood of animals, and on remembering that Ulysses describes the ghosts in the Greek Hades as flocking to drink the sacrificial blood he provides for them, and as being refreshed by it. If, then, blood shed at a funeral was at first meant for the refreshment of the ghost—if when shed on subsequent occasions, as by the sanguinary Dahomans to get the aid of a dead king's ghost in war, it became a blood-offering to a supernatural being for special propitiation; it cannot be doubted that the offering of human blood to a deity with a like motive, is but a further development of the practice. The case of the Mexicans is typical. Their ruling races descended from conquering cannibals; they had cannibal-gods whose idols were fed with human hearts; the priests, when there had not been recent sacrifices, reminded the kings that the idols "were starving with hunger"; war was made, to take prisoners, "because their gods demanded something to eat"; and thousands were for this reason sacrificed annually. When we add the facts that the blood of victims was separately offered; that "the Indians gave the idols, to drink, their own blood, drawn from their ears"; "that the priests and dignified persons also drew blood from their legs and daubed the temples"; and that "the effusion of blood was frequent and daily with some of the priests"; we shall see an obvious filiation. Even in the records of ancient Eastern nations we find blood-offerings common to the two sets of rites. That self-bleedings at funerals occurred among the Hebrews, if not indigenously then by adoption from their neighbours, is proved by the fact that in Deuteronomy they are forbidden to cut themselves for the dead. And that self-bleeding was a religious ceremony among their neighbours, is proved by the fact that in propitiation of their god the prophets of Baal cut themselves "till the blood gushed out of them."

The only question is how far this kind of propitiatory offering has passed into the kind we have now to glance at—the sacrificing a part of the body as a mark of subordination. [There are] many cases of mutilation as a funeral rite, and they might readily be multiplied. Among the Nateotetains of North

America, a woman "cuts off one joint of a finger upon the death of a near relative. In consequence of this practice, some old women may been seen with two joints off every finger on both hands." On the death of a Salish chief, it is the custom for the bravest woman and the man who is to be the succeeding chief, to cut off portions of one another's flesh, and throw them into the fire along with meat and a root. Paralleling these funeral mutilations, we elsewhere in America find mutilations as religious observances. Some of the Mexicans practised circumcision (or something like it), and mutilations much more serious than circumcision, in propitiation of their deities. The Guancavilcas, a Peruvian race, pulled out three teeth from each jaw of their young children, which they thought "very acceptable to their gods"; while, as we before saw, knocking out one of the front teeth is a rite at the funeral of a chief in the Sandwich Islands.

Yet a further mutilation is common to the two classes of observances. Proofs that at funerals the cutting-off of hair is habitual among savages have been given in abundance; and it occurs also as a religious sacrifice. In the Sandwich Islands, on the occasion of the volcanic eruption of 1799, when, to appease the gods, many offerings were made in vain, we are told that at length the king Tamehameha cut off part of his own hair, which was considered sacred, and threw it into the torrent, as the most valuable offering. Daily by the Peruvians, hair was given as an act of worship. "In making an offering they pulled a hair out of their eyebrows," says Garcilasso; and Jos. d'Acosta similarly describes the presentation of eyelashes or eyebrows to the deities. Even among the Greeks we trace a kindred observance: on a marriage the bride sacrificed a lock of her hair to Aphrodite.

Alike, then, in the immolation of human victims, in the offering of blood that flows from the living as well as the dying, in the offering of portions of the body, and even in the offering of hair, we see that funeral rites are paralleled by religious rites.[1]

. . . . . . . . . . . . . . . . . . . . . . . . . . . . . . . . . . . . . .

Thus, evidence abundant in amount and varied in kind justifies the statement made at the close of [my] last chapter [where] it was pointed out that the souls of the dead, conceived by savages sometimes as beneficent agents but chiefly as the causes of evils, might be variously dealt with—might be deceived, resisted, expelled, or might be treated in ways likely to secure good will and mitigate anger. It was asserted that from this last policy all religious observances take their rise. We have seen how they do so.

The original sacred locality, is the locality where the dead are, and which their ghosts are supposed to frequent; the sheltering cave, or house, or other chamber for the dead, becomes the sacred chamber or temple; and that on which the offerings for the dead are placed, becomes the sacred support for offerings—the altar. Food and drink and other things laid for the dead, grow into sacrifices and libations to the gods; while immolations of victims, blood-offerings, mutilations, cuttings-off of hair, originally occurring at the grave, occur afterwards before idols and as marks of fealty to a deity. Fasting as a funeral rite passes into fasting as a religious rite; and lamentations, too, occur under both forms. Praises of the dead, chanted at the burial and afterwards, and recurring at festivals, pass into praises forming parts of religious worship; and prayers made to the dead for aid, for blessing, for protection, become prayers made to divinities for like advantages. Ancestral ghosts supposed to cause diseases, as gods send pestilences, are similarly propitiated by special sacrifices: the ascribed motives of ghosts and gods being the same in kind, and the modes of appealing to those motives the same. The parallelism runs out into various details. There is oversight of conduct by ghosts as there is by deities; there are promises of good behaviour to both; there is penitence before the one as before the other. There is a repetition of injunctions given by the dead, as there is a repetition of divine injunctions. There is a maintenance of fires at graves and in sepulchral chambers, as there is in temples. Burial-places are sometimes, like temples, used as places of refuge. A secrecy is maintained respecting the name of the dead, as in many cases respecting the name of a god. There are pilgrimages to the graves of relatives, and pilgrimages to the graves of supposed divine persons. And in America, certain less-civilized races adopted a method of binding living with dead by seeking to participate in the qualities of the ghost, which a more civilized American race paralleled by a method of binding to a deity through a kindred ceremony for establishing community of nature.

Can so many and such varied similarities have arisen in the absence of genetic relationship? Suppose the two sets of phenomena unconnected— suppose primitive men had, as some think, the consciousness of a Universal Power whence they and all other things proceeded. What probability would there be that towards such a Power they would spontaneously perform an act like that performed by them to the dead body of a fellow savage? And if one such community would not be probable, what would be the probability of two such acts in common? What the probability of four? What of the score communities above specified? In the absence of causal relation the probability against such a correspondence would be almost infinity to one.

Again, if the two sets of rites have a common root, we may see how they come to coexist under forms differing only in their degrees of elaboration. But otherwise, how does it happen that in sundry societies the two sets of rites have been, or are, simultaneously observed in like ways? In Egypt at funerals, and afterwards in tombs, the dead were lauded and sacrificed to as their deities were lauded and sacrificed to. Every day in Mexico there were burial-oblations of food and drink, slayings of servants, offerings of flowers, just as there were daily observances of like kinds to their gods; and representative images of the dead were preserved and worshipped as were the images of the gods. Peruvians poured out human blood on sepulchres and gave it to idols; sacrificed victims to the deceased chief and victims to the deity; cut off their hair for the dead and presented their hair to the Sun; praised and prayed to embalmed bodies, as they praised and prayed to divinities; and made obeisances to the one as to the other. If between the father regarded as ancestor and the father regarded as divinity there is no connection, this community of observances is inexplicable.

Nor is this all. Were there no such origination of religious rites out of funeral rites, it would be impossible to understand the genesis of ceremonies apparently so absurd. How could men possibly have come to think, as did the Mexicans, that a stone bowl full of human blood would please the Sun? or that the Sun would be pleased by burning incense, as the Egyptians thought? In what imaginable way were the Peruvians led to believe that the Sun was propitiated by blowing towards it hairs from their eye-brows; or why did they suppose that by doing the like towards the sea they would mitigate its anger? From what antecedent did there result so strange an idea as that of the Santals, who, worshipping "the Great Mountain," sacrifice to it beasts, flowers, and fruit? Or why should one ancient people think to please the Creator by placing on an altar bread, wine, and incense, which were the very things placed by an adjacent ancient people on altars before their mummies? The assumption that the primitive man gratuitously acts in an irrational way, is quite inadmissible. But if these religious rites, seemingly so irrational, arose from funeral rites, we no longer need wonder at their irrelevance.

We have, then, numerous lines of evidence which, converging to a focus, are by themselves enough to dissipate any doubt respecting this natural genesis of religious observances. Traceable as it is in so many ways, the development of funeral rites into worship of the dead, and eventually into religious worship, becomes clear. We shall find that it becomes still clearer on contemplating other facts under other aspects.

# Note

1.  As it will be at least some years before I come to the division of this work treating of Ceremonial Government, I may as well here briefly indicate the conclusion concerning bodily mutilations in general, which multitudinous facts unite in supporting. All mutilations begin with the taking of trophies in war—trophies carried home by conquerors to prove their prowess. When the conquered man is slain, and either left behind or devoured, the trophy is of course taken without regard to the destructiveness of the mutilation; but when the conquered man is made a slave, the taking of a trophy must neither kill him nor seriously diminish his usefulness. Mutilations of captives, thus at first incident on the taking of trophies, necessarily imply marks borne by the subjugated—signs of subordination. At first distinctive of those taken in war, such marks become signs of subordination in subjected tribes, and in those who are born slaves. Having been

established as badges of submission to a conqueror, and as badges of class-submission, they come into use as badges of submission to the dead, voluntarily inflicted to propitiate their ghosts: first only the ghost of ferocious departed chiefs, who were greatly feared, and thence spreading downwards, as all ceremonial observances do. In the end they become politico-ecclesiastical rites, carrying with them vague notions of submission and sacredness, after their special meanings are lost. And as happens in cases furnished by civilized life, these marks of subordination often grow into sources of pride, and acquire a decorative character. Gashes are so made as to produce admired arrangements of scars, and tattooing develops into ornamental patterns.

# 3

# WILLIAM ROBERTSON SMITH (b. 1846)

A Scottish scholar of Biblical literature and Semitic cultures, William Robertson Smith was raised in a strong protestant family, his father being a minister in the conservative Free Church in Aberdeenshire. Well educated and an accomplished linguist, he worked as a professor in Aberdeen and later in Cambridge. He is well known as the editor and significant contributor to the ninth edition of the *Encyclopaedia Britannica*. His first important essay entitled "Animal Worship and Animal Tribes among the Arabs and in the Old Testament" appeared in 1880, and a book on the Old Testament (1881) and another on the Prophets of Israel (1882) followed. In 1886, Robertson Smith contributed his first work dedicated to sacrifice, an article with that title, to the *Encyclopaedia Britannica*. In 1889, he published his major and most influential work, *Lectures on the Religion of the Semites: The Fundamental Institutions*, a long discussion of sacrifice and its significance for religion.

Several ideas and assumptions inform Robertson Smith's thinking about religion and sacrifice. Like most of his contemporaries (Tylor and Spencer, for example), he believed that all institutions can be explained in terms of their historical development, in terms of varying rates of evolution from a common origin. Accepting the hypothesis of the "psychic unity of mankind," he sought in his work, as he put it, to identify "general causes operating very widely under conditions that were common in primitive times to all races of mankind." For Robertson Smith, determining the earliest and simplest form of religion would reveal the most significant feature of not only contemporary "primitive" but also fully developed modern religious institutions (including Christianity, much to the dismay of several ecclesiastical authorities) as well.

We also find in Robertson Smith's work one of the earliest, and clearly influential, positions emphasizing the primacy of ritual. For him, early forms of religion "were not systems of belief with practical applications," but were instead bodies of "fixed traditional practices, to which every member of society conformed." Religion was not something chosen out of "belief." It was a set of observances marked out for the individual "as part of the general scheme of social obligations and ordinances as a matter of course, by his position in the family and in the nation." We have here a central tenet of what later became the sociology of religion, namely that social solidarity, communal harmony, and shared values are important (perhaps essential, even motivating) byproducts of religious activities, beliefs, and institutions. Later sociologists, such as Durkheim, clearly owe Robertson Smith credit for opening this avenue of investigation. He summarized the position this way: "religion did not exist for the saving of souls but for the preservation and welfare of society."

Totemism was another important concept for Robertson Smith. Following, to some extent, the ideas of his friend J. F. McLennan, namely the thesis about totemism being a universal stage of human society, Robertson Smith suggested that totemism was the earliest and most basic form of religion and that sacrifice was the primary ritual associated with it. He sketched the following scenario. The first notions of deity were local gods as opposed to abstract celestial beings. They were beings fixed to different spheres of nature—plants, animals, and other objects—and as communities of people settled around particular places (in the territories of specific animals, for example), they began to understand themselves as descendants of the gods. "Primitive men" believed, Robertson Smith claimed, that members of their family, particular gods, and certain animals (primarily) are of "one stock." They share a kinship relationship so that the totem, the certain animal (plant, object, etc.) a community or family worships, is treated as an ancestor, ultimately the original progenitor for everyone in the community. Religion, then, was originally a set of practices, and, secondarily, beliefs, where kinship groups maintain a positive relationship with a superhuman being understood to be the source of the social group and its values, and understood to be present in the material form of a specific species or class of objects.

Ordinarily, each totemic group respects actual examples of its totem and refrains from killing these material representations of the god. They are "sacred animals." But when things go wrong (e.g., famines, floods, and other disasters affecting the group), members of the group feel separated from their god, and we have, according to Robertson Smith, the original basis for sacrifice—a repair to this separation, this now flawed relationship between the god and its people. Sacrifice was a means of seeking a re-union with the god. This is accomplished by holding a special occasion where the totem is eaten. Since, Robertson Smith continued, "according to antique ideas," those who eat together "cement and seal a mystic unity with one another," this ritual killing and eating of the totem constitutes a "communion between the god and his worshippers." Sacrifice is essentially a kinship meal shared with a god. Fundamentally, originally, it is a communion.

The diversity of sacrificial phenomena Robertson Smith explains by invoking an evolutionary scheme. At first, during sacrificial rituals, the entire community consumes the whole victim, eating the meat, drinking the blood, and so forth. Gradually, as the victim came to be considered "too powerful to be eaten" and different degrees of "holiness" were attributed to different segments of society, religious specialists (priests) alone would eat the sacrificial animal while its blood (or other parts) would be sprinkled on the people, and later on the god's altar. Finally, with the development of a more abstract celestial god, the sacrifice involved destroying the entire victim in a holocaust. No one eats, for all of the sacrificial offering goes to the god in the form of smoke. In all these cases, however, the significance of sacrifice remains the same for Robertson Smith; it is an act of communion between a social group and a superhuman being.

Still, there are well-known Biblical examples of sacrifice that appear to endorse the understanding of "sacrifice as gift" and which have little to do with a desire to commune with a deity. Recognizing this, Robertson Smith argued that the notion of sacrifice as a gift, as a tribute to the god, is in fact a later development and therefore, contrary to Tylor, is not original. "Sin-offerings," feelings of guilt, attempts at atonement, the sense of loss that often accompanies piacular offerings, and the "honorific" sacrifices that may be performed on a regular basis—these are all derived from the original form of sacrifice as a communion meal. With the rise of agriculture (and a notion that the god deserves the "first fruit"), the domestication of animals (ready replacements for totems) and a new notion of personal property (as opposed to collective property which was "owned" by the god in the first place), gift sacrifices, according to Robertson Smith, appeared. When the notion of a gift is present in a sacrificial setting, it should not be seen as the governing or original feature.

In the following selection, from *The Religion of the Semites* (1889), we find Robertson Smith's response to the "gift-theory" of sacrifice that prevailed before him. Throughout, there are references to the complex theory of sacrifice he developed earlier in his book (and summarized here). With Robertson Smith's "communion theory" of sacrifice, we have the next major contribution to the history of attempts to understand sacrificial phenomena. Despite the most common criticism leveled against him, that there is little evidence that all religions passed through a totemic stage, his is a lasting contribution with wide influence even today.

# From *The Religion of the Semites:*
# *The Fundamental Institutions*

I N CONNECTION with the later Semitic sacrifices, fire is employed for two purposes, apparently quite independent of one another. Its ordinary use is upon the altar, where it serves to sublimate, and so to convey to deities of an

---

William Robertson Smith, *The Religion of the Semites: The Fundamental Institutions* (London: A. and C. Black, 1894), pages 338–418, 439–40. Reprinted with the permission of A. and C. Black.

ethereal nature, gifts of solid flesh, which are regarded as the food of the gods. But in certain Hebrew piacula the sacrificial flesh is burned without the camp, and is not regarded as the food of the gods. The parts of the victim which in the highest form of piacula are burned outside the camp are the same which in lower forms of the sin-offering were eaten by the priests as representatives of the worshippers, or which in ordinary sacrifices would have been eaten by the worshippers themselves. Here, therefore, the fire seems to play the same part that is assigned to it under the role that, if an ordinary sacrifice is not eaten up within one or two days, the remnant must be burned. All sacrificial flesh is holy, and must be dealt with according to fixed ritual rules, one of which is that it must not be allowed to putrefy. Ordinary sacrificial flesh may be either eaten or burned, but sin-offerings are too holy to be eaten except by the priests, and in certain cases are too holy to be eaten even by them, and therefore must be burned, not as a way of conveying them to the deity, but simply as a way of fitly disposing of them.

It is commonly supposed that the first use of fire was upon the altar, and that the burning outside the camp is a later invention, expressing the idea that, in the case of a sacrifice for sin, the deity does not desire a material gift, but only the death of the offender. The ritual of the Hebrew sin-offering lends itself to such an interpretation readily enough, but it is impossible to believe that its origin is to be explained on any such view. If the sin-offering is merely a symbolical representation of a penal execution, why is the flesh of the victim holy in the first degree? and why are the blood and fat offered upon the altar? But it is unnecessary to press these minor objections to the common view, which is refuted more conclusively by a series of facts that have come before us in the course of the last lecture. There is a variety of evidence that fire was applied to sacrifices, or to parts of sacrifices, as an alternative to their consumption by the worshippers, before the altar became a hearth, and before it came to be thought that what was burned was conveyed, as etherealised food, to the deity. The Hebrew piacula that were burned outside the camp represent an older form of ritual than the holocaust on the altar, and the thing that really needs explanation is the origin of the latter.

Originally all sacrifices were eaten up by the worshippers. By and by certain portions of ordinary sacrifices, and the whole flesh of extraordinary sacrifices, ceased to be eaten. What was not eaten was burned, and in process of time it came to be burned on the altar and regarded as made over to the god. Exactly the same change took place with the sacrificial blood, except that here there is no use of fire. In the oldest sacrifices the blood was drunk by the worshippers, and after it ceased to be drunk it was all poured out at the altar. The tendency evidently was to convey directly to the godhead every portion of a sacrifice that was not consumed by the worshipper; but how did this tendency arise?

I daresay that some of you will be inclined to say that I am making a difficulty of a matter that needs no explanation. Is it not obvious that a sacrifice is a consecrated thing, that consecrated things belong to the god, and that the altar is their proper place? No doubt this seems to be obvious, but it is precisely the things that seem obvious which in a subject like ours require the most careful scrutiny. You say that consecrated things belong to the god, but we saw long ago that this is not the primitive idea of holiness. A holy thing is taboo, i.e., man's contact with it and use of it are subject to certain restrictions, but this idea does not in early society rest on the belief that it is the property of the gods. Again, you say that a sacrifice is a consecrated thing, but what do you mean by this? If you mean that the victim became holy by being selected for sacrifice and presented at the altar, you have not correctly apprehended the nature of the oldest rites. For in them the victim was naturally holy, not in virtue of its sacrificial destination, but because it was an animal of holy kind. So long as the natural holiness of certain animal species was a living element in popular faith, it was by no means obvious that holy things belong to the god, and should find their ultimate destination at the altar.

In later heathenism the conception of holy kinds and the old ideas of taboo generally had become obsolete, and the ritual observances founded upon them were no longer understood. And, on the other hand, the comparatively modern idea of property had taken shape, and began to play a leading part both in religion and in social life. The victim was no longer a naturally sacred thing, over which man had very limited rights and which he was required to treat as a useful friend rather than a chattel, but was drawn from the absolute property of the worshipper, of which he had a right to dispose as he pleased. Before its presentation the victim was a common thing, and it was only by being selected for sacrifice that it became holy. If, therefore, by presenting his sheep or ox at the altar, the owner lost the right to eat or sell its flesh, the explanation could no longer be sought in any other way than by the assumption that he had sur- rendered his right of property to another party, viz. to the god. Consecration was interpreted to mean a gift of man's property to the god, and everything that was withdrawn by consecration from the free use of man was conceived to have changed its owner. The blood and fat of ordinary sacrifices, or the whole flesh in the case of the holocaust, were withdrawn from human use; it was held, therefore, that they had become the property of the god, and were reserved for his use. This being so, it was inevitable that the burning of the flesh and fat should come to be regarded as a method of conveying them to the god; and as soon as this conclusion was drawn, the way was open for the introduction of the modern practice, in which the burning took place on the altar. The transformation of the altar into the hearth, on which the sacrificial flesh was consumed, marks the final establishment of a new view of holiness, based on the doctrine of property, in which the inviolability of holy things is no longer made to rest on their intrinsic supernatural quality, but upon their appropriation to the use and service of the gods. The success of this new view is not surprising, for in every department of early society we find that as soon as the notion of property, and of transfers of property from one person to another, gets firm footing, it begins to swallow up all earlier formulas for the relations of persons and things. But the adaptation of old institutions to new ideas can seldom be effected without leaving internal contradictions between the old and the new, which ultimately bring about the complete dissolution of the incongruous system. The new wine bursts the old bottles, and the new patch tears the old garment asunder.

In the case of ordinary sacrifices, the theory that holy things are the property of the deity, and that the consecration of things naturally common implies a gift from man to his god, was carried out with little difficulty. It was understood that at the altar the whole victim is made over to the deity and accepted by him, but that the main part of the flesh is returned to the worshipper, to be eaten sacrificially as a holy thing at the table of the god. This explanation went well enough with the conception of the deity as a king or great lord, whose temple was the court at which he sat to receive the homage of his subjects and tenants, and to entertain them with princely hospitality. But it did not satisfactorily account for the most characteristic feature in sacrifice, the application of the blood to the altar, and the burning of the fat on the sacred hearth. For these, according to the received interpretation, were the food of the deity; and so it appeared that the god was dependent on man for his daily nourishment, although, on the other hand, all the good things that man enjoyed he owed to the gift and favour of his god. This is the weak point in the current view of sacrifice which roused the indignation of the author of Psalm 1, and afforded so much merriment to later satirists like Lucian. The difficulty might be explained away by spiritualising interpretation, which treated the material altar gift as a mere symbol, and urged that the true value of the offering lay in the homage of the worshipper's heart, expressed in the traditional oblation. But the religion of the masses never took so subtle a view as this, and to the majority of the worshippers even in Israel, before the exile, the dominant idea in the ritual was that the material oblation afforded a physical satisfaction to the god, and that copious offerings were an infallible means of keeping him in good humour. So long as sacrifice was exclusively or mainly a social service, performed by the community, the crassness of this conception found its counterpoise in the ideas of religious fellowship that have been expounded in Lecture VII.[1] But in private sacrifice there was little or nothing to raise the transaction above the level of a mere bargain, in which no ethical consideration was involved, but the good understanding between the worshipper and his god was maintained by reciprocal friendly offices of a purely material kind. This superficial view of religion served very well in times of prosperity, but it could not stand the strain of serious and prolonged adversity, when it became plain that religion had to reckon with the sustained displeasure of the gods. In such circumstances men were forced to conclude that it was useless to attempt to appease the divine wrath by gifts of things which the gods, as lords of the earth, already possessed in abundance. It was not only Jehovah who could say, "I will take no bullock out of thy house, nor he-goats from thy folds; for every beast of the forest is Mine, and the cattle on a thousand hills." The Baalim too were in their way lords of nature, and even from the standpoint of heathenism it was absurd to suppose that they were really dependent on the tribute of their worshippers. In short, the gift-theory of sacrifice was not enough to account for the rule that sacrifice is the sole and sufficient form of every act of worship, even in religions which had not realised, with the Hebrew prophets, that what the true God requires of His worshippers is not a material oblation, but "to do justice, and love mercy, and walk humbly with thy God."

If the theory of sacrifice as a gift or tribute, taken from man's property and conveyed to the deity, was inadequate even as applied to ordinary oblations, it was evidently still more inadequate as applied to the holocaust, and especially to human sacrifice. It is commonly supposed that the holocaust was more powerful than ordinary sacrifices, because the gift to the god was greater. But even in ordinary sacrifices the whole victim was consecrated and made over to the god; only in the holocaust the god kept everything to himself, while in ordinary sacrifices he invited the worshipper to dine with him. It does not appear that there is any good reason, on the doctrine of sacrificial tribute, why this difference should be to the advantage of the holocaust. In the case of human sacrifices the gift-theory led to results which were not only absurd but revolting—absurd, since it does not follow that because a man's firstborn son is dearer to himself than all his wealth, the life of that son is the most valuable gift that he can offer to his god; and revolting, when it came to be supposed that the sacrifice of children as fire-offerings was a gift of food to a deity who delighted in human flesh.[2] So detestable a view of the nature of the gods cannot fairly be said to correspond to the general character of the old Semitic religions, which ought to be judged of by the ordinary forms of worship and not by exceptional rites. If the gods had been habitually conceived as cannibal monsters, the general type of ritual would have been gloomy and timorous, whereas really it was full of joyous and careless confidence. I conclude, therefore, that the child-devouring King of the later Moloch-worship owes his cannibal attributes, not to the fundamental principles of Semitic religion, but to false logic, straining the gift-theory of sacrifice to cover rites to which it had no legitimate application. And this conclusion is justified when we find that, though human sacrifices were not unknown in older times, the ancient ritual was to burn them without the camp—a clear proof that their flesh was not originally regarded as a food-offering to the deity.[3]

On the whole, then, the introduction of ideas of property into the relations between men and their gods seems to have been one of the most fatal aberrations in the development of ancient religion. In the beginnings of human thought, the natural and the supernatural, the material and the spiritual, were confounded, and this confusion gave rise to the old notion of holiness, which turned on the idea that supernatural influences emanated, like an infection, from certain material things. It was necessary to human progress that this crude conception should be superseded, and at first sight we are disposed to see nothing but good in the introduction of the notion that holy things are forbidden to man because they are reserved for the use of the gods, and that the danger associated with illegitimate invasion of them is not due to any deadly supernatural influence, directly proceeding from the holy object, but to the wrath of a personal god, who will not suffer his property to be tampered with. In one direction this modification was undoubtedly beneficial, for the vague dread of the unknown supernatural, which in savage society is so strong that it paralyses progress of every kind, and turns man aside from his legitimate task of subduing nature to his use, receives a fatal blow as soon as all supernatural processes are referred to the will and powers of known deities, whose converse with man is guided by fixed laws. But it was in the last degree unfortunate that these fixed laws were taken to be largely based on the principle of property; for the notion of property materialises everything that it touches, and its introduction into religion made it impossible to rise to spiritual conceptions of the deity and his relations to man on the basis of traditional religion. On the other hand, the more ancient idea of living communion between the god and his worshippers, which fell more and more into the background under the theory of sacrificial gifts, contained an element of permanent truth wrapped up in a very crude embodiment, and to it therefore all the efforts of ancient heathenism towards a better way of converse with the divine powers attach themselves, taking hold of those forms and features of sacrifice which evidently involved something more than the mere presentation to the deity of a material tribute. And as the need for something more than the ordinary altar gifts supplied was not habitually present to men's minds, but forced itself upon them in grave crises of life, and particularly in times of danger, when the god seemed to be angry with his people, or when at any rate it was of importance to make sure that he was not angry, all the aspects of worship that go beyond the payment of gifts and tribute came to be looked upon as having a special atoning character, that is, as being directed not so much to maintain a good understanding with the deity, as to renew it when it was interrupted.

When the idea of atonement is taken in this very general form, there is obviously no sharp line between atoning and ordinary sacrifices; for in ordinary life the means that are used to keep a man in good humour will often suffice to restore him to good humour, if they are sedulously employed. On this analogy a mere gift, presented at a suitable moment, or of greater value than usual, was often thought sufficient to appease the divine wrath; a general atoning force was ascribed to all sacrifices, and the value of special piacula was often estimated simply by the consideration that they cost the worshipper more than an everyday offering. We have seen that even human sacrifices were sometimes considered from this point of view; and in general the idea that every offence against the deity can be appraised, and made good by a payment of a certain value, was not inconsistent with the principles of ancient law, which deals with offences against persons on the doctrine of retaliation, but admits to an almost unlimited extent the doctrine that the injured party may waive his right of retaliation in consideration of a payment by the offender. But it is not the doctrine of ancient law that an injured party can be compelled to accept material compensation for an offence; and therefore, even on ordinary human analogies, no religious system could be regarded as complete which had not more powerful means of conjuring the divine displeasure than were afforded by the mere offer of a gift or payment. In point of fact, all ancient religions had sacrificial ceremonies of this more powerful kind, in which the notion of pleasing the god by a gift either found no expression at all, or evidently did not exhaust the significance of the ritual; and these are the sacrifices to which the distinctive name of *piacula* is properly applied.

It is sometimes supposed that special piacula did not exist in the older Semitic religions, and were invented for the first time when the gift-theory of sacrifice began to break down. But this supposition is incredible in itself, and is not consistent with the historical evidence. It is incredible that a gift should have been the oldest known way of reconciling an offended god, for in ordinary life atonement by fine came in at a relatively late date, and never entirely superseded the *lex talionis*; and it is certain, from what we have learned by observing the old form of piacular holocausts, that these sacrifices were not originally regarded as payments to the god, but arose on quite different lines, as an independent development of the primitive sacrifice of communion, whose atoning efficacy rested on the persuasion that those in whose veins the same life-blood circulates cannot be other than friends, bound to serve each other in all the offices of brotherhood.

It has appeared in the course of our inquiry that two kinds of sacrifice, which present features inconsistent with the gift-theory, continued to be practised by the ancient Semites; and to both kinds there was ascribed a special efficacy in persuading or constraining the favour of the gods. The first kind is the mystic sacrifice, represented by a small class of exceptional rites, in which the victim was drawn from some species of animals that retained even in modern times their ancient repute of natural holiness. Sacrifices of this sort could never fall under the gift-theory, for creatures naturally holy are not man's property, but, so far as they have an owner at all, are the property of the god. The significance attached to these sacrifices and the nature of their peculiar efficacy, has already received sufficient attention. The other kind of offering which was thought of as something more than a mere gift, consisted of holocausts and other sacrifices, whose flesh was not conveyed to the god and eaten at his table, but burned without the camp, or buried, or cast away in a desert place. This kind of service we have already studied from a formal point of view, considering the way in which its ritual was differentiated from the old communion sacrifice, and also the way in which most sacrifices of the kind were ultimately brought under the class of sacrificial gifts, by the introduction of the practice of burning the flesh on the altar or burying it in the *ghabghab*; but we have not yet considered how these successive modifications of ritual were interpreted and made to fit into the general progress of social institutions and ideas. Some notice of this side of the subject is necessary to complete our study of the principles of ancient sacrifice, and to it the remainder of the present lecture will be devoted.

It must, however, be remembered that in ancient religion there was no authoritative interpretation of ritual. It was imperative that certain things should be done, but every man was free to put his own meaning on what was done. Now the more complicated ritual prestations, to which the elaborate piacular services of later times must be reckoned, were not forms invented, once for all, to express a definite system of ideas, but natural growths, which were slowly developed through many centuries, and in their final form bore the imprint of a variety of influences, to which they had been subjected from age to age under the changing conditions of human life and social order. Every rite therefore lent itself to more than one interpretation, according as this or that aspect of it was seized upon as the key to its meaning. Under such circumstances we must not attempt to fix a definite interpretation on any of the developments of ancient ritual; all that we can hope to do is to trace in the ceremonial the influence of successive phases of thought, the presence of which is attested to us by other movements in the structure of ancient society, or conversely to show how features in ritual, of which the historical origin had been forgotten, were accounted for on more modern principles, and used to give support to new ideas that were struggling for practical recognition.

From the analysis of the ritual of holocausts and other piacula given in the last two lectures, it appears that through all the varieties of atoning ceremony there runs a common principle: the victim is sacrosanct, and the peculiar value of the ceremony lies in the operation performed on its life, whether that life is merely conveyed to the god on the altar, or is also applied to the worshippers by the sprinkling of the blood, or some other lustral ceremony. Both these features are nothing more than inheritances from the most primitive form of sacramental communion; and in the oldest sacrifices their meaning is perfectly transparent and unambiguous, for the ritual exactly corresponds with the primitive ideas, that holiness means kinship to the worshippers and their god, that all sacred relations and all moral obligations depend on physical unity of life, and that unity of physical life can be created or reinforced by common participation in living flesh and blood. At this earliest stage the atoning force of sacrifice is purely physical, and consists in the reintegration of the congenital physical bond of kinship, on which the good understanding between the god and his worshippers ultimately rests. But in the later stage of religion, in which sacrifices of sacrosanct victims and purificatory offerings are exceptional rites, these antique ideas were no longer intelligible; and in ordinary sacrifices those features of the old ritual were dropped or modified which gave expression to obsolete notions, and implied a physical transfer of holy life from the victim to the worshippers. Here, therefore, the question arises why that which had ceased to be intelligible was still preserved in a peculiar class of sacrifices. The obvious answer is that it was preserved by the force of use and precedent.

It is common, in discussions of the significance of piacular ritual, to begin with the consideration that piacula are atonements for sin, and to assume that the ritual was devised with a view to the purchase of divine forgiveness. But this is to take the thing by the wrong handle. The characteristic features in piacular sacrifice are not the invention of a later age, in which the sense of sin and divine wrath was strong, but are features carried over from a very primitive type of religion, in which the sense of sin, in any proper sense of the word, did not exist at all, and the whole object of ritual was to maintain the bond of physical holiness that kept the religious community together. What we have to explain is not the origin of the sacrificial forms that later ages called piacular, but the way in which the old type of sacrifice came to branch off into two distinct types. And here we must consider that, even in tolerably advanced societies, the distinction between piacular and ordinary offerings long continued to be mainly one of ritual, and that the former were not so much sacrifices for sin, as sacrifices in which the ceremonial forms, observed at the altar, continued to express the original idea that the victim's life was sacrosanct, and in some way cognate to the life of the god and his worshippers. Thus, among the Hebrews of the pre-prophetic period, it certainly appears that a peculiar potency was assigned to holocausts and other exceptional sacrifices, as a means of conjuring the divine displeasure; but a certain atoning force was ascribed to all sacrifices; and, on the other hand, sacrifices of piacular form and force were offered on many occasions when we cannot suppose the sense of sin or of divine anger to have been present in any extraordinary degree. For example, it was the custom to open a campaign with a burnt-offering, which in old Israel was the most solemn piaculum; but this did not imply any feeling that war was a divine judgment and a sign of the anger of Jehovah.[4] It appears rather that the sacrifice was properly the consecration of the warriors; for the Hebrew phrase for opening war is "to consecrate war" ( קדש מלחמה ), and warriors are consecrated persons, subject to special taboos.[5] Here, therefore, it lies near at hand to suppose that the holocaust is simply the modification, on lines which have been already explained, of an ancient form of sacramental communion.[6] The Greeks in like manner commenced their wars with piacular sacrifices of the most solemn kind; indeed, according to Phylarchus,[7] a human victim was at one time customary, which is certainly not true for historical times; but I have no doubt that the statement of Phylarchus corresponds to a wide-spread tradition such as might easily arise if the offerings made on occasion of war were of the exceptional and sacrosanct character with which legends of actual human sacrifice are so frequently associated.[8] One illustration of Phylarchus's statement will occur to everyone, viz. the sacrifice of Iphigenia; and here it is to be noted that, while all forms of the legend are agreed that Agamemnon must have committed some deadly sin before so terrible an offering was required of him, there is no agreement as to what his sin was. It is not therefore unreasonable to think that in the original story the piaculum was simply the ordinary preliminary to a campaign, and that later ages could not understand why such a sacrifice should be made, except to atone for mortal guilt.[9]

If, now, it be asked why the ordinary preliminary to a campaign was a sacrifice of the exceptionally solemn kind which in later times was deemed to have a special reference to sin, the answer must be that the ritual was fixed by immemorial precedent, going back to the time when all sacrifices were of the sacramental type, and involved the shedding of a sacrosanct life. At that time every sacrifice was an awful mystery, and not to be performed except on great occasions, when it was most necessary that the bond of kindred obligation between every member of the community, divine and human, should be as strong and fresh as possible. The outbreak of war was plainly such an occasion, and it is no hazardous conjecture that the rule of commencing a campaign with sacrifice dates from the most primitive times.[10] Accordingly the ceremonial to be observed in sacrifice on such an occasion would be protected by well-established tradition, and the victim would continue to be treated at the altar with all the old ritual forms which implied that its blood was holy and akin to man's, long after the general sanctity of all animals of sacrificial kind had ceased to be acknowledged in daily life. And in the same way sacrifices of exceptional form, in which the victim was treated as a human being, or its blood was applied in a primitive ceremonial to the persons of the worshippers, or its flesh was regarded as too sacred to be eaten, would continue to be offered on all occasions which were marked out as demanding a sacrifice, by some very ancient rule, dating from the time when the natural sanctity of sacrificial kinds was still recognised. In such cases the ancient ceremonial would be protected by immemorial custom; while, on the other hand, there would be nothing to prevent a more modern type of ritual from coming into use on occasions for which there was no ancient sacrificial precedent, e.g., on such occasions as arose for the first time under the conditions of agricultural life, when the old sanctity of domestic animals was very much broken down. Sacrifices were vastly more frequent with the agricultural than with the pastoral nations of antiquity, but, among the older agricultural Semites, the occasions that called for sacrifices of exceptional or piacular form were not numerous, and may fairly be regarded as corresponding in the main to the rare occasions for which the death of a victim was already prescribed by the rules of their nomadic ancestors.

This, it may be said, is no more than a hypothesis, but it satisfies the conditions of a legitimate hypothesis, by postulating the operation of no unknown or uncertain cause, but only of that force of precedent which in all times has been so strong to keep alive religious forms of which the original meaning is lost. And in certain cases, at any rate, it is very evident that rites of exceptional form, which later ages generally connected with ideas of sin and atonement, were merely the modern representatives of primitive sacraments, kept up through sheer force of habit, without any deeper meaning corresponding to the peculiar solemnity of their form. Thus the annual piacula that were celebrated, with exceptional rites, by most nations of antiquity, are not necessarily to be regarded as having their first origin in a growing sense of sin or fear of divine wrath—although these reasons operated in later times to multiply such acts of service and increase the importance attached to them—but are often nothing more than survivals of ancient annual sacrifices of communion in the body and blood of a sacred animal. For in some of these rites, as we have seen in Lecture VIII,[11] the form of communion in flesh too holy to be eaten except in a sacred mystery is retained; and where this is not the case, there is at least some feature in the annual piaculum which reveals its connection with the oldest type of sacrifice. It is a mistake to suppose that annual religious feasts date only from the beginnings of agricultural life, with its yearly round of seedtime and harvest; for in all parts of the world annual sacraments are found, and that not merely among pastoral races, but even in rude hunting tribes that have not emerged from the totem stage.[12] And though some of these totem sacraments involve actual communion in the flesh and blood of the sacred animal, the commoner case, even in this primitive stage of society, is that the theanthropic victim is deemed too holy to be eaten, and therefore, as in the majority of Semitic piacula, is burned, buried, or cast into a stream.[13] It is certainly illegitimate to connect these very primitive piacula with any explicit ideas of sin and forgiveness; they have their origin in a purely naturalistic conception of holiness, and mean nothing more than that the mystic unity of life in the religious community is liable to wear out, and must be revived and strengthened from time to time.

Among the annual piacula of the more advanced Semites which, though they are not mystical sacrifices of an "unclean" animal, yet bear on their face the marks of extreme antiquity, the first place belongs to the Hebrew Passover, held in the spring month Nisan, where the primitive character of the offering appears not only from the details of the ritual,[14] but from the coincidence of its season with that of the Arabian sacrifices in the month Rajab. Similarly in Cyprus, on the first of April, a sheep was offered to Astarte (Aphrodite) with ritual of a character evidently piacular.[15] At Hierapolis, in like manner, the chief feast of the year was the vernal ceremony of the Pyre, in which animals were burned alive—an antique ritual which has been illustrated in the last lecture. And again, among the Harranians, the first half of Nisan was marked by a series of exceptional sacrifices of piacular colour.[16]

So remarkable a concurrence in the season of the great annual piacular rites of Semitic communities leaves little doubt as to the extreme antiquity of the institution. Otherwise the season of the annual piacula is not material to our present purpose, except in so far as its coincidence with the yeaning time appears to be connected with the frequent use of sucking lambs and other very young animals as piacular victims. This point, however, seems to be of some importance as an indirect evidence of the antiquity of annual piacula. The reason often given for the sacrifice of very young animals, that a man thus got rid of a sacred obligation at the very cheapest rate, is not one that can be seriously maintained; while, on the other hand, the analogy of infanticide, which in many savage countries is not regarded as murder if it be performed immediately after birth, makes it very intelligible that, in those primitive times when a domestic animal had a life as sacred as that of a tribesman, new-born calves or lambs should be selected for sacrifice. The selection of an annual season of sacrifice coincident with the yeaning time may therefore be plausibly referred to the time when sacrificial slaughter was still a rare and awful event, involving responsibilities which the worshippers were anxious to reduce, by every device, within the narrowest possible limits.

The point which I took a little time ago, that sacrifices of piacular form are not necessarily associated with a sense of sin, comes out very clearly in the case of annual piacula. Among the Hebrews, under the Law, the annual expiation on the great Day of Atonement was directed to cleanse the people from all their sins,[17] i.e., according to the Mishnic interpretation, to purge away the guilt of all sins, committed during the year, that had not been already expiated by penitence, or by the special piacula appointed for particular offences;[18] but there is little trace of any such view in connection with the annual piacula of the heathen Semites; and even in the Old Testament this interpretation appears to be modern. The Day of Atonement is a much less ancient institution than the Passover; and in the Passover, though the sprinkled blood has a protecting efficacy, the law prescribes no forms of humiliation and contrition, such as are enjoined for the more modern rite. Again, the prophet Ezekiel, whose sketch of a legislation for Israel, on its restoration from captivity, is older than the law of Leviticus, does indeed provide for two annual atoning ceremonies, in the first and in the seventh month;[19] but the point of these ceremonies lies in an elaborate application of the blood to various parts of the temple, with the object of "reconciling the house." This reference of the sacrifice reappears also in Lev. xvi; the sprinkling of the blood on the great Day of Atonement "cleanses the altar, and makes it holy from all the uncleanness of the children of Israel."[20] Here an older and merely physical conception of the ritual breaks through, which has nothing to do with the forgiveness of sin; for uncleanness in the Levitical ritual is not an ethical conception. It seems that the holiness of the altar is liable to be impaired, and requires to be annually refreshed by an application of holy blood—a conception which it would be hard to justify from the higher teaching of the Old Testament, but which is perfectly intelligible as an inheritance from primitive ideas about sacrifice, in which the altar-idol on its part, as well as the worshippers on theirs, is periodically re-consecrated by the sprinkling of holy (i.e., kindred) blood, in order that the life-bond between the god it represents and his kindred worshippers may be kept fresh. This is the ultimate meaning of the yearly sprinkling with a tribesman's blood, which, as Theophrastus tells us, was demanded by so many altars of antiquity,[21] and also of the yearly sprinkling where the victim was not a man, but a sacrosanct or theanthropic animal.

Of all this, however, the later ages of antique religion understood no more than that ancient tradition prescribed certain annual rites of peculiar and sometimes of awful character as indispensable to the maintenance of normal relations between the gods and the worshipping community. The neglect of these rites, it was believed, entailed the wrath of the gods; the Carthaginians, for example, in their distress in the war with Agathocles, believed that Cronus was angry because slaves had been substituted for the noble boys that were his proper victims. But it does not appear that they looked behind this and concluded that the god could not demand periodical sacrifices of such price except as an atonement for the ever-recurring sins of the nation. Ancient religion was so entirely ruled by precedent, that men did not deem it necessary to have an adequate moral explanation even of the most exorbitant demands of traditional ritual; they were content to explain them by some legend that told how the ritual first came to be set up. Thus Diodorus, when he mentions the Carthaginian human sacrifices, suggests the probability that they preserve the memory of Cronus devouring his children;[22] and the Phoenicians themselves appear, from the fragments of Philo Byblius, to have traced back the custom of sacrificing children to a precedent set by the God El, whom the Greeks identify with Cronus.[23]

Indeed, among the Semites the most current view of annual piacula seems to have been that they commemorate a divine tragedy—the death of some god or goddess.[24] The origin of such myths is easily explained from the nature of the ritual. Originally the death of the god was nothing else than the death of the theanthropic victim; but when this ceased to be understood it was thought that the piacular sacrifice represented an historical tragedy in which the god was killed. Thus at Laodicea the annual sacrifice of a deer in lieu of a maiden, which was offered to the goddess of the city, is associated with a legend that the goddess was a maiden who had been sacrificed to consecrate the foundation of the town, and was thenceforth worshipped as its Fortune, like

Dido at Carthage; it was therefore the death of the goddess herself that was annually renewed in the piacular rite. The same explanation applies to such scenic representations as were spoken of in the last lecture,[25] where the deity is annually burned in effigy, since the substitution of an effigy for a human sacrifice, or for a victim representing a god, is very common in antique and barbarous religions.[26] And in like manner the annual mourning for Tammuz or Adonis, which supplies the closest parallel in point of form to the fasting and humiliation on the Hebrew Day of Atonement, is the scenic commemoration of a divine tragedy in which the worshippers take part with appropriate wailing and lamentation. That the rites of the Semitic Adonia[27] were connected with a great sacrificial act, may safely be inferred on general principles; and that the sacrifice was piacular in form, follows from Lucian's account of the ritual of Byblus: "When they have done wailing they first burn a sacrifice[28] to Adonis as to one dead"—the offering therefore was a holocaust as in other annual piacula, and probably corresponds to the annual sacrifice of swine on April 2, at Cyprus, which Joannes Lydus connects with the Adonis legend.[29]

The Adonia therefore seem to me to be only a special form of annual piaculum, in which the sacrifice has come to be overshadowed by its popular and dramatic accompaniments.[30] The legend, the exhibition of the dead god in effigy,[31] the formal act of wailing, which filled all the streets and was not confined to the sanctuary, took much greater hold of the imagination than the antique piaculum at the temple, and became one of the most deeply rooted parts of popular religion.[32] Late in the Middle Ages, in AD 1064 and again in 1204, the Arabic historian Ibn al-Athīr[33] records sporadic revivals, on a great scale, of the ancient lament for the dead god. In the former case a mysterious threat was circulated from Armenia to Chuzistan, that every town which did not lament the dead "king of the Jinn" should utterly perish; in the latter a fatal disease raged in the parts of Mosul and Irac, "and it was divulged that a woman of the Jinn called Umm 'Uncūd (Mother of the grape-cluster) had lost her son, and that everyone who would not make lamentation for him would fall a victim to the epidemic." In this case the form of the lamentation is recorded: "O Umm 'Uncūd, excuse us, 'Uncūd is dead, we knew it not."

It seems to me that one characteristic feature in these late observances is entirely true to the spirit of the old Semitic heathenism. The mourning is not a spontaneous expression of sympathy with the divine tragedy, but obligatory and enforced by fear of supernatural anger. And a chief object of the mourners is to disclaim responsibility for the god's death—a point which has already come before us in connection with theanthropic sacrifices, such as the "ox-murder at Athens."

When the original meaning of the theanthropic ritual was forgotten, and the death of the god was explained by legendary history as a thing of the far past, the obligatory mourning at the annual piaculum was continued by force of usage, and presumably gave rise to various speculations which can only be a matter of conjecture to us. But it is reasonable to suppose that ceremonies which were currently interpreted as the commemoration of a mythical tragedy could not suggest to the mass of the worshippers any ethical ideas transcending those embodied in the myth. The legends of the deaths of Semitic gods that have come down to us are singularly devoid of moral significance, and it is difficult to believe that they could excite any deeper feeling than a vague senti-mental sympathy, or a melancholy conviction that the gods themselves were not exempt from the universal law of suffering and death. And with the common crowd I apprehend that the main feeling involved was generally that which we have seen to survive in the latest manifestations of heathen sentiment—the feeling that a bereaved deity is an angry deity, who may strike blindly all round at those who are not careful to free themselves from the suspicion of blame.

Among the agricultural Semites, where the Baal was mainly worshipped as the giver of vegetative increase and the quickening spirit of vegetative life, the annual mourning for the dead god seems often to have been brought into relation to agriculture and the cycle of agricultural feasts. In the Baal religion all agricultural operations, but particularly the harvest and vintage, are neces-sarily viewed as in some degree trenching on the holy things of the god, and must be conducted with special religious precautions.[34] Thus among the Hebrews the spring piaculum of the Passover, which in its origin belongs to the pre-agricultural stage of Semitic society, was connected in the Pentateuchal system with the opening of the corn-harvest, and in like manner the great Day of Atonement precedes the vintage feast. Mr. Frazer has brought together a good deal of evidence connecting the Adonia—or rather certain forms of the Adonia[35]—with the corn-harvest; the death of the god being held to be annually repeated in the cutting of the divine grain.[36] Similarly the wailing for 'Uncūd, the divine Grape-cluster, seems to be the last survival of an old vintage piaculum. I can only touch on this point here, since the developments of religion connected with agriculture lie beyond the scope of the present volume. The dread of the worshippers, that the neglect of the usual ritual would be followed by disaster, is particularly intelligible if they regarded the necessary operations of agriculture as involving the violent extinction of a particle of divine life. Here, in fact, the horror attending the service is much the same as in the case of the original theanthropic sacrifice, only it is a holy fruit that suffers instead of a holy animal.

In the brighter days of Semitic heathenism, the annual celebration of the god's death hardly suggested any serious thought that was not presently drowned in an outburst of mirth saluting the resurrection of the Baal on the following morning; and in more distressful times, when the gloomier aspects of religion were those most in sympathy with the prevailing hopelessness of a decadent nation—such times as those in which Ezekiel found the women of Jerusalem mourning for Tammuz—the idea that the gods themselves were not exempt from the universal law of death, and had ordered this truth to be com-memorated in their temples by bloody, or even human sacrifices, could only favour the belief that religion was as cruel as the relentless march of adverse fate, and that man's life was ruled by powers that were not to be touched by love or pity, but, if they could be moved at all, would only be satisfied by the sacrifice of man's happiness and the surrender of his dearest treasures. The close psychological connection between sensuality and cruelty, which is familiar to students of the human mind, displays itself in ghastly fashion in the sterner aspects of Semitic heathenism; and the same sanctuaries which, in prosperous times, resounded with licentious mirth and carnal gaiety, were filled in times of distress with the cowardly lamentations of the worshippers, who to save their own lives were ready to give up everything they held dear, even to the sacrifice of a firstborn or only child.

On the whole the annual piacula of Semitic heathenism appear theatrical and unreal, when they are not cruel and repulsive. The stated occurrence of gloomy rites at fixed seasons, and without any direct relation to human conduct, gave the whole ceremony a mechanical character, and so made it inevitable that it should be either accepted as a mere scenic tragedy, whose meaning was summed up in a myth, or interpreted as a proof that the divine powers were never thoroughly reconciled to man, and only tolerated their worshippers in consideration of costly atonements constantly renewed. I apprehend that even in Israel the annual piacula, which were observed from an early date, had little or no share in the development of the higher sense of sin and responsibility which characterises the religion of the Old Testament. The Passover is a rite of the most primæval antiquity; and in the local cults, annual mournings, like the lamentation for Jephthah's daughter—which undoubtedly was connected with an annual sacrifice, like that which at Laodicea commem-orated the mythical death of the virgin goddess—had been yearly repeated from very ancient times. Yet, only after the exile, and then only by a sort of afterthought, which does not override the priestly idea that the annual atonement is above all a reconsecration of the altar and the sanctuary, do we find the annual piaculum of the Day of Atonement interpreted as a general atonement for the sins of Israel during the past year. In the older literature, when exceptional and piacular rites are interpreted as satisfactions for sin, the offence is always a definite one, and the piacular rite has not a stated and periodical character, but is directly addressed to the atonement of a particular sin or course of sinful life.

The conception of piacular rites as a satisfaction for sin appears to have arisen after the original sense of the theanthropic sacrifice of a kindred animal was forgotten, and mainly in connection with the view that the life of the victim was the equivalent of the life of a human member of the religious community. We have seen that when the victim was no longer regarded as naturally holy, and equally akin to the god and his worshippers, the ceremony of its death was still performed with solemn circumstances, not appropriate to the slaughter of a mere common beast. It was thus inevitable that the victim should be regarded either as a representative of the god, or as the representative of a tribesman, whose life was sacred to his fellows. The former interpretation predominated in the annual piacula of the Baal religions, but the latter was that naturally indicated in such atoning sacrifices as were offered on special emergencies and did not lend themselves to a mythical interpretation. For in old times the circumstances of the slaughter were those of a death which could only be justified by the consent, and even by the active participation, of the whole community, i.e., of the judicial execution of a kinsman.[37] In later times this rule was modified, and in ordinary sacrifices the victim was slain either by the offerer, or by professional slaughterers, who formed a class of inferior ministers at the greater sanctuaries.[38] But communal holocausts and piacula continued to be slain by the chief priests, or by the heads of the community or by their chosen representatives, so that the slaughter retained the character of a solemn public act.[39] Again, the feeling that the slaying involves a grave responsibility, and must be justified by divine permission, was expressed by the Arabs, even in ordinary slaughter, by the use of the *bismillah*, i.e., by the slaughterer striking the victim in the name of his god.[40] But in many piacula this feeling was carried much further, and care was taken to slay the victim without bloodshed, or to make believe that it had killed itself.[41] Certain holocausts, like those of the Pyre-festival at Hierapolis, were burned alive; and other piacula were simply pushed over a height, so that they might seem to kill themselves by their fall. This was done at Hierapolis, both with animals and with human victims; and, according to the Mishna, the Hebrew scapegoat was not allowed to go free in the wilderness, but was killed by being pushed over a precipice.[42] The same kind of sacrifice occurs in Egypt, in a rite which is possibly of Semitic origin,[43] and in Greece, in more than one case where the victims were human.[44]

· · · · · · · · · · · · · · · · · · · · · · · · · · · · · · · · · · · · · ·

On the whole it is apparent, from the somewhat tedious discussion which I have now brought to a close, that the various aspects in which atoning rites presented themselves to ancient worshippers have supplied a variety of religious images which passed into Christianity, and still have currency. Redemption, substitution, purification, atoning blood, the garment of righteousness, are all terms which in some sense go back to antique ritual. But in ancient religion all these terms are very vaguely defined; they indicate impressions produced on the mind of the worshipper by features of the ritual, rather than formulated ethico-dogmatical ideas; and the attempt to find in them anything as precise and definite as the notions attached to the same words by Christian theologians is altogether illegitimate. The one point that comes out clear and strong is that the fundamental idea of ancient sacrifice is sacramental communion, and that all atoning rites are ultimately to be regarded as owing their efficacy to a communication of divine life in the worshippers, and to the establishment or confirmation of a living bond between them and their god. In primitive ritual this conception is grasped in a merely physical and mechanical shape, as indeed, in primitive life, all spiritual and ethical ideas are still wrapped up in the husk of a material embodiment. To free the spiritual truth from the husk was the great task that lay before the ancient religions, if they were to maintain the right to continue to rule the minds of men. That some progress in this direction was made, especially in Israel, appears from our examination. But on the whole it is manifest that none of the ritual systems of antiquity was able by mere natural development to shake itself free from the congenital defect inherent in every attempt to embody spiritual truth in material forms. A ritual system must always remain materialistic, even if its materialism is disguised under the cloak of mysticism.

# Notes

1. *Supra,* p. 263 *sqq.*
2. Ezek. xvi. 20, xxiii. 37.
3. Compare the remarks on the sacrifice of the firstborn, *infra, Additional Note* E.
4. The burnt-offering at the opening of a campaign appears in Judg. vi. 20 (cf. ver. 26), xx. 26; 1 Sam. vii. 9, xiii. 10. In Judg. xi. 31 we have, instead of a sacrifice before the war, a vow to offer a holocaust on its successful termination. The view taken by the last redactor of the historical books (Judg., Sam., Kings), that the wars of Israel with its neighbours were always chastisements for sin, is not ancient; cf. Gen. xxvii. 29, xlix. 8; Num. xxiv. 24; Deut. xxxiii. 29.
5. Isa. xiii. 3; Jer. vi. 4, li. 28; Joel iv. [iii.] 9; Mic. iii. 5. See *supra,* p. 158, and *Additional Note* C.
6. I conjecture that the form of gathering warriors together by sending round portions of a victim that has been hewn into pieces (1 Sam. xi. 7; cf. Judg. xix. 29) had originally a sacramental sense, similar to that expressed by the covenant form in which the victim is cut in twain; cf. *Additional Note* H, and the Scythian custom noticed by Lucian, *Toxaris,* § 48. A covenant by hewing an ox into small pieces was also in use among the Molossians; Zenobius, ii. 83.
7. *Ap.* Porph., *De Abst.* ii. 56.
8. Even in the palmy days of Hellenic civilisation we find evidence of a deeply rooted belief in the potency of human sacrifice to ensure victory in war. So late as the time of Pelopidas, the propriety of such sacrifice was formally discussed, and upheld by historical as well as mythical precedents (Plutarch, *Pelopidas,* 21). But the historical precedents reduce themselves, on closer examination, to the single and wholly exceptional case of the sacrifice of three captives before the battle of Salamis. On the other hand, additions might easily be made to the list of legendary precedents, e.g., the case of Bombus (Zenobius, ii. 84).

9. The opening of a campaign appears also in Africa as one of the rare occasions that justify the slaughter of a victim from the tribal herds; see above, p. 297.

10. There is also some reason to think that in very ancient times a sacrifice was appointed to be offered after a victory. See *Additional Note* M, *Sacrifice by Victorious Warriors.*

11. *Supra,* p. 290 *sqq.*

12. For examples of annual sacraments by sacrifice of the totem, see Frazer, *Totemism,* p. 48, and *supra,* p. 295, note 2.

13. I apprehend that in most climates the vicissitudes of the seasons are certainly not less important to the savage huntsman or to the pastoral barbarian than to the more civilised tiller of the soil. From Doughty's account of the pastoral tribes of the Arabian desert, and also from what Agatharchides tells us of the herdsmen by the Red Sea, we perceive that in the purely pastoral life the seasons when pasture fails are annual periods of semi-starvation for man and beast. Among still ruder races, like the Australians, who have no domestic animals, the difference of the seasons is yet more painfully felt; so much so, indeed, that in some parts of Australia children are not born except at one season of the year; the annual changes of nature have impressed themselves on the life of man to a degree hardly conceivable to us. In pastoral Arabia domestic cattle habitually yean in the brief season of the spring pasture (Doughty, i. 429), and this would serve to fix an annual season of sacrifice. Camels calve in February and early March; Blunt, *Bed. Tribes,* ii. 166.

14. *Supra,* p. 344. Note also that the head and the inwards have to be eaten, i.e. the special seats of life (Ex. xii. 9).

15. Lydus, *De Mens.* iv. 45; cf. *Additional Note* G. The χώδιον marks the sacrifice as piacular, whether my conjecture χωδίῳ ἐσχεπασμένοι for χωδίῳ ἐσχεπασμένον is accepted or not.

16. *Fihrist,* p. 322. Traces of the sacredness of the month Nisan are found also at Palmyra (*Enc. Brit.* xviii. 199, note 2), and among the Nabatæans, as Berger has inferred from a study of the inscriptions of Madāïn Ṣāliḥ.

17. Lev. xvi. 30.

18. *Yoma,* viii. 8, 9.

19. Ezek. xlv. 19, 20 (LXX.).

20. Lev. xvi. 19; cf. ver. 33, where the atonement extends to the whole sanctuary.

21. Examples of annual human sacrifice in the Semitic field at Carthage, Porph., *De Abst.* ii. 27 (from Theophrastus), Pliny, *H. N.* xxxvi. 29; at Dumætha, or Duma, in Arabia, *De Abst.* ii. 56. At Laodicea in Syria the annual sacrifice of a deer was held to be a substitute for the more ancient sacrifice of a virgin. (See below, *Additional Note* G.)

22. Diod. xx. 14.

23. Euseb., *Præp. Ev.* i. 10. 21, 33. Thus it would seem that even the unenlightened Israelites addressed in Mic. vi. 7 had a profounder sense of sin than was current among the heathen Semites.

24. I have not noted any Semitic example of another type of explanatory legend of which there are various instances in Greece, viz. that the annual piaculum was appointed as the punishment of an ancient crime for which satisfaction had to be made from generation to generation: Pausan. ix. 8. 2 (at Potniæ), vii. 19 *sq.* (at Patræ in Achaia). In both cases, according to the legend, the sacrifice was originally human.

25. *Supra*, p. 364 *sqq.*
26. Thus the Romans substituted puppets of rushes or wool for human offerings in the Argea and the worship of Mania. In Mexico, again, human victims were habitually regarded as incarnations of the deity, but also paste images of the gods were made and eaten sacramentally.
27. I use this word as a convenient general term describing a particular type of ritual, without committing myself to the opinion that all rites of the type were in connection with the worship of the same god. It is not even certain that there was a god Adonis. What the Greeks took for a proper name is perhaps no more than a title, *Adon*, "lord," applicable to various deities, *CIL*. viii. 1211.
28. Καταγίζουσι; for the sense of the word compare Lucian, *De Luctu*, 19.
29. *Supra*, p. 290 *sq*. If this be so, the Cyprian Adonis was originally the Swine-god, and in this as in many other cases the sacred victim has been changed by false interpretation into the enemy of the god. Cf. Frazer, *The Golden Bough*, ii. 50.
30. In Greece, where the Adonia were no part of the State religion, the celebration seems to have been limited to these.
31. This is part of the genuine Semitic ritual, not merely Greek or Alexandrian; see Lampridius, *Heliog.* vii. : "Salambonam etiam omni planctu et iactatione Syriaci cultus exhibuit." As it is not disputed that Salambo or Salambas = צלם בעל, "the image of Baal," it is strange that scholars should have been misled by Hesychius and the *Etym. Magn.* into making Salambo a name of the Oriental Aphrodite.
32. *Dea Syria*, 6 (Byblus); Ammianus, xx. 9. 15 (Antioch).
33. Ed. Tornberg, x. 27; cf. Bar Hebræus, *Chron. Syr.* ed. Bedjan, p. 242.
34. *Supra*, p. 158.
35. The rites of Byblus cannot be connected either with vintage or harvest, for both of these fall in the dry season, and the Byblian god died when his sacred river was swollen with rain. Here the pre-agricultural spring piaculum seems to have retained its old place in the yearly religious cycle.
36. *The Golden Bough*, chap. iii. § 4. The evidence adduced by Mr. Frazer is not all applicable without limitation to the Semitic Adonia—Greek and Alexandrian forms of the mourning were probably coloured by Greek and Egyptian influences. The Semitic evidence points to Babylonia as the source of the Semitic corn piaculum; it is therefore worth noting that Bezold finds Tammuz and the following month Ab designated as the harvest months of N. Babylonia in the fifteenth century B.C. (*Tell el-Amarna Tablets*, Brit. Mus. 1892, p. xxix).
37. *Supra*, p. 284 *sq.*
38. In *CIS*. No. 86, the ministers of the temple include a class of slaughterers ( זבחם ), and so it was at Hierapolis (*Dea Syria*, xliii.). Among the Jews, at the second temple, the Levites often acted as slaughterers; but before the captivity the temple slaughterers were uncircumcised foreigners (Ezek. xliv. 6 *sqq.* ; cf. *O.T. in J. Ch.* 2nd ed., p. 260 *sqq.*).
39. Thus in the Old Testament we find young men as sacrificers in Ex. xxiv. 5; the elders in Lev. iv. 15, Deut. xxi. 4; Aaron in Lev. xvi. 15; cf. *Yoma*, iv. 3. All sacrifices, except the last named, might, according to the Rabbins, be killed by any Israelite.

    The choice of "young men," or rather "lads," as sacrificers in Ex. xxiv is curiously analogous to the choice of lads as executioners. Judg. viii. 20 is not an isolated case, for Nilus also (p. 67) says that the Saracens charged lads with the execution of their captives.

40. The same feeling is expressed in Lev. xvii. 11; Gen. viii. 3 *sqq.*
41. The blood that calls for vengeance is blood that falls on the ground (Gen. iv. 10). Hence blood to which vengeance is refused is said to be trodden under foot (Ibn Hishām, p. 79, *ult.,* p. 861, 1. 5), and forgotten blood is covered by the earth (Job xvi. 18). And so we often find the idea that a death in which no blood is shed, or none falls upon the ground, does not call for vengeance; while, on the other hand, a simple blow calls for blood-revenge, if it happens to draw blood through the accident of its falling on a sore (Moffaḍḍal al-Ḍabbī, *Amthāl,* p. 10, ed. Constant. AH. 1300). Infanticide in Arabia was effected by burying the child alive; captive kings were slain by bleeding them into a cup, and if one drop touched the ground it was thought that their death would be revenged (*supra,* p. 369, note 1). Applications of this principle to sacrifices of sacrosanct and kindred animals are frequent; they are strangled or killed with a blunt instrument (*supra,* p. 343; note also the club or mallet that appears in sacrificial scenes on ancient Chaldean cylinders, Menant, *Glyptique,* i. 151), or at least no drop of their blood must fall on the ground (Bancroft, iii, 168).
42. *Dea Syria,* lviii.; *Yoma,* vi. 6.
43. Plutarch, *Is. et Os.* § 30; cf. *Additional Note* F.
44. At the Thargelia, and in the Leucadian ceremony.

# 4

# JAMES G. FRAZER (b. 1854)

James George Frazer, historian, classicist and anthropologist, was born in Glasgow and raised in a devout Presbyterian family. He studied at the University of Glasgow and at Trinity College in Cambridge where, after writing a dissertation on Plato, he became professor of classical languages and literature. Already familiar with Tylor's work on animism and cultural comparison, Frazer met and became good friends with William Robertson Smith. The two became virtual collaborators, sharing data and encouraging each other's theoretical projects. For example, Smith asked Frazer to write two important articles, on "Taboo" and on "Totemism," for the *Encyclopaedia Britannica* which he was editing at the time. In 1887, Frazer published a small book on totemism, a work that Robertson Smith cites with approval, and that tapped and helped define the growing anthropological interest in that topic. In 1890, though, Frazer published the first edition of what became his most famous and influential work, *The Golden Bough*, an immense (ultimately 12 volumes) comparative study of culture, religion, and folklore organized under a broad-ranging theory about the origin and nature of religion. Working with a vast array of ethnographic accounts gathered by travelers around the world (Frazer himself never conducted field research and thus has been criticized as an "armchair anthropologist"), this book is certainly one of the "great achievements of English literature and scholarship," as E. E. Evans-Pritchard once put it.

Perhaps the most famous contribution Frazer made in the *Golden Bough* is his definition of the nature and significance of magic. Briefly, magic is a way of acting based on a particular "principle of thought." It is a way of thinking that leads to a way of understanding, and thereby acting in, the world. Frazer called this principle of thought the "Law of Sympathy," and defined it as an assumption that mental and historical associations retain real-world material influences. This law "resolves" itself into two more specific laws: 1) the "Law of Similarity," the assumption that resemblances can affect each other, that imitations affect what they imitate, that "like produces like" and 2) the "Law of Contiguity," the assumption that things once in contact (a part of a whole, for example) continue to affect each other even at a distance. These then are the two basic forms of magic—"imitative" (or "homeopathic") magic and "contagious" magic—and all specific magical acts, Frazer claimed, derive from one or both of these two. In *The Golden Bough*, he collected a massive amount of ethnographic data to support this understanding of magic. Equally significant though is Frazer's claim that this "Law of Sympathy" at the core of "sympathetic magic" is false, that magical acts are based on faulty thinking, on errors.

Like Tylor, Spencer, and Robertson Smith before him, Frazer adopted the dominant intellectual framework of his day and proposed an evolutionary theory of religion. He too sought to explain religion by identifying its origin and then revealing a trajectory of development that has produced the vast diversity of religious phenomena known today. For Frazer, the historical movement from "low" to "high," from the "savage" to the "civilized," was a gradual transition (albeit with a great deal of overlap) from the earliest form, magic, to religion and finally to science. Magic was the first attempt by "primitive" peoples to understand and control their world, to ensure success in the face of natural uncertainties. Thinking, acting, and judging according to the Law of Sympathy, primitives were steeped in magic. As certain individuals exhibited a special ability to perform magic (to develop and implement applications of its principles), as they demonstrated this power to control magical effects, they gained social status and became leaders. The first kings, then, were magicians, according to Frazer. The "Age of Religion" arose when the need to explain failed magical acts became urgent, when for example the rate of such failures increased to a troubling level. The solution, Frazer hypothesized, was to posit the existence of personal, conscious agents who control nature and the course of human life. Now instead of the determined, uniform laws of magic, mankind believed in personal supernatural beings or gods, and now instead of controlling or manipulating laws, human beings must persuade personal deities. Now in place of a magician, the king is a priest, a person with a special ability to propitiate or conciliate divine powers. Despite this advance, though, like magic, religion is also a fallacy, according to Frazer. Both magic and religion misapply the principles of association and result in illegitimate practices. Science, however, correctly understands these principles and applies them without error, and thereby leads to "freedom and truth."

This linear evolutionary scheme allows Frazer to explain a number of religious phenomena. Of these, the notion of a "divine king" is particularly important because Frazer's title, *The Golden Bough*, refers to an example of divine kingship from classical Roman mythology, but also because it leads him to a theory of sacrifice. Frazer explained that once a priest/king demonstrated the power to communicate with a particular god and gain real benefits for his community, he may be understood to possess aspects of the god, perhaps even *be* the god in human form. Throughout the world, Frazer notes, there are examples of kings who are treated as gods, as individuals who manifest divine power, essential embodiments of the source of the community's prosperity. Of even further significance for Frazer, these societies with divine kings tend also to believe that the health, strength, and well-being of their king is directly correlated with that of the entire community as well. If the king were to die, this would be disastrous and crops would fail, game would disappear, rain would cease, and perhaps the entire community would die. Consequently, Frazer notes, these societies do everything they can to protect and preserve their divine kings. The most startling example of such attempts to sustain the power of the divine king occurred when he became old or weak (sexually impotent, for example)—he was killed. Very often, Frazer observes, the ritual installation of a new replacement king included some technique of physically transferring something of the old king to the new king, by consuming a certain body part for example.

The complex of beliefs and practices surrounding divine kingship, while initially puzzling or even troubling, allowed Frazer to demonstrate the explanatory power of his theory of religion, for he understood much of it as a survival of "primitive magical beliefs." A community believing its king's health is directly correlated with its prosperity is an example of homeopathic magic, the "Law of Similarity" clearly at work. Then, attempting to transfer divine power between a king and his successor by retaining a part of the old king can be understood as an example of contagious magic and the "Law of Contiguity." For Frazer, these mistaken notions, these erroneous ways of thinking, are essentially forms of magic.

Frazer understood sacrifice as an application of magic as well. In the case of human sacrifice, the explanation derives from the model of divine kingship. It is an example of regicide, the killing of a human believed to manifest a particular divine power. In examples where the human victim is not a king, for example the sacrifice of slaves, Frazer sees these as derivative, as later developments employing yet another form of magic—substitution. The motivation, in any case, is to retain or rejuvenate the god and thereby to ensure expected divine benefits. Frazer explains animal sacrifice by invoking the notion of totemism and the idea that a particular species of animal represents, for some, the deity of the clan. Periodically, the clan will sacrifice an animal of its totemic species in order to revive the species (i.e., which includes its human kin, the members of the community) as a whole. Here too contagious magic is at work, destroying a part to sustain the whole. Likewise, the totemic meal can be understood as a desire to distribute the power of the god, embodied in the animal killed, to all those members of the clan, each consuming a portion of the animal. First-fruit, harvest, and other vegetable or plant sacrifices are similarly examples of killing a representative of the divine. In this way, claims that dividing the victim and distributing its parts will disperse the god's power of fertility are, for Frazer, still other applications of magical thinking. Burying parts of a sacrificial victim in a field to ensure its productivity, to ensure the field and its produce be rejuvenated (revived) with the new season, is a clear variation on the practice of regicide Frazer interpreted in other cultural contexts. Piacular sacrifices intended to eliminate illness or other misfortune, for example the practice of banishing or killing a "scapegoat" that can "carry" away the misfortune, can also be understood as a variation of regicide. Here, too, the victim represents the god and the misfortune indicates the need for the god's rejuvenation. Like the divine king who begins to show weakness, killing him can transfer his power to a successor. Only later, Frazer claims, were these magical impulses substituted in some cases by ethical concepts of sin, thereby transforming sacrificial behaviors into acts of atonement and expiation. Similarly, Frazer admits that the notion of sacrifice as gift may later, for some groups, "overshadow" ideas that the object sacrificed, whether it be human, animal, or vegetable, is a manifestation of the god.

Reprinted here is a short excerpt from *The Golden Bough: A Study in Magic and Religion*, the abridged version of Frazer's massive opus. Being a work quite impossible to summarize adequately in only a few pages, the selection here briefly discusses "kings killed when their strength fails," "the sacrament of first-fruits," and "killing the divine animal." Frazer is subject to the same criticisms of his contemporaries—the problems of relying on mostly secondary sources, of positing overly intellectualistic understandings of religion, and of endorsing a single unilinear evolutionary scheme—and he is often overlooked in discussions of sacrifice, but with his emphasis on magic (the mode of thinking it reveals), his attention to the vast variety of ritual phenomena, and his dedication to cross-cultural comparison, he nevertheless provides, with what could be called his "magic theory" of sacrifice, a viable theoretical model that can explain a great deal of sacrificial phenomena.

# From *The Golden Bough:*
# *A Study in Magic and Religion*

## Kings Killed When Their Strength Fails

If the high gods, who dwell remote from the fret and fever of this earthly life, are yet believed to die at last, it is not to be expected that a god who lodges in a frail tabernacle of flesh should escape the same fate, though we

James George Frazer, *The Golden Bough: A Study in Magic and Religion* (London: Macmillan and Co., Ltd. 1911–15), pages 309–10, 312–13, 556–7, 578–80. Reprinted with the permission of A. P. Watt Ltd. on behalf of The Council of Trinity College Cambridge.

hear of African kings who have imagined themselves immortal by virtue of their sorceries. Now primitive peoples, as we have seen, sometimes believe that their safety and even that of the world is bound up with the life of one of these god-men or human incarnations of the divinity. Naturally, therefore, they take the utmost care of his life, out of a regard for their own. But no amount of care and precaution will prevent the man-god from growing old and feeble and at last dying. His worshippers have to lay their account with this sad necessity and to meet it as best they can. The danger is a formidable one; for if the course of nature is dependent on the man-god's life, what catastrophes may not be expected from the gradual enfeeblement of his powers and their final extinction in death? There is only one way of averting these dangers. The man-god must be killed as soon as he shows symptoms that his powers are beginning to fail, and his soul must be transferred to a vigorous successor before it has been seriously impaired by the threatened decay. The advantages of thus putting the man-god to death instead of allowing him to die of old age and disease are, to the savage, obvious enough. For if the man-god dies what we call a natural death, it means, according to the savage, that his soul has either voluntarily departed from his body and refuses to return, or more commonly that it has been extracted, or at least detained in its wanderings, by a demon or sorcerer. In any of these cases the soul of the man-god is lost to his worshippers, and with it their prosperity is gone and their very existence endangered. Even if they could arrange to catch the soul of the dying god as it left his lips or his nostrils and so transfer it to a successor, this would not effect their purpose; for, dying of disease, his soul would necessarily leave his body in the last stage of weakness and exhaustion, and so enfeebled it would continue to drag out a languid, inert existence in any body to which it might be transferred. Whereas by slaying him his worshippers could, in the first place, make sure of catching his soul as it escaped and transferring it to a suitable successor; and, in the second place, by putting him to death before his natural force was abated, they would secure that the world should not fall into decay with the decay of the man-god. Every purpose, therefore, was answered, and all dangers averted by thus killing the man-god and transferring his soul, while yet at its prime, to a vigorous successor.

The mystic kings of Fire and Water in Cambodia are not allowed to die a natural death. Hence when one of them is seriously ill and the elders think that he cannot recover, they stab him to death. The people of Congo believed, as we have seen, that if their pontiff the Chitomé were to die a natural death, the world would perish, and the earth, which he alone sustained by his power and merit, would immediately be annihilated. Accordingly when he fell ill and seemed likely to die, the man who was destined to be his successor entered the pontiff's house with a rope or a club and strangled or clubbed him to death. The Ethiopian kings of Meroe were worshipped as gods; but whenever the priests chose, they sent a messenger to the king, ordering him to die, and alleging an oracle of the gods as their authority for the command. This command the kings always obeyed down to the reign of Ergamenes, a contemporary of Ptolemy II, King of Egypt. Having received a Greek education which emancipated him from the superstitions of his countrymen, Ergamenes ventured to disregard the command of the priests, and, entering the Golden Temple with a body of soldiers, put the priests to the sword.

Customs of the same sort appear to have prevailed in this part of Africa down to modern times. In some tribes of Fazoql the king had to administer justice daily under a certain tree. If from sickness or any other cause he was unable to discharge this duty for three whole days, he was hanged on the tree in a noose, which contained two razors so arranged that when the noose was drawn tight by the weight of the king's body they cut his throat.

A custom of putting their divine kings to death at the first symptoms of infirmity or old age prevailed until lately, if indeed it is even now extinct and not merely dormant, among the Shilluk of the White Nile, and in recent years it has been carefully investigated by Dr. C. G. Seligman. The reverence which the Shilluk pay to their king appears to arise chiefly from the conviction that he is a reincarnation of the spirit of Nyakang, the semi-divine hero who founded the dynasty and settled the tribe in their present territory. It is a fundamental article of the Shilluk creed that the spirit of the divine or semi-divine Nyakang is incarnate in the reigning king.

. . . . . . . . . . . . . . . . . . . . . . . . . . . . . . . . . . . . .

Like Nyakang himself, their founder, each of the Shilluk kings after death is worshipped at a shrine, which is erected over his grave, and the grave of a king is always in the village where he was born. The tomb-shrine of a king resembles the shrine of Nyakang, consisting of a few huts enclosed by a fence; one of the huts is built over the king's grave, the others are occupied by the guardians of the shrine. Indeed the shrines of Nyakang and the shrines of the kings are scarcely to be distinguished from each other, and the religious rituals observed at all of them are identical in form and vary only in matters of detail, the variations being due apparently to the far greater sanctity attributed to the shrines of Nyakang. The grave-shrines of the kings are tended by certain old men or women, who correspond to the guardians of the shrines of Nyakang. They are usually widows or old men-servants of the deceased king, and when they die they are succeeded in their office by their descendants. Moreover, cattle are dedicated to the grave-shrines of the kings and sacrifices are offered at them just as at the shrines of Nyakang.

In general the principal element in the religion of the Shilluk would seem to be the worship which they pay to their sacred or divine kings, whether dead or alive. These are believed to be animated by a single divine spirit, which has been transmitted from the semi-mythical, but probably in substance historical, founder of the dynasty through all his successors to the present day. Hence, regarding their kings as incarnate divinities on whom the welfare of men, of cattle, and of the corn implicitly depends, the Shilluk naturally pay them the greatest respect and take every care of them; and however strange it may seem to us, their custom of putting the divine king to death as soon as he shows signs of ill-health or failing strength springs directly from their profound veneration for him and from their anxiety to preserve him, or rather the divine spirit by which he is animated, in the most perfect state of efficiency; nay, we may go further and say that their practice of regicide is the best proof they can give of the high regard in which they hold their kings. For they believe, as we have seen, that the king's life or spirit is so sympathetically bound up with the prosperity of the whole country, that if he fell ill or grew senile the cattle would sicken and cease to multiply, the crops would rot in the fields, and men would perish of widespread disease. Hence, in their opinion, the only way of averting these calamities is to put the king to death while he is still hale and hearty, in order that the divine spirit which he has inherited from his predecessors may be transmitted in turn by him to his successor while it is still in full vigour and has not yet been impaired by the weakness of disease and old age. In this connexion the particular symptom which is commonly said to seal the king's death-warrant is highly significant; when he can no longer satisfy the passions of his numerous wives, in other words, when he has ceased, whether partially or wholly, to be able to reproduce his kind, it is time for him to die and make room for a more vigorous successor. Taken along with the other reasons which are alleged for putting the king to death, this one suggests that the fertility of men, of cattle, and of the crops is believed to depend sympathetically on the generative power of the king, so that the complete failure of that power in him would involve a corresponding failure in men, animals, and plants, and would thereby entail at no distant date the entire extinction of all life, whether human, animal, or vegetable. No wonder, that with such a danger before their eyes the Shilluk should be most careful not to let the king die what we should call a natural death of sickness or old age. It is characteristic of their attitude towards the death of the kings that they refrain from speaking of it as death: they do not say that a king has died but simply that he has "gone away" like his divine ancestors Nyakang and Dag, the two first kings of the dynasty, both of whom are reported not to have died but to have disappeared. The similar legends of the mysterious disappearance of early kings in other lands, for example at Rome and in Uganda, may well point to a similar custom of putting them to death for the purpose of preserving their life.

On the whole the theory and practice of the divine kings of the Shilluk correspond very nearly to the theory and practice of the priests of Nemi, the Kings of the Wood, if my view of the latter is correct. In both we see a series of divine kings on whose life the fertility of men, of cattle, and of vegetation is believed to depend, and who are put to death, whether in single combat or otherwise, in order that their divine spirit may be transmitted to their successors in full vigour, uncontaminated by the weakness and decay of sickness or old age, because any such degeneration on the part of the king would, in the opinion of his worshippers, entail a corresponding degeneration on mankind, on cattle, and on the crops.

. . . . . . . . . . . . . . . . . . . . . . . . . . . . . . . . . . . . . . . .

## The Sacrament of First-Fruits

We have now seen that the corn-spirit is represented sometimes in human, sometimes in animal form, and that in both cases he is killed in the person of his representative and eaten sacramentally. To find examples of actually killing the human representative of the corn-spirit we had naturally to go to savage races; but the harvest-suppers of our European peasants have furnished unmistakable examples of the sacramental eating of animals as representatives of the corn-spirit. But further, as might have been anticipated, the new corn is itself eaten sacramentally, that is, as the body of the corn-spirit. In Wermland, Sweden, the farmer's wife uses the grain of the last sheaf to bake a loaf in the shape of a little girl; this loaf is divided amongst the whole household and eaten by them. Here the loaf represents the corn-spirit conceived as a maiden; just as in Scotland the corn-spirit is similarly conceived and represented by the last sheaf made up in the form of a woman and bearing the name of the Maiden. As usual, the corn-spirit is believed to reside in the last sheaf; and to eat a loaf made from the last sheaf is, therefore, to eat the corn-spirit itself. Similarly at La Palisse, in France, a man made of dough is hung upon the fir-tree which is carried on the last harvest-waggon. The tree and the dough-man are taken to the mayor's house and kept there till the vintage is over. Then the close of the harvest is celebrated by a feast at which the mayor breaks the dough-man in pieces and gives the pieces to the people to eat.

In these examples the corn-spirit is represented and eaten in human shape. In other cases, though the new corn is not baked in loaves of human shape, still the solemn ceremonies with which it is eaten suffice to indicate that it is partaken of sacramentally, that is, as the body of the corn-spirit. For example, the following ceremonies used to be observed by Lithuanian peasants at eating the new corn. About the time of the autumn sowing, when all the corn had been got in and the threshing had begun, each farmer held a festival called Sabarios, that is, "the mixing or throwing together." He took nine good handfuls of each kind of crop—wheat, barley, oats, flax, beans, lentils, and the rest; and each handful he divided into three parts. The twenty-seven portions of each grain were then thrown on a heap and all mixed up together. The grain used had to be that which was first threshed and winnowed and which had been set aside and kept for this purpose. A part of the grain thus mixed was employed to bake little loaves, one for each of the household; the rest was mixed with more barley or oats and made into beer. The first beer brewed from this mixture was for the drinking of the farmer, his wife, and children; the second brew was for the servants. The beer being ready, the farmer chose an evening when no stranger was expected. Then he knelt down before the barrel of beer, drew a jugful of the liquor and poured it on the bung of the barrel, saying, "O fruitful earth, make rye and barley and all kinds of corn to flourish." Next he took the jug to the parlour, where his wife and children awaited him. On the floor of the parlour lay bound a black or white or speckled (not red) cock and a hen of the same colour and of the same brood, which must have been hatched within the year. Then the farmer knelt down, with the jug in his hand, and thanked God for the harvest and prayed for a good crop next year. Next all lifted up their hands and said, "O God, and thou, O earth, we give you this cock and hen as a free-will offering." With that the farmer killed the fowls with the blows of a wooden spoon, for he might not cut their heads off. After the first prayer and after killing each of the birds he poured out a third of the beer. Then his wife boiled the fowls in a new pot which had never been used before. After that, a bushel was set, bottom upwards, on the floor, and on it were placed the little loaves mentioned above and the boiled fowls. Next the new beer was fetched, together with a ladle and three mugs, none of which was used except on this occasion. When the farmer had ladled the beer into the mugs, the family knelt down round the bushel. The father then uttered a prayer and drank off the three mugs of beer. The rest followed his example. Then the loaves and the flesh of the fowls were eaten, after which the beer went round again, till every one had emptied each of the three mugs nine times. None of the food should remain over; but if anything did happen to be left, it was consumed the next morning with the same ceremonies. The bones were given to the dog to eat; if he did not eat them all up, the remains were buried under the dung in the cattle-stall.

. . . . . . . . . . . . . . . . . . . . . . . . . . . . . . . . . . . . . . . . . .

## Killing the Divine Animal

In the preceding chapters we saw that many communities which have progressed so far as to subsist mainly by agriculture have been in the habit of killing and eating their farinaceous deities either in their proper form of corn, rice, and so forth, or in the borrowed shapes of animals and men. It remains to show that hunting and pastoral tribes, as well as agricultural peoples, have been in the habit of killing the beings whom they worship. Among the worshipful beings or gods, if indeed they deserve to be dignified by that name, whom hunters and shepherds adore and kill are animals pure and simple, not animals regarded as embodiments of other supernatural beings. Our first example is drawn from the Indians of California, who living in a fertile country under a serene and temperate sky, nevertheless rank near the bottom of the savage scale. The Acagchemem tribe adored the great buzzard, and once a year they celebrated a great festival called *Panes* or bird-feast in its honour. The day selected for the festival was made known to the public on the evening before its celebration and preparations were at once made for the erection of a special temple (*vanquech*), which seems to have been a circular or oval enclosure of stakes with the stuffed skin of a coyote or prairie-wolf set up on a hurdle to represent the god Chinigchinich. When the temple was ready, the bird was carried into it in solemn procession and laid on an altar erected for the purpose. Then all the young women, whether married or single, began to run to and fro, as if distracted, some in one direction and some in another, while the elders of both sexes remained silent spectators of the scene, and the captains, tricked out in paint and feathers, danced round their adored bird. These ceremonies being concluded, they seized upon the bird and carried it to the principal temple, all the assembly uniting in the grand display, and the captains dancing and singing at the head of the procession. Arrived at the temple, they killed the bird without losing a drop of its blood. The skin was removed entire and preserved with the feathers as a relic or for the purpose of making the festal garment or *paelt*. The carcase was buried in a hole in the temple, and the old women gathered round the grave weeping and moaning bitterly, while they threw various kinds of seeds or pieces of food on it, crying out, "Why did you run away? Would you not have been better with us? you would have made *pinole* (a kind of gruel) as we do, and if you had not run away, you would not have become a *Panes*," and so on. When this ceremony was concluded, the dancing was resumed and kept up for three days and nights. They said that the *Panes* was a woman who had run off to the mountains and there been changed into a bird by the god Chinigchinich. They believed that though they sacrificed the bird annually, she came to life again and returned to her home in the mountains. Moreover, they thought that "as often as the bird was killed, it became multiplied; because every year all the different Capitanes celebrated the same feast of *Panes*, and were firm in the opinion that the birds sacrificed were but one and the same female."

The unity in multiplicity thus postulated by the Californians is very noticeable and helps to explain their motive for killing the divine bird. The notion of the life of a species as distinct from that of an individual, easy and obvious as it seems to us, appears to be one which the Californian savage cannot grasp. He is unable to conceive the life of the species otherwise than as an individual life, and therefore as exposed to the same dangers and calamities which menace and finally destroy the life of the individual. Apparently he imagines that a species left to itself will grow old and die like an individual, and that therefore some step must be taken to save from extinction the particular species which he regards as divine. The only means he can think of to avert the catastrophe is to kill a member of the species in whose veins the tide of life is still running strong and has not yet stagnated among the fens of old age. The life thus diverted from one channel will flow, he fancies, more freshly and freely in a new one; in other words, the slain animal will revive and enter on a new term of life with all the spring and energy of youth. To us this reasoning is transparently absurd, but so too is the custom. A similar confusion, it may be noted, between the individual life and the life of the species was made by the Samoans. Each family had for its god a particular species of animal; yet the death of one of these animals, for example an owl, was not the death of the god, "he was supposed to be yet alive, and incarnate in all the owls in existence."

The rude Californian rite which we have just considered has a close parallel in the religion of ancient Egypt. The Thebans and all other Egyptians who worshipped the Theban god Ammon held rams to be sacred, and would not sacrifice them. But once a year at the festival of Ammon they killed a ram, skinned it, and clothed the image of the god in the skin. Then they mourned over the ram and buried it in a sacred tomb. The custom was explained by a story that Zeus had once exhibited himself to Hercules clad in the fleece and wearing the head of a ram. Of course the ram in this case was simply the beast-god of Thebes, as the wolf was the beast-god of Lycopolis, and the goat was the beast-god of Mendes. In other words, the ram was Ammon himself. On the monuments, it is true, Ammon appears in semi-human form with the body of a man and the head of a ram. But this only shows that he was in the usual chrysalis state through which beast-gods regularly pass before they emerge as full-blown anthropomorphic gods. The ram, therefore, was killed, not as a sacrifice to Ammon, but as the god himself, whose identity with the beast is plainly shown by the custom of clothing his image in the skin of the slain ram. The reason for thus killing the ram-god annually may have been that which I have assigned for the general custom of killing a god and for the special Californian custom of killing the divine buzzard. As applied to Egypt, this explanation is supported by the analogy of the bull-god Apis, who was not suffered to outlive a certain term of years. The intention of thus putting a limit to the life of the human god was, as I have argued, to secure him from the weakness and frailty of age. The same reasoning would explain the custom— probably an older one—of putting the beast-god to death annually, as was done with the ram of Thebes.

# 5

# HENRI HUBERT and
# MARCEL MAUSS
# (both b. 1872)

Henri Hubert and Marcel Mauss were both French ethnologists and sociologists who, working alongside Emile Durkheim, made several important contributions to the comparative study of religions. The two collaborated on a number of publications for *L'Année sociologique*, the journal of sociology founded by Durkheim in 1898. Both men helped establish the journal from its beginning, each serving as a contributing editor. Mauss was born to Jewish parents (Hubert was raised as a Catholic), studied philosophy and languages, including Russian and Sanskrit, and later joined the faculty at the Ecole Pratique des Hautes Etudes in Paris, an institution that employed Hubert as well. Hubert, like his friend Mauss and his mentor Durkheim, was primarily interested in Religion, particularly the relationship between ritual and social realities. While Mauss is best known for his work "Essai sur le don" (1925, later translated as "The Gift"), Hubert is remembered mostly for the collaborative work he undertook with Mauss on the topic of sacrifice. Their "Essai sur la nature et la fonction du sacrifice" originally appeared in the second issue of *L'Année sociologique,* and since its publication in 1898, has served as a reference point for the majority of subsequent studies of sacrificial phenomena.

A number of background assumptions inform the work of Hubert and Mauss, the most important of which is the sociological understanding of religion shared with their mentor Emile Durkheim. Even as their essay on sacrifice precedes the publication of Durkheim's masterwork, *The Elementary Forms of the Religious Life*, there is a clear attention to the trend, articulated earlier by Robertson Smith, that social matters and religious matters are inextricably linked. While it would take some time to work out the nature of that link—the mechanism of it—Hubert and Mauss believe that religious ideas are "social facts," and that ritual ultimately has a "social function," for it helps define and maintain social solidarity by working to reinforce shared values and collective conceptions.

The heart of this sociological position is a distinction Hubert and Mauss make between the "sacred" and the "profane." This is a distinction between the "ordinary" and the "religious," the sacred being a certain quality or character added to particular things, individuals, places, and so forth. Early in the life of *L'Année sociologique*, the group of scholars involved understood religious beliefs and practices primarily in terms of their "obligatory character," that is as distinguishable by virtue of their being imposed upon individuals by society. Certain actions are prohibited and others are mandatory, for example, and for this reason Hubert and Mauss describe the sacred as that which is "set apart," or "isolated" from the profane. Religious beliefs and practices are all based on this distinction. They function to maintain it. At the same time, Hubert and Mauss note how religious people attribute to the sacred sphere a kind of life-sustaining "power" or "current." They see it as "the very source of life." It is the domain of "divine forces" that religious people believe defines the "conditions" of their "existence," and as such is a realm with which they desire a "relationship." Inevitably people find themselves in situations where they wish to "improve their lot," and at these times they believe, Hubert and Mauss suggest, this can be accomplished through a complex set of interactions with the sacred realm, that is, through religion. Religious people face a problem, however. How do they, ordinary human beings, have a "relation-ship" with the sacred if it is by definition something that must remain absolutely separate from the profane? Direct contact with the sacred is a "fearful thing" for ordinary human beings for it is believed, Hubert and Mauss note, the powers of the sacred realm are so "intense" they will destroy any profane object that attempts such contact. How then can human beings tap "the very source of life" (the sacred), while avoiding the deadly consequences of "desecration," disregarding the sacred/profane opposition?

The answer is sacrifice. In sacrificial rituals, the victim serves as an "intermediary" between the sacred and profane. Hubert and Mauss claim sacrificial practices, while being employed for a diversity of purposes, share a common logic—they are a way of creating a link "between the sacred and profane worlds through the mediation of a victim, that is, of a thing that in the course of the ceremony is destroyed." Working with the etymology of the word "sacrifice" ("to make sacred"), Hubert and Mauss argue that sacrifices do indeed make something sacred (consecrated), namely the object sacrificed (what they call the "victim"). The victim gains a sacred quality by virtue of it being employed as an intermediary between the sacred and profane realms, for it serves as a conduit of sorts for moving religious power in either direction between the human and divine realms. Whether intended to benefit an individual or a group, the "religious state" of the "sacrifier" ("the subject to whom the benefits of sacrifice accrue") is altered by channeling sacred power through a victim. Some sacrifices are intended to "increase the religiosity of the sacrifier." These are sacrifices of "sacralization," and thus move a sacred power from the victim to the sacrifier. Likewise, there are sacrifices that aim to "rid the sacrifier of an impurity," so-called sacrifices of "desacralization" where power is moved from the sacrifier to the victim. The two types can at times be combined, but their point is that sacrifice allows the sacred and profane worlds to establish a variety of relationships, hence for a variety of purposes (e.g., expiation, communion, etc.), yet remain distinct.

Unlike the theorists that came before them, Hubert and Mauss avoid questions about the origin of sacrifice. They work more with concepts than data, and seek to sketch a general "sacrificial schema" that will hold what they believe is an essential logic to religious beliefs and practices generally. Instead of a gift-, ghost-, communion-, or magic-based explanation of sacrifice, Hubert and Mauss offer a theory built upon the notion of mediation. While ideas of gift, abnegation, and communion are important for many examples of sacrifice, Hubert and Mauss, recognizing this, do not see them as truly essential in the logical sense or primary in the historical sense. Later scholars have, to varying degrees, found ways to agree and disagree with Hubert and Mauss, but clearly they have had a profound effect on the scholarly project of understanding sacrifice.

Reproduced here are important pages from the "Essai sur la nature et la fonction du sacrifice" (translated as *Sacrifice: Its Nature and Function*) by Hubert and Mauss. Here is their definition of sacrifice, the terminology they coin for the participants of sacrificial rituals, and their concluding chapter where most of their argument is summarized.

# From *Sacrifice: Its Nature and Function*

## Definition and Unity of the Sacrificial System

It is important, before proceeding further, to give an overall definition of the facts that we designate under the heading of sacrifice.

The word "sacrifice" immediately suggests the idea of consecration, and one might be tempted to believe that the two notions are identical. It is indeed certain that sacrifice always implies a consecration; in every sacrifice an object passes from the common into the religious domain; it is consecrated. But not

Henri Hubert, and Marcel Mauss, *Sacrifice: Its Nature and Function*, translated by W. D. Halls (Chicago: University of Chicago Press, 1964), pages 9–13, 95–103. Reprinted with permission from the University of Chicago Press, and from Taylor and Francis Books, Ltd.

all consecrations are of the same kind. In some the effects are limited to the consecrated object, be it a man or a thing. This is, for example, the case with unction. When a king is consecrated, his religious personality alone is modified; apart from this, nothing is changed. In sacrifice, on the other hand, the consecration extends beyond the thing consecrated; among other objects, it touches the moral person who bears the expenses of the ceremony. The devotee who provides the victim which is the object of the consecration is not, at the completion of the operation, the same as he was at the beginning. He has acquired a religious character which he did not have before, or has rid himself of an unfavourable character with which he was affected; he has raised himself to a state of grace or has emerged from a state of sin. In either case he has been religiously transformed.

*We give the name "sacrifier" to the subject to whom the benefits of sacrifice thus accrue, or who undergoes its effects.*[1] This subject is sometimes an individual,[2] sometimes a collectivity[3]—a family, a clan, a tribe, a nation, a secret society. When it is a collectivity it may be that the group fulfils collectively the function of the sacrifier, that is, it attends the sacrifice as a body;[4] but sometimes it delegates one of its members who acts in its stead and place. Thus the family is generally represented by its head,[5] society by its magistrates.[6] This is a first step in that succession of representations which we shall encounter at every one of the stages of sacrifice.

There are, however, cases where the effects of the sacrificial consecration are exerted not directly on the sacrifier himself, but on certain things which appertain more or less directly to his person. In the sacrifice that takes place at the building of a house,[7] it is the house that is affected by it, and the quality that it acquires by this means can survive longer than its owner for the time being. In other cases, it is the sacrifier's field, the river he has to cross, the oath he takes, the treaty he makes, etc. We shall call those kinds of things for whose sake the sacrifice takes place *objects of sacrifice*. It is important, moreover, to notice that the sacrifier himself is also affected through his presence at the sacrifice and through the interest or part he takes in it. The ambit of action of the sacrifice is especially noteworthy here, for it produces a double effect, one on the object for which it is offered and upon which it is desired to act, the other on the moral person who desires and instigates that effect. Sometimes even it is only of use provided it brings about this twofold result. When the father of a family offers a sacrifice for the inauguration of his house, not only must the house be capable of receiving his family, but they must be fit to enter it.[8]

We see what is the distinctive characteristic of consecration in sacrifice: the thing consecrated serves as an intermediary between the sacrifier, or the object which is to receive the practical benefits of the sacrifice, and the divinity to whom the sacrifice is usually addressed. Man and the god are not in direct contact. In this way sacrifice is distinguished from most of the facts grouped under the heading of blood covenant, in which by the exchange of blood a direct fusion of human and divine life is brought about.[9] The same will be said about certain instances of the offering of hair. Here again, the subject who sacrifices is in direct communication with the god through the part of his person which is offered up.[10] Doubtless there are connexions between these rites and sacrifice; but they must be distinguished from it.

But this first characteristic is not enough, for it does not allow us to distinguish sacrifice from those acts, inadequately defined, which may fittingly be termed offerings. There is indeed no offering in which the object consecrated is not likewise interposed between the god and the offerer, and in which the latter is not affected by the consecration. But if every sacrifice is in effect an oblation, there are oblations of different kinds. Sometimes the object consecrated is simply presented as a votive offering; consecration can assign it to the service of the god, but it does not change its nature by the mere fact that it is made to pass into the religious domain. Those oblations of the firstfruits which were merely brought to the temple, remained there untouched and belonged to the priests. On the other hand, in other cases consecration destroys the object offered up; if an animal is offered on the altar, the desired end is reached only when its throat has been cut, or it is cut to pieces or consumed by fire, in short, *sacrificed*. The object thus destroyed is the *victim*. It is clearly for oblations of this kind that the name sacrifice must be reserved. We may surmise that the difference between these two kinds of operation depends upon their different degrees of solemnity and their differing efficacy. In the case of sacrifice, the religious energy released is stronger. From this arises the havoc it causes.

In these conditions we must designate as sacrifice any oblation, even of vegetable matter, whenever the offering or part of it is destroyed, although usage seems to limit the word sacrifice to designate only sacrifices where blood is shed. To restrict the meaning of the name in this way is arbitrary. Due allowance having been made, the mechanism of consecration is the same in all cases; there is consequently no objective reason for distinguishing between them. Thus the Hebrew *minha* is an oblation of flour and cakes[11] which accompanies certain sacrifices. Yet it is so much a sacrifice like these other sacrifices that Leviticus does not distinguish between them.[12] The same rites are observed. A portion is destroyed on the altar fire, the remainder being eaten entirely or in part by the priests. In Greece[13] only vegetable oblations were permitted on the altar of certain gods;[14] thus there were sacrificial rites which did not involve animal oblations. The same may be said of libations of milk, wine, or other liquids.[15] They are subject in Greece[16] to the same distinctions as sacrifices;[17] on occasion they can even replace them.[18] The identity of these different operations was so clearly felt by the Hindus that the objects offered up in these different cases were themselves considered identical. They are all considered as equally living, and are treated as such. Thus in a sacrifice considered to be of sufficient solemnity, when the grains are crushed they are implored not to avenge themselves upon the sacrifier for the hurt done them. When the cakes are placed upon the potsherds to bake, they are requested not to break;[19] when they are cut, they are entreated not to injure the sacrifier and the priests. When a libation of milk is made—and all Hindu libations are made with milk or a milk product—it is not something inanimate that is offered up, but the cow itself, in its liquid essence, its sap, its fertility.[20]

Thus we finally arrive at the following definition: *Sacrifice is a religious act which, through the consecration of a victim, modifies the condition of the moral person who accomplishes it or that of certain objects with which he is concerned.*[21]

For brevity of exposition we shall call those sacrifices in which the personality of the sacrifier is directly affected by the sacrifice *personal sacrifices*, and those in which objects, real or ideal, receive directly the sacrificial action *objective sacrifices*.

. . . . . . . . . . . . . . . . . . . . . . . . . . . . . . . . . . . .

## Conclusion

It can now be seen more clearly of what in our opinion the unity of the sacrificial system consists. It does not come, as Smith believed, from the fact that all the possible kinds of sacrifice have emerged from one primitive, simple form. Such a sacrifice does not exist. Of all the procedures of sacrifice, the most general, the least rich in particular elements, that we have been able to distinguish, are those of sacralization and desacralization. Now actually in any sacrifice of desacralization, however pure it may be, we always find a sacralization of the victim. Conversely, in any sacrifice of sacralization, even the most clearly marked, a desacralization is necessarily implied, for otherwise the remains of the victim could not be used. The two elements are thus so closely interdependent that the one cannot exist without the other.

Moreover, these two kinds of sacrifice are still only abstract types. Every sacrifice takes place in certain given circumstances and with a view to certain determined ends. From the diversity of the ends which may be pursued in this way arise varying procedures, of which we have given a few examples. Now there is no religion in which these procedures do not coexist in greater or lesser number; all the sacrificial rituals we know of display a great complexity. Moreover, there is no special rite that is not complex in itself, for either it pursues several ends at the same time, or, to attain one end, it sets in motion several forces. We have seen that sacrifices of desacralization and even expiatory sacrifices proper become entangled with communion sacrifices. But many other examples of complexity might be given. The Amazulu, to bring on rain, assemble a herd of black bullocks, kill one and eat it in silence, and then burn its bones outside the village; which constitutes three different themes in one operation.[22]

In the Hindu animal sacrifice this complexity is even more marked. We have found shares of the animal attributed for expiation purposes to evil spirits, divine shares put on one side, shares for communion that were enjoyed by the sacrifier, shares for the priest that were consumed by them. The victim serves equally for bringing down imprecations on the enemy, for divination, and for vows. In one of its aspects sacrifice belongs to the theriomorphic cults, for the soul of the animal is dispatched to heaven to join the archetypes of the animals and maintain the species in perpetuity. It is also a rite of consumption, for the sacrifier who has laid the fire may not eat meat until he has made such a sacrifice. Lastly it is a sacrifice of redemption, for the sacrifier is consecrated: he is in the power of the divinity, and redeems himself by substituting the victim in his place. All this is mixed up and confused in one and the same system, which, despite its diversity, remains none the less harmonious. This is all the more the case with a rite of immense purport like the sacrifice to Soma, in which, over and above what we have just described, is realized the case of the sacrifice of the god. In a word, just like a magic ceremony or prayer, which can serve at the same time as an act of thanksgiving, a vow, and a propitiation, sacrifice can fulfil a great variety of concurrent functions.

But if sacrifice is so complex, whence comes its unity? It is because, fundamentally, beneath the diverse forms it takes, it always consists in one same procedure, which may be used for the most widely differing purposes. *This procedure consists in establishing a means of communication between the sacred and the profane worlds through the mediation of a victim, that is, of a thing that in the course of the ceremony is destroyed.* Now, contrary to what Smith believed, the victim does not necessarily come to the sacrifice with a religious nature already perfected and clearly defined: it is the sacrifice itself that confers this upon it. Sacrifice can therefore impart to the victim most varied powers and thereby make it suitable for fulfilling the most varied functions, either by different rites or during the same rite. The victim can also pass on a sacred character of the religious world to the profane world, or vice versa. It remains indifferent to the direction of the current that passes through it. At the same time the spirit that has been released from the victim can be entrusted with the task of bearing a prayer to the heavenly powers, it can be used to foretell the future, to redeem oneself from the wrath of the gods by making over one's portion of the victim to them, and, lastly, enjoying the sacred flesh that remains. On the other hand, once the victim has been set apart, it has a certain autonomy, no matter what may be done. It is a focus of energy from which are released effects that surpass the narrow purpose that the sacrifier has assigned to the rite. An animal is sacrificed to redeem a *dikshita*; an immediate consequence is that the freed spirit departs to nourish the eternal life of the species. Thus sacrifice naturally exceeds the narrow aims that the most elementary theologies assign to it. This is because it is not made up solely of a series of individual actions. The rite sets in motion the whole complex of sacred things to which it is addressed. From the very beginning of this study sacrifice has appeared as a particular ramification of the system of consecration.

There is no need to explain at length why the profane thus enters into a relationship with the divine: it is because it sees in it the very source of life. It therefore has every interest in drawing closer to it, since it is there that the very conditions for its existence are to be found. But how is it that the profane only draws nearer by remaining at a distance from it? How does it come about that the profane only communicates with the sacred through an intermediary? The destructive consequences of the rite partly explain this strange procedure. If the religious forces are the very principle of the forces of life, they are in themselves of such a nature that contact with them is a fearful thing for the ordinary man. Above all, when they reach a certain level of intensity, they cannot be concentrated in a profane object without destroying it. However much need he has of them, the sacrifier cannot approach them save with the utmost prudence. That is why between these powers and himself he interposes intermediaries, of whom the principal is the victim. If he involved himself in the rite to the very end, he would find death, not life. The victim takes his place. It alone penetrates into the perilous domain of sacrifice, it dies there, and indeed it is there in order to die. The sacrifier remains protected: the gods take the victim instead of him. *The victim redeems him.* Moses had not circumcised his son, and Yahweh came to "wrestle" with him in a hostelry. Moses was on the point of death when his wife savagely cut off the child's foreskin and, casting it at Yahweh's feet, said to him: "Thou art for me a husband of blood." The destruction of the foreskin satisfied the god; he did not destroy Moses, who was redeemed. There is no sacrifice into which some idea of redemption does not enter.

But this first explanation is not sufficiently general, for in the case of the offering, communication is also effected through an intermediary, and yet no destruction occurs. This is because too powerful a consecration has grave drawbacks, even when it is not destructive. All that is too deeply involved in the religious sphere is by that very fact removed from the sphere of the profane. The more a being is imbued with religious feeling, the more he is charged with prohibitions that render him isolated. The sacredness of the Nazir paralyses him. On the other hand, all that enters into a too-intimate contact with sacred things takes on their nature and becomes sacred like them. Now sacrifice is carried out by the profane. The action that it exerts upon people and things is destined to enable them to fulfil their role in temporal life. None can therefore enter with advantage upon sacrifice save on condition of being able to emerge from it. The rites of exit partly serve this purpose. They weaken the force of the consecration. But by themselves alone they could not weaken it sufficiently if it had been too intense. It is therefore important that the sacrifier or the object of sacrifice receive the consecration only when its force has been blunted, that is to say, indirectly. This is the purpose of the intermediary. Thanks to it, the two worlds that are present can interpenetrate and yet remain distinct.

In this way is to be explained a very particular characteristic of religious sacrifice. In any sacrifice there is an act of abnegation since the sacrifier deprives himself and gives. Often this abnegation is even imposed upon him as a duty. For sacrifice is not always optional; the gods demand it. As the Hebrew ritual declares, worship and service is owed them; as the Hindus say, their share is owed them. But this abnegation and submission are not without their selfish aspect. The sacrifier gives up something of himself but he does not give himself. Prudently, he sets himself aside. This is because if he gives, it is partly in order to receive. Thus sacrifice shows itself in a dual light; it is a useful act and it is an obligation. Disinterestedness is mingled with self-interest. That is why it has so frequently been conceived of as a form of contract. Fundamentally there is perhaps no sacrifice that has not some contractual element. The two parties present exchange their services and each gets his due. For the gods too have need of the profane. If nothing were set aside from the harvest, the god of the corn would die; in order that Dionysus may be reborn, Dionysus' goat must be sacrificed at the grape-harvest; it is the *soma* that men give the gods to drink that fortifies them against evil spirits. In order that the sacred may subsist, its share must be given to it, and it is from the share of the profane that this apportionment is made. This ambiguity is inherent in the very nature of sacrifice. It is dependent, in fact, on the presence of the intermediary, and we know that with no intermediary there is no sacrifice. Because the victim is distinct from the sacrifier and the god, it separates them while uniting them: they draw close to each other, without giving themselves to each other entirely.

There is, however, one case from which all selfish calculation is absent. This is the case of the sacrifice of the god, for the god who sacrifices himself gives himself irrevocably. This time all intermediaries have disappeared. The god, who is at the same time the sacrifier, is one with the victim and sometimes even with the sacrificer. All the differing elements which enter into ordinary sacrifice here enter into each other and become mixed together. But such mixing is possible only for mythical, that is, ideal beings. This is how the concept of a god sacrificing himself for the world could be realized, and has become, even for the most civilized peoples, the highest expression and, as it were, the ideal limit of abnegation, in which no apportionment occurs.

But in the same way as the sacrifice of the god does not emerge from the imaginary sphere of religion, so it might likewise be believed that the whole system is merely a play of images. The powers to whom the devotee sacrifices his most precious possession seem to have no positive element. The unbeliever sees in these rites only vain and costly illusions, and is astounded that all mankind has so eagerly dissipated its strength for phantom gods. But there are perhaps true realities to which it is possible to attach the institution in its entirety. Religious ideas, because they are believed, exist; they exist objectively, as social facts. The sacred things in relation to which sacrifice functions, are social things. And this is enough to explain sacrifice. For sacrifice to be truly justified, two conditions are necessary. First of all, there must exist outside the sacrifier things which cause him to go outside himself, and to which he owes what he sacrifices. Next, these things must be close to him so that he can enter into relationship with them, find in them the strength and assurance he needs, and obtain from contact with them the benefits that he expects from his rites. Now this character of intimate penetration and separation, of immanence and transcendence, is distinctive of social matters to the highest degree. They also exist at the same time both within and outside the individual, according to one's viewpoint. We understand then what the function of sacrifice can be, leaving aside the symbols whereby the believer expresses it to himself. It is a social function because sacrifice is concerned with social matters.

On the one hand, this personal renunciation of their property by individuals or groups nourishes social forces. Not, doubtless, that society has need of the things which are the materials of sacrifice. Here everything occurs in the world of ideas, and it is mental and moral energies that are in question. But the act of abnegation implicit in every sacrifice, by recalling frequently to the conscious-ness of the individual the presence of collective forces, in fact sustains their ideal existence. These expiations and general purifications, communions and sacralizations of groups, these creations of the spirits of the cities give—or renew periodically for the community, represented by its gods—that character, good, strong, grave, and terrible, which is one of the essential traits of any social entity. Moreover, individuals find their own advantage in this same act. They confer upon each other, upon themselves, and upon those things they hold dear, the whole strength of society. They invest with the authority of society their vows, their oaths, their marriages. They surround, as if with a protective sanctity, the fields they have ploughed and the houses they have built. At the same time they find in sacrifice the means of redressing equilib-riums that have been upset: by expiation they redeem themselves from social obloquy, the consequence of error, and re-enter the community; by the appor-tionments they make of those things whose use society has reserved for itself, they acquire the right to enjoy them. The social norm is thus maintained without danger to themselves, without diminution for the group. Thus the social function of sacrifice is fulfilled, both for individuals and for the community. And as society is made up not only of men, but also of things and events, we perceive how sacrifice can follow and at the same time reproduce the rhythms of human life and of nature; how it has been able to become both periodical by the use of natural phenomena, and occasional, as are the momentary needs of men, and in short to adapt itself to a thousand purposes.

Moreover we have been able to see, as we have proceeded, how many beliefs and social practices not strictly religious are linked to sacrifice. We have dealt in turn with questions of contract, of redemption, of penalties, of gifts, of abnegation, with ideas relating to the soul and to immortality which are still at the basis of common morality. This indicates the importance of sacrifice for sociology. But in this study we have not had to follow it in its development or all its ramifications. We have given ourselves only the task of attempting to put it in its place.

# Notes

1.   The *yajamana* of the Sanskrit texts. Note the use of this word, the present participle middle voice of the verb *yaj*, to sacrifice. For the Hindu writers the sacrifier is the person who expects the effect of his acts to react on himself. (Compare the Vedic formula, "We who sacrifice for ourselves," the *ye yajamahe* of the Avestan formula *yazamaide* (Alfred Hillebrandt, *Ritual Litteratur*, Strasbourg, 1897, p. 11).) These *benefits* of the sacrifice are, in our view, the necessary consequences of the rite. They are not to be attributed to the free divine will that theology has gradually interpolated between the religious act and its consequences. Thus it will be understood that we have neglected a certain number of questions which imply the hypothesis of the sacrifice-gift, and the intervention of strictly personal gods.

2.   This is normally the case with the Hindu sacrifice, which is, as nearly as possible, an individual one.

3.   e.g., *Iliad*, I, 313f.

4.   This is particularly the case with true totemic sacrifices, and with those in which the group itself fulfils the role of sacrificer, and kills, tears apart, and devours the victim; finally, it is also the case with a good number of human sacrifices, above all those of endo-cannibalism. But often the mere fact of being present is enough.

5.   In ancient India the master of the house (*grihapati*) sometimes sacrifices for the whole family. When he is only a participant in the ceremonies, his family and his wife (the latter is present at the great sacrifices) receive certain effects from the sacrifice.

6.   According to Ezekiel, the prince (*nasi* = exilarch) had to pay the costs of sacrifice at festivals, to provide the libations and the victim. Cf. Ezek. xlv, 17; II Chron. xxxi, 3.

7.   See below, p. 65.

8.   See below, p. 65, n. 378. We shall cite especially the sacrifices celebrated at the entrance of a guest into the house: H. C. Trumbull, *The Threshold Covenant* (Edinburgh, 1896), pp. 1ff.

9.   On the blood covenant and the way it has been linked to sacrifice, see Smith, *Religion of the Semites*, Lecture IX; H. C. Trumbull, *The Blood Covenant* (London, 1887).

10.   On the consecration of hair, see G. A. Wilken, "Über das Haaropfer und einige andere Trauergebräuche bei den Volkern Indonesiens," *Revue coloniale internationale*, 1884.

11.   Lev. ii, 1ff; vi, 7ff; ix, 4ff; x, 12ff; Exod. xxiii, 18; xxxiv, 25; Amos iv, 5. The *minha* so far fulfils the function of any other sacrifice that a *minha* without oil

and incense replaces a *hattat* and bears the same name. (Cf. Lev. v, 11.) *Minha* is often used with the general meaning of sacrifice (e.g., I Kings xviii, 29, etc.). Conversely, in the Marseilles inscription the word *zebah* is applied like *minha* to vegetable oblations: *C.I.S.* 165, 1, 12; 1, 14; cf. *ibid.*, 167, li. 9 and 10.

12. Lev. ii.

13. Aristophanes, *Plutus*, ll. 659ff. Stengel, *Die Griechischen Kultusalterthümer*, pp. 89ff.

14. Porphyry, *De abstinentia*, ii, 29. Diogenes Laertius, viii, 13 (Delos). Stengel, *Die Griechischen Kultusalterthümer*, p. 92. Pliny, *Nat. Hist.*, xviii, 7. Scholium on Persius, ii, 48.

15. Smith, *Religion of the Semites*, pp. 230ff. He sees even in the libations of wine and oil of the Semitic rituals equivalents of the blood of animal victims.

16. K. Bernhardi, *Trankopfer bei Homer*, Programm des königlichen Gymnasiums zu Leipzig, 1885. H. von Fritze, *De libatione veterum Graecorum*, Berlin, 1893.

17. νηϋάλια and μελίχρατον. See Stengel, *Die Griechischen Kultusalterthümer*, pp. 93 and 111. J.G. Frazer, *Pausanias* (1898), III, p. 583.

18. Stengel, *Die Griechischen Kultusalterthümer*, p. 99. A libation of spirits has sometimes replaced, in modern practice, the ancient sacrifices. See P. Bahlmann, *Münsterlandische Märchen* (Münster, 1898), p. 341. Cf. Paul Sartori, 'Über das Bauopfer', *Zeitschr. für Ethnologie*, vol. 30 (1898), p. 25.

19. See the texts cited by A. Hillebrandt, *Das Altindische Neu- und Vollmondsopfer*, pp. 42, 43.

20. Were these vegetable offerings substituted for bloody sacrifices, as was implied in the Roman formula, *in sacris simulata pro veris accipi* (Servius, *Ad Aeneid.*, II, 116; Festus, 360b)? It was doubtless convenient to imagine a steady progress from human to animal sacrifice, then from animal sacrifice to figurines representing animals, and thence, finally, to the offering of cakes. It is possible that in certain cases, which moreover are little known, the introduction of new rituals brought about these substitutions. But there is no authority for applying these facts to make generalizations. The history of certain sacrifices presents rather a reverse process. The animals made from dough that were sacrificed at certain agricultural festivals are images of agrarian evil spirits and not simulacra of animal victims. The analysis of these ceremonies later will give the reason for this.

21. It follows from this definition that between religious punishment and sacrifice (at least, expiatory sacrifice) there are both analogies and differences. Religious punishment also implies a consecration (*consecratio bonorum et capitis*); it is likewise a destruction and is wrought by this consecration. The rites are similar enough to those of sacrifice for Robertson Smith to have seen in them models of expiatory sacrifice. Only, in the case of punishment, the manifestation in a violent fashion of the consecration affects directly the one who has committed the crime and who is himself expiating it; in the case of expiatory sacrifice, on the other hand, substitution takes place, and it is upon the victim, and not upon the guilty one, that expiation falls. However, as society is contaminated by the crime, the punishment is at the same time a means for it to rid itself of the contamination with which it is sullied. Thus, in respect of society, the guilty one fulfils the part of an expiatory victim. It may be said that there is punishment and sacrifice at one and the same time.

22. H. Callaway, *Religious System of the Amazulu*, p. 59, cf. p. 92.

# 6

# EDWARD A. WESTERMARCK
## (b. 1862)

Edward Alexander Westermarck, sociologist and anthropologist, was born in Helsinki, Finland. His mother was a librarian and his father a professor of Latin. After earning his Ph.D. in 1890 from the University of Helsinki, he held a post as a professor of Moral Philosophy at the same institution for the next 40 years. During the spring terms between 1907 and 1930 he taught sociology at the London School of Economics, where he influenced Bronislaw Malinowski. Later Malinowski placed Westermarck alongside Durkheim and S. R. Steinmetz as the founders of social anthropology. Westermarck deserves much praise for he was one of the first social scientists to conduct field research (several visits to Morocco over the course of nine years) as well as utilize data collected from secondary sources.

Westermarck is remembered for three main areas of writing and research. The first, and perhaps most influential, is his work on cross-cultural notions of marriage. In 1891 he published his doctoral dissertation in a three-volume work entitled *The History of Human Marriage*, a work that took up an argument based on the notion of natural selection, and claimed monogamy, and not "primitive promiscuity" (the more common assumption of his time), was the original form of marriage. In this work he also concluded that the incest taboo (expressed often with the marriage rule of exogamy) originates from a natural, gut-level, aversion to sex between close relatives (precisely the opposite view Freud later presents). The second notable area of Westermarck's research is his contribution to ethnographic studies of Morocco. He published no fewer than four books on the religion and culture of this area, including *Ritual and Belief in Morocco* (two volumes) in 1926. Finally, Westermarck contributed work on comparative ethics. He wrote two books on this subject—*The Origin and Development of the Moral Ideas* (1906–8), and *Ethical Relativity* (1932). From these comparative studies he asserted that moral judgments arise from emotions and not from the intellect. Consequently, universally valid moral truths do not exist. Instead, psychological (e.g., feelings of altruism) and sociological (e.g., awareness of approval) influences combine, and over a period of development, create the diversity of morals, customs, and laws that vary from group to group.

# E. A. *Westermarck*: from *The Origin and Development of the Moral Ideas*

Westermarck devotes one chapter of *The Origin and Development of the Moral Ideas* to accounts of human sacrifice gathered from around the world. He wishes to explain why some groups have moral laws that include sanctions for killing human beings, why some people believe offering human life is gratifying to "superhuman beings." This is an important though complex endeavor because examples of human sacrifice have appeared on almost every continent, and not simply among "savage races." He briefly considers several native explanations for the practice—the gods "have an appetite for human flesh," the gods require human attendants in the spirit world, and the gods are angry and want to punish a wrongdoer—but finds these inadequate. Westermarck settles instead on a psychological explanation. He speculates that individuals from these sacrificing groups believe, during moments when they feel so threatened they might die, the gods must, for whatever reason, want human life. After all, the gods are ultimately the source of such dangers. As they give life, they can take it. Human sacrifice, therefore, is an attempt to persuade the gods, to avert what appears to be certain death, by offering a different life. Human sacrificial victims are essentially substitutes for the lives of the living, and human sacrifice, Westermarck concludes, "is essentially a method of life-insurance."

Looking at the various circumstances when human sacrifices occur, Westermarck finds support for his claim. He considers a number of situations when different cultures have felt compelled to sacrifice human beings, for example: during times of war, during epidemics, famines, floods, barrenness, illness of an important person (e.g., a king), the construction of buildings, and so forth. In each of these, the victim stands for, what Hubert and Mauss call, the sacrifier. The sacrifier, whether it be an entire community or an individual, seeks relief from a trouble-making god, seeks salvation from death, by offering it a particular human victim. In a later phase of development, Westermarck suggests, people grew reluctant to sacrifice human beings and therefore began to substitute effigies and animals—a substitute for a substitute, but one that follows the original logic. Later still, practices of bleeding and mutilation, where parts are destroyed while the whole is saved, took the place of complete human sacrifice.

Westermarck agrees with Frazer that sacrificial victims (human, animal, and vegetable) are representatives, but he disagrees over what they represent. So while both theorists rely on a theory of symbolism, for Frazer the victim embodies the god, and for Westermarck it stands for the sacrifier. All subsequent motives for sacrifice—to prevent failure, to obtain favors, to expiate sins, to restore harmony, to repay generosity, and so forth—derive, according to Westermarck, from the original psychological mechanism he identifies. Refusing to see the victim as a representative of a god, Westermarck also avoids the controversy surrounding totemism. Instead, he aligns himself with a form of "gift-theory," beginning, as he does, with the notion that gods can be "gratified." His claim relies on the idea of exchange, that human beings can transfer something, namely a "life," to superhuman beings, and that this transfer has a beneficial effect on the relationship between the two.

Reprinted here is a portion of Westermarck's "Human Sacrifice" chapter from his *The Origin and Development of the Moral Ideas*. Dealing with the particular case of human sacrificial victims, it summarizes a wide variety of examples and offers a theoretical claim, an explanation of sacrifice that may be labeled an "exchange theory" of sacrifice.

ᏁᏁᎫᎬᏋ

# From *The Origin and Development of the Moral Ideas*

IT STILL REMAINS for us to consider some particular cases in which destruction of human life is sanctioned by custom or law.

Men are killed with a view to gratifying the desires of superhuman beings. We meet with human sacrifice in the past history of every so-called Aryan race.[1] It occurred, at least occasionally, in ancient India, and several of the modern Hindu sects practised it even in the last century.[2] There are numerous indications that it was known among the early Greeks.[3] At certain times it prevailed in the Hellenic cult of Zeus;[4] indeed, in the second century after Christ men seem still to have been sacrificed to Zeus Lycaeus in Arcadia.[5] To the historic age likewise belongs the sacrifice of the three Persian prisoners of war whom Themistocles was compelled to slay before the battle of Salamis.[6] In Rome, also, human sacrifices, though exceptional, were not unknown in historic times.[7] Pliny records that in the year 97 BC a decree forbidding such sacrifices was passed by the Roman Senate,[8] and afterwards the Emperor Hadrian found it necessary to renew this prohibition.[9] Porphyry asks, "Who does not know that to this day, in the great city of Rome, at the festival of Jupiter Latiaris, they cut the throat of a man?"[10] And Tertullian states that in North Africa, even to the proconsulship of Tiberius, infants were publicly sacrificed to Saturn.[11] Human sacrifices were offered by Celts,[12] Teutons,[13] and Slavs;[14] by the ancient Semites[15] and Egyptians;[16] by the Japanese in early days;[17] and, in the New World, by the Mayas[18] and, to a frightful extent, by the

---

Edward A. Westermarck, *The Origin and Development of the Moral Ideas*, 2 volumes (London: Macmillan and Co. Ltd.; 1912), pages 434–52, 466–76. In the public domain.

Aztecs. "Scarcely any author," says Prescott in his "History of the Conquest of Mexico," "pretends to estimate the yearly sacrifices throughout the empire at less than twenty thousand, and some carry the number as high as fifty thousand."[19] The same practice is imputed by Spanish writers to the Incas of Peru, and probably not without good reason.[20] Before their rule, at all events, it was of frequent occurrence among the Peruvian Indians.[21] It also prevailed, or still prevails, among the Caribs[22] and some North American tribes;[23] in various South Sea islands, especially Tahiti and Fiji;[24] among certain tribes in the Malay Archipelago;[25] among several of the aboriginal tribes of India;[26] and very commonly in Africa.[27]

From this enumeration it appears that the practice of human sacrifice cannot be regarded as a characteristic of savage races. On the contrary, it is found much more frequently among barbarians and semi-civilised peoples than among genuine savages, and at the lowest stages of culture known to us it is hardly heard of. Among some peoples the practice has been noticed to become increasingly prevalent in the course of time. In the Society Islands "human sacrifices, we are informed by the natives, are comparatively of modern institution: they were not admitted until a few generations antecedent to the discovery of the islands";[28] and in ancient legends there seems to be certain indications that they were once prohibited in Polynesia.[29] In India human sacrifices were apparently much rarer among the Vedic people than among the Brahmanists of a later age.[30] We are told that such sacrifices were adopted by the Aztecs only in the beginning of the fourteenth century, about two hundred years before the conquest, and that, "rare at first, they became more frequent with the wider extent of their empire; till, at length, almost every festival was closed with this cruel abomination."[31] Of the Africans Mr. Winwood Reade remarks, "The more powerful the nation the grander the sacrifice."[32]

Men offer up human victims to their gods because they think that the gods are gratified by such offerings. In many cases the gods are supposed to have an appetite for human flesh or blood.[33] The Fijian gods are described as "delighting in human flesh."[34] Among the Ooryahs of India the priest, when offering a human sacrifice to the war-god Manicksoro, said to the god, "The sacrifice we now offer you must eat."[35] Among the Iroquois, when an enemy was tortured at the stake, the savage executioners leaped around him crying, "To thee, Arieskoi, great spirit, we slay this victim, that thou mayest eat his flesh and be moved thereby to give us henceforth luck and victory over our foes."[36] Among the ancient nations of Central America the blood and heart of the human victims offered in sacrifice were counted the peculiar portion of the gods.[37] Thus, in Mexico, the high-priest, after cutting open the victim's breast, tore forth the yet palpitating heart, offered it first to the sun, threw it then at the feet of the idol, and finally burned it; sometimes the heart was placed in the mouth of the idol with a golden spoon, and its lips were anointed with the victim's blood.[38]

But the human victim is not always, as has been erroneously supposed,[39] intended to serve the god as a food-offering. The Tshi-speaking peoples of the Gold Coast, as Major Ellis observes, maintain that their gods require not only food, but attendants; "the ghosts of the human victims sacrificed to them are believed to pass at once into a condition of ghostly servitude to them, just as those sacrificed at the funerals of chiefs are believed to pass into a ghostly attendance."[40] Cieza de Leon mentions the prevalence of a similar belief among the ancient Peruvians. At the hill of Guanacaure, "on certain days they sacrificed men and women, to whom, before they were put to death, the priest addressed a discourse, explaining to them that they were going to serve that god who was being worshipped."[41]

Moreover, an angry god may be appeased simply by the death of him or those who aroused his anger, or of some representative of the offending community, or of somebody belonging to the kin of the offender. Among the Ewe-speaking peoples of the Slave Coast, "in the case of human victims the gods are not believed to devour the souls; and as these souls are, by the majority of the natives, believed to proceed to Dead-land like all others, the object of human sacrifice seems to be to gratify or satiate the malignancy of the gods at the expense of chosen individuals, instead of leaving it to chance— the victims are in fact slain for the benefit of the community at large."[42] One reason why the human victims are so frequently criminals, is no doubt the intention of appeasing the god by offering up to him an individual who is hateful to him. The Sandwich Islanders "sacrifice culprits to their gods, as we sacrifice them in Europe to justice."[43] Among the Teutons the execution of a criminal was, in many cases at least, a sacrifice to the god whose peculiar cult had been offended by the crime.[44] Thus the Frisian law describes as an immolation to the god the punishment of one who violates his temple.[45] In ancient Rome the corn thief, if he was an adult, was hanged as an offering to Ceres;[46] and Ovid tells us that a priestess of Vesta who had been false to her vows of chastity was sacrificed by being buried alive in the earth, Vesta and Tellus being the same deity.[47] In consequence of the sacrilege of Menalippus and Comætho, who had polluted a temple of Artemis by their amours, the Pythian priestess ordained that the guilty pair should be sacrificed to the goddess, and that, besides, the people should every year sacrifice to her a youth and a maiden, the fairest of their sex.[48] The Hebrew *cherem*, or ban, was originally applied to malefactors and other enemies of Yahveh, and sometimes also to their possessions. "*Cherem*," says Professor Kuenen, "is properly dedication to Yahveh, which in reality amounted to destruction or annihilation. The persons who were 'dedicated,' generally by a solemn vow, to Yahveh, were put to death, frequently by fire, whereby the resemblance to an ordinary burnt-offering was rendered still more apparent; their dwellings and property were also consumed by fire; their lands were left uncultivated for ever. Such punishments were very common in the ancient world. But in Israel, as elsewhere, they were at the same time religious acts."[49] The sacrifice of offenders has, in fact, survived in the Christian world, since every execution performed for the purpose of appeasing an offended and angry god may be justly called a sacrifice.[50]

It is impossible to discover in every special case in what respect the worshippers believe the offering of a fellow-creature to be gratifying to the deity. Probably they have not always definite views on the subject themselves. They know, or believe, that on some certain occasion, they are in danger of losing their lives; they attribute this to the designs of a supernatural being; and, by sacrificing a man, they hope to gratify that being's craving for human life, and thereby avert the danger from themselves. That this principle mainly underlies the practice of human sacrifice appears from the circumstances in which such sacrifices generally occur.

Human victims are often offered in war, before a battle, or during a siege.

Cæsar wrote of the Gauls, "They who are engaged in battles and dangers either sacrifice men as victims, or vow that they will sacrifice them . . .; because they think that unless the life of a man be offered for the life of a man, the mind of the immortal gods cannot be rendered propitious."[51] The Lusitanians sacrificed a man and a horse at the commencement of a military enterprise.[52] Before going to war, or before the beginning of a battle, or during a siege, the Greeks offered a human victim to ensure victory.[53] When hard-pressed in battle, the King of Moab sacrificed his eldest son as a burnt offering on the wall.[54] In times of great calamities, such as war, the Phenicians sacrificed some of their dearest friends, who were selected by votes for this purpose.[55] During a battle with king Gelo of Syracuse, the general Hamilcar sacrificed innumerable human victims, from dawn to sunset;[56] and when Carthage was reduced to the last extremities, the noble families were compelled to give up two hundred of their sons to be offered to Baal.[57] In Hindu scriptures and traditions success in war is promised to him who offers a man in sacrifice.[58] In Jeypore "the blood-red god of battle" is propitiated by human victims. "Thus, on the eve of a battle, or when a new fort, or even an important village is to be built, or when danger of any kind is to be averted, this sanguinary being must be propitiated with human blood."[59] In Great Benin human blood was shed in a case of common danger when an enemy was at the gate of the city.[60] The Yorubas sacrifice men in times of national need.[61] Among the Ewe-speaking peoples of the Slave Coast, such sacrifices "are ordinarily only made in time of war, pestilence, or great calamity."[62] The Tahitians offered human sacrifices in seasons of war, or when war was in agitation.[63]

After a victory, captured enemies are sacrificed to the god to whose assistance the success is ascribed. This sacrifice has been represented as a thank-offering;[64] but, in many cases at least, it seems to be offered either to fulfil a vow previously made, or to induce the god to continue his favours for the future.[65] Among the Kayans of Borneo it is the custom that, when captives are brought to an enemy's country, "one should suffer death, to bring prosperity and abolish the curse of the enemy in their lands."[66]

Human sacrifices are offered for the purpose of stopping or preventing epidemics.

The Phenicians sacrificed "some of their dearest friends," not only in war, but in times of pestilence.[67] In similar circumstances the ancient Greeks had recourse to human sacrifices.[68] In seasons of great peril, as when a pestilence was raging, the ancient Italians made a vow that they would sacrifice every living being that should be born in the following spring.[69] In West Gothland, in Sweden, the people decreed a human sacrifice to stay the *digerdöd*, or Plague, hence two beggar children, having just then come in, were buried alive.[70] In Fur, in Denmark, there is a tradition that, for the same purpose, a child was interred alive in the burial ground.[71] Among the Chukchi, in 1814, when a sudden and violent disease had broken out and carried off both men and reindeer, the Shamans, after having had recourse in vain to their usual conjurations, determined that one of the most respected chiefs must be sacrificed to appease the irritated spirits.[72] In Great Benin, "when the doctors declared a man had died owing to Ogiwo, if they think an epidemic imminent, they can tell Overami [the king] that Ogiwo vex. Then he can take a man and a woman, all the town can fire guns and beat drums. The man and woman are brought out, and the head Jujuman can make this prayer: 'Oh, Ogiwo, you are very big man; don't let any sickness come for Ado. Make all farm good, and every woman born man son.'"[73] In the same country twelve men, besides various animals, were offered yearly on the anniversary of the death of Adolo, king Overami's father. King Overami, calling his father loudly by name, spoke as follows: "Oh, Adolo, our father, look after all Ado [that is, Great Benin], don't let any sickness come to us, look after me and my people, our slaves, cows, goats, and fowls, and everything in the farms."[74]

The sacrifice of human victims is resorted to as a method of putting an end to a devastating famine.

Instances of this practice are reported to have occurred among the ancient Greeks[75] and Phenicians.[76] In a grievous famine, after other great sacrifices, of oxen and of men, had proved unavailing, the Swedes offered up their own king Dómaldi.[77] Chinese annals tell us that there was a great drought and famine for seven years after the accession of T'ang, the noble and pious man who had overthrown the dynasty of Shang. It was then suggested at last by some one that a human victim should be offered in sacrifice to Heaven, and prayer be made for rain, to which T'ang replied, "If a man must be the victim I will be he."[78] Up to quite recent times, the priests of Lower Bengal have, in seasons of scarcity, offered up children to Siva; in the years 1865 and 1866, for instance, recourse was had to such sacrifices in order to avert famine.[79]

For people subsisting on agriculture a failure of crops means starvation and death,[80] and is, consequently, attributed to the murderous designs of a superhuman being, such as the earth spirit, the morning star, the sun, or the rain-god. By sacrificing to that being a man, they hope to appease its thirst for human blood; and whilst some resort to such a sacrifice only in case of actual famine, others try to prevent famine by making the offering in advance. This I take to be the true explanation of the custom of securing good crops by means of human sacrifice, of which many instances have been produced by Dr. Frazer.[81] There are obvious links between this custom and that of the actual famine-sacrifice. Thus the ancient Peruvians sacrificed children after harvest, when they prepared to make ready the land for the next year, not every year, however, but "only when the weather was not good, and seasonable."[82] In Great Benin, "if there is too much rain, then all the people would come from farm and beg Overami [the king] to make juju, and sacrifice to stop the rain. Accordingly, a woman was taken, a prayer made over her, and a message saluting the rain god put in her mouth, then she was clubbed to death and put up in the execution tree so that the rain might see . . . In the same way if there is too much sun so that there is a danger of the crops spoiling, Overami can sacrifice to the Sun God."[83] The principle of substitution admits of a considerable latitude in regard to the stage of danger at which the offering is made; the danger may be more imminent, or it may be more remote. This holds good of various kinds of human sacrifice, not only of such sacrifices as are intended to influence the crops. I am unable to subscribe to the hypothesis cautiously set forth by Dr. Frazer, that the human victim who is killed for the purpose of ensuring good crops is regarded as a representative of the corn-spirit and is slain as such. So far as I can see, Dr. Frazer has adduced no satisfactory evidence in support of his supposition; whereas a detailed examination of various cases mentioned by him in connection with it indicates that they are closely related to human sacrifices offered on other occasions, and explicable from the same principle, that of substitution.

"The best known case of human sacrifices, systematically offered to ensure good crops," says Dr. Frazer, "is supplied by the Khonds or Kandhs." The victims, or Meriahs, are represented by our authorities[84] as being offered to propitiate the Earth goddess, Tari Pennu or Bera Pennu, but from their treatment both before and after death it appears to Dr. Frazer that the custom cannot be explained as merely a propitiatory sacrifice. The flesh and the ashes of the Meriah, he observes, were believed to possess a magic power of fertilising the land, quite independent of the indirect efficacy which they might have as an offering to secure the goodwill of the deity. For, though a part of the flesh was offered to the Earth Goddess, the rest of it was buried by each householder in his fields, and the ashes of the other parts of the body were scattered over the fields, laid as paste on the granaries, or mixed with the new corn. The same intrinsic power was ascribed to the blood and tears of the Meriah, his blood causing the redness of the turmeric and his tears producing rain; and magic power as an attribute of the victim appears also in the sovereign virtue believed to reside in anything that came from his person, as his hair or spittle. Considering further that, according to our authorities, the Meriah was regarded as "something more than mortal," or that "a species of reverence, which it is not easy to distinguish from adoration, is paid to him," Dr. Frazer concludes that he may originally have represented the Earth deity or perhaps a deity of vegetation, and that he only in later times came to be regarded rather as a victim offered to a deity than as himself an incarnate deity.[85]

The premise on which Dr. Frazer bases his argument appears to me quite untenable. It is an arbitrary supposition that the ascription of a magical power to the Meriah "indicates that he was much more than a mere man sacrificed to propitiate a deity."[86] A sacrifice is very commonly believed to be endowed with such a power, not as an original quality, but in consequence of its contact or communion with the supernatural being to which it is offered. Just as the Meriah of the Kandhs is taken round the village, from door to door, and some pluck hair from his head, while others beg for a drop of his spittle, so, among the nomadic Arabs of Morocco, at the Muhammedan "Great Feast," a man dressed in the bloody skin of the sheep which has been sacrificed on that occasion, goes from tent to tent, and beats each tent with his stick so as to confer blessings on its inhabitants. For he is now endowed with *l-baraka del-ʿid*, "the benign virtue of the feast"; and the same power is ascribed to various parts of the sacrificed sheep, which are consequently used for magical purposes. If Dr. Frazer's way of arguing were correct we should have to conclude that the victim was originally the god himself, or a representative of the god, to whom it is now offered in sacrifice. But the absurdity of any such inference becomes apparent at once when we consider that, in Morocco, every offering to a holy person, for instance to a deceased saint, is considered to participate in its sanctity. When the saint has his feast, and animals and other presents are brought to his tomb, it is customary for his descendants—who have a right to the offerings—to distribute some flesh of the slaughtered animals among their friends, thereby conferring *l-baraka* of the saint upon those who eat it; and even candles which have been offered to the saint are given away for the same purpose, being instinct with his *baraka*. Of course, what holds good of the Arabs in Morocco does not necessarily hold good of the Kandhs of Bengal; but it should be remembered that Dr. Frazer's argument is founded on the notion that the ascription of a magic power to a victim which is offered in sacrifice to a god indicates that the victim was once regarded as a divine being or as the god himself; and the facts I have recorded certainly prove the arbitrariness of this supposition.

This is by no means the only objection which may be raised against Dr. Frazer's hypothesis. In his description of the rite in question he has emphasised its connection with agriculture to a degree which is far from being justified by the accounts given by our authorities. Mr. Macpherson states that the human sacrifice to Tari Pennu was celebrated as a public oblation by tribes, branches of tribes, or villages, both at social festivals held periodically, and when special occasions demanded exceptional propitiations. It was celebrated "upon the occurrence of an extraordinary number of deaths by disease; or should very many die in childbirth; or should the flocks or herds suffer largely from disease, or from wild beasts; or should the greater crops threaten to fail"; while the occurrence of any marked calamity to the families of the chiefs, whose fortunes were regarded as the principal indication of the disposition of Tari towards their tribes, was held to be a token of wrath which could not be too speedily averted.[87] Moreover, besides these social offerings, the rite was performed by individuals to avert the wrath of Tari from themselves and their families, for instance, if a child, when watching his father's flock, was carried off by a tiger.[88] So, also, Mr. Campbell observes that the human blood was offered to the Earth goddess, "in the hope of thus obtaining abundant crops, averting calamity, and inspiring general prosperity";[89] or that it was supposed "that good crops, and safety from all disease and accidents, were ensured by this slaughter."[90] According to another authority, Mr. Russell, the assembled multitude, when dancing round the victim, addressed the earth in the following words, "O God, we offer this sacrifice to you; give us good crops, seasons, and health."[91] Nor was the magic virtue of the Meriah utilised solely for the benefit of the crops. According to one account, part of the flesh was buried near the village idol as an offering to the earth, and part on the boundaries of the village;[92] whilst in the invocation made by the priest, the goddess was represented as saying, "Let each man place a shred of the flesh in his fields, in his grain-store, and in his yard."[93] The ashes, again, were scattered over the fields, or "laid as paste over the houses and granaries."[94] It is also worth noticing that, among the Kandhs of Maji Deso, the offering was not at all made for the special purpose of obtaining cereal produce, "but for general prosperity, and blessings for themselves and families";[95] and that in the neighbouring principality, Chinna Kimedy, inhabited for the most part by Ooryahs, the sacrifice was not offered to the earth alone, "but to a number of deities, whose power is essential to life and happiness," especially to the god of war, the great god, and the sun god.[96] Now, whilst all these facts are in perfect agreement with the theory of substitution, they certainly do not justify the supposition that the Meriah was the representative of a deity of vegetation.

The same may be said about other cases mentioned by Dr. Frazer, when more closely examined. "The Indians of Guayaquil, in Ecuador," he says, "used to sacrifice human blood and the hearts of men when they sowed their fields."[97] But our authority, Cieza de Leon, adds that those Indians also offered human victims when their chiefs were sick "to appease the wrath of their gods."[98] "The Pawnees," Dr. Frazer writes, "annually sacrificed a human victim in spring when they sowed their fields. The sacrifice was believed to have been enjoined on them by the Morning Star, or by a certain bird which the Morning Star had sent to them as its messenger . . . They thought that an omission of this sacrifice would be followed by the total failure of the crops of maize, beans, and pumpkins."[99] James, to whom Dr. Frazer refers, and other authorities say that the human sacrifice was a propitiatory offering made *to* that star,[100] a planet which especially with the Skidi—the only section of the Pawnees who offered human sacrifices—was an object of superstitious veneration.[101] Sickness, misfortune, and personal mishaps of various kinds were often spoken of as attributable to the incurred ill-will of the heavenly bodies;[102] and the object of the sacrifice to the morning star is expressly said to have been "to avert the evil influences exerted by that planet."[103] According to Mr. Dunbar, whose important[104] article dealing with the subject has escaped Dr. Frazer's notice, "the design of the bloody ordeal was to conciliate that being and secure a good crop. Hence," he continues, "it has been supposed that the morning star was regarded by them as presiding over agriculture, but this was a mistake. They sacrificed to that star because they feared it, imagining that it exerted malign influence if not well disposed. It has also been stated that the sacrifice was made annually. This, too, was an error. It was made only when special occurrences were interpreted as calling for it."[105] At the present day the Indians speak of the sacrifice as having been made to Ti-ra'-wa, the Supreme Being or the deity "who is in and of everything."[106] In the detailed account of the rite, which was given to Mr. Grinnell by an old chief who had himself witnessed it several times, it is said:—"While the smoke of the blood and the buffalo meat, and of the burning body, ascended to the sky, all the people prayed to Ti-ra'-wa, and walked by the fire and grasped handfuls of the smoke, and passed it over their bodies and over those of their children, and prayed Ti-ra'wa to take pity on them, and to give them health, and success in war, and plenteous crops . . . This sacrifice always seemed acceptable to Ti-ra'-wa, and when the Skidi made it they always seemed to have good fortune in war, and good crops, and they were always well."[107] According to this description, then, the human sacrifice of the Pawnees, like that of the Kandhs, was not an exclusively agricultural rite, but was performed for the purpose of averting dangers of various kinds. And this is also suggested by Mr. Dunbar's relation of the last instance of this sacrifice, which occurred in April, 1838. In the previous winter the Skidi, soon after starting on their hunt, had a successful fight with a band of Oglala Dacotahs, and fearing that the Dacotahs would retaliate by coming upon them in overwhelming force, they returned for safety to their village before taking a sufficient number of buffaloes. "With little to eat, they lived miserably, lost many of their ponies from scarcity of forage, and, worst of all, one of the captives proved to have the small-pox, which rapidly spread through the band, and in the spring was communicated to the rest of the tribe. All these accumulated misfortunes the Ski'-di attributed to the anger of the morning star; and accordingly they resolved to propitiate its favour by a repetition of the sacrifice, though in direct violation of a stipulation made two years before that the sacrifice should not occur again."[108]

Nor is there any reason whatever to suppose that the Brahman boys whom the Gonds of India used to kidnap and keep as victims to be sacrificed on various occasions,[109] were regarded as representatives of a spirit or god. They were offered up to Bhímsen, the chief object of worship among the Gonds, represented by a piece of iron fixed in a stone or in a tree,[110] now "to sanctify a marriage, now to be wedded to the soil, and again to be given away to the evil spirit of the epidemic raging," or "on the eve of a struggle."[111]

Dr. Frazer writes:—"At Lagos in Guinea it was the custom annually to impale a young girl alive soon after the spring equinox in order to secure good crops . . . A similar sacrifice used to be annually offered at Benin."[112] But Dr. Frazer omits an important fact—mentioned or alluded to by the two authorities he quotes—which gives us the key to the custom, without suggesting that it has anything to do with the corn-spirit. Adams states that the young woman was impaled "to propitiate the favour of the goddess presiding over the rainy season, that she may fill the horn of plenty."[113] And M. Bouche observes, "Au Bénin, on a conservé jusqu'à présent un usage qui régnait jadis à Lagos et ailleurs: celui d'empaler une jeune fille, au commencement de la saison des pluies, afin de rendre les orichas propices aux récoltes."[114] From these statements it appears that the sacrifice was intended to influence the rain, on which the crops essentially depend. That its immediate object was to produce rain is expressly affirmed by Sir R. Burton. At Benin he saw "a young woman lashed to a scaffolding upon the summit of a tall blasted tree and being devoured by the turkey-buzzards. The people declared it to be a 'fetish,' or charm for bringing rain."[115] We have previously noticed that the people of Benin also have recourse to a human sacrifice if there is too much rain, or too much sun, so that the crops are in danger of being spoiled.[116] The theory of substitution accounts for all these cases.

The practice of offering human victims for the purpose of preventing drought and famine by producing rain is apparently not restricted to West Africa. In the beginning of their year, the ancient Mexicans sacrificed many prisoners of war and children who had been purchased for that purpose, to the gods of water, so as to induce them to give the rain necessary for the crops.[117] The Pipiles of Guatemala celebrated every year two festivals which were accompanied by human sacrifices, the one in the beginning of the rainy season, the other in the beginning of the dry season.[118] In India, among the aboriginal tribes to the south-west of Beerbhoom, Sir W. W. Hunter "heard vague reports of human sacrifices in the forests, with a view to procuring the early arrival of the rains."[119] Without venturing to express any definite opinion on a very obscure subject which has already led to so many guesses,[120] I may perhaps be justified in here calling attention to the fact that Zeus Lycæus, in whose cult human sacrifices played a prominent part, was conceived of as a god who sent the rain.[121] It appears from ancient traditions or legends that the idea of procuring rainfall by means of such sacrifices was not unfamiliar to the Greeks.

A certain Molpis offered himself to Zeus Ombrios, the rain-god, in time of drought.[122] Pausanias tells us that once, when a drought had for some time afflicted Greece, messengers were sent to Delphi to inquire the cause, and to beg for a riddance of the evil. The Pythian priestess told them to propitiate Zeus, and that Aeacus should be the intercessor; and then Aeacus, by sacrifices and prayers to Panhellenian Zeus, procured rain for Greece.[123] But Diodorus adds that the drought and famine, whilst ceasing in all other parts of the country, still continued in Attica, so that the Athenians once more resorted to the Oracle. The answer was now given them that they had to expiate the murder of Androgeus, and that this should be done in any way his father, Minos, required. The satisfaction demanded by the latter was, that they every nine years should send seven boys and as many girls to be devoured by the Minotaur, and that this should be done as long as the monster lived. So the Athenians did, and the calamity ceased.[124]

As an instance of the close relationship which exists between human sacrifices offered for agricultural purposes and other human sacrifices, the following case may also be mentioned. According to Strachey, the Indians in some part of Virginia had a yearly sacrifice of children. These sacrifices they held so necessary that if they should omit them, they supposed their gods "would let them no deare, turkies, corne, nor fish," and, besides, "would make a great slaughter amongst them."[125]

Men require for their subsistence not only food, but drink. Hence when the earth fails to supply them with water, they are liable to regard it as an attempt against their lives, which can be averted only by the sacrifice of a human substitute.

In India, in former times, human victims were offered to several minor gods "whenever a newly excavated tank failed to produce sufficient water."[126] In Kâthiâwâr, for instance, if a pond had been dug and would not hold water, a man was sacrificed; and the Vadala lake in Bombay "refused to hold water till the local spirit was appeased by the sacrifice of the daughter of the village headman."[127] There is a legend that, when the bed of the Saugor lake remained dry, the builder "was told, in a dream, or by a priest, that it would continue so till he should consent to sacrifice his own daughter, then a girl, and the young lad to whom she had been affianced, to the tutelary god of the place. He accordingly built a little shrine in the centre of the valley, which was to become the bed of the lake, put the two children in, and built up the doorway. He had no sooner done so than the whole of the valley became filled with water."[128] When Colonel Campbell was rescuing Meriahs among the Kandhs, it was believed by some that he was collecting victims for the purpose of sacrificing them on the plains to the water deity, because the water had disappeared from a large tank which he had constructed.[129] According to a story related by Pausanias, the district of Haliartus was originally parched and waterless, hence one of the rulers went to Delphi and inquired how the people should find water in the land. "The Pythian priestess commanded him to slay the first person he should meet on his return to Haliartus. On his arrival he was met by his son Lophis, and, without hesitation, he struck the young man with his sword. The youth had life enough left to run about, and where the blood flowed water gushed from the ground. Therefore the river is called Lophis."[130]

. . . . . . . . . . . . . . . . . . . . . . . . . . . . . . . . . . . .

I do not affirm that the practice of human sacrifice is in every case based on the idea of substitution; the notion that a certain god has a desire for such sacrifices may no doubt induce his worshippers to gratify this desire for a variety of purposes. But I think there is sufficient evidence to prove that, when men offer the lives of their fellow-men in sacrifice to their gods, they do so as a rule in the hopes of thereby saving their own. Human sacrifice is essentially a method of life-insurance—absurd, no doubt, according to our ideas, but not an act of wanton cruelty. When practised for the benefit of the community or in a case of national distress, it is hardly more cruel than to advocate the infliction of capital punishment on the ground of social expediency, or to compel thousands of men to suffer death on the battle-field on behalf of their country. The custom of human sacrifice admits that the life of one is taken to save the lives of many, or that an inferior individual is put to death for the purpose of preventing the death of somebody who has a higher right to live. Sometimes the king or chief is sacrificed in times of scarcity or pestilence, but then he is probably held personally responsible for the calamity.[131] Very frequently the victims are prisoners of war or other aliens, or slaves, or criminals, that is, persons whose lives are held in little regard. And in many cases these are the only victims allowed by custom.

This was generally the case among the ancient Teutons,[132] though they sometimes deemed a human sacrifice the more efficacious the more distinguished the victim, and the nearer his relationship to him who offered the sacrifice.[133] The Gauls, says Cæsar, "consider that the oblation of such as have been taken in theft, or robbery, or any other offence, is more acceptable to the immortal gods; but when a supply of that class is wanting, they have recourse to the oblation of even the innocent."[134] Diodorus Siculus states that the Carthaginians in former times used to sacrifice to Saturn the sons of the most eminent persons, but that, of later times, they secretly bought and bred up children for that purpose.[135] The chief aim of the wars of the ancient Mexicans was to make prisoners for sacrificial purposes; other victims were slaves who were purchased for this object, and many criminals "who were condemned to expiate their crimes by the sacrifice of their lives."[136] The Yucatans sacrificed captives taken in war, and only if such victims were wanting they dedicated their children to the altar "rather than let the gods be deprived of their due."[137] In Guatemala the victims were slaves or captives or, among the Pipiles, illegitimate children from six to twelve years old who belonged to the tribe.[138] In Florida the human victim who was offered up at harvest time was chosen from among the Spaniards wrecked on the coast.[139] Of the Peruvian Indians before the time of the Incas, Garcilasso de la Vega states that "besides ordinary things such as animals and maize, they sacrificed men and women of all ages, being captives taken in wars which they made against each other."[140] Among the Tshi-speaking peoples of the Gold Coast, "the persons ordinarily sacrificed to the gods are prisoners of war or slaves. When the latter, they are usually aliens, as a protecting god is not so well satisfied with the sacrifice of his own people."[141] In Great Benin, according to Captain Roupell, the people who were kept for sacrifice were bad men, or men with bad sickness, and they were all slaves.[142] In Fiji the victims were generally prisoners of war, but sometimes they were slaves procured by purchase from other tribes.[143] In Nukahiva "the custom of the country requires that the men destined for sacrifice should belong to some neighbouring nation, and accordingly they are generally stolen."[144] In Tahiti "the unhappy wretches selected were either captives taken in war, or individuals who had rendered themselves obnoxious to the chiefs or the priests."[145] The Muruts of Borneo "never sacrifice one of their own people, but either capture an individual of a hostile tribe, or send to a friendly tribe to purchase a slave for the purpose."[146] It is said to be contrary to the Káyán custom to sell or sacrifice one of their own nation.[147] The Gãro hill tribes "generally select their victims out of the Bengali villages in the plains."[148] The Kandhs considered that the victim must be a stranger. "If we spill our own blood," they said, "we shall have no descendants";[149] and even the children of Meriahs, who were reared for sacrificial purposes, were never offered up in the village of their birth."[150]

We find that various peoples who at a certain period have been addicted to the practice of human sacrifice, have afterwards, at a more advanced stage of civilisation, voluntarily given it up. The cause of this is partly an increase, or expansion, of the sympathetic sentiment, partly a change of ideas. With the growth of enlightenment men would lose faith in this childish method of substitution, and consequently find it not only useless, but objectionable; and any sentimental disinclination to the practice would by itself, in the course of time, lead to the belief that the deity no longer cares for it, or is averse to it. Brahmanism gradually abolished the immolation of human victims, incompatible as it was with the precept of *ahimsâ*, or respect for everything that has life; "the liberation of the victim, or the substitution in its stead and place of a figure made of flour paste, both of which were at first matter of sufferance, became at length matter of requirement."[151] According to the Mahabharata, the priest who performs a human sacrifice is cast into hell.[152] In Greece, in the historic age, the practice was held in horror at least by all the better minds, though it was regarded as necessary on certain occasions.[153] It was strongly condemned by enlightened Romans. Cicero speaks of it as a "monstrous and barbarous practice" still disgracing Gaul in his day;[154] and Pliny, referring to the steps taken by Tiberius to stop it, declares it impossible to estimate the debt of the world to the Romans for their efforts to put it down.[155]

The growing reluctance to offer human sacrifice led to various practices intended to replace it.[156] Speaking of the Italian custom of dedicating as a sacrifice to the gods every creature that should be born in the following spring, Festus adds that, since it seemed cruel to kill innocent boys and girls, they were kept till they had grown up, then veiled and driven beyond the boundaries.[157] Among various peoples human effigies or animals were offered instead of men.

Among the Malays of the Malay Peninsula dough models of human beings, actually called "the substitutes," are offered up to the spirits on the sacrificial trays; and in the same sense are the directions of magicians, that "if the spirit craves a human victim a cock may be substituted."[158] We are told that, in Egypt, King Amosis ordered three waxen images to be burned in the temple of Heliopolis in lieu of the three men who in earlier times used to be sacrificed there.[159] The Romans offered dolls;[160] and in old Hindu families belonging to the sect of the Vámácháris a practice still obtains of sacrificing an effigy instead of a living man.[161] In India, Greece, and Rome, animals, also, were substituted for human victims.[162] Of a similar substitution there is probably a trace in the Biblical story of Isaac being exchanged for a ram, and in the paschal sacrifice.[163] On the Gold Coast the human victim who was formerly sacrificed to the god of the Prah is nowadays replaced by a bullock which is specially reserved and fattened for the purpose.[164]

In other cases human sacrifices have been succeeded by practices involving the effusion of human blood without loss of life. We are told that, in Laconia, Lycurgus established the scourging of lads at the altar of Artemis Orthia, in place of the sacrifice of men, which had previously been offered to her;[165] and Euripides represents Athena as ordaining that, when the people celebrate the festival of Artemis the Taurian goddess, the priest, to compensate her for the sacrifice of Orestes, "must hold his knife to a human throat, and blood must flow to satisfy the sacred claims of the goddess, that she may have her honours."[166] There are also many instances of bleeding or mutilation practised for the same purpose as human sacrifice, probably according to the principle of *pars pro toto*, though it is impossible to decide whether they really are survivals of an earlier sacrifice.

Besides the ceremony of *nawgia*, already described,[167] the Tonga Islanders had another ceremony called *tootoo-nima*, or cutting off a portion of the little finger, as a sacrifice to the gods, for the recovery of a superior relation who was ill; and so commonly was this done that, in Mariner's days, there was scarcely a person living in the Tonga Islands who had not lost one or both little fingers, or at least a considerable portion of them.[168] In Chinese literature there are frequently mentioned instances of persons cutting off flesh from their bodies to cure parents or paternal grandparents dangerously ill. In most cases it remains unmentioned how the flesh was prepared; but it is sometimes stated that porridge or broth was made of it, or that it was mixed with medicine. Dr. de Groot maintains that it was in the first place the ascription of therapeutic virtues to parts of the human body that prompted such filial self-mutilation. But he adds that "often also we read of thigh-cutters invoking Heaven beforehand, solemnly asking this highest power to accept their own bodies as a substitute for the patients' lives they wanted to save; their mutilation thus assuming the character of self-immolation."[169] According to the testimony of a native writer, there is scarcely a respectable house in all Bengal, the mistress of which has not at one time or other shed her blood, under the notion of satisfying the goddess Chandiká by the operation. "Whenever her husband or a son is dangerously ill, a vow is made that on the recovery of the patient, the goddess would be regaled with human blood . . . The lady performs certain ceremonies, and then bares her breast in the presence of the goddess, and with a nail-cutter (*naruna*) draws a few drops of blood from between her breasts and offers them to the divinity."[170] Garcilasso de la Vega states that, whilst some of the Peruvian Indians before the time of the Incas sacrificed men, there were others who, though they mixed human blood in their sacrifices, did not obtain it by killing anyone, but by bleeding the arms and legs, according to the importance of the sacrifice, and, in the most solemn cases, by bleeding the root of the nose where it is joined by the eyebrows.[171]

There is one form of human sacrifice which has outlived all others, namely, the penal sacrifice of offenders. There can be no moral scruples in regard to a rite which involves a punishment regarded as just. Indeed, this kind of human sacrifice is even found where the offering of animals or lifeless things has fallen out of use or become a mere symbol. For this is the only sacrifice which is intended to propitiate the deity by the mere death of the victim; and gods are believed to be capable of feeling anger and revenge long after they have ceased to have material needs. The last trace of human sacrifice has disappeared only when men no longer punish offenders capitally with a view to appeasing resentful gods.

Human beings are sacrificed not only to gods, but to dead men, in order to serve them as companions or servants, or to vivify their spirits, or to gratify their craving for revenge.

From various quarters of the world we hear of the immolation of men for the service of the dead, the victims generally being slaves, wives, or captives of war, or, sometimes, friends.[172] This rite occurs or has occurred, more or less extensively, in Borneo[173] and the Philippine Islands,[174] in Melanesia and Polynesia,[175] in many different parts of Africa,[176] and among some American tribes.[177] In America, however, it was carried to its height by the more civilised nations of Central America and Mexico, Bogota and Peru.[178] There is evidence to show that the funeral ceremonies of the ancient Egyptians occasionally included human sacrifice at the gate of the tomb, although the practice would seem to have been exceptional, at any rate after Egypt had entered upon her period of greatness.[179] It has been suggested that in China the burial of living persons with the dead dates from the darkest mist of ages, and that the cases on record in the native books are of relatively modern date only because in high antiquity the custom was so common, that it did not occur to the annalists and chroniclers to set down such everyday matters as anything remarkable.[180] In the fourteenth century of our era, the funeral sacrifice of men was abolished, even for emperors and members of the imperial family,[181] but it has assumed a modified shape under which it still maintains itself in China. "Daughters, daughters-in-law, and widows especially imbued with the doctrine that they are the property of their dead parents, parents-in-law, and husbands, and accordingly owe them the highest degree of submissive devotion, often take their lives, in order to follow them into the next world." And though it has been enacted that no official distinctions shall be awarded to such suttees, whereas honours are granted to widowed wives, concubines, and brides who, instead of destroying themselves, simply abjure matrimonial life for good, sutteeism of widows and brides still meets with the same applause as ever, and many a woman is no doubt prevailed upon, or even compelled, by her own relations, to become a suttee.[182] Professor Schrader observes that "it is no longer possible to doubt that ancient Indo-Germanic custom ordained that the wife should die with her husband."[183] It has been argued, it is true, that the burning of widows begins rather late in India;[184] yet, though the modern ordinance of suttee-burning be a corrupt departure from the early Brahmanic ritual, the practice seems to be, not a new invention by the later Hindu priesthood, but the revivial of an ancient rite belonging originally to a period even earlier than the Veda.[185] In the Vedic ritual there are ceremonies which obviously indicate the previous existence of such a rite.[186] From Greece we have the instances of Evadne throwing herself into the funeral pile of her husband,[187] and of the suicide of the three Messenian widows mentioned by Pausanias.[188] Sacrifice of widows occurred, as it seems as a regular custom, among the Scandinavians,[189] Heruli,[190] and Slavonians.[191] "The fact," says Mr. Ralston, "that, in Slavonic lands, a thousand years ago, widows used to destroy themselves in order to accompany their dead husbands to the world of spirits, seems to rest on incontestable evidence"; and if the dead was a man of means and distinction, he was also solaced by the sacrifice of his slaves.[192] Funeral offerings of slaves occurred among the Teutons[193] and the Gauls of Cæsar's time;[194] and in the Iliad we read of twelve captives being laid on the funeral pile of Patroclus.[195]

According to early notions, men require wives and servants not only during their life-time, but after their death. The surviving relatives want to satisfy their needs, out of affection or from fear of withholding from the dead what belongs to them—their wives and their slaves. The destruction of innocent life seems justified by the low social standing of the victims and their subjection to their husbands or masters. However, with advancing civilisation this sacrifice has a tendency to disappear, partly, perhaps, on account of a change of ideas as regards the state after death, but chiefly, I presume, because it becomes revolting to public feelings. It then dwindles into a survival. As a probable instance of this may be mentioned a custom prevalent among the Tacullies of North America: the widow is compelled by the kinsfolk of the deceased to lie on the funeral pile where the body of her husband is placed, whilst the fire is lighting, until the heat becomes intolerable.[196] In ancient Egypt little images of clay, or wood, or stone, or bronze, made in human likeness and inscribed with a certain formula, were placed within the tomb, presumably in the hopes that they would there attain to life and become the useful servants of the dead.[197] So also the Japanese[198] and Chinese, already in early times, placed images in, or at, the tombs of their dead as substitutes for human victims; and these images have always been considered to have no less virtual existence in the next world than living servitors, wives, or concubines. In China the original immolations were, moreover, replaced by the custom of allowing the nearest relatives and slaves of the deceased simply to settle on the tomb, instead of entering it, there to sacrifice to the manes, and by prohibiting widows from remarrying.[199]

The practice of sacrificing human beings to the dead is not exclusively based on the idea that they require servants and companions. It is extremely probable that the funeral sacrifice of men and animals in many cases involves an intention to vivify the spirits of the deceased with the warm, red sap of life.[200] This seems to be the meaning of the Dahoman custom of pouring blood over the graves of the ancestors of the king.[201] So, also, in Ashanti "human sacrifices are frequent and ordinary, to water the graves of the Kings."[202] In the German folk-tale known under the name of "Faithful John," the statue said to the King, "If you, with your own hand, cut off the heads of both your children, and sprinkle me with their blood, I shall be brought to life again."[203] According to primitive ideas, blood is life; to receive blood is to receive life; the soul of the dead wants to live, and consequently loves blood. The shades in Hades are eager to drink the blood of Odysseus' sacrifice, that their life may be renewed for a time.[204] And it is all the more important that the soul should get what it desires as it otherwise may come and attack the living. The belief that the bloodless shades leave their graves at night and seek renewed life by drawing the blood of the living, is prevalent in many parts of the world.[205] As late as the eighteenth century this belief caused an epidemic of fear in Hungary, resulting in a general disinterment, and the burning or staking of the suspected bodies.[206] It is also possible that the mutilations and self-bleedings which accompany funerals are partly practised for the purpose of refreshing the departed soul.[207] The Samoans called it "an offering of blood" for the dead when the mourners beat their heads with stones till the blood ran.[208]

Finally, as offenders are sacrificed to gods in order to appease their wrath, so manslayers are in many cases killed in order to satisfy their victims' craving for revenge.

# Notes

1. See Hehn, *Wanderings of Plants and Animals from their First Home*, p. 414 *sqq.*
2. Weber, *Indische Streifen*, i, 54 *sqq.* Wilson, "Human Sacrifices in the Ancient Religion of India," in *Works*, ii, 247 sqq. Oldenberg, *Religion des Veda*, p. 363 *sqq.* Barth, *Religions of India*, p. 57 *sqq.* Monier Williams, *Brahmanism and Hinduism*, p. 24. Hopkins, *Religions of India*, pp. 198, 363. Rájendralála Mitra, *Indo-Aryans*, ii, 69 *sqq.* Crooke, *Popular Religion and Folk-Lore of North India*, ii, 167 *sqq.* Chevers, *Manual of Medical Jurisprudence for India*, p. 396 *sqq.*
3. See Geusius, *Victimæ Humanæ, passim*; von Lasaulx, *Sühnopfer der Griechen und Römer, passim*; Farnell, *Cults of the Greek States*, i, 41 *sqq.*; Stengel, *Die griechischen Kultusaltertümer*, p. 114 *sqq.*
4. *Cf.* Farnell, *op. cit.*, i, 93; Stengel, *op. cit.*, p. 116.
5. Pausanias, viii, 38. 7.
6. Plutarch, *Themistocles*, 13.
7. Plutarch, *Questiones Romanæ*, 83. See Landau, in *Am Ur-Quell*, iii, 1892, p. 283 *sqq.*
8. Pliny, *Historia naturalis*, xxx, 3.
9. Porphyry, *De abstinentia ab esu animalium*, ii, 56.
10. *Ibid.*
11. Tertullian, *Apologeticus*, 9 (Migne, *Patrologiæ cursus*, i, 314).
12. Cæsar, *De bello gallico*, vi, 16. Tacitus, *Annales*, xiv, 30. Diodorus Siculus, *Bibliotheca*, v. 31, p. 354. Pliny, *Historia naturalis*, xxx, 4. Strabo, iv, 5, p. 198. Joyce, *Social History of Ancient Ireland*, i, 281 *sqq.*
13. Tacitus, *Germania*, 9. Adam of Bremen, *Gesta Hammaburgensis ecclesiæ pontificum*, iv, 27 (Migne, *op. cit.*, cxlvi. 644). Grimm, *Teutonic Mythology*, i, 44 *sqq.* Vigfusson and Powell, *Corpus Poeticum Boreale*, i, 409 *sq.* Freytag, "Riesen und Menschenopfer in unsern Sagen und Märchen," in *Am Ur-Quell*, i, 1890, pp. 179–183, 197 *sqq.*
14. Mone, *Geschichte des nordischen Heidenthums*, i, 119, quoted by Frazer, *Golden Bough*, ii, 52. Krauss, in *Am Ur-Quell*, vi, 1896, p. 137 *sqq.* (Servians).
15. Ghillany, *Die Menschenopfer der alten Hebräer, passim.* Robertson Smith, *Religion of the Semites*, p. 362 *sqq.* Wellhausen, *Reste arabischen Heidentums*, p. 115 sq. Von Kremer, *Studien zur vergleichenden Culturgeschichte*, i, 42 *sqq.* Chwolsohn, *Die Ssabier und der Ssabismus*, ii, 147 *sqq.*
16. Amélineau, *L'Evolution des idées morales dans l'Egypte Ancienne*, p. 12.
17. Griffis, *Religions of Japan*, p. 75. Lippert, *Seelencult*, p. 79.
18. Bancroft, *Native Races of the Pacific States*, ii, 704, 725.
19. Prescott, *History of the Conquest of Mexico*, p. 38. *Cf.* Clavigero, *History of Mexico*, i, 281; Acosta, *Natural and Moral History of the Indies*, ii, 346.
20. Acosta, *op. cit.*, ii, 344. De Molina, "Fables and Rites of the Yncas," in *Narratives of the Rites and Laws of the Yncas*, pp. 55, 56, 59. According to Cieza de Leon (*Segunda parte de la Crónica del Perú*, p. 100), the practice of human sacrifice has been much exaggerated by Spanish writers, but he does not deny its existence among the Incas; nay, he gives an account of such sacrifices (*ibid.*, p. 109 *sqq.*). Sir Clements Markham seems to attach undue importance to the statement of Garcilasso de la Vega that human victims were never sacrificed by the Incas (*First Part of the Royal Commentaries of the Yncas*, i, 130, 131, 139 *sqq.* n. †). *Cf.* Prescott, *History of the Conquest of Peru*, p. 50 *sq.*, n. 3.

21. Garcilasso de la Vega, *op. cit.*, i, 50, 130.
22. Müller, *Geschichte der Amerikanischen Urreligionen*, p. 212 *sq.*
23. *Ibid.*, p. 142 *sqq.* Réville, *Religions des peuples non-civilisés*, i, 249 *sq.* Dorman, *Origin of Primitive Superstitions*, p. 208 *sqq.*
24. Schneider, *Naturvölker*, i, 191 *sq.* Fornander, *Account of the Polynesian Race*, i, 129. Ellis, *Polynesian Researches*, i, 106, 346–8, 357 (Society Islanders). Williams, *Missionary Enterprises in the South Sea Islands*, p. 548 *sq.* (especially the Hervey Islanders and Tahitians). Von Kotzebue, *Voyage of Discovery*, iii, 248 (Sandwich Islanders). Lisiansky, *Voyage round the World*, p. 81 *sq.* (Nukahivans), 120 (Sandwich Islanders). Gill, *Myths and Songs from the South Pacific*, p. 289 *sqq.* (Mangaians). Williams and Calvert, *Fiji*, pp. 188, 195; Wilkes, *Narrative of the U.S. Exploring Expedition*, iii, 97; Hale, *U.S. Exploring Expedition, vol. VI, Ethnography and Philology*, p. 57 (Fijians). Codrington, *Melanesians*, p. 134 *sqq.*
25. Ling Roth, *Natives of Sarawak and British North Borneo*, ii, 215 *sqq.* Bock, *Head-Hunters of Borneo*, p. 218 *sq.* (Dyaks).
26. Woodthorpe, in *Jour. Anthr. Inst.*, xxvi, 24 (Shans, etc.). Colquhoun, *Amongst the Shans*, p. 152 (Steins inhabiting the south-east of Indo-China). Lewin, *Wild Races of South-Eastern India*, p. 244 (Pankhos and Bunjogees). Godwin-Austen, in *Jour. Anthr. Inst.*, ii, 394 (Gāro hill tribes). Dalton, *Descriptive Ethnology of Bengal*, pp. 147 (Bhúiyas), 176 (Bhúmij), 281 (Gonds), 285 *sqq.* (Kandhs). Hislop, *Aboriginal Tribes of the Central Provinces*, p. 15 *sq.* (Gonds). Macpherson, *Memorials of Service in India*, p. 113 *sq.*; Campbell, *Wild Tribes of Khondistan*, *passim* (Kandhs).
27. Schneider, *Religion der afrikanischen Naturvölker*, p. 118. Reade, *Savage Africa*, p. 52 (Dahomans, etc.). Ling Roth, *Great Benin*, p. 63 *sqq.* Ellis, *Ewe-speaking Peoples of the Slave Coast*, p. 117 *sqq.* Idem, *Yoruba-speaking Peoples of the Slave Coast*, p. 296. Idem, *Tshi-speaking Peoples of the Gold Coast*, p. 169 *sqq.* Cruickshank, *Eighteen Years of the Gold Coast*, ii, 173. Schoen and Crowther, *Expedition up the Niger*, p. 48 *sq.* (Ibos). Arnot, *Garenganze*, p. 75 (Barotse). Arbousset and Daumas, *Exploratory Tour to the North-East of the Colony of the Cape of Good Hope*, p. 97 (Marimos, a Bechuana tribe). Macdonald, *Africana*, i, 96 *sq.* (Eastern Central Africans). Ellis, *History of Madagascar*, i, 422; Sibree, *The Great African Island*, p. 303 (Malagasy).
28. Ellis, *Polynesian Researches*, i, 106.
29. Fornander, *op. cit.*, i, 129.
30. Wilson, *Works*, ii, 268 *sq.*
31. Prescott, *History of the Conquest of Mexico*, p. 36.
32. Reade, *Savage Africa*, p. 52.
33. See Lippert, *Seelencult*, p. 77 *sqq.*; Schneider, *Naturvölker*, i, 190.
34. Williams and Calvert, *op. cit.*, p. 195.
35. Campbell, *Wild Tribes of Khondistan*, p. 211. Cf. Macpherson, *Memorials of Service in India*, p. 120 (Kandhs).
36. Müller, *Geschichte der Amerikanischen Urreligionen*, p. 142.
37. Bancroft, *op. cit.*, ii, 307, 310, 311, 707 sqq.
38. Clavigero, *op. cit.*, i, 279.
39. Réville, *Hibbert Lectures on the Native Religions of Mexico and Peru*, p. 75. *sq.* Idem, *Prolegomena of the History of Religions*, p. 132. Trumbull, *Blood*

Covenant, p. 189. Steinmetz, *Endokannibalismus*, p. 60, n. 1. Schrader, *Reallexikon der indogermanischen Altertumskunde*, p. 603.

40. Ellis, *Tshi-speaking Peoples of the Gold Coast*, p. 169.
41. Cieza de Leon, *Segunda parte de la Crónica del Perú*, p. 109.
42. Ellis, *Ewe-speaking Peoples of the Slave Coast*, p. 119.
43. Von Kotzebue, *op. cit.*, iii, 248. Cf. Lisiansky, *op. cit.*, 120.
44. Von Amira, in Paul's *Grundriss der germanischen Philologie*, ii, pt. ii, 177. Brunner, *Deutsche Rechtsgeschichte*, ii, 587, 684 *sq.* Vigfusson and Powell, *op. cit.*, i, 410. Gummere, *Germanic Origins*, p. 463.
45. *Lex Frisionum*, Additio sapientium, 12.
46. Granger, *Worship of the Romans*, p. 260.
47. Ovid, *Fasti*, vi, 457 *sq.* Cf. Mommsen, *Römisches Strafrecht*, p. 902.
48. Pausanias, vii, 19. 4.
49. Kuenen, *Religion of Israel*, i, 290 *sq.*
50. See *supra*, p. 197 *sq.* For various instances of expiatory human sacrifice, involving vicarious atonement, see *supra*, p. 66 *sq.*
51. Cæsar, *De bello gallico*, vi, 16.
52. Livy, *Epitome*, 49.
53. Pausanias, iv, 9. 4 *sqq.*; ix, 17. 1. Plutarch, *Themistocles*, 13. *Idem, Aristides*, 9. *Idem, Pelopidas*, 21 *sq.* Lycurgus, *Oratio in Leocratem* (ch. 24) 99. Apollodorus, *Bibliotheca*, iii, 15. 4. Porphyry, *De abstinentia ab esu animalium*, ii, 56. Geusius, *op. cit.*, i, ch. 16 *sq.* Stengel, *op. cit.*, p. 115 *sq.*
54. 2 *Kings*, iii, 27.
55. Porphyry, *op. cit.*, ii, 56.
56. Herodotus, vii, 167.
57. Diodorus Siculus, xx, 14.
58. Chevers, *op. cit.*, p. 399.
59. Campbell, *Wild Tribes of Khondistan*, p. 52.
60. Ling Roth, *Great Benin*, p. 72
61. Ellis, *Yoruba-speaking Peoples of the Slave Coast*, p. 296.
62. *Idem, Ewe-speaking Peoples of the Slave Coast*, p. 117.
63. Ellis, *Polynesian Researches*, i, 276 *sqq.*, 346.
64. Diodorus Siculus, xx, 65 (Carthaginians). De Molina, *loc. cit.*, p. 59 (Incas); etc.
65. Ellis, *Tshi-speaking Peoples*, p. 170. Cruickshank, *op. cit.*, ii, 173. Dubois, *Character, Manners, and Customs of the People of India*, p. 488. Jordanes, *De origine actibusque Getarum*, 5 (41). Cf. Jephthah's vow (*Judges*, xi, 30 *sqq.*).
66. Brook, *Ten Years in Saráwak*, ii, 304 sq.
67. Porphyry, *op. cit.*, ii, 56.
68. Geusius, *op. cit.*, i, ch. 13. Stengel, *op. cit.*, p. 116. Frazer, *Golden Bough*, iii, 125 *sq.*
69. Festus, *De verborum significatione*, "Ver sacrum," Müller's edition, p. 379. Nonius Marcellus, *De proprietate sermonis*, "Versacrum," p. 522. Servius, *In Virgilii Æneidos*, vii, 796.
70. Afzelius, *Swenska Folkets Sago-Häfder*, iv, 181.
71. Nyrop, *Romanske Mosaiker*, p. 69, n. 1.
72. Von Wrangell, *Expedition to the Polar Sea*, p. 122 *sq.*
73. Moor and Roupell, quoted by Read and Dalton, *Antiquities from the City of Benin*, p. 7; also by Ling Roth, *Great Benin*, p. 71 *sq.*

74. Moor and Roupell, quoted by Ling Roth, *op. cit.*, p. 70 *sq.*; also by Read and Dalton, *op. cit.*, p. 6.

75. Pausanias, vii, 19. 3 *sq.* Diodorus Siculus, iv. 61. 1 *sqq.* Geusius, *op. cit.*, i, ch. 14.

76. Porphyry, *op. cit.*, ii, 56.

77. Snorri Sturluson, "Ynglingasaga," 15, in *Heimskringla*, i, 30.

78. Legge, *Religions of China*, p. 54.

79. Hunter, *Annals of Rural Bengal*, i, 128.

80. *Cf.* Sleeman, *Rambles and Recollections*, i, 204 *sqq.*:—"In India, unfavourable seasons produce much more disastrous consequences than in Europe . . . More than three-fourths of the whole population are engaged in the cultivation of the land, and depend upon its annual returns for subsistence . . . Tens of thousands die here of starvation, under calamities of season, which in Europe would involve little of suffering to any class."

81. Frazer, *Golden Bough*, ii, 238 *sqq.*

82. Herrera, *op. cit.*, ii, III.

83. Moor and Roupell, quoted by Read and Dalton, *op. cit.*, p. 7; also by Ling Roth, *Great Benin*, p. 71.

84. Campbell, *Wild Tribes of Khondistan.* Macpherson, *Memorials of Service in India.*

85. Frazer, *op. cit.*, ii, 245 *sq.*

86. *Ibid.*, ii, 246.

87. Macpherson, *op. cit.*, p. 113 *sq.* See, also, *ibid.*, pp. 120, 128 *sqq.*

88. *Ibid.*, p. 113 sq.

89. Campbell, *op. cit.*, p. 51.

90. *Ibid.*, p. 56. *Cf. ibid.*, p. 73.

91. Russell, quoted *ibid.*, p. 54.

92. Russell, quoted *ibid.*, p. 55.

93. Macpherson, *op. cit.*, p. 122 *sq.*

94. *Ibid.*, p. 128.

95. Campbell, *op. cit.*, p. 181.

96. *Ibid.*, p. 120. *Cf. ibid.*, p. 197:—Among the Ooryahs human sacrifice is "performed on important occasions, such as going to battle, building a fort in an important village, and to avert any threatened danger."

97. Frazer, *op. cit.*, ii, 238.

98. Cieza de Leon, *La Crónica del Perú* [parte primera], ch. 55 (*Biblioteca de autores españoles*, xxvi, 409).

99. Frazer, *op. cit.*, ii, 238.

100. James, *Expedition from Pittsburg to the Rocky Mountains*, i, 357. Grinnell, *Pawnee Hero Stories and Folk-Tales*, p. 357. Dunbar, "Pawnee Indians," in *Magazine of American History*, viii, 738.

101. Dunbar, *loc. cit.*, p. 738.

102. *Ibid.*, p. 736.

103. Grinnell, *op. cit.*, p. 357.

104. Mr. Dunbar is "born and reared among the Pawnees, familiar with them until early manhood, a frequent visitor to the tribe in later years" (Grinnell, *op. cit.*, p. 213).

105. Dunbar, *loc. cit.*, p. 738 *sq.*

106. Grinnell, *op. cit.*, pp. 357, 358, xvii.

107. *Ibid.*, p. 367.
108. Dunbar, *loc. cit.*, p. 740.
109. Frazer, *op. cit.*, ii, 241.
110. *Panjab Notes and Queries*, § 550, vol. ii, 90.
111. *Ibid.*, § 721, vol. ii, 127 *sq.*
112. Frazer, *op. cit.*, ii, 239.
113. Adams, *Sketches taken during Ten Voyages to Africa*, p. 25.
114. Bouche, *Sept ans en Afrique occidentale*, p. 132.
115. Burton, *Abeokuta*, i, 19 n.*
116. *Supra*, p. 443 *sq.*
117. Sahagun, *Historia general de las cosas de Nueva España*, i, 50. Torquemada, *Monarchia Indiana*, ii, 251. Clavigero, *op. cit.*, i, 297.
118. Stoll, *Ethnologie der Indianerstänime von Quatemala*, p. 46.
119. Hunter, *Annals of Rural Bengal*, i, 128.
120. See Immerwahr, *Die Kulte und Mythen Arkadiens*, i, 16 *sqq*. Professor Robertson Smith suggests ("Sacrifice," in *Encyclopædia Britannica*, xxi, 136) that the human sacrifices offered to Zeus Lycæus were originally cannibal feasts of a wolf tribe.
121. Pausanias, viii, 38. 4. Farnell, *op. cit.*, i, 41.
122. Farnell, *op. cit.*, i, 42.
123. Pausanias, ii, 29. 7 *sq.*
124. Diodorus Siculus, *op. cit.*, iv, 61. 1 *sqq.*
125. Strachey, *History of Travaile into Virginia Britannia*, p. 95 *sq.*
126. Rájendralála Mitra, *op. cit.*, ii, 111.
127. Crooke, *Popular Religion of Northern India*, ii, 174.
128. Sleeman, *Rambles*, i, 129 sq.
129. Campbell, *Wild Tribes of Khondistan*, p. 129.
130. Pausanias, ix, 33. 4.
131. *Cf.* Frazer, *Golden Bough*, i, 15 *sq.*
132. Grimm, *Teutonic Mythology*, i, 45.
133. Holtzmann, *Deutsche Mythologie*, p. 232.
134. Cæsar, *De bello gallico*, vi, 16.
135. Diodorus Siculus, xx, 14.
136. Clavigero, *op. cit.*, i, 282.
137. Bancroft, *op. cit.*, ii, 704.
138. Stoll, *op. cit.*, p. 40.
139. Bry, *op. cit.*, p. 11.
140. Garcilasso de la Vega, *op. cit.*, i, 50.
141. Ellis, *Tshi-speaking Peoples*, p. 170.
142. Ling Roth, *Great Benin*, p.70.
143. Hale, *U.S. Exploring Expedition, vol. VI. Ethnography and Philology*, p. 57. *Cf.* Wilkes, *op. cit.*, iii, 97.
144. Lisiansky, *op. cit.*, p. 81 *sq.*
145. Ellis, *Polynesian Researches*, i, 346.
146. Denison, quoted by Ling Roth, *Natives of Sarawak*, ii, 216.
147. Burns, in *Jour. of Indian Archipelago*, iii, 145.
148. Godwin-Austen, in *Jour. Anthr. Inst.*, ii, 394.
149. Macpherson, *Memorials of Service in India*, p. 121.
150. Campbell, *Wild Tribes of Khondistan*, p. 53.

151. Barth, *Religions of India*, p. 97.
152. *Supra*, p. 458.
153. Stengel, *op. cit.*, p. 117. *Cf.* Donaldson, *loc. cit.*, p. 464.
154. Cicero, *Pro Fonteio*, 10 (21).
155. Pliny, *Historia naturalis*, xxx, 4 (1).
156. *Cf.* Krause, "Die Ablösung der Menschenopfer," in *Kosmos*, 1878, iii, 76 *sqq.*
157. Festus, *op. cit.*, "Ver sacrum," p. 379.
158. Skeat, *Malay Magic*, p. 72.
159. Porphyry, *op. cit.*, ii, 55.
160. Leist, *Græco-italische Rechtsgeschichte*, p. 272 *sqq.*
161. Rájendralála Mitra, *op. cit.*, ii, 109 *sq.*
162. Leist, *Græco-italische Rechtsgeschichte*, p. 267 *sqq.* Frazer, *Golden Bough*, ii, 38, n. 2. Pausanias, ix. 8. 2. For various modifications of human sacrifice in India, see Wilson, *Works*, ii, 267 *sq.*; Crooke, *Popular Religion of Northern India*, ii, 175 *sq.*
163. See *supra*, p. 458.
164. Ellis, *Tshi-speaking Peoples*, p. 66.
165. Pausanias, iii, 16. 10
166. Euripides, *Iphigenia in Tauris*, 1458 *sqq.*
167. *Supra*, p. 455.
168. Mariner, *op. cit.*, ii, 222.
169. De Groot, *Religious System of China*, vol. iv, book ii, 386 *sq.*
170. Rájendralála Mitra, *op. cit.*, i, 111 *sq.*
171. Garcilasso de la Vega, *op. cit.*, i, 52.
172. See Tylor, *Primitive Culture*, i, 458 *sqq.*; Spencer, *Principles of Sociology*, i, 203 *sqq.*,; Liebrecht, *Zur Volkskunde*, p. 380 *sq.*, Schneider, *Naturvölker*, i, 202 *sqq.*; Hehn, *op. cit.*, p. 416 *sqq.*; Westermarck, *History of Human Marriage*, p. 125 *sq.*; Frazer, *Pausanias*, iii, 199 *sq.*
173. Brooke, *Ten Years in Saráwak*, i, 74. Hose and McDougall, "Relations between Men and Animals in Sarawak," in *Jour. Anthr. Inst.*, xxxi, 207 *sq.* Bock, *Head-Hunters of Borneo*, pp. 210 n., 219 *sq.*
174. Blumentritt, "Der Ahnencultus und die religiösen Anschauungen der Malaien des Philippinen-Archipels," in *Mittheilungen d. Geograph. Gesellsch. in Wien*, xxv, 152 *sq.*
175. Westermarck, *op. cit.*, p. 125 *sq.* Brenchley, *op. cit.*, p. 208 (natives of Tana). Williams and Calvert, *op. cit.*, p. 161 *sq.* (Fijians). Lisiansky, *op. cit.*, p. 81 (Nukahivans). Mariner, *op. cit.*, ii, 220 *sq.* (Tonga Islanders). Taylor, *Te Ika a Maui*, p. 218 (Maoris). Von Kotzebue, *op. cit.* iii, 247 (Sandwich Islanders).
176. Rowley, *Africa Unveiled*, p.127. *Idem, Religion of the Africans*, p. 102 *sq.* Schneider, *Religion der afrikanischen Naturvölker*, p. 118 *sqq.* Westermarck, *op. cit.*, p. 125. Ramseyer and Kühne, *Four Years in Ashantee*, p. 50. Mockler-Ferryman, *British Nigeria*, pp. 235, 259 *sqq.* Burton, *Mission to Gelele*, ii, 19 *sqq.* (Dahomans). *Idem, Abeokuta*, i, 220 *sq. Idem, Lake Regions of Central Africa*, i, 124 (Wadoe); ii, 25 *sq.* (Wanyamwezi). Wilson, *Western Africa*, pp. 203, 219. Ellis, *Tshi-speaking Peoples of the Gold Coast*, p. 159 *sqq. Idem, Ewe-speaking Peoples of the Slave Coast*, pp. 117, 118, 121 *sqq.* Nachtigal, *Sahara und Sudan*, ii, 687 (Somraï and Njillem). Baker, *Ismaïlia*, p. 317 *sq.* (Wanyoro). Casati, *Ten Years in Equatoria*, i, 170 (Mambettu). Callaway, *Religious System of the Amazulu*, p. 212 *sq.*

177. Spencer, *Principles of Sociology,* i, 204. Dorman, *op. cit.,* p. 210 *sqq.* Westermarck, *op. cit.,* p. 125. Macfie, *Vancouver Island and British Columbia,* p. 448. Charlevoix, *Voyage to North America,* ii, 196 *sq.* (Natchez). Rochefort, *Histoire naturelle et morale des Iles Antilles,* p. 568 *sq.* (Caribs).

178. Tylor, *Primitive Culture,* i, 461. Spencer, *Principles of Sociology,* i, 205. Dorman, *op. cit.,* p. 12 *sqq.* Acosta, *op. cit.,* ii, 313, 314, 344 (Peruvians).

179. Wiedemann, *Ancient Egyptian Doctrine of the Immortality of the Soul,* p. 62 n.

180. De Groot, *op. cit.,* vol. ii, book i, 721.

181. *Ibid.,* vol. ii, book i, 724.

182. *Ibid.,* vol. ii, book i, 735, 754, 748.

183. Schrader, *Prehistoric Antiquities of the Aryan Peoples,* p. 391.

184. Hopkins, *op. cit.,* p. 274.

185. Tylor, *Primitive Culture,* i, 465 *sqq.* Zimmer, *Altindisches Leben,* p. 331.

186. *Rig-Veda,* x, 18. 8 *sq.* Macdonell, *Vedic Mythology,* p. 165. Hillebrandt, "Eine Miscelle aus dem Vedaritual," in *Zeitschr. d. Deutschen Morgenländ. Gesellsch,* xl, 711. Oldenberg, *Religion des Veda,* p. 587.

187. Euripides, *Supplices,* 1000 *sqq.*

188. Pausanias, iv, 2. 7.

189. Grimm, *Deutsche Rechtsalterthümer,* p. 451.

190. Procopius, *op. cit.,* ii, 14.

191. Dithmar of Merseburg, *Chronicon,* viii, 2 (Pertz, *Monumenta Germaniæ historica,* v, 861). Zimmer, *op. cit.,* p. 330.

192. Ralston, *Songs of the Russian People,* p. 327 *sq.*

193. Grimm, *op. cit.,* p. 344.

194. Cæsar, *De bello gallico,* vi, 19. In the ancient annals of the Irish there is one trace of human sacrifice being offered as a funeral rite (Cusack, *History of the Irish Nation,* p. 115 n.\*).

195. *Iliad,* xxiii, 175.

196. Wilkes, *U.S. Exploring Expedition,* iv, 453.

197. Wiedemann, *Ancient Egyptian Doctrine of the Immortality of the Soul,* p. 63.

198. Tylor, *Primitive Culture,* i, 463.

199. De Groot, *op. cit.,* vol. ii, book i, 794 *sqq.*

200. *Cf.* Spencer, *Principles of Sociology,* i, 288 *sq.*; Rockholz, *Deutscher Glaube und Brauch,* i, 55; Sepp, *Völkerbrauch bei Hochzeit, Geburt und Tod,* p. 154; Trumbull, *Blood Covenant,* p. 110 *sqq.*

201. Reade, *Savage Africa,* p. 51 *sq.*

202. Bowdich, *Mission from Cape Castle to Ashantee,* p. 289.

203. Grimm, *Kinder- und Hausmärchen,* p. 29 *sq.*

204. *Odyssey,* xi, 153.

205. Trumbull, *Blood Covenant,* p. 114 *sq.*

206. Farrer, *Primitive Manners and Customs,* p. 23 *sq.*

207. *Cf.* Spencer, *Principles of Sociology,* i, 181 *sq.*

208. Turner, *Nineteen Years in Polynesia,* p. 227.

# 7

# EMILE DURKHEIM (b. 1858)

Emile Durkheim was born in northeastern France to a line of rabbis. Well educated, he studied history, philosophy, psychology, and ethnology, and earned his Ph.D. from the Ecole Normale Supérieure in 1882. Five years later he became a professor of sociology and education in Bordeaux and over the next fifteen years wrote several of his more important books—*The Division of Labor in Society* (1893), *Rules of the Sociological Method* (1896), and *Suicide* (1897). In these works, he defined society as a structure of interdependent parts, something that should be studied scientifically by collecting and classifying data, as something inherently ordered. Durkheim founded the journal *L'Année sociologique* in 1898, an immensely influential publication that continued for twelve issues producing seminal essays on such topics as the family, ethics, magic, religion, classification, and sacrifice (Hubert and Mauss, 1899) for the growing discipline of sociology. Then in 1902, Durkheim took a new professorship at the Sorbonne where he fostered a spirit of collaboration among several younger scholars (e.g., Robert Hertz, his nephew Marcel Mauss, and others), continued work on his journal, and in 1912 published his greatest work on religion, originally in French but soon translated into English as *The Elementary Forms of the Religious Life*. Working with ethnographic studies of Australian and American indigenous groups and drawing upon many of the basic theories and methods of sociology he and his colleagues had been refining, Durkheim fashioned a masterpiece theory of religion with this book. It has come to inform, to some degree, virtually all subsequent sociological studies of religion. With the advent of the first World War in 1914 and the great damage it caused—many of his students and younger colleagues were killed—Durkheim's writing and teaching career declined, he suffered several heart attacks, and died in 1917.

At the center of Durkheim's work, and particularly his understanding of religion, is his claim that society is a primary fact, that one's group is fundamental, basic, and not derivative of psychological processes. People are born into a collective world, one which determines the nature of cultural conceptions, language, morals, even apparently individual phenomena like values and feelings. All of these combine to constitute a sense of reality for individuals, one which they adopt by virtue of being a member of a social group, and therefore, Durkheim stressed, this essence of reality is collective. In this way, members of early communities (somewhat less so in modern societies) share a *"conscience collective,"* a common understanding of the world, an understanding that can be analyzed as a set of "collective representations" (e.g., ideas of time, space, number, class, etc.) organized into "institutions." By virtue of it being unanimous, this collective understanding gains a quality of factuality for individuals and is thereby endowed with a sense of obligation, a power of coercion to structure not just the actions but also the thinking of individuals. Being beyond the simply personal, collective representations appear objectively real even as they are, Durkheim asserted, merely a product of society. Built into the workings of society, its structure (division of labor for example) and general practices, are the very mechanisms that ensure its solidarity.

Religion, in Durkheim's opinion, is one such set of collective representations (expressed as "beliefs and practices") that functions to bolster social solidarity, to encourage group cohesiveness. He shares this opinion with Robertson Smith, but Durkheim goes further and postulates an overall theory of religion that eschews evolutionary assumptions in favor of uncovering logically essential principles and processes. His definition of religion serves as the foundation for this project. Religion, Durkheim explains, is the social institution of organized beliefs and practices related to "sacred things." Like his colleagues Hubert and Mauss, Durkheim advocated the view that religion is built upon a distinction between "sacred" and "profane," a distinction that serves as a basic system of classification for religious people. By "sacred" Durkheim means a quality of "superior dignity and power" added to ordinary things, people, places, times, etc. that requires they be "set apart," respected, and often forbidden with respect to mundane use or contact. The source of this added quality is society itself. Put differently, sacred things are those which are "wholly collective," unanimous, socially undeniable, and un-negotiable. They concern the entire community. The profane, of course, is the exact opposite of the sacred. It refers to those individual and personal things (activities, concerns, etc.) that fail to be wholly collective, that are not shared by the group because they are smaller in scale, confined to a more limited context, or are simply accidental. It is clear then how religion functions to strengthen social bonds—it preserves attention to sacred things, which, by Durkheim's definition, are essentially collective. Finally, Durkheim offered an explanation for *how* something acquires the added value of being sacred, for why there is a power to being wholly collective. He suggested that when individuals gather together under extraordinarily unified conditions (for shared purposes, shared activities, shared thoughts, and so forth), they experience "collective effervescence," that is, a bubbling up of a feeling that they are in the presence of something beyond themselves, something powerful and pervasive. The feelings produced when together as a group are feelings of something greater than the self, and according to Durkheim, this should be expected because, despite what specific religious beliefs might claim, the something that is greater than the self is nothing other than society, the collection of people organized into a group.

To illustrate his theory of religion, Durkheim, like Robertson Smith and Frazer, turns to ethnographies of Australian groups and suggests totemism represents the "most primitive" form of religion. The religious principles of totemism are for Durkheim the "elementary forms" which are the logical root of all other more complex and later forms of religion. Totemism deserves this status because it so clearly illustrates the distinction between the sacred and profane as Durkheim conceives it. The totem, as a species respected by a clan and set apart, as something wholly collective, is clearly sacred. It is endowed with a power, what Durkheim calls "the totemic principle," that sustains the (past and continued) existence of the group, and as such is worshipped as a god. Yet, the "totemic principle," he continues, is in fact a product of "collective effervescence," of the group itself. Thus we have Durkheim's famous and controversial claim that the totem, the god of the clan, is "nothing else than the clan itself, personified and represented to the imagination under the visible form of the animal or vegetable which serves as the totem."

Durkheim's understanding of sacrifice derives from his overall position with respect to ritual. Religious rituals are group events, collective activities set apart from the ordinary, that generate a sense of "collective effervescence" for participants. They are symbolic expressions of social realities that serve to strengthen, maintain, and revive group solidarity. Durkheim divides rituals into two main types: the "positive" and the "negative." Negative rituals, what he calls "the negative cult," are actions designed to keep the sacred separate from the profane, to distinguish clearly between the two. These are prohibitions and taboos, forbidden activities, or behaviors restricted to certain contexts (e.g., always in temples or never in temples, and so forth). The "positive cult" is the opposite; it aims to bring the sacred and the profane into temporary contact. The example Durkheim uses as an illustration is the Australian ritual called the *Intichiuma*, an annual set of ceremonies that includes killing the totem and all the members of a clan eating a portion of it. The clan believes that it must periodically perform this ritual to perpetuate the totem, to assure its prosperity, a crucial concern considering the clan itself depends for its survival on the ongoing health of the totemic species. This is a seasonal re-congregation, a regular reassembly of clan members reminding them of their collective identity in and through the totem. Durkheim explains the need for this repetition first by noting that totem species often do decline (migrate, and so forth) in a seasonal pattern, and thus a ceremony designed to restore a clan's totem would vary likewise, but more importantly, he notes that the sense of "collective effervescence" produced by fully collective action is a temporary state. Once individuals return to their personal, economic, utilitarian, mundane business, they lose a sense of the power of the group, of the "totemic principle." Being assembled as a group cannot be constant, so it must be periodic. On a regular basis, social solidarity must be reestablished.

Following Robertson Smith, but in certain ways disagreeing with him, Durkheim sees the *intichiuma* as the clearest expression of the nature of sacrifice. First, he agrees with Robertson Smith that this group of ceremonies, particularly the segment where the totem is eaten in a collective meal, constitutes a communion between the people and their god (the totem). By eating parts of the sacrificial victim, they "assimilate" the "sacred principle residing in it." The people and the god are thus regenerated. For Durkheim, though, the eating is a secondary expression of the more essential fact that the communion is truly established through the assembling of the clan members. They gather together as a group and thereby commune with their god, which, according to Durkheim, is essentially the group itself. In this way, all religious rituals that involve such an assembly are always a communion as well. In opposition to Robertson Smith, however, Durkheim does not exclude from the *intichiuma* notions of gift-giving, nor place them at a later stage of development. Instead, the very notion that these ceremonies benefit the totem is tantamount to their being a gift. Performing the ritual is effectively a gift of life for the totem, for failing to perform the ritual would risk its destruction. In sum, Durkheim advocates a theory of sacrifice that understands it as both a communion and a gift.

The short selection of Durkheim reprinted here is taken from *The Elementary Forms of the Religious Life* and the chapter entitled "The Positive Cult." It discusses why sacrifice in its "most primitive" form should be understood as both a communion and a gift. It is an excellent example of Durkheim's clear logic and sharp argument.

# From *The Elementary Forms of the Religious Life*

B UT ON ANOTHER POINT the new facts at our disposal invalidate the theories of Smith.

According to him, the communion was not only an essential element of the

Emile Durkheim, *The Elementary Forms of the Religious Life*, translated by Joseph Ward Swain, pp. 381–92. Copyright © 1965 by The Free Press. Reprinted with the permission of The Free Press, a division of Simon and Schuster, Inc. and the permission of Taylor and Francis Books, Ltd.

sacrifice, but at the beginning, at least, it was the unique element. Not only is one mistaken when he reduces sacrifice to nothing more than a tribute or offering, but the very idea of an offering was originally absent from it; this intervened only at a late period and under the influence of external circumstances; so instead of being able to aid us in understanding it, it has rather masked the real nature of the ritual mechanism. In fact, Smith claimed to find in the very notion of oblation an absurdity so revolting that it could never have been the fundamental reason for so great an institution. One of the most important functions incumbent upon the divinity is to assure to men that food which is necessary for life; so it seems impossible that the sacrifice, in its turn, should consist in a presentation of food to the divinity. It even seems self-contradictory that the gods should expect their food from a man, when it is from them that he gets his. Why should they have need of his aid in order to deduct beforehand their just share of the things which he receives from their hands? From these considerations Smith concluded that the idea of a sacrifice-offering could have been born only in the great religions, where the gods, removed from the things with which they were primitively confused, were thought of as sorts of kings and the eminent proprietors of the earth and its products. From this moment onwards, the sacrifice was associated with the tribute which subjects paid to their prince, as a price of the rights which were conceded to them. But this new interpretation was really an alteration and even a corruption of the primitive conception. For "the idea of property materializes all that it touches"; by introducing itself into the sacrifice, it denatured it and made it into a sort of bargain between the man and the divinity.[1]

But the facts which we have described overthrow this argumentation. These rites are certainly among the most primitive that have ever been observed. No determined mythical personality appears in them; there is no question of gods or spirits that are properly so called; it is only vaguely anonymous and impersonal forces which they put into action. Yet the reasoning which they suppose is exactly the one that Smith declared impossible because of its absurdity.

Let us return to the first act of the Intichiuma, to the rites destined to assure the fecundity of the animal or vegetable species which serves the clan as totem. This species is the preeminently sacred thing; in it is incarnated that which we have been able to call, by metaphor, the totemic divinity. Yet we have seen that to perpetuate itself it has need of the aid of men. It is they who dispense the life of the new generation each year; without them, it would never be born. If they stopped celebrating the Intichiuma, the sacred beings would disappear from the face of the earth. So in one sense, it is from men that they get their existence; yet in another way, it is from them that men get theirs; for after they have once arrived at maturity, it is from them that men acquire the force needed to support and repair their spiritual beings. Thus we are able to say that men make their gods, or, at least, make them live; but at the same time, it is from them that they live themselves. So they are regularly guilty of the circle which, according to Smith, is implied in the very idea of a sacrificial tribute: they give to the sacred beings a little of what they receive from them, and they receive from them all that they give.

But there is still more to be said: the oblations which he is thus forced to make every year do not differ in nature from those which are made later in the rites properly called sacrifices. If the sacrificer immolates an animal, it is in order that the living principles within it may be disengaged from the organism and go to nourish the divinity. Likewise, the grains of dust which the Australian detaches from the sacred rock are so many sacred principles which he scatters into space, so that they may go to animate the totemic species and assure its renewal. The gesture with which this scattering is made is also that which normally accompanies offerings. In certain cases, the resemblance between the two rites may be followed even to the details of the movements effected. We have seen that in order to have rain the Kaitish pour water over the sacred stone; among certain peoples, the priest pours water over the altar, with the same end in view.[2] The effusions of blood which are usual in a certain number of Intichiuma are veritable oblations. Just as the Arunta or Dieri sprinkle the sacred rock or the totemic design with blood, so it frequently happens that in the more advanced cults, the blood of the sacrificed victim or of the worshipper himself is spilt before or upon the altar.[3] In these cases, it is given to the gods, of whom it is the preferred food; in Australia, it is given to the sacred species. So we have no ground for saying that the idea of oblation is a late product of civilization.

A document which we owe to Strehlow puts this kinship of the Intichiuma and the sacrifice clearly into evidence. This is a hymn which accompanies the Intichiuma of the Kangaroo; the ceremony is described at the same time that its expected effects are announced. A morsel of kangaroo fat has been placed by the chief upon a support made of branches. The text says that this fat makes the fat of the kangaroos increase.[4] This time, they do not confine themselves to sprinkling sacred dust or human blood about; the animal itself is immolated, or sacrificed as one might say, placed upon a sort of altar, and offered to the species, whose life it should maintain.

Now we see the sense in which we may say that the Intichiuma contains the germs of the sacrificial system. In the form which it takes when fully consti-tuted, a sacrifice is composed of two essential elements: an act of communion and an act of oblation. The worshipper communes with his god by taking in a sacred food, and at the same time he makes an offering to this god. We find these two acts in the Intichiuma, as we have described it. The only difference is that in the ordinary sacrifice[5] they are made simultaneously or else follow one another immediately, while in the Australian ceremony they are separated. In the former case, they are parts of one undivided rite; here, they take place at different times, and may even be separated by a rather long interval. But, at bottom, the mechanism is the same. Taken as a whole, the Intichiuma is a sacrifice, but one whose parts are not yet articulated and organized.

The relating of these two ceremonies has the double advantage of enabling us to understand better the nature of the Intichiuma and that of sacrifice.

We understand the Intichiuma better. In fact, the conception of Frazer, which made it a simple magic operation[6] with no religious character at all, is now seen to be unsupportable. One cannot dream of excluding from religion a rite which is the forerunner of so great a religious institution.

But we also understand what the sacrifice itself is better. In the first place, the equal importance of the two elements entering into it is now established. If the Australian makes offerings to his sacred beings, there is no reason for supposing that the idea of oblation was foreign to the primitive organization of the sacrificial institution and later upset its natural arrangement. The theory of Smith must be revised on this point.[7] Of course the sacrifice is partially a communion; but it is also, and no less essentially, a gift and an act of renouncement. It always presupposes that the worshipper gives some of his substance or his goods to his gods. Every attempt to deduce one of these elements from the other is hopeless. Perhaps the oblation is even more permanent than the communion.[8]

In the second place, it ordinarily seems as though the sacrifice, and especially the sacrificial oblation, could only be addressed to personal beings. But the oblations which we have met with in Australia imply no notion of this sort. In other words, the sacrifice is independent of the varying forms in which the religious forces are conceived; it is founded upon more profound reasons, which we shall seek presently.

In any case, it is clear that the act of offering naturally arouses in the mind the idea of a moral subject, whom this offering is destined to please. The ritual acts which we have described become more intelligible when it is believed that they are addressed to persons. So the practices of the Intichiuma, while actually putting only impersonal forces into play, prepare the way for a different conception.[9] Of course they were not sufficient to form the idea of mythical personalities by themselves, but when this idea had once been formed, the very nature of these rites made it enter into the cult; thus, taking a more direct interest in action and life, it also acquired a greater reality. So we are even able to believe that the cult favoured, in a secondary manner, no doubt, but nevertheless one which is worthy of attention, the personification of the religious forces.

But we still have to explain the contradiction in which Robertson Smith saw an inadmissible logical scandal.

If the sacred beings always manifested their powers in a perfectly equal manner, it would appear inconceivable that men should dream of offering them services, for we cannot see what need they could have of them. But in the first place, in so far as they are confused with things, and in so far as they are regarded as principles of the cosmic life, they are themselves submitted to the rhythm of this life. Now this goes in oscillations in contrary directions, which succeed one another according to a determined law. Sometimes it is affirmed in all its glory; sometimes it weakens to such an extent that one may ask himself whether it is not going to fade away. Vegetation dies every year; will it be reborn? Animal species tend to become extinguished by the effect of natural and violent death; will they be renewed at such a time and in such a way as is proper? Above all, the rain is capricious; there are long periods during which it seems to have disappeared for ever. These periodical variations of nature bear witness to the fact that at the corresponding periods, the sacred beings upon whom the plants, animals, rain, etc., depend are themselves passing through grave crisis; so they, too, have their periods of giving way. But men could not regard these spectacles as indifferent spectators. If he is to live, the universal life must continue, and consequently the gods must not die. So he seeks to sustain and aid them; for this, he puts at their service whatever forces he has at his disposition, and mobilizes them for this purpose. The blood flowing in his veins has fecundating virtues; he pours it forth. From the sacred rocks possessed by his clan he takes those germs of life which lie dormant there, and scatters them into space. In a word, he makes oblations.

The external and physical crises, moreover, duplicate internal and mental crises which tend toward the same result. Sacred beings exist only when they are represented as such in the mind. When we cease to believe in them, it is as though they did not exist. Even those which have a material form and are given by sensible experience, depend upon the thought of the worshippers who adore them; for the sacred character which makes them objects of the cult is not given by their natural constitution; it is added to them by belief. The kangaroo is only an animal like all others; yet, for the men of the Kangaroo, it contains within it a principle which puts it outside the company of others, and this principle exists only in the minds of those who believe in it.[10] If these sacred beings, when once conceived, are to have no need of men to continue, it would be necessary that the representations expressing them always remain the same. But this stability is impossible. In fact, it is in the communal life that they are formed, and this communal life is essentially intermittent. So they necessarily partake of this same intermittency. They attain their greatest intensity at the moment when the men are assembled together and are in immediate relations with one another, when they all partake of the same idea and the same sentiment. But when the assembly has broken up and each man has returned to his own peculiar life, they progressively lose their original energy. Being covered over little by little by the rising flood of daily experiences, they would soon fall into the unconscious, if we did not find some means of calling them back into consciousness and revivifying them. If we think of them less forcefully, they amount to less for us and we count less upon them; they exist to a lesser degree. So here we have another point of view, from which the services of men are necessary to them. This second reason for their existence is even more important than the first, for it exists all the time. The intermittency of the physical life can affect religious beliefs only when religions are not detached from their cosmic basis. The intermittency of the social life, on the other hand, is inevitable; even the most idealistic religions cannot escape it.

Moreover, it is owing to this state of dependency upon the thought of men, in which the gods find themselves, that the former are able to believe in the efficacy of their assistance. The only way of renewing the collective representations which relate to sacred beings is to retemper them in the very source of the religious life, that is to say, in the assembled groups. Now the emotions aroused by these periodical crises through which external things pass induce the men who witness them to assemble, to see what should be done about it. But by the very fact of uniting, they are mutually comforted; they find a remedy because they seek it together. The common faith becomes reanimated quite naturally in the heart of this reconstituted group; it is born again because it again finds those very conditions in which it was born in the first place. After it has been restored, it easily triumphs over all the private doubts which may have arisen in individual minds. The image of the sacred things regains power enough to resist the internal or external causes which tended to weaken it. In spite of their apparent failure, men can no longer believe that the gods will die, because they feel them living in their own hearts. The means employed to succour them, howsoever crude these may be, cannot appear vain, for everything goes on as if they were really effective. Men are more confident because they feel themselves stronger; and they really are stronger, because forces which were languishing are now reawakened in the consciousness.

So we must be careful not to believe, along with Smith, that the cult was founded solely for the benefit of men and that the gods have nothing to do with it: they have no less need of it than their worshippers. Of course men would be unable to live without gods, but, on the other hand, the gods would die if their cult were not rendered. This does not have the sole object of making profane subjects communicate with sacred beings, but it also keeps these latter alive and is perpetually remaking and regenerating them. Of course it is not the material oblations which bring about this regeneration by their own virtues; it is the mental states which these actions, though vain in themselves, accompany or reawaken. The real reason for the existence of the cults, even of those which are the most materialistic in appearance, is not to be sought in the acts which they prescribe, but in the internal and moral regeneration which these acts aid in bringing about. The things which the worshipper really gives his gods are not the foods which he places upon the altars, nor the blood which he lets flow from his veins: it is his thought. Nevertheless, it is true that there is an exchange of services, which are mutually demanded, between the divinity and its worshippers. The rule *do ut des,* by which the principle of sacrifice has sometimes been defined, is not a late invention of utilitarian theorists: it only expresses in an explicit way the very mechanism of the sacrificial system and, more generally, of the whole positive cult. So the circle pointed out by Smith is very real; but it contains nothing humiliating for the reason. It comes from the fact that the sacred beings, though superior to men, can live only in the human consciousness.

But this circle will appear still more natural to us, and we shall understand its meaning and the reason for its existence still better if, carrying our analysis still farther and substituting for the religious symbols the realities which they represent, we investigate how these behave in the rite. If, as we have attempted to establish, the sacred principle is nothing more nor less than society transfigured and personified, it should be possible to interpret the ritual in lay and social terms. And, as a matter of fact, social life, just like the ritual, moves in a circle. On the one hand, the individual gets from society the best part of himself, all that gives him a distinct character and a special place among other beings, his intellectual and moral culture. If we should withdraw from men their language, sciences, arts, and moral beliefs, they would drop to the rank of animals. So the characteristic attributes of human nature come from society. But, on the other hand, society exists and lives only in and through individuals. If the idea of society were extinguished in individual minds and the beliefs, traditions, and aspirations of the group were no longer felt and shared by the individuals, society would die. We can say of it what we just said of the divinity; it is real only in so far as it has a place in human consciousness, and this place is whatever one we may give it. We now see the real reason why the gods cannot do without their worshippers any more than these can do without their gods; it is because society, of which the gods are only a symbolic expression, cannot do without individuals any more than these can do without society.

Here we touch the solid rock upon which all the cults are built and which has caused their persistence ever since human societies have existed. When we see what religious rites consist of and towards what they seem to tend, we demand with astonishment how men have been able to imagine them, and especially how they can remain so faithfully attached to them. Whence could the illusion have come that with a few grains of sand thrown to the wind, or a few drops of blood shed upon a rock or the stone of an altar, it is possible to maintain the life of an animal species or of a god? We have undoubtedly made a step in advance towards the solution of this problem when we have discovered, behind these outward and apparently unreasonable movements, a mental mechanism which gives them a meaning and a moral significance. But we are in no way assured that this mechanism itself does not consist in a simple play of hallucinatory images. We have pointed out the psychological process which leads the believers to imagine that the rite causes the spiritual forces of which they have need to be reborn about them; but it does not follow from the fact that this belief is psychologically explicable that it has any objective value. If we are to see in the efficacy attributed to the rites anything more than the product of a chronic delirium with which humanity has abused itself, we must show that the effect of the cult really is to recreate periodically a moral being upon which we depend as it depends upon us. Now this being does exist: it is society.

Howsoever little importance the religious ceremonies may have, they put the group into action; the groups assemble to celebrate them. So their first effect is to bring individuals together, to multiply the relations between them and to make them more intimate with one another. By this very fact, the contents of their consciousness is changed. On ordinary days, it is utilitarian and individual avocations which take the greater part of the attention. Every one attends to his own personal business; for most men, this primarily consists in satisfying the exigencies of material life, and the principal incentive to economic activity has always been private interest. Of course social sentiments could never be totally absent. We remain in relations with others; the habits, ideas, and tendencies which education has impressed upon us and which ordinarily preside over our relations with others, continue to make their action felt. But they are constantly combated and held in check by the antagonistic tendencies aroused and supported by the necessities of the daily struggle. They resist more or less successfully, according to their intrinsic energy: but this energy is not renewed. They live upon their past, and consequently they would be used up in the course of time, if nothing returned to them a little of the force that they lose through these incessant conflicts and frictions. When the Australians, scattered in little groups, spend their time in hunting and fishing, they lose sight of what concerns their clan or tribe: their only thought is to catch as much game as possible. On feast days, on the contrary, these preoccupations are necessarily eclipsed; being essentially profane, they are excluded from these sacred periods. At this time, their thoughts are centred upon their common beliefs, their common traditions, the memory of their great ancestors, the collective ideal of which they are the incarnation; in a word, upon social things. Even the material interests which these great religious ceremonies are designed to satisfy concern the public order and are therefore social. Society as a whole is interested that the harvest be abundant, that the rain fall at the right time and not excessively, that the animals reproduce regularly. So it is society that is in the foreground of every consciousness; it dominates and directs all conduct; this is equivalent to saying that it is more living and active, and consequently more real, than in profane times. So men do not deceive themselves when they feel at this time that there is something outside of them which is born again, that there are forces which are reanimated and a life which reawakens. This renewal is in no way imaginary and the individuals themselves profit from it. For the spark of a social being which each bears within him necessarily participates in this collective renovation. The individual soul is regenerated too, by being dipped again in the source from which its life comes; consequently it feels itself stronger, more fully master of itself, less dependent upon physical necessities.

We know that the positive cult naturally tends to take periodic forms; this is one of its distinctive features. Of course there are rites which men celebrate occasionally, in connection with passing situations. But these episodic practices are always merely accessory, and in the religions studied in this book, they are almost exceptional. The essential constituent of the cult is the cycle of feasts which return regularly at determined epochs. We are now able to understand whence this tendency towards periodicity comes; the rhythm of the social life, and results from it. Society is able to revivify the sentiment it has of itself only by assembling. But it cannot be assembled all the time. The exigencies of life do not allow it to remain in congregation indefinitely; so it scatters, to assemble anew when it again feels the need of this. It is to these necessary alternations that the regular alternations of sacred and profane times correspond. Since the apparent object, at least, of the cult was at first to regularize the course of natural phenomena, the rhythm of the cosmic life has put its mark on the rhythm of the ritual life. This is why the feasts have long been associated with the seasons; we have seen this characteristic already in the Intichiuma of Australia. But the seasons have only furnished the outer frame-work for this organization, and not the principle upon which it rests; for even the cults which aim at exclusively spiritual ends have remained periodical. So this periodicity must be due to other causes. Since the seasonal changes are critical periods for nature, they are a natural occasion for assembling, and consequently for religious ceremonies. But other events can and have successfully fulfilled this function of occasional cause. However, it must be recognized that this frame-work, though purely external, has given proof of a singular resistive force, for traces of it are found even in the religions which are the most fully detached from all physical bases. Many Christian celebrations are founded, with no break of continuity, on the pastoral and agrarian feasts of the ancient Hebrews, although in themselves they are neither pastoral nor agrarian.

Moreover, this rhythm is capable of varying in different societies. Where the period of dispersion is long, and the dispersion itself is extreme, the period of congregation, in its turn, is very prolonged, and produces veritable debauches of collective and religious life. Feasts succeed one another for weeks or even for months, while the ritual life sometimes attains to a sort of frenzy. This is what happens among the Australian tribes and many of the tribes of North-western America.[11] Elsewhere, on the contrary, these two phases of the social life succeed one another after shorter intervals, and then the contrast between them is less marked. The more societies develop, the less they seem to allow of too great intermittences.

# Notes

1. Smith, *The Religion of the Semites,* pp. 390 ff.
2. Smith cites some cases himself in *Religion of the Semites,* p. 231.
3. For example, see Exodus xxix. 10–14; Leviticus ix. 8–11; it is their own blood which the priests of Baal pour over the altar (1 Kings xviii. 28).
4. Strehlow, III, p. 12, verse 7.
5. At least when it is complete: in certain cases, it may be reduced to one of its elements.
6. Strehlow says that the natives "regard these ceremonies as a sort of divine service, just as a Christian regards the exercises of his religion" (III, p. 9).
7. It should be asked, for example, whether the effusions of blood and the offerings of hair which Smith regards as acts of communion are not real oblations (see Smith, *Religion of the Semites,* pp. 320 ff.)
8. The expiatory rites, of which we shall speak more fully in the fifth chapter of this same book, are almost exclusively oblations. They are communions only secondarily.
9. This is why we frequently speak of the ceremonies as if they were addressed to living personalities (see, for example, texts by Krichauff and Kemp, in Eylmann, p. 202).
10. In a philosophical sense, the same is true of everything, for nothing exists except in representation. But as we have shown, this proposition is doubly true for religious forces, for there is nothing in the constitution of things which corresponds to sacredness.
11. See Mauss, *Essai sur les variations saisonnières des sociétés Eskimos,* in *Année sociol.,* IX, pp. 96 ff.

# 8

# SIGMUND FREUD (b. 1856)

Psychologist Sigmund Freud is credited with being the founder of psychoanalytic theory and, for some, one of the most important and influential thinkers of the twentieth century. He was born in Moravia (now the Czech Republic) to Jewish parents, and at the age of four moved to Vienna, where he lived for almost the rest of his life. Freud proved to be a talented young student, excelling in language study, classics, and science. He eventually pursued a degree in medicine, married, and had six children, and early in his career developed an interest in neurology and mental illnesses. Freud became friends with another Viennese physician and psychiatrist, Joseph Breuer, a man who was having success treating certain "nervous disorders" with hypnosis. The two men collaborated and defined a technique for therapy that encouraged patients to recall (by "free association") forgotten memories (from the "unconscious") and thereby benefit from a cathartic re-experience of past trauma (the "cathartic method"). Later Freud outlined the psychological mechanism that explained why this technique was effective at treating certain disorders. Freud had a long career of research and writing. He is best known for his theory of personality and the wide variety of individual and social phenomena it seeks to explain. Most importantly for the study of religion, he wrote *The Interpretation of Dreams* (1900), *Totem and Taboo* (1913), *The Future of an Illusion* (1927), *Civilization and Its Discontents* (1930), and *Moses and Monotheism* (1938). Freud's complete works total over twenty-four large volumes. Praised by some, and despised by others, Freud rarely fails to intrigue, challenge, and impress.

The structure of the human personality is, according to Freud, comprised of a dynamic system of three "forces," three components that compete for control over an individual's thoughts and behaviors. At the center of everyone's personality is an ongoing struggle bétween three different drives or needs. The first is a biological component, what Freud calls the "id," a collection of instinctual drives inherited from pre-human times. These are "primary processes" that operate to discharge tensions, avoid pain, and obtain pleasure. The id motivates the individual to satisfy needs and gratify wishes. The second component of the personality Freud calls the "ego." It is responsible for realistic thinking, for deciding how the individual should interact with the objective world, with reality. Using higher mental processes it evaluates an individual's needs and then orchestrates how best to satisfy them. The third component, the "super-ego," is the moral center of the personality. Instead of reality, it is concerned with social values and ideals. Instead of seeking pleasure, it strives for perfection. The super-ego develops in response to parental and social pressures, their rewards and punishments (and attendant feelings of pride and guilt), and it functions to inhibit the drives of the id and to persuade the ego to adopt moral ideals over the demands of reality.

The content of the id particularly interested Freud. It was here that he worked out his controversial theory of "infant sexuality." Freud believes that the id's drive to obtain pleasure is active from the moment of birth, but that the source of that pleasure changes over time migrating from the mouth (eating), to the anus (excreting), and finally to the genitals (sexual desires). During the genital phase, Freud continues, children naturally find themselves sexually attracted to their parent of the opposite sex and consequently are forced into a position of rivalry with their same-sex parent, even to the point of wanting to kill that parent. This phenomenon Freud calls the "Oedipus complex" after the Greek tragedy of king Oedipus who unknowingly murders his father and marries his mother. These impulses create for children great feelings of anxiety because in addition to the love and protection parents provide, there now is also a threat of punishment—a "castration anxiety" for boys, and for girls a fear of injury from intercourse with the father. Ordinarily, parental prohibitions (one aspect of the super-ego) effectively negotiate this conflict and children learn to submit to the authority of their parents, to depend upon yet fear them. Ultimately, the father becomes the locus for these resolved feelings.

As people live their lives, they struggle to balance the social and the biological in response to the real world. They seek at all times ways to balance the three components of the personality, but Freud hypothesized that when imbalanced, individuals experience different forms of anxiety. "Realistic anxiety" occurs when dangers in the external world, the realities of death (disease for example) impinge and a person feels helpless or weak. "Neurotic anxiety" arises when the drives of the id, its sexual or aggressive character for example, threaten to run out of control and dominate the personality. For example, a person can become "fixated" in a certain stage of sexual development and suffer from the constant fear that he or she will act on that impulse. "Moral anxiety," the last variant, occurs when the super-ego governs the personality and the individual is tormented with feelings of guilt or fears of condemnation.

Healthy individuals deal with these three forms of anxiety by recognizing their cause and returning the personality to a balanced, dynamic state. Traumatic experiences are processed and incorporated. All too often, however, individuals adopt unhealthy defense mechanisms to avoid or ignore psychic discomfort, and consequently the personality remains out of balance and mental illness is the result. The most common such defense mechanism is "repression," simply forcing the disturbing anxiety out of mind, or as Freud hypothesized, pushing it into the unconscious. In this way, abnormal compulsions, obsessions, and other behaviors are manifestations of the unconscious mind. "Regression" is another damaging defense mechanism. Here, the individual deals with anxiety by retreating to an earlier stage of development that somehow provided a solution to the anxiety, offering some protection from it. For this reason, the protective role of the father is highly significant. Finally, Freud identified "projection" as another harmful defense mechanism for individual anxieties. He noticed that sometimes people attribute the source of their anxiety to some external, often imaginary, figure. To calm fears, to fulfill desires and wishes, individuals may resort to inventing (dreaming up) illusory solutions.

Religion, according to Freud, is in fact a collective neurosis, a social defense mechanism for individual anxieties. Troubled by feelings of helplessness and a desire for protection in the world, religious people, despite the content of their beliefs, have chosen to address their anxiety by "regressing" to that period of their infancy when their father provided love and security, and by "projecting" the existence of a divine father-figure who can be worshipped and respected. All of the features of father–child relations felt by children—love, fear, awe, guilt, obedience, even rebellion—are the psychological building blocks of religious attitudes and impulses. These are the unconscious psychological processes behind people's continual allegiance to religious traditions. For Freud, in other words, the workings of the mind explain religion.

Freud also, however, has a theory about the origin of religious traditions, a theory that relies, as the title of his book (*Totem and Taboo*) on this subject indicates, on the notion of totemism. Inspired by Frazer, Robertson Smith, Lang and McLennan, and their use of Australian ethnographic materials, Freud agrees that totemism represents the earliest stage of religion and as such can be used as a model for later religious traditions. Insights gained into the nature of totemism, he assumed, would be useful in interpreting modern religions. Freud, like other authors before him, described totemism generally as a collection of beliefs and practices centered on the "totem" of a group, usually a species of plant or animal. Thought to be the progenitor of the entire clan, the totem was "set apart" and forbidden from contact ("taboo"), especially from being killed, except on very special occasions. Also, and of particular interest to Freud, the totem, which represents the entire clan and accordingly the whole kin-group, defines the rule of incest for clan members. Sex within the clan is forbidden (or exogamy is required). Adhering to these requirements, the members of a totemic group expect the totem to protect them and provide them prosperity.

Freud's contribution to this discussion is to provide a psychological explanation for the origin of totemism. After agreeing that the totem is the father (of each individual and the clan as a whole), Freud recognizes that the two prohibitions of totemism— against killing the totem and against having sexual relations with clan members—coincide precisely with the two crimes committed by Oedipus, murder and incest. This parallel allows Freud to argue that the Oedipal complex and the psychological mechanisms of infantile sexuality are the true root of totemism. He suggests that totemism arose following an original act of murder. A band of brothers, regressing to an infantile stage, enact their Oedipal urges, kill their father to have sexual access to their mothers, eat the father to appropriate his power, but immediately feel guilty for doing so. This "primal horde" sets up a totem as a projection of the father, but institutes a regular ceremony that, part celebration and part mourning, serves as a cathartic release of the "primal guilt" members share. Totemic ceremonies commemorate that primal event.

Freud's understanding of sacrifice parallels his understanding of totemism, much like it does for Robertson Smith as well. The features of modern sacrificial rituals, indeed of religion generally, can be traced to the original form of religion, totemism. Sacrifice, as a ritual that revolves around killing, prohibitions, and consumption, is for Freud simply an explicit manifestation of what all religious beliefs and practices share, namely the unconscious, infantile desires of human beings. The cathartic release of feelings toward the father provided by the totemic meal are reproduced in sacrificial rituals, because, Freud claims, the sacrificial victim represents the father (and the god). The very same Oedipal urges that drove the primal horde to act, ultimately to create a totem, also created the first sacrifice, but, more importantly, continue to drive human beings to act sacrificially. As they compel people to be religious, they motivate sacrificial behavior. Freud is offering what could be called a "guilt theory" of sacrifice.

Reprinted here is a selection from part four of Freud's *Totem and Taboo*, the part entitled "The Return of Totemism in Childhood." Concluding that the Christian Eucharist is "essentially a fresh elimination of the father, a repetition of the guilty deed," Freud summarizes his position on sacrificial rituals. It provides only a small example of Freud's work on religion, and only hints at the lasting influence his thought has had on the study of religion.

# From *Totem and Taboo: Some Points of Agreement between the Mental Lives of Savages and Neurotics*

A GREAT NUMBER of powerful motives restrain me from any attempt at picturing the further development of religions from their origin in totemism to their condition to-day. I will only follow two threads whose course I can trace with especial clarity as they run through the pattern: the theme of the totemic sacrifice and the relation of son to father.[1]

Robertson Smith has shown us that the ancient totem meal recurs in the original form of sacrifice. The meaning of the act is the same: sanctification through participation in a common meal. The sense of guilt, which can only be allayed by the solidarity of all the participants, also persists. What is new is the clan deity, in whose supposed presence the sacrifice is performed, who participates in the meal as though he were a clansman, and with whom those who consume the meal become identified. How does the god come to be in a situation to which he was originally a stranger?

The answer might be that in the meantime the concept of God had emerged—from some unknown source—and had taken control of the whole of religious life; and that, like everything else that was to survive, the totem meal had been obliged to find a point of contact with the new system. The psycho-analysis of individual human beings, however, teaches us with quite special insistence that the god of each of them is formed in the likeness of his father, that his personal relation to God depends on his relation to his father in the flesh and oscillates and changes along with that relation, and that at bottom God is nothing other than an exalted father. As in the case of totemism, psycho-analysis recommends us to have faith in the believers who call God their father, just as the totem was called the tribal ancestor. If psycho-analysis deserves any attention, then—without prejudice to any other sources or meanings of the concept of God, upon which psycho-analysis can throw no light—the paternal element in that concept must be a most important one. But in that case the father is represented twice over in the situation of primitive sacrifice: once as God and once as the totemic animal victim. And, even granting the restricted number of explanations open to psycho-analysis, one must ask whether this is possible and what sense it can have.

Sigmund Freud, *Totem and Taboo: Some Points of Agreement between the Mental Lives of Savages and Neurotics*, translated by James Strachey, pp. 146–55. Copyright 1950 by Routledge and Kegan Paul, Ltd. Reprinted with the permission of W. W. Norton and Co. Inc. and Taylor and Francis Books Ltd.

We know that there are a multiplicity of relations between the god and the sacred animal (the totem or the sacrificial victim). (1) Each god usually has an animal (and quite often several animals) sacred to him. (2) In the case of certain specially sacred sacrifices—'mystic' sacrifices—the victim was precisely the animal sacred to the god (Smith, 1894, 290). (3) The god was often worshipped in the shape of an animal (or, to look at it in another way, animals were worshipped as gods) long after the age of totemism. (4) In myths the god often transforms himself into an animal, and frequently into the animal that is sacred to him.

It therefore seems plausible to suppose that the god himself was the totem animal, and that he developed out of it at a later stage of religious feeling. But we are relieved from the necessity for further discussion by the consideration that the totem is nothing other than a surrogate of the father. Thus, while the totem may be the *first* form of father-surrogate, the god will be a later one, in which the father has regained his human shape. A new creation such as this, derived from what constitutes the root of every form of religion—a longing for the father— might occur if in the process of time some fundamental change had taken place in man's relation to the father, and perhaps, too, in his relation to animals.

Signs of the occurrence of changes of this kind may easily be seen, even if we leave on one side the beginning of a mental estrangement from animals and the disrupting of totemism owing to domestication. There was one factor in the state of affairs produced by the elimination of the father which was bound in the course of time to cause an enormous increase in the longing felt for him. Each single one of the brothers who had banded together for the purpose of killing their father was inspired by a wish to become like him and had given expression to it by incorporating parts of their father's surrogate in the totem meal. But, in consequence of the pressure exercised upon each participant by the fraternal clan as a whole, that wish could not be fulfilled. For the future no one could or might ever again attain the father's supreme power, even though that was what all of them had striven for. Thus after a long lapse of time their bitterness against their father, which had driven them to their deed, grew less, and their longing for him increased; and it became possible for an ideal to emerge which embodied the unlimited power of the primal father against whom they had once fought as well as their readiness to submit to him. As a result of decisive cultural changes, the original democratic equality that had prevailed among all the individual clansmen became untenable; and there developed at the same time an inclination, based on veneration felt for particular human individuals, to revive the ancient paternal ideal by creating gods. The notion of a man becoming a god or of a god dying strikes us to-day as shockingly presumptuous; but even in classical antiquity there was nothing revolting in it.[2] The elevation of the father who had once been murdered into a god from whom the clan claimed descent was a far more serious attempt at atonement than had been the ancient covenant with the totem.

I cannot suggest at what point in this process of development a place is to be found for the great mother-goddesses, who may perhaps in general have preceded the father-gods. It seems certain, however, that the change in attitude to the father was not restricted to the sphere of religion but that it extended in a consistent manner to that other side of human life which had been affected by the father's removal—to social organization. With the introduction of father-deities a fatherless society gradually changed into one organized on a patriarchal basis. The family was a restoration of the former primal horde and it gave back to fathers a large portion of their former rights. There were once more fathers, but the social achievements of the fraternal clan had not been abandoned; and the gulf between the new fathers of a family and the unrestricted primal father of the horde was wide enough to guarantee the continuance of the religious craving, the persistence of an unappeased longing for the father.

We see, then, that in the scene of sacrifice before the god of the clan the father *is* in fact represented twice over—as the god and as the totemic animal victim. But in our attempts at understanding this situation we must beware of interpretations which seek to translate it in a two-dimensional fashion as though it were an allegory, and which in so doing forget its historical strati-fication. The two-fold presence of the father corresponds to the two chronologically successive meanings of the scene. The ambivalent attitude towards the father has found a plastic expression in it, and so, too, has the victory of the son's affectionate emotions over his hostile ones. The scene of the father's vanquishment, of his greatest defeat, has become the stuff for the representation of his supreme triumph. The importance which is everywhere, without exception, ascribed to sacrifice lies in the fact that it offers satisfaction to the father for the outrage inflicted on him in the same act in which that deed is commemorated.

As time went on, the animal lost its sacred character and the sacrifice lost its connection with the totem feast; it became a simple offering to the deity, an act of renunciation in favour of the god. God Himself had become so far exalted above mankind that He could only be approached through an intermediary—the priest. At the same time divine kings made their appearance in the social structure and introduced the patriarchal system into the state. It must be confessed that the revenge taken by the deposed and restored father was a harsh one: the dominance of authority was at its climax. The subjugated sons made use of the new situation in order to unburden themselves still further of their sense of guilt. They were no longer in any way responsible for the sacrifice as it now was. It was God Himself who demanded it and regulated it. This is the phase in which we find myths showing the god himself killing the animal which is sacred to him and which is in fact himself. Here we have the most extreme denial of the great crime which was the beginning of society and of the sense of guilt. But there is a second meaning to this last picture of sacrifice which is unmistakable. It expresses satisfaction at the earlier father-surrogate having been abandoned in favour of the superior concept of God. At this point the psycho-analytic interpretation of the scene coincides approximately with the allegorical, surface translation of it, which represents the god as overcoming the animal side of his own nature.[3]

Nevertheless it would be a mistake to suppose that the hostile impulses inherent in the father-complex were completely silenced during this period of revived paternal authority. On the contrary, the first phases of the dominance of the two new father-surrogates—gods and kings—show the most energetic signs of the ambivalence that remains a characteristic of religion.

In his great work, *The Golden Bough*, Frazer (1911, 2, Chap. 18) puts forward the view that the earliest kings of the Latin tribes were foreigners who played the part of a god and were solemnly executed at a particular festival. The annual sacrifice (or, as a variant, self-sacrifice) of a god seems to have been an essential element in the Semitic religions. The ceremonials of human sacrifice, performed in the most different parts of the inhabited globe, leave very little doubt that the victims met their end as representatives of the deity; and these sacrificial rites can be traced into late times, with an inanimate effigy or puppet taking the place of the living human being. The theanthropic sacrifice of the god, into which it is unfortunately impossible for me to enter here as fully as into animal sacrifice, throws a searching retrospective light upon the meaning of the older forms of sacrifice (Smith, 1894, 410 f.). It confesses, with a frankness that could hardly be excelled, to the fact that the object of the act of sacrifice has always been the same—namely what is now worshipped as God, that is to say, the father. The problem of the relation between animal and human sacrifice thus admits of a simple solution. The original animal sacrifice was already a substitute for a human sacrifice—for the ceremonial killing of the father; so that, when the father-surrogate once more resumed its human shape, the animal sacrifice too could be changed back into a human sacrifice.

The memory of the first great act of sacrifice thus proved indestructible, in spite of every effort to forget it; and at the very point at which men sought to be at the farthest distance from the motives that led to it, its undistorted reproduction emerged in the form of the sacrifice of the god. I need not enlarge here upon the developments of religious thought which, in the shape of rationalizations, made this recurrence possible. Robertson Smith, who had no thought of our derivation of sacrifice from the great event in human prehistory, states that the ceremonies at the festivals in which the ancient Semites celebrated the death of a deity "were currently interpreted as the commemoration of a mythical tragedy" (*ibid.*, 413). "The mourning," he declares, "is not a spontaneous expression of sympathy with the divine tragedy, but obligatory and enforced by fear of supernatural anger. And a chief object of the mourners is to disclaim responsibility for the god's death—a point which has already come before us in connection with theanthropic sacrifices, such as the 'ox-murder at Athens'" (*ibid.*, 412). It seems most probable that these "current interpretations" were correct and that the feelings of the celebrants were fully explained by the underlying situation.

Let us assume it to be a fact, then, that in the course of the later development of religions the two driving factors, the son's sense of guilt and the son's rebelliousness, never became extinct. Whatever attempt was made at solving the religious problem, whatever kind of reconciliation was effected between these two opposing mental forces, sooner or later broke down, under the combined influence, no doubt, of historical events, cultural changes and internal psychical modifications.

The son's efforts to put himself in the place of the father-god became ever more obvious. The introduction of agriculture increased the son's importance in the patriarchal family. He ventured upon new demonstrations of his incestuous libido, which found symbolic satisfaction in his cultivation of Mother Earth. Divine figures such as Attis, Adonis, and Tammuz emerged, spirits of vegetation and at the same time youthful divinities enjoying the favours of mother goddesses and committing incest with their mother in defiance of their father. But the sense of guilt, which was not allayed by these creations, found expression in myths which granted only short lives to these youthful favourites of the mother-goddess and decreed their punishment by emasculation or by the wrath of the father in the form of an animal. Adonis was killed by a wild boar, the sacred animal of Aphrodite; Attis, beloved of Cybele, perished by castration.[4] The mournings for these gods and the rejoicings over their resurrection passed over into the ritual of another son-deity who was destined to lasting success.

When Christianity first penetrated into the ancient world it met with competition from the religion of Mithras and for a time it was doubtful which of the two deities would gain the victory. In spite of the halo of light surrounding his form, the youthful Persian god remains obscure to us. We may perhaps infer from the sculptures of Mithras slaying a bull that he represented a son who was alone in sacrificing his father and thus redeemed his brothers from their burden of complicity in the deed. There was an alternative method of allaying their guilt and this was first adopted by Christ. He sacrificed his own life and so redeemed the company of brothers from original sin.

The doctrine of original sin was of Orphic origin. It formed a part of the mysteries, and spread from them to the schools of philosophy of ancient Greece (Reinach, 1905–12, vol. II, 75 ff.). Mankind, it was said, were descended from the Titans, who had killed the young Dionysus-Zagreus and had torn him to pieces. The burden of this crime weighed on them. A fragment of Anaximander relates how the unity of the world was broken by a primaeval sin,[5] and that whatever issued from it must bear the punishment. The tumultuous mobbing, the killing and the tearing in pieces by the Titans reminds us clearly enough of the totemic sacrifice described by St. Nilus (*ibid.*, vol. II, 93)—as, for the matter of that, do many other ancient myths, including, for instance, that of the death of Orpheus himself. Nevertheless, there is a disturbing difference in the fact of the murder having been committed on a *youthful* god.

There can be no doubt that in the Christian myth the original sin was one against God the Father. If, however, Christ redeemed mankind from the burden of original sin by the sacrifice of his own life, we are driven to conclude that the sin was a murder. The law of talion, which is so deeply rooted in human feelings, lays it down that a murder can only be expiated by the sacrifice of another life: self-sacrifice points back to blood-guilt.[6] And if this sacrifice of a life brought about atonement with God the Father, the crime to be expiated can only have been the murder of the father.

In the Christian doctrine, therefore, men were acknowledging in the most undisguised manner the guilty primaeval deed, since they found the fullest atonement for it in the sacrifice of this one son. Atonement with the father was all the more complete since the sacrifice was accompanied by a total renunciation of the women on whose account the rebellion against the father was started. But at that point the inexorable psychological law of ambivalence stepped in. The very deed in which the son offered the greatest possible atonement to the father brought him at the same time to the attainment of his wishes *against* the father. He himself became God, beside, or, more correctly, in place of, the father. A son-religion displaced the father-religion. As a sign of this substitution the ancient totem meal was revived in the form of communion, in which the company of brothers consumed the flesh and blood of the son—no longer the father—obtained sanctity thereby and identified themselves with him. Thus we can trace through the ages the identity of the totem meal with animal sacrifice, with theanthropic human sacrifice and with the Christian Eucharist, and we can recognize in all these rituals the effect of the crime by which men were so deeply weighed down but of which they must none the less feel so proud. The Christian communion, however, is essentially a fresh elimination of the father, a repetition of the guilty deed. We can see the full justice of Frazer's pronouncement that "the Christian communion has absorbed within itself a sacrament which is doubtless far older than Christianity."[7]

# Notes

1.  Cf. the discussion by C. G. Jung (1912), which is governed by views differing in certain respects from mine.
2.  "To us moderns, for whom the breach which divides the human and the divine has deepened into an impassable gulf, such mimicry may appear impious, but it was otherwise with the ancients. To their thinking gods and men were akin, for many families traced their descent from a divinity, and the deification of a man probably seemed as little extraordinary to them as the canonization of a saint seems to a modern Catholic" (Frazer, 1911a, II, 177f.).
3.  It is generally agreed that when, in mythologies, one generation of gods is overcome

by another, what is denoted is the historical replacement of one religious system by a new one, whether as a result of foreign conquest or of psychological development. In the latter case myth approximates to what Silberer (1909) has described as "functional phenomena" (Cf. Freud, 1900, English translation, 1932, 464 ff.). The view maintained by Jung (1912) that the god who kills the animal is a libidinal symbol implies a concept of libido other than that which has hitherto been employed and seems to me questionable from every point of view.

4.  Fear of castration plays an extremely large part, in the case of the youthful neurotics whom we come across, as an interference in their relations with their father. The illuminating instance reported by Ferenczi (1913) has shown us how a little boy took as his totem the beast that had snapped at his little penis (See page 130 f.). When our children come to hear of ritual circumcision, they equate it with castration. The parallel in social psychology to this reaction by children has not yet been worked out, so far as I am aware. In primaeval times and in primitive races, where circumcision is so frequent, it is performed at the age of initiation into manhood and it is at that age that its significance is to be found; it was only as a secondary development that it was shifted back to the early years of life. It is of very great interest to find that among primitive peoples circumcision is combined with cutting the hair and knocking out teeth or is replaced by them, and that our children, who cannot possibly have any knowledge of this, in fact treat these two operations, in the anxiety with which they react to them, as equivalents of castration.

5.  "*Une sorte de péché proethnique*" (Reinach, 1905-12, vol. II, 76).

6.  We find that impulses to suicide in a neurotic turn out regularly to be self-punishments for wishes for someone else's death.

7.  Frazer (1912, vol. II, 51). No one familiar with the literature of the subject will imagine that the derivation of Christian communion from the totem meal is an idea originating from the author of the present essay.

# References

Ferenczi, S. (1913). "Ein kleiner Hahnemann," *Int. Z. Psychoanal.*, 1, 240. (Trans.: "A Little Chanticleer", *Contributions to Psycho-Analysis*, 1916, 240.)

Frazer, J. G. (1910). *Totemism and Exogamy* (4 vols.), London.

Frazer, J. G. (1911). *The Golden Bough*, (3rd edn., Part I), London.

Freud, S. (1900). *Die Traumdeutung*, Vienna. (*G.S.*, 2–3; *G.W.*, 2–3) (Trans.: *The Interpretation of Dreams*, rev. edn., London, 1932.)

Hubert, H., and Mauss, M. (1899). "Essai sur la nature et la fonction du sacrifice," *Année sociolog.*, 2, 29.

Jung, C. G. (1912). "Wandlungen und Symbole der Libido," *Jb. psychoanal. psychopath. Forsch.*, 3, 120 and 4, 162. (Trans.: *Psychology of the Unconscious*, London, 1919.)

Marillier, L. (1898). "La place du totemisme dans l'évolution religieuse," *Rev. Hist. Relig.*, 37, 204.

Reinach, S. (1905–12). *Cultes, mythes et religions* (4 vols.), Paris.

Silberer, H. (1909). "Bericht über eine Methode, gewisse symbolische Halluzinations-Erscheinungen hervorzurufen und zu beobachten," *Jb. psychoanal. psychopath. Forsch.*, 1, 513.

Smith, W. Robertson (1894). *Lectures on the Religion of the Semites*, new [2nd] edn., London. (1st edn., 1889.)

# 9

# GERARDUS VAN DER LEEUW
# (b. 1890)

Gerardus van der Leeuw was a Dutch theologian and historian of religions. Born in the Hague, and educated in Leiden, he earned his doctorate in 1916 with a concentration in the history of religions. He was an active and committed member of the Dutch Reformed church, and for two years he served as a minister in that denomination. Then in 1918 he accepted a post as Professor of History at the University of Gronigen where he grappled with methodological issues in the study of religion (e.g., the relationship between theology and the comparative study of religions) and taught a wide variety of courses, including Christian theology, Egyptian religion, philosophy, history, comparative religions, and phenomenology. Van der Leeuw is best known for his major work on the phenomenology of religion, published first in German (1933) and later translated into English as *Religion in Essence and Manifestation: A Study in Phenomenology*. Influenced greatly by his teacher P. D. Chantepie de la Saussaye, Rudolf Otto, Wilhelm Dilthey, and others, this book develops a comprehensive phenomenological frame, and presents a systematic, highly organized account of a wide variety of religious phenomena. Even while attracting a fair amount of criticism, this book remains a landmark in the history of studying religions.

Phenomenology is a method of approaching "manifestations," or of what "appears." It seeks to describe and classify without interfering with the "intentionality" of "phenomena," without reducing it, through a process of explanation, to something it is not. This requires the researcher to suspend his or her judgment, to "bracket" preconceptions, in service of maintaining an empirical and historical approach when collecting and classifying data. Van der Leeuw is known for emphasizing an epistemological point in his phenomenology. He points out that whenever a phenomenon appears, the quality of this "appearance refers equally to what appears and to the person to whom it appears." Every phenomenon, in other words, arises through an encounter between subject and object. It depends upon both and constitutes a mutually dependent relationship for both. As such, a phenomenon is neither pure subject nor object. Different from earlier phenomenologists (e.g., C. Tiele, W. B. Kristensen, and others), van der Leeuw claims that the "essence" of phenomena becomes available through this interaction of subject and object, and that therefore "understanding" a phenomenon, "intuiting" its "meaning," always involves a "participation" in it.

# G. van der Leeuw: from *Religion in Essence and Manifestation*

When he turns his attention to religion and applies this method of phenomenology, van der Leeuw finds the notion of "power" to be central. His *Religion in Essence and Manifestation* can be read as a systematic elaboration of this notion and its various appearances in the history of religions. By "power" van der Leeuw means "that something" which human beings seek when they do "not accept the life given," when they "endeavor to find some meaning in life." Religion, then, springs from this impulse, and religions are cultural and historical examples of the ways human beings have in fact encountered the "power" they sought. Put differently, religious phenomena are the products of human beings seeking power in their lives. Power is the subject of religion, but in agreement with Rudolf Otto, van der Leeuw declares power is also the object of religion. It is that "sacred," "holy," "mysterious," "awesome" focus for religious experience and action. Like the phenomenological method's observation that appearances gain their reality through the interplay of subject and object, van der Leeuw argues that religious phenomena are equally interdependent. The phenomenological method is perfectly suited then to examine religion for it too is a hermeneutical endeavor, one dedicated to forwarding understandings of life and the world, or, to use van der Leeuw's language, to understanding appearances of "power."

In part three of *Religion in Essence and Manifestation*, the part entitled "Object and Subject in their Reciprocal Operation," van der Leeuw devotes a chapter to sacrifice. He employs Marcel Mauss's essay, "The Gift," to argue that sacrificial rites gain their significance by virtue of their gift-like qualities and the fact that gifts are inherently "powerful." The gift-giving event (giving, receiving, return giving) creates a "binding force" between all those who participate, linking together the sacrificer, the thing offered (the "pivot of the sacrificial act"), and the receiver so that it becomes "quite impossible" to distinguish between the donor and the recipient. In this way, van der Leeuw claims sacrifice, while beginning as a gift and an offering between a subject (human beings) and object (divine beings), is also a means of communion. What we have here is an understanding of sacrifice that combines a form of gift-theory with communion-theory. Van der Leeuw shares this combination with Durkheim even as he understands the nature of the gift quite differently. Finally, when referring to the practice of the sacrificial meal, van der Leeuw follows Robertson Smith but puts a slight twist on his notion that consuming a sacred animal binds the community together. He emphasizes that this sharing the meal (giving it to one another) is in fact a distribution of the community's power, something that "constitutes and strengthens" the community itself.

While the phenomenology of religion in general and van der Leeuw's work in particular have been the subject of serious critique, there remain useful elements. For example, the sacrifice chapter from *Religion in Essence and Manifestation*, reprinted below, does in fact make a contribution to the history of sacrifice theory. With its attention to the dynamics of gift-giving, it foreshadows a number of later authors, and offers one additional perspective in understanding sacrifice.

# From *Religion in Essence and Manifestation: A Study in Phenomenology*

**1.** THE TERMS "soul" and "sacrifice" must be included among those presenting the greatest variety of meaning in the whole history of religion; and in both cases we may doubt the advisability of estimating such utterly different phenomena, as are comprised under these words, as being diverse instances of that single self-revelation which will be further discussed in the *Epilegomena*. With respect to these two ideas, nevertheless, and as indeed I hope that I have already shown with regard to the soul, the phenomena prove to constitute a fundamental unity. Usually, however, a distinction is made between the sacrificial gift or the sacrifice of homage, and the sacramental meal; in the latter case it is either the god himself who is consumed, or he is looked upon as a table companion who receives his due share. But even with this classification of the phenomena, justice has not been accorded to all the instances. For in many sacrificial ceremonies it is extremely difficult to point to the presence of the "god" at all.[1] In these circumstances, therefore, it would be quite impossible to maintain that old principle of explanation of sacrifice, the rule of *do-ut-des*[2]—"I give that thou mayest give"—which had in fact been formulated in classical times: "Bribes, believe me, buy both gods and men; Jupiter himself is appeased by the offering of gifts";[3] while the brahminic ritual expresses it equally clearly: "here is the butter; where are thy gifts?"[4] In his famous work, *The Religion of the Semites*, however, Robertson Smith has shown that besides this idea of *do-ut-des* there was at least one other that was quite different and yet was the basis of sacrifice—the idea of a communal meal at which the god is either a participant, or else is identical with the sacrifice, that is with the food consumed.[5]

---

Gerardus van der Leeuw, *Religion in Essence and Manifestation: A Study in Phenomenology* (Princeton: Princeton University Press, 1986), pp. 350–60. Copyright © by Princeton University Press. Reprinted with permission of Princeton University Press.

It appears therefore that we must have interpreted the "gift," which is thus supposed to be the basis of sacrifice, in far too European and modern a sense; we have allowed ourselves to be led away by Ovid, and forgotten what "to give" actually means.[6] "To give" is believed to be "more blessed than to receive";[7] but for this maxim the *do-ut-des* theory leaves no scope whatever. It presupposes quite a different view of giving, or rather a wholly contrasted interpretation of "I give . . . " For it is contestable that this kind of argument is, very frequently, the actual ground of sacrifice. But *dare* does not mean merely to dispose of some arbitrary object with a quite indefinite intention; the word *dare* means, rather, to place oneself in relation to, and then to participate in, a second person by means of an object, which however is not actually an "object" at all, but a part of one's own self. "To give," then, is to convey something of oneself to the strange being, so that a firm bond may be forged. Mauss refers, together with other writers, to Emerson's fine essay, *Gifts,* with respect to this "primitive" view of giving: "The only gift is a portion of thyself. Thou must bleed for me. Therefore the poet brings his poem; the shepherd, his lamb; the farmer, corn; the miner, a gem." . . . "The gift, to be true, must be the flowing of the giver unto me, correspondent to my flowing unto him." In fact, giving demands a gift, not however in the sense of any commercial rationalism, but because the gift allows a stream to flow, which from the moment of giving runs uninterruptedly from donor to recipient and from receiver to giver: "the recipient is in the power of the giver."[8] "As a rule, certainly, the receiver of the present appears to gain and the donor to lose, but secretly the gift demands a gift in return. Whoever receives gifts unites himself to the one who bestows them: the accepted gift can bind."[9] We ourselves, in fact, continue to recognize this power whenever we give an employee his "earnest," and that presents maintain friendship we know quite as well as the East African natives who said to Livingstone: "Thou claimest to be our friend; but how are we to know that, so long as thou hast not given us any of thy food and hast not tasted ours? Give us an ox; we will give thee in return everything thou mayest demand, and then we shall be bound to each other by genuine affection."[10] With many primitive peoples, again, refusal to bestow or receive a gift amounts to a declaration of war: it means that community is declined;[11] for the gift is powerful; it has binding force: it has *mana.* Gifts therefore can destroy the recipient; but they can also assist him, and in any event they forge an indissoluble bond. Thus the Maori speak of the *hau* (spirit) of the gift: I give what I have received from thee to a third person, and from him I receive a return gift. This I must now give to thee since it is actually thy gift; the *hau* of thy gift persists in it.[12] "The object received is not a dead thing. Even when it has been handed over by the giver it always retains something pertaining to him." To offer somebody something, then, is to offer someone a part of oneself; similarly, to accept a thing from another person is to receive some portion of his spiritual being, of his soul;[13] and under these circumstances the reciprocal nature of giving is quite obvious.

The *Havamal* expresses all this most forcibly: "Friends should cheer each other with presents of weapons and raiment . . . Those who repay with gifts, and those who respond in the same way, remain friends longest, provided that there is time for matters to turn out well. If you wish to know when you have a friend whom you can trust absolutely, and if you desire to be treated well by him, you must blend your own sentiments with his, interchange gifts with him, and often travel to visit him." In all this there is doubtless an element of calculation: here is the butter, where are the gifts? But there is also involved a just apprehension of friendship; and thirdly, there is something more: a mystic power attached to the gift which establishes *communio*.[14] Or to express this in Lévy-Bruhl's terms: giver and receiver participate in the gift and therefore in each other. Here, too, economic life has its roots; on the Trobriand Islands in Melanesia, for example, the dignified trade in *kula* is distinguished from the ordinary business in *gimwali*; in the first it is not so much a matter of exchange as of the distribution of gifts.[15] The Indian tribes of North-west America, again, practice the "potlatch" system, consisting in two tribes or chiefs engaging in a competition of prodigality; whoever is the richer gives the most and even destroys his own possessions if necessary. All this, however, in order that he himself may prosper,[16] since in this manner he shows that he has power; and we have already observed that the primitive king also demonstrated his power by giving presents. But here, as always, the "power" is just as secular (to use our paltry expression) as it is "sacred," the "potlatch" system being simultaneously religious and economic, social and legal;[17] and a wealthy Maori has *mana*, which is at the same time credit, influence and power. Thus "to buy" is a magical action; and according to Mauss the three obligations of the "potlatch" system are to give, to receive, and to give in return;[18] the one always has the other as a condition. For whoever buys receives something of the owner's being together with his purchase, and that would be dangerous if an exchange gift did not follow: buying must therefore always be accompanied by a return gift;[19] for objects sold are never completely detached from their possessor.[20]

Under such conditions we can hardly be astonished at *money* also having a sacramental origin; and the oldest Greek measure of value was the ox, the sacred sacrificial animal, the money being the tribute that must be paid to the deity. Thus the sacrificial meal, in the course of which the meat was equally divided, was the "germ of public financial administration." Later, coin appeared instead of the sacrifice;[21] but that the coin was money, that is valid, was also due to its originating in the sphere of sacrifice and bringing with it its powerfulness, or as we should say, its credit.[22] Here we meet with the same relationship as was discerned in the case of retaliation (punishment) and revenge:[23] a stream is released, one motion always setting the other free; therefore just as the evil deed must be balanced by revenge or punishment, so must the gift be "requited" by a gift in return or, in modern terms, be paid for.[24]

Sacrifice, then, and in the first place as the sacrificial gift, has now taken its place within a very much wider connotation. It is no longer a mere matter of bartering with gods corresponding to that carried on with men, and no longer homage to the god such as is offered to princes: it is an opening of a blessed source of gifts. We both give and receive, and it is quite impossible to say who is actually donor and who recipient. For both participate in the powerfulness of what is being presented, and hence it is neither the giver nor the receiver, even though he be a god or a divine being, who occupies the focal point of the action. The pivot of the sacrificial act, its power centre, is always the gift itself: it must be given, that is to say, be set in motion. As a rule it is given to another person who may be one's neighbour, or may be some god; but it may also be divided among the members of the community. It may, again, be "given" without any "addressee" at all. For the principal feature is not that someone or other should receive something, but that the stream of life should continue to flow. From this point of view, therefore, not only are gift and communion sacrifices not antitheses but, still further, the sacrifice is transplanted into the very midst of life. It is no *opus supererogatorium*, but the working of the power of life itself. And thus instead of the rationalistic *do-ut-des*, we must say: *do ut possis dare*—"I give in order that thou mayest be able to give": I give thee power that thou mayest have power, and that life may not stagnate because of any lack of potency.

2. "I discern a reference to such a reciprocal effect as this in the Roman sacrificial formula 'Hail to thee'; e.g. '*Iuppiter dapalis,* hail to thee by the offering of thy feast: hail to thee by the wine placed before thee.'[25] Probably this can have no other meaning than: 'Hail to thee! with these sacrificial gifts, which I now offer to thee; be strong through these my gifts.' Such an invocation in a fixed formula, in *verbis certis*, however, was never a merely arbitrary form of speech. For the view certainly prevailed at one time that the gods could be rendered capable of bestowing power only by the constant nourishing of their own strength . . . The Roman, for example, sacrificed to the hearth, to Vesta, by throwing small gifts into the fire, while he was at the same time wholly dependent on this hearth fire, and worshipped it as the essence of the divine fullness of life."[26] Thus the relationship of dependence between god and man, which appears to us to be perfectly obvious, need by no means be actually present; or rather: the dependence certainly subsisted, but it was reciprocal, and may be compared to the status of the Catholic priest in popular piety: "no creature other than he has the 'power' to create God Himself in transubstantiation, to call Him down from His heavenly throne to the altar by his word of consecration."[27]

If however man gives in order that he may also receive, nevertheless he externalizes part of himself in the gift. Here again I believe that I can deepen a certain rationalist viewpoint, so as to be able to set it in its correct connection with life: that namely of so-called vicarious sacrifice. Usually it is maintained that vicarious sacrifice is a *pis aller*, just as the substitute formerly was in military service: no one ever sacrifices himself willingly, and therefore one sacrifices one's children, and later a slave or prisoner, finally an animal, and if that be too costly, a cake in animal form. In fact, we know how human sacrifice was actually replaced by that of animals, for example in the story of Isaac,[28] and also that the sacrificial cake very often retained the form of the animal whose place it had taken.[29] We recall again that the Toradja native, if he tells a lie while travelling by water, quickly pulls a hair from his head and throws it into the stream with the words: "I am guilty, I give this instead of myself."[30] But all this is not merely some acute business deal transacted with the powers. He who "gives," who sacrifices, *always* gives something of himself with it: whether it be his child which he is giving as a building sacrifice, or his hair that he is tendering as an atonement, or his grain offered as first-fruits, it is always a portion of himself.[31] He who makes a sacrifice sacrifices his property, that is, himself.[32] Just as he chooses, therefore, he can replace a part of himself, of his possessions, by something else, since all that he has has a part in him, and participates reciprocally. Certainly this substitution of something different for the gift can arise purely from a desire for comfort or from greed. But it may also be actuated by humanitarian motives; and it may even conduce to indifference so far as the value of the sacrifice is concerned: "the sacrifice of a fowl has the same value in the eyes of the god as the sacrifice of an ox," say the South African Baronga.[33] And from this attitude the path leads on to the standpoint of the prophet demanding obedience and not sacrifice.

But here yet another highly important idea is born: the sacrifice takes the place of the person offering it. With him it is essentially connected; the sacrificer gives himself in and with his offering, and in this surrender the offering assists him. Thus a different light is cast upon the sacrifice of women, slaves, etc., who follow their masters to death. The Hindu burning of widows is universally familiar, while in Nubia slaves and prisoners were slain to accompany the dead man;[34] and the primary purpose of all this was not that the retainers should serve their master in the world beyond. That they must already do, since by their own death and rebirth they facilitated their lord's decease and rebirth. Here then it was a matter of suffering and dying together, whence new life arose. For the broad stream of life, the eternal flux of power, is assured by the greatest possible "expenditure"; and since sacrificer and sacrifice participate in each other, giver and gift can interchange their roles. The idea of the vicarious sacrifice of Christ should therefore be interpreted from this viewpoint, not in the light of some juristic theory: the sacrifice demanded from man being accomplished by Him Who is simultaneously sacrificer and sacrifice, *sacerdos et hostia*.

3. Still further, sacrifice preserves the cycle of power. The stream of gifts (that is, of power), not only assures community between man and man, between man and god, but can also be conducted through all kinds of difficulties and can avert these by absorbing them within the community. Thus the *building sacrifice* removes the risks of construction: taking possession of the piece of ground, and the expulsion of the foreign demonic power residing in the soil, are rendered harmless by the *communio* of the sacrifice; only in this way can the house become a piece of property. The atoning sacrifice, again, removes the sin impeding the stream of life; life's power is set in motion in favour of the person offering the sacrifice. "In this respect it is somewhat indifferent whether this vital power resides in a god and, by means of the sacred food replete with the strength of life, is compelled to circulate by the maker of the sacrifice, or whether it subsists within the sacrifice itself and is consumed as food at first hand by the sacrificer. Originally the food, on which life depended, was probably eaten in the religious sense, that is, in accordance with later ideas, sacramentally.[35] . . . Then the primitive fare, venerated of old (milk and honey, the Roman *mola salsa*, etc.[36]) became the food of the gods or of their realm. But it might also be regarded as itself divine; and then the meal became a sacrifice."[37]

Pre-eminently does the sacramental meal, brought into prominence by Robertson Smith, now become comprehensible. Some sacred substance, an animal or other kind of nourishment, is divided among the members of a community and consumed by them: thus it becomes the sacred that subsists in common,[38] producing a strengthening of the community's power and binding its members more firmly to each other. The custom of dividing an animal into pieces, thereby effecting unity, is familiar in Saul's conduct during the siege of the town of Jabesh;[39] and perhaps this implied a sacrifice also. The significance of the sacrificial meal, however, becomes quite clear to us in the case of the Ainu, the primitive inhabitants of Japan.[40] The Ainu celebrate a bear feast; a very young bear is captured, suckled and carefully reared by a woman, pampered and spoilt for several years and finally killed; in the slaying the whole community participates, at least symbolically; it is then sincerely mourned, and consumed ceremonially in a communal meal. It is the animal of the community; and this follows from the fact that it can be a sacrificial animal only if it has grown up in the tribe, so that a wild bear would be useless for the purpose; it is as it were the child of the woman who brought it up, and who laments it.[41] A vestige of a similar communal meal occurred in Latin antiquity; the Latin League celebrated the *feriae latinae* on the Alban Mount: there the delegates from the Latin towns ate together a white steer; each town received its share, the ceremonial being called *carnem petere*.[42] And again, in a different way, the so-called *epulum Jovis* celebrated at the Ides of September, in which three gods took part;[43] thus in this instance the sacrifice and the god were not identical, the deity being numbered among the guests. But by both methods alike community among the participants was effected or strengthened;[44] and only from the point of view of such community can we comprehend the laments over the sacrifice, and the prayers for forgiveness, met with among so many peoples. This becomes most obvious when totemistic connections with the sacrificial animal predominate. Thus the Zuni of Arizona mourn for the turtle which has been sacrificed: "Ah! my poor dear lost child or parent, my sister or brother to have been! Who knows which? Maybe my own great-grandfather or mother."[45] The sacrifice belongs to the community, indeed *is* the community, constitutes and strengthens it. The community is being sacrificed, "given up," in order to be sustained. And in this sense too only what has been lost can be gained.[46]

4. "This view of sacrifice has been developed in the most magnificent and logical manner in India. There the sacrifice (the ancient Vedic sacrifice of the horse) became a process which was executed with automatic precision: 'Events are apprehended just as they were in the most primitive type of prehistoric ideas of the Universe, as resting on the play of those forces which rule the Universe, and whose mode of operation, remotely comparable to the order of Nature which constitutes the modern concept of the world, the knower is able to calculate and to direct just as he will. But this knower is man himself.'[47] Here sacrifice has become a world process in the literal sense, and man understands how to dominate it. The centre of life's power lies in himself; he is the transitional point of the potencies that move the Universe. Here, then, gods are just as superfluous as they were in the primitive stage."[48]

Actually the sacrifice, as such, is always a sacrament. But where it is expressly called so, that is in Christianity, the concept of the stream of gifts has fused in a marvellous way with the concept of a personal God, and of a Saviour Who is not only the sacrifice, not only the priest, but also a historic personage. Here the danger certainly threatens that owing to the repetition inherent in all cult, the historic-concrete and uniquely given element in the Saviour's sacrifice would be transformed repeatedly into that autocratic automatism which we have just discerned in India. It is true that the bloodless reiteration of the bloody sacrifice of Golgotha, as this is prescribed according to the decisions of the Council of Trent,[49] need repeal neither the unique sacrificial deed of Christ nor the making of the thank-offering on the church's part, which is possible only in the concrete situation. Nevertheless a *soupçon* of the idea of the luxuriantly flowing stream of grace—but without God's act of volition and also without the church's gratitude—once again makes itself constantly perceptible here: Power is striving with Will and Form. If however the struggle just referred to is not carried on one-sidedly, and in favour of a pure dynamism or a mere symbolism, but persists as a living tension, then the Christian Eucharist implies, indeed, an intensification of the mystic and primitive idea of *do-ut-des*. For I cannot perceive any contradiction, such as

Luther did,[50] in the fact that the same entity is simultaneously received and offered. On the contrary, it is precisely the essence of all sacrifice that it should be at the same time an offering and a receiving. The centurion, whose words occur in the mass before communion, says that he is not worthy that the Lord should enter under his roof; nonetheless at the same moment he does enter under the Lord's roof; "I am not worthy that thou shouldest come under my roof", and "Then will I go unto the altar of God,"[51] are *one* celebration and *one* act of God. This in fact found expression in the ancient Christian liturgy when, in the anamnesis, the people appear offering thanks to the Lord with the words "What is His own from what is His own";[52] and it has been most beautifully interpreted in Paul Gerhardt's *Christmas Hymn*:

> Here stand I at Thy manger,
> O little Jesus, my very life.
> I come to bring and give to Thee
> What Thou hast given to me.

# Notes

1. Cf. an enumeration of the forms of sacrifice in Pfleiderer's *Philosophy of Religion*, IV, 186 ff.
2. G. van der Leeuw, *Do-ut-des-Formel, passim.*
3. Ovid, *Ars amatoria*, III, 653 (Mozley); cf. further Alviella, *Idée de Dieu*, 89, where the ancient Hindu formula is quoted: "Give thou to me, I shall give to thee; bring thou to me and I shall bring to thee"; also Jevons, *Introduction*, 69 ff. Grimm, *Schenken und Geben, Kl. Schriften*, II, 174 and note.
4. *RGG*, Article *Opfer* i,
5. Cf. further Reinach who, being the sound evolutionist he is, places the latter type, as the more enigmatical, at the beginning, and sacrificial gifts, as quite clearly comprehensible, at the close of the development.
6. Grönbech in Chantepie, *op. cit.*, II, 581; Laum, *Heiliges Geld*, 32; Grimm, *loc. cit.*
7. *Acts* xx. 35.
8. Grönbech, *loc. cit.*, III, 3.
9. Grimm, *loc. cit.*, 174.
10. Cited by R. Kreglinger, *Grondbeginselen der godsdienstwetenschap*, 68; cf. further Grönbech, III, 112.
11. Mauss, "Essai sur le don, forme archaique de l'échange," *Année sociologique*, N.S., I, 1925, 51.
12. Mauss, *ibid.*, 45f.
13. *Ibid.*, 47 ff.
14. Chap. 32.
15. Mauss, *ibid.*, 64 ff.
16. *Ibid.*, 93 ff.
17. Mauss, *op. cit.*, 99.

18. *Ibid.*, 100.
19. F. D. E. van Ossenbruggen, *Tydschrift van het Ned. Aardr. Genootschap. 2. Reeks*, 47, 1930, 221 ff. Cf. J. C. van Eerde, *ibid.*, 230 ff. These considerations place such a custom as bride purchase in an entirely new light; cf. H. Th. Fischer, *Der magische Charakter des Brautpreises* (*Weltkreis*, 1932, 3, 3).
20. Mauss, *ibid.*, 87.
21. Is Laum correct in suggesting that the *obol* is really the *obelos*—that is, the roasting-spit? *Op. cit.*, 106 ff.
22. Laum.
23. Chap. 23.
24. Cf. A. Olrik, *Ragnarök*, 1922, 460, and the typical Old Norse expression for "revenge," *uphaevelse*, that is, "setting the slain up again."
25. Cato, *Agri cultura*, 132; *mactus* originally means "increased, strengthened," then "honoured"; cf. R. Wünsch, *Rhein. Mus.* 69, 1913, 127 ff.; a similar expansion of meaning to that of the concepts *augeo, auctoritus*.
26. G. van der Leeuw, *Do-ut-des-Formel*, 244f.
27. Heiler, *Katholizismus*, 181.
28. A parallel from Samoa may be found in *Tales from old Fiji* (L. Fison), 1907, 41.
29. Cakes shaped like stags were offered to Artemis Elaphebolos; Nilsson, *Griech. Feste*, 224; cf. 202; Samter, *Religion der Griechen*, 47.
30. Kruyt, *Animisme*, 32 f.
31. Cf. Will, *Le culte*, I, 111.
32. Chap. 33.
33. Will, *ibid.*, I, 101.
34. Cf. G. A. Reisner, *Zeitschrift für ägypt. Sprache und Altertumskunde*, 52, 1915, 34 ff.; A. Wiedemann, *AR*. 21, 1922, 467.
35. "Every meal places man in connection with life's creative forces and with the eternal life of Deity"; Kristensen, *Livet*, 44.
36. Heiler, *Prayer*, 66. Wide, in *Handbuch der klassischen Altertumswissenschaft*, II, 4, 1931, 74.
37. G. van der Leeuw, *Do-ut-des-Formel*, 251 f.
38. Chap. 32.
39. I *Sam.* xi. 7; cf. *Judges* xix; Schwally, *Der heilige Krieg*, 53.
40. Haas, *Bilderatlas*, No. 8.
41. Cf. further Frazer, *Golden Bough*, VIII (*Spirits of the Corn*, II), 101 ff.
42. Warde Fowler, *The Religious Experience of the Roman People*, 172. Wissowa, *Religion und Kultus der Römer*, 124 ff. During the festival the *pax deorum* was maintained—a general tabu.
43. Fowler, *Roman Festivals*, 218 f.
44. Thomsen, *Der Trug des Prometheus*, AR. 12, 1909, 464.
45. Frazer, *Spirits of the Corn*, II, 175 ff. (*Golden Bough*, VIII).
46. It may be said that the stream of powerfulness evoked by the sacrifice vivifies all the participants therein, whether men or gods. It may, however, also be expressed thus:—that this stream flows from the god, or again from some one participant, to man or to another member, through the sacrifice. The altar then becomes the point of transition—the theory of Hubert and Mauss (*Mélanges d'histoire des religions*). But the sacrifice is far more than such a transitional point; it is itself sacredness, power-stuff; cf. the Greek rule οὐκ ἐκφορά—nothing may remain over

of the sacred food—a regulation very frequently encountered in sacrificial practice; cf. Thomsen, *Der Trug des Prometheus, AR.*12, 1909, 466 ff.

47. Oldenberg, *Lehre der Upanishaden,* 16 f.
48. G. van der Leeuw, *Do-ut-des-Formel,* 252.
49. Will, *Le culte,* I, 96 f.
50. *Of the Babylonian Captivity of the Church:* the contradiction "that the mass should be a sacrifice, because we receive the promise, but give the sacrifice. But one and the same object can neither be simultaneously received and offered, nor simultaneously given and received, by the same person."
51. *Matt.* viii, 8; *Ps.* xliii. 4.
52. τά σὰ ἐκτῶν σῶν σοὶ προσφέροντες κατὰ πάντα καὶ διὰ πάντα. H. Lietzmann, *Messe und Herrenmahl,* 1926, 51.

# References

Alfred Bertholet, *Der Sinn des kultischen Opfers* (Abh. preuz. Akad. d. Wiss., 1942, Phil. Hist. Kl. 2).

J. Grimm, *Schenken und Geben (Kl. Schriften,* II, 1865, 173 ff.).

H. Hubert and M. Mauss, *Mélanges d'histoire des religions,* 1909.

B. Laum, *Heiliges Geld,* 1924.

G. van der Leeuw, *Die Do-ut-des-Formel in der Opfertheorie (AR.* 20, 1920–21, 241 ff.).

A. Lods, *Examen de quelques hypothèses modernes sur les origines du sacrifice (Revue d'histoire et de littérature rel.,* 1921, 483 *ff.*).

A. Loisy, *Essai historique sur le sacrifice,* 1920.

B. Malinowski, *Argonauts of the Western Pacific,* 1932.

M. Mauss, "Essai sur le don, forme archaique de l'échange" (*Année sociologique, N.S.,* I, 1925).

S. Reinach, *Cultes, Mythes et Religions,* I, 1905.

W. Robertson Smith, *The Religion of the Semites,* 1927.

Ada Thomsen, *Der Trug des Prometheus (AR.* 12, 1909, 460 ff.).

# 10

# GEORGES BATAILLE (b. 1897)

French philosopher, novelist, and essayist Georges Bataille was born in Billon, central France. After a troubled childhood, he converted to Catholicism early in life, contemplated becoming a priest, but left the Church in 1920. He served briefly in the military but was discharged for health reasons, the first of many problems due to ill health. Bataille received degrees from Epernay College (1914) and the Ecole de Chartres in Paris (1922), and for a short time studied in Madrid. His first professional position was as a librarian at the Bibliothèque Nationale in Paris, a profession he continued later in Provence, and finally in Orleans. Early in his career, Bataille became involved with the Surrealist movement and began to write both fiction and nonfiction that emphasized themes of excess, irrationality, eroticism, and transgression. He is well known for establishing the journal *Critique*, a renowned publication that circulated the early work of important thinkers such as Barthes, Foucault, and Derrida. Bataille is remembered for his novels and his philosophical essays, some of which are now considered classics in a number of fields. These include: *Histoire de l'oeil* (1928, *The Story of the Eye*), *L'Expérience intérieure* (1943, *The Inner Experience*), *Le Coupable* (1944, *The Guilty*), *Sur Nietzsche* (1945, *On Nietzsche*), *Théorie de la religion* (1948, *Theory of Religion*), and *La Part maudite* (1949, *The Accursed Share*).

One of Bataille's main intellectual concerns was the interplay between the rational, ordered, constrained aspects of human knowledge and experience, and the more "base elements," the hidden and obscure. As rational individuals who live under the influence of moral society, most human beings remain blind to the freedom of their true "subject-hood." They exist as objects in pre-given worlds, living under a spell of future-oriented principles that deny the potentiality of the immediate. Bataille suggested, however, that certain moments offer opportunities to express these "base materials," to realize the otherness they represent. Certain human experiences—encounters with the erotic, death, and chance, for example—uncover a certain "intimacy" beneath ordinary social life. Indeed, religion itself, for Bataille, "is the search for lost intimacy." It is a strategy for "detaching from the real order, from the poverty of things, and [for] restoring the divine order." Religion provides avenues through which to seize the essential meaning of human consciousness. It is a quest to tap the "intimacy of life."

Religious sacrifice is a practice particularly suited for this quest. Bataille considers the nature of sacrifice in a number of his writings, but the first volume of *The Accursed*

*Share* offers the most complete formulation of a theory of sacrifice. In this essay on "general economy," Bataille begins by observing that living organisms naturally produce more energy than they need to survive, and that this excess energy, this surplus, must be used somehow. This drives the organism to find an outlet for the surplus, most commonly by applying it to growth. The very character of the organism, its history and abilities, is determined by how it channels this excess energy. Bataille next took the very intriguing step of arguing that society is subject to these same processes, that the general economy of a social group revolves around the nature of its surpluses and the different modes of consumption it employs. Sacrifice is one such mode. It is the violent consumption, the utter destruction, of surplus use. The sacrificial "victim is a surplus taken from the mass of useful wealth," and as it is chosen for destruction, it is an "accursed share." This profitless consumption has a profound effect however. By denying the possibility of using the victim in the future, something clearly the case following its destruction, sacrifice runs counter to the process of degradation social operations entail, the making of servile "things" from true subjects. The sacrificial victim and the sacrificer(s), by negating their utilitarian relationship, rediscover their true "intimate participation." Both, in the context of the sacrificial ritual, "withdraw from the real order" and the sacrificers momentarily escape the "cold calculation" that weighs them down.

The selection reprinted here comes from *The Accursed Share*. In it, Bataille examines features of Aztec sacrifice and develops what could be called his "consumption theory" of sacrifice. It is a fascinating and original explanation for why sacrificial victims are destroyed, why they must be considered valuable, and why people are motivated to sacrifice at all. It is an understanding of sacrifice far too many scholars have neglected.

# From *The Accursed Share:*
# *An Essay on General Economy*

## Society of Consumption and Society of Enterprise

I will describe sets of social facts manifesting a general movement of the economy.

I want to state a principle from the outset: By definition, this movement, the effect of which is prodigality, is far from being equal to itself. While there

Georges Bataille, *The Accursed Share: An Esssay on General Economy*, translated by Robert Hurley, vol. I (New York: Zone Books, 1991) pp. 45–61. Copyright © by Urzone, Inc. Reprinted with permission of Zone Books.

is an excess of resources over needs (meaning real needs, such that a society would suffer if they were not satisfied), this excess is not always consumed to no purpose. Society can grow, in which case the excess is deliberately reserved for growth. Growth regularizes; it channels a disorderly effervescence into the regularity of productive operations. But growth, to which is tied the development of knowledge, is by nature a transitory state. It cannot continue indefinitely. Man's science obviously has to correct the perspectives that result from the historical conditions of its elaboration. Nothing is more different from man enslaved to the operations of growth than the relatively free man of stable societies. The character of human life changes the moment it ceases to be guided by fantasy and begins to meet the demands of undertakings that ensure the proliferation of given works. In the same way, the face of a man changes if he goes from the turbulence of the night to the serious business of the morning. The serious humanity of growth becomes civilized, more gentle, but it tends to confuse gentleness with the value of life, and life's tranquil duration with its poetic dynamism. Under these conditions the clear knowledge it generally has of things cannot become a full self-knowledge. It is misled by what it takes for full humanity, that is, humanity at work, living in order to work without ever fully enjoying the fruits of its labor. Of course, the man who is relatively idle or at least unconcerned about his achievements—the type discussed in both ethnography and history—is not a consummate man either. But he helps us to gauge that which we lack.

## Consumption in the Aztec Worldview

The Aztecs, about whom I will speak first, are poles apart from us morally. As a civilization is judged by its works, their civilization seems wretched to us. They used writing and were versed in astronomy, but all their important undertakings were useless: Their science of architecture enabled them to construct pyramids on top of which they immolated human beings.

Their worldview is singularly and diametrically opposed to the activity-oriented perspective that we have. Consumption loomed just as large in their thinking as production does in ours. They were just as concerned about *sacrificing* as we are about *working*.

The sun himself was in their eyes the expression of sacrifice. He was a god resembling man. He had become the sun by hurling himself into the flames of a brazier.

The Spanish Franciscan Bernardino de Sahagún, who wrote in the middle of the sixteenth century, reports what some old Aztecs told him:

It is said that before the light of day existed, the gods assembled at the place called Teotihaucan . . . and spoke among themselves, saying: "Who will take it upon himself to bring light to the world?" On hearing these words, a god called Tecuciztecatl presented himself and replied: "I will be the one. I will bring light to the world." The gods then spoke again and said: "Who else among you?" They looked at one another then, wondering who this would be, and none dared accept the charge; all were afraid and made excuses. One of the gods who usually went unnoticed did not say anything but only listened to what the other gods were saying. The others spoke to him, saying, "Let it be you, *bubosito*." And he gladly accepted, replying: "I receive your order gratefully; so be it." And the two that were chosen began immediately to do penance, which lasted four days. Then a fire was lit in a hearth made in a rock . . . The god named Tecuciztecatl only offered costly things. Instead of branches he offered rich feathers called *quetzalli*; instead of grass balls he offered gold ones; instead of maguey spines he offered spines made with precious stones; and instead of bloodied spines he offered spines of red coral. And the copal he offered was of a very high quality. The *buboso*, whose name was Nanauatzin, offered nine green water rushes bound in threes, instead of ordinary branches. He offered balls of grass and maguey spines bloodied with his own blood, and instead of copal he offered the scabs of his *bubas*.

A tower was made for each of these two gods, in the form of a hill. On these hills they did penance for four nights . . . After the four nights of penance were completed, the branches and all the other objects they had used were thrown down there. The following night, a little before midnight, when they were to do their office, Tecuciztecatl was given his adornments. These consisted of a headdress of *aztacomitl* feathers and a sleeveless jacket. As for Nanauatzin, the *buboso*, they tied a paper headdress, called *amatzontli*, on his hair and gave him a paper stole and a paper rag for pants to wear. When midnight had come, all the gods gathered round the hearth, which was called *teotexcalli*, where the fire had burned for four days.

They separated into two lines on the two sides of the fire. The two chosen ones took their places near the hearth, with their faces to the fire, in the middle of the two lines of gods. The latter were all standing and they spoke to Tecuciztecatl, saying: "Go on, Tecuciztecatl. Cast yourself into the fire!" Hearing this, he started to throw himself into the flames, but the fire was burning high and very hot, and he stopped in fear and drew back. A second time he gathered his strength and turned to throw himself into the fire, but when he got near he stopped and did not dare go further; four times he tried, but could not. Now, it had been ordered that no one could try more than four times, so when the four attempts had been made the gods addressed Nanauatzin, saying: "Go on, Nanauatzin. It is your turn to try!" As soon as these words were said, he shut his eyes and, taking courage, went forward and threw himself into the fire. He began at once to crackle and sizzle like something being roasted. Seeing that he had thrown himself into the fire and was burning, Tecuciztecatl also cast himself into the flames and burned. It is said that an eagle went into the fire at the same time and burned, and this is why the eagle has scorched-looking and blackened feathers. An ocelot followed thereafter but did not burn, only being singed, and this is why the ocelot remains spotted black and white.[1]

A short while later, having fallen on their knees, the gods saw Nanauatzin, "who had become the sun," rising in the East. "He looked very red, appearing to sway from side to side, and none of them could keep their eyes on him, because he blinded them with his light. He shone brightly with his rays that reached in all directions." The moon in turn rose up over the horizon. Because he had hesitated, Tecuciztecatl shone less brightly. Then the gods had to die; the wind, Quetzalcoatl, killed them all: The wind tore out their hearts and used them to animate the newborn stars.

This myth is paralleled by the belief that not only men but also wars were created "so that there would be people whose hearts and blood could be taken so that the sun might eat."[2] Like the myth, this belief obviously conveys an extreme value placed on consumption. Each year, in honor of the sun, the Mexicans observed the four days of fasting that were observed by the gods. Then they immolated lepers who were like the *buboso* with his skin disease. For in their minds thought was only an exposition of actions.

## The Human Sacrifices of Mexico

We have a fuller, more vivid knowledge of the human sacrifices of Mexico than we do of those of earlier times; doubtless they represent an apex of horror in the cruel chain of religious rites.

The priests killed their victims on top of the pyramids. They would stretch them over a stone altar and strike them in the chest with an obsidian knife. They would tear out the still-beating heart and raise it thus to the sun. Most of the victims were prisoners of war, which justified the idea of wars as necessary to the life of the sun: Wars meant consumption, not conquest, and the Mexicans thought that if they ceased the sun would cease to give light.

"Around Easter time," they undertook the sacrificial slaying of a young man of irreproachable beauty. He was chosen from among the captives the previous year, and from that moment he lived like a great lord. "He went through the whole town very well dressed, with flowers in his hand and accompanied by certain personalities. He would bow graciously to all whom he met, and they all knew he was the image of Tezcatlipoca [one of the greatest gods] and prostrated themselves before him, worshipping him wherever they met him."[3] Sometimes he could be seen in the temple on top of the pyramid of Quauchxicalco: "Up there he would play the flute at night or in the daytime, whichever time he wished to do it. After playing the flute, he too would turn incense toward the four parts of the world, and then return home, to his room."[4] Every care was taken to ensure the elegance and princely distinction of his life. "If, due to the good treatment he grew stout, they would make him drink saltwater to keep slender."[5] "Twenty days previous to the festival they gave this youth four maidens, well prepared and educated for this purpose. During those twenty days he had carnal intercourse with these maidens. The four girls they gave him as wives and who had been reared with special care for that purpose were given names of four goddesses . . . Five days before he was to die they gave festivities for him, banquets held in cool and gay places, and many chieftains and prominent people accompanied him. On the day of the festival when he was to die they took him to an oratory, which they called Tlacuchcalco. Before reaching it, at a place called Tlapituoaian, the women stepped aside and left him. As he got to the place where he was to be killed, he mounted the steps by himself and on each one of these he broke one of the flutes which he had played during the year."[6] "He was awaited at the top by the satraps or priests who were to kill him, and these now grabbed him and threw him onto the stone block, and, holding him by feet, hands and head, thrown on his back, the priest who had the stone knife buried it with a mighty thrust in the victim's breast and, after drawing it out, thrust one hand into the opening and tore out the heart, which he at once offered to the sun."[7]

Respect was shown for the young man's body: It was carried down slowly to the temple courtyard. Ordinary victims were thrown down the steps to the bottom. The greatest violence was habitual. The dead person was flayed and the priest then clothed himself in this bloody skin. Men were thrown into a furnace and pulled out with a hook to be placed on the executioner's block still alive. More often than not the flesh consecrated by the immolation was eaten. The festivals followed one another without interruption and every year the divine service called for countless sacrifices: Twenty thousand is given as the number. One of the victims incarnating a god, he climbed to the sacrifice surrounded, like a god, by an attendance that would accompany him in death.

## Intimacy of Executioners and Victims

The Aztecs observed a singular conduct with those who were about to die. They treated these prisoners humanely, giving them the food and drink they asked for. Concerning a warrior who brought back a captive, then offered him in sacrifice, it was said that he had "considered his captive as his own flesh and blood, calling him son, while the latter called him father."[8] The victims would dance and sing with those who brought them to die. Efforts were often made to relieve their anguish. A woman incarnating the "mother of the gods" was consoled by the healers and midwives who said to her: "Don't be sad, fair friend; you will spend this night with the king, so you can rejoice." It was not made clear to her that she was to be killed, because death needed to be sudden and unexpected in her case. Ordinarily the condemned prisoners were well aware of their fate and were forced to stay up the final night, singing and dancing. Sometimes they were made to drink until drunk or, to drive away the idea of impending death, they were given a concubine.

This difficult wait for death was borne better by some victims than by others. Concerning the slaves who were to die during one of the November festivals, we are told that "they went to the homes of their masters to bid them good-bye . . . They were singing in a very loud voice, so loud that it seemed to split their breast, and upon reaching the house of their masters they dipped both hands in the bowls of paint or of ink and put them on the lintels of the doors and the posts of the houses, leaving their imprint in colors; the same they did in the houses of their relatives. Some of them who were lion-hearted would eat as usual, others could not eat thinking of the death they soon would have to suffer."[9] A slave who represented the goddess Illamatecutli was dressed entirely in white, adorned with white and black feathers, and her face was painted half black and half white. "Previous to being killed, this woman had to dance, and the old men played the tune for this dance, and the singers sang the songs; and while she danced she cried, sighed and worried, knowing that her death was so close at hand."[10] In the autumn women were sacrificed in a temple called Coatlan. "Some of them, upon climbing the steps, were singing, others screamed, and still others cried."[11]

## The Religious Character of the Wars

These sacrifices of prisoners cannot be understood apart from the conditions that made them possible: wars and the assumed risk of death. The Mexicans shed blood only provided that they risked dying.

They were conscious of this enchantment of war and sacrifice. The midwife would cut the umbilical cord of the newborn baby boy and say to him:

I cut your navel in the middle of your body. Know and understand that the house in which you are born is not your dwelling . . . It is your cradle, the place where you lay your head . . . Your true land is elsewhere; you are promised for other places. You belong to the countryside where battles are fought; you were sent to go there; your function and your skill is warfare; your duty is to give the sun the blood of your enemies to drink and to supply the earth with the bodies of your enemies to eat. As for your native land, your legacy and your happiness, you will find them in the house of the sun in the sky . . . You will be fortunate to be found worthy of dying on the battlefield, decorated with flowers. What I now cut from your body and from the middle of your stomach rightly belongs to Tlatecutli who is the earth and the sun. When war begins to seethe and the soldiers assemble, we shall put it in the hands of those who are valorous soldiers, so that they might give it to your father and mother, the earth and the sun. They will bury it in the middle of the field where the battles are fought: This will be the proof that you are offered and promised to the earth and the sun; this will be the sign that you profess this office of warfare, and your name will be written in the field of battle so that your name and your person will not be forgotten. This precious offering collected from your body is like the offering of a maguey spine, of reeds for smoking and *axcoyatl* branches. Through it your vow and sacrifice are confirmed . . .[12]

The individual who brought back a captive had just as much of a share in the sacred office as the priest. A first bowl of the victim's blood, drained from the wound, was offered to the sun by the priests. A second bowl was collected by the sacrificer. The latter would go before the images of the gods and wet their lips with the warm blood. The body of the sacrificed was his by right; he would carry it home, setting aside the head, and the rest would be eaten at a banquet, cooked without salt or spices—but eaten by the invited guests, not by the sacrificer, who regarded his victim as a son, as a second self. At the dance that ended the feast, the warrior would hold the victim's head in his hand.

If the warrior had himself been overcome instead of returning a victor, his death on the field of battle would have had the same meaning as the ritual sacrifice of his prisoner: It would also have satisfied the hungry gods.

This was said in the prayer to Tezcatlipoca for the soldiers: "In truth, you are not wrong to want them to die in battle, for you did not send them into this world for any other purpose than to serve as food for the sun and the earth, with their blood and their flesh."[13]

Satiated with blood and flesh, the sun gave glory to the soul in his palace. There the war dead mingled with the immolated prisoners. The meaning of death in combat was brought out in the same prayer: "Make them bold and courageous; remove all weakness from their hearts so that they may not only receive death joyfully, but desire it and find charm and sweetness therein; so that they do not fear arrows or swords but rather consider them a pleasant thing, as if they were flowers and exquisite dishes of food."

## From the Primacy of Religion to the Primacy of Military Effectiveness

The value of warfare in Mexican society cannot mislead us: It was not a *military* society. Religion remained the obvious key to its workings. If the Aztecs must be situated, they belong among the warrior societies, in which pure, uncalculated violence and the ostentatious forms of combat held sway. The reasoned organization of war and conquest was unknown to them. A truly *military* society is a venture society, for which war means a development of power, an orderly progression of empire.[14] It is a relatively mild society; it makes a custom of the rational principles of enterprise, whose purpose is given in the future, and it excludes the madness of sacrifice. There is nothing more contrary to military organization than these squanderings of wealth represented by hecatombs of slaves.

And yet the extreme importance of warfare had brought about a significant change for the Aztecs, in the direction of the *rationality* of enterprise (which introduces, together with the concern for results and for effective force, a beginning of humanity) as against the cruel *violence* of consumption. While "the king remained in his palace," the court favored the victim (who was given "the honors of a god") with one of the most solemn sacrifices of the year. There is no possibility of a mistake here: This was a sacrifice of substitution. A softening of the ritual had occurred, shifting onto others the internal violence that is the moral principle of consumption. To be sure, the movement of violence that animated Aztec society was never turned more within than without; but internal and external violences combined in an economy that put nothing in reserve. The ritual sacrifices of prisoners commanded the sacrifices of warriors; the sacrificed victims represented at least the sumptuary expenditure of the sacrificer. The substituting of a prisoner for the king was an obvious, if inconsequent, abatement of this sacrificial frenzy.

## Sacrifice or Consumption

This softening of the sacrificial process finally discloses a movement to which the rites of immolation were a response. This movement appears to us in its logical necessity alone and we cannot know if the sequence of acts conforms to it in detail; but in any case its coherence is evident.

Sacrifice restores to the sacred world that which servile use has degraded, rendered profane. Servile use has made a *thing* (an *object*) of that which, in a deep sense, is of the same nature as the *subject*, is in a relation of intimate participation with the subject. It is not necessary that the sacrifice actually destroy the animal or plant of which man had to make a *thing* for his use. They must at least be destroyed as things, that is, *insofar as they have become things*. Destruction is the best means of negating a utilitarian relation between man and the animal or plant. But it rarely goes to the point of holocaust. It is enough that the consumption of the offerings, or the *communion*, has a meaning that is not reducible to the shared ingestion of food. The victim of the sacrifice cannot be consumed in the same way as a motor uses fuel. What the ritual has the virtue of rediscovering is the intimate participation of the sacrificer and the victim, to which a servile use had put an end. The slave bound to labor and having become the property of another is a *thing* just as a work animal is a thing. The individual who employs the labor of his prisoner severs the tie that links him to his fellow man. He is not far from the moment when he will sell him. But the owner has not simply made a *thing*, a commodity, of this property. No one can make a *thing* of the second self that the slave is without at the same time estranging himself from his own intimate being, without giving himself the limits of a *thing*.

This should not be considered narrowly: There is no perfect operation, and neither the slave nor the master is entirely reduced to the *order of things*. The slave is a thing for the owner; he accepts this situation which he prefers to dying; he effectively loses part of his intimate value for himself, for it is not enough to be this or that: One also has to be for others. Similarly, for the slave the owner has ceased to be his fellow man; he is profoundly separated from him; even if his equals continue to see him as a man, even if he is still a man for others, he is now in a world where a man can be merely a *thing*. The same poverty then extends over human life as extends over the countryside if the weather is overcast. Overcast weather, when the sun is filtered by the clouds and the play of light goes dim, appears to "reduce things to what they are." The error is obvious: What is before me is never anything less than the universe; the universe is not a *thing* and I am not at all mistaken when I see its brilliance in the sun. But if the sun is hidden I more clearly see the barn, the field, the hedgerow. I no longer see the splendor of the light that played over the barn; rather I see this barn or this hedgerow like a screen between the universe and me.

In the same way, slavery brings into the world the absence of light that is the separate positing of each *thing*, reduced to the *use* that it has. Light, or brilliance, manifests the intimacy of life, that which life deeply is, which is perceived by the subject as being true to itself and as the transparency of the universe.

But the reduction of "that which is" to the *order of things* is not limited to slavery. Slavery is abolished, but we ourselves are aware of the aspects of social life in which man is relegated to the level of *things*, and we should know that this relegation did not await slavery. From the start, the introduction of *labor* into the world replaced intimacy, the depth of desire and its free outbreaks, with rational progression, where what matters is no longer the truth of the present moment, but, rather, the subsequent results of *operations*. The first labor established the world of *things*, to which the profane world of the Ancients generally corresponds. Once the world of things was posited, man himself became one of the things of this world, at least for the time in which he labored. It is this degradation that man has always tried to escape. In his strange myths, in his cruel rites, man is *in search of a lost intimacy* from the first.

Religion is this long effort and this anguished quest: It is always a matter of detaching from the *real* order, from the poverty of *things*, and of restoring the *divine* order. The animal or plant that man *uses* (as if they only had value *for him* and none for themselves) is restored to the truth of the intimate world; he receives a sacred communication from it, which restores him in turn to interior freedom.

The meaning of this profound freedom is given in destruction, whose essence is to consume *profitlessly* whatever might remain in the progression of useful works. Sacrifice destroys that which it consecrates. It does not have to destroy as fire does; only the tie that connected the offering to the world of profitable activity is severed, but this separation has the sense of a definitive consumption; the consecrated offering cannot be restored to the *real* order. This principle opens the way to passionate release; it liberates violence while marking off the domain in which violence reigns absolutely.

The world of *intimacy* is as antithetical to the *real* world as immoderation is to moderation, madness to reason, drunkenness to lucidity. There is moderation only in the object, reason only in the identity of the object with itself, lucidity only in the distinct knowledge of objects. The world of the subject is the night: that changeable, infinitely suspect night which, in the sleep of reason, *produces monsters. I submit that madness itself gives a rarefied idea of the free "subject," unsubordinated to the "real" order and occupied only with the present.* The *subject* leaves its own domain and subordinates itself to the *objects* of the *real* order as soon as it becomes concerned for the future. For the *subject* is consumption insofar as it is not tied down to work. If I am no longer concerned about "what will be" but about "what is," what reason do I have to keep anything in reserve? I can at once, in disorder, make an instantaneous consumption of all that I possess. This useless consumption is *what suits me*, once my concern for the morrow is removed. And if I thus consume immoderately, I reveal to my fellow beings that which I am *intimately*: Consumption is the way in which *separate* beings communicate.[15] Everything shows through, everything is open and infinite between those who consume intensely. But nothing counts then; violence is released and it breaks forth without limits, as the heat increases.

What ensures the return of the *thing* to the *intimate* order is its entry into the hearth of consumption, where the violence no doubt is limited, but never without great difficulty. It is always the purpose of sacrifice to give destruction its due, to save the rest from a mortal danger of contagion. All those who have to do with sacrifice are in danger, but its limited ritual form regularly has the effect of protecting those who offer it.

Sacrifice is heat, in which the intimacy of those who make up the system of common works is rediscovered. Violence is its principle, but the works limit it in time and space; it is subordinated to the concern for uniting and preserving the commonality. The individuals break loose, but a breaking-loose that melts them and blends them indiscriminately with their fellow beings helps to connect them together in the operations of secular time. It is not yet a matter of *enterprise*, which absorbs the excess forces with a view to the unlimited development of wealth. The works in question only aim at continuance. They only predetermine the limits of the festival (whose renewal is ensured by their fecundity, which has its source in the festival itself). But the community is saved from ruination. The *victim* is given over to violence.

## The Victim, Sacred and Cursed

The victim is a surplus taken from the mass of *useful* wealth. And he can only be withdrawn from it in order to be consumed profitlessly, and therefore utterly destroyed. Once chosen, he is the *accursed share*, destined for violent consumption. But the curse tears him away from the *order of things*; it gives him a recognizable figure, which now radiates intimacy, anguish, the profundity of living beings.

Nothing is more striking than the attention that is lavished on him. Being a thing, he cannot truly be withdrawn from the real order, which binds him, unless destruction rids him of his "thinghood," eliminating his usefulness once and for all. As soon as he is consecrated and during the time between the consecration and death, he enters into the closeness of the sacrificers and participates in their consumptions: He is one of their own and in the festival in which he will perish, he sings, dances, and enjoys all the pleasures with them. There is no more servility in him; he can even receive arms and fight. He is lost in the immense confusion of the festival. And that is precisely his undoing.

The victim will be the only one in fact to leave the real order entirely, for he alone is carried along to the end by the movement of the festival. The sacrificer is divine only with reservations. The future is heavily reserved in him; the future is the weight that he bears as a thing. The official theologians[16] whose tradition Sahagún collected were well aware of this, for they placed the voluntary sacrifice of Nanauatzin above the others, praised warriors for being consumed by the gods, and gave divinity the meaning of consumption. We cannot know to what extent the victims of Mexico accepted their fate. It may be that in a sense certain of them "considered it an honor" to be offered to the gods. But their immolation was not voluntary. Moreover, it is clear that, from the time of Sahagún's informants, these death orgies were tolerated because they impressed foreigners. The Mexicans immolated children that were chosen from among their own. But severe penalties had to be decreed against those who walked away from their procession when they went up to the altars. Sacrifice comprises a mixture of anguish and frenzy. The frenzy is more powerful than the anguish, but only providing its effects are diverted to the exterior, onto a foreign prisoner. It suffices for the sacrificer to give up the wealth that the victim could have been for him.

This understandable lack of rigor does not, however, change the meaning of the ritual. The only valid excess was one that went beyond the bounds, and one whose consumption appeared worthy of the gods. This was the price men paid to escape their downfall and remove the weight introduced in them by the avarice and cold calculation of the real order.

# Notes

1. Bernardino de Sahagún, *Historia general de las cosas de Nueva España*, Mexico City: Porrúa, 1956, book VII, ch. 2.
2. *Historia de los Mexicanos por sus pinturas*, ch. 6.
3. Sahagún, *Historia*, book II, ch. 5.
4. *Ibid.*, appendix of book II.
5. *Ibid.*, book II, ch. 24.
6. *Ibid.*, book II, ch. 5.
7. *Ibid.*, book II, ch. 24.
8. *Ibid.*, book II, ch. 21.
9. *Ibid.*, book II, ch. 34.
10. *Ibid.*, book II, ch. 36.
11. *Ibid.*, book II, ch. 33.
12. *Ibid.*, book II, ch. 31.
13. *Ibid.*, book II, ch. 3.
14. I am basing myself on the views of Marcel Granet and Georges Dumézil.
15. I wish to emphasize a basic fact: The separation of beings is limited to the real order. It is only if I remain attached to the order of *things* that the separation is *real*. It *is* in fact *real*, but what is real is *external*. "Intimately, all men are one."
16. In the simple sense of a knowledge of the *divine*. It has been said that the texts that I refer to show a Christian influence. This hypothesis seems pointless to me. The substance of Christian beliefs is itself drawn from the previous religious experience and the world depicted by Sahagún's informants has a coherence all its own. If need be, the voluntary poverty of Nanauatzin could be interpreted as a Christianization. But this opinion appears to me to be based on a contempt for the Aztecs, which, it must be said, Sahagún seems not to have shared.

# 11

# ADOLF E. JENSEN (b. 1899)

Adolf Ellegard Jensen was born in Kiel, Germany, studied mathematics and philosophy, and, after receiving his doctorate in 1922, began working in the field of ethnology and the history of religions with Leo Frobenius at the Institute for Cultural Morphology in Munich. Frobenius was the principal advocate and an early architect of an anthropological position known as "culture circles" (*Kulturkreislehre*). He, and under his influence Jensen as well, thought cross-cultural similarities could be explained by identifying geographical "circles" organized around some central set of criteria that, while diffused throughout a number of different cultural groups within the circle, share a common origin and constitute an organic whole. Jensen, again like Frobenius, held a teaching position at the University of Frankfurt after the Institute for Cultural Morphology moved there in 1925. Jensen conducted field research in a number of countries, including several in Africa and later in the East Indies on Ceram. He wrote a number of anthropological accounts of his expeditions, but is best known for his book on religion entitled *Mythos und Kult bei Naturvölkern* (1951), later translated into English as *Myth and Cult among Primitive Peoples* (1969). In this book, Jensen presents a sustained theoretical argument that explains the nature of religious myth and ritual. He commands a diversity of ethnographic sources, and offers one means of "intercultural comprehensibility" through what has become a classic statement of the *Kulturkreislehre* approach to comparative religions.

Arguing against those scholars who postulated a "primitive mentality" distinct from modern modes of thought, Jensen frames his theory of religion with a claim about all people—contemporary "primitives," pre-historic peoples, and modern people alike—sharing a common drive. All human beings, he claims, seek to understand the broader world and their proper place in it. The thinking associated with this search for understanding, he continues, is the basis for how people believe they should act in the world. Thus, thoughts and behaviors are linked, and when turned toward the question of understanding human beings in relationship to the world, religion is the product. Myths and rituals, in other words, are produced from human attempts to think about, and act with respect to, the meaning and value of their lives.

Myths and rituals arise differently in two distinct phases of cultural development.

Jensen argues that human beings once existed in a primal period of "mythic creativity" when immediate experiences of undeniable emotional and physical realities (like birth, death, eating, sex, and so forth) led to "spontaneous expression." People were "seized" by the "mystery of life" and were compelled thereby to think and act accordingly. In other words, they received a "sacred vision" that permitted understanding, and that would be "expressed" in myths and rituals (thoughts and actions). Jensen insists, however, that this process of expression is not a product of human intentionality or utilitarian concerns, and is free of human "purposes." In fact with increased utilitarian and secular concerns, human societies entered a second phase, one not of "expressions," but of "applications." As political and economic "purposes" grow, the human drive to understand remains, but now instead of a spontaneous encounter with a "sacred vision," people inherit "formalizations," reconfigured cultural contents derived from those "expressed" in the previous, primal phase. These later contents are degenerates, secondary products of a "law of semantic depletion." Naturally, Jensen sees that most of the ethnographic data modern scholars observe would be this derived form. Accordingly, the task of inter-preting religious myths and rituals of this second phase is a matter of seeking how they relate to those myths and rituals of the primal phase. For Jensen, meaning resides in original expression, not in subsequent application.

Fortunately for modern interpreters, certain essential features of the primal phase have been preserved. Vestiges of the original expression do exist in certain myths and rituals. After comparing myths from around the world, Jensen believes originally there were two basic myths or myth-complexes, two original "expressions" during that first primal phase. All subsequent myths (and their concomitant rituals) are semantic depletions of these two. The first of these Jensen names the "Hainuwele mythologem" following a particular myth he encountered in Ceram. This myth, common among root-crop cultivating peoples, is the story of how the primordial time ended following the killing of a deity. It tells how a group of Dema (ancestral beings) killed the deity, dismembered its body, and scattered the pieces, which became the very tubers that serve as food for the group. This myth recounts how a primordial killing created the shape of the current world, the existence of mortal beings, and their food. The second mythologem, Jensen notes, is common among grain cultivators. The model here is the story of Prometheus, the story of a hero that steals valuable commodities from the sky, in this case fire, but also the first seeds to plant. Here too this story recounts the origin of a particular cultural world (one based on grain cultivation), the introduction of certain foods, but also the arrival of death. Jensen also remarks that in certain examples the hero is killed or driven away from the community following a new sense of sin or remorse, so like the Hainuwele mythologem, killing plays an important role.

With this theoretical background, it is a small step to take for Jensen to explain the phenomenon of sacrifice. As one form of ritual, sacrifice is simply a re-actualizing of primordial events, as it happens, a killing that re-enacts an original killing. The first rituals were "spontaneous expressions" (via action) accompanying the two basic mythologems, and since, as Jensen claims, all modern rituals are semantically depleted "survivals" that draw upon that original form, sacrifice is no different. For Jensen, sacrifice is not an offering, or a petition, or a communication. Nor is it essentially a communion (though social solidarity may be one of its effects). It is a commemoration. Turning to specifically expiatory sacrifices, sacrifices that ask for atonement, Jensen believes they represent another "application" of the original meaning of sacrifice. Misdeeds occur when people transgress the "order of things," when they forget the moral order that was established at the beginning. Expiation, then, requires the guilty to remember. As an act of commemoration, ritual, including ritual sacrifice, accomplishes exactly that. It restores the "world order" returning the guilty to their proper place.

In support of his thesis, Jensen uses the fact that archaic hunting and gathering peoples lacked the practice of ritual killing. While the hunt certainly ended with a kill, for these earliest hunters the killing itself was part of the natural order of things (it was required for survival) and needed no explanation. But with the development of agriculture, a new and less violent way of producing food, killing became a problem. It took on significance and impacted people because it was no longer necessary for survival, and because it differed so clearly from agricultural activity. This new awareness of killing provided an opportunity, Jensen continues, for people to realize that human life itself stems ultimately from the destruction of other life, whether it be plant or animal. With the rise of agriculture, in other words, there was a new question of "why must we kill to live?" The myth of Hainuwele provides the answer. Her killing, as it established the world, also established killing as central to the human condition.

The complexity of Jensen's theory is impossible to summarize with a single selection from his writings. Reprinted here, though, is the core of his treatment of sacrifice, as he presents it in *Myth and Cult among Primitive Peoples*. Jensen is oftentimes neglected in discussions of sacrifice, but his "commemoration theory," while somewhat controversial and certainly open to critique, does make a valuable contribution to the overall trajectory of attempts to understand sacrifice.

# From *Myth and Cult among Primitive Peoples*

## Ritual Killing and Blood-Sacrifice[1]

The killing of human beings and animals, more than any other cultic practice, has lent weight to accusations of barbarity in early cultures. Not only human sacrifice and head-hunting but the ceremonial killing of animals seems repulsive to us. The killing, however, is an unavoidable concomitant of the respective acts, while the true motives of the ceremonies may be sought in other contexts. In many instances there can be no doubt that the killing is essential, that it constitutes an important, even decisive, part of the event.

Wherever we know of animal sacrifices—almost exclusively of domestic animals, for they all occur in agricultural cultures—eating of the flesh or offering certain portions to a deity is part of the total event, and the animal is always brought to the cult place alive to be killed there. That this is no accident, at least for some primitive culture strata, becomes clear in the glorification of the killing and its presentation as a deed necessary for the preservation of the world order.

In the discussion of man hunts attention has generally been focused up to now on the trophy to be won—usually heads or genitalia—and the motivation has been sought in the acquisition of potent magical substances or the like. Important as the ceremonies may be in connection with the collected trophies—they do, in fact, usually get preferred mention in the description of the events—we should not be deluded into the belief that the act of killing is of primary importance to primitive man. There are differences, for instance, between head- or genitalia-hunting and the so-called human or animal sacrifices. For example, in head-hunting the killing cannot be performed at the cultic center. The specific importance of the act of killing is underlined. Successful participation in a head-hunt often is the prerequisite for marriage for a young man and, in this respect, it does not matter whether he is in actual possession of a trophy or not. The fact that he has killed is alone decisive. Among some Ethiopian peoples there is a "counting-up of killings" in conjunction with religious festivals in which each killing is assigned a point value; the value varies with the tribal affiliation of the victims, but even the killing of animals is included in the count. Actual possession of the trophy is not decisive.

The number of examples attesting the importance of the act of killing within

Adolf E. Jensen, *Myth and Cult among Primitive Peoples*, translated by M. T. Choldin (Chicago: University of Chicago Press), pp. 162–74. Reprinted with the permission of the University of Chicago Press.

a given cultural configuration is very large. The most telling formulation of the idea may be in an Ethiopian song reported by Cerulli (II, 125 ff.). Enumerating the things worthy of special praise, the song says: "My Gada is a Gada of abundance . . . of riches . . . of peace . . . may your milk vessel be full . . . your mead vessel shall run over. May your calf grow so large that it excells the bull. *He who has not yet killed, shall kill.* She who has not yet borne, shall bear" (emphasis added).

# 1. The Attitude Toward Killing in Hunting Cultures

These and many other examples do not come from cultures which count among the oldest in the history of mankind. Killing is glorified especially by the older and the younger root-crop cultivators, who are also the chief exponents of such phenomena as man hunts, head-hunting, and cannibalism. Early archaic high cultures did not reject ritual killing, which may certainly be traced to its "cultivator" component.

With regard to our moral scruples, we must keep in mind that the act of killing should not be confused with unrestrained carnage. Murder is no less a punishable offense in primitive cultures than in ours. The permissible act of killing is strictly regulated by religious rite. It is not a deed which sets aside moral scruples or does not know of any (cf. chap. 9). Our perplexity remains, however, insofar as it seems to us an aberration that the idea of the divine should be related to man in ways which find expression in such acts. This problem will be discussed later.

First we shall deal with a phenomenon significant in connection with the act of killing itself. It is the fact that ritual killing not only is completely absent in the oldest known strata of culture, that is among the hunting-and-gathering peoples, but that here we encounter a totally different mental attitude. The hunter kills, as it were, for professional reasons; to be a successful hunter, i.e., to kill much game, is a natural wish dictated by the urge of self-preservation. In stark contrast to the naturalness of killing, however, a major part of the hunter's ceremonial is oriented, not to glorify the act of killing, but to nullify and negate the unavoidable deed. We find corresponding customs in all regions where hunting peoples still live, at the southern reaches of the ecumene as well as in the Arctic.

We hear, for instance, that the successful hunter will try to shift the blame by telling the slain animal his arrow "had lost its way" or that not they, the hunters, but "the toad" or "the sun" had killed it. At the same time, as we have seen, the "Master of the animals" watches that no more game than necessary is killed. The customs and ideas show clearly that killing is not viewed as a desirable or laudable act but as an encroachment into a non-human realm, forced upon man by the struggle for sustenance. These examples may suffice to support the assertion that ritual killing is not only absent in the earliest period of man's history but that we must assume for it a different, often opposite mental attitude (cf. here Friedrich, "Jägertum," 21 ff.).

## 2. A Pseudo-Rationale for Ritual Killing

If peoples at the oldest cultural and economic stage of history did not practice ritual killing of animals, incisive events indeed must have introduced such cruel practices. What are the causes of animal sacrifice? Tylor, for instance, explains ritual killing as a desire for the liberation of souls (II, 42). He refers in particular to the widespread retainer killings, performed on the occasion of the death of a king or nobleman whose soul proceeds to a world where the souls of his wives, servants, and slaves are to be of perpetual service to him. This interpretation has the advantage of being supported by native statements. There is no doubt that very concrete concepts about the potential separate existence of souls are current in certain primitive cultures. The idea that such souls might be put to some service was also present obviously. Yet we find this idea only in relatively late cultures which are characterized by state organization and complex political power structures, while it is absent in the stratum of archaic cultivators.

The question arises whether ritual killing in both strata is attributable to the same concept at all or if retainer killing may not have originated in a complex of ideas quite distinct from that which produced, for instance, head-hunting. In my opinion it is not difficult to furnish proof that this custom goes back to the same root as the ritual killing of men and beasts in the archaic cultivator stratum. The fact that (in America as well as Africa) the respective cultures are not only geographically adjacent to archaic cultivator cultures but have carefully preserved their ideology in myths and cults suggests this. If, however, the two sets of customs are connected, the later form, naturally, cannot give us any hint of the *original* concepts behind ritual killing. Later cultures took over killing as an established trait from former times and restructured it in line with other sets of concepts to become a sacrificial death of the king's retainers.

In another form of ritual killing, i.e., blood-sacrifice, the meaning has been thought to lie in an idea of sacrifice to a deity. The term "sacrifice" always connoted an offering to the god, and in this sense it was widely distributed, even throughout the latest archaic high cultures. It is described to us as an essential part of religion in India as well as in ancient Greece, though it will forever remain incomprehensible why it should give the gods pleasure to see man engaged in killing and subsequently in feasting. The Greeks themselves noticed the disparity in the allotment of portions of the sacrificial animals and traced it back to a ruse of Prometheus. Very like the sacrificial death of the king's retainers this leaves a residue of unsolved problems which makes it impossible to ascertain the "origin" of the curious feature from adduced motives.

The archaic cultivator cultures did not have the concept of blood-sacrifice. The act of killing is not a gift to the deity. Just like other sacrifice, it is a religiously founded ethical action. This already seems to me to bespeak a common root of sacrifice and ritual killing; it would mean that blood-sacrifice draws its essential meaning from this common root and that the transformation into an "offering" is a relatively incidental, late, and rationalistic reinterpretation. The nexus between killing-ritual and sacrifice will be taken up again later, and at that occasion we shall revert to an earlier idea (cf. chap. 4, sec. 4): the relation between the older Dema-deities and the polytheistic gods of the archaic high cultures.

One further element should be considered from which the act of killing seems inseparable and which is therefore regarded as the motive par excellence for the origin of the ritual: heroic mentality, which to our day constitutes the ethical imperative of masculinity. Soldierly bearing in war or in duels in defense of one's honor constitutes high values in ancient cultures as well as in ours; in the oldest of the archaic root-crop cultures these are not notable characteristics of the killing-rituals. Here and there in songs of praise for successful head-hunters we may hear verses in which courage and bravery are stressed. In fact, the act of killing, whether in battle with other men or savage beasts, is hardly to be accomplished without a display of courage and thus its mention is quite natural. But the heroic orientation toward courage and bravery is almost totally lacking in the ancient cultures, though, among the Nordic peoples of the period of the Sagas, it led to an extensive battle code (injunction of killing by might and of attack on the defenseless). Killing is often done in a manner most unheroic; it would have to be called cowardly if such an evaluation were called for. The defenseless as well as women and children are killed, and raids are conducted as perfidiously as possible to insure success and reduce personal danger to a minimum. The glorification of killing is therefore more likely to stress the fact of having killed than the courage exhibited in the act, though there is an occasional intimation of that idea.

One thing the head-hunter and the Teutonic heroes have in common, however: their deed and success meet with the approval of the community which even demands the deed as part of the divine order. The creative event which engendered their attitude toward killing and which has shown such tenacity in maintaining itself at the center of significance in manifold transmutations must be sought in the most archaic cultivator strata.

# 3. Ritual Killing in Root-Crop Cultures
## (Hainuwele Mythologem)

At another place I have attempted to clarify the original meaning of killing-rituals from the world view of the cultivators (cf. "Weltbild"). I shall therefore give a brief résumé only and limit myself to highlights of the data.

The world view of the archaic cultivators in general may be concluded from a number of accounts which describe the ceremonial life of some decidedly archaic cultivator populations and contain at the same time—and this is most important—an extensive collection of their myths. Reference of the cults to the myths has been stressed by several researchers. The accounts deal with peoples of India, eastern Indonesia, New Guinea, and the Americas. The lack of corresponding reports from Africa is undoubtedly an accidental lacuna in field research; there are enough clues to show that the same forces must have been at work in Africa also. But the area outside of Africa from which we have clear statements is large enough to demonstrate that the cultural homogeneity, borne out in religious utterance, must be credited to world-wide diffusion of one of the most magnificent cultural epochs in the history of mankind. All these peoples know the idea of a mythic primal past which antedates the world as it exists today. Not men, but Dema lived then on earth; sometimes they are thought to have human form, sometimes the form of animals or plants. Prominent among them are the Dema-deities (cf. chap. 4, sec. 2). Always central to the myth is the slaying of the Dema-deity, but the reason remains obscure. In Ceram (eastern Indonesia) the slain deity is Hainuwele. I proposed to call the mythic theme of the murdered deity and of the origin of crop plants the Hainuwele mythologem.

For the present we must take it for granted that the deity is killed by the Dema, an event with which the primal era ends and today's world begins. The Dema become men, mortal and propagating—this is a main point; the deity henceforth exists in the realm of the dead or transforms itself into the house of death. From the body of the deity originate crop plants so that the eating of the plants is, in fact, an eating of the deity. Since the supreme deity often also had animal shape—especially that of the pig—the killing of pigs, too, qualifies as a "representation" of the deeply disturbing primeval event. Its repetition means no less to mankind than a constant remembrance of the divine act which stands at the beginning and from which all things stem.

This ever renewing reminiscence constitutes the charter of a whole series of cultic activities which become typical of this culture. Diverse as they seem at first glance, they are related to the same primeval event and try to make this prototype live again. Puberty rites are reminders of the act of procreation which originated in conjunction with the first mythic act of killing and of the fact that mortality is inevitably a part of this. The death ceremonials which refer to the journey to the land of the dead are commemorative celebrations, since every death journey repeats the journey of the Dema-deity. Most important is the constant re-enactment of the killing itself. It does not matter here whether men or certain animals considered "identical" with the deity are slain. Thus the human and animal sacrifices (to which head-hunts belong) are the most frequently recurring motive; cannibalism is the festive remembrance of the realization that the eating of crop plants in reality is an eating of the deity in its transmutation.

In our context, these are the fundamental features of a religion in which everything of significance to the bearers of the culture is traceable to institution by a deity, whose unmotivated slaying constitutes the basic idea of the mythology. It turns out that the human and animal sacrifices carry none of the connotations of "sacrifice" for the genuine representatives of the culture which they have assumed in later cultures. For them it is neither more nor less than the festive reformulation of a primeval event; the sacred event is made to occur again, primarily for commemoration but also to initiate another generation into the order of all things. To this extent the slain being—man or animal— represents, of course, the deity itself in the sense in which an actor represents King Lear on the stage and is "identical" with him for the duration of the play. The deity is not "sacrificed to itself" as it has been put on occasion. It would be more cautious and more correct if the term "sacrifice" were entirely avoided in respect to these specific acts of killing among the genuine archaic cultivators. It can be shown that among cultivators in particular even killings that take place in definite ceremonies—regarding the fertility of the fields, rain-making, the curse of barrenness in man or beast—are not rain sacrifices, fertility sacrifices, etc., but re-enactments to keep alive the memory of primeval events.

## 4. The Change in Significance of Ritual Killing in Younger Cultures

If we admit the validity of the mythic world view, the killing ritual appears reasonable. Now we shall ask to what extent the mythically expressed propositions are comparable with other, for instance, scientific statements and their "truths." First we shall look at the mythic justification of ritual killing in the most archaic root-crop culture, where the slain deity offered the prototype. Thereby killing became a cultic, i.e., religious-ethical activity. Ritual killing, however, occurs not only in that stratum but in similar forms in younger cultures also, where they are usually designated as blood-sacrifices. We ask then to what extent there may be a genetic connection between these forms of killing in the various culture strata and also whether significatory changes did perhaps occur.

In treating this topic, we are dealing with three major epochs of culture history. Living forms of the two older ones, the cultures of the root-crop and cereal cultivators, still confront us on almost all continents; the younger is known to us through numerous sources of the archaic high cultures. All three epochs knew ritual killing. It is especially notable that the occasions at which the killings take place, besides some variations, show remarkable similarities. Such occasions might be the death of a chief or a nobleman; the construction of a house, especially a temple; rain-making; observances to insure fertility; the suppression of epidemics; reconciliation ceremonies after a war; expiation of a transgression, etc.

Whatever may have caused the great restructurings in the history of mankind which make us speak of epochs—vexing, in any case, for culture history—we shall leave undiscussed. We can, however, distinguish epochs by a proper set of criteria.

It is not the killing ritual alone that runs through all three epochs; it seems to me that many fundamental traits of the religious world view can be ascertained in them, often in different dress but never so changed that one cannot recognize the material from which the dress was made. Problems of culture history are not the real topic of this book, which strives to discover the original meanings of phenomena. But to find the meaning of cultural configurations we must also consider changes in that meaning. Therefore it may be permissible to speculate on relationships, on the one hand, between the cultivators' idea of the Dema-deity and the divine figures of the polytheistic high cultures, and, on the other hand, between legitimate killing rituals and semantically depleted blood-sacrifices.

The term "sacrifice," in the sense of an offering, has been carried over in scientific usage from the archaic high cultures to similar though more primitive manifestations. In accounts of head-hunting expeditions, however, the word would be rarely found, if for no other reason than that the external course of events is more evocative of "war" or "chase" than of "offering." The word may be employed, however, when a pig is killed and eaten in a death ritual of a head-hunting tribe. But, as I have shown at another place ("Weltbild," 54), the killing of the pig is fully equivalent to the head-hunt in the mythic frame of reference. Thus "sacrificial offering" in the sense of a sacred act (sacrifice) should either be extended to include head-hunting or be dropped entirely. The designation "ritual killing" emphasizes precisely that which the archaic cultivators stress. We ask, then, whether sacrificial offerings in the younger cultures signify something completely different and perhaps stem from different roots, or whether they are semantically depleted "survivals" of ancient ritual killings.

With respect to peoples with stratified societies it can hardly be doubted that blood-sacrifice is no more than the persistence of ritual killing in a degenerated form. Head-hunting expeditions become formal wars whose aim is to take as many prisoners as possible, to make them slaves, and to kill them at the cult site (or temple), as was formerly done with the sacrificial animals. That the slaves are also exploited economically is a very characteristic culture trait; for the first time, the idea was grasped that man, too, can be "utilized," thus instituting social stratification.[2] Degeneration of the original concept of ritual killing is evidenced especially by the emphasis on the number of victims. We have already seen (chap. 4, sec. 9) the expectation of some future good functioning as a major factor in the process of semantic depletion. If killing is a sacred act which involves rewards, its root meaning will be corrupted by the primitive (though human) deduction that the more killed the more benefits are engendered. This corruption through adoption of a quantitative principle is observable throughout the younger cultures. Here belong the "feasts of merit" which increase the recompense in accordance with the number of animals killed.

Another factor contributing to the degeneration is the primitive substantialization of the idea of the death journey. The archaic cultivator did not know the association of ideas which makes the slain victim servant to his conqueror, if for no other reason than the absence of the concept "servant." The claim that the magical powers of the victim become the victor's spoils, as it were, has been advanced by the advocates of the hypothesis of pre-animistic magic, and whenever it is made there is the suspicion that it derives from that very source. In the younger archaic high cultures, already at the threshold of literacy, killings at the death of a noble are explicitly justified by services the sacrificial victims are to render their master in the beyond. This is a very natural conclusion among peoples that have such concrete ideas of a continuation of life after death (cf. chap. 14, sec. 2). Yet this is also a gross oversimplification or else a clumsy embroidering of the sublime concept of a journey into death— typical "application-thinking," compared to the "expressive thinking" of the older culture stratum.

The above applies more or less to all socially stratified cultures. I should like to advance the following idea, though as an assertion only: the world view of this epoch is based almost exclusively on the mythic insights of the archaic root-crop culture without addition of essentially new ideas. Just as exclusively, the cultural configurations are "applications" of those mythic concepts and thereby very "successful" elaborations of social, technological, or economic life. But, weighed ideologically, the "successful developments" constitute pauperization and semantic depletion. By the same token, there is no concept by which the offerings could be differentiated from the ritual killings among archaic cultivators, and there is nothing that would suggest separate origin. Such ideas, supported by like arguments and often in a like form, are found only in the head-hunt or in the genitalia-hunt, as we are tempted to call it by analogy, since genitalia or foreskins are brought home as trophies as in northeast Africa (Jensen, 1936, 437 ff.) and as already told in the Old Testament (II Sam. 23:8 ff.).

As we stated before, the term "sacrifice" was transposed from the archaic high cultures to primitive situations. But how can we ever understand—in spite of any theory—that it can be satisfying to any god or many gods that men or animals be killed and eaten for their glorification? By comparing it with this old and familiar practice, primitive actions do not become one whit more comprehensible. We get further if we go in the opposite direction and accept per se the meaning-filled and therefore understandable ritual killing which the cultivators practiced as the more ancient and original rite; the sacrificial offerings of the high cultures would then assume their place as no-longer-understood, depleted "survivals." This view, applied to the sacrifices of the Greeks, was held by K. Meuli in an article (1945) which adduces material so convincingly that doubt of his basic contentions seems hardly possible. His attention is mainly directed toward details of sacrificial ritual, and he shows us how among the Greeks, to whom the sense and meaning of these sacrifices already appeared doubtful, such rituals corresponded to those of the Asiatic pastoralists down to minutiae. But even among Asiatic pastoralists the strictly observed rites attendant upon the eating of the animals were only survivals from a much older hunting culture which had carried out the very same commandments in the killing of animals. We have to go back to the hunters to find act and meaning in a one-to-one relationship. To the hunter, resurrection—the regeneration by the "Master of the animals"—is an important (almost too practical) but in any case natural concern, and the rules strictly followed serve this regeneration. That, at least, is the impression that emerges from the data. Where the hunting cultures are concerned, we do best to hold back on a definitive judgment, for the ultimate sense of many actions has not yet revealed itself.

According to Meuli, the practices associated with offerings in archaic high cultures reach back into earlier periods of history than we had contemplated. Regarding the ritualistic handling of the several sections of the offering, comparison with the hunters seems to be confirmed; we have much material to corroborate it. However, significant features of the "sacrifice" are lacking among hunters, and in particular those that make of it a sacred act. The fact that the killing of an animal is associated with the deity at all (irrationally as a present, as a gift), the fact that many peoples never kill or eat their domestic stock outside the ritual setting, not even by subsequently elevating the action from a meal to a religious feast, the fact that animals are actually killed and eaten only at truly religious occasions, the fact that the killing of animals can expiate an ethical infraction—all this receives its intrinsic meaning only through making reference to the mythic slaying of a deity. The relationship of man to the fact of killing is, as we have seen, an important element in the hunter's intellectual quest for an understanding of his environment, in a quite idiosyncratic sense, however, from which the later idea of sacrifice can hardly be derived.

In any event, the killing and eating of a "sacrificial victim" makes sense only if it constitutes a sacred act, i.e., a cultic re-enactment of divinely creative events and is both commemoration and internalization. How, otherwise, are we to understand expiatory sacrifices? How can guilt be atoned by the killing and eating of an animal? It can make sense only if the guilt itself consists in the fact that the internalization and commemoration have not taken place on some occasion which should properly have evoked it, so that guilt must be consciously revived. This, in fact, constitutes "ethical guilt" in the religious world view of the archaic cultivators. The entire existing world order and with it actions that have to conform to this order were the result of that event, and any infraction of the order—the disregarding of a taboo—is a guilt of omission, of forgetfulness. Such forgetfulness, however, is expiated by a particularly intensified act of commemoration (cf. chap. 9, sec. 3).

An expiatory sacrifice is meaningful only, then, if linked to a primeval event in which killing is an intrinsic element. It is the same with sacrificial offerings at a house raising, which we encounter in their most meaning-filled form in the archaic head-hunter cultures but which have persisted throughout all the archaic high cultures and into latest occidental history; it neither preserved its original, nor did it gain any new or comprehensive significance. Here, too, the genuine meaning is given in the Hainuwele mythologem: the slain deity is the first being to embark upon the death journey and is transformed into the realm of the dead, represented on earth by the cult edifice, and constructed to this day according to the indications of the myth (cf. Landtman, 1927, 9 ff.). The temple, as representation of the land of the dead, and the original slaying, as inception of the world order, are mythologically very closely linked, so that it is not astonishing if among occasions for cultic re-enactments of the primeval drama the erection of a sacred edifice is frequently mentioned.

If we are willing to concede the original, true, and understandable sense of blood-sacrifice only in connection with the Hainuwele mythologem, it may be objected that a phenomenon which first appeared in a specific context often enough persists, completely changed in significance, in some other cultural setting. This is not to be denied, but sacrificial offering is mentioned as one of the—actually rather plentiful—examples where cultic acts were taken over from the older, truly religious practices and were carried on without a paralleling world view. In these instances, the activities were not meaningfully integrated in the new perception of the world. This would hardly have been possible, considering the wide distribution of sacrificial offering, if ritual killing had not long before degenerated to a fixed but no longer understood routine throughout a lengthy process of semantic depletion.

# Notes

1. This term is used throughout the book. It might be more correct to speak of "bloody sacrifices," as R. H. Lowie does in *Primitive Religion*, for not blood but an animal is sacrificed, at the killing of which blood is shed.
2. Trimbon suggested this in a conversation.

# References

Cerulli, Enrico (1927–8). *Etiopia occidentale*. Vols. I and II. Rome.

Friedrich, Adolf (1939). "Die Forschung über das frühzeitliche Jägertum." In *Paideuma*, vol. VI. Stuttgart.

Jensen, A. E. (1936). *Im Lande des Gada. Wanderungen zwischen Volkstrümmern Südabessiniens*. Stuttgart.

Jensen, A. E. (1948). "Das religiöse Weltbild einer frü hen Kultur." In *Studien zur Kulturkunde*, vol. IX. Stuttgart.

Landtman, Gunnar (1927). *The Kiwai Papuans of British New Guinea*. London.

Meuli, Karl (1945). "Griechische Opferbräuche." In *Phyllobolia für Peter von der Mühll*. Basel.

# 12

# EDWARD E. EVANS-PRITCHARD
## (b. 1902)

British anthropologist Edward Evan Evans-Pritchard was born in Sussex to a Christian family, his father a clergyman in the Church of England. He studied history at Oxford, and in 1923 entered a graduate program in anthropology at the London School of Economics studying under Charles Seligman, an Africanist who advocated the importance of field research in anthropology. Evans-Pritchard spent many years doing fieldwork, living among a number of different ethnic groups in north and east Africa, most notably the Azande and the Nuer, but also the Shilluk, Anuak, and Luo peoples. Over the course of ten years (1926–36), Evans-Pritchard made no fewer than six major expeditions to the Sudan in northeast Africa. From this research, he published his first ethnography, *Witchcraft, Oracles, and Magic among the Azande* (1937), a book that has become a standard within anthropological literature, and later, *The Nuer: A Description of the Modes of Livelihood and Political Institutions of a Nilotic People* (1940), the first book of what became a trilogy devoted to the Nuer. Following World War II, during which he served in the British army, Evans-Pritchard returned to England, taught at Cambridge for a year, but then in 1946 accepted a position teaching social anthropology at Oxford. There he settled down and accomplished a great deal of writing, publishing no fewer than eight books and scores of articles. His third book on the Nuer, *Nuer Religion* (1956), and his ethnography on Azande witchcraft have been his most influential works within the field of religious studies.

Evans-Pritchard should be included in the list of British anthropologists (e.g., Daryll Forde, Max Gluckman, and Meyer Fortes) who approached culture as a structured system of interconnected functioning parts. Following Alfred Radcliffe-Brown and Bronislaw Malinowski, this theory of "structural functionalism" saw societies as integrated wholes comprised of different institutions (e.g., religious, political, kinship, economic, etc.) that function to meet individual and social needs. This was a position that recognized the insights of French sociologists like Emile Durkheim, particularly the importance of social organization and solidarity, but also served as a corrective to the evolutionary and overly intellectualistic theories that dominated the late nineteenth and early twentieth centuries. While not adopting the strong explanatory role of functionalism, Evans-Pritchard did approach his fieldwork seeking to discover what amounts to a local logic, a clear account of how all the details of a society's life fit together. For this reason, studying any human phenomenon, including religion, must begin with describing the interrelated character of each cultural component involved. Only then can the meaning of a particular belief or practice be demonstrated, and demonstrated, at best, for that particular socio-cultural group.

These methodological assumptions help explain why Evans-Pritchard, different from the other theorists previously considered in this anthology, is not promoting a universal theory of sacrifice, one that would apply to all religious groups and all examples of sacrificial ritual. Instead, he insists his conclusions be limited to the narrow cultural confines of the particular group he studies, in this case, the Nuer. This is not to say that Evans-Pritchard is simply interested in description, for to the contrary, he is well versed in anthropological theory and does ultimately want to understand Nuer society, its religious beliefs and practices. What he provides is a case study that grapples with theoretical issues and offers culturally specific conclusions.

The Nuer are a small, semi-nomadic, cattle-herding ethnic group that live in the savanna region of the upper Nile (southern Sudan). Organized into patrilinear clans, a great deal of their cultural life is based upon their cattle. Cattle are extremely valuable, for as they provide milk, meat, skins, dung, and tools, they are necessary for survival, and as they serve for trade, marriage exchanges, and markers of lineage divisions and prestige, they are necessary for society as well. Cattle, Evans-Pritchard tells us, are the most precious thing the Nuer possess. Furthermore, the Nuer have the custom of "ox-names," the practice of giving a young boy a nickname derived from the ox he receives upon initiation into adulthood. This practice effectively extends the social group by "identifying" each member with their herds. It creates an idealized "intimacy" between men and cattle whereby, for example, individual men or even entire clans can be "saluted by reference to their cow." Finally, as we shall see, cattle are for the Nuer essential to their religious life as well. They are the quintessential victim for sacrifice. In fact, no matter what is actually sacrificed on a particular occasion, whether it be an ox, some other animal, or even a vegetable, the Nuer refer to it as a "cow." Socially, economically, and religiously, cattle are central to the Nuer.

Nuer religion revolves around the nature of many superhuman agents and their relationship to human beings. Evans-Pritchard explains the center of Nuer religion is "Spirit" (or "God"), a high god "of the sky" who reveals himself through natural phenomena but is said to be the "giver and sustainer of life," a loving fatherly "protector," the omnipotent, invisible, ubiquitous being who is the "explanation of everything." Consequently, human beings are "dependent on God" and are "helpless without his aid." God is also the ultimate judge, upholding moral standards, punishing faults (misconduct, and forms of "disrespect") and by extension rewarding proper behavior. The Nuer also recognize a number of lesser deities, totemic spirits, and nature spirits more immanent than the High God, and hence the subject of more ceremonial attention, for example in divination, possession states, hymns, prophecy, and so forth. Still, Evans-Pritchard insists that these other deities are "in essence one deity" and not truly separate from the High God. They are "refractions of God" in relation to particular activities, natural phenomena, persons, and social groups—different "manifestations of Spirit."

Evans-Pritchard claims sacrifice is the primary mode of religious activity for the Nuer. Along with prayers and a few more informal actions, it is the main way human beings address the spiritual realm. The Nuer make sacrifices for two main reasons. The first Evans-Pritchard labels "confirmatory" because it is associated with confirming social relations as they change during marriages, births, and other rites of passage. These are collective sacrifices designed to benefit a group. They ask God to validate new social standings, to draw closer and show approval, and as such Evans-Pritchard sees them as examples of what Hubert and Mauss called sacrifices of "sacralization." The second general reason the Nuer sacrifice is in many ways the opposite of the first. Instead of confirmation and benefiting entire groups, here individuals sacrifice for piacular reasons, to atone for some fault or expiate a perceived sin. Since God is ultimately the cause of misfortunes (sickness, barrenness, other moments of danger), since Spirit is interfering with human affairs, he must be propitiated so that the interference (and resultant misfortune) will end. Hence Evans-Pritchard labels these piacular rituals sacrifices of "desacralization."

Most Nuer sacrificial rituals proceed through a series of four acts: (1) an initial "presentation" of the victim that involves tethering the ox to a peg in the ground; (2) a "consecration" that requires the sacrificer to rub ashes on the back of the animal thereby, Evans-Pritchard suggests, establishing a "link" between man and beast; (3) an "invocation," a prayer addressing God stating the intention of the sacrifice; and (4) the killing itself where the animal is speared and its blood runs out on the ground. The Nuer say that God "takes" the "life" of the animal (symbolized by its blood and breath), while the sacrificer takes the flesh and eats it, though Evans-Pritchard claims this meal is not part of the sacrificial ritual itself.

The Nuer refer to piacular sacrifice, the most common type, using a number of revealing words that combine to hint at the meaning of the rite. Evans-Pritchard discusses these at length, but they include notions of gift, bargain, homage, purification, compensation, exchange, and covenant. Ultimately, though, he believes the notion of "substitution" can summarize the meaning of sacrifice for the Nuer. With a small nod to Westermarck, Evans-Pritchard believes sacrifice is a ritual where the life of an animal is substituted for the life of an individual or group of human beings, "*vita pro vita.*"

Reprinted here is an essay on the meaning of Nuer sacrifice that Evans-Pritchard republished as a chapter in his book *Nuer Religion.* In it, we learn the reasons he settles on "substitution" as the core of Nuer sacrifice. Part of his decision comes from rejecting the "gift-theory" of Tylor, the "communion theory" of Robertson Smith, and the "mediation theory" of Hubert and Mauss. We see Evans-Pritchard struggle with the issues that are by now quite familiar in theories of sacrifice—the nature of the victim, the intentions of the sacrificer, the symbolism of the ritual accoutrements, the status of the recipient, the treatment of the victim's body, and the broader religious and social context for the rite. In the end, this essay remains a model study of a particular cultural example of sacrificial practice. It demonstrates the complexity of sacrificial phenomena, but also how central it can be in the religious lives of certain people.

# "The Meaning of Sacrifice among the Nuer"

THE MAIN CONCLUSIONS reached in earlier accounts of Nuer sacrifice (Crazzolara 1949; Evans-Pritchard 1951, 1953*a*, *b*) are as follows: (1) There are two broad types of sacrifice, the confirmatory type which is chiefly concerned with social relations—changes of social status and the interaction of social groups—and the piacular type which is concerned rather with the moral and physical welfare of the individual. Our attention is here mostly directed to the second, the piacular, type because of its greater importance for an understanding of Nuer religion, but it is not possible to keep the two classes entirely apart. The ritual configuration is the same in both and no rigid line of demarcation between them can be based on intention alone. Moreover, in seeking to grasp the significance of some of the chief features of the sacrificial rite, symbolic content has to be discussed at the collective as well as at the individual level. (2) The piacular sacrifices are performed in situations of danger arising from the intervention of Spirit in human affairs, often thought of as being brought about by some fault. In such sacrifices ideas of propitiation and expiation are prominent and their purpose is described by

E. E. Evans-Pritchard, "The Meaning of Sacrifice among the Nuer," *Journal of the Royal Anthropological Institute*, vol. 84 (1954), pp. 21–33. Reprinted with the permission of Blackwell Publishers.

words which have the sense of bargain, exchange, and purpose. They centre, however, in the general idea of substitution of lives of oxen for lives of men. (3) Almost all sacrifices consist of four movements—formal presentation, consecration, invocation, and slaughter. It is particularly in the invocation and consecration that we must look for the meaning of the whole drama. The invocation states the intention of the sacrifice, and it is made with the spear in the right hand. The spear, being an extension of the right hand, represents the virtue and vitality of the officiant and through it, as well as by speech, he throws his whole self into the intention. In symbol, the spear is the man. When a whole lineage or clan is concerned in the sacrifice the spear is that of the ancestor of the lineage or clan and represents the whole group which, through its representative, offers up the victim. (4) The consecration by placing ashes on the back of the victim with the right hand is also, at any rate in the piacular sacrifices, a gesture of identification of man with victim; and this is a special and emphatic expression within the sacrificial situation of an identification which has also a more general denotation, perhaps arising from that situation, for in sacrifice man and ox can be said to be really equivalent. Thus Nuer have an identification with the oxen given to them, together with a spear, by their fathers at their initiation to manhood, and the collective counterpart to this is the identification of the lineage with its ancestral herd; and all cattle are reserved for sacrifice. So if in symbol the sacrificial spear is the man, so also is the sacrificial victim.

We may now ask ourselves what light is shed by what we have discovered about Nuer sacrifice on theories of sacrifice put forward by anthropologists and others, and attempt, with the aid of these theories, and in terms of them, to reach some general conclusions about the meaning sacrifice has among the Nuer. Much has been written about the nature of sacrifice, and this is not surprising in view of the central position it has had in the Hebrew and Christian religions and in the religions of pagan Greece and Rome. These writings are for the most part doctrinal, devotional, or philosophical, or are more concerned with historical and exegetical interpretations of ancient texts of one or other religion than with a comparative study of sacrifice. Much of what has been written is, however, of general importance, especially the work of Old Testament scholars. It is true that these scholars had to rely solely on documents both the date and meaning of which are often doubtful, so that there is still much uncertainty, which can in no way be dispelled, about the significance of the various forms of Hebrew sacrifice at different, and especially in the earlier, periods of the history of Israel, for ideas associated with sacrifice changed in the course of centuries in Israel, just as they did in Greece or in the Hindu religion from Vedic times till today. Nevertheless, much is known about sacrifice in these ancient religions and such theories of sacrifice as have been put forward have been mostly based on studies of their sacred texts.

As is well known, there have been two main theories of sacrifice, the communion theory and the gift theory. The communion theory, which seems to have been first put forward by Sykes (1748) in his *Essay on the Nature, Design, and Origin of Sacrifices*, was given wide currency by Robertson Smith (1889) in his *Lectures on the Religion of the Semites*, a book which had a powerful, and in some ways unfortunate, influence on other writers—Frazer, Jevons, Reinach, Durkheim, Sydney Hartland, Freud, Oesterley, Gayford, Willoughby, and many others. Briefly, his theory was that primitive sacrifice, and particularly early Semitic sacrifice, is a feast in which the god and his worshippers eat together. It is a communion or act of social fellowship—not a gift, not a tribute, not a covenant, not an expiation, not a propitiation. All these ideas are either much later or, if present in the earliest forms of sacrifice, are secondary or even merely germinal. Moreover, the sacrificial victim is a sacred beast, not in virtue of being set apart or consecrated for sacrifice, but intrinsically. It is the totem of the clan and hence of the same blood as the people who slew it and ate it. But in a sense it is also the god himself, for the god is the ancestor of the clan and therefore kin to both his worshippers and their totemic victim. By sacramentally eating their god, the theanthropic and theriomorphic victim, the worshippers acquired spiritual strength.

The totemic part of this theory is unacceptable, since there is almost no evidence that can be adduced in support of it, either from the literature concerning the early Hebrews, with whom Robertson Smith was chiefly concerned, or from accounts of primitive peoples, to which he made appeal. The eating of the totem-god was more than even Sir James Frazer, a sympathetic commentator, could accept (Frazer, 1931, 198 ff.), and he tells us that Robertson Smith himself had second thoughts about this part of his theory (Frazer, 1927, 278–90). It was undoubtedly the influence of McLennan which led him in this and some of his other writings of the unsupportable conclusion that the early Semitic societies were totemic clans, a conclusion which Père Lagrange (1903, ch. 7), and others showed to be baseless. He was further led astray by the German so-called Higher Criticism, and especially by Wellhausen (1885, ch. 2), who supposed that pre-exilic Hebrew sacrifices were little more than social meals or feasts. W. L. Baxter (1895, *passim*) had no difficulty in showing this supposition to be false. Indeed, I think that every competent Old Testament scholar would today admit the accuracy of Buchanan Gray's conclusions that the idea of gift and not, or at any rate rather than, that of communion is predominant in even the earliest sacrifices known to us, that the ideas of expiation and propitiation are present in these earliest sacrifices, and that by the time of Deuteronomy it is clear that a eucharistic intention is present (Gray, 1925, 1–82). Even, therefore, in its more reasonable form, minus the totemic character of the victim, Robertson Smith's attempt to show that festal communion between worshippers and their gods was the original form of Semitic sacrifice could only be a highly speculative hypothesis for times for which records, and hence evidences, are totally lacking.

It is true that, in this less extravagant form, it appears to receive some support from ethnographic sources. The Rev. W. C. Willoughby, for example, our chief authority on Bantu religions, tells us that their sacrifices are communion feasts at which the ghosts of the dead, whom he calls "the gods," and their living kinsmen are thought to feed together on the victim, the ghosts consuming the essence of the flesh and the living its material substance: "the animal is slaughtered to provide a feast for gods [ghosts] and men, and its death seems to carry no other significance" (Willoughby, 1928, 396 ff.), a statement difficult to reconcile with what he says about the need for confession and disposition of the will. But though Willoughby's testimony that Bantu sacrifices are sacramental communions shows, if he is correct, that primitive sacrifices may have this significance it does little to strengthen Robertson Smith's contentions about the early Hebrews, for the Bantu religions are predominantly manistic and the recipients of their offerings are, though ghosts, both men and kin, while early Hebrew religion was theistic and its sacrifices were made to God. It is true that Robertson Smith held that the gods of the early Semites were regarded as ancestors of the clans which worshipped them, but the evidence in favour of such a view is negligible. It has yet to be shown that the idea of sacramental communion between gods and men is common in those primitive religions which are also dominantly theistic.

The communion theory as held by Robertson Smith and those who have accepted his interpretations gives us little aid towards understanding the nature of Nuer sacrifices to God, and they do not lend it support. The idea is excluded by definition in the case of their holocausts. The flesh of other victims can only be said to be in any sense sacred in such sacrifices as those in which parts of it may not be eaten by the sacrificers. In their common sacrifices of wild cucumbers the victims are in any case inedible. In none of their sacrifices is there, to my knowledge, any suggestion that God partakes of the essence of the sacrificial flesh. What goes to him is the life, and it would be to extend the communion theory beyond legitimate bounds to say that his taking—not consuming—the life and man's eating of the flesh constitute a communion in the sense given to the idea of communion by its upholders. Moreover, though men eat the carcase, their eating of it, however important socially this festal side to sacrifice may be, is not a sacramental meal but an ordinary commensal act of family or kin which, moreover, falls outside the sacrificial rites. Those who eat the flesh are not thought to gain spiritual strength by doing so. In the etymological sense of the word "sacrifice" it is the life which is made *sacer* by the consecration, not the flesh which the sacrificers eat.

It is only in a mystical, and not in a material, sense that Nuer sacrifice might be called a communion, in the sense that through sacrifice man communicates with God who is invoked to be present to receive the life of the consecrated victim and to hear what it is that those who make the sacrifice desire of him. It is communion in this sense of union, of a *communio* established through the victim, that H. Hubert and M. Mauss were speaking of in their "Essai sur la nature et la fonction du sacrifice" when they said that in sacrifice a communication is established between the sacred and the profane by the intermediation of a victim (1898, 133). We may readily accept that the victim is an intermediary between God and man, in that they are brought together in the offering of its life. The fourth-century Neo-Platonist Sallustius (*De diis et mundo* §xvi) already saw that two living objects which are distant from each other can be brought into union (συναφή) only by means of an intermediary (μεσότης) of the same order, a third life (Nock tr., 1926, pp. 28–31).

We have, nevertheless, to bear in mind that the purpose of Nuer piacular sacrifices is to establish communication with God rather in order to keep him away or get rid of him than to establish union or fellowship with him. What Georges Gusdorf (1948, 78) says of religious sacrifice in general, that it is made not only to the gods but against the gods, is very true for the Nuer, in whose piacular sacrifices prophylactic and apotropaic features are very evident. They are made in times of trouble, present or feared, and the trouble comes from God and is evidence of his intervention in human affairs. Sacrifice is made to persuade him to turn away from men and not to trouble them any more. It is made to separate God and man, not to unite them. In a sense they are already in contact in the sickness or other trouble. The sacrifice is intended to rid the sufferer of the spiritual influence whose activity is apparent in the sickness. There is here a paradox. God is separated from man by an act which brings them together. The solution of the paradox would seem to lie in a distinction between two kinds of union, union on a material plane which is to be dissolved in the moment of sacrifice by bringing about union on a moral plane. This is consistent with the Nuer representation of sickness in which the sickness itself, the moral state of the sufferer, and the action of Spirit form a complex whole. I return to this point later. It also reflects the essential ambiguity of their conception of God as the source of good and ill.

Much older than the communion theory of sacrifice is the gift theory, supported among anthropological writers by Sir Edward Tylor and Herbert Spencer. For Tylor (1913, ch. 18) sacrifices are gifts made to a deity as if he were a chief, and to take the abnegation theory as representing the primitive intention of sacrifice would be "to turn history upside down." For Herbert Spencer (1882, 102) sacrifice has developed from the placing of offerings on the graves of the dead to please their ghosts. Other writers who regard sacrifice as being essentially a gift to gods stress other motives: to nourish the gods, to obtain favours from them, to propitiate their wrath, to draw nearer to them, to create harmony between God and man, to expiate sins, or with eucharistic, commemorative, or other intentions. Now Nuer sacrifice is clearly a gift of some sort. They say that they are giving God a thing, a gift. But it is a gift which is immolated, it is that which makes the offering a sacrifice. And the gift must be a life or something which stands for a life. Moreover, a gift is a far from simple idea. It is a symbol which may have many different meanings and shades of meaning. We have to determine what sense or senses it has in Nuer sacrifices. We shall attempt to do so after a short discussion of some other theories of sacrifice which deserve our consideration.

Hubert and Mauss, in their well-known essay on sacrifice, recognize that sacrifices are generally in some degree gifts but they do not consider that their significance lies in that fact. Sacrificial intentions are too mixed and variable to permit classification by reference to them alone. A sacrifice may be a gift or a communion or it may be both, and these meanings may be combined with yet others; and the emphasis varies from rite to rite and even in the same rite. We should rather be seeking for the core, the basic mechanism, of all sacrificial acts, and this is best done, our authors think, by examining some typical examples, mostly those found in Sanscritic and Old Testament texts.

They define sacrifice as "a religious act which, by the consecration of a victim, modifies the state of the moral person who performs it or of certain objects in which he is interested" (Hubert and Mauss, 1898, 41),[1] the conse-cration consisting in the destruction of the victim in the rite. The sacred and the profane meet in the victim, which represents, is fused and identified with, the person of the sacrificer. Whence it follows that there are two main types of sacrifice distinguished by a difference of orientation. In the first the sacred forces are transmitted through the victim to the sacrificer, who gains, often by partaking of its flesh, a sacred character he lacked before the sacrifice. These are sacrifices of sacralization. The other type of sacrifice is that of desacraliza-tion. In these the sacred forces are transmitted through the victim away from the sacrificer. They do not make sacred the profane but they make profane what is sacred. The sacrificer has in him religious forces which are harmful or dangerous to him and the rites get rid of them. This second type of sacrifice is therefore expiatory. Sickness and other misfortunes come from faults so that healing and expiatory rites are the same, sickness and sin being eliminated by the same procedure (as in Nuer piacular sacrifices); and in this sense the sinner is sacred. Religious forces operate for ill as well as for good. They have this double aspect, and thus the central religious act of sacrifice bears the same ambiguity (as is the case among the Nuer). But what is common to all sacrifices, what underlies their complexities and their diversities of form, is the procedure, which is always the same, of establishing communication between the sacred and the profane.

But divine beings are an illusion and sacrifice therefore a shadow play. Why, then, should so macabre a drama be so widespread and persistent? Because it is a symbolic enactment of the relation in which the individual stands to society. From society, for which the god is a symbol, the individual draws the strength and assurance he needs in his undertakings and the redemption of his faults;

and in return he renounces his possessions, the value of the renunciation being not in the worth of the possessions but in the act of submission and abnegation before the collective personality of the social group. The act recalls to individual minds the presence of collective forces and serves to maintain them.

There is much of value in this essay, but it is too abstract. This is partly due to the argument's being based on Brahmanic interpretations of Vedic sacrifice, not on the living drama of sacrifice but on its rubrics, its stage-directions. It is also partly due to treating sacrifice as a mechanical rite and without reference to religious thought and practice as a whole, without regard to what men conceive their own nature and the nature of the gods to be. How fatal to compare Hebrew and Hindu sacrifices outside the contexts of these two religions which are so entirely different! Both weaknesses derive from the Durkheimian sociologistic metaphysic.

Alfred Loisy tells us little that Hubert and Mauss had not already told us. He says in his *Essai historique sur le sacrifice* (Loisy, 1920) that the sacrifices of primitive and semi-civilized peoples are essentially magical rites. What characterizes them is not gift as such but the efficacy of the rite which is regarded as physical and immediate. There are two general forms, or aspects, of the rites, the negative and the positive, the elimination of harmful influences and the regulation of useful forces. These two aspects may, nevertheless, be combined in the same rite. In the higher religions, the national cults, and the religions of salvation, the negative aspect has developed into the idea of expiation and the positive aspect into the idea of divine service; and sacrificial intentions have become much more mixed and complex. In primitive religions there is nothing more to sacrifice than magical efficacy, and some element of this idea persists even in the higher religions. Loisy's treatment of the subject rests on his conviction that the beings to whom sacrifices are made do not exist and that even if they did exist the action taken would not attain the results aimed at. His distinction between primitive sacrifice and the sacrifices of the higher religions might, therefore, be said to be less one between magic and religion than one between pure magic and sublimated magic. He admits, however, that though all religions are futile dreams, taken as wholes, including their sacrifices, they have had some useful social functions. They have given men confidence in life, they have strengthened social ties, and they have, by means of the tributes and prohibitions they have imposed, created morality.

We may now return to the Nuer. In their piacular sacrifices to God, which I consider first, they give something to him to get rid of some danger or misfortune, usually sickness. The general idea underlying such sacrifices is that of substitution, the life of a beast being taken by God in the place of the life of a man, or the life of a beast being given in exchange for the life of a man. The ideas of purchase, redemption, ransom, exchange, bargain, and payment are very evident in Nuer sacrifices, as the words by which they refer to them indicate; and they are not peculiar in this, for, as Hubert and Mauss (1898, 134–5) rightly emphasize, there is probably no sacrifice in which there is not some idea of redemption and something of the nature of a contract. As in the reciprocity of all giving and receiving, as Mauss (1923, 53–60) points out also in his "Essai sur le don," sacrifice establishes a contractual relationship between persons, those who give and those who receive. We can say definitely that a relationship of this kind, based on a sort of exchange, is involved in Nuer sacrifices; but if they include, they go beyond the dialectic of exchange and contract, even when thought of in terms of persons and not of things, for we can hardly speak of simple exchange or contract when one side in reality gets nothing and the other side may get nothing too.

This is an old problem. Since in most Nuer sacrifices men eat the carcase of the victim, what is God supposed to receive? It was partly on this point, that the offerings were enjoyed by those who offered them and not by God, that the prophets of the Old Testament criticized bloody sacrifice and that it was held up to ridicule by the Greek comic poets whose writings on the subject were collected by Clement of Alexandria (Wilson tr., 1872, 426 ff.). But it may be said, and it is said by the Nuer, that God gets the life. But what advantage is that to him? All the beasts of the field are his and the cattle on a thousand hills. So he gets nothing. The Nuer also sense this. The victim already belongs to God before it is slain. And it is not his only in the sense that it is no longer man's because man has dedicated or consecrated it to him, so that in the sacrificial invocation the officiant tells God to take "thy cow" and not "my cow" or "our cow," sometimes putting his hand on the beast or pointing at it with his spear as he does so to direct attention to the devoted animal, and uses the expressions *kam yang*, to give a beast in the sense of delivering what is due, and *kan yang*, to take a beast in the sense of taking what is the right of the taker. Nor is it only his in the wider sense that all beasts of the flocks and herds are in a general way of speaking devoted to him, being reserved for sacrifice to him, so that they ought not to be killed for any other purpose. The victim is always his in a yet more general religious sense which extends beyond, and is not derived from, the sacrificial situation, in the sense, that is, that everything belongs to him. In giving a beast to God man without doubt loses something but God, to whom it belonged anyhow, gains nothing. But though this sense of God's ownership may be general it is not unprecise. Thus, Nuer do not complain when a beast is killed by lightning or sickness for God has a right to take his own, and here also they speak to God about it as "*yangdu*," "thy cow," so the expression is not determined by formal consecration, which merely gives greater emphasis to it. All life belongs to God. It comes from him and to him it returns, and when he wants it he takes it. Indeed, his taking of a beast by lightning or sickness has a certain similarity to sacrifice in that Nuer say that God takes the life of the beast in the place of the life of its master, the beast, as they say, in this manner shielding the man; but it differs otherwise from true sacrifice where man makes an offering of his own accord, and what he offers is a consecrated life.

If God gains nothing, have we then to interpret Nuer sacrifice in terms of what man loses, in the sense of abnegation the word "sacrifice" has come to have in our own language? Is it that man deprives himself of something that should take the emphasis? This also is an old problem. Would God have gained anything by Isaac's death? Assuredly not, but Abraham would have lost what was most precious to him. It cannot be denied that, although there is no sacrificial tariff, Nuer feel that the greater the crisis the greater should be the offering. At least some cattle should be slaughtered to stay a plague, and their carcases are abandoned. In mortuary ceremonies oxen, and even cows, must be sacrificed. In cases of serious sin or grave sickness it is desirable to sacrifice an ox if one can be spared. In lesser crises a goat or a sheep suffices, or even a cucumber. All this suggests that the greater the danger the higher should be the payment, the more valuable the gift or substitute and the more complete the surrender of it. But the matter is not so simple as that. It is of course true that cattle are by far the most valuable possessions of the Nuer, and there is no need to emphasize their economic, social, religious, and emotional significance or that their herds are small, but, though doubtless their high value is an important consideration, we have to remember that it is not merely a question of relative value but also one of religious tradition and convention. Men and oxen have a symbolic equivalence in the logic of sacrifice, so that whatever is sacrificed is an "ox." If there were enough oxen one might always sacrifice an ox, and in symbol and by surrogate one does so, but as there are not enough, other offerings have to take their place and oxen be kept for the greater crises and those important ceremonial occasions when quantity of meat is a primary consideration. When an ox is sacrificed it is not just a matter of making the highest bid for divine favour when it is most needed, on the principle that the greater the gift the greater will be the return. This is evident from the fact that the victims in marriage ceremonies must be oxen, for here the ideas of substitution and exchange are least in evidence and the purpose of sacrifice is social rather than religious. Nor, in piacular sacrifices, should the holocaust be taken as evidence that it is simply a matter of the greater the need the greater must be the surrender, for when the carcases of victims are abandoned to stave off plagues and murrains there is the idea of the evils entering into their bodies, and since the sacrifices are made on behalf of everybody no one can eat them. They are holy or taboo for all and not, as in some other sacrifices where one half of the victim is abandoned, only for certain persons.

But valuable though his beasts are to a Nuer and great the loss of them— even though he may feast on their carcases after they have been sacrificed he still loses them—Nuer themselves freely explain that it is not so much what is sacrificed that is important as the intention of those who sacrifice. If a man is poor he will sacrifice a goat, or even a cucumber, in the place of an ox, and

God will accept it. A man should give according to his circumstances and the sacrifice is not less efficacious because it is a small thing. We can perhaps, therefore, understand why it is that whereas the Bantu often belittle the sacrifices they make to their ghosts, calling an ox a calf or a goat a kid (Willoughby, 1928, 343, 371), the Nuer in their sacrifices to God do the opposite, calling a goat or a cucumber a cow. The emphasis in the first case is on the receiving. The ghosts are flattered by the suggestion that the gifts made to them would be small things in their eyes. In the second case it is on the giving, on the sincerity of intention. It is a question, Nuer say, of the heart or, as we would say, of disposition. It is clear, indeed, that if God is prepared to accept a cucumber instead of an ox it is not merely the thing itself which is significant, for a cucumber can have no use or value for him. We should fix our attention on the suppliant as well as on what he offers, for what he offers is not only whatever it may happen to be but also the expression of an interior state. If a cucumber costs man nothing and benefits God not at all, we have surely to seek deeper into the ideas of payment, substitution, or exchange for the meaning of sacrificial gifts.

All gifts are symbols of inner states, and in this sense one can only give oneself; there is no other kind of giving. This has often been said,[2] and in the sense in which it is said it is true. But the idea is a very complex one, for, as Mauss (1923, 50–3 *et passim*) says in his "Essai sur le don," in giving possessions, in which the personality participates, one not only surrenders part of it to another but to that extent one possesses him and he can only free himself by making return. An exchange of gifts is thus more than a reciprocity in things. It is the creation and maintenance of a relationship. When Nuer give their cattle in sacrifice they are very much, and in a very intimate way, giving part of themselves. What they surrender are living creatures, gifts more expressive of the self and with a closer resemblance to it than inanimate things, and these living creatures are the most precious of their possessions, so much so that they may be said to participate in them to the point of identification.

But it is not only in this rather general sense of identification of men with cattle that Nuer can be said to offer up themselves in offering up their cattle in sacrifice. We have seen that one of the chief features of their sacrifices is the rubbing of ashes along the backs of the victims. It is true that this may be regarded as an act of consecration but it is also, to a greater or lesser degree, an act of identification.

Philo (*De sacrificiis*, 136) tells us that in sacrifice what is offered up is not the victim but the mind and purpose of the sacrificer (Colson tr., 1929, 193), and identification of sacrificer with victim is a common interpretation by writers on the subject, including modern students of sacrifice.[3] Indeed, it is quite explicit in some religions, in particular in certain Vedic, Hebrew, and Muslim rites, that what one consecrates and sacrifices is always oneself, and this is sometimes symbolically represented, by laying of hands on the victims. It is an interpretation which makes good sense for Nuer piacular sacrifices. I have not, it is true, heard Nuer say that this is what the laying on of hands means to them—it is our interpretation, what it means to us—but I have given reasons elsewhere, in describing Nuer acts of dedication and consecration and in discussing their spear symbolism and the role of cattle in their religion (Evans-Pritchard, 1953a, b), for my conclusion that this meaning is implicit in their sacrifices also, and I do not think that their piacular sacrifices, where the life of an animal is substituted for the life of a man, are intelligible unless this is granted. It is quite explicit among the neighbouring Shilluk people. The Rev. D. S. Oyler (1920, 298) describes how in a sacrifice by their king he says in his invocation over the victim "the flesh of this animal is as my flesh, and its blood is the same as my blood."

But if man gives himself in sacrifice he does so only in the symbolism of sub-stitution, in what Loisy calls a *figuration*: he is only acting a part in a drama. It is the ox which dies, not he. Once again, this is an old problem. In trying to solve it we must recall that the purpose of Nuer piacular sacrifices is either to get rid of some present evil or to ward off some threatening evil, and also that the evil is very often, perhaps always in some degree, connected with the ideas of sin, fault, and error, and hence with feelings of guilt. The notions of elim-ination, expulsion, protection, purification, and propitiation and expiation cannot easily be separated out in these sacrifices, though in any particular sacrifice it may be possible to say that one or other notion is most in evidence. The sense of fault is clearly expressed in the sacrificial rites, in the confession of grievances and resentments, which is a feature of some sacrifices, and also in the sacrificial invocations, which must state a true account of everything which has led up to the crisis. But it is most clearly and dramatically expressed by the common practice of all present placing ashes on the back of a beast and then either washing them off or slaughtering it. Nuer say that what they are doing is to place all evil in their hearts on to the back of the beast and that it then flows into the earth with the water or the blood. This is not done in most piacular sacrifices, but in almost all such sacrifices someone places ashes on the victim's back on behalf of those for whom the sacrifice is being made, and a Nuer says of the sacrifice that whatever evil has occasioned it is placed on the back of the victim and flows away with its blood into the earth. We have also noted how in some animal sacrifices, and always when a cucumber is sacrificed, the evil is said to go into the left half of the victim, which is therefore abandoned, and how in the case of other offerings they are entirely abandoned for the same reason. They are asking God to take away the evil and that the evil may be ransomed or expiated or wiped out with the victim. It is clear, therefore, that the laying on of hands is not only a consecration and an identification but also a transference of the evil which troubles the sacrificer on to the victim. It is put on to the victim and destroyed with it. The victim thus has the role of scapegoat. This does not mean that the victim is made responsible for the evil.

There is no suggestion of *poena vicaria*. The ox is not punished in the place of the man but is a substitute for him in the sense of representing him. In the laying on of hands the ideas of consecration, identification, and transference seem to be blended in the representation of a substitute. If this is so it would follow that what the sacrificer is doing is to identify himself with the victim within the meaning of the transference. In other words, he identifies that part of himself which is evil with the victim so that in its death that part may be eliminated and flow away in its blood. As Gusdorf (1948, 178), quoting Nietzsche, aptly remarks, "en morale, l'homme ne se traite pas comme un *individuum*, mais comme un *dividuum*."

The same idea is expressed when in danger Nuer throw away as an offering to God something representing themselves and in substitution for themselves— a bead, a tassel, or some other small object of personal adornment or a lump of tobacco—that the evil may depart with it and they be spared. Dr P. P. Howell has recorded a most interesting, and as far as I know unique, act of self-mutilation for the same purpose. An elder of some social standing committed an act of bestiality with a cow and was so overcome by shame and remorse that, in addition to sacrificing a beast, "as an act of expiation he cut off one of his own fingers with a spear" (personal communication).[4]

In sacrifice, then, some part of man dies with the victim. It can therefore be regarded both as an absolution and a rebirth; and also, as the psycho-analysts say, as akin to suicide (Money-Kyrle, 1930, 248, 252, *et passim*).[5] Fundamentally, however, if we have to sum up the meaning of Nuer piacular sacrifice in a single word or idea I would say that it is a substitution—a life for a life. If it were not so it would be difficult to understand at all why offerings to God should be immolated. The life can only be given by its liberation through death, as Professor E. O. James (1933, *passim*) emphasizes in his *Origins of Sacrifice*.[6] Substitution, a common enough interpretation of sacrifice,[7] is the central meaning of the rites—they are a giving or exchange or an expiation in that sense—whatever other ideas are mixed up in it or become attached to it. But ultimately it eludes reason altogether. That is why it is so difficult to write about.

But to sum up the meaning of Nuer piacular sacrifices in a single word scarcely does justice to the very complex set of ideas they express. We have found it necessary to use a variety of words in speaking of them: communion, gift, apotropaic rite, bargain, exchange, ransom, elimination, expulsion, purification, expiation, propitiation, substitution, abnegation, homage, and others. According to situation and particular purpose, one element in this complex of meaning may be stressed in one rite and another element in another rite, or there are shifts in emphasis from one part of the sacrificial rite to another. The matter becomes yet more complicated and resistant to precise definition when we take into consideration the scale on which Spirit is figured to Nuer at different levels, and also what I have called their confirmatory sacrifices, for so far I have been discussing only sacrifices to God and only those made to him which belong to the piacular class.

In piacular sacrifices to God the *do-ut-des* notion, some sort of exchange or bargain, may never be entirely absent but it appears in a refined and sublimated form. The favour requested does not follow automatically the sacrifice, *ex opere operato*. God is not compelled by the sacrifice to grant it. It is indeed obvious, to the Nuer as well as to us, that, apart from there being no means by which bargaining with God can be conducted, it is no use trying to haggle with him because he is master of everything and can want nothing. The favour that God gives the sacrificer is what Nuer call *muc*, a free will gift that does not depend on reciprocity. Nor is there any idea that God is at fault if he does not give what is asked for in a sacrifice. In his dealings with man, God always has the *cuong*, is always in the right. But when we examine sacrifices to spirits of the air and of the earth, the relations between spirit and man are somewhat different and colour the meaning of sacrifices accordingly. The lesser spirits are in competition and if one of them has a cow or an ox dedicated to it its prestige is thereby increased. They do not, as God does, own all the beasts anyhow, but only those men give to them. This is why one dedicates beasts to the spirits but only rarely and in very special circumstances to God, for there is little point in giving him what is his already. Likewise, a sacrificed life, which is God's anyhow, is something spirits are thought to gain. Further, since God needs nothing he does not ask for anything. He does not require sacrifices of men and cause them ill if they are not made. The spirits do. They demand attention, and they are not to be satisfied with cucumbers. They demand bloody offerings. And if they are not given animal sacrifices they seize their devotees and make them sick. Nuer, therefore, do not hesitate to bargain with these spirits, speaking through their mediums, in a downright way which astonished me. The sense of the bargain is always the same: if we give you an ox or a sheep or a goat will you leave the sick man alone that he may recover, or what do you require of us this year in sacrifice that we may not be troubled by you? And when the sacrifice is made and the animal twitches in its final agonies the spirit is said to be tugging at its flesh. In the case of fetish spirits they are said to *cam*, to eat, offerings and though the expression is used metaphorically its use nevertheless implies a more material conception of offerings. It is significant that the lower in the scale is the conception of spirit, the more it is thought of as taking delight in what is offered.

Thus even though sacrifices to God and to the spirits may be placed in the same piacular class and though the apotropaic element in both is very evident they cannot have precisely the same meaning. Even in piacular sacrifices to God there may be much variation of meaning, as, for example, between those in which the idea of expiation is most in evidence, such as those made to wipe out some definite sin like incest, and those made so that people may recover from wounds and ailments not attributed to specific offences and which, therefore, do not have the same moral connotation. But in either case the general attitude is the same. Man approaches God through sacrifice and asks for aid. It is man and not God who benefits by the sacrifice. Man's attitude in these sacrifices contrasts with his attitude in the case of sacrifices to spirits who have seized people to exact gifts from them or may do so if they are not satisfied. It is true that men generally have a feeling that the spirits would not have troubled them if they had been given their due and that their devotees have only themselves to blame if they have neglected them, and also that men give to the spirits for the same reason that they often give to God, that they may be left alone. But the psychology of gifts to spirits is different. Here the substitution is blended with the idea of propitiation and satisfaction rather than of expiation or solicitation for aid, and the experience is on a different level of thought. Man does not wrestle with God, but here man and a spirit are pitted against one another, and the huckstering is conducted through a human agency—is, in fact, between humans, between the sacrificer and the representative of a spirit, a prophet and generally a very minor one. God has no such representatives. The leopard-skin priests are men's representatives to him and not his representatives to men. We are here faced with the problem of the one and the many, which I have discussed elsewhere (Evans-Pritchard, 1953c); and we see in these differences of attitude in sacrifices to God and in those made to lesser spirits a counterpart in action to the ambiguity of the idea of spirit, the source of good and ill, as represented in the paradox of unity and plurality.

Thus we see that in Nuer sacrifice there are different shades of meaning. The pattern varies. There are shifts of emphasis. Any attempt to present a general interpretation, to put forward a simple formula, to cover all Nuer sacrifices meets with further difficulty when we turn to the confirmatory sacrifices. Here the intention is clearly different. God, or whichever of his refractions may be involved, is not angry and therefore does not have to be propitiated. No sin has been committed and there is therefore nothing to expiate. Life is not usually endangered so there is no need for substitution. Initiations and weddings are occasions of mirth, and even mortuary ceremonies, though they are solemn occasions, mark the end of mourning and therefore have a joyous side to them. There may always be some element of anxiety in these *rites de passage*, and perhaps also—it is difficult to say—of a feeling of the possibility of fault. In some confirmatory sacrifices, those concerned with death, these elements are manifest, but in others, such as marriage ceremonies, they are not evident and the stress is rather on ensuring the success of a social activity and validating it. As I have said earlier, we cannot make a rigid distinction between the one type of sacrifice and the other. Mortuary sacrifices might be placed in either class, according to the point of view.

But in initiation and marriage ceremonies the sacrifices are only incidents in a succession of ceremonial acts, and they have a maximum of festal, and a minimum of religious, significance. The sacrifice adds strength to what is being accomplished by other means and it provides a meal for those attending what is primarily a social gathering, so much so that those who have a right to the carcase of the victim in marriage sacrifices may demand that a bigger ox be slaughtered than that presented. In these ceremonies we have to distinguish between the religious rite of sacrifice and the secular rites which it accompanies and sacralizes. A boy is initiated into manhood by the making of six incisions across his forehead and by various other acts of a ritual and ceremonial character. The sacrifice is something extra added to these acts which protects the lad from harm, makes God and the ghosts witnesses of his change of status, and provides a feast for the living witnesses, his ever-hungry kinsmen and neighbours. Likewise in marriage, though sacrifices must be made, to make and secure the completion of the stages leading to the full union of man and wife as well as to give the visiting relatives-in-law a meal, the union itself is brought about mainly by other than religious acts: payment of bridewealth, wedding ceremonial and festivities, and so forth. The sacrifices form only a part of the whole series of ritual and other activities, and a part in which the religious content is reduced to a minimum, the movements of the sacrifice being conducted in a perfunctory manner. To indicate the unimportance of the religious element in the total event, one might perhaps compare it among ourselves to grace before a festal meal. There is, therefore, a difference of attitude and hence of meaning between the confirmatory and the piacular sacrifices. We must suppose that in the laying on of hands in the former by representatives of the lineages which offer up the victims the ideas of identification and of transference of evil are not so prominent as in the piacular sacrifices.

Yet we cannot exclude these killings from the general category of sacrifice. They are what Hubert and Mauss call sacrifices of sacralization in contrast to sacrifices of desacralization. We can, nevertheless, say that the most typical confirmatory sacrifices or sacrifices of sacralization, those sacrifices which lack, at any rate to any marked degree, piacular significance are least important for an understanding of the character of Nuer religion. Their religion, it is true, is part of their culture but, as such, its role in the regulation of the social life, its structural role, is subsidiary to its role in the regulation of the individual's relations with God, its personal role. The two roles are of different orders and have different functions, and it is the second which has the greater interest for us, for though Nuer religious activity is part of their social life and takes place within it they conceive it as expressing essentially a relationship between man and something which lies right outside his society, and it is, therefore, within the framework of that conception that our study of their religion has to be made and its central act of sacrifice has to be understood.

# Notes

1. Every English translation of this passage I have seen gives "the moral state of the person," which has, of course, a quite different meaning from the collective sense of "l'état de la personne morale."
2. E.g. by Emerson (1844), Pederson (1926, p. 201), Money-Kyrle (1930, p. 231), van der Leeuw (1938, pp. 35–56), and Gusdorf (1948, pp. 16 ff.).
3. E.g., Hubert and Mauss (1898, pp. 66–7), Gayford (1924, pp. 63, 110–11), Money-Kyrle (1930, p. 248), van der Leeuw (1938, pp. 350 ff.), Gusdorf (1948, pp. 79, 99), Johnson (1949, p. 62), and Nygren (1953, p. 120).
4. For a discussion of similar acts of self-mutilation in various parts of the world see Tylor (1913, pp. 400–1) and Sollas (1924, pp. 412 ff.). Nuer say that only a *yong*, a crazy person, would commit bestiality. I have never come across a case of it myself. I heard of only one case of sodomy, between two lads. A sheep was sacrificed and its entrails were tied round the waists of the partners and then severed.
5. The analysts conclude, as we have, that in piacular sacrifice the victim is a substitute for the offerer, who identifies himself with it, so that in destroying it he destroys part of himself. But their interpretation of its meaning is, of course, very different. It is a "symbolic parricide," and they speak of it also in terms of "super-ego," "trauma of birth," "anal eroticism," and so forth.
6. His interpretation, as I understand it, in terms of the *do-ut-possis-dare* motif does not, however, accord with Nuer ideas. See also Dussaud (1921) and Oesterley (1937).
7. Given, among anthropologists, some emphasis by Edward Westermarck (1908, pp. 616 ff.).

# References

Baxter, W. L. (1895). *Sanctuary and Sacrifice. A Reply to Wellhausen.* Bible Students' Lib. 4. 511 pp. London: Eyre and Spottiswoode.

Colson, F. H. tr. (1929). "On the Birth of Abel and the Sacrifices offered by him and by his Brother Cain (De sacrificiis Abelis et Caini)". In *Philo,* edited with English translation and introductions by F. H. Colson and G. H. Whitaker, 10 vols. (1929–41), II, pp. 88–195, and Appendix, pp. 488–97. Loeb Class. Lib. London: Heinemann.

Crazzolara, J. P. (1949). "Der Gotteskult bei den Nuer. 3. Das Opfer." In *Der Ursprung der Gottesidee,* Wilhelm Schmidt, ed., 9 vols. (1912–49), VIII, pp. 25–32. Münster i.W.: Aschendorffsche Verlagsbuchhandlung.

Dussaud, René (1921). *Les origins cananéennes du sacrifice israélite.* 334 pp. Paris: Ernest Leroux.

Emerson, R. W. (1844). "Gifts." In *Essays,* 2nd ser., with introduction by T. Carlyle, pp. 105–9. London: John Chapman.

Evans-Pritchard, E. E. (1951). "Some Features and Forms of Nuer Sacrifices." *Africa,* 21, pp. 112–21.

Evans-Pritchard, E. E. (1953a). "Nuer Spear Symbolism." *Anthrop.* Q. 26, pp. 1–19.

Evans-Pritchard, E. E. (1953b). "The Sacrificial Role of Cattle among the Nuer". *Africa,* 23, pp. 181–98.

Evans-Pritchard, E. E. (1953c). "The Nuer Conception of Spirit in the Relation to the Social Order." *Amer. Anthrop.* 55, pp. 201–14.

Frazer, Sir James George (1927). *The Gorgon's Head and other Literary Pieces* (new and enlarged ed. of *Sir Roger de Coverley and other Literary Pieces*, London, 1920), with preface by Anatole France. 453 pp. London: Macmillan.

Frazer, Sir James George (1931). *Garnered Sheaves.* 538 pp. London: Macmillan.

Gayford, S.C. (1924). *Sacrifice and Priesthood: Jewish and Christian.* 178 pp. London: Methuen.

Gray, George Buchanan (1925). *Sacrifice in the Old Testament: Its Theory and Practice.* 434 pp. Oxford: Clarendon Press.

Gusdorf, Georges (1948). *L'expérience humaine du sacrifice.* 275 pp. Paris: Presses Universitaires de France.

Hubert, Henri and Mauss, Marcel (1898). "Essai sur la nature et la fonction du sacrifice." *Année social.,* 2, pp. 29–138.

James, Edwin Oliver (1933). *Origins of Sacrifice. A Study in Comparative Religion.* 314 pp. London: Murray.

Johnson, Aubrey R. (1949). *The Vitality of the Individual in the Thought of Ancient Israel.* 107 pp. Cardiff: University of Wales Press.

Lagrange, Marie-Joseph (1903). *Etudes sur les religions sémitiques.* Études bibliques. 430 pp. Paris: Victor Lecoffre.

Leeuw, G. van der (1938). *Religion in Essence and Manifestation. A Study in Phenomenology.* Translation of *Phänomenologie der Religion* (Tübingen, 1933) by J. E. Turner. Sir Halley Stewart Publ. 5. 709 pp. London: Allen & Unwin.

Loisy, Alfred (1920). *Essai historique sur le sacrifice.* 552 pp. Paris: Émile Nourry.

Mauss, Marcel (1923) (1925). "Essai sur le don, forme et raison de l'échange dans les sociétés archaïques." *Année social.,* N.S., 1, pp. 30–186. (English translation by I. G. Cunnison in press. London: Cohen & West.)

Money-Kyrle, R. (1930). *The Meaning of Sacrifice.* Int. Psycho-Anal. Lib. 16. 273 pp. London: Hogarth Press and Institute of Psycho-Analysis.

Nock, Arthur Darby tr. (1926). *Sallustius: Concerning the Gods and the Universe,* edited with prolegomena and translation by Arthur Darby Nock. cxxiii, 48 pp. Cambridge: University Press.

Nygren, Anders (1953). *Agape and Eros.* Translation of *Eros och Agape* (Stockholm, 1930–6) by Philip S. Watson, 2nd ed., revised and partly retranslated. 764 pp. London: S.P.C.K.

Oesterley, W. O. E. (1937). *Sacrifices in Ancient Israel: Their Origin, Purposes and Development.* 320 pp. London: Hodder & Stoughton.

Oyler, D. S. (1920). The Shilluk Peace Ceremony. *Sudan Notes,* 3, pp. 296–9.

Pedersen, Johs. (1926). *Israel: Its Life and Culture,* 2 vols. (1926–40), I. London: Oxford University Press; Copenhagen: Povl Branner.

Smith, Sir William Robertson (1889). *Lectures on the Religion of the Semites,* Ser. I. Burnett Lectures, 1888–9. 488 pp. Edinburgh: Black.

Sollas, W. J. (1924). *Ancient Hunters and their Modern Representatives,* 3rd edn. 354 pp. London: Macmillan.

Spencer, Herbert (1882). *The Principles of Sociology,* 2 vols. (1876–82), II. London: Williams & Norgate.

Sykes, Arthur Ashley (1748). *An Essay on the Nature, Design, and Origin of Sacrifices.* 354 pp. London: Knapton.

Tylor, Edward B. (1913). *Primitive Culture*, 5th edn., 2 vols., II. London: Murray.

Wellhausen, Julius (1895). *Prolegomena to the History of Israel.* Translation of *Geschichte Israels*, I (Berlin, 1878), by J. Sutherland Black and Allan Menzies with preface by W. Robertson Smith. 552 pp. Edinburgh: Black.

Westermarck, Edward (1906). *The Origin and Development of the Moral Ideas*, 2 vols., II. London: Macmillan.

Willoughby, William Charles (1928). *The Soul of the Bantu. A Sympathetic Study of the Magico-Religious Practices and Beliefs of the Bantu Tribes of Africa.* 476 pp. London: Student Christian Movement.

Wilson, William tr. (1869). *The Writings of Clement of Alexandria.* Translated by the Rev. William Wilson, 2 vols. (1867–9), II. Ante-Nicene Christian Lib. 12. Edinburgh: Clark.

# 13

# WALTER BURKERT (b. 1931)

German classicist Walter Burkert was born in the town of Neuendettelsau in Bavaria, studied classical history and philosophy at the Universities of Erlangen and Munich, and received his Ph.D. in 1955. He has taught at the University of Erlangen and the Technical University of Berlin in Germany, at Harvard University and the University of California at Berkeley in the United States, and for most of his career at the university of Zürich in Switzerland. Working in the field of classical philology, literature, and culture, Burkert has published numerous articles and books on Greek myth and ritual. Most of these he wrote in German, but they were later translated into English. His most important books include: *Lore and Science in Ancient Pythagoreanism* (1962, 1972), *Homo Necans: The Anthropology of Ancient Greek Sacrificial Ritual and Myth* (1972, 1983), *Greek Religion Archaic and Classical* (1977, 1985), *Structure and History in Greek Myth and Ritual* (1979), *The Orientalizing Revolution* (1984, 1992), and, recently, *Creation of the Sacred: Tracks of Biology in early Religions* (1996). Throughout his work Burkert exhibits impressive scholarship, and presents bold theoretical stances. Working across many academic disciplines—anthropology, history, ethology, literature, and classics, for example—he has challenged scholars of religion to think about their subject quite differently.

Sacrifice has long been a topic of interest for Burkert, many of his writings addressing it directly or placing it within some broader discussion. His most important work on sacrifice is contained in *Homo Necans*, an entire book devoted to the subject. The book is extraordinary because it revisits a project dear to the Victorians (e.g., Tylor, Spencer, Frazer, etc.) writing more than a century ago, the origin of religion, and offers modern readers another explanation deriving religion from sacrifice. Burkert develops a theory of sacrifice that places it at the origin of human religious life. There was no religion before there was sacrifice, so, once again, to understand sacrifice is to understand religion. Burkert works primarily with Greek cultural materials, but unlike Evans-Pritchard, he believes his theory provides an explanation of religion (and sacrifice) in all cultural settings.

Burkert's understanding of sacrifice is a psychosocial, historically evolutionary theory that claims the social needs of Homo Sapiens evolved in parallel with psychological phenomena, and that as these changes occurred, certain effects led to the establishment of sacrificial and religious institutions. Like other evolutionary theorists, Burkert claims that human cultural products can be understood to derive from a common process of development, a unilinear course that began at a common source. Identifying that source and sketching the mechanisms of that development constitute an explanation of the final products, no matter how diverse and apparently unrelated they may be (e.g., Nuer cattle sacrifice and the Christian Eucharist).

Burkert begins his account of this process with what he considers to be the basic animal nature of human beings. During Paleolithic times (approximately 60,000–8,000 B.C.E.), Burkert explains, Homo Sapiens were like chimps; they were food gatherers and not hunters, living in small family units. At the same time, however, there was intense competition and a general atmosphere of "intraspecific aggression" characterized by spontaneous acts of violence. Recognizing Freud's contribution, but also that of animal behaviorist Konrad Lorenz, Burkert believes that the earliest ancestors of human beings were instinctually competitive and aggressive, not truly cooperating or sharing (food, for example) in any significant way.

This all changed, however, with the rise of a very specific form of activity—hunting. Burkert suggests that a successful hunt, one that ends in the killing of an animal, required several new human traits. It required patience, planning, and cooperation among a group of men. In the name of fairness, it required sharing the spoils (the meat, the food) of the hunt. It required the development of weapons and their use to destroy some foreign (to the group) being. It even required certain physical abilities, for example a marked strength, a talent for running, and an upright posture. These new and special human qualities led naturally, Burkert continues, to a sharp sexual differentiation within cooperating bands, with men hunting and women cooking (using fire to prepare newly acquired meat from the hunt) and raising children. All together, these changes constitute the very basis, and thereby the origin, of social life. The rise of hunting was the crucial moment in hominization, in the development of social and cultural patterns that remain today.

Burkert claims there was a psychological development as well. If the hunt is to succeed, cooperation and sharing must prevail, and the deep instincts of aggression and competition must be controlled or channeled. During the hunt, this is accomplished by redirecting aggressions toward the prey, an anthropomorphized being, rather than toward one's fellow hunters. Instead of victory over another human being in competition, there is the thrill of a successful hunt, culminating in an exhilarating moment of the kill itself. This is cathartic for the hunters, and serves as a release of the aggressions they suppressed in their cooperation during the hunt. This catharsis, *cleansing of emotion* however, also includes a "shock" of killing, the hunters suddenly feeling a sense of guilt and remorse for having spilt the blood of another being. This shock and guilt, Burkert believes, led early hunters to develop additional activities that would "compensate" for their "taking" the life of another, e.g., arranging bones, prayers that address the prey or a "Master of Animals," or specific rules for how the hunt must be conducted to ensure respect and fairness to the prey. The hunt, therefore, becomes the locus for several important aspects of human nature—aggression (competition, violence, etc.), guilt (remorse, fault, etc.), and compensation (reparation, fairness, etc.)—that must be addressed and balanced in a working society.

As societies have a constant need for this balancing, for harnessing biological instincts and responding to the demands of cooperative solidarity, they will continually require the benefits of the hunt (and all the preliminary and ensuing actions) even after they evolve past the hunting stage of civilization. Consequently, Burkert concludes, the hunt becomes ritualized. It becomes the first and most basic form of religious ritual—sacrifice. He supports this claim by emphasizing the phenomenological parallels between the features of the hunt (killing, receiving, sharing, giving, repenting, and so forth) and of sacrifice. Beginning with this specific ritual, Burkert wants to derive all other religious phenomena, myths, doctrines, and so forth. Religion itself, then, can be understood as a complex of interactions and communications that arise from early sacrificial rituals, from symbolic enactments of the hunt. By repeating the hunt, albeit in increasingly complicated and/or abstracted religious forms, societies define and maintain a sense of order, stability, and continuity. It is precisely when this sense is absent or threatened, Burkert notes, that societies turn to sacrifice and other religious rituals.

In later works, Burkert does recognize the limits to his thesis and the absence of certain kinds of supporting evidence. He tempers his appeals to the psychology of early human beings and admits that his theory may not simply apply to all forms of sacrifice. He is content, in the end, to argue for its plausibility and not its proof. Despite these qualifications, Burkert's *Homo Necans*, the first few pages of which are reprinted here, his "hunting theory" of sacrifice, remains an important and inspired contribution to the history of understanding sacrifice. It is a challenging, yet ultimately rewarding work.

# From *Homo Necans: The Anthropology of Ancient Greek Sacrificial Ritual and Myth*

## 1. Sacrifice as an Act of Killing

Aggression[1] and human violence have marked the progress of our civilization and appear, indeed, to have grown so during its course that they have

Walter Burkert, *Homo Necans: The Anthropology of Ancient Greek Sacrificial Ritual and Myth*, translated by Peter Bing (Berkeley, Calif.: University of California Press, 1983), pp. 1–29. Reprinted with the permission of the University of California Press and Walter de Gruyter.

become a central problem of the present. Analyses that attempt to locate the roots of the evil often set out with short-sighted assumptions, as though the failure of our upbringing or the faulty development of a particular national tradition or economic system were to blame. More can be said for the thesis that all orders and forms of authority in human society are founded on institutionalized violence. This at least corresponds to the fundamental role played in biology by intraspecific aggression, as described by Konrad Lorenz. Those, however, who turn to religion for salvation from this "so-called evil" of aggression are confronted with murder at the very core of Christianity—the death of God's innocent son; still earlier, the Old Testament covenant could come about only after Abraham had decided to sacrifice his child. Thus, blood and violence lurk fascinatingly at the very heart of religion.

From a classicizing perspective, Greek religion appeared and still appears to some as bright and harmlessly cheerful. Yet those who maintain that the skandalon of the Cross (I Cor. 1:23) is on another level altogether overlook the deeper dimension that accompanies the easy life of the gods as portrayed by Homer. If a man is able to draw near to the gods, as the priest Chryses with Apollo or as Hektor or Odysseus with Zeus, he can do so because he has "burnt many thigh-pieces of bulls" (*Il.* 1.40, 22.170; *Od.* 1.66), for this is the act of piety: bloodshed, slaughter—and eating. It makes no difference if there is no temple or cult-statue, as often occurs in the cult of Zeus. The god is present at his place of sacrifice, a place distinguished by the heap of ashes left from "sacred" offerings burnt there over long periods of time, or by the horns and skulls of slaughtered rams and bulls, or by the altar-stone where the blood must be sprinkled. The worshipper experiences the god most powerfully not just in pious conduct or in prayer, song, and dance, but in the deadly blow of the axe, the gush of blood and the burning of thigh-pieces. The realm of the gods is sacred, but the "sacred" act done at the "sacred" place by the "consecrating" actor consists of slaughtering sacrificial animals, ἱερεύειν τὰ ἱερεια.[2] It was no different in Israel up to the destruction of the temple.[3] It is prescribed that daily "burnt offering shall be on the hearth upon the altar," "all night until the morning" (Lev. 6:2); these offerings, the remnants of two one-year-old lambs cut into pieces, are "a pleasing odor to the Lord." Thus the principal sin of Antiochus Epiphanes against Jerusalem was that he ordered that "the continual burnt offering [be] taken away" (Dan. 8:11). Augustus built an altar to celebrate the establishment of world peace and, together with his family, appears on the reliefs of this Ara Pacis as a sacrificer, preceded by servants carrying the sacrificial axe. Thus, the most refined Augustan art provides a framework for the bloody sacrifices at the center.

Sacrificial killing is the basic experience of the "sacred." *Homo religiosus* acts and attains self-awareness as *homo necans*. [killing man] Indeed, this is what it means "to act," ῥέζειν, *operari* (whence "sacrifice" is *Opfer* in German)—the name merely covers up the heart of the action with a euphemism.[4] The bliss of encountering divinity finds expression in words, and yet the strange and extraordinary events that the participant in the sacrifice is forced to witness are all the more intense because they are left undiscussed.

Thanks to the descriptions in Homer and tragedy, we can reconstruct the course of an ordinary Greek sacrifice to the Olympian gods almost in its entirety. The path that leads to the center of the sacred experience is complex. The preparations include bathing and dressing in clean clothes,[5] putting on ornaments and wreaths;[6] often sexual abstinence is a requirement.[7] At the start, a procession (πομπή),[8] even if still a small one, is formed. The festival participants depart from the everyday world, moving to a single rhythm and singing. The sacrificial animal is led along with them, likewise decorated and transformed—bound with fillets, its horns covered with gold.[9] Generally it is hoped that the animal will follow the procession compliantly or even willingly. Legends often tell of animals that offered themselves up for sacrifice,[10] apparent evidence of a higher will that commands assent. The final goal is the sacrificial stone, the altar "set up" long ago, which is to be sprinkled with blood. Usually a fire is already ablaze on top of it. Often a censer is used to impregnate the atmosphere with the scent of the extraordinary, and there is music, usually that of the flute. A virgin leads the way, "carrying the basket" (κανηφόρος),[11] that is, an untouched girl holding a covered container . . . A water jug must be there as well.

First of all, after arriving at the sacred place, the participants mark off a circle; the sacrificial basket and water jug are carried around the assembly, thus marking off the sacred realm from the profane.[12] The first communal act is washing one's hands as the beginning of that which is to take place. The animal is also sprinkled with water. "Shake yourself," says Trygaios in Aristophanes,[13] for the animal's movement is taken to signify a "willing nod," a "yes" to the sacrificial act. The bull is watered again,[14] so that he will bow his head. The animal thus becomes the center of attention. The participants now take unground barley grains (οὐλαί), the most ancient agricultural product, from the basket. These, however, are not meant for grinding or to be made into food: after a brief silence, the solemn εὐφημεῖν, followed by a prayer out loud—in a way, more self-affirmation than prayer—the participants fling the barley grains away onto the sacrificial animal, the altar, and the earth.[15] They are after another kind of food. The act of throwing simultaneously as a group is an aggressive gesture, like beginning a fight, even if the most harmless projectiles are chosen. Indeed, in some ancient rituals stones were used.[16] Hidden beneath the grains in the basket was the knife, which now lies uncovered.[17] The leader in this incipient drama, the ἱερεύς, steps toward the sacrificial animal, carrying the knife still covered so that the animal cannot see it. A swift cut, and a few hairs from the brow are shorn and thrown into the fire. This is another, though more serious, act of beginning (ἄρχεσθαι),[18] just as the water and the barley grains were a beginning. Blood has not yet been spilled and no pain whatsoever has been inflicted, but the inviolability of the sacrificial animal has been abolished irreversibly.

Now comes the death blow. The women raise a piercing scream: whether in fear or triumph or both at once, the "Greek custom of the sacrificial scream"[19] marks the emotional climax of the event, drowning out the death-rattle. The blood flowing out is treated with special care. It may not spill on the ground; rather, it must hit the altar, the hearth, or the sacrificial pit. If the animal is small it is raised over the altar; otherwise the blood is caught in a bowl and sprinkled on the altar-stone. This object alone may, and must again and again, drip blood.[20]

The "act" is over; its consequences are the next concern. The animal is carved up and disemboweled. Its inner organs are now the main focus, lying revealed, an alien, bizarre, and uncanny sight, and yet common in the same form to men as well, as is known from seeing wounded soldiers. The tradition specifies precisely what must be done with each piece.[21] First of all, the heart, sometimes still beating, is put on the altar.[22] A seer is present to interpret the lobes of the liver.[23] In general, however, the σπλάγχνα—the collective term for the organs—are quickly roasted in the fire from the altar and eaten at once. Thus the inner circle of active participants is brought together in a communal meal, transforming horror into pleasure. Only the bile is inedible and has to be disposed of. Likewise, the bones are not to be used for the subsequent meal, so they are "consecrated" beforehand. The bones, above all the thigh-bones (μηρία) and the pelvis with the tail (ὀσφύς), are put on the altar "in the proper order."[24] From the bones, one can still see exactly how the parts of the living animal fit together: its basic form is restored and consecrated. In Homer, a "beginning," i.e., a first offering, consisting of raw pieces of flesh from every limb, is put on the bones as well, indicating the entirety of the slaughtered animal.[25] The purifying fire then consumes all these remains. The skulls of bulls and rams and goat-horns are preserved[26] in the sacred place as permanent evidence of the act of consecration. The flow of blood is now replaced in its turn by the offerings of the planter, pouring libations of wine into the fire and burning cakes.[27] As the alcohol causes the flames to flare up, a higher reality seems present. Then, as the fire dies down, the pleasing feast gradually gives way to everyday life.[28] The skin of the sacrificial victim is generally sold to benefit the sanctuary, to purchase new votive offerings and new victims: in this way, the cult insures its own continuance.[29]

This rite is objectionable, and was already felt to be so early on, because it so clearly and directly benefits man. Is the god "to whom" the sacrifice is made any more than a transparent excuse for festive feasting? All he gets are the bones, the fat, and the gall bladders. Hesiod says that the crafty Prometheus, the friend of mankind, caused this to be so in order to deceive the gods, and the burning of bones became a standard joke in Greek comedy.[30] Criticism that damned the bloody act per se was far more penetrating. Zarathustra's curse applies to all who lust for blood and slaughter cattle.[31] "I have had enough of burnt offerings of rams and the fat of fed beasts; I do not delight in the blood of bulls or of lambs or of he-goats," says the Lord through Isaiah.[32] In the Greek world, the Pythagoreans and Orphics demanded that the lives of all creatures with souls be spared, and Empedokles was the most vehement of all in attacking the cannibalistic madness of the traditional sacrificial meal, as also in expressing the desire for a realm of non-violent love on the path toward "purification."[33] Philosophy then took up the criticism of blood-sacrifice— above all, Theophrastus, in his influential book *On Piety*. This book explained animal-sacrifice as having replaced cannibalism, which, in turn, had been forced on men because of difficult times.[34] After this, a theoretical defense of sacrificial custom was virtually hopeless.[35] Both Varro and Seneca were convinced that the gods do not demand blood-sacrifice.[36] Judaism in the Diaspora spread more easily because cult practices had become concentrated in one temple in Jerusalem, thus virtually making Judaism outside Jerusalem a religion without animal-sacrifice.[37] This also helped form Christian practice, which could thus take up the traditions of Greek philosophy. On the other hand, it gave the idea of sacrifice a central significance and raised it to a higher status than ever before.[38] The death of God's son is the one-time and perfect sacrifice, although it is still repeated in the celebration of the Lord's Supper, in breaking the bread and drinking the wine.

Folk custom, however, managed to defy even Christianization and was subdued only by modern technological civilization. The German expression *geschmückt wie ein Pfingstochse* ("decked out like an ox at Pentecost") preserves the memory of the ritual slaughter of an ox at the church festival (see n. 9 above). In Soviet Armenia the slaughter of a sheep in front of the church is still a feature of regular Sunday service. Isolated Greek communities in Cappadocia celebrated the ancient sacrificial ritual well into the twentieth century: opposite the conventional altar in the chapel of the saint would be a sacrificial altar-stone, upon which incense was burned when candles were lit; during prayers, it would be decked with wreaths. The sacrificer would bring the animal—a goat or a sheep—into the chapel, leading it three times around the sacrificial stone while children threw grass and flowers onto it. As the priest stood at the altar, the keeper of the animal would make a sign of the cross with his knife three times and then slaughter the animal while praying. The blood was supposed to sprinkle the stone. After this, outside the chapel, the animal would be carved up and the feast prepared. The priest, like his ancient counterpart, received the animal's thigh and skin, as well as its head and feet.[39] Christianity is here no more than a transparent cover for the ancient form that underlies it: that is to say, for the sacred act of blood-sacrifice.

Animal-sacrifice was an all-pervasive reality in the ancient world. The Greeks[40] did not perceive much difference between the substance of their own customs and those of the Egyptians and Phoenicians, Babylonians and Persians, Etruscans and Romans, though ritual details varied greatly among the Greeks themselves.[41] One peculiarity of Greek sacrifice presents a problem for the modern historian: the combination of a fire-altar and a blood-rite, of burning and eating, corresponds directly only with the burnt offerings (*zebah, šelamim*) of the Old Testament[42]—although the details of Ugaritic and Phoenician sacrificial cults are uncertain—and these differ markedly from Egyptians and Mesapotamian, as well as Minoan-Mycenaean, rites, all of which have no altars for burning whole animals or bones.[43] And yet, whatever complexities, layers, and changes in cultural tradition underlie the individual peculiarities, it is astounding, details aside, to observe the similarity of actions and experience from Athens to Jerusalem and on to Babylon. A detailed Babylonian text of which several copies were made describes the sacrifice of a bull whose skin was used as the membrane of a tympanon in the temple:[44] an untouched black bull would be chosen for the secret ceremony, which took place in a room enclosed on all sides by curtains. The complicated preparations included scattering grain, offering breads and libations, and sacrificing a sheep. The bull stood chained on a rush mat until it was time for its mouth to be washed. After this, incantations would be whispered into both its ears, after which it was sprinkled with water, purified with a torch, and surrounded by a circle of grain. Following prayer and song, the bull was killed, the heart burned at once, and the skin and left shoulder sinew removed to string the tympanon. After further libations and offerings, the priest would bend down to the severed head and say, "This deed was done by all the gods; I did not do it." One version of the text says that the cadaver would be buried; an older one forbids at least the head priest from eating the meat. Fifteen days later, in a largely parallel ceremony, with preparatory and closing rites, the newly covered tympanon was brought into the center in place of the bull, thus in-augurating it into its function.

Not even the religious revolution in the Near East, i.e., the emergence of Islam, could eliminate animal-sacrifice. The high point in the life of a Moslem is the pilgrimage to Mecca[45] which still today draws hundreds of thousands of worshippers annually. The central point occurs on the ninth day of the holy month, in the journey from Mecca to Mount Arafat, where the pilgrims stay from noon till sundown praying "before God." This is followed by the Day of Sacrifice. On the tenth day, in Mina, the pilgrim must throw seven pebbles at an old stone monument and then slaughter—usually with his own hands—a sacrificial animal—a sheep, a goat, or even a camel—which is driven up and sold to him by Bedouins. He eats some of the animal, though usually giving most of it away or simply leaving it. Saudi Arabia has resorted to bulldozers to remove the carcasses. After this, the pilgrim is allowed to cut his hair again and remove his pilgrim's robes. Likewise, sexual abstinence ends after his return to Mecca. It is the consecrated man who kills and the act of killing is made sacred. "In the name of Allah" and "Allah is merciful" are the Moslem formulas that accompany even profane slaughter.

Daily routine inevitably made the sacrificial ritual an empty formality.[46] Therefore, in order to stress its importance, especially in the ancient Near East, ordinances were created stipulating countless observances. The Greeks seem to have given most care in the "beginning" stages (ἄρχεσθαι), as if trying to distract attention from the central point, which nonetheless remained permanently fixed. Hubert and Mauss[47] aptly characterized the structure of sacrificial ritual with the concepts of "sacralization" and "desacralization"; that is to say, preliminary rites, on the one hand, and closing rites, on the other, framing a central action clearly marked as the emotional climax by a piercing scream, the "Ololygé." This act, however, is the act of killing, the experience of death. Thus, a threefold rhythm becomes evident in the course of the sacrifice,[48] moving from an inhibited, labyrinthine beginning, through a terrifying midpoint, to a scrupulously tidy conclusion. Vegetable offerings frequently come at the beginning and again at the end of the ceremony, when libations are also especially characteristic. But the offerings can overlap and multiply, enlarging the pattern until a triad of sacrificial festivals emerges which yet adheres to the same unchangeable rhythm: the preliminary sacrifice, the terrifying sacrifice, and the victorious, affirming sacrifice. The core is always the experience of death brought about by human violence, which, in turn, is here subject to predetermined laws. And this is nearly always connected with another human—all too human—action, namely, eating: the festive meal of those who share in the sacred.

## 2. The Evolutionary Explanation: Primitive Man as Hunter

Karl Meuli's great essay on "Griechische Opferbräuche" (1946)[49] added a new dimension to our understanding of sacrifice. He noted striking similarities in the details of Greek sacrifice and the customs of hunting and herding societies, mostly in Siberia. Moreover, he pointed out prehistoric discoveries that seemed to attest to similar customs by Middle Paleolithic times. This powerful step backward about 50,000 years in time admittedly seems to explain *obscurum per obscurius*. Whether the prehistoric evidence may be taken to indicate belief in a supreme being—a kind of primordial monotheism—is a moot question. It seemed less risky to state: "Sacrifice is the oldest form of religious action."[50] But much of the oldest evidence remains controversial.

Meuli relied on the "burial of bears" of Neanderthal times, as described by Bächler and others:[51] they claimed that they had found bears' skulls and bones, especially thigh-bones, carefully set up in caves, and that these corresponded to the "skull-and long bone sacrifice" observed among Siberian hunters, who used to deposit the bones and skulls of their quarry in sacred places.[52] In Greek ritual, too, it is the bones, especially the thigh-bones, that belong to the gods. The bear's special role further appears in the "bear festivals" of northern Eurasian tribes, from the Finns to the Ainus and on to America.[53] Yet the findings of Bächler have come under serious attack: chance assemblage of bones cannot be excluded as an explanation of the alleged bear-burials.[54] It is safer to rely on the evidence of the Upper Paleolithic, the epoch of homo sapiens. At this period, hunters' customs, including the manipulation of animals' bones and skulls, are clearly attested; Meuli's insight about the antiquity of Siberian hunting ritual is basically confirmed, even if still more ancient layers remain in the dark. There are places where stag skulls and deer skeletons were gathered, as well as the bones of bison and mammoths.[55] At a site in Siberia, twenty-seven mammoth skulls were found set up in a circle around a central point where a female statuette lay buried beneath a pile of bones and partially worked tusks.[56] This recalls a frequently reproduced gold ring from Mycenae, on which a row of animal skulls borders the procession to the seated goddess.[57] A stylized pair of horns is the common and omnipresent religious symbol of Minoan-Mycenaean culture. Much earlier, in the household shrines of Çatal Hüyük, there are genuine cow-horns set up in rows or inserted in plaster heads.[58] Upper Paleolithic deer hunters had attached a reindeer skull to a pole near a place where they used to throw young roes into the water, weighted down with stones—a "sacrifice of immersion."[59] There is a life-size clay statue of a bear in the cave of Montespan, which had been covered with a genuine bearskin, including the skull.[60] Similarly, hunters in the Sudan covered a clay figure with the skins of slaughtered lions or leopards, just as farmers in southern Abyssinia did with the skin of a young sacrificial bull. Hermes the cattle-thief and cattle-killer stretched out on a rock the skins of the cows he had slaughtered. This, too, is "one of the many sagas about the origin of sacrifice."[61]

One could, of course, try to cut through these correspondences with conceptual distinctions, and separate hunting and sacrifice on principle.[62] In the hunt, one might argue, killing is not ceremonial but practical and subject to chance; its meaning and goal, both quite profane, lie in obtaining meat for food; a wild beast must be seen in opposition to a tame domestic animal. And yet the very similarity of hunting and sacrificial customs belies such a distinction. Killing can become ceremonial even among hunters. A tame bear, for instance, would have to perform at the bear festival. We also hear of a complete mammoth skeleton found on a high crag, a place to which it could only have been driven by men.[63] On the other hand, the hunting situation is often evoked and acted out in later civilizations, as if one had to catch a wild beast so as to sacrifice it at a predetermined place. Thus, Plato combines the hunt and sacrifice in a semi-barbarous context, his fictitious Atlantis,[64] and in fact bull-hunts are attested in the marginal areas of Greek culture.[65] An Attic myth tells how Theseus subdued the wild bull of Marathon so that it let itself be led to the sacrifice—and this is said to be the legendary origin of the local festival in Marathon, the Hekaleia.[66] Among the Sumerians, a "wild bull" was considered the most eminent sacrificial animal, even though it had long been extinct in Mesopotamia. The consecrated horns in the sanctuaries of Çatal Hüyük were, however, still obtained from genuine wild bulls; bull- and stag-hunting appear on the very impressive wall-paintings there . . .[67] The way in which the leopard and men swarm around the bull and the stag in these paintings is perhaps almost more suggestive of a dance than of hunting. In Egypt, the sacrifice of bulls and hippopotami, performed by the pharaoh, was entirely stylized as a hunt.[68] In many parts of Greece, the animals chosen for sacrifice were "set free for the god," almost as if they were wild beasts on sacred land until the time appointed for the bloody "act."[69]

The continuity between the hunt and sacrificial ritual appears most forcibly in the ritual details that leave no tangible archaeological trace; these have been set out in detail by Meuli. The correspondences extend from the preparations, with their purifications and abstinences, to the closing rites, involving bones, skulls, and skins. In hunting societies accessible to ethnological study, hunters are said to have expressed clear feelings of guilt with regard to the slaughtered animal. The ritual provides forgiveness and reparation, though frequently taking on a scurrilous character which prompted Meuli to coin the phrase "the comedy of innocence." The ritual betrays an underlying anxiety about the continuation of life in the face of death.[70] The bloody "act" was necessary for the continuance of life, but it is just as necessary for new life to be able to start again. Thus, the gathering of bones, the raising of a skull or stretching of a skin is to be understood as an attempt at restoration, a resurrection in the most concrete sense. The hope that the sources of nourishment will continue to exist, and the fear that they will not, determine the action of the hunter, killing to live.

These customs are more than mere curiosities, for the hunt of the Paleolithic hunter is not just one activity among many. The transition to the hunt is, rather, one of the most decisive ecological changes between man and the other primates. Man can virtually be defined as "the hunting ape" (even if "the naked ape" makes a more appealing title.)[71] This statement leads to a second indisputable fact, namely, that the age of the hunter, the Paleolithic, comprises by far the largest part of human history. No matter that estimates range between 95 and 99 percent: it is clear that man's biological evolution was accomplished during this time. By comparison, the period since the invention of agriculture—10,000 years, at most—is a drop in the bucket. From this perspective, then, we can understand man's terrifying violence as deriving from the behavior of the predatory animal, whose characteristics he came to acquire in the course of becoming man.

Our conception of primitive man and his society will always be a tentative construct; still, there are some social and psychological preconditions that cannot have been absent from the situation of the early hunters. The primate's biological makeup was not fit for this new way of life. Man had to compensate for this deficiency by a tour de force of ingenious technology and institutions, that is to say, by his culture, although that culture itself quickly became a means of selection. Of primary importance was the use of weapons, without which man poses virtually no threat to beasts. The earliest weapon that was effective at a distance was the wooden spear hardened by fire.[72] This presupposes the use of fire; earlier, bones had served as clubs.[73] Man's upright posture facilitated the use of weapons. But perhaps more important than all this was the development of a social order leading to sharp sexual differentiation, which has even become a part of our inherited biological constitution. Among human beings, hunting is man's work—in contrast to all animal predators—requiring both speed and strength; hence the male's long, slender thigh. By contrast, since women must bear children with ever larger skulls, they develop round, soft forms. Man's extraordinarily protracted youth, his *neoteny*, which permits the development of the mind through learning and the transmission of a complicated culture, requires long years of security. This is basically provided by the mother at home. The man assumes the role of the family breadwinner—an institution universal to human civilizations but contrary to the behavior of all other mammals.[74]

The success of the "hunting ape" was due to his ability to work cooperatively, to unite with other men in a communal hunt. Thus, man ever since the development of hunting has belonged to two overlapping social structures, the family and the *Männerbund*; his world falls into pairs of categories: indoors and out, security and adventure, women's work and men's work, love and death. At the core of this new type of male community, which is biologically analogous to a pack of wolves, are the acts of killing and eating. The men must constantly move between the two realms, and their male children must one day take the difficult step from the women's world to the world of men. Fathers must accept their sons, educating them and looking after them—this, too, has no parallel among mammals. When a boy finally enters the world of men, he does so by confronting death.

What an experience it must have been when man, the relative of the chimpanzee, succeeded in seizing the power of his deadly enemy, the leopard, in assuming the traits of the wolf, forsaking the role of the hunted for that of the hunter! But success brought its own dangers. The earliest technology created the tools for killing. Even the wooden spear and wedge provided man with weapons more dangerous than his instincts could cope with. His rudimentary killing inhibitions were insufficient as soon as he could kill at a distance; and males were even educated to suppress these inhibitions for the sake of the hunt. Moreover, it is as easy, or even easier, to kill a man as it is to kill a fleeing beast, so from the earliest times men slipped repeatedly into cannibalism.[75] Thus, from the very start, self-destruction was a threat to the human race.

If man nonetheless survived and with unprecedented success even enlarged his sphere of influence, it was because in place of his natural instincts he developed the rules of cultural tradition, thus artificially forming and differentiating his basic inborn behavior. Biological selection rather than conscious planning determined the educational processes that helped form man, so that he could best adapt himself to the role. A man had to be courageous to take part in the hunt; therefore, courage is always included in the conception of an ideal man. A man had to be reliable, able to wait, to resist a momentary impulse for the sake of a long-range goal. He had to have endurance and keep to his word. In these matters men developed behavior patterns that were lacking in anthropoid apes and were more closely analogous to the behavior of beasts of prey.[76] Above all, the use of weapons was controlled by the strictest—if also artificial—rules: what was allowed and necessary in one realm was absolutely forbidden in the other. A brilliant accomplishment in one was murder in the other. The decisive point is the very possibility that man may submit to laws curbing his individual intelligence and adaptability for the sake of societal predictability. The educative power of tradition attempts to bind him in an irreversible process analogous to biological "imprinting."[77]

On a psychological level, hunting behavior was mainly determined by the peculiar interplay of the aggressive and sexual complexes, which thus gave form to some of the foundations of human society. Whereas research on biological behavior, at least in predatory animals, carefully distinguishes intraspecific aggression from the behavior of hunting and eating,[78] this distinction obviously does not hold for man. Rather, these two became superimposed at the time when man unexpectedly assumed behavior of predatory animals. Man had to outdo himself in his transition to the hunt, a transition requiring implementation of all his spiritual reserves. And because this sort of behavior became specific to the male sex, that is to say, "men's work," males could more easily adapt themselves to the intraspecific aggression programmed for courtship fights and the impulses of sexual frustration.

It is not easy for adult males to cooperate, and especially the "naked ape," whose sexuality clearly grew out of proportion in order to bind men to women and thus insure that the family would be supported.[79] The heightened aggressiveness thus aroused could be turned to the service of the community by means of redirection, as has been described by Konrad Lorenz;[80] for it is precisely group demonstration of aggression toward outsiders that creates a sense of close personal community. The *Männerbund* becomes a closed, conspiratorial group through the explosive potential of aggression stored internally. This aggression was released in the dangerous and bloody hunt. The internal and external effects of aggression mutually enhanced the chances of success. Community is defined by participation in the bloody work of men. The early hunter soon subdued the world.

Because the hunter's activity was reinforced by behavior aimed originally at a human partner—that is, through intraspecific aggression—in place of a biologically fixed relationship of beast and quarry, something curious occurred: the quarry became a quasi-human adversary, experienced as human and treated accordingly. Hunting concentrated on the great mammals, which conspicuously resembled men in their body structure and movements, their eyes and their "faces," their breath and voices, in fleeing and in fear, in attacking and in rage. Most of all, this similarity with man was to be recognized in killing and slaughtering: the flesh was like flesh, bones like bones, phallus like phallus, and heart like heart,[81] and, most important of all, the warm running blood was the same. One could, perhaps, most clearly grasp the animal's resemblance to man when it died. Thus, the quarry turned into a sacrificial victim. Many observers have told of the almost brotherly bond that hunters felt for their game,[82] and the exchangeability of man and animal in sacrifice recurs as a mythological theme in many cultures besides the Greek.[83]

In the shock caused by the sight of flowing blood[84] we clearly experience the remnant of a biological, life-preserving inhibition. But that is precisely what must be overcome, for men, at least, could not afford "to see no blood," and they were educated accordingly. Feelings of fear and guilt are the necessary consequences of overstepping one's inhibitions; yet human tradition, in the form of religion, clearly does not aim at removing or settling these tensions. On the contrary, they are purposefully heightened. Peace must reign within the group, for what is called for outside, offends within. Order has to be observed inside, the extraordinary finds release without. Outside, something utterly different, beyond the norm, frightening but fascinating, confronts the ordinary citizen living within the limits of the everyday world. It is surrounded by barriers to be broken down in a complicated, set way, corresponding to the ambivalence of the event: sacralization and desacralization around a central point where weapons, blood, and death establish a sense of human community. The irreversible event becomes a formative experience for all participants, provoking feelings of fear and guilt and increasing desire to make reparation, the groping attempt of restoration. For the barriers that had been broken before are now all the more willingly recognized. The rules are confirmed precisely in their antithetical tension. As an order embracing its opposite, always endangered yet capable of adaptation and development, this fluctuating balance entered the tradition of human culture. The power to kill and respect for life illuminate each other.

With remarkable consistency, myths tell of the origins of man in a fall, a crime that is often a bloody act of violence.[85] The Greeks speculated that this was preceded by a golden age of modest vegetarianism, ending in the "murder" of the plow-ox. Accordingly, anthropologists once saw the peaceful gatherers, or even the planters, as the original form of human civilization. The study of prehistory has changed this picture: man became man through the hunt, through the act of killing. "The greatest danger to life is the fact that man's food consists entirely of souls," said an Eskimo shaman,[86] just as Porphyrios characterized the state of mankind, divorced from the gods and dependent on food, by quoting Empedokles: "Such are the conflicts and groanings from which you have been born." As one of the Old Testament myths seems to tell us, men are the children of Cain. Yet killing, if it was a crime, was salvation at the same time. "You saved us by shedding blood," the Mithraists address their savior-god, Mithras the bull-slayer.[87] What has become a mystic paradox had been just fact in the beginning.

# 3. Ritualization

Although sacrifice began in the hunt, it appeared at its most meticulous and brilliant in the ancient city cultures, and at its most gruesome in Aztec civilization. It maintained its form and perhaps even acquired its purely religious function outside the context in which killing was necessary for life. For the action to be thus redirected and maintained, there had to be ritualization.

The concept of *ritual* has long been used to describe the rules of religious behavior. Biology's recent usurpation of the term appears, however, to confuse the concept, mixing the transcendent with the infra-human. But perhaps these two do indeed meet within the fundamental orders that constitute life. Thus, we deliberately start from the biological definition of ritual, and from there we will soon be led deep into the nature of religion.

Since the work of Sir Julian Huxley and Konrad Lorenz,[88] biology has defined *ritual* as a behavioral pattern that has lost its primary function—present in its unritualized model—but which persists in a new function, that of communication. This pattern in turn provokes a corresponding behavioral response. Lorenz's prime example is the triumph ceremony of a pair of graylag geese, which is no longer prompted by a real enemy. The victory over a nonexistent opponent is meant to demonstrate and draw attention to the couple's solidarity and is confirmed by corresponding behavior in the partner, who understands the ritual communication because of its predetermined stereotypy. In the triumph ceremony, communication is reciprocal and is strengthened by the reactions of each side. But it can also be one-sided, as, for example, when a threatening gesture is answered by ritual submission, which thus upholds a hierarchy. This communicating function reveals the two basic characteristics of ritual behavior, namely, repetition and theatrical exaggeration. For the essentially immutable patterns do not transmit differentiated and complex information but, rather, just one piece of information each. This single piece of information is considered so important that it is reinforced by constant repetition so as to avoid misunderstanding or misuse. The fact of understanding is thus more important than what is understood. Above all, then, ritual creates and affirms social interaction.

Aggressive behavior evokes a highly attentive, excited response. Pretended aggression thus plays a special role in ritual communication. Raising one's hands, waving branches, wielding weapons and torches, stamping the feet while turning from attack to flight, folding the hands or lifting them in supplication, kneeling and prostration: all these are repeated and exaggerated as a demonstration whereby the individual proclaims his membership and place in the community. A rhythm develops from repetition, and auditory signals accompanying the gestures gives rise to music and dance. These, too, are primordial forms of human solidarity, but they cannot hide the fact that they grew out of aggressive tensions, with their noise and beating, attack and flight. Of course, man has many modes of expression that are not of this origin and that can be ritualized. But in ethology, even laughter is thought to originate in an aggressive display of teeth.[89] Gestures of disgust or "purification" are not far removed from the impulses of aggression and destruction. Some of these ritual gestures can be traced with certainty to the primates, from waving branches and rhythmic drumming to phallic display and raising the hand in supplication.[90]

It is disputed to what extent ritual behavior is innate or learned.[91] We will have to wait for further ethological research. There is even a possibility that specific learning or formative experiences may activate innate behavior. Universal modes of behavior suggest an innate stock from which they are drawn. Yet, building upon these, cultural education creates special forms delimiting individual groups almost as if they were "pseudo-species." Fortunately, in studying the effect of rituals as communication in society, the question of their biological roots is comparatively unimportant.

Ever since Emile Durkheim, sociologists have been interested in the role of rites, and especially of religious rituals in society. "It is through common action that society becomes self-aware"; thus "the collective feelings and ideas that determine [society's] unity and character must be maintained and confirmed at regular intervals."[92] A. R. Radcliffe-Brown has been the most thorough in developing this functional perspective: a society can exist only by means of common concepts and feelings which, in turn, are developed through society's effect on the individual. "The ceremonial customs of a society are a means by which the sentiments in question are given collective expression on appropriate occasion."[93] Today one would perhaps replace the term *sentiment* with *thought structure and behavior pattern* but on the whole, ethology has confirmed and reinforced this view. The ritual actualizes social interaction; it dramatizes the existing order. We may call it "status dramatization,"[94] although this is not to say that a rite cannot establish and define a new status.

Besides this functional-behavioristic approach, and apparently contradicting it, is the psychoanalytic concept of ritual based on empirical observation of compulsive behavior. Here, too, we find set behavior patterns that have lost their primary, pragmatic function. In this view, neurosis becomes a kind of private religion, and sacred ritual becomes collective neurosis. Through ritual, the psyche tries to avoid anxieties, fleeing to a world of its own making from a reality it cannot accept and thus negates. Oppressed and wounded by that reality, it seeks to escape utter madness. Thus, religion is seen as an irrational outburst, a "ghost dance."[95]

The contrast, however, is more one of perspective than of substance. Just as in biology one may, on the one hand, observe the formation of a mutation and its physiological effects in terms of causality, while, on the other, gauging its relative advantage or disadvantage from a different environmental perspective, so, too, in studying the formation of private rituals, the sociological-functional approach provides a necessary complement to psychology. We cannot grasp religion as a fixed form if it is merely personal; it becomes a formative construct only over the course of generations. Sacrificial rituals, in any case, are impressive evidence for a continuity spanning thousands of years, and even if they exist only because of certain psychological influences, the continuity is surely due to other factors, factors of biological and social selection.

The first of these factors is negative. A ritual can persist in a community so long as it does not threaten that community with extinction. Some religious developments have indeed tended in this direction. The swift falls of most Gnostic movements and the final fall of Manichaeism were undoubtedly caused by their negation of life, just as the monks of Mount Athos, who were maintained by the outside world's consciousness of sin, are dying out today. If, however, practically all human cultures are shaped by religion, this indicates that religious ritual is advantageous in the process of selection, if not for the individual, then at least for the continuance of group identity.[96] Religion outlives all non-religious communities; and sacrificial ritual plays a special role in this process.

Furthermore, those rituals which are not innate can endure only when passed on through a learning process. The impulse for imitation, which is highly developed in man and especially in children, is decisive here, and it is encouraged by the theatricality of ritual. Children act out weddings and funerals again and again. This alone, however, cannot preserve the form of ritual, which remains rigid and unchanging over long periods of time. For this, the rite must be established as sacred. A religious rite is almost always "serious": some danger is evoked arousing anxiety, which then heightens attentiveness and lifts the subsequent proceedings out of the colorful stream of daily experience. Thus, the learning process leaves an ineradicable impression. By far the greatest impression is made by what terrifies, and it is just this that makes aggressive rituals so significant.

But even this is not enough to guarantee the permanence of the ritual:

226

deviations are corrected by elimination. Ritual was evidently so important for the continuance of human society that it became one of the factors of selection itself for innumerable generations. Those who will not or cannot conform to the rituals of a society have no chance in it. Only those who have integrated themselves can have influence and affect action. Here, the serious character of religious ritual becomes a very real threat. The psychological failure to meet this threat causes personal catastrophe. For instance, a child who consistently laughs during solemn occasions will not survive in a religious community. Appollonios of Tyana once declared such a boy to be possessed by a demon, but luckily the evil spirit quickly left the frightened young rascal.[97] In the Middle Ages, abbots fought the devil with very real cudgels, and up until modern times, a consecrated "devil's whip" always lay ready. This helps to account for the durability of aggressive ritual.

The biological-functional view of ritual has a consequence that is seldom realized, because it seems to go against the intention of humanism, which sees its mission in pursuing a phenomenology of the mind or soul and in disclosing a world of concepts or ideas. Ever since Wilhelm Mannhardt and Robertson Smith, the study of religions has focused on ritual. The evidence of the literary tradition no longer satisfied, since it had become evident that it was secondary. Thus, scholars looked for its roots in "deeper," "more primitive ideas."[98] It was, and is, considered self-evident that ritual, especially religious ritual, must depend on an antecedent "idea,"[99] even though it always turns out that those people whom history has been able to observe still practicing ritual "no longer" understand its "deeper meaning." After the rationalistic bias in the concept *idea* was exposed, scholars looked instead to "experience" or "deep perception"[100] for the roots which, as a creative response, produced ritual. Sociology, however—and, in this case, history—long ago revolutionized this perspective. Ideas do not produce ritual; rather, ritual itself produces and shapes ideas, or even experience and emotions. "Ce ne sont pas des émotions actuelles, ressenties à l'occasion des reunions et des cérémonies, qui engendrent ou perpétuent les rites, mais l'activité rituelle qui suscite les émotions."[101] "A specific practice or belief . . . never represents a direct psychological response of individuals to some aspect of the outer world . . . The source of their beliefs and practices is . . . the historic tradition."[102] It is this, by transmitting the custom as custom, that produces ideas, shapes experiences, excites desires.

This change in perspective, of course, takes us back to a basic assumption of primitive religion which religious studies constantly try to transcend: the source of religious customs is the "ways of our ancestors."[103] Ever since the pre-Socratics, people have stubbornly asked how mankind came to have its religious ideas; and they have done so although all men of the historical era, and certainly countless prehistoric generations, were taught their religious beliefs by the generation immediately preceding them. Plato expressed it thus: children come to believe in the existence of the gods by observing how "their own parents act with utmost seriousness on behalf of themselves and their children" at sacrifice and prayer.[104] Even the most radical innovations in the history of religion proceeded from this basis.

To be cautious, let us say that all human action is accompanied by ideas, surrounded by images and words. Tradition embraces language as well as ritual behavior. Psychoanalysis even speaks of "unconscious ideas." But to what extent these ideas, which are then raised after all into the realm of linguistic presentation, are just hermeneutic accessories or factors that exercise a demonstrable causality is a difficult question, at best answerable only in the context of psychology itself. By means of interpretation, one can attribute ideas to any action. Ritual has an understandable function *within* society—of course, it often has many, and changing, functions, for, as we know, biological selection favors multiple functions. Human beings can usually understand ritual intuitively, at least in its constituent parts. Thus, ritual makes sense in two ways. It is quite right to speak of "ideas" or "insights" which are "contained" in ritual and which it can express and communicate—as, for instance, the reality of a higher, transcendent power or the sacredness of life. However, it is more problematic to say that ritual has some "purpose," since we know that its course is predetermined and that a superimposed purpose cannot change it but can at most provoke it as a whole. There is no justification for viewing the "idea," even in its linguistic manifestation, as anterior to or decisive for ritual. In the history of mankind, ritual is far older than linguistic communication.[105] Neither the ideas and insights that can be extracted as a partial clarification by interpreting the ritual nor the emotions and explanations expressed by participants in the cult are the basis and origin of ritual; they simply accompany it. Thanks to its theatrical, mimetic character and the deep impression that its sacred solemnity can impart, ritual is self-perpetuating.

# Notes

1. S. Freud pointed the way in *Das Unbehagen in der Kultur* (1930), *Ges. Schriften XII* (1934), 27–114 = *Ges. Werke XIV* (1948), 419–506. K. Lorenz (1963) is basic from the standpoint of the behaviorist. The sometimes spirited criticisms of his approach—for instance, M. F. Ashley-Montagu, ed., *Man and Aggression* (1968); A. Plack, *Die Gesellschaft und das Böse* (1969[4]); J. Rattner, *Aggression und menschliche Natur* (1970)—did indeed correct some particulars but sometimes also displayed wishful thinking and partisanship; cf. Eibl-Eibesfeldt's (1970) defensive posture. For application to religious studies see P. Weidkuhn, *Aggressivität, Ritus, Säkularisierung. Biologische Grundformen religiöser Prozesse* (1965).
2. On Greek sacrifice see Stengel (1910), (1920) 95–155; Eitrem (1915); F. Schwenn, *Gebet und Opfer* (1927); L. Ziehen, *RE XVIII* (1939), 579–627, III A (1929),

1669–79; Meuli (1946); Burkert (1966); Nilsson (1955) 132–57; Casabona (1966); E. Forster, "Die antiken Ansichten über das Opferwesen," Diss. Innsbruck, 1952; E. Kadletz, "Animal Sacrifice in Greek and Roman Religion," Diss. University of Washington, 1976; Detienne and Vernant (1979). For the pictorial tradition see G. Rizza, ASSA 37/38 (1959/60), 321–45; Metzger (1965) 107–18. On sacrifice generally see W. R. Smith (1894); H. Hubert and M. Mauss, "Essai sur la nature et la fonction du sacrifice," *Année sociologique* 2 (1898), 29–138 = M. Mauss, *Oeuvres I* (1968), 193–307; A. Loisy, *Essai historique sur le sacrifice* (1920); R. Money-Kyrle, *The Meaning of Sacrifice* (1930) (psychoanalytical); E. M. Loeb, "The Blood Sacrifice Complex," *Mem. Amer. Anthr. Assoc.* 30 (1923); E. O. James, *Sacrifice and Sacrament* (1962); Burkert (1981).

3. R. de Vaux, *Les Sacrifices de l'Ancien Testament* (1964); cf. n. 42 below.

4. The basic meaning of θύειν is "to smoke." Concerning the ancients, Plutarch writes (following Theophrastus?) ταραττόμενοι καὶ δειμαίνοντες "ἔρδειν" μὲν ἐκάλουν καὶ "ῥέζειν," ὥς τι μέγα δρῶντες, τὸ θύειν ἔμψυχον, *Q. conv.* 729 f.; πονεῖσθαι *Il.* 2.409, cf. 1.318; *Hy. Merc.* 436. Likewise in Hebrew and Hittite, the verb *to do* is used in the sense of "to sacrifice"; cf. Casabona (1966) 301–4, who warns against generalizations.

5. E.g., Od. 4.759; Eur. El. 791 and J. D. Denniston's *Commentary* (1939), *ad loc.*; Poll. 1.25; Wächter (1910) 11–12; R. Ginouvès, ΒΑΛΑΝΕΥΤΙΚΗ; *Recherches sur le bain dans l'antiquité grecque* (1962), 299–318.

6. Xen. *Anab.* 7.1.40; Aeschines 3.77; etc.; J. Köchling, *De coronarum apud antiquos vi atque usu* (1913); K. Baus, *Der Kranz in Antike und Christentum* (1940); L. Deubner, *ARW* 30 (1933), 70–104; Blech (1982).

7. Fehrle (1910), esp. 155–8; for the Coan inscription on the sacrifice of a bull for Zeus Polieus see now *SIG*³ 1025 = LS 151 A 41–4.

8. E. Pfuhl, *De Atheniensium pompis sacris* (1910); Wilamowitz (1932) 350–4.

9. Od. 3.432–8. This survived in folk custom until modern times; see U. Jahn, *Die deutschen Opferbräuche bei Ackerbau und Viehzucht* (1884), 136–7, 315–17, on the proverbial "ox at Pentecost"; Megas (1956), 17. On the meaning of ἱερεῖον τέλειον see Arist. fr. 101; Plut. *De def. or.* 437a; Schol. A. Il. 1.66; Eust. 49.35.

10. θεηλάτου βοός δίκην Aesch. Ag. 1297; see Burkert (1966), 107 n. 43; Dio Chrys. Or. 12.51 (Olympia); Porph. *Abst.* 1.25 (Gadeira, Kyzikos); Plut. *Pel.* 22 (Leuktra); Apollon. *Mir.* 13 (Halikarnassos); Arist. *Mir. Ausc.* 844a35 (Pedasia); Philostr. *Her.* 8 p. 294(Rhesos), 17 p. 329 and Arr. *Peripl.* 22 (Leuke); Ael. *Nat. an.* 10.50 (Eryx), 11.4 (Hermione); especially for human sacrifice see Neanthes *FGrHist* 84 F 16 (Epimenides), Serv. *Aen.* 3.57 (Massalia), Paus. 4.9.4 (Messenia); Isaac, according to Hellenistic tradition, see Jos. *Ant. Jud.* 1.232; IV Macc. 13:12, 16:20. Cf. J. Schmitt, *Freiwilliger Opfertod bei Euripides* (1921).

11. J. Schelp, *Das Kanoun, der griechische Opferkorb* (1975); for reproductions see, e.g., Simon (1969), 193; Deubner (1932), pl. 11.1; Nilsson (1955), pl. 32.1.

12. E. g., Aristoph. *Pax* 956–8, Eur. *Iph. Aul.* 1568; Eitrem (1915) 7–29.

13. Aristoph. *Pax* 960; ὃ δ'ἑκούσιον ἂν κατανεύσῃ. . . Porph. *Abst.* 2.9 = Parke and Wormell (1958) II #537; Plut. Q. conv., 729 f., De def. or. 435b–c, 437a; Schol. Il. 1.449; Schol. Aristoph. *Pax* 960; Schol. Apoll. Rhod. 1.425; cf. Meuli (1946), 254, 266; J. G. Frazer, *Pausanias' Description of Greece*, 1898, on Paus. 10.5.7; Ginouvès, ΒΑΛΑΝΕΥΤΙΚΗ, 311–18.

14. Bull-sacrifice for dithyrambic victory: see, e.g., the Munich stamnos 2412 = *ARV²* 1036, 5 in Stengel (1920), pl. V.

15. A. W. H. Adkins, "Εὔχομαι, Εὐχωλή and Εὖχος in Homer," *CQ* 19 (1969), 20-33: "asserting his existence, his value, his claims" (33); this characteristic, a given in Homeric usage, conforms exactly to the position of prayer in the sacrificial ritual, although the prayer qua request can, as Oriental texts show, be far more elaborate.

16. Οὐλοχύτας ἀνέλοντο / προβάλοντο *Il.*, 1.449/458, 2.410/421, and cf. *Od.*, 3.447; χέρνιβα τ' οὐλοχύτας τε κατάρχεσθαι *Od.*, 3.445; cf. Aristoph., *Pax* 961-7. For οὐλαί as the most ancient grain see Theophrastus in Porph. *Abst.*, 2.6 and Schol. *Il.*, 1.449b; Schol., *Od.*, 3.441; *Suda* 0 907; Eust., 1859.48; as an expression of πολυπληθεία and εὐφορία see Schol. A, *Il.*, 1.449, Schol., *Od.*, 3.441. Ψηφῖσιν . . . ἀντί οὐλῶν χρώμενοι Paus., 1.41.9 (cf. III.4 below). For ritual stone-throwing around the altar of Poseidon at the Isthmian sanctuary see O. Broneer, *Hesperia* 28 (1959), 303. Cf. L. Ziehen, *Hermes* 37 (1902), 391–400; Stengel (1910), 13–33; Eitrem (1915) 261–308, who recognized the equivalence with φυλλοβολία and καταχύσματα; Burkert (1966) 107, n. 46.

17. Plat., Com. Fr. 91 (CAF I 626); Aristoph., *Pax* 948 with Schol.; Eur., *El.*, 810, *Iph. Aul.*, 1565; Philostr., *V. Ap.*, 1.1.

18. *Od.*, 3.446, 14.422; Eur., *Alc.*, 74-76, El., 811; Eitrem (1915), 344–72—who, however, erroneously makes the "beginning" into a "selbständige Opfergabe" (413).

19. Ἑλληνικὸν νόμισμα θυστάδος βοῆς Aesch., *Sept.*, 269; *Od.*, 3.450; Aesch., *Ag.*, 595,1118; Hdt. 4.189; L. Deubner, "ololyge und Verwandtes," *Abh. Berlin* (1941), 1.

20. Αἱμάσσειν τοὺς βωμούς Poll., 1.27; Porph., *Abst.*, 1.25; cf. Bacch., 11.111; Aesch., *Sept.*, 275. For vase-paintings see n. 2 above; ἀμνίον *Od.*, 3.444 (cf. Schol.) = σφαγεῖον Poll., 10.65. In place of the altar (βωμός), the hearth (ἑστία, ἐσχάρα) or sacrificial pit (βόθρος) can receive the blood; cf. II.2.n.18 below. Cf. Stengel (1910), 105–25.

21. Stengel (1910), 73–8; Meuli (1946), 246–72; συσπλαγχνεύειν Aristoph. *Pax* 1115; Eup. Fr. 108 (CAF I 286); Ath., 410b.

22. Galen *Plac. Hipp. et Plat.* 2.4 p. 238 K; cf. Cleanthes in Cic. *Nat. deor.* 2.24; *Suda* k 370 (*An. Bekk.* I 275.10; *Et. M.* 492.12); Hsch. καρδιοῦσθαι, καρδιουλκίαι, and cf. Luk., *Sacrif.*, 13; *LSS*, 121.7.

23. G. Blecher, *De extispicio capita tria* (1905); for Near Eastern tradition see J. Nougayrol, "Les rapports des haruspicines étrusque et assyro-babylonienne," *CRAI* (1955), 509–18.

24. Εὐθετίσας Hes., *Th.*, 541. Meuli (1946), 215–17 proved that the μηρία mentioned regularly in Homer are the thigh-bones; ὀστέα λευκά Hes., *Th.*, 540, 557. The comic poets normally mention ὀσφύς and gall; cf. Men., *Dysc.*, 451–2 and cf. Fr., 264, *Sam.*, 399–402; Eub., Fr., 95, 130 (CAF II, 197, 210); Com. Adesp., Fr. 1205 (*CAF*, III 606). Vase-paintings (see n. 2 above) portray the ὀσφύς and tail of the sacrificial animal on the altar; cf. Aristoph., *Pax*, 1054 with Schol.

25. Ὠμοθέτησαν *Il.*, 1.461, 2.424; Od. 3.458, 12.361, 14.427; Dion. Hal., *Ant.*, 7.72.17; Meuli (1946), 218, 256, 262.

26. Theophr., *Char.*, 21.7; Schol. Aristoph., *Plut.*, 943; Eitrem (1917), 34–48; Nilsson (1955), 88, 145. For the accumulation of goat-horns in the temple of

Apollo at Dreros see S. Marinatos, *BCH* 60 (1936), 224–5, 241–4. On the Keraton of Delos see Dikaiarchus fr. 85 W. = Plut. *Thes.*, 21; Callim., *Hy. Ap.*, 58–64; E. Bethe, *Hermes* 72 (1937), 191-94.

27. *Od.*, 3.459–60; καὶ ἐπιθύει ἀλφίτων ἡμίεκτον . . . *LS* 157 A, and cf. 151 A 20 ἐπιθύειν.

28. Often everything must be eaten on the spot (οὐ φορά): see Burkert (1966), 103 n. 36; *LSS* 88, 94.

29. Stengel (1920), 116–17; esp. IG II² 1496 τὸ περιγινόμενον ἀναλίσκειν εἰς ἀναθήματ[α *SIG*³ 1044, 47 = *LSAM* 72, 47; cf. *LSS* 61, 62–7, 23b4; *SIG*³ 982, 23–8; *LS* 69, 85. An exception: τὸ δέρμα ἁγίζετ[αι *LS* 151 D 16; LS 18 Γ 11 τὸ δέρμα καταγίζ(εται), Δ 11 δέρμα καταιγίζε(ται) meaning "is burned" (Sokolowski) or "is torn apart" (Hsch. καταιγίσας and αἰγίζει, *Suda* αι 44; G. Daux, *BCH* 87 [1963], 630)?

30. See note 24 above; A. Thomsen, "Der Trug des Prometheus," *ARW* 12 (1909), 460-90; J. Rudhardt, "Les mythes grecs relatifs à l'instauration du sacrifice," *MH* 27 (1970) 1–15. The basis of the criticism is the concept that τὸ θύειν δωρεῖσθαί ἐστιν τοῖς θεοῖς (Plat., *Euthyphr.*, 14c). Accordingly, tables were set up for the gods (τράπεζαι); σκέλος τὸπρᾶτο βοὸς παρθέντο τοι θιôι *IG* IV 914 = *SIG*³ 998 (Epidaurus, fifth century B.C.); cf. L. Ziehen, *RE* XVIII 615–16; S. Dow and D. H. Gill, "The Greek Cult Table," *AJA* 69 (1965), 103–14. Yet it is possible to slaughter a wild boar "for Zeus and Helios" and then throw the cadaver into the sea (*Il.*, 19.197/268 and cf. 3.104/310; for tortuous hypotheses to save the "offering" –interpretation see Stengel [1910], 19–23). Likewise in the Latin *mactare*, "glorify," the god's glory and exultation derive from the subjection of the *victima*.

31. ESP. Yasna 32.8, 12, 14 (G. Widengren, *Iranische Geisteswelt* [1961], 155; H. Humbach, *Die Gathas des Zarathustra* [1959], I 97–9). It is unclear, however, to what extent blood-sacrifice was rejected on principle, since it continued in practice: see M. Boyce, *JRAS* (1966), 110; G. Widengren, *Die Religionen Irans* (1963), 66, 92, 109.

32. Is. 1:11; cf. 66:3.

33. The Pythagorean tradition is divided, with ἐμψύχων ἀπέχεσθαι against δικαιότατον θύειν (Iambl. V. *Pyth.* 82). Cf. J. Haussleiter, *Der Vegetarismus in der Antike* (1935), 79–163; W. Burkert, *Lore and Science in Ancient Pythogoreanism* (1972), 180–3; Empedokles B 136–9.

34. Porph. Abst. 2.27; J. Bernays, *Theophrastos' Schrift über Frömmigkeit* (1866), 86, 116; W. Pötscher, *Theophrastos* Περὶ εὐσεβείας (1964), 174–5.

35. One way out was to posit inferior, more bloodthirsty demons: see Xenokrates fr. 23–5 Heinze.

36. *Dii veri neque desiderant ea neque deposcunt* Varro in Arnob. 7.1; *deum... non immolationibus nec sanguine multo colendum* Sen. fr. 123 = Lact. *Div. inst.* 6.25.3. Cf. Demonax in Luk. *Dem.* 11; the Sibyl in Clem. *Pr.* 4.62; (Just.) *Coh. ad. Gr.* 16.

37. With the exception of Passover celebrations; cf. J. Jeremias, *Die Passahfeier der Samaritaner* (1923); Th. H. Gaster, *Passover: Its History and Traditions* (1958).

38. Τὸ πάσχα ἡμῶν ἐτύθη Χριστός, I Cor. 5:7. For the rest, I refer the reader to H. D. Wendland and E. Kinder, *RGG*³ IV 1647–56. The Christian Jews still made Paul partake in a sacrifice in Jerusalem (Num. 6:13–21) and finance it; cf. Acts

21:23–6. On the other hand, "Petrus" (Clem. *Hom.* 2.44.2) declares that the sacrificial laws of the Old Testament are forgeries.

39. Megas (1956), 15, and cf. 17, 84, 87, 224. (The name of the sacrifice, γουρπάνι, comes from Islam: Arabic *qurbān*). For animal sacrifice to "Zeus" in Albania see Cook III (1940), 1168-71. See now G. N. Aikaterinides, Νεοελληνικὲς αἱματηρὲς θυσίες (Athens, 1979).

40. Theophrastus (Porph. *Abst.* 2 and cf. n. 34 above), in his study of the development of sacrifice, found it natural to include Egyptians, Syrians, Carthaginians, Etruscans, Thracians, and Scythians. The Tradition that the Cyprians invented sacrifice (Tatian. 1, pp. 1, 6 Schwartz) goes back to Asklepiades of Cyprus, *FGrHist* 752 F 1 = Neanthes, *FGrHist* 84 F 32 = Porph. *Abst.* 4.15.

41. The antithesis between Olympian and Chthonic cult is often regarded as fundamental (Rohde [1898], 148-52; Harrison [1922], 1-31; less schematically, Meuli [1946], 188–211, and cf. Nilsson [1955], 132–3). The antithesis between heavenly gods and gods of the underworld is frequently attested starting with Aeschylus (*Hik.*, 24, 154, *Ag.*, 89); a familiar distinction is that between ἐναγίζειν, "to make tabu," or ἐντέμνειν, "to slaughter into the sacrificial pit" for heroes and the dead, and θύειν (F. Pfister, *Der Reliquienkult im Altertum* II [1912], 466–80; Casabona [1966], 204–8, 225–9). On the different ways of slaughtering see Schol. Apoll. Rhod. 1.587, *Et. Gen.*, p. 115 M = *Et. M.*, 245: 24–6; H. v. Fritze, *JdI* 18 (1903), 58–67. Yet besides the sacrificial pits (βόθροι) there are different kinds of altars (βωμοί, ἐσχάραι, Porph., *Antr.* 6; Schol. Eur., *Phoen.*, 274; Serv., *Buc.*, 5.66; Yavis [1949], 91–5), and the complex of θυσίαι ἄγευστοι (Stengel [1910], 105) does not correspond to the realm of the chthonic: sacrificial meals are familiar to us from the cult of the θεοὶ χθόνιοι (Stengel [1910], 131–3), especially δεῖπνα from hero-cults (A. D. Nock, *HThR* 37 [1944], 141–66). Likewise, σφάγιον and θοίναμα do not mutually exclude each other: see Eur., *Or.*, 815. In the cult of the dead, the meal during which the dead man is offered blood (*Il.*, 23.29–34; αἱμακουρία, cf. I. 6 below) is juxtaposed to a rite of burning (*Il.*, 23.166–76). Burnt offerings alone are rare: They often function as a preliminary, e.g., *LS*, 151, A 29–36 (cf. burnt-offering/thank-offering in I Sam. 10:8, 13:9), just as a single sanctuary will often have both the grave of a hero and the altar of the god: i.e., we are dealing with an antithesis within the ritual, not with two fundamentally different and separate things. Cf. Burkert (1966), 103 n. 36. Likewise, in the Egyptian realm, sacrifice for the dead and that for gods have common roots: see W. Barta, *Die altägyptischen Opferlisten von der Frühzeit bis zur griech. –röm. Epoche* (1963), 153. On roasting/boiling see II.1.n.29.

42. R. K. Yerkes, *Sacrifice in Greek and Roman Religions and Early Judaism* (1952); R. Schmid, *Das Bundesopfer in Israel* (1964), therefore assumed that Israeli burnt-offering was a Mycenaean import via Ugarit (92), but cf. D. Gill, *Biblica* 47 (1966), 255-62: Homer's familiar μηρία καίειν is absent from Mycenaean.

43. Demonstrated by Yavis (1949); cf. K. Galling, *Der Altar in den Kulturen des Alten Orients* (1925). On Mesopotamia see G. Furlani, "Il sacrificio nella religione dei Semiti di Babilonia e Assiria," *Mem. Linc.* VI 4 (1932), 103-370; F. Blome, *Dei Opfermaterie in Babylon und Israel* (1934); Y. Rosengarten, *Le régime des offrandes dans la société sumérienne d'après les textes présargoniques de Lagas* (1960). On Egypt see H. Kees, "Bemerkungen zum Tieropfer der Ägypter und seiner Symbolik," *NGG* (1942), 71-88; Ph. Derchain, *Rites*

*égyptiens I: Le Sacrifice de l'oryx* (1962), concerning which cf. J. Zandee, *Bibl. Or.* 20 (1963), 251–3; W. Barta, *Die altägyptischen Opferlisten* (n.41 above). On Ugarit see B. Janowski, *Ugarit-Forschungen* 12 (1980), 231–59.

For a sacrificial list from Alalakh see D. J. Wiseman, *The Alalakh Tablets* (1953), 126. For a monumental altar for bull-sacrifice at Myrtou Pygades on Cyprus, including horn-symbols, a watering place for cattle, and bull statuettes (ca. 1700/1200 B.C.) see *AA* (1962), 338–9, fig. 84. For a depiction of bull-sacrifice at Pylos see *The Palace of Nestor II* (1969), pl. 119.

The "hearth-house," out of which the Greek temple developed, is a type known already in Helladic times: see H. Drerup, *Archaeologia Homerica* O (1969), 123–8. M. H. Jameson, *AJA* 62 (1958), 223, refers to sacrifice at the hearth in Mycenaean times. Open-air sites for burnt-offering—ash-altars consisting of piles of ashes and bones—are abundantly attested both for Greece (Nilsson [1955], 86–8; cf. II.1 below on Lykaion, II.2 on Olympia) and for bronze-age Europe (W. Krämer, "Prähistorische Brandopferplätze," in *Helvetia antiqua, Festschr. E. Vogt* [1966], 111–22). It does not seem possible at this time to organize various forms of sacrifice at the "hearth-house," the stone altar, and the ash-altar into a historical system.

44. *ANET*, 334–8. The main text is Seleucid; others were copied in the seventh century B.C. from older Babylonian models. They thereby attest to the survival of the ritual over the centuries. On the tympanon and the kalu-priest (= Sum. *galu*), who "laments" "in the language of the female," see E. Dhorme, *Les religions de Babylonie et d'Assyrie* (1949²), 207–9, 217.

45. *Enzyklopädie des Islam* II (1927), 208–13; *Encyclopédie de l'Islam* III (1965), 33-40 *s.v. HADJDJ*; ibid. for the proof that the basic elements of pilgrimage are pre-Islamic.

46. A sacrificial list from Uruk notes 50 rams, 2 bulls, 1 ox, and 8 lambs, among many others, as the daily sacrifice: *ANET*, 344. Croesus had 3,000 animals sacrificed at Delphi: Hdt. 1, 50; 154 cows were brought for a festival on Delos: *IG* II/III² 1635, 35. King Seleukos gave 1,000 ἱερεῖα (sheep) and 12 cows for a sacrifice at Didyma: *OGI* 214, 63.

47. See n. 2.

48. Corresponding to the special case of the initiation rite, as established by Harrison (1927), 15: παιδοτροφία–σπαραγμός–ἀναβίωσις.

49. Nilsson's "durchschlagender Einwand" (1955), 145 n. 2, "dass nur gezähmte Tiere, fast nie wilde geopfert werden," applies only to a problem of historical change (cf. I.5 below) and not to Meuli's basic argument. To be sure, the latter completely overlooked the Neolithic Near Eastern component by making an all-too-direct connection between the Indo-Germanic Greeks and the Eurasian hunters and herders. Against Meuli's allegedly magical interpretation, Müller-Karpe (1966) 227–8 proposes a religious one that proceeds from the experience of a "transcendental power"; but this is precisely what the ritual communicates, and any interpretation of it—even self-interpretation—is secondary (cf. I.3 below).

50. H. Kühn, "Das Problem des Urmonotheismus," *Abh. Mainz* (1950), 22, 17, whose interpretation follows P. W. Schmidt, *Der Ursprung der Gottesidee VI* (1935), 444–54, as well as A. Vorbichler, *Das Opfer auf den heute noch erreichbaren ältesten Stufen der Menschheitsgeschichte* (1956), and Müller-Karpe (1966) 228.

51. E. Bächler, *Das alpine Paläolithikum der Schweiz* (1940); Meuli (1946) 237–9. For additional finds in Central Franken, Silesia, and Siberia, see Müller-Karpe (1966), 226; in Hungary, see I. Trencsényi-Waldapfel, *Untersuchungen zur Religionsgeschichte* (1966), 19 n.17.

52. U. Holmberg, "Uber die Jagdriten der nördlichen Vøolker Asiens und Europas," *J. Société Finno-Ougrienne* 41 (1925). A. Gahs, "Kopf-, Schädel- und Langknochenopfer bei Rentiervölkern," *Festschr. P. W. Schmidt* (1928), 231–68; I. Paulson, "Die Tierknochen im Jagdritual der nordeurasischen Völker," " *Zeitschr. f. Ethnologie* 84 (1959), 270–93; I. Paulson, Å. Hultkrantz, and K. Jettmar, *Die Religionen Nordeurasiens und der amerikanischen Arktis* (1962).

53. A. I. Hallowell, "Bear Ceremonialism in the Northern Hemisphere, " *American Anthropologist* 28 (1926), 1–175; J. M. Kitigawa, "Ainu Bear Festival," *History of Religions* 1 (1961), 95–151; I. Paulson, "Die rituelle Erhebung des Bärenschädels bei arktischen und subarktischen Völkern," *Temenos* 1 (1965), 150–73.

54. Against Bächler's theory, see F. E. Koby, *L'Anthropologie* 55 (1951), 304–8; H. G. Bandi in *Helvetia antiqua* (1966), 1–8; cf. the discussion in J. Maringer, "Die Opfer der paläolithischen Menschen," in *Anthropica* (1968), 249–71; M. Eliade, *Histoire des croyances et des idées religieuses* I (1976), 23–7, 393f.

55. Müller-Karpe (1966), 225–6.

56. Jelisejevici: see Müller-Karpe (1966) 225.

57. *Corpus der minooischen und mykenischen Siegel*, eds. F. Matz and H. Biesantz, I (1964), #17; Nilsson (1955), pl. 17.1; Simon (1969), 181–3. Even if these were meant to represent animal-headed vessels (Simon), they are a further, symbolizing development of the ancient sacrificial structure (see IV.2.n.39).

58. Mellaart (1967), 140–1, 144–55, 181.

59. Müller-Karpe (1966), 224–5, pl. 199.45.

60. Müller-Karpe (1966), 205 pl. 107.1; A. Leroi-Gourhan, *Préhistoire de l'art occidentale* (1965), 313, figs. 646–7. For parallels from the Sudan see L. Frobenius, *Kulturgeschichte Afrikas* (1933), 83; from Abyssinia see A. Friedrich, *Paideuma* 2 (1941), 23–4; Meuli (1946), 241; cf. I. Paulson, *Temenos* 1 (1965), 160–1, on statues of bears as substitutes for actual dead ones, "the soul's residence."

61. W. R. Smith (1894) 306.2; πέτρη ἐπ᾿ ἠλιβάτῳ, *Hy. Merc.* 404, hence probably to be read 124 ἐπὶ (Cdd. ἐνὶ) πέτρῃ. In the myth, the skins apparently turned to stone, like the skin of Marsyas at Kelainai (Hdt., 7.26; Xen., *Anab.*, 1.2.8). The rite was no longer practiced; cf. I.1.n.29 above.

62. See Nilsson's objection, n. 1 above. On the interpretation of hunt and slaughter in Africa see Straube (1955), 199-204.

63. Müller-Karpe (1966), 225 (Gravettien).

64. Plat. Critias, 199d-e; H. Herter, *RhM* 109 (1966), 140–2.

65. For ταυροθηρία in Thessaly see *IG*, IX 2528, 531-37; *Arch. Deltion* 16 (1960), 185, *REG*, 77 (1964), 176; *AP*, 9.543; on this and on the ταυροκαθάψια in Asia Minor see L. Robert, *Les gladiateurs dans l'Orient grec* (1940), 318–19, who also treats the remaining κυνηγέσια and θηρομαχίαι (309-331). For a ἱερὸν κυνηγέσιον in Athens see *Hypoth. Dem.* 25.

66. Soph. fr. 25 P.; Callim. fr. 259-60; 264; Plut., *Thes.*, 14 following Philochoros, *FGrHist* 328, F 109; Paus., 1.27,10. For vase-paintings see Brommer (1960), 192–6.

67. On Sumerian wild bulls see Müller-Karpe (1968), II 338; on Çatal Hüyük see Mellaart (1967) 200–8, pl. 54-7, 61–4; cf. n. 9 above.

68. H. Kees, "Bemerkungen zum Tieropfer der Ägypter und seiner Symbolik," *NGG* (1942), 71–88.

69. Babrius 37 (μόσχος ἄφετος in antithesis to the plow-ox). For herds of Hera in Croton see Levy, 14.3.2, and cf. Nikomachos in Porph. V., *Pyth.*, 24, Iambl. V., *Pyth.*, 61. For the cattle of Argive Hera see III.2.n.25 below; for Διὸς βοῦς at Miletus see Hsch. *s.v.*; for a donkey sacrificed to the winds at Tarentum see Hsch. ἀνεμώτας; for the sheep of Helios at Apollonia/Epirus see Hdt. 9.93; for bulls of Dionysus at Kynaithos see Paus. 8.19.2; for sacred sheep, goats, cattle, and horses at Delphi see *OGI* 345, 15-19; for sacred sheep at Delos see *IG* II/III² 1639, 15; for cattle of "Herakles" in Spain see Diod., 4.18.3; for cattle of the "Meteres" in Sicily see Diod., 4.80.6; for "Persian Artemis'" (Anahita) herds on the Euphrates see Plut., *Luc.* 24; for τὰ θρέμματα τῆς θεοῦ at Kleitor see Polyb., 4.19.4; Scillus, Xen., *Anab.*, 5.3.9; for the herds of Persephone of Kyzikos see Plut., *Luc.*, 10. Cf. further, in myth, Apollo's cattle in Thessaly, *Hy. Merc.*, 70–2; and Helios' cattle, *Od.*, 12. For Atlantis see Plat., *Critias.*, 119d, and cf. *Prot.*, 320a, Aesch., *Prom.*, 666. Similarly, for the Indian Aśvamedha a horse is "set free": see W. Koppers, *Wiener Beitr. z. Kulturgeschichte* 4 (1936), 306.

70. Meuli (1946), 224–52; H. Baumann, "Nyama, die Rachemacht," *Paideuma* 4 (1950), 191–230. For a psychiatric perspective see R. Bilz, "Tiertöter-Skrupulantismus," *Jahrbuch f. Psychologie und Psychotherapie* 3 (1955), 226–44.

71. Morris (1967) 19–49, and cf. C. F. Hocket and R. Ascher, "The Human Revolution," *Current Anthropology* 5 (1964), 135–47, with discussion 148–68; A. Kortlandt, *Current Anthropology* 6 (1965), 320; La Barre (1970) 69–92; R. Ardrey, *The Hunting Hypothesis* (1976). Important points were anticipated by R. Eisler, *Man into Wolf* (1951). In the meantime, organized hunting, with sharing of meat, has been observed in chimpanzees: G. Teleki, *Scientific American* 228/1 (1973), 32–42, and cf. P. J. Wilson, *Man* n.s. 10 (1975), 5–20. Chimpanzees are more human that expected—cf. also A Kortlandt and M. Kooij, *Symp. Zool. Soc. London* 10 (1963), 61–88 —yet they do not use weapons and cannot attack big game.

72. Müller-Karpe (1966), 148; Burkert (1967), 283–7. See generally K. Lindner, *La Chasse préhistorique* (1950).

73. R. A. Dart, *Adventures with the Missing Link* (1950), 191–204; cf. 109–19, "The Antiquity of Murder."

74. Morris (1967), 37–9; La Barre (1970) 79–83. On the role of man as breadwinner see M. Mead, *Male and Female* (1949), 188–94.

75. On the "gesicherten Tatsache von Ritualtötungen" in Paleolithic times see Müller-Karpe (1966), 240 (Ofnet cave), 232–3 (Monte Circeo), 230 (Peking Man). Cannibalism is probable: see la Barre (1970), 404–6, 134 n.30; M. K. Roper, "A Survey of Evidence for Intrahuman Killing in the Pleistocene," *Current Anthropology* 10 (1969), 427–59.

76. A. Kortlandt, *Current Anthropology* 6 (1965), 323: "The evolution of the specifically human type of culture required the combination of the manual dexterity of an arboreal fruit eater with the long-term foresight and perseverance of a highly specialized carnivore." On the human tendency to submit to authority see Eibl-Eibesfeldt (1970), 120–3.

77. On the biological fact of imprinting see K. Lorenz, "Über tierisches und menschliches Verhalten," *Ges. Abh.* I (1965), 139–48, 270–1 (orig. 1935); E. H. Hess,

*Science* 130 (1959), 133–41, who makes the remarkable finding that "the administration of punishment or painful stimulation increases the effectiveness of the imprinting experience" (141) in contrast to the learning process. For the problem of applicability to man see H. Thomae, "Entwicklung und Prägung," *Hdb. D. Psychologie* III (1959), 240–311 (which, as it deals with secular man, ignores religious ritual).

78. Lorenz (1963), 40; Eibl-Eibesfeldt (1970), 7–8, with polemic against R. A. Dart (n. 25 above). On the other hand, La Barre (1970), 130, for instance, speaks of the obviously "necessary aggression of hunting."

79. Morris (1967), 50–102; putting some limitations on his theses, cf. Eibl-Eibesfeldt (1970) 149–87, esp. 170–2.

80. Lorenz (1963) 251–318, Eibl-Eibesfeldt (1970), 187–90.

81. Human and animal σπλάγχνα bore the same names from the earliest times, but whereas the animal's were well known from slaughter, human entrails became visible only in those wounded in war or during human sacrifice. Their visible presence was basic for the consciousness of one's own "subjectivity"—heart, diaphragm, and gall in Greek; liver and kidneys as well in other languages (cf. R. B. Onians, *Origins of European Thought* [1951], esp. 21–43 and 84–9).

82. Meuli (1946), 248–52, and cf. H. Baumann, *Paideuma* 4 (1950), 198, 200; Meuli (1967), 160.

83. For an animal substituted for a man see the story of Abraham and Isaac in Gen. 22:13; Iphigenia in Aulis, Apollod., *Epit.*, 3.22; virgin and goat at Munichia, Zen. Athous, 1.8, p. 350 Miller; Paus. Att., ε 35 Erbse; for Veiovis *immolatur ritu humano capra* Gell., 5.12.11. The reverse situation, that a man dies instead of a sacrificial animal, is a beloved motif in tragedy: see Burkert (1966), 116. Substitution, however, also occurs in ritual: see the βουθυσία instead of human sacrifice at Salamis/Cyprus, Porph., *Abst.*, 2.54; for the frequent substitution of child- and animal-sacrifice at Carthage see G. Charles-Picard, *Les réligions de l'Afrique antique* (1954), 491; for children designated as calves and sacrificed see Luk., *Syr., D.* 58; for a calf treated as a child and sacrificed see Ael., *Nat. an.*, 12.34 (Tenedos).

84. For folkloristic material see H. L. Strack, *Das Blut im Glauben und Aberglauben der Menschheit* (1900[7]); F. Rüsche, *Blut, Leben und Seele* (1930); J. H. Waszink, *RAC* II (1954), 459-73. For a psychological perspective on the shock caused by blood see G. Devereux, *Mohave Ethnopsychiatry and Suicide* (1961), 14, 42–5.

85. For man being created from the blood of a rebellious god see the Enuma Eliš] VI, *ANET,* 68, and cf. *ANET,* 100; for man's παλαιὰ Τιτανικὴ φύσις see Plat., *Leg.*, 701c, probably following the Orphic myth. Aratus, 130–4 links the transition to the Iron age, the flight of Dike, and the sacrifice of the plow-ox. Cf. W. R. Smith (1894), 306–8; B. Gatz, *Weltalter, goldene Zeit und sinnverwandte Vorstellungen* (1967), 165–71.

86. Cited by Meuli (1946), 226; Empedokles, B 124.2 in Porph., *Abst.*, 3.27 (ἔκ τε νεικέων Porph., ἔκ τε στοναχῶν Diels, following the parallel tradition). Plut. *Conv. sept. sap.* 159c-d: ᾧ δ'ἄνευ κακώσεως ἑτέρου τὴν αὑτοῦ σωτηρίαν ἀμήχανον ὁ θεὸς πεποίηκε, τούτῳ τὴν φύσιν ἀρχὴν ἀδικίας προσέθεικεν. A. E. Jensen's treatment, "Über das Töten als kulturgeschichtliche Erscheinung," *Paideuma* 4 (1950), 23–8 = *Mythos und Kult bei Naturvölkern* [1951], 197–229, is fundamental and rich in source material. His thesis that this is an expression of

man's basic realization that he is dependent on organic food can be made more specific from an historical perspective: it is the ideology of the hunter, still maintained in the planter's culture. Cf. Straube (1955) 200–4.

87. *Et nos servasti* [ . . . ] *sanguine fuso*: inscription in the Mithraeum of Santa Prisca, Rome: M. J. Vermaseren and C. C. van Essen, *The Excavations in the Mithraeum of the Church of Santa Prisca in Rome* (1965), 217–20. In the lacuna, *eternali* had been read, but this cannot have been there: S. Panciera in U. Bianchi, ed., *Mysteria Mithrae* (1979), 103ff.

88. Sir Julian Huxley, *Proc. Zool. Soc.* (1914), 511–15 on "ceremonies" of the Great Crested Grebe; Lorenz (1963), 89–127; "A Discussion on Ritualization of Behavior in Animals and Man," *Philos. Trans. Roy. Soc. London* B251 (1966), 247–526, with articles by Huxley, Lorenz, and others; Eibl-Eibesfeldt (1970), 60–70; P. Weidkuhn, *Aggressivität, Ritus, Säkularisierung* (1965). In defining ritual as "action re-done or pre-done," J. Harrison (*Epilegomena to the Study of Greek Religion* [1921], xliii) recognized the displacement of behavior but not the communicatory function. Now E. R. Leach, for example, finds that "communicative behavior" and "magical behavior" in ritual are not basically different (*Philos. Trans. Roy. Soc. London* B251 [1966], 403–4).

89. Lorenz (1963), 268–70; cautiously, Eibl-Eibesfeldt (1970), 197.

90. Burkert (1979), 39–45. On drumming see Eibl-Eibesfeldt (1970), 40; on phallic display see 1.7 below; on the outstretched hand see Eibl-Eibesfeldt (1970), 204–5; Morris (1967) 157, 166.

91. On the socially learned behavior of the primate see, for instance, L. Rosenkötter, *Frankfurter Hefte* 21 (1966), 523–33, and cf. I.1.n. 1 above.

92. E. Durkheim, *Les Formes élémentaires de la vie religieuse* (1912; 1960⁴), 598: "c'est par l'action commune qu'elle [sc. la société] prend conscience de soi"; 610: "entretenir et raffermir, à intervalles réguliers, les sentiments collectifs et les idées collectives qui font son unité et sa personnalité."

93. A. R. Radcliffe-Brown, *The Andaman Islanders* (1933²), 234.

94. For the term see F. W. Young, *Initiation Ceremonies: A Cross-Cultural Study of Status Dramatization* (1965).

95. It is sufficient to refer to La Barre's comprehensive treatment (1970). See S. Freud, "Zwangshandlungen und Religionsübungen," *Ges. Schr.* 10 (1924), 210–20 = *Ges. Werke* 7 (1941), 129–39.

96. So already O. Gruppe, *RML* Suppl., "Geschichte der klassischen Mythologie und Religionsgeschichte" (1921), 243. Group selection is not accepted by the modern theory of evolution—see R. Dawkins, *The Selfish Gene* (1976)—but it is still granted that "a grudger's strategy" is "evolutionarily stable": ibid. 199-201.

97. Philostr., *V. Ap.*, 4.20. On the *Teufelspeitsche* see A. Jacoby, *Schweiz. Archiv. f. Volkskunde* 28 (1928), 81-105. Cf. the story of the "witch's child" in Gottfried Keller's *Der grüne Heinrich* (1854), I, ch. 5.

98. For instance, Mannhardt (1875), 603 states his conclusion as follows: "Als Überlebsel der Primitivisten Entwickelungszustände des menschlichen Geistes hat sich . . . die Vorstellung von der Gleichartigkeit des Menschen und des Baumes gerettet. Die Überyeugung 'der Baum hat eine Seele wie der Mensch,' und der Wunsch zu Wachsen und zu blühen wie ein Baum, sind . . . die Eltern eines weitverzweigten Glaubens und mannigfacher Gebräuche gewesen"; that is, the conception and wish give rise to the custom. W. R. Smith speaks of the ideas

expressed in the ritual tradition, "Ideen, die im traditionellen Ritual zum Ausdruck kommen" ([1894], 20, etc.) and of the fundamental idea of the conception grasped in the ritual (439). H. Usener (*Götternamen* [1895, 1948³], 330) sought behind the varying names "eine Geschichte der Vorstellungen" as the building blocks of an "Entwicklungsgeschichte des menschlichen Geistes."

99. E. g., Nilsson (1955), 2: "Es gibt Glaubenssätze . . . aus ihnen entspriessen . . . die religiösen Handlungen"; we are obliged "die allgemeinen Vorstellungen zuerst auf Grund der religiösen Handlungen herauszuarbeiten."

100. H. Usener, *Vorträge und Aufsätze* (1907), 42, for instance, spoke of "religiöser Empfindung" which finds expression "in Vorstellungen und in Handlungen." Likewise, Meuli looks to "den natürlichen, spontanen Ausdruck," "die lebendige Empfindung" as the "Grundlage," "Vorbild" and "Formgeber" of the custom ([1946], 202, and cf. 250; *Schweiz. Archiv f. Volkskunde* 43 [1946], 91–109, in which, however, he is fully aware of the rite's demonstrative character).

101. C. Lévi-Strauss, *Le totémisme aujourd'hui* (1962), 102f.

102. A. I. Hallowell, *American Anthropologist* 28 (1926), 19. M. Mead, *Male and Female* (1949), 61, stresses that even childhood experiences bear the stamp of the adult world, "a process of transmission, not of creation."

103. Cf. Preface n. 7.

104. Plat. *Leg.* 887d.

105. There is the thesis that Neanderthal man could not yet produce articulate speech in our form due to his physiology. See Ph. Lieberman, "On the Evolution of Human Language," *Proc. Seventh Int. Congr. Phonetic Sciences* (Leiden, 1972), 258–72; see also Ph. Lieberman, E. S. Crelin, and D. H. Klatt, *American Anthropologist* 74 (1972), 287–307; "Origins and Evolution of Language and Speech," *Annals New York Acad. Sciences* 280 (1976). Yet there was hunting, cannibalism, and burial—but no pictorial art—in the Lower Paleolithic: this points to a human society based on ritual before the final evolution of language. Lieberman's thesis, though, is controversial.

# 14

# RENÉ GIRARD (b. 1923)

Cultural theorist and literary critic René Girard was born in Avignon, France. He studied Medieval history at the Ecole de Chartres in Paris, but in 1947 he entered Indiana University in the United States, later earning his Ph.D. there in 1950. He began a long career of teaching literature at a number of American institutions, including Duke University, Bryn Mawr College, the State University of New York at Buffalo, and Johns Hopkins University. In 1981, he received an appointment to teach French Language, Literature, and Civilization at Stanford University, where he remained until his retirement in 1995. Girard's research and writing focus on the insights comparative literature provide for the understanding of religion and culture. In his first major work, *Deceit, Desire and the Novel: Self and Other in Literary Structure* (1965, originally in French, *Mensonge romantique et vérité romanesque*, 1961) he examined several great romantic novels and discovered a surprising pattern of human relations he later called "mimetic desire." Turning from this literary project to the anthropology of religion, Girard wrote his most famous and controversial book, *Violence and the Sacred* (1972, 1977), in which he developed several new important concepts in his thought: the broad significance of violence, and the "scapegoat mechanism." Employing these concepts, he then focused his attention on Biblical literature and wrote *Things Hidden since the Foundation of the World* (1978, 1987), an account of how Christianity undermines the scapegoat mechanism, but also offers a different solution to cycles of violence. Girard's work has generated a substantial following of supporters, and his ideas are still discussed regularly in a journal (with the title, *Contagion*) devoted to his ideas. Historians of religions, anthropologists, critical theorists, literary critics and others have found his thinking inspiring, even as others have rejected it.

Girard's book *Violence and the Sacred* develops a bold theory of religion built around a theory of sacrifice. Drawing upon psychological contents and social facts, he presents a psychosocial explanation for what he describes as the "violence" of religion. Ultimately, much like Burkert's *Homo Necans* (which was published in the same year), Girard argues that all religious phenomena have their origin in sacrificial activity, that understanding the nature and origin of sacrifice will provide an explanation of religion as well. The violence associated with ritual killing is the key to the origin of the sacred.

Girard begins with the notion of desire and a crucial observation that beyond an individual's intrinsic needs, desire is often "mimetic" in the context of a group. A person may want something, in other words, simply because another person values or possesses it, whether it be a tangible object or intangible character trait. Rivalry is inevitable with "mimetic desire," however, for as one person desires what another has, even to the point of wanting to *be* that other, there is resistance, perhaps anger. This is an unstable tension, a "monstrous double" Girard calls it, of both admiration and rejection. It is a tension that cannot be sustained and therefore leads to violence, the individual simply "taking" what he or she desires against the will of the rival. Now though, the roles are reversed and mimetic desire generates an arena of vengeance, which if unchecked escalates, feeding back upon itself, and leads to the murder of one of the parties. Here too, because revenge is possible, a cycle of uncontrolled killing will spread along lines of allegiance throughout the group, and threaten to destroy the fabric of society. This psychological phenomenon, for Girard, is an undeniable fact.

Societies, Girard continues, have discovered a means to end the cycle of violence caused by mimetic desire. They have discovered the "mechanism of the surrogate-victim," the practice of transferring the interior violence of the group (social chaos, sense of sin, evil, impurity) to a surrogate, a scapegoat, who can be expelled from (i.e., killed by) the community. This scapegoat, Girard notes, must be unable to retaliate and thereby extend the cycle of violence; it must be somewhat marginalized from the group, not fully a member but not completely foreign either. Domesticated animals, non-human community members, are ideal victims. Active in this mechanism is a "mob mentality," one that blames some innocent figure for social evil and that believes salvation (the return of stability and order) will come from eliminating that figure. By virtue of an unconscious process, "bad violence" threatening the very order of society is removed with an act of "good violence." Curiously, Girard continues, when the mechanism of the surrogate victim works, and the community is essentially saved from itself, members may look back and understand the victim as a savior. Whoever was at first worthy of blame is later remembered as beneficent, as the being who helped (perhaps even voluntarily—choosing to die) the community overcome a dangerous crisis. Being the locus of both good and bad violence, the victim acquires an air of mystery, of awesome power, potentially dangerous but generous, transcendent but nearby—all characteristics, in short, of the sacred. Girard concludes, the surrogate victim becomes, for the community, a divine being, a power to be worshipped, a founding ancestor who continues to protect and provide, bless and punish.

Girard claims this scapegoat mechanism accounts for the origin of religion. Very simply, religion arose when a group first discovered the means to deflect its own internal violence onto an innocent victim, when it chose, that is, to sacrifice a surrogate to restore social harmony. The original religious act was a sacrifice, a collective response to the violence generated by mimetic desire. All subsequent sacrifices, these acts of "good violence," simply repeat this mechanism in response to every new "sacrificial crisis," to moments of social chaos (any "loss of distinctions"), or situations of actual communal violence. Such crises arise repeatedly because the impulses of mimetic desire are relentless. There will always be a need to address aggressions, jealosy, disorder, (and later) guilt, and thus there will always be a need for ritual. Indeed, religious myths and rituals, according to Girard, are "recollections" of the scapegoat mechanism, each driven by a constant need to insure the proper control over, the right "distance" from, violence. A group's myths and rituals (beliefs and practices) function to maintain for its members a proper relationship with the sacred (violence), with what can destroy them, but also saves them. Later in the development process, societies may suddenly become conscious of the scapegoat mechanism and it will fail (Biblical literature demonstrates this process, Girard claims, with Christianity finally exposing the "truth" of scapegoating). Modern secular societies are left with their judicial systems to protect against the violent conse-quences of the mimetic impulse.

Girard claims that the "whole of human culture" is unified by this single psy-chosocial mechanism. With such a sweeping theory, it is no wonder that he has attracted both devoted followers and highly vocal critics. In terms of sacrifice theory, Girard offers a "scapegoat theory," a version of a "substitution" theory—the victim accepting the violence that members of society would otherwise inflict upon each other. Identifying the nature (the content and context) of this substitution, empha-sizing the notion of violence, and demonstrating how it impacts other aspects of culture, is Girard's major contribution to studies of sacrifice.

Reprinted below is the first chapter of Girard's *Violence and the Sacred*. It presents his initial thoughts on sacrifice, his definition of sacrifice, and the significance of violence for religions generally.

mimetic : stimulating the action or effect of.

# From *Violence and the Sacred*

IN MANY RITUALS the sacrificial act assumes two opposing aspects, appearing at times as a sacred obligation to be neglected at grave peril, at other times as a sort of criminal activity entailing perils of equal gravity.

To account for this dual aspect of ritual sacrifice—the legitimate and the illegitimate, the public and the all but covert—Henri Hubert and Marcel Mauss, in their "Essay on the Nature of Function of Sacrifice,"[1] adduce the sacred character of the victim. Because the victim is sacred, it is criminal to kill him— but the victim is sacred only because he is to be killed. Here is a circular line of reasoning that at a somewhat later date would be dignified by the sonorous term *ambivalence*. Persuasive and authoritative as that term still appears, it has been so extraordinarily abused in our century that perhaps we may now recognize how little light it sheds on the subject of sacrifice. Certainly it provides no real explanation. When we speak of ambivalence, we are only pointing out a problem that remains to be solved.

If sacrifice resembles criminal violence, we may say that there is, inversely, hardly any form of violence that cannot be described in terms of sacrifice—as Greek tragedy clearly reveals. It has often been observed that the tragic poets cast a glimmering veil of rhetoric over the sordid realities of life. True enough— but sacrifice and murder would not lend themselves to this game of reciprocal substitution if they were not in some way related. Although it is so obvious that it may hardly seem worth mentioning, where sacrifice is concerned first appearances count for little, are quickly brushed aside—and should therefore receive special attention. Once one has made up one's mind that sacrifice is an institution essentially if not entirely symbolic, one can say anything whatsoever about it. It is a subject that lends itself to insubstantial theorizing.

Sacrifice contains an element of mystery. And if the pieties of classical humanists lull our curiosity to sleep, the company of the ancient authors keeps it alert. The ancient mystery remains as impenetrable as ever. From the manner in which the moderns treat the subject of sacrifice, it would be hard to know whether distraction, detachment, or some sort of secret discretion shapes their thinking. There seems to be yet another mystery here. Why, for example, do we never explore the relationship between sacrifice and violence?

Recent studies suggest that the physiology of violence varies little from one individual to another, even from one culture to another. According to Anthony Storr, nothing resembles an angry cat or man so much as another angry cat or man.[2] If violence did indeed play a role in sacrifice, at least at one particular stage of the ritual, we would have a significant clue to the whole subject. Here would be a factor to some extent independent of those

René Girard, *Violence and the Sacred*, pp. 1–38. © 1977. The Johns Hopkins University Press. Reprinted with the permission of The Johns Hopkins University Press and the Athlone Press Ltd.

cultural variables that are often unknown to us, or only dimly known, or perhaps less familiar than we like to think.

Once aroused, the urge to violence triggers certain physical changes that prepare men's bodies for battle. This set toward violence lingers on; it should not be regarded as a simple reflex that ceases with the removal of the initial stimulus. Storr remarks that it is more difficult to quell an impulse toward violence than to rouse it, especially within the normal framework of social behavior.

Violence is frequently called irrational. It has its reasons, however, and can marshal some rather convincing ones when the need arises. Yet these reasons cannot be taken seriously, no matter how valid they may appear. Violence itself will discard them if the initial object remains persistently out of reach and continues to provoke hostility. When unappeased, violence seeks and always finds a surrogate victim. The creature that excited its fury is abruptly replaced by another, chosen only because it is vulnerable and close at hand.

There are many indications that this tendency to seek out surrogate objects is not limited to human violence. Konrad Lorenz makes reference to a species of fish that, if deprived of its natural enemies (the male rivals with whom it habitually disputes territorial rights), turns its aggression against the members of its own family and destroys them.[3] Joseph de Maistre discusses the choice of animal victims that display human characteristics—an attempt, as it were, to deceive the violent impulse: "The sacrificial animals were always those most prized for their usefulness: the gentlest, most innocent creatures, whose habits and instincts brought them most closely into harmony with man . . . From the animal realm were chosen as victims those who were, if we might use the phrase, the most *human* in nature."[4]

Modern ethnology offers many examples of this sort of intuitive behavior. In some pastoral communities where sacrifice is practiced, the cattle are intimately associated with the daily life of the inhabitants. Two peoples of the Upper Nile, for example—the Nuers, observed by E. E. Evans-Pritchard, and the Dinka, studied at a somewhat later date by Godfrey Lienhardt—maintain a bovine society in their midst that parallels their own and is structured in the same fashion.[5]

The Nuer vocabulary is rich in words describing the ways of cattle and covering the economic and practical, as well as the poetic and ritualistic, aspects of these beasts. This wealth of expression makes possible a precise and finely nuanced relationship between the cattle, on the one hand, and the human community on the other. The animals' color, the shape of their horns, their age, sex, and lineage are all duly noted and remembered, sometimes as far back as five generations. The cattle are thereby differentiated in such a way as to create a scale of values that approximates human distinctions and represents a virtual duplicate of human society. Among the names bestowed on each man is one that also belongs to the animal whose place in the herd is most similar to the place the man occupies in the tribe.

The quarrels between various subgroups of the tribes frequently involve cattle. All fines and interest payments are computed in terms of head of cattle, and dowries are apportioned in herds. In fact, Evans-Pritchard maintains that in order to understand the Nuer, one must *"chercher la vache"*—"look to the cows." A sort of "symbiosis" (the term is also Evans-Pritchard's) exists between this tribe and their cattle, offering an extreme and almost grotesque example of the closeness that characteristically prevails between pastoral peoples and their flocks.

Fieldwork and subsequent theoretical speculation lead us back to the hypothesis of substitution as the basis for the practice of sacrifice. This notion pervades ancient literature on the subject—which may be one reason, in fact, why many modern theorists reject the concept out of hand or give it only scant attention. Hubert and Mauss, for instance, view the idea with suspicion, undoubtedly because they feel that it introduces into the discussion religious and moral values that are incompatible with true scientific inquiry. And to be sure, Joseph de Maistre takes the view that the ritual victim is an "innocent" creature who pays a debt for the "guilty" party. I propose an hypothesis that does away with this moral distinction. As I see it, the relationship between the potential victim and the actual victim cannot be defined in terms of innocence or guilt. There is no question of "expiation." Rather, society is seeking to deflect upon a relatively indifferent victim, a "sacrificeable" victim, the violence that would otherwise be vented on its own members, the people it most desires to protect.

The qualities that lend violence its particular terror—its blind brutality, the fundamental absurdity of its manifestations—have a reverse side. With these qualities goes the strange propensity to seize upon surrogate victims, to actually conspire with the enemy and at the right moment toss him a morsel that will serve to satisfy his raging hunger. The fairy tales of childhood in which the wolf, ogre, or dragon gobbles up a large stone in place of a small child could well be said to have a sacrificial cast.

Violence is not to be denied, but it can be diverted to another object, something it can sink its teeth into. Such, perhaps, is one of the meanings of the story of Cain and Abel. The Bible offers us no background on the two brothers except the bare fact that Cain is a tiller of the soil who gives the fruits of his labor to God, whereas Abel is a shepherd who regularly sacrifices the first-born of his herds. One of the brothers kills the other, and the murderer is the one who does not have the violence-outlet of animal sacrifice at his disposal. This difference between sacrificial and nonsacrificial cults determines, in effect, God's judgment in favor of Abel. To say that God accedes to Abel's sacrificial offerings but rejects the offerings of Cain is simply another way of saying—from the viewpoint of the divinity—that Cain is a murderer, whereas his brother is not.

A frequent motif in the Old Testament, as well as in Greek myth, is that of brothers at odds with one another. Their fatal penchant for violence can only be diverted by the intervention of a third party, the sacrificial victim or victims.

Cain's "jealousy" of his brother is only another term for his one characteristic trait: his lack of a sacrificial outlet.

According to Moslem tradition, God delivered to Abraham the ram previously sacrificed by Abel. This ram was to take the place of Abraham's son Isaac; having already saved one human life, the same animal would now save another. What we have here is no mystical hocus-pocus, but an intuitive insight into the essential function of sacrifice, gleaned exclusively from the scant references in the Bible.

Another familiar biblical scene takes on new meaning in the light of our theory of sacrificial substitution, and it can serve in turn to illuminate some aspects of the theory. The scene is that in which Jacob receives the blessing of his father Isaac.

Isaac is an old man. He senses the approach of death and summons his eldest son, Esau, on whom he intends to bestow his final blessing. First, however, he instructs Esau to bring back some venison from the hunt, so as to make a "savory meat." This request is overheard by the younger brother, Jacob, who hastens to report it to his mother, Rebekah. Rebekah takes two kids from the family flock, slaughters them, and prepares the savory meat dish, which Jacob, in the guise of his elder brother, then presents to his father.

Isaac is blind. Nevertheless Jacob fears he will be recognized, for he is a "smooth man," while his brother Esau is a "hairy man." "My father peradventure will feel me, and I shall seem to him as a deceiver; and I shall bring a curse upon me, not a blessing." Rebekah has the idea of covering Jacob's hands and the back of his neck with the skins of the slaughtered goats, and when the old man runs his hands over his younger son, he is completely taken in by the imposture. Jacob receives the blessing that Isaac had intended for Esau.

The kids serve in two different ways to dupe the father—or, in other terms, to divert from the son the violence directed toward him. In order to receive his father's blessing rather than his curse, Jacob must present to Isaac the freshly slaughtered kids make into a "savory meat." Then the son must seek refuge, literally, in the skins of the sacrificed animals. The animals thus interpose themselves between father and son. They serve as sort of insulation, preventing the direct contact that could lead only to violence.

Two sorts of substitution are telescoped here: that of one brother for another, and that of an animal for a man. Only the first receives explicit recognition in the text: however, this first one serves as the screen upon which the shadow of the second is projected.

Once we have focused attention on the sacrificial victim, the object originally singled out for violence fades from view. Sacrificial substitution implies a degree of misunderstanding. Its vitality as an institution depends on its ability to conceal the displacement upon which the rite is based. It must never lose sight entirely, however, of the original object, or cease to be aware of the act of transference from that object to the surrogate victim; without that awareness no substitution can take place and the sacrifice loses all efficacy. The biblical passage discussed above meets both requirements. The narrative does not refer directly to the strange deception underlying the sacrificial substitution, nor does it allow this deception to pass entirely unnoticed. Rather, it mixes the act of substitution with another act of substitution, permitting us a fleeting, sidelong glimpse of the process. The narrative itself, then, might be said to partake of a sacrificial quality; it claims to reveal one act of substitution while employing this first substitution to half-conceal another. There is reason to believe that the narrative touches upon the mythic origins of the sacrificial system.

The figure of Jacob has long been linked with the devious character of sacrificial violence. In Greek culture Odysseus plays a similar role. The story of Jacob's benediction can be compared to the episode of the Cyclops in the *Odyssey*, where a splendidly executed ruse enables the hero to escape the clutches of a monster. *deceptive maneuver*

Odysseus and his shipmates are shut up in the Cyclops' cave. Every day the giant devours one of the crew; the survivors finally manage to blind their tormentor with a flaming stake. Mad with pain and anger, the Cyclops bars the entrance of the cave to prevent the men from escaping. However, he lets pass his flock of sheep, which go out daily to pasture. In a gesture reminiscent of the blind Isaac, the Cyclops runs his hands over the back of each sheep as it leaves the cave to make sure that it carries no passenger. Odysseus, however, has outwitted his captor, and he rides to freedom by clinging to the thick wool on the underside of one of the rams.

A comparison of the two scenes, one from Genesis and the other from the *Odyssey*, lends credence to the theory of their sacrificial origins. In each case an animal intervenes at the crucial moment to prevent violence from attaining its designated victim. The two texts are mutually revealing: the Cyclops of the *Odyssey* underlines the fearful menace that hangs over the hero (and that remains obscure in the Genesis story); and the slaughter of the kids in Genesis, along with the offering of the "savory meat," clearly implies the sacrificial character of the flock, an aspect that might go unnoticed in the *Odyssey*.

Sacrifice has often been described as an act of mediation between a sacrificer and a "deity." Because the very concept of a deity, much less a deity who receives blood sacrifices, has little reality in this day and age, the entire institution of sacrifice is relegated by most modern theorists to the realm of the imagination. The approach of Hubert and Mauss leads to the judgment of Claude Lévi-Strauss in *La Pensée sauvage*: because sacrificial rites have no basis in reality, we have every reason to label them meaningless.

The attempt to link sacrifice to a nonexistent deity brings to mind Paul Valéry's description of poetry as a purely solipsistic activity practiced by the more able solely out of love for art, while the less able persist in the belief that they are actually communicating with someone!

The two ancient narratives examined above make unmistakable reference to the act of sacrifice, but neither makes so much as a passing mention of a deity. If a god had intervened in either incident, its significance would have been diminished rather than increased, and the reader would have been led to conclude, in accordance with the beliefs common to late antiquity and to the modern world, that sacrifice has no real function in society. Divine intervention would have meant the elimination of the pervasive aura of dread, along with its firmly structured economy of violence. We would have then been thrown back upon a formalistic critical approach that would in no way further our understanding.

As we have seen, the sacrificial process requires a certain degree of *misunderstanding*. The celebrants do not and must not comprehend the true role of the sacrificial act. The theological basis of the sacrifice has a crucial role in fostering this misunderstanding. It is the god who supposedly demands the victims; he alone, in principle, who savors the smoke from the altars and requisitions the slaughtered flesh. It is to appease his anger that the killing goes on, that the victims multiply. Interpreters who think they question the primacy of the divine sufficiently by declaring the whole affair "imaginary" may well remain the prisoners of the theology they have not really analyzed. The problem then becomes, how can a real institution be constructed on a purely illusory basis? It is not to be wondered at if the outer shell finally gives way, bringing down with it even the most solid aspects of the institution.

Instead of rejecting the theological basis outright, qua abstraction (which is the same, in effect, as passively accepting it), let us expose its assumptions to a critical examination. Let us try to uncover the societal conflicts that the sacrificial act and its theological interpretations at once dissimulate and appease. We must break with the formalistic tradition of Hubert and Mauss.

The interpretation of sacrifice as an act of violence inflicted on a surrogate victim has recently been advanced once again. Godfrey Lienhardt (in *Divinity and Experience*) and Victor Turner (in a number of works, especially *The Drums of Affliction*), drawing from fieldwork, portray sacrifice as practiced among the Dinka and the Ndembu as a deliberate act of collective substitution performed at the expense of the victim and absorbing all the internal tensions, feuds, and rivalries pent up within the community.

Sacrifice plays a very real role in these societies, and the problem of substitution concerns the entire community. The victim is not a substitute for some particularly endangered individual, nor is it offered up to some individual of particularly bloodthirsty temperament. Rather, it is a substitute for all the members of the community, offered up by the members themselves. The sacrifice serves to protect the entire community from *its own* violence; it prompts the entire community to choose victims outside itself. The elements of dissension scattered throughout the community are drawn to the person of the sacrificial victim and eliminated, at least temporarily, by its sacrifice.

If we turn our attention from the theological superstructure of the act—that is, from an interpretive version of the event that is often accepted as the final statement on sacrifice—we quickly perceive yet another level of religious discourse, in theory subordinated to the theological dimension, but in reality quite independent of it. This has to do with the social function of the act, an aspect far more accessible to the modern mind.

It is easy to ridicule a religion by concentrating on its more eccentric rites, rites such as the sacrifices performed to induce rain or bring fine weather. There is in fact no object or endeavor in whose name a sacrifice cannot be made, especially when the social basis of the act has begun to blur. Nevertheless, there is a common denominator that determines the efficacy of all sacrifices and that becomes increasingly apparent as the institution grows in vigor. This common denominator is internal violence—all the dissensions, rivalries, jealousies, and quarrels within the community that the sacrifices are designed to suppress. The purpose of the sacrifice is to restore harmony to the community, to reinforce the social fabric. Everything else derives from that. If once we take this fundamental approach to sacrifice, choosing the road that violence opens before us, we can see that there is no aspect of human existence foreign to the subject, not even material prosperity. When men no longer live in harmony with one another, the sun still shines and the rain falls, to be sure, but the fields are less well tended, the harvests less abundant.

The classic literature of China explicitly acknowledges the propitiatory function of sacrificial rites. Such practices "pacify the country and make the people settled...It is through the sacrifices that the unity of the people is strengthened" (CH'U YU II, 2). The *Book of Rites* affirms that sacrificial ceremonies, music, punishments, and laws have one and the same end: to unite society and establish order.[6]

In attempting to formulate the fundamental principles of sacrifice without reference to the ritualistic framework in which the sacrifice takes place, we run the risk of appearing simplistic. Such an effort smacks strongly of "psychologizing." Clearly, it would be inexact to compare the sacrificial act to the spontaneous gesture of the man who kicks his dog because he dares not kick his wife or boss. However, there are Greek myths that are hardly more than colossal variants of such gestures. Such a one is the story of Ajax. Furious at the leaders of the Greek army, who refused to award him Achilles' weapons, Ajax slaughters the herd of sheep intended as provisions for the army. In his mad rage he mistakes these gentle creatures for the warriors on whom he means to vent his rage. The slaughtered animals belong to a species traditionally utilized by the Greeks for sacrificial purposes; but because the massacre takes place outside the ritual framework, Ajax is taken for a madman. The myth is not, strictly speaking, about the sacrificial process; but it is certainly not irrelevant to it. The institution of sacrifice is based on effects analogous to those produced by Ajax's anger—but structured, channeled and held in check by fixed laws.

In the ritualistic societies most familiar to us—those of the Jews and of the Greeks of the classical age—the sacrificial victims are almost always animals. However, there are other societies in which human victims are substituted for the individuals who are threatened by violence.

Even in fifth century Greece—the Athens of the great tragedians—human sacrifice had not, it seems, completely disappeared. The practice was perpetuated in the form of the pharmakos, maintained by the city at its own expense and slaughtered at the appointed festivals as well as at a moment of civic disaster. If examined closely for traces of human sacrifice, Greek tragedy offers some remarkable revelations. It is clear, for example, that the story of Medea parallels that of Ajax on the sacrificial level, although here we are dealing with human rather than with animal sacrifice. In Euripides' *Medea* the principle of human substitution of one victim for another appears in its most savage form. Frightened by the intensity of Medea's rage against her faithless husband, Jason, the nurse begs the children's tutor to keep his charges out of their mother's way:

> I am sure her anger will not subside until it has found a victim. Let us pray that the victim is at least one of our enemies![7]

Because the object of her hatred is out of reach, Medea substitutes her own children. It is difficult for us to see anything resembling a religious act in Medea's insane behavior. Nonetheless, infanticide has its place among ritualistic practices; the practice is too well documented in too many cultures (including the Jewish and the ancient Greek) for us to exclude it from consideration here. Medea's crime is to ritual infanticide what the massacre of sheep in the *Ajax* is to animal sacrifice. Medea prepares for the death of her children like a priest preparing for a sacrifice. Before the fateful act, she issues the traditional ritual announcement: all those whose presence might in any way hinder the effectiveness of the ceremony are requested to remove themselves from the premises.

Medea, like Ajax, reminds us of a fundamental truth about violence; if left unappeased, violence will accumulate until it overflows its confines and floods the surrounding area. The role of sacrifice is to stem this rising tide of indiscriminate substitutions and redirect violence into "proper" channels.

*Ajax* has details that underline the close relationship between the sacrificial substitution of animals and of humans. Before he sets upon the flock of sheep, Ajax momentarily contemplates the sacrifice of his own son. The boy's mother does not take this threat lightly; she whisks the child away.

In a general study of sacrifice there is little reason to differentiate between human and animal victims. When the principle of the substitution is *physical resemblance* between the vicarious victim and its prototypes, the mere fact that both victims are human beings seems to suffice. Thus, it is hardly surprising that in some societies whole categories of human beings are systematically reserved for sacrificial purposes in order to protect other categories.

I do not mean to minimize the gap that exists between the societies that practice human sacrifice and those that do not. However, this gap should not prevent us from perceiving what they have in common. Strictly speaking, there is no essential difference between animal sacrifice and human sacrifice, and in many cases one is substituted for the other. Our tendency to insist on differences that have little reality when discussing the institution of sacrifice—our reluctance, for example, to equate animal with human sacrifice—is undoubtedly a factor in the extraordinary misunderstandings that still persist in that area of human culture.

This reluctance to consider all forms of sacrifice as a single phenomenon is nothing new. Joseph de Maistre, having defined the principle of sacrificial substitution, makes the bold and wholly unsubstantiated assertion that this principle does not apply to human sacrifice. One cannot, he insists, kill a man to save a man. Yet this assertion is repeatedly contradicted by Greek tragedy, implicitly in a play like *Medea*, and explicitly elsewhere in Euripides.

In Euripides' *Electra*, Clytemnestra explains that the sacrifice of her daughter Iphigenia would have been justified if it had been performed to save human lives. The tragedian thus enlightens us, by way of Clytemnestra, on the "normal" function of human sacrifice—the function de Maistre had refused to acknowledge. If, says Clytemnestra, Agamemnon had permitted his daughter to die:

> . . . in order to prevent the sack of the city, to help his home, to rescue his children, sacrificing one to save the others, I could then have pardoned him. But for the sake of brazen Helen . . . !

Without ever expressly excluding the subject of human sacrifice from their research—and indeed, on what grounds could they do so?—modern scholars, notably Hubert and Mauss, mention it but rarely in their theoretical discussions. On the other hand, the scholars who do concern themselves with human sacrifice tend to concentrate on it to the exclusion of everything else, dwelling at length on the "sadistic" or "barbarous" aspects of the custom. Here, again, one particular form of sacrifice is isolated from the subject as a whole.

This dividing of sacrifice into two categories, human and animal, has itself a sacrificial character, in a strictly ritualistic sense. The division is based in effect on a value judgment, on the preconception that one category of victim—the human being—is quite unsuitable for sacrificial purposes, while another category—the animal—is eminently sacrificeable. We encounter here a survival of the sacrificial mode of thinking that perpetuates a misunderstanding about the institution as a whole. It is not a question of rejecting the value judgment on which this misunderstanding is based, but of putting it, so to speak, in parentheses, of recognizing that as far as the institution is concerned, such judgments are purely arbitrary. All reduction into categories, whether implicit or explicit, must be avoided; all victims, animal or human, must be treated in the same fashion if we wish to apprehend the criteria by which victims are selected (if indeed such criteria exist) and discover (if such a thing is possible) a universal principle for their selection.

We have remarked that all victims, even the animal ones, bear a certain *resemblance* to the object they replace; otherwise the violent impulse would remain unsatisfied. But this resemblance must not be carried to the extreme of complete assimilation, or it would lead to disastrous confusion. In the case of animal victims the difference is always clear, and no such confusion is possible. Although they do their best to empathize with their cattle, the Nuers never quite manage to mistake a man for a cow—the proof being that they always sacrifice the latter, never the former. I am not lapsing into the trap of Lévy Bruhl's "primitive mentality." I am not saying that primitive man is less capable of making distinctions than we moderns.

In order for a species or category of living creature, human or animal, to appear suitable for sacrifice, it must bear a sharp resemblance to the *human* categories excluded from the ranks of the "sacrificeable," while still maintaining a degree of difference that forbids all possible confusion. As I have said, no mistake is possible in the case of animal sacrifice. But it is quite another case with human victims. If we look at the extremely wide spectrum of human victims sacrificed by various societies, the list seems heterogeneous, to say the least. It includes prisoners of war, slaves, small children, unmarried adolescents, and the handicapped; it ranges from the very dregs of society, such as the Greek pharmakos, to the king himself.

Is it possible to detect a unifying factor in this disparate group? We notice at first glance beings who are either outside or on the fringes of society: prisoners of war, slaves, pharmakos. In many primitive societies children who have not yet undergone the rites of initiation have no proper place in the community; their rights and duties are almost nonexistent. What we are dealing with, therefore, are exterior or marginal individuals, incapable of establishing or sharing the social bonds that link the rest of the inhabitants. Their status as foreigners or enemies, their servile condition, or simply their age prevents these future victims from fully integrating themselves into the community.

But what about the king? Is he not at the very heart of the community? Undoubtedly—but it is precisely his position at the center that serves to isolate him from his fellow men, to render him casteless. He escapes from society, so to speak, via the roof, just as the pharmakos escapes through the cellar. The king has a sort of foil, however, in the person of his fool. The fool shares his master's status as an outsider—an isolation whose literal truth is often of greater significance than the easily reversible symbolic values often attributed to it. From every point of view the fool is eminently "sacrificeable," and the king can use him to vent his own anger. But it sometimes happens that the king himself is sacrificed, and that (among certain African societies) in a thoroughly regulated and highly ritualistic manner.[8]

It is clearly legitimate to define the difference between sacrificeable and nonsacrificeable individuals in terms of their degree of integration, but such a definition is not yet sufficient. In many cultures women are not considered full-fledged members of their society; yet women are never, or rarely, selected as sacrificial victims. There may be a simple explanation for this fact. The married woman retains her ties with her parents' clan even after she has become in some respects the property of her husband and his family. To kill her would be to run the risk of one of the two groups' interpreting her sacrifice as an act of murder committing it to a reciprocal act of revenge. The notion of vengeance casts a new light on the matter. All our sacrificial victims, whether chosen from one of the human categories enumerated above or, *a fortiori*, from the animal realm, are invariably distinguishable from the non-sacrificeable beings by one essential characteristic: between these victims and the community a crucial social link is missing, so they can be exposed to violence without fear of reprisal. Their death does not automatically entail an act of vengeance.

The considerable importance this freedom from reprisal has for the sacrificial process makes us understand that sacrifice is primarily an act of violence without risk of vengeance. We also understand the paradox—not without its comic aspects on occasion—of the frequent references to vengeance in the course of sacrificial rites, the veritable obsession with vengeance when no chance of vengeance exists:

> For the act they were about to commit elaborate excuses were offered; they shuddered at the prospect of the sheep's death, they wept over it as though they were its parents. Before the blow was struck, they implored the beast's forgiveness. They then addressed themselves to the species to which the beast belonged, as if addressing a large family clan, beseeching it not to seek vengeance for the act that was about to be inflicted on one of its members. In the same vein the actual murderer was punished in some manner, either beaten or sent into exile.[9]

It is the entire species *considered as a large family clan* that the sacrificers beseech not to seek vengeance. By incorporating the element of reprisal into the ceremony, the participants are hinting broadly at the true function of the rite, the kind of action it was designed to circumvent and the criteria that determined the choice of victim. The desire to commit an act of violence on those near us cannot be suppressed without a conflict; we must divert that impulse, therefore, toward the sacrificial victim, the creature we can strike down without fear of reprisal, since he lacks a champion.

Like everything that touches on the essential nature of the sacrificial act, the true distinction between the sacrificeable and the nonsacrificeable is never clearly articulated. Oddities and inexplicable anomalies confuse the picture. For instance, some animal species will be formally excluded from sacrifice, but the exclusion of members of the community is never mentioned. In constantly drawing attention to the truly maniacal aspects of sacrifice, modern theorists only serve to perpetuate an old misunderstanding in new terms. Men can dispose of their violence more efficiently if they regard the process not as something emanating from within themselves, but as a necessity imposed from without, a divine decree whose least infraction calls down terrible punishment. When they banish sacrificial practices from the "real," everyday world, modern theorists continue to misrepresent the violence of sacrifice.

The function of sacrifice is to quell violence within the community and to prevent conflicts from erupting. Yet societies like our own, which do not, strictly speaking, practice sacrificial rites, seem to get along without them. Violence undoubtedly exists within our society, but not to such an extent that the society itself is threatened with extinction. The simple fact that sacrificial practices, and other rites as well, can disappear without catastrophic results should in part explain the failure of ethnology and theology to come to grips with these cultural phenomena, and explain as well our modern reluctance to attribute a real function to them. After all, it is hard to maintain that institutions for which, as it seems, we have no need are actually indispensable.

It may be that a basic difference exists between a society like ours and societies imbued with religion—a difference that is partially hidden from us by rites, particularly by rites of sacrifice, that play a compensatory role. This difference would help explain why the actual function of sacrifice still eludes us.

When internal strife, previously sublimated by means of sacrificial practices, rises to the surface, it manifests itself in interfamily vendettas or blood feuds. This kind of violence is virtually nonexistent in our own culture. And perhaps it is here that we should look for the fundamental difference between primitive societies and our own; we should examine the specific ailments to which we are immune and which sacrifice manages to control, if not to eliminate.

Why does the spirit of revenge, wherever it breaks out, constitute such an intolerable menace? Perhaps because the only satisfactory revenge for spilt blood is spilling the blood of the killer; and in the blood feud there is no clear distinction between the act for which the killer is being punished and the punishment itself. Vengeance professes to be an act of reprisal, and every reprisal calls for another reprisal. The crime to which the act of vengeance addresses itself is almost never an unprecedented offense; in almost every case it has been committed in revenge for some prior crime.

Vengeance, then, is an interminable, infinitely repetitive process. Every time it turns up in some part of the community, it threatens to involve the whole social body. There is the risk that the act of vengeance will initiate a chain reaction whose consequences will quickly prove fatal to any society of modest size. The multiplication of reprisals instantaneously puts the very existence of a society in jeopardy, and that is why it is universally proscribed. *prohibited*

Curiously enough, it is in the very communities where the proscription is most strictly enforced that vengeance seems to hold sway. Even when it remains in the background, its role in the community unacknowledged, the specter of vengeance plays an important role in shaping the relationships among individuals. That is not to say that the prohibition against acts of vengeance is taken lightly. Precisely because murder inspires horror and because men must be forcibly restrained from murder, vengeance is inflicted on all those who commit it. The obligation never to shed blood cannot be distinguished from the obligation to exact vengeance on those who shed it. If men wish to prevent an interminable outbreak of vengeance (just as today we wish to prevent nuclear war), it is not enough to convince their fellows that violence is detestable—for it is precisely because they detest violence that men make a duty of vengeance.

In a world still haunted by the specter of vengeance it is difficult to theorize about vengeance without resorting to equivocations or paradoxes. In Greek tragedy, for instance, there is not—and cannot be—any consistent stand on the subject. To attempt to extract a coherent theory of vengeance from the drama is to miss the essence of tragedy. For in tragedy each character passionately embraces or rejects vengeance depending on the position he occupies at any given moment in the scheme of the drama.

Vengeance is a vicious circle whose effect on primitive societies can only be surmised. For us the circle has been broken. We owe our good fortune to one of our social institutions above all: our judicial system, which serves to deflect the menace of vengeance. The system does not suppress vengeance; rather, it effectively limits it to a single act of reprisal, enacted by a sovereign authority specializing in this particular function. The decisions of the judiciary are invariably presented as the final word on vengeance.

Vocabulary is perhaps more revealing here than judicial theories. Once the concept of interminable revenge has been formally rejected, it is referred to as *private* vengeance. The term implies the existence of a *public* vengeance, a counterpart never made explicit. By definition, primitive societies have only private vengeance. Thus, public vengeance is the exclusive property of well-policed societies, and our society calls it the judicial system.

Our penal system operates according to principles of justice that are in no real conflict with the concept of revenge. The same principle is at work in all systems of violent retribution. Either the principle is just, and justice is therefore inherent in the idea of vengeance, or there is not justice to be found anywhere. He who exacts his own vengeance is said to "take the law into his own hands." There is no difference of principle between private and public vengeance; but on the social level, the difference is enormous. Under the public system, an act of vengeance is no longer avenged; the process is terminated, the danger of escalation averted.

The absence of a judicial system in primitive societies has been confirmed by ethnologists. Malinowski concludes that "the 'criminal' aspect of law in savage communities is perhaps even vaguer than the civil one; the idea of 'justice' in our sense [is] hardly applicable and the means of restoring a disturbed tribal equilibrium [are] slow and cumbersome."[10]

Radcliffe-Brown's conclusions are identical, and summon up, as such conclusions must, the specter of perpetual vengeance: "Thus, though the Andaman Islanders had a well-developed social conscience, that is, a system of moral notions as to what is right and wrong, there was no such thing as punishment of a crime by the society. If one person injured another it was left to the injured one to seek vengeance if he wished and if he dared. There were probably always some who would side with the criminal, their attachment to him overcoming their disapproval of his actions."[11]

The anthropologist Robert Lowie speaks of the "administering of justice" in reference to primitive societies. He distinguishes two types of societies, those that possess a "central authority," and those that do not. Among the latter it is the parental group, he declares, that exercises the judicial power, and *this group confronts the other group in the same way that a sovereign state confronts the outside world.* There can be no true "administering of justice," no judicial system without a superior tribunal capable of arbitrating between even the most powerful groups. Only that superior tribunal can remove the possibility of blood feud or perpetual vendetta. Lowie himself recognizes that this condition is not always met: "From the supreme law of group solidarity it follows that when an individual has injured a member of another group, his own group shield him while the opposing group support the injured man's claims for compensation or revenge. Thence there may develop blood-feuds and civil wars . . . The Chukchi generally make peace after the first act of retribution, but among the Ifugao the struggle may go on almost interminably . . . "[12]

To speak here of the "administering of justice" is to abuse the meaning of the words. The desire to find in primitive societies virtues equal or superior to our own as regards the control of violence must not lead us to minimize the differences. Lowie's terminology simply perpetuates a widely accepted way of thinking by which the right to vengeance *takes the place* of a judicial system wherever such a system is lacking. This theory, which seems securely anchored to common sense, is in fact erroneous and gives rise to an infinite number of errors. Such thinking reflects the ignorance of a society—our own—that has been the beneficiary of a judicial system for so many years that it is no longer conscious of the system's real achievements.

If vengeance is an unending process it can hardly be invoked to restrain the violent impulses of society. In fact, it is vengeance itself that must be restrained. Lowie bears witness to the truth of this proposition every time he gives an example of the "administering of justice," even in those societies that, according to him, possess a "central authority." It is not the lack of any abstract principle of justice that is important, but the fact that the so-called legal reprisals are always in the hands of the victims themselves and those near to them. As long as there exists no sovereign and independent body capable of taking the place of the injured party and taking upon itself the responsibility for revenge, the danger of interminable escalation remains. Efforts to modify the punishment or to hold vengeance in check can only result in a situation that is precarious at best. Such efforts ultimately require a spirit of conciliation that may indeed be present, but may equally well be lacking. As I have said, it is inexact to speak of the administering of justice, even in connection with such institutional concepts as "an eye for an eye" or the various forms of trial by combat. In such cases it seems wise to adhere to Malinowski's conclusion: "The means of restoring a disturbed tribal equilibrium [are] slow and cumbersome . . . . We have not found any arrangement or usage which could be classed as a form of 'administration of justice,' according to a code and by fixed methods."[13]

If primitive societies have no tried and true remedies for dealing with an outbreak of violence, no certain cure once the social equilibrium has been upset, we can assume that *preventive* measures will play an essential role. Here again I return to the concept of sacrifice as I earlier defined it: an instrument of prevention in the struggle against violence.

In a universe where the slightest dispute can lead to disaster—just as a slight cut can prove fatal to a hemophiliac—the rites of sacrifice serve to polarize the community's aggressive impulses and redirect them toward victims that may be actual or figurative, animate or inanimate, but that are always incapable of propagating further vengeance. The sacrificial process furnishes an outlet for those violent impulses that cannot be mastered by self-restraint; a partial outlet, to be sure, but always renewable, and one whose efficacy has been attested by an impressive number of reliable witnesses. The sacrificial process prevents the spread of violence by keeping vengeance in check.

In societies that practice sacrifice there is no critical situation to which the rites are not applicable, but there are certain crises that seem to be particularly amenable to sacrificial mediation. In these crises the social fabric of the community is threatened; dissension and discord are rife. The more critical the situation, the more "precious" the sacrificial victim must be.

It is significant that sacrifice has languished in societies with a firmly established judicial system—ancient Greece and Rome, for example. In such societies the essential purpose of sacrifice has disappeared. It may still be practiced for a while, but in diminished and debilitated form. And it is precisely under such circumstances that sacrifice usually comes to our notice, and our doubts as to the "real" function of religious institutions are only reinforced.

# R. Girard: from *Violence and the Sacred*

Our original proposition stands: ritual in general, and sacrificial rites in particular, assume essential roles in societies that lack a firm judicial system. It must not be assumed, however, that sacrifice simply "replaces" a judicial system. One can scarcely speak of replacing something that never existed to begin with. Then, too, a judicial system is ultimately irreplaceable, short of a unanimous and entirely voluntary renunciation of all violent actions.

When we minimize the dangers implicit in vengeance we risk losing sight of the true function of sacrifice. Because revenge is rarely encountered in our society, we seldom have occasion to consider how societies lacking a judicial system of punishment manage to hold it in check. Our ignorance engages us in a false line of thought that is seldom, if ever, challenged. Certainly we have no need of religion to help us solve a problem, runaway vengeance, whose very existence eludes us. And because we have no need for it, religion itself appears senseless. The efficiency of our judicial solution conceals the problem, and the elimination of the problem conceals from us the role played by religion.

The air of mystery that primitive societies acquire for us is undoubtedly due in large part to this misunderstanding. It is undoubtedly responsible for our extreme views of these societies, our insistence on portraying them alternately as vastly superior or flagrantly inferior to our own. One factor alone might well be responsible for our oscillation between extremes, our radical evaluations: the absence in such societies of a judicial system. No one can assess with certainty the amount of violence present in another individual, much less in another society. We can be sure, however, that in a society lacking a judicial system the violence will not appear in the same places or take the same forms as in our own. We generally limit our area of inquiry to the most conspicuous and accessible aspects of these societies. Thus, it is not unnatural that they should seem to us either horribly barbarous or blissfully utopian.

In primitive societies the risk of unleashed violence is so great and the cure so problematic that the emphasis naturally falls on prevention. The preventive measures naturally fall within the domain of religion, where they can on occasion assume a violent character. Violence and the sacred are inseparable. But the covert appropriation by sacrifice of certain properties of violence—particularly the ability of violence to move from one object to another—is hidden from sight by the awesome machinery of ritual.

Primitive societies are not given over to violence. Nor are they necessarily less violent or less "hypocritical" than our own society. Of course, to be truly comprehensive we ought to take into consideration *all* forms of violence, more or less ritualized, that divert a menace from nearby objects to more distant objects. We ought, for instance, to consider war. War is clearly not restricted to one particular type of society. Yet the multiplication of new weapons and techniques does not constitute a fundamental difference between primitive and modern warfare. On the other hand, if we compare societies that adhere to a judicial system with societies that practice sacrificial rites, the difference between the two is such that we can indeed consider the absence or presence of these institutions as a basis for distinguishing primitive societies from "civilized" ones. These are the institutions we must scrutinize in order to arrive, not at some sort of value judgment, but at an objective knowledge of the respective societies to which they belong.

In primitive societies the exercise of preventive measures is not confined exclusively to the domain of religion. The way in which these measures are made manifest in normal social intercourse made a lasting impression on the minds and imaginations of the first European observers and established a prototype of "primitive" psychology and behavior which, if not universally applicable, is still not wholly illusory.

When the least false step can have dire consequences, human relationships may well be marked by a prudence that seems to us excessive and accompanied by precautions that appear incomprehensible. It is in this sense that we must understand the lengthy palavers that precede any undertaking not sanctified by custom, in this sense that we must understand primitive man's reluctance to engage in nonritualized games or contests. In a society where every action or gesture may have irreparable consequences it is not surprising that the members should display a "noble gravity" of bearing beside which our own demeanor appears ridiculous. The commercial, administrative, or ideological concerns that make such overwhelming demands on our time and attention seem utterly frivolous in comparison to primitive man's primary concerns.

Primitive societies do not have built into their structure an automatic brake against violence; but we do, in the form of powerful institutions whose grip grows progressively tighter as their role grows progressively less apparent. The constant presence of the restraining force allows modern man safely to transgress the limits imposed on primitive peoples without even being aware of the fact. In "policed" societies the relationships between individuals, including total strangers, is characterized by an extraordinary air of informality, flexibility, and even audacity.

Religion invariably strives to subdue violence, to keep it from running wild. Paradoxically, the religious and moral authorities in a community attempt to instill nonviolence, as an active force into daily life and as a mediating force into ritual life, through the application of violence. Sacrificial rites serve to connect the moral and religious aspects of daily life, but only by means of a lengthy and hazardous detour. Moreover, it must be kept in mind that the efficacy of the rites depends on their being performed in the spirit of *pietas*, which marks all aspects of religious life. We are beginning to understand why the sacrificial act appears as both sinful and saintly, an illegal as well as a legitimate exercise of violence. However, we are still far from a full understanding of the act itself.

Primitive religion tames, trains, arms, and directs violent impulses as a defensive force against those forms of violence that society regards as inadmissible. It postulates a strange mixture of violence and nonviolence. The same can perhaps be said of our own judicial system of control.

There may be a certain connection between all the various methods employed by man since the beginning of time to avoid being caught up in an interminable round of revenge. They can be grouped into three general categories: (1) preventive measures in which sacrificial rites divert the spirit of revenge into other channels; (2) the harnessing or hobbling of vengeance by means of compensatory measures, trials by combat, etc., whose curative effects remain precarious; (3) the establishment of a judicial system—the most efficient of all curative procedures.

We have listed the methods in ascending order of effectiveness. The evolution from preventive to curative procedures is reflected in the course of history or, at any rate, in the course of the history of the Western world. The initial curative procedures mark an intermediary stage between a purely religious orientation and the recognition of a judicial system's superior efficiency. These methods are inherently ritualistic in character, and are often associated with sacrificial practices.

The curative procedures employed by primitive societies appear rudimentary to us. We tend to regard them as fumbling efforts to improvise a judicial system. Certainly their pragmatic aspects are clearly visible, oriented as they are not toward the guilty parties, but toward the victims—since it is the latter who pose the most immediate threat. The injured parties must be accorded a careful measure of satisfaction, just enough to appease their own desire for revenge but not so much as to awaken the desire elsewhere. It is not a question of codifying good and evil or of inspiring respect for some abstract concept of justice; rather, it is a question of securing the safety of the group by checking the impulse for revenge. The preferred method involves a reconciliation between parties based on some sort of mutual compensation. If reconciliation is impossible, however, an armed encounter can be arranged in such a manner that the violence is wholly self-contained. This encounter can take place within an enclosed space and can involve prescribed regulations and specifically designed combatants. Its purpose is to cut violence short.

To be sure, all these curative measures are steps in the direction of a legal system. But the evolution, if indeed evolution is the proper term, is not continuous. The break comes at the moment when the intervention of an independent legal authority becomes *constraining*. Only then are men freed from the terrible obligations of vengeance. Retribution in its judicial guise loses its terrible urgency. Its meaning remains the same, but this meaning becomes increasingly indistinct or even fades from view. In fact, the system functions best when everyone concerned is least aware that it involves retribution. The system can—and as soon as it can it will—reorganize itself around the accused and the concept of guilt. In fact, retribution still holds sway, but forged into a principle of abstract justice that all men are obliged to uphold and respect.

We have seen that the "curative" measures, ostensibly designed to temper the impulse toward vengeance, become increasingly mysterious in their workings as they progress in efficiency. As the focal point of the system shifts away from religion and the preventive approach is translated into judicial retribution, the aura of misunderstanding that has always found a protective veil around the institution of sacrifice shifts as well, and becomes associated in turn with the machinery of the law.

As soon as the judicial system gains supremacy, its machinery disappears from sight. Like sacrifice, it conceals—even as it also reveals—its resemblance to vengeance, differing only in that it is not self-perpetuating and its decisions discourage reprisals. In the case of sacrifice, the designated victim does not become the object of vengeance because he is a replacement, is not the "right" victim. In the judicial system the violence does indeed fall on the "right" victim; but it falls with such force, such resounding authority, that no retort is possible.

It can be argued that the function of the judicial system is not really concealed; and we can hardly be unaware that the judicial process is more concerned with the general security of the community than with any abstract notion of justice. Nonetheless, we believe that the system is founded on a unique principle of justice unknown to primitive societies. The scholarly literature on the subject seems to bear out this belief. It has long been assumed that the decisive difference between primitive and civilized man is the former's general inability to identify the guilty party and to adhere to the principle of guilt. Such an assumption only confuses the issue. If primitive man insists on averting his attention from the wrongdoer, with an obstinacy that strikes us as either idiotic or perverse, it is because he wishes above all to avoid fueling the fires of vengeance.

If our own system seems more rational, it is because it conforms more strictly to the principle of vengeance. Its insistence on the punishment of the guilty party underlines this fact. Instead of following the example of religion and attempting to forestall acts of revenge, to mitigate or sabotage its effects or to redirect them to secondary objects, our judicial system *rationalizes* revenge and succeeds in limiting and isolating its effects in accordance with social demands. The system treats the disease without fear of contagion and provides a highly effective technique for the cure and, as a secondary effect, the prevention of violence.

This rationalistic approach to vengeance might seem to stem from a peculiarly intimate relationship between the community and the judicial system. In fact, it is the result not of any familiar interchange between the two, but of the recognition of the sovereignty and the independence of the judiciary, whose decisions no group, not even the collectivity as a body, can challenge. (At least, that is the principle.) The judicial authority is beholden to no one. It is thus at the disposal of everyone, and it is universally respected. The judicial system never hesitates to confront violence head on, because it possesses a monopoly on the means of revenge. Thanks to this monopoly, the system generally succeeds in stifling the impulse to vengeance rather than spreading or aggravating it, as a similar intervention on the part of the aggrieved party would invariably do.

In the final analysis, then, the judicial system and the institution of sacrifice share the same function, but the judicial system is infinitely more effective. However, it can only exist in conjunction with a firmly established political power. And like all modern technological advances, it is a two-edged sword, which can be used to oppress as well as to liberate. Certainly that is the way it is seen by primitive cultures, whose view on the matter is indubitably more objective than our own.

If the function of the system has now become apparent, that is because it no longer enjoys the obscurity it needs to operate effectively. A clear view of the inner workings indicates a crisis in the system; it is a sign of disintegration. No matter how sturdy it may seem, the apparatus that serves to hide the true nature of legal and illegal violence from view eventually wears thin. The underlying truth breaks through, and we find ourselves face to face with the specter of reciprocal reprisal. This is not a purely theoretical concept belonging to the intellectual and scholarly realm, but a sinister reality; a vicious circle we thought we had escaped, but one we find has tightened itself, all unsuspected, around us.

The procedures that keep men's violence in bounds have one thing in common: they are no strangers to the ways of violence. There is reason to believe that they are all rooted in religion. As we have seen, the various forms of prevention go hand in hand with religious practices. The curative procedures are also imbued with religious concepts—both the rudimentary sacrificial rites and the more advanced judicial forms. *Religion* in its broadest sense, then, must be another term for that obscurity that surrounds man's efforts to defend himself by curative or preventative means against his own violence. It is that enigmatic quality that pervades the judicial system when that system replaces sacrifice. This obscurity coincides with the transcendental effectiveness of a violence that is holy, legal, and legitimate successfully opposed to a violence that is unjust, illegal, and illegitimate.

In the same way that sacrificial victims must in principle meet the approval of the divinity before being offered as a sacrifice, the judicial system appeals to a theology as a guarantee of justice. Even when this theology disappears, as has happened in our culture, the transcendental quality of the system remains intact. Centuries can pass before men realize that there is no real difference between their principle of justice and the concept of revenge.

Only the transcendental quality of the system, acknowledged by all, can assure the prevention or cure of violence. This is the case no matter what the consecrating institution may be. Only by opting for a sanctified, legitimate form of violence and preventing it from becoming an object of disputes and recriminations can the system save itself from the vicious circle of revenge.

A unique generative force exists that we can only qualify as religious in a sense deeper than the theological one. It remains concealed and draws its strength from this concealment, even as its self-created shelter begins to crumble. The acknowledgement of such a force allows us to assess our modern ignorance—ignorance in regard to violence as well as religion. Religion shelters us from violence just as violence seeks shelter in religion. If we fail to understand certain religious practices it is not because we are outside their sphere of influence but because we are still to a very real extent enclosed within them. The solemn debates on the death of God and of man are perhaps beside the point. They remain theological at bottom, and by extension sacrificial; that is, they draw a veil over the subject of vengeance, which threatens to become quite real once again, in the form not of a philosophical debate but of unlimited violence, in a world with no absolute values. As soon as the essential quality of transcendence—religious, humanistic, or whatever—is lost, there are no longer any terms by which to define the legitimate form of violence and to recognize it among the multitude of illicit forms. The definition of legitimate and illegitimate forms then becomes a matter of mere opinion, with each man free to reach his own decision. In other words, the question is thrown to the winds. Henceforth there are as many legitimate forms of violence as there are men to implement them; legitimacy as a principle no longer exists. Only the introduction of some transcendental quality that will persuade men of the fundamental difference between sacrifice and revenge, between a judicial system and vengeance, can succeed in bypassing violence.

All this explains why our penetration and demystification of the system necessarily coincides with the disintegration of that system. The act of demystification retains a sacrificial quality and remains essentially religious in character for at least as long as it fails to come to a conclusion—as long, that is, as the process purports to be nonviolent, or less violent than the system itself. In fact, demystification leads to constantly increasing violence, a violence perhaps less "hypocritical" than the violence it seeks to expose, but more energetic, more virulent, and the harbinger of something far worse—a violence that knows no bounds.

While acknowledging the differences, both functional and mythical, between vengeance, sacrifice, and legal punishment, it is important to recognize their fundamental identity. Precisely because these three institutions are essentially the same they tend to adopt the same types of violent response in times of crisis. Seen in the abstract, such an assertion may seem hyperbolic or simply unbelievable. It can only be appreciated by means of concrete examples. Only then will the utility of the comparison become apparent; customs and institutions that have remained incomprehensible, unclassifiable, and "aberrant" heretofore make sense when seen in the light of this identity.

Robert Lowie, discussing collective reactions to an act of violence, brings out a fact well worth noting here: "The Chukchi generally make peace after the first act of retribution . . . While the Ifugao tend to protect a kinsman under almost all circumstances, the Chukchi often avert a feud by killing a member of the family."[14]

Whether it be through sacrificial killing or legal punishment, the problem is to forestall a series of reprisals. As the above quotation shows, Lowie is well aware of this aspect. In killing one of their own, the Chukchi abort the issue; by offering a victim to their potential enemies they enjoin them not to seek vengeance, not to commit an act that would constitute a fresh affront and oblige the other side to seek further retribution. This expiatory procedure brings to mind the sacrificial process; the fact that the victim is someone other than the guilty party drives the resemblance home.

The Chukchi practice cannot, however, be classified as sacrificial. A properly conducted ritual killing is never openly linked to another bloodletting of irregular character. It never allows itself to pass as a deliberate act of retribution. Because this link is consistently missing, the meaning of the sacrificial process has always eluded us, and the relationship between sacrifice and violence has remained obscure. Now the meaning is made clear, and in a manner too spectacular for the act to be mistaken for mere ritual.

Should one then classify this custom among legal punishments? Can one properly refer to it as an "execution of justice?" Probably not; after all, the victim of the second murder was in no way responsible for the first. To be sure, Lowie invokes the concept of "collective responsibility," but this is not a satisfactory explanation. Collective responsibility never specifically excludes the true culprit, and this is precisely what is being done here. Even if this exclusion is not clearly spelled out, there is sufficient evidence for us to assume that in many instances the true culprit is systematically spared. As a cultural attitude, this certainly demands attention.

To refer in this context to the so-called primitive mentality, to some "possible confusion between the individual and the group," is to hedge the issue. If the Chukchi choose to spare the culprit it is not because they cannot distinguish where the guilt lies. On the contrary, they perceive it with the utmost clarity. It is precisely because they see that the guilty party is guilty that they choose to spare him. The Chukchi believe that they have good reasons to act as they do, and it is these reasons we must now examine.

To make a victim out of the guilty party is to play vengeance's role, to submit to the demands of violence. By killing, not the murderer himself, but someone close to him, an act of perfect reciprocity is avoided and the necessity for revenge by-passed. If the counterviolence were inflicted on the aggressor himself, it would by this very act participate in, and become indistinguishable from, the original act of violence. In short, it would become an act of pure vengeance, requiring yet another act of vengeance and transforming itself into the very thing it was designed to prevent.

Only violence can put an end to violence, and that is why violence is self-propagating. Everyone wants to strike the last blow, and reprisal can thus follow reprisal without any true conclusion ever being reached.

In excluding the actual guilty party from reprisals the Chukchi hope to avoid the vicious cycle of revenge. They try to cover their tracks—but not entirely, for they do not want to deprive their act of its primordial meaning as a response to an initial killing, as the payment of a debt contracted by one of their number. To quell the passions aroused by this crime an act is required that bears some resemblance to the vengeance sought by the plaintiffs but that does not quite qualify as an act of revenge. The act resembles both a legal punishment and a sacrifice, and yet it cannot be assimilated to either. The act described here resembles a legal punishment in that it constitutes an act of reparation, a violent retribution; and the Chukchi show no hesitation in imposing on themselves the same loss they have inflicted on others. Their action resembles a sacrifice in that the victim of the second murder is not responsible for the first.

So flagrant a disregard of the principle of guilt strikes us as absurd. We hold that principle in such high esteem that any deviation from it appears to us an aberration of the intellect or malfunction of the senses. Yet our line of reasoning is rejected by the "primitives" because it involves too strict an application of the doctrine of vengeance and is thus fraught with peril.

When we require a direct link between guilt and punishment we believe that we adhere to a fundamental truth that has somehow eluded the primitive mind. In fact, we are ignoring a problem that poses a very real threat to all primitive societies: escalating revenge, unleashed violence—a problem the seeming extravagances of their customs and the violence of their religious practices are specifically designed to meet.

In Greek culture in particular, physical contact with the anathema is avoided. Behind this peculiar prohibition lurks a fear perhaps analogous to the one that inspires the Chukchi custom. To do violence to a violent person is to be contaminated by his violence. It is best, therefore, to arrange matters so that nobody, except perhaps the culprit himself, is directly responsible for his death, so that nobody is obliged to raise a finger against him. He may be abandoned without provisions in mid-ocean, or stranded on top of a mountain, or forced to hurl himself from a cliff. The custom of exposure, as a means of getting rid of malformed children, seems to find its origin in this same fear.

All such customs may appear to us unreasonable and absurd. In fact they adhere to a coherent logic. All of them concern themselves with formulating and practicing a form of violence incapable of serving as a connecting link between the violent act that preceded and the one that must follow. The aim is to achieve a radically new type of violence, truly decisive and self-contained, a form of violence that will put an end once and for all to violence itself.

Primitive peoples try to break the symmetry of reprisal by addressing themselves directly to the question of form. Unlike us, they perceive recurrent patterns, and they attempt to halt this recurrence by introducing something different into the picture. Modern man has long since lost his fear of reciprocal violence, which, after all, provides our judicial system with its structure. Because the overwhelming authority of the judiciary prevents its sentence from becoming the first step in an endless series of reprisals, we can no longer appreciate primitive man's deep-seated fear of pure, unadulterated vengeance. The Chukchi's behavior or the Greeks' cautious treatment of the anathema strike us as puzzling.

Of course, the Chukchi solution is not to be confused with retaliatory vengeance, ritual sacrifice, or legal punishment. And yet it is reminiscent of all these institutions. Their solution seems to occur at the point where all three intersect. Unless the modern mind can cope with the fact that the three are indeed capable of intersecting, it is not likely to shed much light on the questions that concern us here.

The Chukchi solution is fraught with psychological implications, all of rather limited interest. For example, it can be said that in choosing to kill someone close to the culprit rather than the culprit himself the Chukchi are trying to be conciliatory without risking a loss of face. That is indeed possible, but there are many other possibilities as well. It is easy to lose one's way in a maze of psychological speculation. The religious structure clearly transcends all "psychological" interpretations; it neither requires nor contradicts them.

The essential religious concern here is ritual impurity. And the cause of ritual impurity is violence. In many cases, this fact seems self-evident.

Two men come to blows; blood is spilt; both men are thus rendered impure. Their impurity is contagious, and anyone who remains in their presence risks becoming a party to their quarrel. The only sure way to avoid contagion is to flee the scene of violence. There is no question here of duty or morality. Contamination is a terrible thing, and only those who are already contaminated would wilfully expose themselves to it.

If even an accidental contact with a "contaminated" being can spread the impurity, it goes without saying that a violent and hostile encounter will guarantee infection. Therefore, the Chukchi reason, whenever violence is inevitable, it is best that the victim be *pure*, untainted by any involvement in the dispute. As we can see, these notions of impurity and contagion play an active role in social relations and are firmly rooted in reality. It is precisely this basis in reality that scholars have long denied. Modern observers—particularly Frazer's contemporaries and disciples—were totally blind to the reality that lay behind these ideas, because it was not *their* reality and because primitive religion succeeded in camouflaging its social function. Concepts such as impurity and contagion, because they translate human relations into material terms, provide a sort of camouflage. The peril that overshadows all human relations and that stems from these relations is presented either in a purely material or in a wholly otherworldly guise. The notion of ritual impurity can degenerate until it is nothing more than a terror-stricken belief in the malevolent results of physical contact. Violence has been transformed into a sort of seminal fluid that impregnates objects on contact and whose diffusion, like electricity or Balzacian "magnetism," is determined by physical laws. Far from dissipating the ignorance that surrounds these concepts, modern thinking only reinforces the confusion. By denying religion any basis in reality, by viewing it as a sort of bedtime story for children, we collaborate with violence in its game of deception.

In many religious communities—among the ancient Greeks, for instance—when a man has hanged himself, his body becomes impure. So too does the rope from which he dangles, the tree to which the rope is attached, and the field where the tree stands. The taint of impurity diminishes, however, as one draws away from the body. It is as if the scene of a violent act, and the objects with which the violence has been committed, send out emanations that penetrate everything in the immediate area, growing gradually weaker through time and space.

When a town has undergone a terrible bloodletting, and emissaries from that town are sent to another community, they are considered impure. Every effort is made to avoid touching them, talking to them, remaining in their presence any longer than necessary. After their departure rites of purification are undertaken: sacrifices offered, lustral water sprinkled about.

While Frazer and his disciples tend to view this fear of infection by the "impure" as a prime example of the "irrational" and "superstitious" element of religious thought, other observers regard it as an anticipation of sound scientific principles. They point out the striking resemblance between the precautions that modern medicine takes against bacterial infection and the ritualistic avoidance of pollution.

In some societies contagious diseases—smallpox, for instance—have their own particular gods. During his illness the patient is dedicated to the god; that is, he is isolated from the community and put under the supervision of an "initiate," or priest of the god, someone who has contracted the illness and survived it. This man now partakes of the god's power; he is immune to the effects of the divine violence.

It is easy to see why some observers have concluded that these impurity rituals reveal some sort of vague intuitive knowledge of microbiology; that the rituals, in short, are grounded in fact. Against this view it is argued that the procedures that are supposed to protect the believers from ritual impurity often disregard, or even flout, the principles of modern hygiene. This argument is not wholly satisfactory, however, for it fails to take into account the possible parallels between ritualistic precautions and the first tentative measures taken in the early days of public hygiene—in the nineteenth century, for example.

The theory that regards religious terrors or taboos as a sort of protoscience has hit on something of real interest, but too indefinite and limited to be of much use in our investigation. Such a theory can only arise in a culture that regards *sickness* as the sole fatal influence, the sole enemy man has to conquer. Clearly, medical considerations are not excluded from the primitive concept of contagion, and the prevention of epidemics plays a definite role in the impurity rites. But these factors play only a minor role in primitive culture. They arouse our interest precisely because they offer the sole instance in which the modern scientific notion of contagion, which is exclusively pathological, coincides with the primitive concept, which is far broader in scope.

The aspects of religion in which contagion seems to have some reality for us are hard to distinguish from those in which it ceases to have any reality. That is not to say that primitive religion is afflicted with the sort of "confusion" that Frazer or Levy-Bruhl attributed to it. The assimilation of contagious diseases and all forms of violence—the latter also regarded as contagious in nature—is based on a number of complementary inferences that combine to form a strikingly coherent picture.

A primitive society, a society that lacks a legal system, is exposed to the sudden escalation of violence. Such a society is compelled to adopt attitudes we may well find incomprehensible. Our incomprehension seems to stem from two main factors. In the first place, we know absolutely nothing about the contagion of violence, not even whether it actually exists. In the second place, the primitive people themselves recognize this violence only in an almost entirely dehumanized form; that is, under the deceptive guise of the *sacred*.

Considered all together, the ritual precautions against violence are firmly rooted in reality, absurd though some of them may appear to our own eyes. If the sacrificial catharsis actually succeeds in preventing the unlimited propagation of violence, a sort of *infection* is in fact being checked.

From the outset of this study, after all, I have regarded violence as something eminently communicable. The tendency of violence to hurl itself on a surrogate if deprived of its original object can surely be described as a contaminating process. Violence too long held in check will overflow its bounds—and woe to those who happen to be nearby. Ritual precautions are intended both to prevent this flooding and to offer protection, insofar as it is possible, to those who find themselves in the path of ritual impurity—that is, caught in the floodtide of violence.

The slightest outbreak of violence can bring about a catastrophic escalation. Though we may tend to lose sight of this fact in our own daily lives, we are intellectually aware of its validity, and are often reminded that there is something infectious about the spectacle of violence. Indeed, at times it is impossible to stay immune from the infection. Where violence is concerned, intolerance can prove as fatal an attitude as tolerance, for when it breaks out it can happen that those who oppose its progress do more to assure its triumph than those who endorse it. There is no universal rule for quelling violence, no principle of guaranteed effectiveness. At times all the remedies, harsh as well as gentle, seem efficacious; at other times, every measure seems to heighten the fever it is striving to abate.

Inevitably the moment comes when violence can only be countered by more violence. Whether we fail or succeed in our effort to subdue it, the real victor is always violence itself. The *mimetic* attributes of violence are extraordinary—sometimes direct and positive, at other times indirect and negative. The more men strive to curb their violent impulses, the more these impulses seem to prosper. The very weapons used to combat violence are turned against their users. Violence is like a raging fire that feeds on the very objects intended to smother its flames.

The metaphor of fire could well give way to metaphors of tempest, flood, earthquake. Like the plague, the resemblance violence bears to these natural cataclysms is not limited to the realm of poetic imagery. In acknowledging that fact, however, we do not mean to endorse the theory that sees in the sacred a simple transfiguration of natural phenomena.

The sacred consists of all those forces whose dominance over man increases or seems to increase in proportion to man's effort to master them. Tempests, forest fires, and plagues, among other phenomena, may be classified as sacred. Far outranking these, however, though in a far less obvious manner, stands human violence—violence seen as something exterior to man and henceforth as a part of all the other outside forces that threaten mankind. Violence is the heart and secret soul of the sacred.

We have yet to learn how man succeeds in positing his own violence as an independent being. Once he has accomplished this feat, however, the sacred presence invades his universe, mysteriously infects, without participating in it, and buffets him about rather in the manner of a plague or other natural disaster. Once all this has occurred, man is confronted with a group of phenomena that, despite their heterogeneous appearance, exhibit remarkable similarities.

As a general practice, it is wise to avoid contact with the sick if one wishes to stay healthy. Similarly, it is wise to steer clear of homicides if one is eager not to be killed.

As we see it, these are two distinct types of "contagion." Modern science concerns itself with one type, and has established its reality beyond all dispute. However, the other type could well be of greater importance to the members of a society that we have defined as primitive—that is, a society lacking legal sanctions.

Religious thought encompasses a large body of phenomena under the heading of ritual impurity—phenomena that seem disparate and absurd from the viewpoint of modern science but whose relationship and reality become perfectly clear when tested for the presence of basic violence, the prime ingredient and ultimate resource of the whole system.

There are undeniable similarities, for instance, between a bout of serious illness and an act of violence wilfully perpetrated by an enemy. The sufferings of the invalid are analogous to those of the wounded victim; and if the invalid runs the risk of dying, so too do all those who are involved in one fashion or another, whether actively or passively, in a violent action. Death is nothing more than the worst form of violence that can befall a man. It is no less reasonable, therefore, to lump together all the possible causes of death, pathological and otherwise, than it is to create a separate category for only one of them: sickness.

To understand religious thought requires an empirical approach. The goal of religious thinking is exactly the same as that of technological research— namely, practical action. Whenever man is truly concerned with obtaining concrete results, whenever he is hard pressed by reality, he abandons abstract speculation and reverts to a mode of response that becomes increasingly cautious and conservative as the forces he hopes to subdue, or at least to outrun, draw ever nearer.

In its simplest, perhaps most elementary form, religion manifests little curiosity about the origins of those terrible forces that visit their fury on mankind but seems to concentrate its attention on determining a regular sequential pattern that will enable man to anticipate these onslaughts and take measures against them.

Religious empiricism invariably leads to one conclusion: it is essential to keep as far away as possible from sacred things, always to avoid direct contact with them. Naturally, such thinking occasionally coincides with medical empiricism or with scientific empiricism in general. This is why some observers insist on regarding religious empiricism as a preliminary stage of science.

This same empiricism, however, can sometimes reach conclusions so utterly foreign to our own way of thinking and can show itself so narrow, inflexible and myopic in its attitudes that we are tempted to attribute its functioning to some sort of psychological malaise. Such a reaction leads us to regard primitive society as an "ailing" society, beside which our "civilized" society presents a picture of radiant health.

The adherents of this theory show no hesitation in standing these categories on their heads, however, whenever the need arises. Thus, on occasion, it is "civilization" that is sick; and because civilized society is the antithesis of primitive society, it now appears that the primitive sphere must be the healthy one. Manipulate them as one will, it looks as if the concepts of sickness and health are not very useful in clarifying the relationship between primitive societies and our own.

Ritual precautions that appear lunatic or at least highly exaggerated in a modern context are in fact quite reasonable when viewed in their proper context—that is, in the context of religion's complete unawareness of the violence it makes sacred. When men believe that they can actually feel the breath of the Homeric Cyclops at their backs, they are apt to resort to all means at their disposal, to embrace all possible precautions. It seems safer to overreact than to underreact.

This religious attitude is not dissimilar to that of medicine when suddenly confronted with an unknown disease. An epidemic breaks out; the doctors and scientists are unable to isolate the pathogenic agent. Under the circumstances, what should they do? Clearly they must adopt, not *some* of the precautionary measures employed against familiar diseases, but *all* of them, without exception. Ideally, they would invent entirely new measures, since the enemy they are fighting is itself employing new weapons.

Once the microbe has been identified, it is seen that some of the measures employed were completely useless and should be abandoned in any future dealings with the disease. Yet it must be admitted that as long as the cause of the illness was unknown, their use was fully justified.

We must be careful not to push our metaphor too far. Neither primitive nor modern man has yet succeeded in identifying the microbe responsible for the dread disease of violence. Western civilization is hindered in its efforts to isolate and analyze the causes and to examine them in any but the most superficial manner because it has enjoyed until this day a mysterious immunity from the most virulent forms of violence—an immunity not, it seems, of our society's making, but one that has perhaps resulted in the making of our society.

Among primitive taboos the one that has perhaps been most analyzed is the taboo surrounding menstrual blood. Menstrual blood is regarded as impure; menstruating women are segregated from the community. They are forbidden to touch any objects of communal usage, sometimes even their own food, for risk of contamination.

If we wish to understand why menstruation is considered "impure," we must consider it within the general category of bloodletting. Most primitive people take the utmost care to avoid contact with blood. Spilt blood of any origin, unless it has been associated with a sacrificial act, is considered impure. This universal attribution of impurity to spilt blood springs directly from the definition we have just proposed: wherever violence threatens, ritual impurity is present. When men are enjoying peace and security, blood is a rare sight. When violence is unloosed, however, blood appears everywhere—on the ground, underfoot, forming great pools. Its very fluidity gives form to the contagious nature of violence. Its presence proclaims murder and announces new upheavals to come. Blood stains everything it touches the color of violence and death. Its very appearance seems, as the saying goes, to "cry out for vengeance."

Any bloodletting is frightening. It is only natural, therefore, that menstrual bleeding should awaken fear. However, there is another, complicating element at work here. Although menstrual bleeding can be readily distinguished from blood spilt in a murder or an accident and can thus be dissociated from those virulent forms of violence, it is in many societies regarded as the most impure of impurities. We can only assume that this extreme reaction has to do with the sexual aspect of menstruation.

Sexuality is one of those primary forces whose sovereignty over man is assured by man's firm belief in his sovereignty over it. The most extreme forms of violence can never be directly sexual because they are collective in nature. The group is quite capable of perpetrating a single, coherent act of violence, whose force is increased with the addition of each individual quotient of violence; but sexuality is never truly collective. That fact alone explains why sexual interpretations of the sacred invariably ignore or play down the role of violence, whereas an interpretation based on violence readily grants sexuality the prominent place it occupies in all primitive religions. We are tempted to conclude that violence is impure because of its relation to sexuality. Yet only the reverse proposition can withstand close scrutiny. Sexuality is impure because it has to do with violence.

Such an idea seems to run counter to the spirit of contemporary humanism, which has settled into a friendly accord with the pan-sexualism of the psycho-analysts and remains unruffled even by the death-wish theory. Nonetheless, the signs are too numerous and too clear to be ignored. We have conceded that menstrual blood has a direct relationship to sexuality; we also contend that its relationship to unleashed violence is even closer. The blood of a murdered man is impure. This impurity cannot be derived from the impurity attributed to menstrual blood. On the other hand, to understand the impurity of menstrual blood we must trace its relationship to blood spilt by violence, as well as to sexuality. The fact that the sexual organs of women periodically emit a flow of blood has always made a great impression on men; it seems to confirm an affinity between sexuality and those diverse forms of violence that invariably lead to bloodshed.

To understand the nature and extent of this affinity we must return to the solid core of "common sense" that plays a far greater role in religious thinking than fashionable theorists are willing to acknowledge. In fact, the notion that the beliefs of all mankind are a grand mystification that we alone have succeeded in penetrating is a hardy perennial—as well as being, to say the least, somewhat arrogant. The problem at hand is not the arrogance of Western science nor its blatant "imperialism," but rather its sheer inadequacy. It is precisely when the need to understand becomes most urgent that the explanations proposed in the domain of religion become most unsatisfactory.

The connection between sexuality and religion is a heritage common to all religions and is supported by an impressive array of convergent facts. Sex and violence frequently come to grips in such direct forms as abduction, rape, defloration, and various sadistic practices, as well as in indirect actions of indefinite consequences. Sex is at the origin of various illnesses, real or imaginary; it culminates in the bloody labors of childbirth, which may entail the death of mother, child, or both together. Even within the ritualistic framework of marriage, when all the matrimonial vows and other interdictions have been conscientiously observed, sexuality is accompanied by violence; and as soon as one trespasses beyond the limits of matrimony to engage in illicit relationships—incest, adultery, and the like—the violence, and the impurity resulting from this violence, grows more potent and extreme. Sexuality leads to quarrels, jealous rages, mortal combats. It is a permanent source of disorder even within the most harmonious of communities.

In refusing to admit an association between sexuality and violence—an association readily acknowledged by men over the course of several millennia—modern thinkers are attempting to prove their broadmindedness and liberality. Their stance has led to numerous misconceptions. Like violence, sexual desire tends to fasten upon surrogate objects if the object to which it was originally attracted remains inaccessible; it willingly accepts substitutes. And again like violence, repressed sexual desire accumulates energy that sooner or later bursts forth, causing tremendous havoc. It is also worth noting that the shift from violence to sexuality and from sexuality to violence is easily effected, even by the most "normal" of individuals, totally lacking in perversion. Thwarted sexuality leads naturally to violence, just as lovers' quarrels often end in an amorous embrace. Recent scientific findings seem to justify the primitive perspective on many points. Sexual excitement and violent impulses manifest themselves in the same manner. In both instances, the majority of discernible bodily reactions are identical.[15]

Before we attempt to explain away the taboo on menstrual blood by means of some all-inclusive, generalized interpretation—before, for example, we invoke those "phantasms" that play the same role in our consciousness as do "the enchanters' tricks" in Don Quixote's—we should make quite sure that we have first exhausted all direct avenues to comprehension. In fact, there is nothing incomprehensible about the viewpoint that sees menstrual blood as a physical representation of sexual violence. We ought, however, to go further: to inquire whether this process of symbolization does not respond to some half-suppressed desire to place the blame for all forms of violence on women. By means of this taboo a transfer of violence has been effected and a monopoly established that is clearly detrimental to the female sex.

The taint of impurity cannot always be avoided; even the most careful precautions are no security against it. And the least contact with the infection can contaminate the entire community.

How can one cleanse the infected members of all trace of pollution? Does there exist some miraculous substance potent enough not only to resist infection but also to purify, if need be, the contaminated blood? Only blood itself, blood whose purity has been guaranteed by the performance of appropriate rites—the blood, in short, of sacrificial victims—can accomplish this feat.

Behind this astonishing paradox, the menace of violent action can be discerned. All concepts of impurity stem ultimately from the community's fear of a perpetual cycle of violence arising in its midst. The menace is always the same and provokes the same set of responses, the same sacrificial gestures designed to redirect the violence onto inconsequential victims. The idea of ritual purification is far more than mere shadow play or illusion.

The function of ritual is to "purify" violence; that is, to "trick" violence into spending itself on victims whose death will provoke no reprisals. Because the secret of this mechanism is unknown to the participants in the rites, religion tries to account for its own operation metaphorically, using for that purpose the objects and materials involved in that operation. The properties of blood, for example, vividly illustrate the entire operation of violence. We have already spoken of blood spilt by mischance or malice. Blood that dries on the victim soon loses its viscous quality and becomes first a dark sore, then a roughened scab. Blood that is allowed to congeal on its victim is the impure product of violence, illness, or death. In contrast to this contaminated substance is the fresh blood of newly slaughtered victims, crimson and free flowing. This blood is never allowed to congeal, but is removed without trace as soon as the rites have been concluded.

The physical metamorphosis of spilt blood can stand for the double nature of violence. Some religious practices make elaborate use of this duality. Blood serves to illustrate the point that the same substance can stain or cleanse, contaminate or purify, drive men to fury and murder or appease their anger and restore them to life.

We are not dealing here with one of Gaston Bachelard's "material metaphors," a poetic recreation of little real consequence. Nor does Laura Makarius's suggestion that the ambiguous character of blood is in fact the ultimate reality behind the constant reversals of primitive religion seem wholly apposite here.[16] Both authors lose sight of a crucial point: the paradoxical nature of violence. Although religion grasps this paradox—and that only tentatively—mostly by means of such symbolic representations as that of blood, it differs radically from modern theory, which speaks of "phantasms" and "poetry" and does not even realize how real the sacrificial process can be and how appropriate the major metaphors and symbols through which it is expressed.

Even the wildest aberrations of religious thought still manage to bear witness to the fact that evil and the violent measures taken to combat evil are essentially the same. At times violence appears to man in its most terrifying aspect, wantonly sowing chaos and destruction; at other times it appears in the guise of peacemaker, graciously distributing the fruits of sacrifice.

The secret of the dual nature of violence still eludes men. Beneficial violence must be carefully distinguished from harmful violence, and the former continually promoted at the expense of the latter. Ritual is nothing more than the regular exercise of "good" violence. As we have remarked, if sacrificial violence is to be effective it must resemble the nonsacrificial variety as closely as possible. That is why some rites may seem to us nothing more than senseless inversions of prohibited acts. For instance, in some societies menstrual blood is regarded as a beneficial substance when employed in certain rites but retains its baleful character in other contexts.

The two-in-one nature of blood—that is, of violence—is strikingly illustrated in Euripides' *Ion*. The Athenian queen, Creusa, plots to do away with the hero by means of an exotic talisman: two drops of blood from the deadly Gorgon. One drop is a deadly poison, the other a miraculous healing agent. The queen's old slave asks her the origin of this substance:

> *Creusa:* When the fatal blow was struck a drop spurted from the hollow
> vein . . .
> *Slave:* How is it used? What are its properties?
> *Creusa:* It wards off all sickness and nourishes life.
> *Slave:* And the other drop?
> *Creusa:* It kills. It is made from the Gorgon's venomous serpents.
> *Slave:* Do you carry them mixed together or separate?
> *Creusa:* Are good and evil to be mixed together? Separate, of course.

Nothing could seem more alike than two drops of blood, yet in this case nothing could be more different. It is only too easy to blend them together and produce a substance that would efface all distinction between the pure and the impure. Then the difference between "good" and "bad" violence would be eliminated as well. As long as purity and impurity remain distinct, even the worst pollution can be washed away; but once they are allowed to mingle, purification is no longer possible.

# Notes

1. Hubert, H. and Mauss, M. (1968). *Sacrifice: Its Nature and Function*. Chicago.
2. Storr, A. (1968). *Human Aggression*. New York.
3. Lorenz, K. (1966). *On Aggression*, trans. Majorie Kerr Wilson. New York.
4. de Maistre, J. (1890). "Eclaircissement sur les sacrifices," *Les Soirées de Saint-Petersbourg*. Lyons, 2: 341–2. Here, and throughout the book, translations are by Patrick Gregory unless an English-language reference is cited.
5. Evans-Pritchard, E. E. (1940). *The Nuer*. Oxford; Lienhardt, G. (1961). *Divinity and Experience: The Religion of the Dinka*. Oxford.

6. Radcliffe-Brown, A. R. (1952). *Structure and Function in Primitive Society.* Glencoe, Ill., p. 158.
7. Here, and throughout the book, quotations from the Greek plays have been translated by Patrick Gregory, from the original Greek.
8. Cf. Chapter 4, pp. 104–10.
9. Hubert and Mauss, *Sacrifice,* p. 33.
10. Malinowski, B. (1967). *Crime and Custom in Savage Society.* Totowa, N.J., p. 94.
11. Radcliffe-Brown, A. R. (1964). *The Andaman Islanders.* New York, p. 52.
12. Lowie, R. (1970). *Primitive Society.* New York, p. 400.
13. Malinowski, *Crime and Custom in Savage Society,* pp. 94, 98.
14. Lowie, *Primitive Society,* p. 400.
15. Storr, *Human Aggression,* pp. 18–19.
16. Cf. Makarius, L. (1968). "Les Tabous du forgeron," *Diogène* 62, April-June.

# 15

# JAN VAN BAAL (b. 1909)

Dutch anthropologist Jan van Baal began his career as a colonial official rather than an academic. He studied at Leyden University, wrote an ethnographic dissertation on southern New Guinea, and received his Ph.D. in 1934. Two years later he became a civil servant working as the Assistant District Commissioner in the Dutch colony of New Guinea. In 1949, after the second World War, during which he was briefly detained by the Japanese, van Baal became the Director of the Bureau of Native Affairs for the Dutch government in New Guinea. In this position, he conducted his own field research, and became a strong advocate of "applied anthropology," the notion that an understanding of local customs should inform political and economic development decisions. Between 1952 and 1958, van Baal served as the Governor of Dutch New Guinea. A year later he accepted a professorship at the Royal Tropical Institute of Amsterdam in the Anthropology department, and later was named a full professor at the University in Utrecht. One of van Baal's earliest books, and now his best known, is *Dema. Description and Analysis of Marind-anim Culture* (1966), a detailed Irian Jaya ethnography. This book was the first of several focusing on the nature of religion. His others include: *Symbols for Communication: An Introduction to the Anthropological Study of Religion* (1971), *Reciprocity and the Position of Women: Anthropological Papers* (1975), and *Man's Quest for Partnership: The Anthropological Foundations of Ethics and Religion* (1981).

Throughout his work, van Baal develops a notion that religious beliefs and practices constitute a fundamental response to certain facts of the human condition, in particular an undeniable need to "communicate" with the broader world, with an ordered cosmos. This communication, while perhaps including the exchange of messages, is more a matter of creating a meaningful relationship between the communicating parties. Religion is an expression of an innate human desire to "participate" in the universe, to overcome uncertainty and feel "at home" and included. Belief in supernatural beings, and all of the behaviors related to the supernatural realm—festivals, prayers, burial practices, healing ceremonies, ethical codes, etc.—provide comfort, and "lend meaning to human existence."

Van Baal's contribution to sacrifice theory appears in his essay "Offering, Sacrifice and Gift," a revised paper he presented at a conference in 1975. In the very first sentence he defines "offering" as an "act of presenting something to a supernatural being," and defines sacrifice as a special type of offering, one that includes killing the object offered. Hence understanding the nature of religious offerings will, van Baal believes, be a first step toward understanding sacrifice as well. The key to both phenomena is the notion of gift-giving. This essay is an extended examination of gift giving, its structure and consequences in a religious context. He criticizes Tylor for portraying gift-giving in "magical and mystical" terms, for transforming it into a "bribe," and he praises Marcel Mauss' treatment of gift-giving (in "Essai sur le don") for raising attention to the obligation of reciprocity it includes. Van Baal goes further, however, and argues that a more fundamental motivation is at work in religious offerings.

He begins with a distinction between "low-intensity rites," more routine expressions of belief and worship, and "high-intensity rites," the more occasional responses to misfortune and disasters. He notes how most understandings of gift-giving fail to account for both types. For example, he questions how low-intensity offerings to gods can simply be "to win divine favors," and how offerings brought under high-intensity conditions (those for penitence and expiation) can be magical attempts to transfer the sinner's "faults" to the victim. Instead of these, van Baal suggests that gift-giving in all these religious contexts can be understood as a particularly "effective means of communication" with the universe. In this way, sacrifice too, as a particular form of gift-giving, is a way for human beings to communicate with the divine realm. Destroying the sacrificial victim, killing it, eliminating its material presence, provides an "unshakable factuality" to the ritual event. It marks the reality of the communication.

While van Baal is most remembered for his ethnographic work, what could be called his "communication theory" of sacrifice should also be recognized as an important contribution. Reprinted here is van Baal's complete essay on sacrifice.

# "Offering, Sacrifice and Gift"

IN THIS PAPER[1] I call an offering any act of presenting something to a supernatural being, a sacrifice an offering accompanied by the ritual killing of the object of the offering. This definition does not permit the use of the term

Jan van Baal, "Offering, Sacrifice, Gift," *Numen*, Vol. XXIII (1976): 161–78. Reprinted with the permission of E. J. Brill Academic Publishers.

sacrifice for killing rituals (a term introduced by Jensen, 1951) that are neither preceded nor followed by the presentation of the object of the rite to a supernatural being.

Among the distinctive features of offering and sacrifice I do not include their sacred nature, considered to be their most essential characteristic by Hubert and Mauss, the authors of the *Essai sur la Nature et la Fonction sociale du Sacrifice* (1899). Founding their argument on data derived from Hebrew and Vedic sources, they concluded that the confrontation with the sacred is the awe-inspiring heart and core of the sacrificial act. However, the authors of these sources were native theologians, representing the views held by a priestly elite caste in a fairly highly developed society. Modern ethnographic research in simpler societies gives evidence that here the victims of a sacrifice are relatively rarely held to be sacred. Under certain circumstances they may, indeed, be tabooed but the rule is that these victims are primarily appreciated as meat. Even the parts more specifically dedicated to the gods are so little sacred that sometimes the children are condoned to snatch up the (mostly small) portions set aside for divine use. The sacred nature of the victim is too accidental a feature to be used as the foundation for the construction of a theory on the origin and development of sacrifice. To that end we have to turn to that general characteristic that sacrifice and offering have in common, that of being gifts. It is all the more desirable to concentrate on this common feature because a sacrifice is not necessarily a more deeply religious ceremony than an offering. Some of the really elaborate East Indonesian sacrifices are more typically social than religious affairs as is well borne out by their markedly potlatch-like character. Reversely, an offering can be a highly impressive religious ceremony without including a sacrifice. Quite a variety of Balinese temple feasts do not include any form of ritual killing, the decorated dishes (the meat included) being prepared at home, afterwards to be carried by the assembled villagers in a colourful ceremonial procession to the temple where they devoutly place the offerings at the foot of one of the shrines, to be dedicated by the priest who, on a raised platform, says his prayers and *mantras* and rings his bell. Of course, the combination of the rite with a killing ceremony may add to the grandeur of the event but, when all is said and done, the possibility to stage such a killing ceremony is not primarily a matter of greater religious devotion, but of wealth, a form of ceremony that only livestock-breeding peoples can afford. Apart from human beings the only animals that let themselves be sacrificed, i.e. killed on the spot chosen for the celebration, are domestic animals. The ritual killing of game is necessarily restricted to very exceptional circumstances and occasions.

The problem is whether this emphasis on the gift-character of offering and sacrifice can help us anyway better understand their meaning. It has been tried before with decidedly poor results, such as the interpretation of offerings as implements in a cunning game of *do-ut-des* with deities and ancestors dull enough to let themselves occasionally be cheated by the presentation of small titbits, or even of symbolic gifts such as that of a chicken for a real bull. However, such interpretations do not derive from undue stress on the fact that offerings are gifts, but from a fundamental misconception of the proper nature of the gift.

The confusion started with Tylor's definition of sacrifice (to him synonymous with offering): "As prayer is a request made to a deity as if he were a man, so sacrifice is a gift made to a deity as if he were a man. The human types of both may be studied unchanged in social life to this day. The suppliant who bows before his chief, laying a gift at his feet and making his humble petition, displays the anthropomorphic model and origin at once of sacrifice and prayer" (1871, II, 375). The metaphor is thoroughly misleading, as appears when Tylor's human types are transposed to more modern conditions. The suppliant then changes into the petitioner standing, not before a chief, but before the window-counter of the licence office, underhand pushing a banknote across the desk to the clerk whom he wishes to hand him the licence he desires. Tylor's human types did not offer a gift, but a bribe. His *do-ut-des* theory of sacrifice is its necessary consequence. The bribe is given to induce the deities to go out of their way to meet the "suppliant's" desires. To ensure this the offering must be substantial, and if it is not (as in the case of a titbit or a symbolic offering) Tylor accuses the sacrificer of cheating. Of course he does; having founded his notions of gift and sacrifice on corruption, he has to persist to the very end.

Tylor's theory of sacrifice has been rejected (and rightly so) on the ground that it is incompatible with the spirit and meaning of religion. Unfortunately, Tylor's adversaries did not find fault with Tylor's notion of the gift but with the gift as such. Even the appearance in 1924 of Marcel Mauss' "Essai sur le don" failed to lead to more than at best a partial reappraisal of the gift as the founding notion of offering and sacrifice. Typical in this respect is the position taken by van der Leeuw in his *Phaenomenologie der Religion* (§ 50). Admitting that an offering is a gift, he emphasizes the "magical" effect of the gift and thus succeeds in combining some aspects of the gift as described by Mauss with old concepts borrowed from the *do-ut-des* theory and more recent notions stressing the magical and mystical implications of sacrifice and offering. The theory is too much a mixture of everything to be convincing, but we cannot blame van der Leeuw for stressing the magical aspects. It was Mauss himself who had kept him on this track.

The problem underlying the "Essai sur le don" is the Durkheimian problem of the origin of the moral obligation faithfully to fulfill one's part in a contractual agreement. Historically the gift is older than the contract from which it differs primarily by the absence of any explicit agreement stipulating the nature, time, or form of the return gift. Gift and return gift are not the free and voluntary acts as they seem to be. There are no really free gifts. The analysis undertaken by Mauss disclosed that the gift involves three distinct obligations, those to give, to accept (one cannot refuse a gift) and to reciprocate. The obligation to reciprocate, the gift has in common with the contract, and it is to this aspect that Mauss paid specific attention. Why reciprocity? Although he did not formulate a comprehensive theory (the "Essai" is primarily a pheno-menological description and analysis) he did make a few suggestions, the most important among them being that something pertaining to the personality of the giver adheres to the object given away as a present, inducing the receiver to give something in return. A case in point is the Maori belief that a sizable gift has a *hau*, a kind of mana, compelling the donee to reciprocate lest the *hau* make him fall ill and die (Mauss, 1950, 158f.).

It is evident that this Maori belief simply reflects the compulsive power of the obligation as experienced by a Maori. It is a secondary interpretation of the obligation without any explanatory value because reciprocity is as strictly mandatory where such beliefs are unknown (cf. also Cl. Lévi-Strauss in Mauss, 1950, xxxix). To van der Leeuw, however, the belief was precisely what suited his own preferences for "magical" explanations and encouraged him to apply them in his theory of sacrifice.

Mauss had still another problem, one that he did not solve but that he analyzed beautifully. The reciprocity of the gift is anything but mechanical. It is deeply affected by status differences between exchange partners. The superior gives more than the inferior. A man of low status who gives lavishly is braggish, a rich man who fails in magnificence is mean. Therefore the return gift of the man of low status is small, of a man of high status is big. This has important implications on the practice of sacrifice and offering. The sacrificer is by definition always the lesser of the deities whom he offers his gift. His offering is, naturally, small, and Mauss dryly remarks: "Car ces dieux qui donnent et rendent sont là pour donner une grande chose à la place d'une petite" (1950, 169). Mauss did not comment any further on matters of sacrifice and so his remark did not get the attention it deserves. Yet, it once and for all disproved Tylor's disdainful comments on small offerings. Offerings are small naturally, and the real problem of sacrifice is not the small but the big offering. We shall have to return to this later; for the moment our concern is primarily with the absence of a theory explaining the characteristics of the gift. Mauss raised the problems without solving them.

A major problem of the gift is that of the inconsistencies of its reciprocity. Reciprocity itself had been recognized as a principle of universal significance even before Mauss. Malinowski expounded its importance for all forms of exchange in his *Argonauts of the Western Pacific* in 1922. In 1926 he gave further substance to the thesis that reciprocity is a principle of universal validity by applying it to the rules of civil and penal law (*Crime and Custom in Savage Society*). Later (1949) Lévi-Strauss called reciprocity one of the funda-mental structures of the human mind (1967, 98), a principle always and everywhere spontaneously recognized and applied in social institutions. Yet, the stronger the stress on reciprocity as a principle of universal validity, the more urgent the problems created by deviating institutions and customs. An absorbing discussion of the ins and outs of disbalanced reciprocity was presented by Marshall Sahlins in his essay "On the Sociology of Primitive Exchange" (1965). It is not only that reciprocity is sometimes unbalanced as in gift-exchange between partners of unequal status, but reciprocity can also be muddled, unclear, a principle held in latency as a weapon in reserve against persons who fail to comply with reasonable expectations. Muddled reciprocity prevails in the give-and-take characterizing the interaction between members of the small group. Here every member contributes to capacity, the strong and the clever producing the bulk of the group's material necessities, whereas the weak and the infirm have little more to offer than their good intentions. Up to an extent the relation is of a similar nature as that between high-status and low-status givers, but it differs in that it is perfectly informal. However, though reciprocity is not explicitly mentioned, it is not forgotten. It is implicit. When a member fails to cooperate to the degree he is expected to do, he will immediately be reminded of the rule of reciprocity and its implications.

I shall not enter into a discussion of the theoretical explanations forwarded by Sahlins and others. A major weakness of all of them is the lack of distinction between the diverging forms of exchange, an astonishing omission because some of the differences are so obvious. To give an example: the reciprocity obligatory in gift-exchange is not protected by law, but the obligations incurred in contracts and trade agreements are. Or another example: a gift must be accepted but a commercial offer not. Considerations of this kind induced me to a renewed review of the relevant facts by grouping them into two pairs of opposites, *viz.* gift-exchange versus trade, and punishment versus revenge, the latter in connection with reciprocity in succ. penal and civil law. The results concerning gift-exchange and trade I summarized in the following table (from van Baal, 1975, 50):

| *Trade* | *Gift-exchange* |
|---|---|
| Traders functionally each other's equals | Participants not always equals |
| Social relations weak, exhausted by completed exchange | Social relations strong, strengthened by completed exchange |
| Aims at the other one's goods | Aims at the other one's person |
| Goods exchanged often lowly valued | Goods exchanged often highly valued |
| Strict reciprocity, balanced | Reciprocity not always balanced |
| No obligation to trade or to accept an offer | Obligation to give and to accept a gift |
| Contracts (trade-relations) protected by law | Gift-exchange not protected by law |
| Trade does not bind participants | Gifts bind, turn participants into partners |

With regard to punishment and revenge I note that both involve a harm inflicted on the wrongdoer, but inflicted for radically different purposes. A punishment aims at restoring the delinquent to his proper place in the group by his atonement and his acceptance of the harm delivered to him. To the contrary revenge sees at the personal satisfaction and the restoration of the damaged status of the delinquent's victim by the severance and denial of social ties between the parties concerned. Punishment and revenge have in common that they normally are incommensurate to the crime but they are this in different ways. In punishment reciprocity tends to be muddled, less severe than a strict balance requires. In revenge it is clearly disbalanced. A thrashing must be repaid with a superior return-gift of blows to restore the initial victim's status.[2] In general, revenge sees at the elimination of the delinquent, punishment at his person and its salvation for society. This is why, in penal law-suits, the administering of justice tends to be characterized by muddled reciprocity, whereas in the settlement of civil law-suits dealing with goods and material interests, reciprocity is carefully balanced. The parallelism (mostly a parallelism in reverse) between these differences and some of those between gift-exchange and trade, is striking.

The principal difference between the two categories of exchange of goods is that in gift-exchange participants aim at the other one's person, in trade at the other one's goods. The gift holds a message to the donee, that of "I, donor, regard you as a partner, appreciate you as a friend, as one who belongs to us." The gift transfers this message not with empty words but with the unshakable factuality of its material presence. Thus the gift is an answer to the fundamental problem of the human condition, that of man's uncertainty about himself as a part of his universe from which, as a subject, he differs and is perennially separate.

In *Symbols for Communication* I argued that the dialectics of the human condition, the combination of being a part and yet a subject, a subject and yet a part of one's universe, make communication an urgent necessity, a communication, however, that is not merely an exchange of messages, but a communication which implies that whole world of feeling that conveys the comforting awareness of the reality of one's participation and "Zuhausesein," being at home, in one's universe. I shall not repeat the argument and confine myself to stating that the gift has the power to persuade a homesick waif or a suspicious soul that he is counted in, that he belongs to the group. Who could refuse a gift or fail to reciprocate? The gift is a godsend.

In all this there is no magic at all and yet it explains a lot. It even explains why the gift can be misused and taken advantage of for selfish purposes. The gift is an attractive and persuasive form for establishing contacts and ameliorating relations. It can be used to persuade a donee to do things he would not think of doing otherwise. We then speak of a bribe. Another misuse is the distribution of gifts as a means to enhance one's status, a possibility exploited in the Kwakiutl potlatch to such an extreme that in some cases gift-giving is turned into a form of controlled warfare instead of a friendly game. All this should not divert us from appreciating what and how a gift really is.

The gift is directed at the other one's person. Consequently, the latter's status and accidental circumstances must be taken account of. The gifts presented to a man in mourning differ from those given to a bridegroom. The gift must be adapted to social conditions. When there is a feast or a public crisis ostentatious giving is called for, but when things are running smoothly, as usually is the case in the small group that is a closely knit unit, it takes the unobtrusive form of a purely informal give-and-take with no other book-keeping of everyone's contributions than the sincerity of his intentions. It is the intentions that count in actions directed at the other one's person.

The many forms of offering and sacrifice could, like those of the gift, be grouped in ostentatious and unobtrusive forms. More meaningful, however, is a classification according to differences in religious situation by discerning between low-intensity and high-intensity rites. I owe the use of this distinction to the courtesy of Mr. J. G. Platvoet of the Theological Faculty of Utrecht University who introduced it in an inedited paper in which he opposed low-intensity communication to high-intensity communication. Low-intensity communication, he argued, is the ideal form for man's relations with the super-natural. When things run smoothly and anxiety is absent, simple rites suffice to keep up good relations with the gods, inspiring confidence in the persistence of their benevolence and protection. To the contrary, when misfortune or disaster persuade the faithful that there is something wrong with these relations, other rites are called for, those of the high-intensity type.

The opposition as introduced by Mr. Platvoet is, of course, not an absolute one, but it certainly is meaningful. It paves the way to due attention to what is so often neglected in our discipline, the religious practice of the simple faithful who is just pious without problems or fuss. One might call it routine piety provided it be understood that this routine is a mark of its sincerity. It is not a mean thing that, in some cultures, in every household on every day a minuscule gift of food is set aside on the simple house-shrine dedicated to the ancestors. Elsewhere such customs are restricted to special occasions like festive meals or the first dish of the beans or corn of the new harvest. When beer has been brewed a few drops are spilled or a small gourd is set aside under thanksgiving. The offerer does not mind who ultimately eats or drinks his offering. What counts is that he expresses his faith in the nearness of his gods and ancestors who, because of this nearness, must be remembered as co-residents of the compound. Our western culture is a word-culture. Accordingly the material sharing of food has been reduced to the thanksgiving of saying grace. Yet, it serves the same purpose, the inner realization of the Lord's comforting presence. The impact of a food offering is best illustrated by a remarkable custom of an Australian people, the Murngin, as little given to praying and offering as any Australian tribe. Celebrating their rites for the dead, they publicly take a meal of which nothing is set aside for the deceased with the explicit aim that his spirit will understand that he does no longer belong to the circle of the living and has to leave (Warner, 1957, 417). Sharing food is communicating.

Among the low-intensity rites we must include the sacrifices and offerings made on the occasion of ostentatious, potlatch-like celebrations like those for the inauguration of a new subclan or the commemoration of a deceased chief in East Indonesia. When the Ngad'a of Flores celebrate such a feast scores of buffaloes are slaughtered after having been presented ceremonially to the gods (for a summary see van Baal, 1971, 250–8). It is a great social event because all the meat must be distributed among the numerous guests, the share allotted to the gods and ancestors being really minimal, a detail rationalized on the eastern part of the island by stating that what little is to us, is much to the gods and reversely (Arndt, 1951, 2, 18, 106). The guests display greater interest in the distribution of the meat than in the religious part of the ceremony. Yet, the ancestors are not really ignored. Actually, they participate in every aspect of Ngad'a life. They all have their sanctuaries in the village, where the dead are buried in the stone walls separating the terraces on which, in these mountain-villages, the houses are built. Every house has its special niches where the forefathers of the inmates abide and where they receive small food offerings every time there is a festive dish. These small offerings are brought without any ceremonial. We even do not know whether the bringer of the food addresses the ancestors or that he just puts the food down at the intended place. But an official ceremony like an inauguration calls for an official invocation. One of the interesting features of such an invocation is the emphasis on the desirability of the presence, the nearness even, of gods and ancestors. They are invited to descend to accept the beasts that shall be sacrificed in their honour, but also to sit on their people's shoulders and necks and to protect them like a stone wall against disaster and sickness.

The address to the gods invariably includes a prayer for health, prosperity, and a long life. Although such prayers are common enough, the combination with an offering should surprise us for the simple reason that it is bad form for the donor of a gift to request anything in return, let alone to specify his desires. This deviation from the ordinary pattern of gift-giving is all the more conspicuous because on a feast of this size and magnificence there is not the slightest reason to pray for prosperity. The whole feast is a demonstration of the feast-giver's undoubted prosperity. If ever there is a wrong moment to ask for it, it is on this day of abundance. And yet they pray for it as well as for many other things about which the assembled merry-makers do not visibly worry. What makes it all the more interesting is that this is not a specifically Ngad'a idiosyncrasy: sacrifices are attended by prayers everywhere, whether there is a reason for praying or not. An interesting parallel is presented by the custom of Protestant Christians to say grace before meals. Though dimly aware that a thanksgiving is a poor occasion for asking favours, they strongly feel that irrespective of all rational considerations something ought to be requested anyhow. They decide to ask for a blessing. Nobody knows exactly what this stands for, and this apparently makes it easier to pray for it.

The irrationality of the usage cautions us not to look for its basic motivations in the aims overtly and consciously pursued, i.e., in the things prayed for, but in the structure of the prayer situation as such. It is the address of a man offering something to his god, a discourse between two beings separated by the maximal status difference imaginable. Vis-à-vis the almighty humility is called for, not merely in words but in deeds as well. Requesting is both the most simple and the most decisive act of self-humiliation, the recognition at once of the requestrant's dependence and of the addressee's power. Confronted to his god, asking is the most effective confession of a man's belief and worship. What cannot be done when offering a gift to a fellow-man, asking for something, must be done when offering a gift to a god. To do otherwise would be braggish. And this is where a gift differs from an offering.

All this is pertinent to low-intensity situations in which the relations between a man and his gods are normal and need nothing more or less than being kept up. Such relations are akin to those prevailing in the small and closely knit group with its continuous give-and-take, where intentions count more and better than the physical contributions made by each member individually. The offerings made in this situation are vehicles of intentions. Everyone knows that, just like everyone knows that the gods do not really eat the offerings presented to them, but that the mice and the ants do, or, as the case may be, the children. No one minds; the giving is a symbolic act of communication and so is the disappearance of the food a symbol of the participation of the gods and credulously ascribed to their acceptance. It is the symbol that counts. It is all very simple and there is no question of magic. The notion that offering and sacrifice are sacral acts hardly plays a role. Even in Hebrew religion, where the holiness of the Lord and everything pertaining to him is so strongly emphasized in the priestly precepts, the sacrifices of which the main part goes to the sacrificer are less sacred than the others. Some of them (the offering for a vow and the voluntary offering mentioned in Lev. 7) may even be eaten on the day after the sacrifice, an exceptional latitude in this purity ridden complex of regulations.

The picture changes as soon as situations present themselves requiring action for high-intensity communication: illness, epidemics, calamities, or mortal sin. The means applied may include sacrifice and offering, but the *schema* of gift-exchange is affected by other considerations to such an extent that it has to give way to wholly different forms such as those pertinent to penitence and expiation, or to communication with the gods by identification with their mythical activities. The sacrificial rituals that must answer the requirements of high-intensity situations are of such extreme diversity that I must confine myself to a few cases to illustrate my point, beginning with those in which the *schema* of the gift is dominant and then turning to those in which it has lost its relevance.

My first case is that of the payment of vows. Vows are made in prayers sent up by a barren woman desiring a child, by a family for the recovery of a sick father or son, by a dismissed official for a new job, etc. If the prayer is heard a sacrifice shall be brought at a certain sanctuary on the day appointed for such occasions. The procedure followed at the sanctuary is a perfectly normal one. The beast is presented to the deity whom thanks are brought for his bene-volence. Then the victim is slaughtered, the meat divided among the guests, and a small portion set aside for the deity if this is thought to be proper at all (it can fail to turn up, for example, if the blood flowing away is regarded as the divine share). The celebration is a feast where gratitude and merriness prevail. Yet, it is also a payment. Vows must be paid and woe befalls him who fails to do so. But it is a payment of a particular nature. Although the vow resembles a condition in a contract, it differs from a contractual condition in that it does not oblige the other party to the deliverance of any good, but only the maker of the vow. The deity remains perfectly free to hear or not to hear the suppliant. The latter binds only himself. The stage set by the vow is that the fulfilment of the prayer shall be seen as a gift, a completely free gift of the deity. If that gift be made then, of course, the beneficiary owes a countergift, the countergift stipulated in the vow. The reciprocity of the gift is binding. That the whole procedure is defined by the *schema* of the gift is confirmed by the fact that feelings of gratitude define the spiritual atmosphere of the celebration.

A more or less comparable case is that of the sacrifice brought for a sick man whose illness is ascribed to the wrath of neglected ancestors who did not receive all the sacrifices that a wise man should make on their behalf. The ancestors are nearby, often even inmates of the house, and the rules of the gift imply the obligation to give, primarily to those who are kinsmen. The negligence of the obligation has to be made good by a bigger gift than usual. The *do-ut-des* of the transaction that must lead to the patient's recovery is not contrary to the *schema* of the gift anyway. The same holds true of the sacrifices brought for the reconciliation of injuries committed against living persons, injuries discovered since the delinquent fell ill. Reparations are made and social bonds restored. Payments, indeed, but payments made in the form of gifts with deities or ancestors as the ever present participants of the celebration. Again, the prevalence of the *schema* of the gift is evident. It is confirmed by the fact that the victim of the sacrifice is cut up and the meat distributed among those present, as usual. It is neither sacred nor taboo.

A sacrifice for the expiation of mortal sin is completely different. The relevant procedure has been elaborately discussed by Hubert and Mauss. The scene is well known: the sinner puts his hand on the victim's back to express his intrinsic relation with the beast, and then, after the dedication, follows the complete destruction of the animal by fire. The victim is God's, i.e., it is sacred. It is also the bearer of the sacrificer's impurity and sin which are taken away by its destruction. That the victim is the vehicle of the sinner's impurity is high-lighted by the sacrifice brought on the Day of Atonement: one goat is burned, the other brought to the desert and set free. It is the goat for Azazel (Lev. 16: 10), carrying the people's impurity with it, just like the bird set free for the recovered leper (Lev. 14: 5ff.) takes the latter's impurity with it. In both cases the priest explicitly transfers the impurity to the beast by symbolic acts.

Although there is not the slightest doubt that after consecration the victims, whether burned or set free, are sacred, it is fully justified to doubt the wisdom of stressing this sacredness too much, i.e., beyond its function of being a symbol of the proper meaning of the ritual. In other words, I object against a reification of the symbolic content by interpreting it as a magical act. It is a misjudgment of the fundamental meaning of the expiatory sacrifice as an act of atonement, an act ruled not by magic but by the *schema* of the punishment, namely, a public confession combined with the suffering of a penalty which make the confessor acceptable to return to his place in society and in the normal relationships between gods and men. Earlier in this paper I referred to certain parallels between the *schema* of the gift and that of punishment. They explain why a sacrifice, more often a form of the gift, can be used also as a form of punishment. Because a punishment it is: the public confession of a sin but also the loss of a precious article of wealth that is not used for any good but for destruction, the destruction of its owner's guilt.

Expiatory sacrifices are reported from many parts. In East Indonesia, where holocausts are rare, the southern Toradja will bring one in case a man has committed incest with his sister or a full cousin. It is a mortal sin that makes the land hot so that prolonged drought must be feared. A buffalo is dedicated to the supreme being by the priest who addresses the god with his face turned westward (the ordinary posture is eastward). The beast is then killed and cut into pieces that are burned. In one part of the area the offender himself must tether the beast and address the god while holding the rope with his hand. The act of atonement and the punishment are clear. Yet, in this case there is more to it than this alone. Just like the sin has cosmic consequences, making the land hot, so has the holocaust. The smoke-clouds that go up from the burning sacrifice will in time turn into rain-clouds that cool the earth.[3]

Two things here are combined. On the one hand sin, punishment, and atonement, and on the other hand the belief that human acts can have cosmic consequences. The belief makes part of a worldview to which the visible things hold a mystery of their own by which they are more than they are or seem to be. Although to the Toradja the supreme being is the ultimate source and ruler of all hidden powers, human beings have a responsibility and power of their own. One may call this magic but I think that mystic knowledge is a better word, doing more justice to the notions of reverence inherently implied, as well as to the fact that this belief refers to another form of communication with the universe, *viz.* that by symbolic identification.

Expiatory sacrifices are not always holocausts. The Nuer of the East African Sudan have other ways to deal with serious cases of incest. An ox, dedicated by a priest, is killed and divided from nose to tail into two halves, one for the priests, the other for the sacrificer and his family who will consume the meat of their half. But the blood is for God and they closely observe that it runs away into the soil because it carries the delinquent's sin with it and makes for complete atonement and purification. Up to an extent the sacrificer is identical with the victim; before it is killed he rubs its back with ashes, expressing their togetherness (Evans-Pritchard, 1956, 189, 216, 298). The identification of a man and his ox is a recurrent theme in Nuer culture. In a sacrifice as here discussed it takes mystic dimensions in the identification of the sacrificer's sin with the victim's blood, and in the bisection of the carcass. If one prefers that term, one might call it magic, provided it be recognized that the act is primarily one of punishment and atonement: a public confession of sin and the loss of a highly valued animal, at the very least of the half of it that goes to the priests. That the punishment is not harder than this is because the Nuer do not condemn incest as severely as the Toradja do.

The Nuer celebrate holocausts for other purposes. When there is impending danger of pest or murrain they "go out to meet it." They slaughter a number of oxen in the bush where the carcasses are left behind "as a wall." The sacrifice is made to God, but the dead beasts are left to the evil spirits of illness. They may not be touched by anyone and the idea seems to be "that the evil has entered them through the sacrificial act" (Evans-Pritchard, 1956, 220). The magical effect of the rite is obvious; something dedicated to God must stop the peril. The "wall" of dead beasts has a power derived from the sacrifice, in part perhaps also from the notion that oxen are so near to man. In fact, this holocaust is a deed of despair. The Nuer are cattle loving people and nothing but the gravest danger can persuade them to part with their oxen in this manner. It is impossible to classify this holocaust either as a gift or as a penitence. There are some elements of penitence in it, but certainly not of the gift. Yet, if penitence has suggested the form, it still has a distant character, that of coming to terms with evil spirits who must be propitiated by a desperate act that comes nearer to a bribe than anything.

We noted in passing that cattle are so near to man. As a matter of fact, cattle are extremely inviting vehicles for identification, primarily for identification with man, but also for identification with the gods. Cattle are wealth, the most important item of wealth among many peoples. They are tended with care and devotion. Among cattle breeders strong feelings of togetherness between a man and his beasts prevail. An interesting case is that of the Ngad'a of Flores. They hold the view that *Déva*, the supreme being, herds mankind like the Ngad'a herd their buffaloes. Next to *Déva* there are a host of minor *déva*, particularizations of the great one. Father Arndt noted a statement to the effect that, when the *déva* above kill a buffalo a man dies on earth, and when the people on earth slaughter a buffalo a *déva* dies in heaven. The statement as such is no more than an intriguing case of pious speculation; it has no effect whatsoever on ritual. But the close relation between *déva*, man, and buffalo also finds expression in myth. All three are associated symbolically with the moon, and in a few myths a *déva* appears in the shape of a buffalo (van Baal, 1971, 252).

From here it is only one step to the identification of the sacrificed buffalo with the deity. The point of interest is that this step is not taken, not by the Ngad'a, not by the Nuer, nor by any of the Indonesian and African cattle breeding peoples I know of. As I did not make special enquiries into this matter, it would be rash to say that it does not occur at all. The possibility lying so near at hand, it would be surprising if it did not do somewhere. Nevertheless, the probability of an identification of victim and deity is considerably smaller that it must seem in the light of theories such as those by Frazer or by Hubert and Mauss on the god-victim of the agrarian sacrifice. These sacrifices, symbolizing the death of the corn-mother or the revival of the tree-spirit, derive from a radically different climate of religious thinking than the sacrifices associated with gift-exchange or with penalty and atonement. The proper content of the agrarian sacrifice is the re-enactment of the divine drama of death and resurrection, of life born by death. The drama of the gods is the drama of nature as well as that of the main means of subsistence, the corn. It is also the drama of mankind. Re-enacting its major events the actors identify themselves with the gods like the Australian aborigines do when they repeat the deeds of their ancestors by having these dream-time beings personified by men who are held to be physically their reincarnations. They thus give shape to the mysterious intentions that are the hidden essence of visible reality, identifying themselves with them, and through them with that whole world of mysterious intentions that is the secret essence of their universe. Communication with that universe is realized by acts of identification with the ancestors, the incarnations of its mystery, by direct participation in the mythical events and divine deeds. It is a form of communication that differs fundamentally from the person-to-person type of communication through discourse or the exchange of gifts between man and his gods.

The sacrifice of the god-victim is an effort at communication through identification. In this climate of thinking the question arises whether the victim should not more properly be a man than a beast symbolizing the god. In Mexico a thoroughly pessimistic worldview inspired a violent realism that found its fulfilment in the most diverse forms of human sacrifice. To many historians of religion the barbarism of the New World forms of sacrifice held a corroborant of the veridity of the numerous accounts of comparable atrocities committed in the ancient civilizations of the Old World. I must raise a *caveat* here. Modern anthropological research suggests that the proper secret of many secret rituals is not the supposedly esoteric meaning of the ritual, but, contrari-wise, the technique how to operationalize this esoteric meaning. A good case is that of the Marind-anim of South New Guinea (West-Irian). One section of the tribe periodically celebrated an initiation ritual called *ezam-uzum*, husband-wife. Before the beginning of the rites a contraption was constructed consisting of a long tree-trunk, resting on the ground with one end, and with the other at man's height on a simple scaffolding. Toward the end of the rites all the neophytes had to copulate one after another with a certain girl lying on a mat under the elevated end of the trunk. While the last of the neophytes was doing his duty the scaffolding was suddenly torn down, and the trunk crushed the copulating pair who were roasted and eaten. Obviously, they personified *ezam* and *uzum*, and a more convincing case of eating the deity is hardly imaginable. Later research confirmed the truth of the construction of the elevated tree trunk and also that at a certain moment the scaffolding was torn down, but not of the story of the copulating pair. All that was crushed were two coconuts, roughly decorated as a man's and a woman's head, and this did not even happen under the tree but a little way off. The story of the pair killed under the tree is the story told to the non-initiated. That it contains esoteric truth is confirmed by the more elaborate initiation rituals of the coastal divisions of the tribe. There, too, stories were told about a pair or a woman killed and eaten at the end of the rites. These stories were veritable myths giving significant infor-mation on the cosmological meaning of the rites. The non-initiated were allowed to know them, but not how the death of the deities concerned was operationalized by means of a perfectly innocent symbolism (cf. van Baal, 1966, 540 f., ch. 10, 11).

There is ample reason to keep this in mind when studying ancient records of human sacrifice. These sacrifices might have occurred less frequently than these records suggest. But I shall not enter deeper into this. Instead, another question must be raised. Are we really justified to call these rituals sacrifices? If they go combined with an offering or a dedication to a deity, we certainly are, but not if this element is lacking and the ritual is confined to the re-enactment of a mythical drama. In that case we had better use a more appropriate term, either the one of drama, or the term once proposed by Jensen, that of killing ritual (1951). I have no preferences in this matter, but I do object against the use of the term sacrifice for rituals in which every element of the gift or atonement is utterly absent. Giving is important, far more important than our theories thus far have been willing to recognize, erroneously substituting bribing for giving.

True giving is participating, participating in the life and work of the donee, participating in one's universe as a sympathizing member. No one can partici-pate without giving first. Giving is essential for a meaningful existence. The simple food-offering set aside for the gods, the clumsy prayer before meals, and the give-and-take characteristic of mutual care in the small group, are the most effective means of communication, cementing togetherness and confirming security. All communication begins with giving, offering.

## Notes

1.  Originally read at the 13th Congress of the International Association for the History of Religions, Lancaster, August 1975.
2.  A special form of revenge is capital punishment. Formally it is not a punishment because it does not begin with its execution, but ends with it. And materially it aims at the convict's elimination from society (cf. van Baal, 1975, pp. 58 ff.).
3.  I thank Dr. Hetty Nooy-Palm for this information.

## References

Arndt, Paul, s.v.d. (1951). *Religion auf Ost Flores, Adonare und Solor.* Studia Instituti Anthropos, vol. I. Wien-Mödling: Missionsdruckerei St. Gabriel.

Baal, J. van (1966). *Dema. Description and Analysis of Marind-anim Culture.* The Hague: Nijhoff.

Baal, J. van (1971). *Symbols for Communication.* Assen: Van Gorcum.

Baal, J. van (1975). *Reciprocity and the Position of Women.* Anthropol. Papers. Assen: Van Gorcum.

Evans-Pritchard, E. E. (1956). *Nuer Religion.* Oxford: Clarendon Press.

Hubert, H. and Mauss, M. (1899). "Essai sur la nature et la fonction sociale du sacrifice." *Année sociologique* II: 29–138 (Reprinted in *Mélanges d'Histoire des Religions,* 1–130, Paris, 1909).

Jensen, A. E. (1951). *Mythos und Kult bei Naturvölkern.* Wiesbaden: Steiner Verlag.

Leeuw, G. van der (1933). *Phaenomenologie der Religion.* Tübingen: Mohr. References to rev. edn. 1956.

Lévi-Strauss, Claude (1947/67). *Les Structures élémentaires de la Parenté.* Paris: Presses Univ. de France. References to 2nd edn., La Haye, Mouton, 1967.

Lévi-Strauss, Claude (1950) "Introduction à l'œuvre de Marcel Mauss". In Mauss, 1950, 9–52.

Malinowski, Bronislaw (1922). *Argonauts of the Western Pacific.* New York: Dutton; London: Routledge and Kegan Paul.

Malinowski, Bronislaw (1926). *Crime and Custom in Savage Society.* London: Kegan Paul, French Trubner; New York: Harcourt Brace.

Mauss, Marcel (1924). "Essai sur le don". In *Année sociologique,* nouv. série I: 30–186. Reprint in Mauss 1950.

Mauss, Marcel (1950). *Sociologie et Anthropologie par M. Mauss.*

Sahlins, Marshall D. (1965). "On the Sociology of primitive Exchange". In Michael Banton (ed.), *The Relevance of Models for Social Anthropology,* ASA Monographs I. London: Tavistock.

Tylor, E. B. (1871). *Primitive Culture,* 2 vols. London: Murray. References to 4th edn.

Warner, W. Lloyd (1957). *A Black Civilization.* Rev. edn. New York: Harper.

# 16

# VICTOR TURNER (b. 1920)

Victor Turner was born in Glasgow, Scotland, studied poetry and classics at University College in London, and after a five-year interruption for military service during World War II, received a B.A. in anthropology at the age of twenty-nine. He earned his Ph.D. in anthropology from the University of Manchester after a four-year period of fieldwork studying the Ndembu, a forest-dwelling people of Zambia. In 1957, he published his dissertation as *Schism and Continuity in African Society*, a study of the role of conflict and the resolution of conflict within social organization. Turner began his teaching career at the University of Manchester, but in 1963 he accepted a position in the anthropology department at Cornell University, the first of several American institutions where he would work, the others being the University of Chicago and the University of Virginia. Throughout his career he published widely on the topics of religion, ritual, symbolism, social dynamics, and later, performance theory. Much of this work has been broadly influential in the fields of anthropology and comparative religion. His most well-known books include: *The Forest of Symbols: Aspects of Ndembu Ritual* (1967), *The Drums of Affliction: A Study of Religious Processes among the Ndembu of Zambia* (1968), *The Ritual Process: Structure and Anti-Structure* (1969), and *Dramas, Fields, and Metaphors: Symbolic Action in Human Society* (1974).

Trained in the shadow of British structural-functionalism, Turner understood cultures as systematic structures comprising a social order, and religion, particularly ritual, as a key agent employed to establish this order. Different from most of his predecessors however, Turner insisted that social order was not static, but was instead dynamic, dramatic, and changing. Societies should be analyzed, he suggested, in terms of "social dramas," phases of public action and re-action. Cultures have a local history comprised of various crises, disturbances, and imbalances in the social order, but also ritual responses and attempts to redress problems. In this way, cultures are "episodic," never fully in equilibrium, with social meanings and values negotiated through ritual processes.

The ideas of French folklorist Arnold van Gennep, specifically his notion of "rites of passage," helped inspire Turner to develop this notion of social process. Van Gennep observed that religions often employ certain rituals (or clusters of rituals) when individuals undergo biological and social changes, for example during birth, puberty, marriage, and death. He suggested that these rituals of transition accomplish a transformation for the individual participant, clearly marking new social identities and status. Most importantly for Turner, van Gennep observed that these "rites of passage" ordinarily follow a sequence of three different phases or stages: a separation phase, an intermediate "liminal" phase, and a final reintegration phase. The middle phase, characterized by "liminality," became a key concept for Turner. He claimed that not just individuals, but whole communities move through such phases, experience liminality, and undergo transformations. Turner coined the word "communitas" to describe this social form of liminality. Being "betwixt and between," communitas refers to periods when normal social structures (hierarchies, divisions, limits, heterogeneity) dissolve allowing egalitarian impulses and feelings of unity and freedom to predominate. Throughout much of his work, Turner understood ritual processes (e.g., pilgrimages, new year festivals, divination practices, etc.) in relation to communitas, as either preceding, constituting, or following it. He revealed a number of important insights by applying this interpretive model, that is, by identifying the role of communitas in social processes, and recognizing the movement from structure, to anti-structure, to new structure.

Ritual is symbolic activity, for Turner. It is an acting with and through symbols. He understands symbols as "polysemous," "multivocal," units that paradoxically condense multiple meanings. Ritual links together otherwise polarized meanings, specifically social (ideological, moral, and normative) meanings and personal (emotional, sensory, and desirable) meanings. Consequently, the full meaning of ritual symbols is never simply fixed. Ritual is instead a creative process that defines and re-defines semantic units, that moves between different "levels of meaning" (what Turner calls "operational," "positional," and "exegetical" levels), and therefore supporting the fundamental mechanism of cultural life as process.

Turner treats sacrifice as one form of ritual, and as such understands it as a transformative process within the broader context of cultural processes. Like other types of ritual, sacrifice revolves around negotiating phases of structure and liminality (communitas). Turner claims that many of the common features of sacrificial activity (honoring gods, gift giving, the expiation of sins, communication between the sacred and profane, and so forth), can be understood as embodying some part of this negotiation. In his article, "Sacrifice as Quintessential Process: Prophylaxis or Abandonment?", he develops this approach to sacrifice and discusses how it tends to respond to the structure/liminality dynamic in two different ways: as "abandonment" and as "prophylaxis." Using Ndembu material he notes that sacrifice often seeks to generate communitas, to create a context of liminality where social and personal problems (suffering, failure, disease, and so forth) can be dissolved. Problems can be "abandoned" by involving them in a transformative ritual action, that is, one that welcomes communitas and the subsequent restoration of order it provides.

Conversely, sacrificial rites may also be employed as a means of maintaining or protecting social order and structure. Rather than responding to a crisis, these rituals are concerned with demarcating limits, preventing disorder, and reestablishing hierarchies. Turner observes certain literate, complex, agriculturally based societies perform these "prophylactic" rites on a regular basis. For both abandonment and prophylaxis, sacrifice transforms the "moral state" of the participants. As the sacrificial victim is destroyed, Turner suggests, the balance between structure and anti-structure (including the power each represents) is altered, and the dynamic nature of the social order is redefined.

Sacrifice for Turner is one method by which human beings can engage the symbolic character of their world. During moments of crisis and the opposite, during ordinary celebrations, religious ritual allows individuals and groups to respond creatively to the changing needs of their experience, to the dynamic nature of their sense of reality. Sacrifice, by virtue of the radical change it inflicts upon a victim, namely its death or destruction, adds an additional level of symbolic efficacy in the effort to alter the moral condition of the social order. Ultimately, Turner presents what could be called a "transformation theory" of sacrifice. Relying on his general notion of ritual and its overall significance for society, he emphasizes how sacrifice may be the "quintessential" ritual practice.

Reprinted here is a brief selection from Turner's article "Sacrifice as Quintessential Process: Prophylaxis or Abandonment?" It provides an example of his thinking about ritual in general, as well as a glimpse into how he understands sacrifice.

# From "Sacrifice as Quintessential Process: Prophylaxis or Abandonment?"

ONE CAN hardly imagine a system more different from the Ndembu than the Iguvian. Structuration prevails over flow in many ways. The major religious ceremonies take place on fixed dates in the annual cycle—Ndembu rituals are not calendrically connected. The procedures of each Iguvian ritual

Victor Turner, "Sacrifice as Quintessential Process: Prophylaxis or Abandonment?", *History of Religions*, vol. 16, no. 3 (1977): pp. 208–15, with the permission of the publisher.

are fixed in written rubrics and must be performed in a set order, though there is a fallback mechanism of ritual redress in case of error or failure in the performance. Rituals involve a hierarchy of deities, each of whom has his or her sacrificial beasts and prescribed forms of worship. But the main difference perhaps is in the Iguvian stress on limits and boundaries and in the association of sacrifices with such fines. Sacrifice for Ndembu and many other African peoples is dominantly associated with the termination of flow—with the sharp cutting off of a social process, the ending of a relationship in a form that had become unviable. Iguvian and other Umbrian and Latin sacrifice is linked with the demarcation of frameworks in space and time. It is a cultural mapping device for establishing contours, limits, and bounded spaces. Perhaps this "plotting and piecing" is appropriate for a culture of skilled and committed farmers. In the Roman case, certainly, the methodical farming style was made over to the political realm just as Mars, originally an agricultural numen, became primarily associated with war in the religion of the state. Death enters both the African and Iguvian forms, but in the former symbolic death as expressed in sacrificial acts punctuates, as it were, the behavioral "speech" of changing social relations, while in the latter it imposes sacred legitimacy on the ritually discriminated, one might almost say "constructed," social and cultural orders seen as expressions of the invisible divine order. Sacrifices express discontinuities and thus create structure in this ritual system dedicated to demarcating, separating, and framing.

An example of this structuring or restructuring sacrificial ritual may be found in the *lustratio* of the sacred mount or citadel of Iguvium, known as the Arx Fisia. In Latin and Umbrian ritual a *lustratio* was a ritual process aimed at affecting purification and protection from evil or inauspicious influences—indeed it began with taking the auspices, an observation of the position of birds entering a *templum* or rectangular space in which the augur sits looking southward for favorable avian indications (flight or song) on the east or unfavorable on the west. The *lustratio* consists essentially of a solemn procession around the thing to be purified, whether city, fields, army, or flocks, and the offering of prayer and sacrifice at certain points. Vergil describes such a lustration, after the funeral rites for Misenus, in the *Aeneid* 6. 229. The Iguvian tablets mention that in the lustration of the citadel three gates and two shrines form successive places of sacrifice. Sacrifices are made first before each gate then behind it. Any structuralist worth his salt would be delighted by this highly formalized process. I will not give all the details but cannot refrain from mentioning that each of the eight sacrifices is offered to a different deity and that each consists of the slaughter of three animals. Each performance is associated with the worship of a separate deity and has five stages thrice repeated: libation; invocation; a long prayer; slaughter of an animal; and an offering of the *exta* or vital organs of the animal, a cake of spelt (a primitive species of wheat with grains that do not thresh free of the chaff) and a flour cake, with wine or posea (inferior soured wine). The *exta* are offered in a litter. The whole sacrificial process is terminated by a prayer recited in low tones generally summarizing the sacrifice.

Before the Trebulan Gate three oxen are sacrificed to Iuppiter Grabovius; behind it three pregnant sows to Trebus Iovia. Before the Tesenacan Gate three oxen are offered to Mars Grabovius (then mainly an agricultural deity); behind it three suckling pigs to Fisus Sancius. Before the Porta Veia three oxen with white foreheads are offered to Vofionus (or Vofio) Grabovius; behind it three lambs to Tefer Iovius. The seventh sacrifice is made at the Jovian shrine, three bull calves to Mars Hodius. The eighth and last stop of the circuit is made at the shrine of Coredius for the sacrifice of three bull calves to Hontus Cerifius. Details of minor offerings vary slightly from site to site. "The inscription states that if any fault is committed by any omission in the prescribed ritual, then the sacrifices are vitiated. It will be necessary to observe the birds again, to return to the Porta Trebulana, and to begin the entire sacrifice and procession anew."[1]

Followers of Dumézil will have already noted the triads in sacrifice: the numbers of beasts slain on each occasion, the triad of gods with the title Grabovius, Jupiter, Mars, and Vofionus—"to make whom a triad in the technical sense, only a common shrine is lacking."[2] Kretschmer has derived the term Grabovius applied as adjective to three deities, Iuppiter, Mars, and Vofionus, from the Slavic *grabz*, an oak tree, considering it to have been borrowed by the Umbrians from the Illyrian, with the meaning of "belonging to oaks, oak god."[3] The association of Jupiter and the Greek Zeus with sacred oak groves used for oracular purposes (for example, Dodona) is well known. But I will not here go into the fascinating detail of these rites. Enough data have been presented to show that they are concerned with general processes of inclusion and exclusion, of delimiting, of protecting the known against the unknown, and presenting models of symmetry and hierarchy. They impose cosmos on the city at regular, calendrical intervals. They also have a strong prophylactic intention, they prevent or guard against pollution or inauspicious intervention. Whereas the Ndembu and other African rituals responded to crises, these Umbrian rites ward them off. The words of the invocation and prayer made in front of the Trebulan gate (one of the ingresses into the citadel, thus constituting a potentially dangerous threshold of *limen*) make this clear:

> Iuppiter Grabovius, I invoke thee with this ox, a rich expiatory offering, for the Fisian hill, for the Iguvian State, for the name of this hill, for the name of this state. Iuppiter Grabovius, honored with this, if on the Fisian Hill a fire had broken out, if in the Iguvian State the due rites are omitted, overlook it. Iuppiter Grabovius, if there is any fault in thy sacrifice, any offense, any diminution, any neglect, any defect, any fault seen or unseen, Iuppiter Grabovius, if it is permitted, let it be expiated with this ox, the rich expiatory offering. Iuppiter Grabovius, purify the Fisian Hill, purify the

Iguvian State, the nobles, the rites, the men, the cattle, the fields, and the fruits of the Fisian Hill. Be propitious, be favorable with thy peace to the Fisian Hill, to the Iguvian State, to the name of the hill, to the name of the state. Iuppiter Grabovius, preserve safe the Fisian Hill, preserve safe the Iguvian State . . .[4]

The *lustratio* rites, like all other Iguvian rites recorded in the tablets, are frame-maintenance rites. The city or the state has taken over the sacrificial system, and acting through its twelve Fratres Atiedii, the priestly college, has elaborated and systematized the material of sacrifice as perhaps it was known in earlier times among the Umbrian tribes. In so doing, sacrifice has been put directly at the service of the overarching cosmological and political structures, losing to a great extent its interior quality and its sensitive responsiveness to important changes in specific personal and social relationships. The formed has been made to prevail over the forming, law over the living, in these sacrifices.

Now let us return to the Ndembu sacrifices at Chihamba in which the deity Kavula first allows himself to be sacrificed then, in a new mode of being, sacrifices the former sacrificers, the candidates for admission to his cult, who are also patients aspiring to be cured of illness or ill luck brought about by neglect or transgression of the kinds of rules binding on a localized moral community of living and dead kin. Here there is some sense of abandonment, not merely prophylaxis. You will recall how Hubert and Mauss in the final pages of their seminal essay, while characterizing sacrifice as a mingling of dis-interestedness and self-interest,[5] since "no sacrifice [does not have] some *contractual* element," made one exception.[6] "This is the case of the sacrifice of the god, for the god who sacrifices himself gives himself irrevocably. This time all intermediaries have disappeared. The god who is at the same time the 'sacrifier' [by which the translator, W. D. Halls, means the sponsor of the sacrifice] is one with the victim and sometimes even with the 'sacrificer' [that is, the officiant or priest]. All the differing elements which enter into ordinary sacrifice here enter into each other and become mixed together. But such mixing is possible [Hubert and Mauss insist] only for mythical, that is, ideal beings. This is how the concept of a god sacrificing himself for the world could be realized, and has become, even for the most civilized peoples, the highest expression and, as it were, the ideal limit of abnegation, in which no appor-tionment occurs."[7] The French scholars seem to have only the high historical religions in mind, but we have seen the same principle of total mutual identifi-cation in death and rebirth of god, victim, sacrifice, and sacrificer operating in the religion of a remote West Central Bantu-speaking tribe of Zambian forest dwellers. There is no question of "totemism" here,[8] except in the Lévi-Straussian sense that an "animal code" (the sacrifice of fowls) is used as part of the sacrificial process, and that the real death of fowls is homologous with the symbolic death of adepts and candidates. But the whole process suggests that it is only by "losing one's life" that one will find life more abundantly, only by entrusting oneself to the invisible powers that one will renew one's own visible social existence. But I do not want to fall into Hubert and Mauss's trap: that of blithely identifying what they call "the *sacred* things in relation to which sacrifice functions" as "*social* things," a statement which they say "is enough to explain sacrifice."[9] "This character of intimate penetration and separating," they say, "of immanence and transcendence, is distinctive of social matters to the highest degree. They also exist at the same time within and outside the individual, according to one's viewpoint. Sacrifice . . . is a social function because sacrifice is concerned with social matters."[10]

Here one would have to say that if sacrifice is "ambiguous," the school of Durkheim has not resolved its ambiguity by invoking the *deus ex machina*, "society," whom they have placed on the throne of the God who is dead— murdered one supposes, not sacrificed, since sacrifice presupposes a resurrection or at least a regeneration. Society may perhaps better be thought of in this idiom as Augustine's "terrene city" or "social structure," in which the person is masked in the *persona*, subjugated to the rules and customs hedging about his status role and group membership, and driven by self-interest, enlightened or otherwise, to maximize his gratifications at the expense of his fellows. Here the dynamic principle is *Amor sui*, "Love of self." Or it may be Augustine's "heavenly city" of disinterested communitas that is being presented as the model of postsacrificial behavior, where persons unmask themselves and freely become friends and lovers, where William Blake's formulation prevails: "Mutual Forgiveness of each Vice, Such are the Gates of Paradise."[11] Sacrifice, too, relates to these opposed models for "society": the lamb may be slaughtered to maintain the structured order, as in the system maintained at Iguvium by the priestly college. Or it may be an indicator of the dissolution of all structural *fines* or boundaries, an annihilator of artificial distances, restorative of communitas however transiently.

In the sacrifice of abandonment, the classical theological notions of sin, redemption, and atonement all find their places as phases in a process which seeks personal and social renewal through the surgical removal, interiorly in the will, exteriorly by the immolation of a victim, of the pollution, corruption, and division brought about by mere participation in the domain of social structure. Sacrifice is here regarded as a *limen*, or entry into the domain of communitas where all that is and ever has been human and the forces that have caused humanity to be are joined in a circulation of mutual love and trust. In the sacrifice of prophylaxis, structure certainly is cleansed, but left intact; here enlightened self-interest prevails. Hubert and Mauss put the matter very well:

The two parties present [gods and men] exchange their services and each gets his due. For the gods too have need of the profane. If nothing were set aside from the harvest, the god of the corn would die; in order that

Dionysus may be reborn, Dionysus' goat must be sacrificed at the grape harvest; it is the *soma* that men give the gods that fortifies them against evil spirits. In order that the sacred may subsist, its share must be given to it, and it is from the share of the profane that this apportionment is made . . . we know that with no intermediary there is no sacrifice. Because the victim is distinct from the sacrificer and the god, it separates them while uniting them: they draw close to each other, without giving themselves to each other entirely.[12]

Major religions, such as Christianity, move between these poles of the sacrificial process, between Chihamba and *Lustratio arcis*, so to speak, which themselves correspond to the dual nature of "the social," communitas and structure. On the one hand Jesus, at Gethsemane, "abandons" himself: "Not my will but Thine be done." On the other hand, theologians, beginning with Saint Paul, draw out all the implications of the ransom or redemption metaphor, with its structural implications of slavery and the market. At one pole self is immolated for the other, at the opposite pole the other is immolated for self. Between the poles there are many gradations of offering: part of self may be offered for some others; part of the other may be offered for the whole self. These nuances may be coded in many ways: in the type and quantity of victims, in the manner of immolation, in the kind of officiant, in the time and place of the sacrificial occasion.

In summary, anthropology knows many theories of sacrifice, including those of the evolutionists, diffusionists, functionalists, and structuralists. Each has tended to focus on a component act, object, relationship, or concept of what is, in reality, a complex ritual process, verbal and nonverbal, which has to be grasped from the outset as a totality. Gift exchange, tribute, propitiation, penitence, atonement, submission, purification, communion, symbolic parricide or filiocide, impetration, and many more ideas or practices have been advanced as clues, even keys, to its understanding. Sacrifice, as we have seen, may be performed by or for individuals, groups, or types of persons. It may involve the offering of a gift or the immolation of a victim—which may be partially or totally destroyed, consumed totally or as a special portion by officiants, or eaten by all present, often after special preparation. Prayers as well as objects are offered. Most sacrifices, whether embedded in seasonal, curative, life-crisis, divinatory, lustrational, or other kinds of rituals, or performed as isolable ritual sequences, are intended to transform the moral state of those who offer them, through the intermediacy of a victim, as Hubert and Mauss have eloquently shown.

The sacrificial process, especially when it involves the immolation of something highly valued (directly or figuratively), posits the antinomy of an unblemished self (directly and spontaneously related to other such selves) and a blemished self (or, in most non-Western contexts, multiple selves) closed or distanced from each other by conflicts and jealousies attendant upon the occupancy of positions in the social structure. Two notions of power are contrasted: power based on force, wealth, authority, status, tradition, or competitive achievement; and power released by the dissolution of systemic and structural bonds. The sacrifice of abandonment collapses hierarchical and segmentary differentiations. The first kind of power is offered and abandoned; the second, sometimes thought of as deriving from God, the gods, *numina*, spirits, ancestors, or other types of generous "Invisibles," is tapped to purify and simplify relations among group members and the "mental sets" of individuals. The structural self is immolated to liberate the antistructural identity. Of course, different types of sacrifices deal with this process in different ways, some stressing total renunciation of the structural order both subjectively and objectively, others its cleansing and renovation. In the majority of public sacrifices, the order of social structure is ultimately reinstated or reconstituted on the understanding that it must pass periodically, wholly or segment by segment, under the knife or through the fires of sacrifice, dying to be reborn in symbol, surrogate, or ordeal. *Renunciatory* sacrifices stress the interiority of the act, *prophylactic* sacrifices the performative, institutionalized details. And while the former uses the imagery of sharp, almost surgical death to bring about the rebirth of the identity and the existential communitas, the agapic feast of identities, the latter employ the metaphor of death to establish or reestablish the limits, boundaries, and frames of legitimately constituted structures of society and culture, within which orderly life may be lived. One destructures, the other restructures, soul and city. Both renew, both respond to the human condition, oscillant and liminal between the Visible and the Invisible, the Many and the One.

# Notes

1. W. Ward Fowler, *The Religious Experience of the Roman People* (1911), p. 29.
2. Irene Rosenzweig, *Ritual and Cults of Pre-Roman Iguvium* (1937), p. 67.
3. *Ibid.*, p. 68.
4. *Ibid.*, p. 32.
5. Hubert and Mauss, *Essay on Sacrifice* (1964), p. 100.
6. *Ibid.*, p. 101.
7. *Ibid.*
8. A system of beliefs centered on the notion that an animal or natural object is consanguineally related to a given family, clan, or moiety and taken as its emblem or symbol.
9. Hubert and Mauss, p. 101.
10. *Ibid.*, p. 120.
11. William Blake, *Poetry and Prose*, ed. D. Erdman (New York: Doubleday and Co., 1965), p. 256.
12. Hubert and Mauss, p. 100.

# 17

# LUC DE HEUSCH (b. 1927)

Belgian anthropologist and cultural historian of Africa, Luc de Heusch studied at both the Université Libre de Bruxelles (1944–9) and the Sorbonne in Paris (1951–2). After three years of field research in the former Belgian Congo, he earned his Ph.D. in anthropology from Brussels University. During this time he became interested in filmmaking, and over the course of his career produced several ethnographic films, including *Fête chez les Hamba* (1955), a glimpse into the ritual life of the Hamba of Kasai, *Sur les Traces du Renard Pâle* (1983), a collaboration with Germaine Dieterlen on the Dogon, and several others on Rwandan society. De Heusch served as a professor at the Université Libre de Bruxelles for his entire academic teaching career (1955–92), accepting several visiting appointments in France, Canada, and the United States. His research focused mostly on political anthropology and the anthropology of religion in Africa. He has published a number of articles and books, the best known of which include, *Why Marry Her?: Society and Symbolic Structures* (1971, 1981), *The Drunken King, or, The Origin of the State* (1972, 1982), and *Sacrifice in Africa: A Structuralist Approach* (1985). His work presents an abundance of ethnographic detail, and offers strong theoretical statements and analyses.

De Heusch adopts "structuralist" methods in much of his work. Like many French-speaking intellectuals of his time (e.g., Jacques Lacan, Jean-Pierre Vernant, Germaine Dieterlen, and many others), he was influenced by recent developments in the field of linguistics, a new turn away from historical approaches to language that saw linguistic elements having intrinsic value, and a turn toward an approach that sought meanings by identifying how the relations between elements constitute a structured system. Swiss linguist Ferdinand de Saussure, particularly his emphasis on the relational concept of "difference," is usually credited for inspiring this move toward studying the structure of language. He suggested that linguistic signs are meaningful by virtue of their place within a system of "horizontal" (syntagmatic combinations) and "vertical" (paradigmatic selections) relations, and that this system underlies, unifies, and explains the diversity of linguistic events. Taking up this notion of the "differential" character of language, Russian linguist Roman Jakobson argued that phonemes are always distinguished from each other according to a finite set of oppositions, that, in other words, the structure of language is comprised, at its most basic level, of "binary oppositions." Claude Lévi-Strauss, heavily influenced on this point by Marcel Mauss' *The Gift*, extended these insights from linguistics to establish a method of "structural anthropology," one that understands cultural phenomena as governed by an underlying logical structure. Like linguistic elements, single cultural details are significant in their relations to the overall cultural system. Lévi-Strauss argued that a "structuring pattern of binary oppositions"—oppositions like male/female, raw/cooked, dry/wet, hard/soft, nature/culture, humans/animals, and life/death—a system of "contrasts and intermediaries," constitutes a universal logic that codes all cultural phenomena. The task of analysis, therefore, becomes recognizing the binary oppositions structuring a people's sense of social and cultural order. Understanding religious myths and rituals is, in this way, a matter of sensing not only their role in defining and maintaining local understandings of reality, but also the essential (unconscious, inter-subjective) structured system of relations they manifest.

The classicists Marcel Detienne and Jean-Pierre Vernant have offered an example of a structuralist treatment of sacrifice, an example that influences Luc de Heusch's work. Over the course of many writings, Detienne and Vernant have examined Greek material and identified a complex network of parallel relations linking together sacrifice, marriage, and agriculture (of cereal grains). These three aspects of Greek culture, all of which are implicated in the myth of Prometheus and/or the slaying of Dionysus, stand "at the center" of a system of oppositions (e.g., above/below, raw/burned, beasts/gods, seduction/virginity, etc.). The practice of ritual sacrifice and the myth of Prometheus establish "just the right distance" between the oppositions. Remembered and enacted by human beings, this myth and ritual recall distinctions that make cultural life possible. The point here, one at the heart of any structuralist analysis, is that the meaning of any single ethnographic detail (mythic event, ritual performance, etc.) springs from its position within a field of relations. While sacrifice may function to "conform group cohesion," its meaning, for Detienne and Vernant, resides in its relation to a larger system of structured relations.

Luc de Heusch, in his book *Sacrifice in Africa: A Structuralist Approach*, notes that certain aspects of this Greek "cooking model" of sacrifice, or certain "variants" of it, can contribute to an overall understanding of sacrificial practices in Africa. In this study, de Heusch considers materials from several different African ethnic groups—in particular, the Bambara, Dogon, Zulu, Thonga, and Swazi. In each case, he shows how sacrificial rituals follow one of two "sacrificial schema," two different organized symbolic systems: "royal, cosmogonic sacrificial practices" and "domestic, culinary practices." This first is a topic Frazer already associated with sacrifice, the phenomenon of "sacred kingship" with its cluster of common features (e.g., complex prohibitions surrounding the king, regicide, and so forth). The death of the sacrificial victim is a substitute for the king/god, who when killed is reborn along with the cosmos itself. The second schema, the domestic and culinary, involves the killing of an animal, its ritual cooking, and a meal. Here, the relations between human beings and divine beings (whether in need of "conjunction" or "disjunction") are attached to the nature of the victim and the culinary/alimentary events surrounding its treatment. Both schemas include sets of oppositions according to which each particular cultural example of sacrifice can be classified, and charted, as is common in structural analyses. At the same time, de Heusch strays slightly from his structuralist project when he concludes that sacrifice is "primarily" an attempt "to outwit death," that an "existential emptiness" (experienced quite variously) drives human beings to destroy part of what they "have" to preserve what is essential—who they are (their "being"). In sacrifice, putting it differently, the victim is a payment of a "sacrificial debt," a payment of life to sustain life.

Reprinted below are the last few pages from de Heusch's *Sacrifice in Africa*. They provide some examples of the structuralist approach he employs throughout his book, and they contain his overall conclusions for the entire study. With critical references to Hubert and Mauss, Evans-Pritchard, and Girard, de Heusch provokes in this book a number of important questions regarding the nature of the sacrificial victim. As a "structuralist theory" (or "relations theory,") of sacrifice, it suggests that there are a finite number of relations constituting the nature of sacrificial phenomena, and that knowing these allows us to gain an understanding of these phenomena.

# From *Sacrifice in Africa:*
# *A Structuralist Approach*

TRADITIONAL LABELS only minimize and oversimplify this problem. Let us try, rather, to set up the structural frameworks that are developed around sacrifice. As the central phenomenon of the royal problematic as well as of the cosmogonic myths, human sacrifice bears a maximum load. It triggers new energies, short-circuiting or destroying dangerous powers which were

Luc de Heusch, *Sacrifice in Africa: A Structuralist Approach*, translated by L. O'Brien and A. Morton (Bloomington: Indiana University Press, 1985), pages 206–16. Reprinted with the permission of Indiana University Press and the author.

previously rampant. It often incites horror. The Bambara accept the sacrifice of the albino, the king's substitute, as a necessary evil; it is the "bad sacrifice" *par excellence*. It is not the result of murderous blind fury as war is. The Aztecs, in implementing the monstrous conjunction of war and human sacrifice, were convinced that they were obeying the relentless laws of the universe. Frazer, too anxious to relegate human sacrifice to a barbarous stage in human evolution, curiously neglected to point out that the drama of the Passion, re-enacted on Christian altars, is a universal theme. Christianity's greatness lies in knowing how to present the political assassination perpetrated in Judea by the Roman colonizer, as the ultimate sacrifice, and in having tried to build on this schema—at the price of a metaphysical illusion—a society of peace and brotherhood. That message can never again be forgotten.

Yet a blind man's soft voice, which would not have been heard outside Dogon country if Griaule had not been so attentive, also deserves to be considered as a profession of sacrificial faith, based on the hope of a more humane, more balanced world than that dreamed of by the solitary Fox: the sacrifice circulates "a word," destined for all, says the old Ogotémmeli.

It can be argued, if you will, that the absolute supremacy of Christianity lies in its being a religion of love. However, let us not forget Freud's diagnosis ". . . a religion, even if it calls itself the religion of love, must be hard and unloving to those who do not belong to it. Fundamentally, indeed, every religion is in this same way a religion of love for all those whom it embraces; while cruelty and intolerance towards those who do not belong to it are natural to every religion" (Freud, 1951, 50–1). Let us moderate this rather severe judgement. Intolerance of nonbelievers is evidently the paradoxical privilege of religions said to be "universal" which consider themselves "superior." An "archaic" ethnic religion, made to measure for a people, does not pretend to impose its truth on neighbouring societies, which seem to take pleasure in upsetting its foundations, in changing it, without risking dangerous reprisals.

We shall borrow from Hubert and Mauss the notion of a "sacrificial schema" to designate that primary structural pattern which is centred on the death of a king or a god. Frazer had the insight to detect it, but did not completely understand all its complexity. However, we shall be careful not to see it as a historical transformation of an older and more general schema, engendered by a so called development of mythology, as did Hubert and Mauss. Rather, we propose to contrast it with the area of domestic sacrifice which, as we shall show, obeys in its turn a bipolar topological conception.

We have seen that this second schema, not reducible to the first, takes its form through ritual cooking as practised by such different people as the ancient Greeks, the Mofu of Cameroon, the Zulu and the Thonga of southern Africa. The victim is always an animal. It is the point at which men and gods meet, or confront, each other. The social function predominates. However, the cutting up of the animal, the ways of cooking, and the disposition intended for the various parts outline a cosmological space. A human community marks out its territory at a greater or lesser distance from the invisible world. The joyful intimacy of the Zulu or Mofu family, grouped around the domestic hearth with the ancestors invited to share a meal (if only metaphorically) contrasts with the situation of the Greek citizens grouped around the spit and cauldron, facing the distant gods of Olympus, who merely breathe in the smoke. In one case a lineage community tightens its bonds with its dead, who never cease to participate in the circle of life, in the other a city asserts its cohesion by showing its dependence on the immortal gods who do not share man's fate.

The killing of an animal and its ritual cooking establish a division of space just as much as they do a communication. The Thonga's collective sacrifices occupy a remarkable position in this set of homogeneous practices: in a crisis, the extended family can only communicate with its own ancestors, who are excluded from the familial stew, through the intermediary of the uterine nephews, who roast the ancestors' share in a space outside the village (see Chapter IV).

Nuer and Lugbara sacrifices can be integrated with this pattern of culinary rites provided we take into consideration a certain number of transformations. The sacrificial practice of these two societies does not imply any positive communication with the invisible world; the sacrificer is repaying a personal debt to the ancestors or to the spirits of the air. Among the Lugbara, this debt involves his entire lineage. No more than in the case of the Greeks is there a true alimentary sharing. Here ritual cooking contrasts the *raw* part, reserved for the ancestors, and the *cooked* part, reserved for the Lugbara men. The Nuer's decision is even more radical: the air spirits' portion does not include any meat, but only chyme, chyle, and blood. All alimentary communion is completely missing. The territory of the ancestors (Lugbara) or of the air spirits (Nuer) is absolutely distinct from human territory. The Lugbara isolate the sacrificer from the community through an encirclement rite, and he undergoes a veritable rite of passage. However, this procedure is far from being intrinsically linked with the sacrificial schema, as Hubert and Mauss thought.

Among the Nuer, chyme is found in the inedible portion reserved for the air spirits, and among the Lugbara, in the raw part intended for the ancestors. In both cases it obviously points up the lack of commensality between mankind and the gods. The Thonga use chyme as an agent of separation, of transformation or expulsion. The Zulu use it to purify the place of sacrifice, to ward off the actions of witchcraft that come from without. In highly differing African civilizations, chyme belongs to rawness, to a space exterior to the human area characterized by the cooking of food.

In this respect, the Mofu's ritual cooking occupies a unique position. Though like the Zulu they invite their ancestors to partake in the meal, they also sprinkle chyme over their altars, "literally encrusted with remains of the preceding sacrifices" (Vincent, 1976, 194). Why? One of Vincent's informants replies that not only will the ancestors be in no hurry to demand a new sacrifice, but what is more, sorcerers will hesitate to enter a home where the ancestors are satisfied, and thus very vigilant. This symbolic position of chyme, here considered in the light of its resistance to rot, could be considered a remarkable synthesis of the purifying function attributed to it by the Zulu, and the separating role accorded to it by the Lugbara (to maintain the ancestors at a distance).

We might be criticized for mixing together indiscriminately different sacrificial cuisines belonging to highly different cultural areas. It should be noted, however, that the topology of these rites is situated along one continuous axis, from the alimentary communion to which the Zulu unreservedly abandon themselves, to the absolute separation of raw and cooked meat (characterizing the relations of the Lugbara with their ancestors).

## Heat or Coolness

Sacrifice involves not only the dialectic of the raw and the cooked. It can also develop an opposition of coolness and heat.

The Zulu call on the ancestors to settle themselves at the domestic hearth and there consume their share of the sacrificial feast. But in order for this conjunction of the dead and the living to be realized, all the participants must be in a moral condition of "coolness"; the fire of discord must be extinguished in their hearts. Coolness is an attribute of social harmony; it constitutes a preliminary to the sacrifice, a procedure in the course of which the ancestors leave their aquatic dwelling in order to come and warm themselves again, to play with the fire, to promote female fertility.

The reverse situation characterizes the Lugbara sacrificial system. The sacrificer is accountable for an offence, and he exists in a dangerous state of "heat" even after the illness which struck him has been cured. The role of the sacrifice is to "cool him off" and the ancestors are given only the raw part of the sacrificial victim (Middleton, 1979).

I compare these two approaches in Figure 1.

|  | *Recipient* | *Sacrifier* |
| --- | --- | --- |
| Zulu (conjunctive sacrifice) | Close to the fire | Is in a favourable condition of coolness |
| Lugbara (disjunctive sacrifice) | Kept away from the fire | Is in an inauspicious condition of heat |

**Figure 1**

Let us examine from this perspective a Chad tribe, the Massa, whose rites have been described for us by Fr. Dumas-Champion (Dumas-Champion, 1979). The sacrifice is performed to drive away a threatening spirit. The sacrifier is in an "overheated" condition. This dangerous heat passes into the body of a victim whose blood is a "cooling vector" (Dumas-Champion, 1979). The bloody flux allows the escape of the evil which was to be expelled. The Massa world-vision is dramatized: "the ancestors and the supernatural powers, *fuliana*, feed on blood and seek to make men die so as to satisfy their urges" (Dumas-Champion, 1979). But these voracious ancestors are not exactly vampires; what they want is to force their kin to join them. The Massa thus seem to move the conjunctive point of the spirits and the living into a frightening hereafter. The peaceful finality of the Zulu sacrifice is here reversed: the Massa drive away those dangerous, greedy creatures, the ancestors.

This new sort of relationship with the supernatural world is aggravated in popular Hinduism, which is practised by certain Dravidian societies (Herrenschmidt, 1978). Meat-eating goddesses as opposed to a vegetarian god, demand ceaseless tributes of domestic animals; chiefly male goats and rams. But, "basically there is only one perfect victim: man himself" (Herrenschmidt, 1978, 128). Certain of these goddesses act as sovereigns, ruling a territory. But others are so dangerous and voracious that the sacrificial rite seeks, purely and simply, to drive them away. Their demands keep increasing: they claim the entire range of domestic animals, from the baby chick to the buffalo. In this haunted universe, it is the recipient of the sacrifice who now finds herself in a terrifying state of "heat." The meat offering excites the goddess even further; that is why they offer her, immediately afterwards, cooling foods (milk, yogurt, etc.). Thus thermal regulation takes place this time in the course of the sacrificial sequence, thanks to the opposition between the elements of the offering.

One should recall, here, that classic Brahman sacrifice implies the heating up of the sacrifier (by self-cooking), delivering him up to Agni, the god of the devouring fire.

## To Eat or Be Eaten

The alimentary/culinary question dominates our second sacrificial schema. The Greeks vigorously rejected the idea that the gods could consume whatever part of the victim they chose. The Nuer and the Lugbara maintain a division between the raw and the cooked. The Zulu and Mofu invite their ancestors to share cooked meat. Sometimes, as we have just seen, the gods become cannibals. In Massa country, the water genie and the genie of death have a preference for the dog, because of the human qualities of its blood, described as "bitter." But such a victim is never eaten by men; it is thrown away, for eating a dog would be a veritable act of anthropophagy (Dumas-Champion, 1979).

The question is reversed, however, when one considers the other sacrificial schema. The dog, as a substitute for a human being, is eaten by the Nya initiates who, in Minyanka country, constitute a kind of collective royal body. This manducation, however, does bring to mind somewhat the sorcerer's transgression (as does the cult as a whole). When the king is the designated sacrificial victim, the substitute animal is handled with infinite precaution. Such is the case among the Swazi, where the young men designated to eat the flesh of the black ox during the annual ritual of Ncwala must undergo a rigorous purification. In Dogon country only the "impure" can eat the goat, representing the ancestor Lebe during the sowing festival. The absorption of this sacrificial flesh is particularly dangerous for other men because Lebe had transgressed. Yet, at the limit, any animal sacrifice, for the Dogon, implies theophagy. Every Dogon animal sacrifice re-enacts the stages of the death and rebirth of the god Nommo. The sacrifier eats the victim's liver, filled with vital energy. Throwing this organ on the altar and sharing the body among the participants re-enacts, respectively, the rebirth and the dismembering of the divine body (see p. 148). A cannibalistic theme runs through the myth, indeed, through Dogon sacrificial practice. The albino, sacrificed three years after the enthronement of the religious chief (the hogon) was eaten. According to one version of the myth the ancestors devoured the body of their seventh sibling, Nommo's terrestrial incarnation, after having sacrificed him. When the victim was reborn as a snake, he in turn swallowed the ancestor Lebe and then vomited him (see p. 132). The only source of this mythic or ritual cannibalism, which contrasts sharply with the peaceful, social institutions and their respect for human life, is metaphysical. We must remember that the Dogon consider every birth, every germination, as an "externalization" of words. However, this metaphor implies an inverse and complementary representation of ingestion, the eating of seeds, and of sacrificial victims, which are themselves supports for the Word and for humanity. Life is, so to speak, constantly swallowed and spat out. The victim, destroyed and ingested, sets free a life force which constitutes the very denial of death. Theophagy, the absorption of the god's vital force, is based on this illusion. Catholic communion, in which the bread and wine "are," according to the strictest of dogma, the flesh and blood of Christ, the source of immortal life, belongs to the same order of concerns.

Therefore from this point of view, sacrifice seems to offer two alternatives: to be eaten by the god, or to eat him. This opposition, however, is not always so vividly sensed. The Lugbara sacrifier, in debt to the ancestors, does project himself into the animal victim, but the invisible recipients, who receive a raw portion, are in no way cannibalistic, no more than the men who eat its cooked meat. As for the Zulu, they reach an agreement; they join with their ancestors in a "Great Feed." No one—not the sacrifier, not the recipient—is identified with a victim that is "good to eat" from the double viewpoint of gastronomy and metaphysics.

The pleasure principle is not incompatible with the constraints of religious practice. If it is merely a matter of expelling something evil, the cooking is suspended, eating the animal is forbidden, with no further action. However, the expediting system of the scapegoat is peripheral to the sacrificial pattern. It does not constitute the centre of gravity for all sacrifice as René Girard thinks. We found it to be an exception to the Nuer's paradigmatic sacrifice of the ox: a dog with a cut ear takes away the illness, *thiang*, which threatens little children (Chapter I). In the Zulu rite the young girls by means of a goat expel the "blackness" threatening their statute when one of them has broken a sexual interdiction. However, such a sacrifice has nothing to do with the culinary treatment to which the Zulu submit an animal offered to the ancestors. On the contrary, the victim is abandoned without being eaten, and the only symbolic operator is the purifying chyme (see Chapter III). From a topological point of view, the "scapegoat-victim" is relegated to an empty space at the limits of human territory. It is in a deserted location that the Rwanda sacrifice black goats and human monsters, signs of "unproductivity" which threaten the rainfall; in Rwanda as well, these "scapegoats" may be sent into enemy territory, that is, into a place the Rwanda would like to devastate (Chapter V). Yet here, as elsewhere, these exceptional acts differ radically from the sacrifice of cattle to the royal ancestors or to the god Ryangombe. In most cases, elaborate, complicated relations between men and the supernatural powers are bound up with the animal and the culinary issue. Among the Nuer, the sacrifier's guilt does not take away his appetite once he has paid his debt to the air spirits. After all, the Nuer rarely eat beef except at sacrifices. There is as much enjoyment and feasting in the atonement for an offence (Nuer) as in a communal meal (Zulu).

All this leads us to question, once again, the very reason for raising animals. A certain positivist history would have us believe that the domestication of animals and agriculture are part of the same undertaking. These two "neolithic" techniques surfaced at almost the same time in the Middle East and a new division of labour developed among peoples, with some providing meat, others cereals. No doubt this schema is generally applicable. It does, however, neglect a number of problems. The populations we have reviewed, a differing mix of farmers and herdsmen, use domestic animals with varying degree of reservation to maintain a sacrificial project. They chose Abel's side against Cain's, even if vegetable offerings sometimes accompany the sacrifice of goats, sheep and oxen. When cattle are used in social life, it is as a matrimonial exchange medium or as a mark of prestige. Barring exceptions, sacrifice is the necessary condition of butchery. It was the absolute rule among those great beef-lovers and sharp merchants, the Greeks. Among the Diola, sacrificial death is the very purpose of breeding. A Brahman adage expresses it just as strongly: "Meat-eating goes with sacrifice" (Biardeau, 1976, 53). It is the "interiorization of sacrifice", the asceticism required of the Brahman in a later period that explains the appearance of vegetarianism in classic Hinduism, whereas the warriors (*ksatriya*) continued to be associated with violence and meat-eating (Biardeau, 1976, 81). It is not surprising that the cattle's sacrificial function lessens when it is used in politico-economic strategies, when it becomes the stakes of a dominant class, a cumulative capital. This is the case in traditional Rwanda society, where the possession of large herds, distributed in networks of clientships, guarantees the aristocratic status of the Tutsi. The need to maintain and augment the cattle-capital, the instrument of social domination, surely explains why sacrifice was limited, in principle, to steers and sterile cows. The Tutsi boasted of their ability to nourish themselves exclusively on milk (see Chapter V).

Pastoralist societies are careful to exclude or limit the sacrifice of female animals. This is the case among the Nuer, who sacrifice only oxen, with certain exceptions. However, to cause rainfall, the Swazi do not hesitate to sacrifice a pregnant ewe or a black cow in calf (Kuper, 1947, 171). Among the Diola cattle raising is pure sacrificial loss. The same can be said of the raising of goats among the Thonga, of dogs and chickens among the Minyanka, of sheep, goats, and indeed of cattle among the Gurmantche. It is as if the role of a certain number, if not all, domestic species is to constitute a reserve of wealth for man to draw on so as to tie or untie the ambiguous bonds with the invisible.

The question of "eating to live" shifts to another focal point, where it is a matter of eating with or without the gods, yet always in accord with them. One sometimes also risks being eaten by them, just as they can be eaten to acquire their life force.

## Provisional Conclusions

This long meandering is merely a reconnoitring trip. I have not tried to substitute a new overall theory for that of Hubert and Mauss, which I have challenged, but rather to indicate some new perspectives.

The failure of Hubert and Mauss is rooted in two aporia. Their ambition was to reduce all sacrifice to rite of passage schema based on a vague topology contrasting the "profane" and the "sacred." The two end results which they believed could explain the "sacralization" and "desacralization" of the sacrifier on this universal basis, seemed to me inoperable. For these notions, I prefer to substitute those of the conjunction and the disjunction of spaces, human and nonhuman. I have thus laid out a culinary sacrificial topology. It cannot be reduced to the schema to which are referred all sacrificial practices associated with sacred kingship or with the mythic sovereignty of a god doomed to die in order to be reborn. In this case the sacrificial debt is entirely based on the cosmogonic order upon which, in the last resort, social order depends.

Hubert and Mauss's second aporia consists in placing these two schemas in an evolutionary sequence thereby contradicting their own premises. Indeed, it is incomprehensible how in a certain number of civilizations the god himself could constitute the sacrificial victim when the authors define the latter as a mediator between a "profane" world and a "divine" world which differ radically. They should have explained how the sacrificed god himself could belong to both worlds, even at the risk of destroying the fundamental opposition which was postulated.

Now, many examples indicate that the "sacred" king, whose function is to control both social harmony and cosmological rhythms, incarnates the group as "body territory" while at the same time belonging to the world of the Elsewhere, of mysterious nature, of the "bush" or the sky, haunted by the forces governing life and death. Only a consistent theory of sacred or divine kingship permits us to understand why the sovereign is the victim *par excellence* in such a politico-symbolic configuration. The gods who die and are reborn immortal can be understood in the same way. Nommo, humanity's divine ancestor, is both the Dogon social body and the water genie living in the pond.

These two sacrificial models, far from being united by some mysterious law governing the evolution of religious institutions, are perfectly capable of coexisting in the same society. However, a homogeneous symbolic system must then be agreed on. The Lovedu sacrifice only goats to the ancestors in the domestic realm: they keep the sheep (substituting for a human victim) to be used for sacrifices to bring rain, while waiting for the queen to offer her own life. The Zulu maintain the same division between "sacrifiable" species: the oxen (or goats) are for the ancestors, the sheep for the python genie, the regulator of rainfall.

In all the societies we have examined, the victim is never just any animal. Aside from a determination of a species or sub-species, subtle criteria often play a role in the individual selection. In any case, the possibility of substituting one animal for another (indeed, a vegetable species for an animal species) operates within strict limits. Nowhere does there exist a general system of convertibility for sacrificial values. If the Zulu can choose indifferently between a goat and an ox for a domestic sacrifice, it is because of the common properties of their digestive systems. On the other hand, a goat could never be substituted for a sheep in sacrifices to bring rain except by changing its status: muzzled, it symbolically acquires the docile nature of that silent animal, a token of the sky.

Many questions have not been dealt with. Specifically, the symbolism of the seed in relation to the animal should have been examined. We have seen (all too rapidly, I fear) that among the Zulu the offering of beer is a type of sacrifice (Chapter III). Let us once again refer back to the Dogon. After the harvest, the officiant re-enacts the different steps in Nommo's sacrifice and rebirth when he successively pours on the (family or collective) altar a mixture of water and flour, first raw, then cooked. The fermentation of the drink is "likened to the resurrection of the seed (killed by the cooking) and at the same time to Nommo's resurrection" (Dieterlen, 1976, 49). The purpose of the libations is to return the seeds to Nommo's collarbones. "It is done", Dieterlen comments, "to avoid any loss of substance from the seeds which stay protected in special granaries until the next seedtime" (Dieterlen, 1976, 49). The rite performed on this occasion restores their "souls" to the seeds, through a reverse procedure.

An unavoidable enigma remains: sacrifice plays with death in a completely different way than do war or hunting. It is a third mysterious term: here the annihilation of a life nourishes a phantasmagoria of want. A want that all the victims in the world would not fulfil. There, at a greater or lesser distance from the gods, society displays its fissures, the hole of death left by the sun in the first Dogons' placenta. It is impossible to penetrate this existential emptiness (or to artificially fill it with violence as Girard does). We can only study sacrifice from the exterior, describe it as a symbolic work and analyse the systems of representations linked with the treatment of the victim. This varies greatly. The animal body can be furiously torn apart, transformed in the hope to reach the signs of the beginning (Gurmantche), or it can be calmly cut up and prepared so that the ancestors can re-inject their own aquatic substance into the woman's vagina, a gaping hole open to death (Zulu). Sacrifice burrows into the deepest part of the animal to extract some meaning. The black bull and black goat the Rwandans expel to the edge of human space along with a breastless woman are also full of meaning, this time as monstrous creatures. However, we must not forget that the killing of a victim is often but one episode among others, within a complex ritual. In all the above-mentioned cases, and whatever the form, sacrifice does nevertheless appear to be an autonomous rite. I hope to have shown that the study of the multiple facets does not lead to the emptiness of a theoretical illusion.

I will readily grant the reader that the division I propose between a set of royal and cosmogonic sacrificial practices on one hand, and a set of domestic and culinary practices on the other, is too absolute. A sacrifice to the ancestors introduces guidelines into the universe; it already sketches out a topology even a cosmology. And reciprocally the sacrifices formerly carried out in Brahman India can be defined as a cosmic cooking, a "cooking of the world." But the Zulu domestic sacrifice does not re-enact the birth of the universe; it no more cooks it than cools it. We are thus justified in distinguishing two sacrificial spheres. Our analysis has pointed up not only difference of emphasis, but indeed different ways of thinking about sacrifice, of organizing symbolic systems. However, it is always a matter of establishing a locus, near or distant—in space or time—where a debt of life is to be paid.

To perform a sacrifice is, primarily, to try to outwit death. Human sacrifice represents the outer limit which many rites—in which the sacrifier is seen to project himself into the animal victim, losing a part of his "having" in order to preserve the essential—strive to reach. This limit is indeed reached when the king, the epitome of "having" and "being," is doomed to immolation for the good of the community. These ritual acts, which are part of a metaphysical calculation of profit and loss, have nothing to do with the violence of war, which undertakes the blind destruction of the "other." When war becomes the servant of sacrifice, when a people decides to appropriate the lives of others in order to incessantly feed its gods, the religious system is lost in madness. We know that this issue disturbed the conscience of the ancient Mexicans at a certain moment in their history. Yet, even then, the victims had to change their status: they ceased to be captives and, themselves, became the gods.

In Africa, human sacrifice is most often only a means of deferring the sacrifice of the king. But it can also denote the perversion of royal power, the illicit means by which a king allows himself to perform an evil deed, a transgression. This is the dark side of sacrifice. To acquire the sacred power, the dreaded *wene*, "emanation of superhuman forces," held by the earth spirits, the Yombe chiefs (Zaire) did not hesitate to carry out a grim procedure: a young girl, captured by the pretender's soldiers, was, while still alive, cut in two with the "knife of power." Her liver was torn out and eaten by the chief (Doutreloux, 1967, 240). Indeed, the great *nkisi* fetishes draw their efficacy from the vital principle (*kinyumba*) of human victims. In this case, the warriors' violence interferes with the quest of sacred royalty by an act which Bantu morality expressly considers an abuse of power. Yet all power, when it calls itself sacred, also becomes terrifying, steeped in sorcery. This is clearly stated by the Bambara when they assimilate the immolation of the albino, which regenerates the king's vigour, with "a bad sacrifice."

Be it the life of an animal, or of a man, that is at stake, the sacrificial rituals form a coherent set when compared with the techniques of the trance; these, through an upsetting conjunction, abolish the distance between the human realm and that of the gods within the very body of the possessed person, without destroying it. Elsewhere I have outlined a structural analysis of these phenomena (de Heusch, 1971). To be sure, possession and sacrifice can both be parts of the same ritual sequence. Among the Minyanka, for example, it is always a man in a trance who seizes the bags of Nya and brings them into the sacrificial enclosure. Possession here constitutes an "adorcism"[1] and necessarily precedes an appeal to Nya's efficacious power, which is brought about through a complex symbolic process by the sacrifice of dogs. On the other hand, the Thonga use sacrificial blood to exorcise those possessed by a violent and dangerous spirit coming from a realm foreign to that of the ancestors. In this case it is a matter of driving away a pathogenic spirit that is responsible for a mental disturbance—in short, to effect a disjunction, and not, as in the case of the Minyanka, a positive conjunction.

This brief summary suggests that the two essential means—sacrifice and possession—that men have at their disposal for establishing a communication with the gods in order to survive—or for breaking it in order not to perish—belong to a more general ritual system for which this book, however fragmentary and incomplete, perhaps provides a few new elements.

# Note

1. I proposed to use this word, as opposed to "exorcism", to designate the positive relation between a possessed man and the possessing spirit.

# References

Biardeau, Madeleine (1976). "Le sacrifice dans l'hindouisme". In Biardeau and Malamoud, *Le Sacrifice dans l'Inde Ancienne*. Paris, pp. 7–154.

Biardeau, Madeleine and Malamoud, Charles (1976). *Le Sacrifice dans l'Inde Ancienne*. Paris.

Dieterlen, Germaine (1976). "Introduction à de nouvelles recherches sur le sacrifice chez les Dogon," in *Systèmes de pensée en Afrique noire*. Vol. 2, *Le Sacrifice* I. Paris: Laboratoire associé 221, CNRS, pp. 43–50.

Doutreloux, Albert (1967). *A l'Ombre des fétiches. Société et culture Yombe*. Louvain and Paris.

Dumas-Champion, Françoise (1979). "Le sacrifice comme procès rituel chez les Massa (Tchad)." In *Systèmes de pensée en Afrique noire*. Vol. 4, *Le Sacrifice* III. Paris, pp. 95–115.

Freud, Sigmund (1951). *Group Psychology and the Analysis of the Ego*. New York (first edn. 1922).

Herrenschmidt, Oliver (1978). "Les formes sacrificielles de l'hindouisme populaire." In *Systèmes de pensée en Afrique noire*. Vol. 3, *Le Sacrifice* II. Paris: CNRS, pp. 115–33.

de Heusch, Luc (1971). *Pourquoi l'épouser? et autres essais*, Paris (English edn.: *Why Marry Her?*, Cambridge, 1981).

Kuper, Hilda (1947). *An African Aristocracy. Rank among the Swazi*. London, New York, Toronto: Oxford University Press.

Middleton, John (1979). "Rites of sacrifice among the Lugbara." In *Systèmes de pensée en Afrique noire*. Vol. 4, *Le Sacrifice* III. Paris, 175–92. Erratum, *Le Sacrifice* IV, 1983, p. 217.

Vincent, Jeanne-Françoise (1976). "Conception et déroulement du sacrifice chez les Mofu." In *Systèmes de pensée en Afrique noire*. Vol. 2, *Le Sacrifice* I. Paris: CNRS, pp. 177–203.

# 18

# VALERIO VALERI (b. 1944)

Anthropologist Valerio Valeri was born in northwest Italy, as a youth lived with his family in Istanbul and Libya, and attended boarding school in Venice. He received a degree in Philosophy at the University of Pisa in 1968, studied for a time with Lévi-Strauss in Paris, and later, under the guidance of Marshall Sahlins and Louis Dumont, received his Ph.D. in ethnology from the University of Paris in 1976. His doctoral dissertation focused on the myths and political organization of Hawaiian society, even as he conducted more than two years of fieldwork in the northern mountains of Seram with the Huaulu. Valeri mastered more than a dozen languages and excelled at both field and archival research. Also in 1976, he took a position teaching in the Anthropology Department at the University of Chicago, remaining there for his entire scholarly career. He is best known for the major study of Hawaiian myth, ritual, and society he published as *Kingship and Sacrifice: Ritual and Society in Ancient Hawaii* (1985). It is a model in its treatment of detailed cultural material and its nuanced theoretical position. During the late 1980s, Valeri returned his attention to his Indonesian research, and conducted further fieldwork among the Huaulu in Seram. Out of this research, again combined with extensive archival work and theoretical knowledge, he fashioned a complex understanding of "taboo" and its relationship to identity. This work appeared, after Valeri's death in 1998, as *The Forest of Taboos: Morality, Hunting, and Identity among the Huaulu of the Moluccas* (2000).

Valeri's *Kingship and Sacrifice* presents a sophisticated analysis of sacrifice in terms of ritual efficacy, its role in articulating the ideas of a community (e.g., its political order) through action. He begins by asserting that ritual is a collective ordering of subjects' consciousness, a process that produces a "conceptual order" for participants. Ritual is inherently a collective "symbolic action," a formal setting where subjects act upon (with respect to) "objectified mental processes." Much in agreement with Durkheim, Valeri suggests symbolic representations are produced, in fact, in ritual contexts, and by being made concrete, allow ritual participants to "experience their truth," to believe them. Religion, therefore, is directly tied to social understandings and relations. It makes "sense" of a subject, and his or her actions, Valeri claims, "by stressing that they are part of a harmonious and hierarchical whole."

Valeri applies this approach to ritual in his analysis of sacrifice in Hawaii, making his first step a definition of sacrifice that identifies the participants (human beings and deities), the motivation for sacrificing (an end sought), actions (an offering), and the objects (the things offered) involved. Each of these components that comprise a sacrificial ritual should be seen as symbolic, and therefore, he believes, interpretation of their symbolic content is central to understanding sacrifice. In the Hawaiian context, the central symbol is the object offered during sacrifice, the victim. He notes that in all cases, the offering represents some aspect of the deity receiving the sacrifice, but at the same time, since deities are essentially "reified representations of certain human properties" and actions, the offering also symbolizes the human sacrifier as well. Certain animals are particularly well suited to carry this multivalence, for example domestic animals, which are part human and part nonhuman. Furthermore, the offering, or some of its components (e.g., its name or physical properties), serves as a symbol of the outcome sought by the sacrifier (a white chicken evoking "purity," for example). When the sacrificial victim is divided, human beings and deities each receive their share (usually eating it), thereby implicating the participants of the sacrifice as well. The significance then for all of these components, Valeri concludes, arises by virtue of their presence in the ritual itself. Their symbolic content is made real for human beings through the sacrificial performance.

After placing sacrifice in this larger frame of symbolic action, Valeri presents a "model of Hawaiian sacrifice." Sacrifice is a particular form of social action that transforms the "relationships of the sacrifier, god, and group by representing them in public," each being changed through the procedure. It involves three stages, he claims. The first occurs when a person is motivated to sacrifice, when, that is, he or she perceives some "lack" or "imperfection that must be overcome." This is a stage of "imperfect humanness," one that includes levels of damaged or imbalanced social relations. The act of killing the sacrificial victim in the presence of an audience and then offering a share to the god constitutes the second stage, and the third occurs when the sacrifier eats the remaining share. Revolving around the material victim, sacrificial events move through these stages so that the symbolic values of every sacrificial element present—concepts, concerns and conduct—are constituted and reconstituted. The very structure of Hawaiian society, its essentially hierarchical character, depends upon it.

Finally, this model of Hawaiian sacrifice allows Valeri to formulate a classificatory scheme of different types of sacrifice. He builds on his claim that Hawaiian deities may be understood as objectified human actions, types of action idealized in relation to certain social contexts, and suggests that there are essentially three types of action, and hence three major types of sacrifice—the "nomocentric," the "ergocentric," and the "genocentric." He demonstrates how the various occasions for sacrifice (first fruits, expiation, life-cycle events, divination, and so forth) can be analyzed in terms of the semiotic changes that occur between the sacrifier, the offering, the god, and the audience.

Reprinted here are several sections from *Kingship and Sacrifice*—Valeri's definition of sacrifice, a summary of his "model of Hawaiian sacrifice," and a brief account of his typology of sacrifice. Ultimately Valeri settles on a "representational theory" of sacrifice. By combining aspects of Frazer and Westermarck (with respect to the significance of the victim) and generalizing notions of gift and communion, he offers important insights into the broader question of how sacrifice accomplishes its work.

# From *Kingship and Sacrifice: Ritual and Society in Ancient Hawaii*

## Preliminary Definition

The most important, most frequently used Hawaiian ritual is sacrifice. By "sacrifice" I mean any ritual action that includes the consecration of an "offering" to a deity. This offering is made up of one or more individuals belonging to species having symbolic values exploited in the course of the ritual. In addition to this principal component, always made up of living and edible beings, the offering may consist of inanimate objects such as bark cloths.

Every sacrifice implies a subject, individual or collective, who performs it or on whose behalf it is performed. Following a usage introduced by Hubert and Mauss (1899), I call this subject the "sacrifier." Sometimes the sacrifier employs a ritual specialist to perform the sacrifice for him. Again following Hubert and Mauss I call this specialist the "sacrificer" (the English word that comes closest to the French *sacrificateur*).

Usually the offering, after having been entirely consecrated to the deity, is divided in two parts: the first goes to the deity alone, the second goes to the sacrifier and the other participants, among whom it is shared according to the order of their rank.

In short, the term "sacrifice" designates a complex ritual action, during

Valerio Valeri, *Kingship and Sacrifice: Ritual and Society in Ancient Hawaii* (Chicago: University of Chicago Press, 1985), pp. 37–8, 70–5, 81–3. Reprinted with the permission of the University of Chicago Press.

which an offering made up of animal, vegetable, or artificial components having symbolic values is consecrated to one or several deities, on certain occasions and with certain ends in view. Thus every sacrifice must be described as a function of the following features: (1) its end and the occasion on which it is made; (2) the deity or deities to whom it is addressed; (3) the content of the offering and its symbolic value; (4) the way the offering is treated and apportioned in the rite.

The ends and occasions of sacrifices, as well as the offerings' symbolic values and treatment, will receive particular emphasis as the features that best make it possible to discover the fundamental principles of sacrificial action.

. . . . . . . . . . . . . . . . . . . . . . . . . . . . . . . . . . . .

## A Model of Hawaiian Sacrifice

Of all the theories of sacrifice just discussed, the one that views it as a complex ritual process, as a "symbolic action" that cannot be reduced to any of the elements ("gift," "communion," "catharsis," etc.) recognized in it by native consciousness or by the interpreter seems the most adequate to me. Thus I believe that Hawaiian sacrificial ritual should be viewed as a "symbolic action" that effects transformations of the relationships of sacrifier, god, and group by representing them in public. This symbolic action consists of three main stages.

It begins with what motivates it: a perceived lack. Thus if a man has transgressed, he is in a state of lack because he is not "in communion" with his group and the god thereof, but is marked off from them by a taboo. Moreover, the transgressor's lack also implies a lack in the god (as we shall see) and in the group, which have lost their integrity because of the transgression.

To take another example: the sacrifice by which a young boy is incorporated into the men's house of his homestead is motivated by his lack: he is not yet considered an adult. But his lack is also a lack of his group, which does not yet have him as a full male member, and of the god, who does not yet receive his cult. A similar state of lack is the starting point of the sacrifices that empower the sacrifier to perform certain technical activities together with a given group of people or on their behalf.

Whether it is due to transgression or to being unable to perform certain acts, the initial state of lack is perceived as an imperfection that must be overcome. This imperfection or even disorder is represented by an aspect of the offering that is emphasized at this stage. Thus, as I have noted, that the pig is a kind of disordered equivalent of a human (cf. Emerson, 1892, 14) may be relevant at this moment. That the offering is a double of the sacrifier opens the possibility of transforming him, both by destroying (and eventually punishing) his present person and by making him a new person. This transformation is represented—in the second main stage of the symbolic action—by the god's devouring the offering.

This devouring is an incorporation of the offering (and therefore of the sacrifier) in the god. It signifies that the sacrifier is now encompassed by the god, is part of his *kuleana*, "domain." This means, concretely, that the sacrifier now corresponds to the concept for which the god stands and that he instantiates it. In other words, the sacrifier views himself and is viewed by the audience as a token of which the god is the type.

In the third stage of the sacrificial action the offering incorporated into the god is divided in two parts: one stays permanently with the god, the other returns to the sacrifier and is partaken of by him and by those who participate in the ritual.

Each part of the offering, which is a double of the sacrifier, signifies a different stage of his. The part that remains with the god signifies the state of the sacrifier when he is intensely conscious of what the god stands for: the concept of the sacrifier's subject. This level of consciousness was in the foreground when the sacrifier's attention was entirely focused on the god and the offering entirely consecrated to him.

The part that is detached from the god signifies the state of the sacrifier's consciousness when his attention is redirected toward the concrete world. Eating this part creates a transition from the previous state of consciousness to the ordinary one and at the same time subordinates the latter to the former, since the two parts are metonymically related. The eating also marks the effects of this subordination: the reproduction of the sacrifier's relationship with his group and of his ability to act in it.

This model of sacrifice presupposes that the rite is the objective form of a process of consciousness that it stimulates. The structure of this process is the triadic one isolated by Hubert and Mauss: the sacrifier moves from state A to state C by passing through state B, which implies being in contact with the god.

But I shall now show that this view of sacrifice is incomplete and that—rather than describing the real process—it focuses on its marked moments only. Moreover, it treats sacrifice as a bilateral relationship between sacrifier and god and fails to stress that the collective judgment of the audience always mediates that relationship. It seems to me that a more adequate description of Hawaiian sacrifice is one that recognizes the constant coexistence and interrelation of four parallel processes, concerning as many terms: the sacrifier; the god; the group (represented by the audience); and the signifiers (principally offerings and imagès).

Let me redescribe the sacrificial process by taking into consideration all four components. In the initial stage, sacrifier, god, and group are in the same state of lack or disorder. This state is represented by signifiers borne by the offering. In addition, the offering as a whole consists for the most part of natural species, which have indexical or incompletely iconic relationships with the predicates personified by the god involved in the sacrifice. Because they are indexical or partially iconic, these signifiers evoke the corresponding predicates less clearly and completely than does a purely iconic signifier such as the anthropomorphic image of the god. Being fully iconic, the image directly represents what it stands for and therefore produces a clearer consciousness of the human type personified by the god.

The first stage of the sacrificial rite, then, is characterized by the following chain of implications: focus on the indexical or partially iconic signifiers of the god ⊃ lesser consciousness of their signifieds ⊃ lesser order in the sacrifier, who realizes less the divine type or is in contrast with it ⊃ lesser order in the group because of the disorder of the sacrifier.

The common feature of all terms at this stage is disorder, imperfect realization of humanness; this feature may be signified by emphasizing the animal or disordered dimension in the offering. In the case of human sacrifice, it is emphasized by the choice of a transgressor as victim.

In the second stage, the natural signifiers are brought into contact (by consecration) with the anthropomorphic signifier (the image). This results in a transformation of the consciousness of what the god stands for: the human type he personifies becomes more evident. Correlatively, the sacrifier is allegedly transformed: he is made perfectly ordered by the presence of the concept in his consciousness. And of course this state of the sacrifier corresponds to a heightened state of order and attention in the audience, that is, the group to which he belongs.

In the next stage, attention and orderliness are lessened by somewhat removing the divine concept from the consciousness and—as we shall see—by reducing the bodily and speech control required during the consecration. This removal is effected by focusing again on the natural offering, that is, on the signifier that evokes the god less clearly. But the share of the offering eaten by sacrifier and group retains an indexical relationship with the god in his most evident human form: therefore, by eating it the sacrifier and his commensals both remove to the background and preserve in a superordinate position their previous state of consciousness. It is in this position that it can influence their actions and make them compatible.

If the four terms of the rite coexist and vary together at every stage, how is it that sacrifice can be described—in the fashion of Hubert and Mauss—as a movement from sacrifier in state A to god and then to sacrifier in state B? The reason is that this description connects the terms that are marked, and therefore most evident, in each of the three stages of the process. But we are not allowed to forget that the unmarked terms are *always* present and *always* presupposed by the process. Thus it would be wrong to view—as Hubert and Mauss do—the god as always identical to what he is when he is a marked term, that is, in the second stage. He is himself transformed in the process. Moreover, the state of the group can never be separated from that of the other terms, since it is the collective judgment of the audience that lends the process much (sometimes most) of its efficacy.

I have used the terms "much" and "most" on purpose. Indeed, having analyzed Hawaiian sacrifice as an objectified process of consciousness, I have implied that its efficacy depends at least to some extent on its ability to induce what it represents in the sacrifier's consciousness.

But this claim may be questioned. Isn't sacrifice efficacious in a purely conventional way? Doesn't its efficacy depend only on the collective recognition that it has been correctly performed? And even if we wish to take the sacrifier's consciousness into account, should we not suppose that the effect of the rite on consciousness (an effect that may be called "understanding") is taken for granted whenever the rite has been correctly performed, so that the relation between rite and effect must be viewed as purely conventional in this case as well?

My answer to these questions is that the effects of sacrifice are related to the correct performance of the rite both conventionally and nonconventionally. In other words, to borrow Austin's (1975) terminology, the rite is performative because of illocutionary (conventionally produced) and perlocutionary (nonconventionally produced) effects at the same time. Moreover, I am prepared to maintain that there is an implicit belief that the results of sacrifice, whatever they are, depend on a previous effect, conventionally produced or not, on the sacrifier's understanding. In other words, the understanding and consequent introjection of what the god stands for is assumed or recognized in every collective judgment as to the efficacy or the rite with regard to its stated aims, which usually are not understanding itself. I maintain this precisely because I claim that the god is essentially a concept of human action: thus a rite that consists in empowering a subject to act in a certain way by reference to the concept of that action must be based on the presupposition that the subject understands that concept (albeit in reified form). Therefore, when a rite of passage is declared successful, and as a result the sacrifier is incorporated into a new group (for instance the group of adult males), it is conventionally supposed that he has "understood," and therefore taken as a guide for his new actions as an adult, the concept of that action as personified by the god. Analogously, in a sacrifice of purification, the sacrifier is effectively reincorporated in his group because the latter assumes that, as a result of the correct performance of the rite, he has understood the rule of the actions of the members of that group relative to one another.

In the two examples I have just given, the effect of the rite is illocutionary. The correct performance of the rite makes it successful because the audience supposes that the sacrifier has "understood," simply by performing the rite, and therefore it accepts him into its fold. But in other cases the effect (both the understanding and its consequences) cannot be considered purely illocutionary. Take, for instance, the numerous sacrifices connected with ergological activities, curing, war, propitiation, and so on. In these cases the efficacy of the rite depends on events that may occur or not occur *after* it has been performed: health recovered, a victory, a good harvest.

It is the occurrence of favorable events, therefore, that makes it possible retrospectively to assess the effectiveness of sacrifice (see Valeri, 1982b, 35, n. 20). The audience's evaluation of the rite at the end of its performance, therefore, is not sufficient to create the event whose attainment the rite represents (in certain offerings) or mentions (in the prayers). In other words, the event is not purely conventional, as a purification or the passage from one status to another (see Valeri, 1981b, 234–7). The audience's assessment of the rite must therefore be viewed as conditional and as a constative rather than a performative statement.

All the audience can say at the end of the performance is that it seems to have had a certain effect on the status of the sacrifier, that it has transformed him, and therefore that his actions should be successful.

It goes without saying that no sacrifice can be viewed as having only illocutionary or only perlocutionary effects, whatever the nature of its effects. Given that every sacrificial rite is multipurpose and multivalent, it has a variety of effects through a variety of mechanisms that are incompletely codified. Thus the empowering of a king may seem a purely illocutionary effect of a rite; but since, as we shall see, this empowering takes place in a rite that has multiple purposes, one of them being, very often, success in war, it is vulnerable to the rite's perlocutionary effects with regard to these purposes. In other words, if the king wins the war that follows the rite, it is retrospectively declared that he has really been made a king by the rite; if he does not win, the judgment that he has been made king may be revised. It is therefore difficult to decide if the collective judgment at the time of the performance must be considered performative or constative. In a sense, it is partly performative and partly constative only, because the establishment of the king's legitimacy does not simply depend on formal criteria.

. . . . . . . . . . . . . . . . . . . . . . . . . . . . . . . . . . . . . . . . .

# Conclusion

It is now possible to relate the classification of the deities to the classification of sacrifices. My discussion has indicated that most deities personify socially recognized or accepted types of action in certain social contexts. Three main kinds of types personified by deities can be distinguished:

1. Types of moral actions that perpetuate a given type of group (kinship group, political group of a certain order, age group, functional group, etc.) or social category (kinship category, hierarchical category, etc.).
2. Types of technical actions that produce artifacts.
3. Types of actions that make certain species available for use, that "produce" them.

Each of these kinds of types corresponds to a different kind of "body" or natural manifestation of the deity. A deity or an aspect of a deity that refers to moral actions and their subjects (groups, hierarchical categories, etc.) tends to be especially associated with natural phenomena that symbolize those actions, the subjects of the latter, or the operations necessary to their realization. The natural correlates of a deity or an aspect of a deity that refer to "technical" actions are phenomena symbolizing the process of work or constituting its substance and results. As for the types that make certain species available, they are symbolized by these species.

To each of these classes of divine types corresponds a class of sacrificial rituals or aspects thereof. The sacrifices that relate to the first class of types include all that concern the relations of the subject with the social group or category in which he is classified or reclassified by the rite. It also includes the sacrifices concerned with the reproduction of a group or category as such. I call all these sacrifices *nomocentric*.

The sacrifices that relate to the second class of divine types include all that concern technical work. Therefore it is appropriate to call them *ergocentric*.

The sacrifices that relate to the third class of divine types are of course first-fruits sacrifices. Since they are directly concerned with natural species as reflections of the human species, I propose to call them *genocentric*.

Classes of sacrifices can also be generated by distinguishing the different kinds of type/token relationship involved in nomocentric and ergocentric sacrifices. Two main kinds of relationships can be distinguished: (1) the sacrifier moves from the status of an inferior token of the deity to the status of superior token of the same deity; (2) the sacrifier moves from the status of token of the deity $x$ to the status of token of the deity $y$, the two deities being sequentially linked as stages of a process of transformation. Alternatively, $x$ and $y$ can be viewed as two aspects or particularizations of the same deity.

The distinction between (1) and (2) is only relative, since the passage from inferior to superior status can be represented both by the passage from one token to another and by the passage from one type to another. The case in which the sacrifier passes from the status in which he has no relationship with a deity to the status in which he has a relationship with it does not deserve separate treatment, since it is usually a particular moment of (2) or an extreme case of (1).

One can immediately see that sacrifices of purification, expiation, propitiation, and in fact all sacrifices connected with rites of passage can be classified on the basis of these two kinds of relationship. For instance, "purification" is nothing else than the reestablishment of the token/type relationship between sacrifier and god. (This, in turn, makes it possible for the sacrifier to be reintegrated into his group.) It can also be seen in relative terms, as a passage from the status of an inferior token to the status of a token that fully displays the properties of the type. Analogously, "expiation" is the destruction of the sacrifier's old self when it is in contrast with the type it should incarnate, and its transformation into a token of this type. A sacrifice of propitiation reinforces the sacrifier's status as a token of the god type, in order to avoid future negative consequences inherent in an inappropriate instantiation.

Thus, on the basis of an abstract system of relations derived from our model of sacrifice, it is possible to deduce the concrete types of sacrifice enumerated at the beginning of this chapter.

Note also that ergocentric and nomocentric sacrifices, on the one hand, and firstfruits sacrifices, on the other, are both different and complementary. They are different because, as indicated, the first two reinforce the semiotic aspect of all the individuals of the natural species they employ, while the third reinforce it only in certain individuals—the firstfruits—in order to suppress it in all others.

This contrast is made evident by the fact that while firstfruits sacrifices exclude eating the offering (the divine part that must be separated from the empirical whole) but make it lawful to eat the species outside the sacrificial context, the other sacrifices require eating some of the offering but forbid eating the species used as offering outside the sacrificial context.

But it is evident that these contrasts derive from a fundamental complementarity. For firstfruits sacrifices dedivinize nature in order to make it "free," available for material appropriation; the other sacrifices divinize man and his implements in order to make him able to effect the material appropriation of nature.

Thus the desacralization of nature implies the sacralization of man. Perhaps, then, it is possible to follow Kojève when he reformulates Hegel's interpretation of sacrifice by writing that in this rite "il faut . . . supprimer une partie du divin pour sanctifier l'homme" (1947, 247).

# References

Austin, John L. (1975). *How to do Things with Words.* 2nd edn. Cambridge: Harvard University Press.

Emerson, Nathaniel B. (1965) [1909]. *Unwritten literature of Hawaii: The Sacred Songs of the Hula, compiled and translated with Notes and an Account of the Hula.* Reprint edn. Rutland, Vt., and Tokyo: Charles E. Tuttle.

Hubert, Henri and Mauss, Marcel (1899). "Essai sur la nature et la fonction du sacrifice." *L'Année sociologique* 2, pp. 29–139. Reprinted in Mauss (1968-69, 1, pp. 193-307).

Hubert, Henri and Mauss, Marcel (1929) [1909]. "Introduction à l'analyse de quelques phénomènes religieux". Preface to *Mélanges d'histoire des religions.* Reprint. Paris: Alcan.

Kojève, Alexandre (1947). *Introduction à la lecture de Hegel.* Paris: Gallimard.

Valeri, Valerio (1981b). "Rito". In *Enciclopedia,* 12, pp. 209-43. Turin: Einaudi.

Valeri, Valerio (1982b). "The transformation of transformation: A structural essay on an aspect of Hawaiian history (1809-1819)." *Social Analysis* 10 (May), pp. 3–41.

# 19

# JONATHAN Z. SMITH (b. 1938)

American historian of religions Jonathan Zittell Smith attended Haverford College as an undergraduate and received his Ph.D. in 1969 from Yale University after writing a dissertation on James G. Frazer and *The Golden Bough*. Employing "the categories of play, the joke and burlesque," Smith argued that Frazer's data, theory, and method of comparison were flawed. Smith has taught at Dartmouth College and the University of California in Santa Barbara, but he has spent most of his scholarly career (since 1973) at the University of Chicago. He has served as the Dean of the Faculty of the College (1977–82), and now coordinates the Religion and Humanities Program and the Program in Early Christian Literature at the College. Smith's primary area of scholarly interest is Hellenistic religions and the religions of late Antiquity, but he also has a persistent interest in questions of method and theory in the academic study (and teaching) of religion. He has published a large body of influential work. In particular he has written numerous articles addressing fundamental issues and ideas within the field of Religious Studies. Many of these are collected now in two books: *Map is not Territory: Studies in the History of Religions* (1978), and *Imagining Religion: From Babylon to Jonestown* (1982). In 1987, Smith published the results of a more extended reflection on the concept of ritual (in *To Take Place: Toward Theory in Ritual*) and in 1990 released further thoughts on the method of comparison (in *Drudgery Divine: On the Comparison of Early Christianities and the Religions of Late Antiquity*). More recently, Smith edited *The Harper-Collins Dictionary of Religion* (1995), working to set a self-conscious theoretical tone throughout, developing a system of cross-referencing of entries, and writing many of its articles.

Many of Smith's writings address methodological problems of comparison. From his earliest work, he recognized the importance of comparison for Religious Studies, but also realized that most examples of comparing religions were unsophisticated and haphazard. Looking at this problem, Smith identified what he called four modes of comparison, four ways scholars have attempted to compare cultural (and religious) data—"ethnographic," "encyclopedic," "morphological," and "evolutionary" comparisons—but in the end found all of them flawed or inadequate. On a number of occasions, Smith has insisted that comparison requires "the postulation of difference" as well as similarity, the stipulation of incongruity as well as pattern. It requires a theoretical position (a claim) to suggest how a particular set of differences amid similarities is interesting or significant. Neglecting "difference" has allowed scholars, unjustifiably, to ignore the theoretical assumptions informing their descriptions and interpretations. Smith argues quite convincingly against this habit.

Smith is also well known for presenting a typology of symbolic systems. With reference to specific historical-cultural examples, he suggests that there are two basic models of symbolic world creation, two basic attitudes toward the mapping of reality, or world-views. Interestingly, these attitudes tend to be expressed through spatial relations, in particular, through the distinction between "center" and "periphery." In this way, one world-view is "locative," as it recognizes the center as the locus of social value, and the other (its opposite) is "utopian," a more open stance that values the periphery. Smith's point here is that human beings orient themselves by mapping cultural and religious values on, among other things, spatial relations. Stipulating spatial boundaries allows concrete conceptual boundaries.

Ritual, for Smith, is a social process that suggests order, continuity, and predictability. It emphasizes repetition, propriety (a sense of "ought") and intentionality and is concerned with meaning, reality, and values. Ritual accomplishes this work by virtue of its inherently discriminatory character. Different from ordinary activity which occurs in "any place," ritual activity always occurs ("takes place") within a controlled context (a "taken place"). In other words, ritual is "social emplacement." It is a process of making proper choices, of setting limits and drawing boundaries, and thereby is a means of defining different physical ("sacred spaces") and conceptual ("sacred beings") places. Ritual is a controlled environment, one where everything involved is intentionally included, where nothing is accidental and everything, by virtue of being selected, is significant. In this way, ritual is what Smith calls a "focusing lens." It marks and reveals meaning by directing attention to the differences between the "things" (e.g., objects, behaviors, individuals, etc.) included in, and excluded from, the ritual context. Through its successful performance, ritual establishes and maintains fundamental social distinctions, for example between the "sacred" and the "profane." Human beings conduct rituals to remember, replace, and return to, these distinctions. Periodically, the ambiguities and accidents of ordinary life can be clarified and contained in ritual performance. The conceptual order aligned with ritual lends meaning to broader categories of human interest and concern.

Smith's understanding of religion follows this notion of ritual. Religion is "a mode of human creativity," a way of acting, that seeks to discover and create a meaningful "place" in which to dwell. Religions are different historical attempts to "inhabit" such places, different constructed worlds of meaning, different demarcated ways of being. Myths, rituals, doctrines, experiences, all the cultural features of religious traditions contribute to this sense of being "situated." They combine to provide human beings materials for thought, building blocks for imagining their proper place in the world.

## *J. Z. Smith:* "The Domestication of Sacrifice"

Sacrifice has not been a regular topic of interest for Smith, but on one occasion, at a conference in 1983, he presented a paper entitled "The Domestication of Sacrifice." In this paper, Smith applies his understanding of ritual to the phenomenon of sacrifice. One particular fact stands out for him, a fact noticed by a number of earlier researchers (e.g., Jensen): "animal sacrifice appears to be, universally, the ritual killing of a domesticated animal." In other words, prior to the rise of agrarian and pastoralist societies and their techniques of breeding domesticated animals, sacrifice did not exist. Sacrifice, Smith therefore suggests, cannot be an original phenomenon, as many have argued (e.g., Girard), for it is a "product of civilization." The key here is the nature of domestication. It is, Smith tells us, a process that requires selection, a matter of choosing specific animals to breed, and therefore is also a kind of discriminative killing (of those not chosen). Sacrifice, then, as it plays on the "artificial," the "selected" nature of a domestic animal (the victim), is a ritual "elaboration" of domestication, a structured "exaggeration" of an important cultural process. Like all rituals, according to Smith, sacrifice is an event that marks difference, in this case, the difference between the domesticated and the wild, the selective kill and the fortuitous kill, and in certain contexts the distinction between human beings and gods, and between nature and culture. As such, sacrifice provides, again like all rituals, a context that "gives rise to thought."

Reprinted here is Smith's article "The Domestication of Sacrifice." Limited to the phenomenon of specifically animal sacrifice, it does not attempt to explain the complete diversity of known sacrificial phenomena. Nevertheless it does provide, with its "elaboration theory" (which becomes "domestication theory" with respect to animal sacrifice), an additional means of understanding sacrifice.

# "The Domestication of Sacrifice"

In their eagerness to plumb ritual's dark symbolic or functional depths, to find in ritual more than meets the eye, anthropologists have, perhaps increasingly, tended to overlook ritual's surface, that which does meet the eye. Yet, it is on its surface, in its form, that we may discern whatever may be peculiar or ritual.

R. A. Rappaport

## I

One consensual element that appears to inform this "conversation on a theory of ritual" is a marked restlessness with the reduction of ritual to myth, and a concomitant concern with "action" as a mode of human expression and experience that has a necessary integrity of its own.[1] In the elaboration of such a point of view, little will be gained by simply inverting past valences,[2] by adopting Goethe's stragem of substituting "in the beginning was the deed" for "was the word." Although such an inversion could be questioned on logical grounds alone, there are other reasons more pressing to the concerns of this conversation. Chief among these is that, in the case of man, speech and action are given together. Neither is prior, in fact or in thought.[3] The connection is both so necessary and so intimate as to challenge all analogies where this duality is lacking (e.g., the animal on the one hand, the computer on the other). If action is not an "acting out" of speech, neither is speech a "secondary rationalization" of deed. In the history of this debate, much mischief has been done by the seemingly one-sided association of speech with thought and rationality, rather than perceiving action and speech, ritual and myth, as being coeval modes of human cognition.

Likewise, little will be gained by reinstating the old hierarchy by way of the back door. I have been struck by the desire of many who hold to the priority of action/ritual to find a story or a "primal scene" at the "origin" (itself, a narrative or mythological notion) of rite, be this expressed as tale or emotion, as articulate or inarticulate. In the one case, action has slid, all too easily, into "drama"; in the other, a consequence has been affirmed, all too readily, as a cause.

In thinking about a "theory of ritual," it would seem more fruitful to focus on the characteristics of those actions that, by one definition or another, *we* designate as "rituals," and to abstain from initial concern for content, which, among other problems, inevitably forces a premature return to myth. For me, in undertaking such an enterprise, the central theoretical works are two:

Jonathan Z. Smith, "The Domestication of Sacrifice," pp. 191–205 in *Violent Origins: Ritual Killing and Cultural Formation*, edited by Robert G. Hamerton-Kelley (Stanford: Stanford University Press, 1987). © 1987 by the Board of Trustees of the Ward Stanford Junior University. Reprinted with the permission of Stanford University Press, www.sup.org.

Freud's brief essay "Zwangshandlungen und Religionsübungen" (1907) and the exasperating and controversial "Finale" to Lévi-Strauss's *L'Homme nu* (1971).

As is well known, Freud, in this first essay on religion, remarked on the resemblance between "what are called obsessive actions in sufferers from nervous afflictions and the observances by means of which believers give expression to their piety." The connection was to be found in the notion of "obsession," in the compulsion to do particular things and to abstain from others. The things done and the things not done are ordinary, "everyday" activities that are elaborated and made "rhythmic" by additions and repetitions. Obsessive acts in both individuals and rituals are described as the overwhelming concern for

> little preoccupations, performances, restrictions and arrangements in certain activities of everyday life which have to be carried out always in the same or in a methodically varied way . . . elaborated by petty modifications [and] little details [accompanied by the] tendency to displacement [which] turns apparently trivial matters into those of great and urgent import.

In this early essay, the defining characteristic of ritual is "conscientiousness [toward] details": "Thus, in slight cases the ceremonial seems to be no more than an exaggeration of an orderly procedure that is customary and justifiable; but the special conscientiousness with which it is carried out . . . stamps the ceremonial as a sacred act."[4]

In Freud's essay, although a set of five summarized cases are offered as examples of individual obsessive behavior, no specific examples of religious ceremonial are provided. In the chapter in Lévi-Strauss, the religious examples are specified as those instances where "a ritual ceremony has been recorded and transcribed in its entirety," which may "fill a whole volume, sometimes a very large one" and take "days" to perform.[5] Lévi-Strauss's characterizations of ritual are drawn from "thick" ethnographic texts, from transcripts of an entire ritual rather than from a brief ethnographic "snapshot." As such, they are to be given particular value.

Lévi-Strauss begins with the two questions that confront any theorist of ritual: how are we to define ritual? how are the actions in ritual to be distinguished from their close counterparts in everyday life? He answers both of these questions (like Freud) by way of a characterization: "In all cases, ritual makes constant use of two procedures: parcelling out [*morcellement*] and repetition." Parcelling out is defined as that activity where, "within classes of objects and types of gesture, ritual makes infinite distinctions and ascribes discriminatory values to the slightest shades of difference" (1981, 672 [1971, 601]). Parcelling out is what he elsewhere describes as the processes of "micro-adjustment" (*micro-péréquation*), which he holds to be the characteristic activity of ritual (1966, 10).

Alongside this "infinite attention to detail" is the second characteristic, that of a "riot of repetition." Lévi-Strauss proposes a further reduction of these two characteristics: "At first glance, the two devices of parcelling out and repetition are in opposition to each other . . . But, in fact, the first procedure is equivalent to the second, which represents, so to speak, its extreme development" (1981, 673). One does not have to be persuaded of the cogency of this reduction to accept the accuracy of the two characteristics.[6]

I have not cited these two theorists in order to urge acceptance of their theories (which are, in fact, thoroughly incompatible), but rather to insist on the accuracy of their complementary characterizations of the surface appearance of ritual. They have presented us with a prima facie case for what is distinctive in ritual. Freely paraphrasing, both insist that ritual activities are an exaggeration of everyday activities, but an exaggeration that reduces rather than enlarges, that clarifies by miniaturizing in order to achieve sharp focus. Collecting their terms, ritual is the realm of the "little," the "petty," the "trivial." It is the realm of "infinite distinctions" and "micro-adjustments." Ritual is primarily a matter not of nouns and verbs, but of qualifiers—of adjectives and adverbs. Ritual precises ambiguities.

While I would derive a host of implications from these characterizations for a "general theory of ritual,"[7] one is of particular importance for this conversation. To put it crudely, ritual is "no big deal."[8] The object of action that receives ritual attention is, more often than not, commonplace. The choice of this or that object for ritual attention often appears arbitrary.[9] But what is of prime importance is its infinite and infinitesimal elaboration in the manner that Freud and Lévi-Strauss have suggested.[10] One cannot single out a highly condensed or dramatic moment from the total ritual ensemble as if this, in some sense, was the "essence" of the ritual.

These considerations underscore the position that a theory of sacrifice (our specific topic for this conversation) cannot be found in a quest for origins, but can only be found through the detailed examination of elaborations. The idioms of sacrifice are diverse; the everyday acts it elaborates are manifold (e.g., butchering, eating, exchanging, gift-giving, greeting, displaying); the contexts in which sacrifice gets applied and rationalized are highly variegated. Until there is an adequate typology, accompanied by "thick descriptions" of exemplary ritual processes and ensembles, little progress will be made. To my knowledge, neither of these preconditions has been adequately fulfilled.

Let me make clear that this is not a request for more data, but a theoretical stance. I have tried to express this stance, in a quite different context, as a denial of

> the privilege given to spontaneity as over against the fixed, to originality as over against the dependent, to the direct as over against the mediated . . . This is expressed in the learned literature in a variety of dichotomies:

330

religion/magic, individual/collective, charisma/routinization, communion/ formalism, the text as direct speech over against the commentary and the gloss, the original or primordial over against the secondary or historical. In elegant form this privilege is expressed in the writings of a scholar such as Adolf Jensen for whom all truth, meaning, and value is located in what he describes as a primal moment of ontic "seizure," a "revelation," a "direct cognition." The first verbal "formulation" of this experience, its first "concretization" is an "intuitive, spontaneous experiencing" which he terms, "expression." All subsequent "formalizations" and "concretizations" are reinterpretations of this primal experience which Jensen terms "applications" (for him, a pejorative). All "applications" fall under the iron "law of degeneration" resulting in the original "spontaneity" becoming a "fixed but no longer understood routine." [In contradistinction, I would propose an enterprise that would insist on] the value of the prosaic, the expository, the articulate. It is to explore the creativity of what I have termed in another context, "exegetical ingenuity," as a basic constituent of human culture. It is to gain an appreciation of the complex dynamics of tradition and its necessary dialectics of self-limitation and freedom. To do these things . . . is to give expression to what I believe is the central contribution that religious studies might make, . . . the realization that, in culture, there is no text, it is all commentary; that there is no primordium, it is all history; that all is application. The realization that, regardless of whether we are dealing with "texts" from literate or non-literate cultures, we are dealing with historical processes of reinterpretation, with tradition. That, for a given group at a given time to choose this or that way of interpreting their tradition is to opt for a particular way of relating themselves to their historical past and their social present.[11]

Despite the above, although a quite different enterprise from my usual agendum, in accommodation to what appears to be one of the dominant concerns of the present conversation, I will venture a highly tentative suggestion on the possible activity that achieved prime elaboration in sacrifice.

## II

From the immense variety of human ritual activities, a few have been lifted out by scholars as privileged examples on which to build theories of ritual—preeminently sacrifice, New Year's scenarios, and male initiatory rites. Each of these three seems to entail quite different consequences for scholarship. The choice of which one is to be taken as exemplary is one of great significance. Having said this much, let me note that, among this small group, animal sacrifice has often appeared to be primus inter pares, primarily because it has seemed (at least to the scholarly imagination) quintessentially "primitive." Perhaps the first question that ought to be asked is, "Is this the case?"[12]

The putative "evidence" for the primitivity of animal sacrifice is far from compelling. Though there are obvious questions of definition, of what counts, I know of no unambiguous instance of animal sacrifice that is not of a domesticated animal. The Paleolithic indications for sacrifice are dubious. I know of no unambiguous instance of animal sacrifice performed by hunters. *Animal sacrifice appears to be, universally, the ritual killing of a domesticated animal by agrarian or pastoralist societies*. Where it occurs in groups otherwise classified, it is still of a domesticated animal, usually in the context of a highly developed "exchange (or display)" ideology.[13] Furthermore, though I am unhappy with many of the interpretative implications developed from the familiar dual typology, where there are articulate native systems of animal sacrifice, they do appear to fall into the categories of gift-offering-display and/or pollution removal. Neither gives comfort to primitivity. The former seems to require a developed notion of property, the latter the complex ideological and social hierarchies of pure/impure. As best as I can judge, sacrifice is not a primitive element in culture. Sacrifice is a component of secondary and tertiary cultures. It is, primarily, a product of "civilization."

Why, then, the preoccupation with the primitivity of sacrifice? Beyond its obvious resonance with elements of our past, with Greco-Roman and Judeo-Christian religious systems and practices, I suspect that sacrifice allows some scholars the notion that here, in this religious phenomenon at least (or at last), is a dramatic encounter with an "other," the slaying of a beast. As I have suggested elsewhere, such a notion rests on an agrarian mythologization of the hunt and is not characteristic of what we can learn of the attitudes of hunting and gathering peoples toward the activities of hunting (1982a, 57–8). This agrarian reinterpretation (interesting and important as it is in itself) has allowed the scholarly fantasy that ritual is an affair of the *tremendum* rather than a quite ordinary mode of human social labor. It has allowed the notion that ritual—and therefore religion—is somehow grounded in "brute fact" rather than in the work and imagination and intellection of culture.

It may well be for these reasons that one of the other privileged modes of ritual, initiation, has not been so vigorously put forth as the exemplum of primitivity. This is surprising in light of the fact that many of those early reports that asserted that this or that primitive group had "no religion" (reports that led, ultimately, to the overdrawn theses of *Urmonotheismus*, particularly in the form of the "otiose High God"; see J. Smith 1982a, Chapter 5) specifically noted no sacrificial practices, but did report (often in lurid terms) the presence of initiatory practices and secret societies. It is my sense, after surveying a wide sample of literature, that sacrifice and initiation stand in an inverse ratio to each other: where there are elaborate initiatory rituals, sacrifice seems relatively undeveloped; where there are complex sacrificial cycles and ideologies, initiation seems relatively undeveloped. Indeed, I am tempted to suggest that initiation is for the hunter and gatherer and primitive agricultural-ist what sacrifice is for the agrarian and pastoralist. But initiation is relentlessly an affair of "culture" rather than "nature," and one of making ordinary what appears to be an experience of the *tremendum*.[14] Furthermore, the temporal dimensions of initiation (at times an affair of twenty years, with highly ambiguous limits),[15] in contrast to the extreme binary compression and irre-versibility of the sacrificial kill, make clear that initiation is an affair more of social labor than of drama.

Given these observations, I hazard the opinion that the starting point for a theory of sacrifice, that which looms largest in a redescription of sacrifice, ought no longer to be the verb "to kill," or the noun "animal," but the adjective "domesticated." Sacrifice is, in part, a meditation on domestication. A theory of sacrifice must begin with the domesticated animal and with the sociocultural process of domestication itself. In such an enterprise, we are aided by a recent rich literature on the historical processes of domestication, and on "domesticity" as a native, taxonomic category.[16]

Following current usage, domestication may be defined as the process of human interference in or alteration of the genetics of plants and animals (i.e., selective breeding). It is frequently, although not necessarily, associated with agriculture, which may be defined as the process of human interference in or alteration of the environment of plants and animals. Such processes of interfer-ence presuppose a variety of social developments and result in a variety of social consequences.

For an understanding of sacrifice (and other agrarian ritual activities), the most important consequence is an alteration of the sense of space and time. The most obvious spatial and temporal reorientation associated with domesti-cation is signaled by the term "sedentary community." This marks a shift from the hunter-and-gatherer's social world of immediacy, skill, and chance to a social world of futurity and planning—of the capacity for continuity of time and place. This is apparent with respect to animals. Here the art of breeding is, as well, the art of selective killing. Some animals must be held separated out for several years until they reach sexual maturity. The bulk of the herd must be slaughtered while immature. In the domesticated situation (as the archaeologi-cal stratigraphy bears out), immature animals will be killed more frequently than mature ones, males more frequently than females, and so forth and so on. For the domesticator, killing is an act of precise discrimination with an eye to the future. It is dependent on the social acceptance of a "delayed payoff," as well as on the social acquisition of the intricate technology of sexuality and the concomitant pattern of settled dwelling.

If this everyday and continual activity of domestication is agrarian and pastoral man's prime mode of relating to the animal, then we can specify with precision the commonplace activity that is elaborated obsessively and intellectually in sacrifice, as well as its difference from the hunter's relationship to game: *sacrifice is an elaboration of the selective kill, in contradistinction to the fortuitous kill.*

Though I do not wish to strain the point, it does appear that the other elements characteristic of domestication have their concomitant elaborations in sacrifice. The notion of the "delayed payoff" is central to any but the most mechanical *do ut des* understanding of the gift structure of some sacrificial systems, but it is present in some pollution systems as well. (For example, in the Israelitic cult, washing with water works for immediate, advertent pollutions, whereas the *hatta'th* is for inadvertent impurities that one may or may not be aware of, or for pollutions that last more than a week.[17]) Furthermore, sacrifice is not fortuitous with respect to either time or place—it is highly determined and presumes a sedentary pattern.[18] Finally, in many sacrificial systems, the complex requirements for the physical and/or behavioral characteristics of a particular animal chosen (bred) for sacrifice, whether before or after the kill, represent to an extreme degree the same kinds of details that are sexually selected for by the breeder.[19]

All of these elements, governed in the majority of cases by elaborate, highly formalized rules, suggest that sacrifice is an exaggeration of domestication, a meditation on one cultural process by means of another. If domestication is a "focusing" on selected characteristics in the animal, a process of sexual "experimentation" that strives to achieve a "perfection" or "rectification" of the natural animal species (these terms, it will be recalled, are key elements in my vocabulary for ritual; see Smith, 1982a, 40–2), then sacrifice becomes a focus on this focus, an experimentation with this experimentation, a perfecting of this perfection, a rectification of this rectification. It can do this precisely because it is a ritual. *Sacrifice, in its agrarian or pastoral context, is the artificial (i.e., ritualized) killing of an ariticial (i.e., domesticated) animal.*[20] Because sacrifice is inextricably related to alimentation and, therefore, to what I have elsewhere described as a basic cultural process of reduction and ingenuity, of food and cuisine (see Smith, 1982a, 40–2), it is, perhaps, especially suited for this sort of meditation.

What has been proposed thus far could be further elaborated with respect to the taxonomies of domesticated animals in relation to humans, on the one hand, and to animals on the other.[21] Just as the role of the mask in initiation ceremonies, as interpreted by Victor Turner (1967, 105–8), where the artificial, radical mixture or juxtaposition of anatomical features from humans and animals serves as an occasion for cultural meditation on difference and relationship; so too in the case of a domesticated animal, which is, in some sense, a hybrid, a fabrication.[22] Furthermore, if the domesticated animal stands, in native taxonomies, between man and the wild animal, then, to invoke a more familiar scholarly idiom for sacrifice, the sacrificial animal stands in an analogous position between man and "the gods." The transactional character of both positions relativizes the apparent absolute difference. (Hence the frequently observed correspondence of kin taxonomies and rules for sexual relations to taxonomies for domesticated animals and rules for their eating or sacrifice.) Sacrifice accomplishes this not by sacramentalism, but by an etiquette of infinite degrees and baroque complexities (for a good example, see Tambiah 1969, 142–3). But to develop such a thesis with any cogency and conviction demands particularities rather than generalities: the comparison of specific exemplary taxonomies of domesticates with specific exemplary sacrificial ensembles. The detail such a discussion would require goes well beyond the bounds of civil "conversation."

If Lévi-Strauss, through a discussion of wild animals in the "totemic" systems of hunters and gatherers, has taught us well that animals are "good to eat" and "good to think," then the domesticated animals in the sacrificial systems of agriculturalists and pastoralists may teach us, in analogous ways, that animals are "goods to eat" and "goods to think."

## A Note on the Primitivity of Animal Sacrifice

As is well known, the observations that "ritual killing is completely absent in the oldest known strata of culture," and that animal sacrifices are "almost exclusively of domestic animals, for they all occur in agricultural cultures" stand at the foundation of A. E. Jensen's theory of sacrifice and ritual killing (1963, esp. 162–90; quotes from 162–3). Jensen uses these observations to reason to a different set of conclusions than those proposed here.

It would require a lengthy monograph to review critically all the putative evidence that has been adduced for the primitivity of animal sacrifice and to cite the evidence for the stark assertions made above. Since the issue of primitivity is without interest for me, someone else will have to provide such a work. (I would propose J. van Baal, the distinguished scholar of *dema*, who has more than once offered a similar assessment, although I share none of his presuppositions. See, among others, van Baal, 1976, esp. 162; 1981, 67–73, 219–25, and passim.) However, some brief indications may be provided:

1. The Paleolithic evidence remains opaque to interpretation. Since the work of F. E. Koby (1951), the evidence for Paleolithic bear sacrifice has been rendered exceedingly doubtful (see Leroi-Gourhan, 1971, 30–6; Burkert, 1979, 167, n. 3). This is extremely important because the only contemporary putative evidence for a wild animal being used in sacrifice is the circum-polar bear festival.

In fact, the bear festival does not fit, although it was used as the hermeneutic key to interpret the Paleolithic remains. (a) The peoples who practice the bear festivals are pastoralists, not hunters. While the figure of the "Master of the Animals" appears to be shared by them and some hunters (especially the Amerindians), among the latter there is no recorded sacrifice of wild game. The conception of the "Master" among the reindeer pastoralists is in the idiom of pastoralism (penning the animals and the like). It is possible that this is a notion independent from that of the "Master" among hunters. If not, it is a radical reinterpretation that forbids any easy synthesis. (b) In the circum-polar bear ritual, the animal is domesticated for a period of years before being slain. (c) In the case of the Ainu (for whom there is the best ethnographic documentation), both the most distinguished native Ainu anthropologist, K. Kindaichi (1949), and the bear festival's most distinguished recent interpreter, J. M. Kitagawa (1961), vigorously deny that the ritual should be classified as a sacrifice, seeing it instead as part of a complex structure of visit-and-return. (See further Smith, 1982a, 59, and the literature cited on p. 144, n. 24.) At the very least, the complex tissue of parallelism, invoked since the pioneering article by W. Koppers (1933), will have to be carefully reevaluated. Both terms of the proposed equation are in difficulty. The equation has been decisive in the literature on the primitivity of animal sacrifice.

2. On the issue of Paleolithic sacrifices, the evaluation of the evidence has been one of steady retreat from confidence to uncertainty. For example, J. Maringer, who confidently declared in 1952 that "the practice of sacrificing the head, skull and long bones of animals survived from earliest times right up to the Upper Paleolithic" (1960, 90), retreated by 1968 to declaring that sacrifice is not evident in Lower and Middle Paleolithic deposits, and that it is possible to speak "with relatively great certainty" (*"mit mehr oder minder grosser Sicherheit"*) of animal sacrifices only in the Upper Paleolithic (1968, 271). Yet even here, strong alternative hypotheses that account for the "evidence" as nonsacrificial have been proposed (e.g. Pohlhausen, 1953), as Maringer acknowledges (1968, 269–70).

3. The fact that sacrifices are invariably of domesticated animals in contrast to wild ones (and hence from a different "sphere" than religious practices associated with hunters or Paleolithic man) was already quite properly insisted upon by L. Franz (1937). Several months of checking in a variety of ethnographic monographs have turned up no exceptions. Here, I distinguish between killing an animal in sacrifice and the postmortem offering of some portion of an animal routinely killed for food. The latter is certainly present among some hunters and gatherers.

There are occasions of the ritual killing and eating of wild animals in connection with initiatory rituals, most particularly initiations into secret societies. The Lele pangolin, made famous by M. Douglas (1957, and other works), would be an obvious example, although she gives no reliable description. I sharply distinguish this from sacrifice, and would classify the bulk of the instances known to me as modes of ordeal.

I would also note the interesting thesis—first developed by E. Hahn, C. O.

Sauer, and others, and recently revived by E. Isaac (1963; 1970, 105–10; and elsewhere)—that animals were first domesticated for the purpose of sacrifice.

4. In the discussion of the primitivity of animal sacrifice, much depends on how one imagines hunters (Paleolithic or contemporary). I join in the consensus that there never was, and certainly is not now, a stage of pure hunting. Hunting is always in combination with gathering, with plant products making up the bulk of the diet (except in unusual cases, such as that of the Eskimos).

It is, of course, impossible to determine the diet of Paleolithic man. Only animal bones, mollusk shells, and the like can be preserved, not soft parts and vegetable substances. For contemporary hunters and gatherers, a figure that approximately 70 percent of their normal diet is vegetable occurs in a variety of cultural locales, from the Amazon to Australia (e.g., Reichel-Dolmatoff, 1971, 11; Meggitt, 1957, 143). Furthermore, if one examines a wide variety of ethnographic reports, it becomes clear that the meat portion of the diet, that which is the result of hunting, is composed largely of small mammals, birds, reptiles, eggs, insects, fish, and mollusks. *Mano a mano* combat with large carnivores is largely unreported. For example, among the Desana, although their mythology is largely concerned with jaguars, Reichel-Domatoff reports that "a man who goes to hunt for two or three days per week obtains approximately three catches, for example, a small rodent, an armadillo, and a few birds. In a month he can get three or four wild guinea pigs, two cavies and a monkey; a deer or a peccary every two months; and a tapir once a year" (1971, 13). If bored-through teeth (trophies?) are any indication of the results of a Paleolithic hunt, 56 percent of a wide sample of such teeth are those of fox and deer, and only 3 percent are of bear or wolf (Leroi-Gourhan 1971, 28).

Finally, as I insisted in "The Bare Facts of Ritual" (1980), we need to recognize the strong ideological component in hunting. Although men routinely gather, and women in some societies routinely hunt (e.g., Efe pygmies, Klamath Indians, Tasmanians, the Australian Tiwi), hunting is strongly marked as a prestigious male activity, even when the males rarely hunt. Though the native descriptions of killing strongly emphasize its *mano a mano* character, in some of those same societies, traps, stampedes, ambushes, and the like are widely employed.

5. I have not raised the issue, widely discussed in some German anthropological circles, that many of our present hunting-and-gathering societies may be derivatives from earlier agricultural societies (e.g., Narr, 1952, esp. 504). But this may need to be taken into account in re-evaluating a particular report, as does the more recent influence of agrarians on pastoralists and hunters and gatherers (especially in Africa and northern Eurasia).

# Notes

1. Although from a theoretical perspective quite different from any adopted by the major participants in this "conversation," see R. A. Rappaport's eloquent formulation (1979, p. 174): "It becomes apparent through a consideration of ritual's form that ritual is not simply an alternative way to express certain things, but that certain things can be expressed only in ritual." The epigraph is from the same page.

2. I am speaking here at the level of theory. There is much to commend the detailed investigations of a variety of scholars from Lévi-Strauss to Tambiah, which have demonstrated that, in a wide variety of cultural situations, myth and rite often stand in an inverse relationship to one another.

3. Here as elsewhere, I mean "social man."

4. Freud (1907, p. 26, 34). In presenting this aspect of Freud, I have deliberately abstained from his genetic account, which is here less important than his characterization, since it is only an analogy that is being proposed. A theory of ritual, in any case, could not be constructed on the basis of the 1907 essay alone. A far more interesting genetic proposal (although equally remote from my concerns) is his late notion of a "compulsion to repeat," as sketched out in *Beyond the Pleasure Principle* (1920). See Gay, 1975; 1979, esp. Chapter 3.

5. Lévi-Strauss's specific examples make clear that he is primarily thinking of the accounts in those thick, green *Reports* of the Bureau of American Ethnology. The documents he has in mind as parallel from Africa and Oceania are not specified.

6. As in the case of Freud, so here I have abstained from accepting the implications that Lévi-Strauss perceives in this characterization of ritual (although they appear highly cogent to me, whereas his appeal to Dumézil does not). If myth (and language) are perceived as dichotomizing and contrastive, then "ritual, by fragmenting operations and repeating them unwearyingly in infinite detail, takes upon itself the laborious task of patching up holes and stopping gaps, and it thus encourages the illusion that it is possible to run counter to myth, and to move back from the discontinuous to the continuous" (Lévi-Strauss, 1981, p. 674). Compare the formulation in Rappaport (1979, p. 206): "The distinctions of language cut the world into bits—into categories, classes, oppositions and contrasts. It is in the nature of language to search out all differences and turn them into distinctions. [It is] in the nature of liturgical orders to unite or reunite . . . Liturgical orders are meta-orders . . . They mend ever again worlds forever breaking apart under the blows of usage and the slashing distinctions of language." (See also pp. 127–8, 204, and passim.)

7. These theoretical presuppositions underlie my attempt to develop a vocabulary for speaking of ritual. The notions of *focus* and *perfection* developed in "The Bare Facts of Ritual" (1980) have been more or less adequately described in Mack's Introduction; the notions of *experimentation* and, especially, *rectification*, developed in "A Pearl of Great Price" (1976), regrettably, were not. (See note 10, below.)

8. As opposed to myth or to the mythology of a ritual, which may very well be a "big deal." (See note 6, above.)

9. See the development of this in "The Bare Facts of Ritual" (1980). The object may, after all, as well be a cucumber as an ox. It is for this reason that I abstain from

all questions about the etiology of the object of ritual attention (*pace* Mack's persistent questions to me on this point). I doubt, in most cases, whether the originating element is recoverable. If it is, it would be without theoretical interest.

10. I have developed this, at some length, as the dynamic of *reduction* and *ingenuity* in "Sacred Persistence" (1982c, esp. pp. 40–2), which is a statement explicitly intended to be read in conjunction with "Bare Facts"—and unfortunately ignored in Mack's summary.

11. J. Smith, 1983, pp. 223–4. This is a fundamental attitude underlying my recent work, as adumbrated in the Foreword to *Imagining Religion* (1982a), as well as in "Sacred Persistence," "Bare Facts," and "A Pearl of Great Price," to mention those essays most directly relevant to our conversation.

12. I have abstained from the question of human sacrifice and other modes of the ritual killing of humans (headhunting, cannibalism, "sacral regicide," etc.), which are often too readily homologized with animal sacrifice. The evidence for these practices is frequently less certain than for animal sacrifice—often being more illustrative of intercultural polemics than cultural facts. Nevertheless, a rapid review would indicate that documented human sacrifice is present only in agricultural or pastoral cultures. The other modes of ritual killing, while requiring their own interpretations where their occurrence appears credible, are not to be classified as "sacrifice" (as Jensen, among others, has quite properly argued).

13. See my "Note on the Primitivity of Animal Sacrifice" at the end of the paper.

14. On initiation as an affair of culture, consider, for example, the lack of correlation between biological puberty and the so-called puberty initiations, already clearly perceived by A. van Gennep (1960, pp. 65–71). On the making ordinary of the experience of the *tremendum*, consider, for example, the frequent phenomenon of the unmasking of the putative deities. (Cf. the survey in di Nola, 1972 and the comments in J. Smith, 1978a, pp. 300–2.)

15. For an extremely detailed description of an elegant example, see Tuzin, 1980.

16. For the historical processes, see, among others, Ucko and Dimbleby 1969; Isaac, 1970. For domestication as a taxonomic category, see, among others, Leach, 1964; Tambiah, 1969. See further J. Smith, 1974.

17. This understanding of this element in the Israelitic system and its implications has been especially well worked out by Jacob Milgrom. See, among other works, Milgrom, 1970; 1976, esp. pp. 766–8.

18. This characteristic was clearly perceived by Jensen (1963, p. 162), who used it as a point of marked contrast to headhunting.

19. Each of these elements, presented here impressionistically, would have to be tested for frequency by means of detailed cross-cultural comparisons.

20. Perhaps this may account for the agrarian mythologization of the hunt, which exaggerates the "otherness" (i.e., the nonfabricated nature) of the wild beast. (See above; and J. Smith, 1982a, pp. 57–8.)

21. See Leach, 1964; Tambiah, 1969. Here is an excellent example of the relation of ritual to myth (see note 6, above). The myths of domestication are relentlessly binary and contrastive. The etiquette and rituals concerning domesticated animals, in relation to both wild animals and humans, reduce this binary and contrastive characteristic by providing instances of almost infinite degrees of difference. Note that this is raised to the level of theory by Leach (1964, pp. 62–3).

22. This is in contradistinction to Lévi-Strauss's understanding of sacrifice as belonging to the "realms of continuity" (1966, Chapter 8, where this notion is developed in a contrast between sacrifice and totemism), which appears to be in contradistinction to his later theory of ritual as described above on the basis of *L'Homme nu.*

# References

Burkert, W. (1979). *Structure and History in Greek Mythology and Ritual.* Berkeley, Calif.

Douglas, M. (1957). "Animals in Lele Religious Symbolism," *Africa* 27, pp. 46–58.

Franz, L. (1937). *Religion und Kunst der Vorzeit.* Prague.

Freud, S. (1907/1924). "Obsessive Acts and Religious Practices," in Vol. 2 of J. Riviere, ed., *Sigmund Freud, M.D., LL.D.: Collected Papers 25–35.* London.

Gay, V. (1975). "Psychopathology and Ritual," *The Psychoanalytic Review* 62, pp. 493–507.

Gay, V. (1979). *Freud on Ritual: Reconstruction and Critique.* Missoula, Mont.

Isaac, E. (1963). "Myths, Cults and Livestock Breeding," *Diogenes* 41, pp. 70–93.

Isaac, E. (1970). *Geography of Domestication.* Englewood Cliffs, N.J.

Jensen, A. E. (1963). *Myth and Cult Among Primitive Peoples.* Trans. Marianna Tax Choldin and Wolfgang Weissleder. Chicago. Originally published in 1951 as *Mythos und Kult bei Naturvölkern: religionswissenschaftliche Betrachtungen* (Wiesbaden).

Kindaichi, K. (1949). "The Concepts Behind the Ainu Bear Festival," *Southwestern Journal of Anthropology,* 5, pp. 345–50.

Kitigawa, J. M. (1961). "Ainu Bear Festival (Iyomante)," *History of Religions* 1, pp. 95–151.

Koby, F. E. (1951). "L'Ours des cavernes et les paléolithiques," *L'Anthropologie* 55, pp. 304–8.

Koppers, W. (1933). "Der Bärenkult in ethnologischer und prähistorischer Beleuchtung," *Palaeobiologica* 6, pp. 47–64.

Leach, E. R. (1964). "Anthropological Aspects of Language: Animal Categories and Verbal Abuse," in E. H. Lenneberg, ed., *New Directions in the Study of Language.* Cambridge, Mass.

Leroi-Gourhan, A. (1971). *Les Religions de la préhistoire: Paléolithique.* 2nd edn. Paris.

Lévi-Strauss, C. (1966). *The Savage Mind.* Chicago. Originally published in 1962 as *La Pensée sauvage* (Paris).

Lévi-Strauss, C. (1981). *The Naked Man.* Trans. J. and D. Weightman. New York. Originally published in 1971 as *L'Homme nu* (Paris).

Maringer, J. (1960). *The Gods of Prehistoric Man.* New York.

Maringer, J. (1968). "Die Opfer des paläolithischen Menschen," *Anthropica: Gedenkschrift zum 100. Geburtstag von P. Wilhelm Schmidt,* pp. 249–71. Vienna.

Meggitt, M. J. (1957). "Notes on the Vegetable Foods of the Walbiri of Central Australia," *Oceania,* 28, pp. 143–5.

Milgrom, Jacob (1970). "The Function of the Hatta't Sacrifice" (in Hebrew), *Tarbiz,* 40, pp. 1–8.

Milgrom, Jacob (1976). "Sacrifice and Offerings, OT," *The Interpreter's Dictionary of the Bible*, supplementary vol. Nashville, Tenn.

Narr, K. J. (1952). "Das Höhere Jägertum: Jüngere Jagd- und Sammelstufe," in F. Valjavec, ed., *Historia Mundi* I, pp. 502–22. Bern.

di Nola, A. (1972). "Demythicization in Certain Primitive Cultures," *History of Religions* 12, pp. 1–27.

Pohlhausen, H. (1953). "Zum Motive der Rentierversenkung," *Anthropos* 48, pp. 987–90.

Rappaport, R. A. (1979). *Ecology, Meaning and Religion*. Richmond, Calif.

Reichel-Dolmatoff, G. (1971). *Amazonian Cosmos: The Sexual and Religious Symbolism of the Tukano Indians*. Chicago. Originally published in 1963 as *Desana: Le Symbolisme universel des Indiens Tukano de Vaupés* (Paris).

Smith, J. Z. (1974). "Animals and Plants in Myth and Legend," *Encyclopædia Britannica*, 15th edn., I, pp. 911–18.

Smith, J. Z. (1976). "A Pearl of Great Price and a Cargo of Yams: A Study of Situational Incongruity," *History of Religions* 16, pp. 1–19. (Reprinted in Smith, 1982a, pp. 90–101.)

Smith, J. Z. (1978a). *Map is Not Territory: Studies in the History of Religion*. Leiden.

Smith, J. Z. (1980). "The Bare Facts of Ritual," *History of Religions* 20, pp. 112–27. (Reprinted in Smith, 1982a, pp. 53–65).

Smith, J. Z. (1982a). *Imagining Religion: From Babylon to Jonestown*. Chicago.

Smith, J. Z. (1982c). "Sacred Persistence." In Smith, 1982a, pp. 36–52.

Smith, J. Z. (1983). "No Need to Travel to the Indies: Judaism and the Study of Religion." In J. Neusner, ed., *Take Judaism For Example*, pp. 215–26. Chicago.

Tambiah, S. J. (1969). "Animals are Good to Think and Good to Prohibit," *Ethnology* 8, pp. 423–59.

Turner, V. (1967). *The Forest of Symbols: Aspects of Ndembu Ritual*. Ithaca, N.Y.

Tuzin, D. F. (1980). *The Voice of the Tambaran*. Berkeley, Calif.

Ucko, P. J., and Dimbleby, G. W. eds. (1969). *The Domestication and Exploitation of Plants and Animals*. Chicago.

van Baal, J. (1976). "Offering, Sacrifice and Gift," *Numen* 23, pp. 161–78.

van Baal, J. (1981). *Man's Quest for Partnership: The Anthropological Foundations of Ethics and Religion*. Assen, The Netherlands.

van Gennep, A. (1960). *Rites of Passage*. Chicago.

# 20

# ROBERT J. DALY (b. 1933)

Robert J. Daly is a Jesuit priest who studied Philosophy, English, and Theology at both Boston College and Catholic University. In 1972, he received his Doctor of Theology degree in Würzburg Germany after writing a dissertation entitled "Christian Sacrifice: The Judeo-Christian Background before Origen." He joined the Theology Faculty at Boston College in 1971, served as its chairperson for fifteen years, and continued to teach there until his recent retirement. Daly was the editor of the journal *Theological Studies* between 1991 and 1995. He is well known for his continued work on the nature and meaning of Christian sacrifice. His most famous book is *The Origins of the Christian Doctrine of Sacrifice* (1978). He has written a number of scholarly articles and edited several books, including a work by Edward J. Kilmartin, *The Eucharist in the West: History and Theology* (1998). His ongoing area of research is the history and theology of Christian sacrifice.

There is a long tradition in Christianity of using sacrificial language when speaking about the death of Jesus. The nature of this language, however—its referents, its relationship to fundamental tenets of the Church, its significance for broader theological questions—has been a matter of debate and controversy. For example, the question of who is "sacrificing" what/whom "to" whom and for what purpose can be answered in a number of ways, even within the context of Christian doctrine. The complexities of the "Christ-event" itself (the death and resurrection of Jesus) and the ritual of the Eucharist (a celebration of the "Christ-event" through a communal meal when the "body and blood" of Christ are consumed) make this a very difficult question to answer definitively.

Robert Daly has devoted many years to thinking about the issue of sacrifice in Christianity, and has identified several helpful distinctions. First, he has highlighted the fact that the Christian meaning of sacrifice has changed throughout the development of the tradition, the earliest form being mostly a joyful celebration accompanied by feelings of thanksgiving and general petition for communal well-being, and later forms turning more toward atonement, expiation and propitiation. Over time these distinctions became blurred as various aspects from earlier times were retained. Next, Daly has distinguished between propitiation and atonement. Propitiation is the act of a human being intended to influence a deity, mostly to soothe the deity's anger or to secure some favor. It is essentially an "anabatic or upward dynamic from creature to God," even as it seeks some particular response from the divine. Atonement, conversely, is the deity acting to forgive sins and other transgressions, a mostly "katabatic or downward dynamic from God to creature," even as it implicates some form of human agency. Here too, ignoring this distinction contributes to the complexity and confusion surrounding the Christian notion of sacrifice. Finally, Daly has noted that Christian sacrifice has followed two divergent trends of development. The first is a process of "spiritualization," a movement from emphasizing the efficacy of ritual performance, to the importance of proper dispositions when offering sacrifice, to the daily, "apostolic works of the Christian life." This constitutes an evolving context in which human beings recognize and enact a "vertical" "Creator-creature relationship." At the same time, there has been an "institutionalizing trend" in the development of Christian sacrifice, a move, paralleling the increasing social organization of the Church, that established the Mass as a sacrifice under the exclusive control of a priest. This represents, according to Daly, a "regression back to the first phase of spiritualization," a horizontal movement along sociopolitical lines of power, and as such has challenged the trend toward a spiritualization of sacrifice.

Ultimately, "authentic Christian sacrifice," Daly claims, is a matter of "self-giving and loving obedience." It is a means to strengthen human-divine relations. Reprinted here is Daly's essay "The Power of Sacrifice in Ancient Judaism and Christianity," in which he outlines his approach to Christian sacrifice. It contributes a theological understanding of sacrifice, one derived from the history and doctrine of a specific religious tradition, Christianity, and as such makes no broader theoretical claim about the meaning of sacrifice in non-Christian traditions. It serves also as an example of how certain understandings of sacrifice can open up studies of non-ritual phenomena, permitting an interpretation of their sacrifice-like character.

# "The Power of Sacrifice in Ancient Judaism and Christianity"

MY TITLE avoids the familiar phrase "Judaeo-Christian tradition" since in my work on the development of Christian concepts of sacrifice (Daly, 1978a, 1978b, 1989), I have not yet undertaken a careful study of the devel-

Robert J. Daly, "The Power of Sacrifice in Ancient Judaism and Christianity," *Journal of Ritual Studies* 4 (1990): pp. 181–98. Reprinted with the permission of the Journal of Ritual Studies and the author.

opments within Judaism after the beginning of the Christian era. My analysis of Christian sacrifice focuses primarily on conceptions derived from Western rather than Eastern Christianity. It should also be noted that the research underlying this paper was undertaken with a specifically theological agenda: to study the development that resulted in Origen's spiritualized Christian theology of sacrifice in the first half of the third century C.E. Accordingly, the typology developed here is more theological than historical. I mention this not to evade the analyses, questions, and challenges of the historian of religions, but simply to point out the relative strengths and weaknesses of my analysis and the direction from which to expect challenges to it.

The sacrificial ritual was the center of the religious life of ancient Israel (Daly, 1978a, 1–207; 1978b, 11–47). In early Christianity, because of its fierce rejection of both Jewish and pagan ritual sacrifice, just the opposite appears to be the case. From New Testament times, however, Christians thought and spoke of Christ's death as sacrificial, of their own community as the new temple in which spiritual sacrifices were to be offered, and of Christian life itself as sacrificial (Daly, 1978a, 208–307; 1978b, 53–83). Before many centuries had passed, the central act of Christian worship, the Eucharist, was referred to as "the sacrifice of Christians" (Augustine, *City* 10.6; Daly, 1978a, 498–508; 1978b, 127–34; 1989, 152–3).

Sacrifice does not of course cover all that is referred to by the theme of ritual and power, but it is a good place to begin. An analysis of sacrifice in terms of the interrelationship of ritual and power invites one to examine in particular the function and effects of sacrifice. What does sacrifice accomplish or do? To whom? For whom? By whom? These questions have both vertical and horizontal implications in that they encompass spiritual (= vertical) as well as socio-political and economic (= horizontal) dimensions of power.

With respect to the specifically spiritual purposes or effects of sacrifice, or of rituals viewed as sacrificial (Daly, 1978b, 4–6), sacrifices that are undertaken to offer homage to the deity or to establish contact with the deity by means of some kind of gift implicitly involve issues of spiritual power in the sense that any such human contact with God strengthens the fundamental Creator-creature relationship. However, the spiritual power of sacrificial rituals is most clearly evident in sacrifices that are undertaken to attain communion with or participation in the life of the deity, or to gain reconciliation with the deity in the form of atonement, forgiveness, propitiation, or expiation. As will be discussed later, atonement, whether seen as remedial, as it usually is, or simply as strengthening an already positive relationship with God, had become so prominent in Jewish conceptions of sacrifice by the beginning of the Common Era that the process of atonement became virtually equated with the sacrificial ritual.

Control over access to the means of atonement inevitably involves issues of sociopolitical and economic power. Questions about the function and purpose of sacrifice must therefore take into account not only the spiritual power involved in strengthening divine-human relationships on a vertical plane, but also the sociopolitical and economic aspects of power on the horizontal plane of human relationships that are established, strengthened, or restored through sacrificial rituals. The following analysis will examine the development of conceptions of sacrifice in ancient Judaism and Christianity in light of the dialectic between spiritual power and the sociopolitical and economic aspects of power.

# Terminology

## Sacrifice

Within the Judaeo-Christian tradition, and even within Christianity itself, the term "sacrifice" has many and at times substantially different meanings, encompassing a range of practices and experiences, and thus considerable effort is required to determine what the term means in any given context. This is even more true when the discussion moves beyond the Judaeo-Christian tradition to a consideration of the multifaceted meaning of sacrifice in other religions. In this context we can no longer afford to indulge in the relatively facile comparisons that characterized the early stages of the comparative study of religions.

The conceptions of sacrifice common in the Mediterranean and Near Eastern world of ancient Judaism and early Christianity are quite different from those found in the modern Western world. In the ancient world sacrifice was understood in almost entirely religious rather than secular terms. It was viewed as a cultic act, a religious ritual, even when serving obviously public purposes, as in the sacrificial ceremonies of Roman army religion to which Christians, sometimes at the cost of their lives, took exception (Helgeland, et al., 1984, 48–55). Such sacrifices were preferably as large as possible and were always offered *to* a god, thus indicating a recognition of the deity's superior status. By early Christian times sacrifices were generally performed joyously as part of a public holiday or celebration and were often associated with sentiments of petition and thanksgiving. There was a strong emphasis on active giving and doing rather than on a more passive sense of giving up or depriving oneself of something. In Jewish sacrifice in particular a passive sense of deprivation usually played no great role. The death or destruction of the thing sacrificed was generally looked on as incidental and not as an inherently significant factor in the sacrifice.

In the secularized modern Western world, in contrast, when one speaks of "making a sacrifice," this does not generally refer to a cultic ritual but rather to a private, secular action, which may assume religious import by transference. Such a sacrifice is preferably as small as possible and is not offered *to* anyone. It is generally performed with regret accompanied by sadness, and the emphasis is on giving up and deprivation. The diminution or loss suffered by the victim—who often is also the agent of the sacrifice—tends to be seen as a necessary and constituent factor, thus making sacrifice something that may indeed be necessary and laudably heroic but that on the whole is viewed as unpleasant and to be avoided as far as possible (Daly, 1978b, 1–4; Yerkes, 1953, 1–8).

While making allowances for the oversimplifications inherent in such a quick comparison, one can see that in the highly religious world of ancient Western civilization the term "sacrifice" was associated with a rich variety of positive connotations, while in the highly secularized modern Western world the term is laden with a broad range of negative connotations. Neglect or ignorance of these differences is problematic even to our own day. For example, a direct result of such ignorance is the common tendency among contemporary Christians to overemphasize the physical aspects of Christ's death to the detriment of the dispositions of self-giving and loving obedience that alone give meaning to the sacrifice of Christ. Consequently, an authentic recovery of what sacrifice meant in the ancient world does not come easily to the citizen of the modern secularized West. Indeed, some pastoral theologians, despairing of the task, suggest that the word "sacrifice" be eliminated altogether from the vocabulary of Christian preachers.

## Atonement and Propitiation

The religious psychology of Judaism from which Christianity arose was characterized by an intensely heightened awareness of the abject frailty and sinfulness of human life over against the transcendent holiness and otherness of God. The sin offering had assumed an importance it apparently did not have in earlier times, and *atonement* had become the dominant idea associated with the sacrificial ritual. An atoning significance had become associated even with other types of sacrifice, such as the whole burnt offering and the banquet-type sacrifice exemplified in the Passover ritual, that originally did not have an atoning significance (Metzinger, 1940, 355; von Rad, 1962, 284; Thompson, 1963, 224; Schmitz, 1910, 60–9,113–18; Büchler, 1967, 429–38). Even the daily *tamid*, the dominant ritual in terms of day-to-day observances, came to have an atoning function associated with it. The schools of Hillel and Shammai apparently agreed on this fact, although they disagreed in their explanation of it (Büchler, 1967, 415, 428, 430, 446, 453). There was thus a tendency to equate sacrifice with the process of atonement, and conversely atonement tended to be viewed as identified with ritual blood sacrifice. The first Christians apparently shared this view, as illustrated, for example, by the assertion in Hebrews 9.22 that "without the shedding of blood there is no forgiveness of sin," and by the insertion of "for the forgiveness of sins" after " . . . my blood of the covenant, which is poured out for many" in the Eucharistic words of institution in Matthew 26.28.

The process of atonement in ancient Judaism and early Christianity served the *positive* function of making persons or things "acceptable" or "pleasing" to God and the *negative* (or apotropaic) function of interrupting or averting the course of evil set loose by sin or transgression. The words "propitiation," "expiation," "forgiveness," and "reconciliation" are often used indiscriminately as synonyms for atonement, but their meanings are at times quite divergent. Since contemporary studies of sacrifice and atonement reflect this lack of clarity and consistency, constructive discussion requires establishing some careful distinctions. Perhaps the most important of these distinguishes between the two quite different dynamics at work in the process of atonement: the anabatic or upward dynamic from creature to God, and the katabatic or downward dynamic from God to creature.

At a certain point in the course of its history ancient Israel came to the understanding that atonement is the free and gracious work of God, not of a human being. In a religious insight similar (and chronologically almost parallel) to the criticism launched against cult religion by Greek philosophy, which reasoned that we do not change or move the unchangeable God by our prayers and sacrifices, ancient Israel came to the conclusion that atonement is the work of God, not of humans. The dynamic of atonement, however much it might also require concomitant human activity, is essentially katabatic, a downward or *creature-directed action of God* in which human beings become the beneficiaries of the positive and negative functions mentioned above (Daly, 1978a, 95–136; 1978b, 25–33; von Rad, 1962, 262–72; Ricoeur, 1967).

*Propitiation,* on the other hand, is essentially anabatic and is thus quite different from atonement.

> Actions of *propitiation* soothe the anger or ill will of the deity and/or secure the deity's favor. This idea originally presupposed a crassly material notion of an arbitrary deity who had to be "bought off" or kept happy. With the growing awareness that the creature cannot exert pressure on the immutable God, this cruder conception tended to give way to the higher religious sentiments of praise, petition, adoration, thanksgiving, and recognition of God's excellence. Propitiation involves the notion of a[n] [anabatic] *God-directed action of the creature.* (Daly, 1978b, 28)

Christianity inherited from Judaism the insight that atonement is the work of God, but it remained a fragile, easily obscured insight, as the heated Reformation debates on the mass as a sacrifice remind us. My own theological judgment that atonement, properly understood, is essentially katabatic rather than anabatic is not intended to reduce the anabatic to the category of the useless or irrelevant. In theological terms the position that I am outlining, which is fundamentally supported by the broad sweep of the biblical and Christian traditions, might be described as the "reformed Catholic" position that has become fairly common in recent decades. On the one hand, it admits the validity of the Reformation insight that salvation is the work of God, not of creatures, and that no human work is the cause of salvation. On the other hand, it insists on the validity of the Catholic insight that prayer and good works are a necessary and integral part of the dynamics of salvation.

## Spiritualization of Sacrifice

In the development of sacrificial conceptions and practices in the Judaeo-Christian tradition, one can distinguish two distinct trends that are at times in tension with one another: a spiritualizing trend and an institutionalizing trend. The trend towards the spiritualization of sacrifice generally tends to arise out of situations of powerlessness. As we shall see, this trend can be most clearly seen in Jewish history in the periods following the Babylonian exile (586 B.C.E.) and the destruction of the Second Temple (70 C.E.) when the Jews, having been stripped of sociopolitical power, were also deprived of their locus of spiritual power, the Temple in Jerusalem, where sacrificial rituals alone could be performed. The trend towards the institutionalization of sacrifice, on the other hand, tends to be fostered by the power structures within the religious community as a means of consolidating their power and authority. As an example of this trend we shall examine in the next section the Roman Catholic church's institutionalization of the "sacrifice of the mass" in which the priest was viewed as the principal agent in whom was invested the spiritual power of the mass, which brought with it a concomitant increase in the sociopolitical and economic power of the priestly class.

The term "spiritualization" is often defined by means of common synonyms such as dematerialization, sublimation, ethicization, rationalization, interiorization, or symbolization. No one of these synonyms is adequate. However, some of them, such as "dematerialization," can be misleading when applied to the Jewish and Christian traditions, for the spiritualization that has taken place in the context of the creational faith of Judaism and the incarnational faith of Christianity has not always been of a dematerializing kind (Daly, 1978a, 3–6, 494–7; 1978b, 6–8; Wenschkewitz, 1932, 70–230; Hermission, 1965; Clements, 1965, 100–22; Gärtner, 1965, 16–46).

Within the spiritualizing trend of the Judaeo-Christian tradition at least four phases can be distinguished (Daly, 1978b, 135–40). The *first phase* is already at work in the early formative years of the Hebrew scriptures, as can be seen, for example, in the tenth century B.C.E. Yahwist accounts of the sacrifices of Cain and Abel (Genesis 4) and of Noah's sacrifice (Genesis 8), which emphasize the religious dispositions required of the one offering the sacrifice. What constitutes the proper dispositions does not remain hidden in the inscrutability of the divine will. It is progressively spelled out in the covenant theology and cult criticism of the early written prophets (eighth to sixth centuries B.C.E.) and in the work of the Deuteronomic historians (sixth century B.C.E.) who redacted Joshua, Judges, 1 and 2 Samuel, and 1 and 2 Kings into their present form. Sacrifice is not rejected; indeed, the dynamic center of sacrifice and locus of its power still seem to be the actual performance of the sacrificial ritual. However, it is made abundantly clear that without the proper dispositions of the offerer the ritual is "not acceptable" or is even "hateful" in God's eyes and is therefore worthless, ineffective, and devoid of power.

In the *second phase* of the spiritualizing trend, which begins in the post-exilic period (fifth century B.C.E. and later), the locus of the sacrifice's power shifts from the external performance of the ritual to the internal dispositions of the one performing it. The religious exigencies of the exile and diaspora apparently accelerated this process in that even after the Temple in Jerusalem was rebuilt those in exile no longer had easy access to the Temple, which was the only place in which valid sacrifices could be offered. The idea gained force that what brought about atonement, reconciliation, and union with God was not the performance of the sacrificial ritual but the fact that the ritual was performed in obedience to the Torah. This development obviously stems from ideas underlying the prophetic dictum "obedience, not sacrifice," which Jesus later quoted.

The *third phase,* a relative short step from the second, was to see, as did the Qumran sectarians in their separation from the Jerusalem Temple, the pious works of the Torah as taking the place of the ritual sacrifices of atonement. After the destruction of the Second Temple in 70 C.E., this became the way most Jews responded to the impossibility of offering sacrifices in the Temple. Philo of Alexandria, who lived only a few decades before the destruction of the Second Temple, provides another example of this phase of spiritualization. However, Philo, drinking from the streams of Greek philosophy, goes even further in attributing only symbolic significance to the performance of the sacrificial rituals.

In a certain sense this third phase rounds out the spiritualization process in the Judaeo-Christian tradition. However, the story is not yet finished. In a *fourth phase*, a specifically Christian development, but one that is also paralleled in post-biblical Judaism, in addition to stressing the importance of proper dispositions a new emphasis is placed on the equally vital importance of "incarnating" these dispositions in practical loving, healing, diaconal, ministerial and apostolic works of authentic Christian living. This constitutes the

Christian culmination of the spiritualization of sacrifice. Christians are called to offer sacrifice with the same dispositions as Christ in obedient self-offering to the Father for the salvation of humanity. In offering "such sacrifices" (Heb. 13.16) Christians participate in the dynamic reality—and hence the power—of the sacrifice of Christ. The "ritual" of this sacrifice, it should be emphasized, is not a liturgical rite in the traditional religious sense, but the liturgy of Christian life itself. Far from being a mere pious thought or flight of homiletic fancy, this conception of Christian sacrifice, or of the sacrifices that Christians offer, is in fact the only conception of Christian sacrifice found in the New Testament (Daly, 1978a, 240–56, 493–6; 1978b, 82–3).

The process of spiritualization thus culminates in what I judge, from a theological perspective, to represent the ideal of Christian spirituality and life. In the actual history and life of Christianity, the reality, not surprisingly, has often fallen far short of this ideal.

## Institutionalization of Sacrifice

In Christianity this falling short of the ideal is in part associated with an institutionalizing trend that began to develop fairly early in tension with the spiritualizing trend just described (Daly, 1978b, 140). In the Christian *ideal*, I would argue, this institutionalizing trend is secondary. In practice, however, it has often been dominant in the experience of Christians, sometimes so dominant as to obscure the primary trend of spiritualization completely. When that happens the Christian church is in danger of no longer constituting the servant church proclaimed by Christ but rather a dominative church, the kind of institution from which the Christ of the Gospels so emphatically distanced himself. This seems to suggest that spiritualization is good and institutionalization is bad, which would be an obvious oversimplification since aberrations can be found in both trends. In Christianity, however, and especially in a contemporary Roman Catholicism newly sensitive to the actual and potential disorder in its own house, the aberrations seem to be more blatant in association with the institutionalizing trend.

In the New Testament, as we have seen, Christian sacrificial activity was spiritual, ethical, or diaconal, but definitely not ritual. However, sacrificial ritual language and imagery were used to describe this spiritualized (Christological, to be precise) activity. In the second century when Christian writers first began to refer to the Eucharist as sacrificial, it was the Eucharistic prayer, not the Eucharistic ritual, that was referred to. However, by the beginning of the third century, especially in Hippolytus, one can detect the beginning of a "regression" back to the first phase of spiritualization: the idea that the performance of the ritual action constitutes a sacrifice (Daly, 1978b, 140).

The Christian church never reverted to material sacrifice, but it nevertheless so thoroughly institutionalized and routinized what came to be called the "sacrifice of the mass" that, especially in popular piety, it absorbed many of the characteristic abuses of a material sacrificial cult. A key development in this process was the gradual replacement of the idea, quite widespread among the fathers of the church, that Jesus Christ is the principal agent in the sacrifice of the mass with the notion that the celebrating priest is the principal agent. The twelfth-century medieval Latin commentaries on the mass provide fairly clear witness to this development (Schaefer, 1983).

From a theological perspective this was a massive aberration from which the Roman Catholic Church still has not yet fully recovered. Its disastrous consequences are known to all familiar with the history of medieval and Reformation Christianity, and they are still at work today, as can be seen, for example, in the debate over women's ordination. An extraordinary power— accompanied in the popular mind, which often enough included the mind of the priest himself, by blatant semi-magical connotations—was put into the hands of the priest: the power to forgive sins through the sacramental ritual of confession and absolution and thus to save from the threat of eternal damnation; and the power through the ritual of the mass to "confect" the Eucharist and make Christ present by changing bread and wine into his body and blood and to offer this sacrifice, in the words of the Council of Trent, as an effective sacrifice of propitiation for the living and the dead (Denzinger and Schönmetzer, 1965, no.1753).

Along with the priest's spiritual power, and because of it, came massive social, political, and economic power. To be fair one must of course admit that at times this highly institutionalized ritual system worked remarkably well. However, even at its best it was, like all such systems, built more on the sands of historically conditioned human needs and desires than on the solid rock of Christ. It is easy for us now to make such judgments, to look back with the clear vision of historical hindsight and see how mistaken it was for Christians on both sides of the Reformation to identify the historically conditioned developments of their own churches with the rock of Christ.

For 450 years the divided Christians of the West have been trying to sort out the sand from the rock. All of these Christian groups, have—and indeed cannot exist without—their institutionalized rituals, which range from the free church (but still ritualistic) ways of celebrating only the Word, to the high church celebrations of the Eucharist as well as the Word. Those who lead or preside over these celebrations are in positions of power: spiritual power and, very often, social, political, and economic power. One is tempted to say that there is a correlation between these two types of power and that sociopolitical and economic power increases in proportion to the degree of sacramentality present in the church. However, the history of Christianity in the United States, and in particular the contemporary phenomenon of TV evangelism, should make one cautious about such facile formulae.

The image evoked by bringing the theme of ritual and power to bear on contemporary Christianity is one of ebbing and flowing among the different phases of the spiritualizing trend. However, at times the reality is also one of fierce tension between the spiritualizing and institutionalizing trends. Persons and institutions are constantly trying, and not always for religious reasons, to harness the power inherent in or flowing from religious ritual. Nevertheless, I would argue that the ritual itself, sometimes independently and in spite of those trying to control it, has a profound transformative effect on those who celebrate it and expose themselves to its power: saving, sanctifying, healing, forgiving, purifying, strengthening, reconciling, unifying, building, people-forming, church-forming, sect-forming—and thus also at times separating and alienating as well as uniting.

## Conclusion: Some Recent Developments

Two twentieth-century developments suggest how far Christian thought has moved away from the Reformational polemic evoked by the words "propitiatory power of sacrifice."

### Ecumenical Rapprochement

One hundred years ago Christian theologians were so divided and bound to their polemically formed ecclesiologies that dialogue on controversial points was impossible. Typical was the work of Lutheran Johann Höfling (1851) and the Roman Catholic Ignaz Döllinger (1826). Each examined the same patristic data and came up with diametrically opposite conclusions on the question of the mass as sacrifice. Today, however, theologians of these two churches (Lehmann and Schlink, 1983, 215–38) as well as of the Anglican Communion (Meyer and Vischer, 1984, 68–77) are in substantial agreement on most aspects of this question, including the hotly contested Reformation claims and counterclaims concerning the propitiatory character of the mass. The term "propitiation" is generally used in this context in the documents of the Council of Trent in the sense of atonement as we defined it earlier. However, it also carries some of the connotations of propitiation that we previously delineated.

A key to this development seems to have been the fundamental insight into *Mysteriengegenwart* (the mystery-presence of Christ or "mystery theology" formulated by Odo Casel): the belief that it is primarily Christ who is present and acting in the Eucharist and other sacraments (Casel, 1928, 145–224; 1962). This insight has enabled representative Roman Catholic, Anglican, and Protestant theologians to formulate in mutually satisfactory ways the sacrificial and hence propitiatory character of the mass. The mass, in this perspective, is not something over which the priest or the church has some kind of quasi-

352

magical control. It is not a new or different sacrifice, but the once-and-for-all perfect sacrifice of Christ now present sacramentally or "in mystery." This interpretation of the mass has in effect "demythologized" many of the controverted claims of a heavily institutionalized or routinized Roman Catholicism by appropriating them in a manner with which non-Roman Catholics also can feel comfortable—that is, through a more profound understanding of the mystery of the presence and activity of Christ in the church.

This development has had the effect of relocating the power of the Eucharistic rite, shifting it away from the institutional realm, with its inevitable sociopolitical and economic associations, towards the spiritual realm where it really belongs, in the mystery of Christ's presence. This development has also enabled Protestants and Catholics to apply basically the same critique to many of the social, political, and economic aspects of the power associated with Christian ritual. One can now more easily criticize and even reject the ways in which ritual has been subjected to the abuse of power, as well as the means of that abuse, without simultaneously seeming to reject an important article of faith. Such developments have also made it possible for representatives of various Christian groups to discuss in amity theories such as those of René Girard.[1]

## Deritualization and Reritualization in Contemporary Christianity

The liturgical renewal of recent decades has been accompanied by an extensive deritualization of contemporary Roman Catholic life and, inchoately at least, a concomitant reritualization of worship in some Protestant communities in the form of reviving liturgical practices previously abandoned in the course of the Reformation. I am not in a position to say much about the Protestant side of this phenomenon, but the Catholic side of it gives rise to a number of interesting observations.

The more obvious manifestations of the process of deritualization in contemporary Roman Catholicism include: the transformation of Sunday mass from a numinous ritual performed silently in an inaccessible language by a distant priest with his back to the congregation, eliciting sentiments of awe and transcendence, to a vernacular community gathering almost totally deprived of its awe-inspiring power to evoke the transcendent; the democratization of the mass liturgy through the addition of lay deacons and lay ministers of the Word and of the Eucharist; the fading of the belief that faithful weekly attendance at mass is an absolute prerequisite for salvation; the abolition of Friday abstinence and the elimination of most of the fasting regulations; the widespread disappearance of the practice of frequent auricular confession. These changes have been accompanied by a great loss of church power in the life of contemporary Roman Catholics. No longer are the faithful so bound to the sacramental ministrations of the priest for the establishment, restoration, or maintenance of their sense of well-being with God. This may account for some of the heated controversies that accompany liturgical reforms and inno- vations, especially when they seem to take place suddenly or arbitrarily. Changes in ritual practice do indeed signify and bring about changes in the relationships of power, both on the vertical plane of spiritual power and on the horizontal plane of sociopolitical and economic power. Church authorities and church members are, implicitly at least, very much aware of this. Deritualiza- tion is not the only reason why Roman Catholicism is no longer the monolithic power it once seemed to be, but it may well be among the most important of these reasons.

# Note

1.    In a series of recent works, René Girard (1977, 1978, 1982, 1985) has presented a social scientific analysis of the power of sacrifice. He analyzes the mimetic psy- chosocial mechanisms, especially the scapegoat mechanism, by which human societies through the use of rituals have been able to defuse the violence that would otherwise have consumed them. Girard's work has helped to demystify, on the horizontal level at least, the power that ritual has had in the life of people of all ages and cultures. The essential components of his theory have been summarized by Schwager (1987, 46–7) as follows.

1. Fundamental human desire is of itself not oriented towards a specific object. It strives after the good that has been pointed out as worthy of effort by someone else's desire. It imitates a model.

2. Imitating the striving of another person (who is also one's model) inevitably leads to conflict, because the other's desire aims at the same object as one's own desire. The model immediately becomes a rival. In the process, the disputed object is forgotten. As desire increases, it focuses more and more exclusively on the other's desire, admires and resents it together. The rivalry tends finally towards violence, which itself begins to appear desirable. Violence becomes the indicator, and hence worthy of imitation, of a successful life.

3. Since all human beings have a tendency towards violence, living together peacefully is anything but natural. Reason and good will (social contract) are not enough. Outbreaking rivalries can easily endanger the existing order, dissolve norms, and wipe out notions of culture. New spheres of relative peace are created, however, when mutual aggressions suddenly shift into the unanimous violence of all against one (scapegoat mechanism).

4. The collective unloading of passion onto a scapegoat renders the victim sacred. He or she appears as simultaneously accursed and life-bringing. Sacred awe emanates from him or her. Around him or her arise taboo rituals and a new social order.

5. The sacrifices subsequently carry out in strictly controlled ritual limits the original collective transfer of violence onto a random scapegoat. Internal aggressions are thus diverted once again to the outside, and the community is saved from self-destruction.

# References

Augustine (1972). *City of God*. Trans. Henry Bettenson. Harmondsworth, Middlesex, England: Penguin.

Büchler, Adolf (1967) [1928]. *Studies in Sin and Atonement in the Rabbinic Literature of the First Century*. Library of Biblical Studies. New York: Ktav.

Casel, Odo (1928). "Mysteriengegenwart," *Jahrbuch für Liturgiewissenschaft* 8, pp. 145–224.

Casel, Odo (1962). *The Mystery of Christian Worship*. Ed. Burkhard Neunheuser. 4th rev. edn. Westminster, Md: Newman.

Clements, R. E. (1965). *God and Temple: The Idea of the Divine Presence in Ancient Israel*. Oxford: Basil Blackwell.

Daly, Robert J. (1978a). *Christian Sacrifice: The Judaeo-Christian Background before Origen*. Washington, D.C.: Catholic University of America Press.

Daly, Robert J. (1978b). *The Origins of the Christian Doctrine of Sacrifice*. Philadelphia: Fortress.

Daly, Robert J. (1989). "Sacrifice in Origen and Augustine: Comparisons and Contrasts," *Studia Patristica* 19, pp. 148–53.

Denzinger, Henricus, and Schönmetzer, Adolfus (1965). *Enchiridion Symbolorum*. 33rd edn. Freiburg: Herder.

Döllinger, Ignaz (1826). *Die Lehre von der Eucharistie in den drei ersten Jahrhunderten*. Mainz.

Gärtner, Bertil (1965). *The Temple and the Community in Qumran and the New Testament*. Cambridge: Cambridge University Press.

Girard, René (1977). *Violence and the Sacred*. Trans. Patrick Gregory. Baltimore: Johns Hopkins University Press.

Girard, René (1978). *Des choses cachées depuis la fondation du monde*. Paris: Grasset.

Girard, René (1982). *Le bouc émissaire*. Paris: Grasset.

Girard, René (1985). *La route antique des hommes pervers*. Paris: Grasset.

Helgeland, John, Daly, Robert J., and Burns, J. Patout (1984). *Christians and the Military: The early Experience*. Ed. Robert J. Daly. Philadelphia: Fortress.

Hermisson, H.-J. (1965). *Sprache und Ritus im altisraelitischen Kult: Zur "Spiritualisierung" der Kultbegriffe im Alten Testament*. Neukirchen-Vluyn: Neukirchener Verlag.

Höfling, Johann (1851). *Die Lehre der ältesten Kirche vom Opfer im Leben und Cultus der Christen*. Erlangen: Palm'sche Verlagsbuchhandlung.

Lehmann, Karl, and Schlink, Edmund (eds.) (1983). *Das Opfer Christi und seine Gegenwart in der Kirche: Klärungen zum Opfercharakter des Herrenmahles*. Freiburg: Herder; Göttingen: Vandenhoeck and Ruprecht.

Metzinger, A. (1940). "Die Substitutionstheorie und das alttestamentliche Opfer mit besonderer Berücksichtigung von Lev. 17, 11," *Biblica* 21, pp. 159–87, 247–72, 353–77.

Meyer, Harding, and Vischer, Lukas (1984). *Growth in Agreement: Reports and Agreed Statements of Ecumenical Conversations on a World Level*. New York and Ramsey: Paulist; Geneva: World Council of Churches.

Rad, Gerhard von (1962, 1965). *Old Testament Theology*. Trans. D. M. G. Stalker. 2 vols. New York: Harper and Row.

Ricoeur, Paul (1967). *The Symbolism of Evil*. Trans. E. Buchanan. New York: Harper and Row.

Schaefer, Mary (1983). "Twelfth Century Latin Commentaries on the Mass: Christological and Ecclesiological Dimensions." Ph.D. Dissertation, University of Notre Dame.

Schmitz, O. (1910). *Die Opferanschauungen des späteren Judentums*. Tübingen.

Schwager, Raymund (1987). *Must There Be Scapegoats? Violence and Redemption in the Bible*. Trans. Maria Assad. San Francisco: Harper and Row.

Thompson, R. J. (1963). *Penitence and Sacrifice in Early Israel outside the Levitical Law: An Examination of the Fellowship Theory of Early Israelite Sacrifice*. Leiden: E. J. Brill.

Wenschkewitz, Hans (1932). "Die Spiritualisierung der Kultusbegriffe: Tempel, Priester und Opfer im Neuen Testament," *Angelos* 4, pp. 70–230.

Yerkes, Royden Keith (1953). *Sacrifice in Greek and Roman Religions and Early Judaism*. London: Adam and Charles Black.

# 21

# BRUCE LINCOLN (b. 1948)

American historian of religions Bruce Lincoln was born in Philadelphia. He graduated from Haverford College in 1970 with a Bachelors degree in religion. He received his Ph.D. in the History of Religions from the University of Chicago in 1976 after writing a dissertation comparing East African and Indo-Iranian religious systems. His advisor was Mircea Eliade. Lincoln taught at the University of Minnesota for eighteen years, and since 1993 has been a professor of the History of Religions at the University of Chicago with joint appointments in the Departments of Anthropology, and Classical Language and Literature, and memberships in several inter-departmental committees including the Committee on the Ancient Mediterranean World, and the Committee on the History of Culture. He is also a member of the Center for Middle Eastern Studies at Chicago. Lincoln's primary areas of research are Indo-European religions, the religious uses of ideology, and questions of method and theory in studying religious and social phenomena. He works competently in more than a dozen languages. He has published prodigiously, contributing articles to journals, edited volumes, and encyclopedias. He has given many public lectures and presented papers at conferences in the United States, Europe and Scandinavia. Lincoln has authored seven books, most recently: *Theorizing Myth: Narrative, Ideology, and Scholarship* (1999), *Authority: Construction and Corrosion* (1994), and *Death, War, and Sacrifice: Studies in Ideology and Practice* (1991).

Central to much of Lincoln's thinking about religion and its role in society is the notion of ideology, the notion that social life—a group's modes of thought, patterns of behavior, and sets of meanings—is constituted of ideas. Human beings understand their world, and hence act in relationship to it, by constructing concepts, representations, artificial semantic structures that by definition reduce, simplify, and bind reality. The very construction of society is a matter of putting things in order, of classifying experience, of including and excluding, of recognizing values, of following conventions, and obeying constraints. These processes of selection ultimately produce, and reproduce, a particular social order that gains hegemonic status. The point, however, is that this hegemony is in fact ideological, that social and cultural elements are not simply natural, universal, or a matter of common sense, despite how they may appear from one historical perspective or another. Social fields are never simply homogeneous, but are instead inherently contested. The dominant discourse, the authoritative view, is actually only one possible narrative, one opinion, that has gained its status at the expense of alternatives. The interests of some (the powerful, those that rank high and gain from the social order) in effect subordinate and oppress these alternative ideas (taxonomies, values, etc), and the individual people and groups that hold them. Studying society and cultural phenomena involves, therefore, not only examining the various processes of persuasion and mystification that allow certain discourses to become hegemonic, but also revealing the consequences of those processes.

Religion, for Lincoln, is a particularly powerful form of ideology. It is a discourse that tends to legitimize other cultural discourses by investing them with a quality of transcendence. Religion frequently contributes to the mystification process behind the production of social hegemony. It is one mechanism for the construction of cultural authority and the preservation of hierarchical systems (of race, gender, or class, for example). Over the course of many writings, Lincoln has found various aspects of religion (e.g. myth, women's initiation rites, divination practices) to be sites that both contain and conceal contested versions of reality, truth, and propriety. The assertions of universal validity and eternal significance claimed with respect to most religious phenomena constitute, when accepted, a misrecognition, something, Lincoln suggests, that serves to establish and maintain differential distributions of power.

Lincoln addresses sacrifice in this context. Working with examples drawn from Indo-European societies, he finds a great deal of evidence for the ideological character of sacrifice. Many scholars have recognized sacrifice to be a central concept for most Indo-European (e.g., Greek, Germanic, Celtic, Indian, and so forth) societies thought and practice. Many of these societies tell how the world was created from the primordial dismemberment of a sacrificial victim, with particular body parts giving rise to different hierarchical classes of society (the head becoming the priestly class, for example). Similarly, these societies often recount how the body of the first human being was formed from corresponding parts of the cosmos (eyes coming from the sun, etc.). Through a system of homologies, pairs of "alloforms" Lincoln calls them, Indo-European societies were able to integrate cosmos and society and to map the entire hierarchical structure onto the human body. Sacrifice, a ritual performed and controlled by the priestly (highest ranking) class, was said to repeat the primordial sacrifice, thereby sustaining, reviving, re-establishing the existing order of things. Indeed, the very life and prosperity of the human and divine worlds required successful sacrifice. The critique of this practice is clear. Like other ideologies, the myths and rituals of sacrifice in Indo-European societies legitimate one particular power structure thereby rewarding some and oppressing others. Those exploited by the social hierarchy become, in a sense, secondary sacrificial victims for they too, in addition to the actual victim, suffer as a result. There are those who benefit from sacrifice and those who clearly do not. Finally, Lincoln highlights the important fact that sacrifice is inherently asymmetrical, one party benefiting from the destruction of another (the victim). Built into the practice itself, this hierarchy, this arrangement of "higher" and "lower" entities, is thereby strengthened and reinforced.

Reprinted here is Lincoln's essay entitled "Debreasting, Disarming, Beheading: Some Sacrificial Practices of the Scyths and Amazons" published originally in his book *Death, War, and Sacrifice: Studies in Ideology and Practice* (1991). It is a brief account of the hierarchical features of one form of sacrifice, and a critique of its ideological character. At the end, Lincoln formulates a definition of sacrifice. The essay provides an "ideology theory" of sacrifice, one that provides an understanding of the political consequences of sacrificial acts.

# "Debreasting, Disarming, Beheading: Some Sacrificial Practices of the Scyths and Amazons"

IN THIS CHAPTER I will be discussing certain practices that are reported for a set of interrelated peoples in antiquity: the Scythians, the Amazons whom certain Scythian youths are said to have married, and the Sauromatians, who supposedly descended from this union.[1] Our information about the practices that concern me comes chiefly from two important texts: the *Histories* of Herodotus and a medical work of the Hippocratic corpus entitled *On Airs, Waters, and Places,* that—like Herodotus—was written in the middle of the fifth century.[2] At the outset, I should note the possibility that some of these practices, like some of these peoples (particularly the Amazons), were more imaginary than actual, although as François Hartog, Page duBois, and others have shown us, this in no way diminishes their interest or importance, for one can learn much from the imaginary practices of an imaginary people, particularly regarding the thoughts and values of those whose imaginations they inhabit.[3]

Bruce Lincoln, "Debreasting, Disarming, Beheading: Some Sacrificial Practices of the Scyths and Amazons," pp. 198–208 in *Death, War, and Sacrifice: Studies in Ideology and Practice* (Chicago: University of Chicago Press, 1991). Reprinted with the permission of the University of Chicago Press and the author.

I should also make clear that rather few of the practices I will discuss were actually called "sacrifices" by the authors who wrote about them or by the people (if any) who performed them. Some of the other practices that interest me here might be called executions, mutilations, tortures, surgical, or even cosmetic procedures. Yet in spite of this broad divergence of terminology, I believe it makes sense to group them together for reasons that should become clear by the end of the chapter. Moreover, this regrouping has the ancillary benefit of raising questions about the category of "sacrifice" itself, which—like all categories—brings some things together by excluding others, thereby simplifying and clarifying some matters, but also precluding alternative conclusions that might otherwise emerge.

## Of Arms, Breasts, and Amazons

There is a great deal more that could be said here, but I would prefer not to get bogged down in talking about theories of sacrifice, theories of theories of sacrifice, or theories of theories.[4] Rather, let me forego such a meta-discourse in favor of more directly engaging the relevant primary sources, beginning somewhat arbitrarily with chapter 17 of the Hippocratic treatise, which provides the earliest and most thorough explanation that we have of how and why it was that the Amazons were supposed to have acquired their characteristic physical mark:[5]

> These women have no right breast, for in their infancy their mothers take a bronze instrument that is constructed for this very purpose, and after making it red-hot, they place it on the [daughter's] right breast and cauterize it *so that its growth is destroyed, and it surrenders all its strength and fullness to the right shoulder and arm.*

Although it is often said elsewhere that this debreasting was done so that in maturity Amazons might be able to draw bowstrings unimpeded across their chests,[6] the passage I have quoted offers a different explanation, one that is less narrowly pragmatic in character. For it is said that they cauterize the breast— and we will have to return and consider why this particular method of debreasting was specified—"so that its growth is destroyed, and it surrenders [*ekdidonai*] all its strength and fullness to the right shoulder and arm."[7] A breast is thus negated for the benefit of the arm, a soft bodily member for one that is hard, and one that is weak, nurturant, and sustaining of life for one that is strong, martial, and—in martial contexts—a bringer of death. In short, a member that is considered to be categorically female is sacrificed to augment the power of one that is similarly regarded as categorically male (see Figure 1).

| Breast | Arm |
| --- | --- |
| Soft | Hard |
| Weak | Strong |
| Nurturant | Martial |
| Life | Death |
| Female | Male |

**Figure 1:** Symbolic associations in the Amazons' mastectomies, as described in the Hippocratic treatise *On Airs, Waters, and Places*, ch. 17.

To the set of binary oppositions that is assembled under the master categories of the breast and the arm there is one more pair that should also be added, for it is absolutely central to the broader concerns of this Hippocratic text, for all that it may strike us as initially opaque.[8] This is the contrast of the moist and the dry, and in order to appreciate its significance for the materials we have been considering, a bit of background is necessary.

The treatise *On Airs, Waters, and Places* is an early work of medical ecology, explicitly devoted to demonstrating that a region's climate shapes the bodies and characters of its residents in the same manner that it shapes the topography itself.[9] At a not-so-very subtextual level, however, this is advanced less as a general theoretical proposition than—in the wake of Greek victories in the Persian wars—as the practical basis for comparing Europeans and Asians (under which category were included all non-Europeans), to the general detriment of the latter.[10] To this end, the text poses the argument that the greater variability of their seasons makes Europeans hardier, more energetic, wilder, and more warlike than Asians, while conversely the greater uniformity of their climate makes Asians milder, gentler, more beautiful, and also more torpid than their European counterparts.[11] Going further, the text observes that Asians are not all alike, and proceeds to subcategorize them according to whether their climates are marked by consistent heat and dryness, as in the case of Egyptians and Libyans,[12] or by an equally consistent cold and moisture, as in that of the Scythians, who "breath[e] a moist, thick air and drink water from snow and frosts," and therefore have bodies that are "thick, fleshy, jointless, moist and slack, and their bowels are the moistest of all bowels" (*On Airs, Waters, and Places*, 19). This system of contrasts, as graphed below in Figure 2, thus identifies the Scythians as that people who are, by virtue of their climate, the moistest of all Asians, which is to say the weakest of the weak, and flabbiest of the mild.

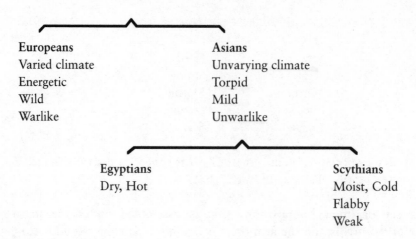

**Europeans**
Varied climate
Energetic
Wild
Warlike

**Asians**
Unvarying climate
Torpid
Mild
Unwarlike

**Egyptians**
Dry, Hot

**Scythians**
Moist, Cold
Flabby
Weak

*Figure 2:* Classification of the world's people in the Hippocratic treatise *On Airs, Waters, and Places.*

If the text sees nature as having made Scythians weak, it also notes that they developed certain techniques for rectifying this unfortunate condition. As chapter 20 of the Hippocratic treatise tells us:

> You will find that the majority of the Scythians . . . have been cauterized on the shoulders, arms, wrists, breasts, hips, and loins, *for no reason other than the moistness and the softness of their bodies.* For they are not able to draw their bows, or to throw their javelins from the shoulder due to their moistness and enervation. But as soon as they cauterize, most of the moisture in the joints is dried up and their bodies become more sinewy, better nourished, and very well knit.

The weakness of the Scythians was thus traced to a bodily moistness that was itself seen as a product of the climate in which they lived, and this moistness was therefore treated—cured—with fire. In contrast, the weakness and moistness of the Amazons was located less in their environment (they being recent immigrants to the north) than in their gender. For like women everywhere, Amazons lactate, something which permitted this text (and others like it) to argue that as a portion of female bodies—the breast—is given over to moisture, females are therefore inherently softer, weaker, and more phlegmatic than men. Unlike other women, however, the Amazons were said to have treated one of their breasts the same way that Scythians treated much of their bodies, cauterizing it in order to dry up its inherent moisture. Cauterization may thus be understood as a medico-physiological practice that was informed by a set of cosmological theories: theories in which, moreover, a racist and patriarchal position was thoroughly embedded. Obviously, one recoils at even the imaginary use of red-hot bronze to negate breasts in favor of arms, but equally offensive—and even more insidious—is the use of purportedly "scientific" discourse to advance the project of negating not just the moist in favor of the dry, but also the female in favor of the male, the Asian in favor of the European, and the weak in favor of the strong.

## Of Arms, Blood, and Enemies

If Amazons and Scyths supposedly took pains to strengthen their arms for use in battle, the latter group is also said to have performed operations designed to take away the strength of their enemies' arms, as may be seen from Herodotus' account of the Scythian sacrifices to Ares, their god of war. Such rituals were celebrated at his shrines, which were found in every Scythian district and took the form of great wooden pyramids surmounted by an ancient iron sword of characteristically Scythian shape that Herodotus says was the god's "image" or "representation" (*agalma*).[13] Vast sacrifices of sheep and horses were brought to this sword on a yearly basis, and there were also other victims. Of these, Herodotus recounts:

> Out of every hundred men whom the Scythians might capture in battle, they sacrifice one man, not in the same manner as they use for sheep, but differently. For they pour wine over the heads of these men, and they cut their throats over a vessel, then bear this vessel up on top of the pile of firewood, and they pour this blood over the sword. They carry this blood atop, and down below, alongside the shrine they do these things: they cut off the right arms of those men whose throats had been cut, together with their hands, and they throw these into the air. And when they have finished with the rest of the victims, they depart. And the hand lies where it has fallen, apart from the body. (Herodotus, 4.62)

At its most basic level, this grisly ceremony may be understood as a theater of cruelty that impressed on its audience, as on its victims, the power of those who staged the performance and who benefited from the fear it inspired. Beyond this, however, the ritual was informed by a whole system of cosmological speculation, as becomes clear from a close reading of its details and central sequences.

To begin, we might note that the victims are described not just as having been killed, but also dismembered, for two very specific parts of their bodies were violently separated from the rest in the course of the ritual. Most obvious is the case of their shockingly literal dis-armament, to which I will shortly return. First, however, there is the curious treatment of their blood, which is particularly striking given the fact that in no other Scythian sacrifices was blood shed, nor were any libations poured.[14] Here, however, the shedding of blood and the pouring of libations form part of a clearly articulated ritual sequence in which wine was first poured over the top of the victims' heads as they stood at the base of the shrine. Next, blood was made to flow from their throats (i.e. the base of their heads) into an *aggos* (a vat or pitcher for holding liquids, especially wine), in which it was then carried to the top of the shrine, where it was poured over the sword's tip (i.e. the "head" of Ares' image). Actions in the above—that is, atop the shrine—thus depended upon actions in the below, to which they also held relations of parallelism and inversion. For whereas the victim and the recipient were both bathed in fluids, that which was poured over the god's head had just been drained from the victim's throat, the wine of the initial libation have been thus transmuted into human blood, which was in turn transmuted into Ares' wine.

Insofar as the Scythians were an Iranian people, it is tempting to connect this ritual sequence with the pattern of creation mythology that is well attested in Iranian sources, as well as those of other ancient peoples who spoke languages of the Indo-European family. Here, the universe—in its cosmic as well as its social manifestation—is said to have been created through a primordial act of sacrifice, in which the victim's dismembered body was transformed into the material substance of all else. With regard to the universe, for example, the victim's flesh is said to have become earth, its hair plants, its eyes the sun, and—according to some variants—its blood to have become wine, which thereafter when drunk served to renew and to fortify the blood.[15] Similarly, with regard to society, it is told how the properly hierarchic social order came from the same victim, whose dismembered head became the class of sovereigns—priests or kings—while his hands and arms became warriors, and his lower bodily parts the mass of the common people.

## Heads of Enemies, Heads of State

The performance of sacrifice among other Iranians was clearly understood as a repetition of the acts of creation, as Marijan Molé was the first to recognize.[16] And in their treatment of the prisoners whom they offered to Ares, it would appear that Scythians gave ritual reenactment to that section of their creation myths which told how the warrior class originated from the dismembered arms of the first victim, thereby seeking to secure the reproduction of their own martial power from the bodies of those who in the recent past had unsuccessfully opposed that same power on the battlefield.

Other Scythian practices show similar concerns and seem to draw on the same mythic ideology. Thus, Scythians who were defeated in single combat are said to have had their right hand cut off,[17] and regarding Scythian warriors' treatment of enemies whom they slew in battle, Herodotus recounts (4.64): "Many of them flay the skin off the right hands of enemy corpses, with the nails still attached, and make these into the sheaths of their quivers." This passage then goes on to state that these same warriors drank the blood of the fallen (as if it were wine),[18] and that they also severed their victims' heads, which they delivered to the Scythian king as a precondition for receiving a share of the booty.[19]

Just as Scythian warriors negated their enemies' arms in practices based on a cosmogonic myth that were designed to augment their own power, Scythian kings thus seem to have done the same with their enemies' heads. Other practices also show that heads were taken from victims with the conscious intent of thereby sustaining the kingship. For not only were enemy soldiers decapitated, but select others who in some fashion stood opposed to the kingship were also treated in like fashion. Thus, beheading was the punishment for anyone convicted of forswearing an "oath" by the royal hearth, for these were the most solemn of all oaths, any violation of which would imperil the health of the king and the well-being of the realm.[20]

Similarly, when the Scythians found that one of their kings, Scyles, had turned apostate by secretly embracing the Mysteries of Dionysus, they deposed him from the kingship and replaced him on the throne with his brother, who then had him beheaded. Here, Scyles figures as something of an antiking: that is, someone who came to the throne, but betrayed his office and was rightly deprived of it, after which the kingship he had damaged was renewed with the offering of his head.[21]

## Coda

In the preceding discussion, I have had occasion to consider the Amazons' debreasting and a wide variety of practices attributed to the Scythians, including their therapeutic cauterizations, their offerings to Ares, their mutilation of opponents slain in battle, their execution of perjurers, and finally their treatment of a deposed king. All of these may be understood—following Franz Kafka even more than Michael Foucault—as various means for writing cosmologically and politically significant messages upon people's bodies in so emphatic a fashion that those bodies (or significant portions thereof) are destroyed in the process.[22]

But are they sacrifices?

If the final word on this deceptively simple question must remain with our sources, then the answer is unambiguously no, for only with reference to the prisoners offered to Ares do the texts we have considered employ any of the standard Greek terminology for "sacrifice." Yet no point of method obligates us to accept the views and categories of those whom we study, however much we *are* obliged to take them seriously. Rather, we do better to treat these indigenous categories as themselves providing data for studies in which we may seek to discover the criteria from which these categories were constructed and the role that they played in organizing the practices of those people who constructed them. Clearly, that which sets the offerings to Ares apart from the other materials, and that which led Herodotus and others to regard it as a "sacrifice," is the presence of a god, which is to say that here and here alone did the acts of violence we have considered find legitimation in the fiction of a divine presence, if only that of the fetishized sword.[23] Most modern students of sacrifice, however, would view the (purported) presence of divine recipients as an accidental rather than an essential feature of sacrifice, i.e. one variable among many, but hardly *sine qua non*.

I should like to suggest a model of sacrifice that is sufficiently broad to cover all the examples I have treated (whose similarities far outweigh their differences), and a variety of other data besides. To that end, I would argue that sacrifice is most fundamentally a logic, language, and practice of transformative negation, in which one entity—a plant or animal, a bodily part, some portion of a person's life, energy, property, or even the life itself—is given up for the benefit of some other species, group, god, or principle that is understood to be "higher" or more deserving in one fashion or another. By this logic, animals are regularly sacrificed for humans (in research as in rituals), humans for gods (including such gods as "freedom," "higher profits," and "the national interest"), perjurers for kings (subversives for the state), breasts for arms (butter for guns), and the moist for the dry (fat for muscle, "no pain, no gain").

There are many distinguished scholars who take a rather benevolent view of sacrifice, stressing the way in which it furthers the construction of community or assists in the canalization of violence, to cite two influential examples.[24] Yet I continue to be troubled by the radical asymmetry that exists between the sacrificer and the sacrificed, or between those who call for sacrifices and those who bear the costs. In theory, the logic, language, and practice of sacrifice are accessible to a great many people for a great many purposes, many of which I could comfortably endorse. Yet more often than not, the calls to sacrifice which prove effective strike me as offensive and the performances that are actually staged seem little short of criminal, particularly when those categories of person who already enjoy disproportionate shares of all that this life has to offer—men, victorious warriors, or kings, e.g.—are able to define themselves and their favored entities as "higher" than others, and to reproduce their power and their privilege through the sacrifice they impose on those other, "lower" beings.

## Notes

1. The classic account of the relations between Amazons and Scyths is found in Herodotus 4.110–17. Among the more important recent scholarship in Western languages on the Amazons, see William Blake Tyrell, *Amazons: A Study in*

*Athenian Mythmaking* (Baltimore: Johns Hopkins University Press, 1984); Page duBois, *Centaurs and Amazons: Women and the Pre-History of the Great Chain of Being* (Ann Arbor: University of Michigan Press, 1982); S. Rocca, "Dalle Amazzoni alla militia Phoebes," in *Misoginia e maschilismo in Grecia e in Roma* (Genoa: Istituto di Filologia Classica e Medievale, 1981), pp. 97–119; Jeannie Carlier, "Voyage en Amazonie grecque," *Acta Antiqua Academiae Scientiarum Hungaricae* 27 (1979): 381–405; "Les Amazones font la guerre et l'amour," *L'Ethnographie* 74 (1980): 18–22; and P. Devambez, "Les Amazones et l'Orient," *Revue archéologique* (1976): 265–80. On the Scyths and Sauromatians, see: François Hartog, *The Mirror of Herodotus: The Representation of the Other in the Writing of History* (Berkeley: University of California Press, 1988); Renate Rolle, *The World of the Scythians* (London: B. T. Batsford, 1989); idem, *Totenkult der Skythen* (Berlin: Walter de Gruyter, 1979); Edmond Lévy, "Les origins du mirage scythe," *Ktema* 6 (1981): 57–68; K. F. Smirnov, "Sauromate et Sarmates," *Dialogues d'histoire ancienne* 8 (1982): 121–41; Georges Dumézil, *Romans de Scythie et d'alentours* (Paris: Payot, 1979); and W. D. Blawatsky and G. A. Kochelenko, "Quelques traits de la religion des scythes," in *Hommages à M. J. Vermaseren,* vol. 1 (Leiden: E. J. Brill, 1978), pp. 60–6. More generally, but with important reference to these peoples and the texts in which they are described, see also Brent D. Shaw, "'Eaters of Flesh, Drinkers of Milk': The Ancient Mediterranean Ideology of the Pastoral Nomad," *Ancient Society* 13–14 (1982-3): 5–31, esp. pp. 8–13; and Michèle Rosellini and Suzanne Saïd, "Usages de femmes et autres *nomoi* chez les 'sauvages' d'Hérodote: Essai de lecture structurale," *Annali della Scuola normale superiore di Pisa* 8 (1978): 949–1005, esp. pp. 998–1003.

2. Also useful is Lucian's *Toxaris,* although it is written much later than the other two sources noted above (2nd century A.D.).

3. That the image of the Amazons was produced for the most part by inverting the givens of Athenian patriarchy has been argued persuasively by Carlier, duBois, Tyrrell, and others. Unlike the Amazons, however, the Scythians were a very real people, with whom Herodotus and the author of *On Airs, Waters, and Places* had direct contact in the Black Sea port of Olbia. Still, Hartog has emphasized the degree to which Herodotus' representations were strongly inflected by the Athenian predisposition to see in Scythian nomadism the antithesis of their own *polis*-life. In general, Hartog's position, like that of others who read ethnographic reports with an eye toward their authors and audiences rather than towards the people whom they purport to describe, seems to me a useful principle but one which can produce oversimplifications. Preferable, in my view, is to understand such reports as suspended by their authors between the audience for whom and the people of whom they write. As such, ethnographic texts are surely conditioned by the interests of the audience and the author, but not wholly determined by them. Rather, within such texts a set of complex negotiations is staged between lives as they are lived by actors, observed by ethnographers, heard about by readers, and imagined by all of the above. Regarding the nature of Greek-Scythian relations, see A. M. Khazanov, "Les Scythes et la civilisation antique: Problèmes des contacts," *Dialogues d'histoire ancienne* 8 (1982), pp. 7–51.

4. The most thorough and incisive review of current debates on the topic of sacrifice is offered by Cristiano Grottanelli, "Uccidere, donare, mangiare: problematiche

attuali del sacrificio antico," in C. Grottanelli and N. F. Parise, eds., *Sacrificio e società nel mondo antico* (Rome: Laterza, 1988), pp. 3–53, a work which deserves much wider notice than it has thus far received. Theories of sacrifice tend to emphasize either the killing or the eating of the victims, and accordingly follow lines of analysis introduced either by Sir James George Frazer on the one hand, or W. Robertson Smith on the other. Yet to stress one of these aspects at the expense of the other is to divorce consumption from production, a move that makes no more sense in studies of ritual than it does in those of political economy.

5. In antiquity the name *Amazōn* was interpreted as derived from a form *a-mazos*, "one without a breast" or "the de-breasted one," with privative *a-* (< Proto-Indo-European *$\eta$-), plus *mazos* (= the Ionian form of *mastos*, "breast"). See, e.g., Diodorus Siculus 2.45.3 and Scholium bT to *Iliad* 3.189. Modern philology tends to treat this as a folk etymology, however, since it fails to account for the final suffix. To date, no alternate interpretation of the term's derivation and significance has gained scholarly acceptance.

6. E.g., Diodorus Siculus 2.45.3; Scholium bT to *Iliad* 3.189; Apollodorus, *Bibliotheca* 2.5.9; Strabo 11.5.1; Justinian, *Epitome* 2.4; Curtius Rufus 6.5.28.

7. Cauterization is also specified as the means of debreasting by Hellanicus, fragment 16 in Jacoby, *Fragmente der griechischen Historiker* 3B45, Diodorus Siculus 2.45.3, Curtius Rufus 6.5.28, and Dionysius Scytobrachion, as quoted in Diodorus Siculus 3.53.3.

8. On this text, see C. Calame, "Environnement et nature humaine. Le racisme bien tempéré d'Hippocrate," in *Sciences et racisme* (Lausanne: Payot, 1986), pp. 75–99; Alain Ballabriga, "Les eunuques scythes et leurs femmes. Stérilité des femmes et impuissance des hommes en Scythie selon le traité hippocratique *des airs*," *Métis* 1 (1986): 121–39; A. Thivel, "L'explication des maladies dans le traité hippocratique *Des airs, des eaux et des lieux*," *Annales de la Faculté des Lettres et Sciences humaines de Nice* 50 (1985): 129–38; Jackie Pigeaud, "Remarques sur l'inné et l'acquis dans le *Corpus Hippocratique*" in F. Lasserre and P. Mudry, eds., *Formes de pensée dans la Collection Hippocratique* (Geneva: E. Droz, 1983), pp. 41–55; S. Frederick, *Hippocratic Heritage: A History of Ideas about Weather and Human Health* (New York: Pergamon Press, 1982); Jacques Jouanna, "Les causes de la défaite des Barbares chez Eschyle, Hérodote et Hippocrate," *Ktéma* 6 (1981): 3–15; and W. Backhaus, "Der Hellenen-Barbaren-Gegensatz und die hippokratische Schrift *Peri aerōn hydatōn topōn*," *Historia* 25 (1976): 170–85.

9. For direct statements of these concerns see, e.g. chapters 1, 2, and 13.

10. Chapter 12 of the Hippocratic treatise announces this as its *topos*: "I plan to show how greatly Asia and Europe differ from each other in every way, and how their peoples differ in [bodily] form, so much so that one resembles the others not at all."

11. See esp. chapters 12, 16, and 24.

12. The situation of the Egyptians and Libyans is discussed briefly in chapter 18 and at the beginning of chapter 13. It seems to have been treated at length in a now-missing portion of chapter 12. The Scythians are discussed in chapters 18–22.

13. Herodotus 4.62. In contrast to his treatment of all other Scythian deities, Herodotus gives no indigenous name for that god he calls by the Greek name of "Ares," whose worship is quite anomalous in numerous ways. See further

Herodotus 4.59 and the discussion of Hartog, *The Mirror of Herodotus*, pp. 188–92. On the distinctive nature of the Scythian sword, see W. Ginters, *Das Schwert der Skythen und Sarmaten in Südrussland* (Berlin, 1928).

14. Herodotus 4.60. Cf. Lucian, *Toxaris* 45, which states that Scythians think it an act of *hybris* to pour libations of wine.

15. On this pattern in general, see Bruce Lincoln, *Myth, Cosmos, and Society: Indo-European Themes of Creation and Destruction* (Cambridge, Mass.: Harvard University Press, 1986). The relations of wine and blood, as described in the Zoroastrian text *Zad Spram* 3.46, are treated at pp. 66 and 196–97.

16. Marijan Molé, *Culte, mythe, et cosmologie dans l'Iran ancien* (Paris: Presses universitaires de France, 1963); see also *Myth, Cosmos, and Society*, esp. pp. 41–64, 141–71.

17. Lucian, *Toxaris* 10, where this treatment is described as a "penalty" (*epitimion*).

18. A number of Scythian practices show that blood and wine were regarded as alloforms of one another, i.e. the macro- and microcosmic shapes taken by the same basic substance. Thus, for example, an annual feast was held in which wine was served only to those who had slain enemies in battle (Herodotus 4.66), and oaths of friendship were taken by drinking a mixture of blood and wine (Herodotus 4.70, Lucian, *Toxaris* 37). Such concerns may also have been involved in the well-known Scythian predilection for drinking their wine unmixed, a practice considered scandalous in antiquity.

19. Herodotus 4.64. Iconographic and archaeological evidence also attests to head-hunting and to the dismemberment of enemy dead. Cf. Rolle, *World of the Scythians*, pp. 82–6.

20. Herodotus 4.68. See, further, Chapter 15, "On the Scythian Royal Burials."

21. Herodotus 4.79–80. A similar story, involving the decapitation of a (foreign) king who had by his conduct shown himself unworthy of his office is told at length by Lucian, *Toxaris* 44–5. Particularly noteworthy is the fact that the king is beheaded in the temple of Ares, as he is about to swear a somewhat questionable oath. See esp. chapter 50.

22. In many ways, Kafka's haunting story "In the Penal Colony" can be read as a precursor of Foucault's *Discipline and Punish*. Both works contain much that is useful for an understanding of sacrifice. Dante, of course, provides a still earlier antecedent, as does Plato, *Gorgias* 525C-E, where one finds the appealing, but mystificatory notion that it is most often the rich and the powerful whose bodies in Hades will have painful lessons written upon them.

23. Lucian, *Toxaris* 38, also describes worship of the Scythian sword but makes no mention of "Ares." Rather, it is there asserted that Wind and Sword are themselves gods (*theoi*) by whom Scythians swear oaths "because Wind is the source of life, and Sword is that which causes to die." Fabio Mora, *Religione e religioni nelle storie di Erodoto* (Milan: Editoriale Jaca, 1985), pp. 125–7, has gone so far as to argue that Herodotus misrecognized the sword as an image of Ares, and consequently further misunderstood this ritual—which Mora prefers to view as a ceremony terminating the annual period of warfare—as a sacrifice.

24. Marcel Mauss and Henri Hubert, *Sacrifice: Its Nature and Function* (Chicago: University of Chicago Press, 1964); René Girard, *Violence and the Sacred* (Baltimore: Johns Hopkins University Press, 1977).

# 22

# NANCY JAY (b. 1929)

Nancy Jay was born in South Africa, grew up in New England, and attended Radcliffe College beginning in 1946. She paused her studies in 1949 to raise a family, but returned to Radcliffe after remarrying, and in 1967 received her B.A. in Anthropology. She studied clinical psychology at Harvard for a short time, and in 1971 enrolled at Brandeis University for graduate studies in Sociology. Throughout the 1970s, Jay's interest in gender issues and religion increased, culminating with her dissertation research on the question of why men tend to dominate in religious contexts. As a sociologist, she sought to explain how such a structure, one based on gender, was maintained. Reading widely in the fields of Anthropology, Sociology, Classics, and Psychology, Jay developed a theory that focused on the nature of sacrifice to explain this social phenomenon. She received her Ph.D. in 1981 under the guidance, primarily, of Egon Bittner and Kurt Wolff. For the next ten years, until her untimely death in 1991, Jay taught sociology courses at Harvard Divinity School and revised her dissertation for publication. During this time she published two important articles: "Sacrifice as Remedy for Having Been Born of Woman" (1985) and "Sacrifice, Descent and the Patriarchs" (1988), the latter in the prestigious journal *Vetus Testamentum*. Her book *Throughout Your Generations Forever: Sacrifice, Religion, and Paternity* was published in 1992 and won an American Academy of Religion award for excellence. In addition to a command of theoretical issues in the social sciences, and a detailed knowledge of diverse ethnographic materials (including Greek, African, Hawaiian, and Biblical), this book demonstrates Jay's moral concern, her true interest in how personal relations are affected by religious and social institutions, in this case how sacrifice affected and continues to affect the lives of women. It is a model for engaged comparative study.

Early in her book Jay makes the important observation that sacrifice has a logic, it both "joins people together in community and separates them from defilement, disease, and other dangers." What may sometimes appear as separate rites (hence the common division between "communion" and "expiation" sacrifices), and what can include incredibly different details, in fact adheres to a common structure. Jay argues that sacrifice is a process that achieves social differentiation; it accomplishes the work of creating (and if repeated, maintaining) artificial social distinctions. In communion sacrifice the victim is usually eaten (shared among members of the community), thereby distinguishing those who eat from those who don't. Those who commune (eat) form the community (social group) distinct from others. In expiation sacrifice, where the victim is usually not eaten but driven away from the community (often destroyed as an embodiment of sin, moral pollution, etc.), the remaining members of the group, all those who were not separated, are united and purified. This act of atonement achieves an "at-one-ment." In both types of sacrifice, acting upon the victim marks and strengthens the collective identity of those participating in the rite, those who eat and those who are not expelled, as the case may be.

This logic of sacrifice takes on particular significance for Jay with respect to a curious anthropological fact: "only adult males—fathers, real and metaphorical—may perform sacrifice." Only non-childbearing women are known to perform sacrifice, and therefore it appears that sacrifice is a social practice that distinguishes between men and women, or more specifically, between fathers and mothers. Put differently, a great deal of ethnographic information indicates the logic of sacrifice is manifest along gendered lines. This information and the logic of sacrifice she identified allow Jay to state her thesis. She suggests that because men lack a "natural" means to reckon paternal relations, cultures have compensated by instituting artificial mechanisms for creating and sustaining patrilineal descent, what Jay calls "male intergenerational continuity." Sacrifice is one such mechanism. Men can employ the logic of sacrifice, very effectively exclude women, and thereby produce and reproduce specifically male descent over the natural descent that follows being born of a woman.

With this thesis in hand, Jay demonstrates its application to the sacrificial practices of several different societies, in particular Greek, African, and Hawaiian societies. These allow her to consider representative examples of the different systems of descent: patrilineal, matrilineal, and bilateral. In each, Jay reveals how sacrifice indexes gender, as well as other distinctions held essential to social order. This explains, for example, why moments of social disorder often call for sacrifice; distinctions need clarification. Likewise, sacrificial practices that revolve around kingship, a hierarchical social institution dominated by males, are explained; sacrifice sets rank. Turning to Biblical literature, she explains the increased concern about sacrifice in the later "P" (priestly) source in comparison to the earlier "J" (Yahwist) source as a growing need to differentiate the male priesthood. Similarly, Jay sees a link between the Catholic Church's emphasis on priestly descent, its hierarchical structure, and its use of sacrificial language with respect to the Eucharist, a language often lacking in Protestant traditions.

Jay's "descent theory" of sacrifice is the first to highlight the role of gender. Her point is that systems of descent are fundamental to human society—they are the basis of marriage rules, for example—but distinguishing male lines requires a social mechanism. Jay has shown that historically many cultures have used ritual sacrifice to satisfy this need, making it a form of religious reproduction. Her theory predicts that as social groups require less distinction, or as social institutions no longer organize around lines of descent, the importance of sacrifice will decrease. Jay's work is challenging and provocative. It makes a sophisticated theoretical contribution to the project of understanding sacrifice.

Reprinted here is Jay's chapter entitled "Sacrifice and Descent." It builds to a clear statement of her understanding of sacrifice as "a remedy for having been born of woman."

*greater the similarities, less importance in sacrifice*

# From *Throughout Your Generations Forever: Sacrifice, Religion, and Paternity*

FOR THE GREEKS, the essential features of their social world (those that distinguished it equally from the natural and the divine realms) were sacrifice, marriage, and agriculture.[1] In myth these all share the same origin: marriage and agricultural production were consequences of Prometheus's sacrifice ending the Golden Age. Turning from the myth to its social context, from Pandora to the world of young Greek brides, marriage takes on a more precise meaning: it is not a voluntary personal relation between two individuals, but a relation for and between family groups:

> Pleasure is not the object of marriage. Its function is quite different: to unite two family groups within the same city, so that a man can have legitimate children who "resemble their father" despite being the issue of their mother's womb, and who will thus be able, on the social and religious level, to continue the line of their father's house to which they belong. (Vernant, 1980, 136)

The unfortunate defect of being "the issue of their mother's womb" is a quality children share with the beasts. Wild animals also have a mother, "to

Nancy Jay, *Throughout Your Generations Forever: Sacrifice, Religion, and Paternity* (Chicago: University of Chicago Press, 1992), pp. 30–40. Reprinted with the permission of the University of Chicago Press.

whom they are linked by the natural animal bond of childbirth; but they have no father. Without marriage there can be no paternal filiation, no male line of descent, no family, all of which presuppose a link which is not natural, but religious and social" (ibid., 138). The sexual promiscuity of the beasts is precisely the absence of the patrilineal family, and the male purity of the Golden Age is the ideal principle of that family carried to a level of absolute perfection. Letting "P" stand for patriliny, the three-tiered structure can be written this way:

| *wild/natural level* | *social/religious level* | *Golden Age (divine level)* |
| --- | --- | --- |
| $-P$ | $+P$ | $P^n$ |
| unregulated sex | regulated sex | male purity |
| death | social continuity | immortality |

This structure encodes mortality just as it does sexuality. The social and religious continuity of the patrilineal family gives males an attenuated form of immortality in the institutionalized succession of fathers and sons. The beasts, recognizing no fathers, have no continuity at all to mitigate individual mortality. On the other hand, if children only resembled their fathers perfectly they would be identical younger versions, cloning younger exact duplicates in their turn, and the Golden Age of male immortality would have returned. It is only mothers, bearing mortal children, who dim this glorious vision of eternal and perfect patriliny. Remember Pandora: because of a woman, men are mortal.

Only in myth is the fatal flaw of having been born of woman overcome. Herakles was sacrificing bulls to his father, Zeus, when the fire ignited a poisoned shirt his wife had given him. In Ovid's account he bears his Latin name, Hercules:

> All that his mother gave him burned away.
> Only the image of his father's likeness
> Rose from the ashes of his funeral pyre . . .
> So Hercules stepped free of mortal being . . .
> And with an air of gravity and power
> Grew tall, magnificent as any god.
> (*Metamorphoses*, 1958, 248)

Purified by the fire (almost like bones and fat), Herakles became a heavenly god. As both mortal hero and immortal god, he received both chthonic and Olympic sacrifice.

That women destroy the ideal of perfect patrilineal continuity has a real foundation in Greek social organization. Women (who fail in such glaring ways to resemble the father) do not contribute to the continuity of their own family line. The above quotation from Vernant needs correction: it is not "legitimate children" but only legitimate sons who "continue the line of their father's house to which they belong." Women marry outside their own family and bear children for the continuity of a different family. Children are born not just of women, but of outsiders. For any boy, "all that his mother gave him" pollutes the purity of the paternal line.

The starkness of the Greek womb/tomb equation is probably unrivaled, but all over the world social structures idealizing "eternal" male intergenerational continuity meet a fundamental obstacle in their necessary dependence on women's reproductive powers. There are various ways to organize over or around this obstacle, to transcend it. Many societies value continuity flowing unilineally from father to son to son's son, and these are probably the most common contexts for intensively sacrificial religions. But they are not the only ones. Even in settings where various kinds of descent through women are valued, and also in social organizations with no actual family base (such as the clerical hierarchy of the Roman Church), sacrificing produces and reproduces forms of intergenerational continuity generated by males, transmitted through males, and transcending continuity through women.

It is important to recognize that all the different ways people create enduring continuity between generations cannot really be sorted into categories like "patrilineal," "matrilineal," or "bilateral." Chapter 2 emphasizes that the terms "communion" and "expiation" do not actually describe any real sacrifice. They are only abstractions, lenses to look through. What is true of sacrificial traditions is true also of kinship traditions: they are so diverse that concrete general categories become impossible. There is not one real statistical typification "patriliny"; there are countless *different* normative ways in which people envision continuity between fathers and sons and value this intergenerational link as especially important for inheritance, political control, and other forms of social organization. There are also all the ways people do not conform to family norms. For example, Greek brides normatively married outside "the line of their father's house." But marriage inside the extended family did sometimes occur in Athens, especially in the case of an heiress, to keep the dowry in the family (Cantarella, 1987, 45). When I use a term like "patrilineal" then, it is only an ideal type, not a real one, a lens for looking at a great variety of different ways of valuing father-son continuity, and even more ways of leading real family lives.[2]

A century ago W. Robertson Smith recognized an affinity between patriliny and sacrifice. In *The Religion of the Semites* they are so closely linked that he could not err about one without simultaneously distorting the other. Following Wellhausen, Robertson Smith believed that all sacrifice was originally clan sacrifice (1972, 284). Rejecting his contemporaries' utilitarian theories of sacrifice as gift (or even bribery: *do ut des*), he claimed that the purpose of sacrifice was to create and maintain relationships of kinship between "men" and their gods. He did not consider that sacrifice might create and maintain kinship between men and men. He took that kinship for granted as "natural." Nor did he distinguish between the "principle of kinship" and the "tie of blood." There was no difference, for him, between consanguineal relatedness and the ordering of society according to the selective, normative systems that actual kinship groups create and maintain. By his "tie of blood" he meant only unilineal descent. But since this was, for him, "natural" kinship, he did not consider that biological descent had already been (socially and religiously) transformed into something else.

In common with most theorists of his time, he believed that originally everyone recognized only descent from mothers. The possibilities for sacrifice in such a society are limited, however, for "the children are of the mother's kin and have no communion of blood religion with the father. In such a society there is hardly any family life, and there can be no sacred household meal" (ibid., 278). At some unspecified time, and in some unknown way, almost everyone but a few very primitive groups switched to patrilineal descent, still considered by Smith only as a natural blood tie, not as an achievement. It is on the father-son relation that the sacrificial relation of deity to worshiper is founded, although it was later expanded to include patron-client, master-servant, and king-subject.

Smith's lengthy treatment of relations between worshiper and deity was limited to consanguineal and derivative relations. He did not consider marriage as a possible model.[3] Nor did he mention relations between affines (persons and groups related to one another by marriage). Smith's kinship systems are so thoroughly unilineal that there are no affines anywhere, and consequently, no problems of affinal relations in unilineal descent.[4] In fact, "the members of one kindred looked on themselves as one living whole, a single animated mass of blood, flesh, and bones" (ibid., 274). Nowhere in *The Religion of the Semites* is there any indication of how these utterly united kin groups are related to, and differentiated from, other such groups.

For Smith, all kinship relations were entirely benign.[5] In spite of Cain and Abel, Jacob and Esau, Joseph and brethren, and many others, this Hebrew Bible scholar was serenely convinced that "those in whose veins the same life-blood circulates cannot be other than friends bound to serve each other in all the offices of brotherhood" (ibid., 398). Kinship relations with deities are equally benign. "The habitual temper of the worshippers is one of joyous confidence in their god, untroubled by any habitual sense of human guilt . . . ancient religion assumes that ordinary acts of worship are all brightness and hilarity" (ibid., 255, 257).

In identifying "natural" kinship with totally homogeneous, affineless unlineal descent, and in purging kin relations of all guilt, envy, hatred, and terror, Smith had already done all the work of sacrifice. His purifying process was so complete before anyone killed a victim that there was nothing left to expiate, to get rid of, from kinship structure or from religious life. The clean had already been wholly separated from the unclean. His preliminary atoning work was so perfect that there was no room left for atonement itself. As he himself said, "There was no occasion and no place for a special class of atoning sacrifices" (ibid., 360). Atonement, expiation, sin offerings, and all the dark side of sacrifice was only a later, secondary development, a consequence of the "Assyrian catastrophe" and the despair that followed the Babylonian exile. As well as being historically inaccurate, this at-one-ment without atonement is logically and sacrificially impossible. Smith had created a Golden Age of his own among the Semites.

A peculiar mixture of error, erudition, and profound insight, *The Religion of the Semites* has been regularly denounced for the last seventy years. Smith has been condemned for leading astray biblical scholars, anthropologists, sociologists, psychoanalysts, and theologians. But bad scholarship is usually forgotten. If his work continued to trouble people, it was because his central idea was partly correct. He was right in linking sacrifice with kinship, even with kinds of kinship rather like what he described: clearly defined patrilineal descent systems, commonly excluding mothers and affines. Although his inattention to kin group differentiation, and to affinal relations, led Smith into absurdities, even his "single animated mass of blood, flesh and bones" has some real basis when the unity is conceived as social, religious, or moral, rather than as physical. (A corporate unilineal descent group, seen from the outside, says Meyer Fortes, "might be defined as a single legal personality."[6]) No matter how corporate, a patrilineage is never "a physical unity of life." Nor is unilineal descent natural, but social and religious. And sacrificing orders relations within and between lines of human fathers and sons, between men and men, at least as effectively as it does relations between men and their divinities.

Maintaining normative modes of family continuity through male or female lines ("unilineal descent")[7] glosses only some of the ways people may order social relations in terms of descent. Descent "systems" are all ideal ways of ordering the social relations of reproduction, and, as is true of all forms of social organization, unilineal descent is associated with specific kinds of economic production. The varieties of enduring intergenerational continuity such groups strive for may be glossed as "lineage" organization. Lineage organization is particularly efficient for control and transmission by inheritance of productive property such as farmland and livestock herds, and also of gainful monopolized skills, including priestly skills and political office. Such enduring descent groups (and blood-sacrificial religions too) are not of significance among people relatively unconcerned with inheritance of important productive property, such as hunter-gatherers, who have little durable property. Nor do they usually survive the introduction of a modern economy with occupational differentiation and monetary media of exchange. Like blood-sacrificial religions, such enduring family groups are concentrated among pre-industrial societies with some degree of technological development, in which rights in durable property are highly valued.[8] The symbolic structure in which the Greeks linked agriculture, patriliny, and sacrifice may be unique, but control of agricultural property by patrilineal descent groups as a material base of sacrificial religion is found around the world and across a wide range of societies. These range from extremely poor subsistence farmers, with no central government at all, to highly sophisticated societies like pre-revolutionary China.[9]

Because these are all family groups, the control of the means of production is inseparably linked with the control of the means of reproduction, that is, the fertility of women. As Fortes says,

> I have several times remarked on the connection generally found between lineage structure and the ownership of the most valued productive property of the society, whether it be land, or cattle, or even the monopoly of a craft like blacksmithing . . . A similar connection is found between lineage organization and control over reproductive resources and relations. (1953, 35)

(For "reproductive resources," read "childbearing women.") "Rights over the reproductive powers of women," says Fortes, "are easily regulated by a descent group system" (ibid., 30).

The social relations of production may be much the same whether inter-generational continuity through men or through women is more highly valued. But the social relations of reproduction will differ between "matrilineages" and "patrilineages," since matrilineages divide men's rights over women's bodies between brothers and husbands, who are ordinarily members of different lineages. In this sense the identity of the group controlling productive and reproductive property is always imperfect in matrilineages.

It should be recognized that although the different kinds of groups glossed as "patrilineages" are patriarchies, "matrilineages" are not matriarchies. Men ordinarily hold the major positions of authority in matrilineages as well as in patrilineages. It is the descent of authority, and of property, which differs: in patrilineages it is from father to son, in matrilineages from uncle to nephew, from mother's brother to sister's son. Both systems are ways of formally connecting men with women as childbearers, that is, ways of organizing inter-generational continuity between men and men in the face of the fact that it is women who give birth and with whom the next generation begins life already in close relation. Both systems are ways in which men regulate rights over women's reproductive powers, but in matrilineal descent systems these rights are divided: the man with rights of sexual access and the man and group with rights in the offspring are not the same.

Although obviously both types of unilineal descent, father to son and mother's brother to sister's son, are equally dependent on women's powers of reproduction for their continuity, this dependence is structurally recognized in matrilineal descent, but transcended in patrilineal descent. Rights of membership in a matrilineage may be determined by birth alone, providing sure knowledge of maternity. Paternity never has the same natural certainty, and birth by itself cannot be the sole criterion for patrilineage membership. No enduring social structure can be built only upon the shifting sands of that uncertain relation, biological paternity. Social paternity and biological paternity may, and often do, coincide, but it is social paternity that determines patrilineage membership. Some sacrificing societies, such as the Romans or the Nuer, distinguish between biological and social paternity in their vocabulary: for example, the Latin distinction between (biological) *genitor* and (social) *pater.* Only the *pater* was significant sacrificially.

Unilineal descent groups are not concerned merely with an existing order, but with its continuity through time, generation succeeding generation. When the crucial intergenerational link is between father and son, for which birth by itself cannot provide sure evidence, sacrificing may be considered essential for the continuity of the social order. What is needed to provide clear evidence of social and religious paternity is an act as definite and available to the senses as is birth. When membership in patrilineal descent groups is identified by rights of participation in blood sacrifice, evidence of "paternity" is created which is as certain as evidence of maternity, but far more flexible.

Consider patrilineal ancestor cults, whose powerful affinity with sacrificial ritual is widely recognized. Ancestral sacrifice ritually indexes patrilineage boundaries (keeps the difference between members and not-members) by distinguishing between those who have rights to participate and those who do not, and at the same time extends the temporal continuity of the lineage beyond its living members to include the dead.

Sacrificial ancestor cults are commonly features of corporate descent groups whose members are tied to a certain locality by inherited farmland, and also often by ancestral graves. Right of participation in sacrifices can also identify patrilineage membership even when the lineage is not a corporate group and is not clearly defined territorially, but in this case there may not be an ancestor cult, and sacrifice, more "spiritual" as the group is less corporate, may be offered to divinities. The Nuer and Dinka are examples. Sacrificing may be the exclusive privilege of only one descent group in a society: a hereditary priesthood, who may keep their own lineage boundaries absolutely clear while other, non-sacrificing descent groups in the same society lose such clearly defined identity. In this case the ideology of eternal genealogical continuity is also centered in the priesthood. The Israelite Aaronid priesthood is an example.

Sacrificing can identify, and maintain through time, not only social structures whose continuity flows through fathers and sons but also other forms of male to male succession that transcend dependence on childbearing women. Because it identifies social and religious descent, rather than biological descent, sacrificing can identify membership in groups with no presumption of actual family descent. This is the case with the sacrifice of the Mass, offered by members of a formally institutionalized "lineage," the apostolic succession of the clergy in the Roman Church. This social organization is a truly perfect "eternal line of descent," in which authority descends from father to father, through the one "Son made perfect forever," in a line no longer directly dependent on women's reproductive powers for continuity. (See chapter 8.)

Sacrificial ritual can serve in various ways as warrant of, and therefore as means of creating, patrilineal descent—as a principle of social organization, not as a fact of nature. When sacrifice works in this performative way it is what Thomas Aquinas called an "effective sign," one that causes what it signifies: in this case, patrilineage membership (*Summa Theologica*, III, Q62, 1). For Thomas, as well as for tribal sacrificers, the effective work of symbolic action is, of course, reflexively dependent on the existence of other structures (social, religious, linguistic, legal, etc.). That is, sacrifice does not "cause" patrilineage membership where there are not patrilineages.

Sacrifice cannot be infallible evidence of begetting and therefore obviously cannot constitute biological paternity. It is the social relations of reproduction, not biological reproduction, that sacrificial ritual can create and maintain. Where the state and the social relations of production are not separable from patrilineally organized social relations of reproduction, the entire social order may be understood as dependent on sacrifice. "Not just the religious cult but the order of society itself takes shape in sacrifice," says Burkert of the Greeks (1983, 84). This is also true of other entirely unrelated societies, such as nineteenth-century West African city states like Benin and Dahomey and twentieth-century subsistence farmers or pastoral cattle herders, without urban development or centralized organization. The particular Greek elaboration of alimentary symbolism is surely unique, but Detienne's observation that "the city as a whole identifies itself by the eating of meat" (1979b, ix) accurately describes sacrificial maintenance of social organization in other traditions and other societies. The Israelite priesthood, for example, identified itself by eating of meat (the "edible" sin offering), and so did and do different kinds of patrilineal groups in Africa, Europe, Asia, and the New World.

When a form of social organization is dependent on sacrifice for its identification and maintenance, it can also be lost by failure to sacrifice, and improper sacrifice can endanger it. As Detienne says, "To abstain from eating meat in the Greek city-state is a highly subversive act" (1979b, 72). Georges Dumézil tells the sad story of the end of a Roman family. An official named Appius Claudius persuaded the family to sell its private sacrificial cult to the state for public use.

According to Festus . . . Appius Claudius went blind, and within the year all members of the selling family died . . . Thenceforth it was the urban proctor who each year made the offering of an ox (or a heifer) in the name of Rome. (1970, 435)

According to Dumézil, "Some think . . . that we must understand [this account] by reversing the order of events." That is, the state only assumed control of the cult because the proprietary family had already died out. But the story's order of events (although not their speed) is quite possibly correct. Having lost its ritual means of identification, and with it the ritual entail of its property, the family line itself disappeared—not as a number of biological individuals but as the particular kind of social organization it was.

Consider a cautionary tale from M. Herskovits about the problems of maintaining patrilineal descent in the West African kingdom of Dahomey. Only certain ritual specialists could touch victims which had been offered to the ancestors and hope to survive the contact. Without these specialists there could be no sacrifice, but training them involved a long course of rituals in a specially constructed cult house for the dead. This course of training was undertaken as seldom as possible because of the great danger involved, both from the intensity of relations with the ancestral dead and also from the possibility of committing a fatal ritual error. The royal ancestor cult was the apex of the hierarchy of all ancestor cults in the kingdom, and consequently it was the duty of the king to officiate in the centralized training of the kingdom's ancestor cult specialists. After French colonizers ended the monarchy, the head of the royal patrilineal descent group, or sib, continued in the ritual position of the king. In the early thirties, when Herskovits was in Dahomey, the head of the royal sib had neglected to perform his ritual duty of building the cult house because, even if he did not die at once as a consequence of committing some ritual error, he would in any case die soon from such prolonged and intense contact with the dead.

The last cult house for the ancestors of the entire kingdom . . . was established so many years ago that most of those who received this training are dead, and it is urgent that another soon be instituted, though it is believed that this will hasten the death of the head of the royal family. In the last one, it is said, some three thousand initiates came from . . . each sib all over the kingdom . . . [When the last of these, now old] die, there will be no one able to touch a sacrificial animal, and thus will even greater evil befall all Dahomeans, and the entire royal family will die out. (1938, vol. 1, 228)

This final prophecy of doom is not mere superstition. If the cult house were not built, if the prerequisite for continued sacrifice were not met, the royal sib might indeed die out. The biological individuals forming its membership need not die, but the royal sib, as a social organization constituted and maintained by sacrifice, dependent on repeated sacrifice for its "eternal" continuity, would decay with the end of sacrificing. Evils would befall all Dahomeans because all Dahomean kinship organization was sacrificially maintained and was organized in relation to the royal sib.

Only the Aztecs outdid the Dahomeans in volume, compulsiveness, and cruelty of sacrificing. Dahomean religion was not representative of sacrificial religion, it was an exaggeration of it, a concentration and intensificiation of many features which occur selectively and less starkly in many other sacrificing societies. In Dahomey, says Herskovits, a child "legally stands in no relation whatever to his mother's kin" (ibid., 153). This is certainly unusual, as is also the degree of continuity with the dead and the desperateness of dependence on sacrifice for maintenance of the social order. But all these are only exaggerations of what could be called a common sacrificial principle: that it is by the participation in the rule-governed (moral, not biological) relatedness of father and son in a ritually defined social order, enduring continuously through time, that birth and death (continually changing the membership of the "eternal" lineage) and all other threats of social chaos may be overcome.

Man born of woman may be destined to die, but man integrated into an "eternal" social order to that degree transcends mortality. I use the word "man" advisedly, for in sacrificially maintained descent groups, "immortality," which may be no more than the memory of a name in a genealogy, is commonly a masculine privilege. It is through fathers and sons, not through mothers and daughters, that "eternal" social continuity is maintained. Daughters, who will marry out, are not members of the lineage in the same way as their brothers, nor do mothers have full membership in their husbands' and sons' lineage. Where participation in "eternal" social continuity is a paternal inheritance, mortality itself may be phrased as a maternal inheritance. (As Job said [14. 1,4], "Man that is born of women is of few days, and full of trouble . . . Who can bring a clean thing out of an unclean?")

Exogamous patrilineal groups whose members find wives from outside the group, are utterly dependent on alien women for their continuity. But if descent from these women were given full social recognition, the patrilineage would have no boundaries, no identity, and no recognizable continuity. The integration of any unilineal descent group, its continuity through time as the same, as one, can only be accomplished by differentiation from other such groups. There is necessarily an "either/or" about lineage membership (members must be distinguished from not-members), and for patriliny, this either/or requires transcending descent from women.

The twofold movement of sacrifice, integration and differentiation, communion and expiation, is beautifully suited for identifying and maintaining patrilineal descent. Sacrifice can expiate, get rid of, the consequences of having been born of woman (along with countless other dangers) and at the same time integrate the pure and eternal patrilineage. Sacrificially constituted descent, incorporating women's mortal children into an "eternal" (enduring through generations) kin group, in which membership is recognized by participation in sacrificial ritual, not merely by birth, enables a patrilineal group to transcend mortality in the same process in which it transcends birth. In this sense, sacrifice is doubly a remedy for having been born of woman.

# Notes

1. "Sacrifice and marriage appear to occupy the same position at the center of the system, this being exactly compared to that of cereals which, placed between the wet rawness of grasses on the one hand (the food of animals) and the incorruptible dryness of the aromatic plants (the food of the gods) on the other, represent the midway position, the human norm" (Vernant, 1980, p. 150).

2. Kuper (1982) very usefully and critically reviews the issue of "descent theory" in anthropology, stressing its inadequacies as a model. Comaroff (1987) extends this critique to issues of "gender" and "kinship," stressing the work of construction that has gone into these terms in Western society and especially in anthropology. I am indebted to John Comaroff for these references.
   A good deal of deconstructionist work has been done recently by anthropologists critically examining these and related anthropological concepts. I suggest that "sacrifice," exhibiting a unified logic in its action that transcends cultural boundaries, provides a context for reexamining the *sociological* utility of such concepts as "gender," "lineage," and "descent" critically but less dismissively.

3. This may seem remarkable since Smith was concerned ultimately with Israelite sacrifice and the covenant relation between the Israelites and Yahweh is often phrased as marriage. He was correct in his choice however. The Israelites did not use marriage as a model of sacrificial relations with Yahweh. That would have put the sacrificers in the position of married women.

4. There was probably a real ground in Semitic patrilineal endogamy for Smith's ignoring of affines and related difficulties. Nevertheless he had to forget, for example, all the tension between Jacob and his father-in-law, Laban.

5. Why did Freud, who relied on Smith so heavily and so indiscriminately for *Totem and Taboo*, not suspect something here?

6. Fortes (1953, p. 26) is here discussing "collective responsibility in blood vengeance." Smith based his notion of kinship as a "physical unity of life" primarily on his understanding of collective blood vengeance.

7. I am using the term "unilineal descent group" as a gloss covering a variety of different unilineal descent structures: clan, sib, lineage (maximal and minimal), etc.

8. This account draws on Meyer Fortes, "The Structure of Unilineal Descent Groups" (1953, p. 24).

9. Modern capitalist corporations have certain resemblances to corporate lineages, in ownership of property, enduring continuity, etc. (As Sir Henry Maine said, "Corporations never die.") But when there is no longer even a metaphor of descent in conceptions of legal or moral corporate unity, sacrificial ritual is wholly irrelevant.

# References

Burkert, Walter (1983). *Homo Necans: The Anthropology of Ancient Greek Sacrificial Ritual and Myth*. Translated by Peter Bing. Berkeley, Los Angeles, London: University of California Press.

Cantarella, Eva (1987). *Pandora's Daughter: The Role and Status of Women in Greek and Roman Antiquity*. Translated by Maureen B. Fant. Baltimore, Md. and London: Johns Hopkins University Press.

Comaroff, John L. (1987). "Sui Genderis: Feminism, Kinship Theory, and Structural 'Domains.'" In *Gender and Kinship: Essays toward a Unified Analysis*. Edited by Jane Fishburne Collier and Sylvia Junko Yanagisako. Stanford, Calif.: Stanford University Press.

Detienne, Marcel (1977). *The Gardens of Adonis: Spices in Greek Mythology*. Translated by Janet Lloyd. Atlantic Highlands, N. J.: Humanities Press.

Detienne, Marcel (1979) *Dionysos Slain*. Translated by Mireille Muellner and Leonard Muellner. Baltimore, Md. and London: Johns Hopkins University Press.

Dumézil, Georges (1970). *Archaic Roman Religion*. Translated by Philip Krapp. Chicago and London: University of Chicago Press.

Fortes, Meyer (1953). "The Structure of Unilinear Descent Groups." *American Anthropologist*, n.s. 55: 17-41.

Herskovits, Melville Jean (1938). *Dahomey, an Ancient West African Kingdom*. 2 vols. New York: J. J. Augustin.

Kuper, Adam (1982). "Lineage Theory: A Critical Retrospect." In *Annual Review of Anthropology 1982*. Palo Alto, Calif.: Annual Reviews, Inc.

Smith, W. Robertson (1972). *The Religion of the Semites: The Fundamental Institutions*. New York: Schocken Books.

Vernant, Jean-Pierre (1980). *Myth and Society in Ancient Greece*. Translated by Janet Lloyd. Sussex: Harvester Press; Atlantic Highlands, N. J.: Humanities Press.

# 23

# WILLIAM BEERS (b. 1948)

Born in Baltimore, Maryland, William Beers attended Gettysburg College (graduating in 1971) and received a Masters of Divinity degree in 1975 from the Episcopal Divinity school in Cambridge, Massachusetts. He studied religion and the social sciences at the University of Chicago under Peter Homans, and received his Ph.D. in 1989 after earning a mark of distinction for his dissertation entitled "Women and Sacrifice: Male Narcissism and the Psychology of Religion." He served for ten years as the director of chaplaincy services at the Rockville General Hospital in Connecticut, and taught Sociology courses for eight years at the University of Connecticut. He taught religion at James Madison University between 1996 and 1997, and now is the Director of Pastoral Care at St. Clare Hospital in Baraboo, Wisconsin. Beers travels frequently working with a large international humanitarian relief organization, and is completing work on a novel.

Beers published his doctoral dissertation under the same title in 1992. It is a work that applies the psychoanalytical theories of Heinz Kohut to cultural phenomena, particularly ritual sacrifice. With reference to an early article written by Nancy Jay ("Sacrifice as Remedy for Having Been Born of Woman," 1985), Beers believes the key to understanding sacrifice is the fact that only men perform sacrifices. He suggests that psychological differences between men and women explain this fact. Put differently, aspects of being male lead men to sacrifice. Specifically, sacrifice "embodies and conceals" a form of anxiety that can be traced to male infant experiences revolving around the formation of the self. Combing the theories of Heinz Kohut and Ilene Philipson, Beers suggests that male (and not female) infants, by virtue of being a different gender than their mothers, experience an "omnipotent maternal self-object as Other." The inability to identify with this idealized (even omnipotent) self-object results in a male sense of self-esteem that is weaker, fraught with anxiety, and more easily threatened. Ultimately, men develop "more rigid ego boundaries" and throughout their lives seek reinforcement in the form of prestige and power—all the while carrying a "need for, resentment of, and envy of" the maternal self-object, which they unconsciously associate with women. Men suffer from this "narcissistic anxiety" (which includes both desire and disgust) whenever they are faced with some form of "marginality," some experience of potential or actual self-disintegration. In response, they turn to sacrifice. As a symbolic process that can be both "conjunctive" and "disjunctive," sacrifice is well suited to realize both a "desire for merger with an idealized self-object" and a need for differentiation and separation in the face of personal and social chaos. The violence of sacrificial ritual is an expression of the rage men feel following their failure to identify with this idealized self-object, but also in other contexts, their failure to maintain rigid ego boundaries.

Sacrifice, for Beers, can be traced to a psychological mechanism, one that forms in the earliest phases of male infant development. Like Freud, he offers a psychoanalytical theory of sacrifice, one that posits the motivations for sacrificial behavior in the realm of the unconscious. He illustrates this theory through two different applications. In one, he explains the sacrificial practices described in several Melanesian ethnographies, and argues that these practices rise from "the male need for prestige and their fear of women." In the second example, Beers demonstrates how his theory of male narcissistic anxiety explains many traditional attitudes toward women in the Episcopal Church, attitudes toward sex, abortion, ordination of women, creationism, and the Eucharist. Here too, unconscious male needs for power and prestige are active.

The following selection is the central theoretical chapter from Beers' book. It presents what could be called his "narcissism theory" of sacrifice. It briefly summarizes the psychological model and then turns to the task of explaining sacrifice. It is difficult for this selection (as is true for others in this book) to convey the full complexity and subtlety of the theory, but it does present the core structure of Beer's claims about why men sacrifice.

⌘

# From *Women and Sacrifice: Male Narcissism and the Psychology of Religion*

FROM AN anthropological point of view, the cultural context of sacrifice includes the conflicts and contradictions that arise both naturally (logically) or deliberately out of symbolic classificatory systems. These systems are constructed around a sacred order that reflects and protects the inclusive structures

---

William Beers, *Women and Sacrifice: Male Narcissism and the Psychology of Religion* (Detroit: Wayne State University Press, 1992), pp. 137–47. Reprinted with the permission of Wayne State University Press and the author.

of social reality. The historical foundation of social reality is the kinship system. Like most classificatory systems, kinship systems are based on binary oppositions. The kinship surrounding the vast majority of sacrificial systems is patriliny. The binary opposition of the patrilineal kinship system is based on a father/mother, male/female dichotomy.

In qualifying Lévi-Strauss's claim that the mind innately classifies reality through binary oppositions, I have argued that binary or bipolar constructions of reality have their psychological origins in the early narcissistic period of life. MacCormick notes that "the first distinction all new-born humans make is that between self and nurturing other" (1980, 2–3). She goes on to ask, "What is the exact relationship between the organizing work of the unconscious and the conceptual domain of social structure, political relations, and so forth?" (3). Any answer to that question requires a developmental model of the mind.

Through the review of anthropological and dynamic psychological theory in Parts I and II, I developed the thesis that ritual blood sacrifice embodies male and male-identified anxiety and men's symbolic efforts to control and acquire the experienced power of women. In this chapter I want to present a gender-specific psychoanalytic theory of sacrifice using Kohut's model of the mind. One advantage to Kohut's psychology of the self for anthropology is that it diminishes the bothersome nature/nurture argument. The question of whether nature or culture is the basis for this or that human characteristic becomes irrelevant, because without adequate empathic and mirroring self-objects, humans never develop the psychological structure necessary to internalize the social and cultural world. As noted earlier, Mary Douglas wrote that "the only one who holds nothing sacred is the one who has not internalized the norms of any community" (1975, xv). Geertz (1973) says as much when he asserts that without the symbolic systems mediated to the developing psychological apparatus through the parent(s), a human being would remain a formless monster. From a psychoanalytic point of view, this means that parental self-objects begin to provide normative structures for transforming the grandiose self and idealized parent imago into socially realistic ambitions and ideals, mediated by individual talents and skills.

The formation of the bipolar self through the grandiose and idealized self-objects can, even under optimal conditions, become fraught with anxiety, which can be experienced throughout life. The anxiety centers around esteem issues and is marked by intense hunger for the idealized self-object. It is also marked by disintegration anxiety (the fear of fragmentation of the grandiose self). Because the maternal self-object (the idealized parent imago) provides the initial ideals and mirroring for the developing psychological apparatus, subsequent identification and internalization necessary for the continued socialization of an individual is built on this original bipolar structure, and the boundaries of the self continue to be narcissistically related to the internalized social structure.

If, as I have been arguing, gender plays an important part in the self-structuring of male and female psychological apparatuses, men will be more likely to feel threatened by factors affecting their grandiose sense of self-esteem, prestige, and power because they have experienced the omnipotent maternal self-object as Other, rather than experiencing themselves as subjective extensions of the self-object, as will be the case with women. Likewise, they are unable throughout life to ever fully identify with that self-object as woman the way that women can. And, as Philipson (1985) notes, because women have more fluid ego boundaries, they are less likely to feel overly anxious or threatened by marginality—the states of ambiguity that exist amidst all social structures. Indeed, women (and their children) are themselves the primary marginal people in a patrilineal society.

For men, periods of marginality threaten their more rigid ego boundaries. I believe this is true for several related reasons. The male sense of self is based on the maintenance of distinctions. René Girard went so far as to claim that distinctions maintain peace while the loss of distinctions leads to rivalry and violence. This need for distinctions has its origins in the self/self-object period of early narcissism, when the male psychological apparatus is distinguishing from the maternal self-object and structuring the self. Marginality is an intrusion into a social structure that reflects and maintains the structure of the self. A male-determined, patrilineal social structure confronted with marginality (e.g., sacred pollution) is equivalent to an individual man experiencing a narcissistic intrusion of an archaic (maternal) self-object. Indeed, from the point of view of the self-object function, the two are indistinguishable.

I need to say something more about the narcissistic anxiety arising during structural marginality. Anxiety is the psychological place where men and women most differ with regards to marginality. Because of the gender-specific quality of the maternal self-object's emphatic mirroring, when confronted with marginality, women are more likely to identify with the marginality. They have the compensatory structures that allow for merger and equilibrium (a kind of "I am not helpless because I am connected"). Men, on the other hand, will respond to marginality in a different way, via the activation of the grandiose self ("I am not helpless because I am the most powerful"). Geertz clearly shows how the grandiosity works in the Balinese cockfights. Although Kohut uses the term *fear*, marginal anxiety is much more than fear. In truth, anxiety lacks the object that fear has. I prefer the term *dread* to describe the narcissistic experience of marginality. With dread there is both desire and disgust. The ambiguity of distinctions, which marginality offers, creates both the desire for and disgust of merger, as well as the desire for and disgust of the self as separate. The dread of margins is, in fact, desire and disgust on both sides of the ambiguous boundary.

Kierkegaard (1946) was the first modern thinker to articulate the dual side of narcissistic (he termed it *aesthetic*) dread, and his analysis is psychoanalytically correct. On the one side, dread has no object. In fact, dread is the destruction of subject and object. And on the other side, dread is the possibility of the self being constituted (in Kohut's terms, through the transmuting internalization of the self-objects). Kierkegaard's discussion of the aesthetic stage and the concept of dread are remarkably parallel to many of Kohut's discussions of narcissistic personality disorders. Marginal anxiety, then, is the place where the self either transforms the self-objects (via identification and internalization) or is fragmented by them.

As I have indicated, on the one hand, women appear more able to identify with and internalize marginal states. Communitas is one result of marginal anxiety, and it is perhaps psychologically more available to women. I really do not want to say much more about women; they can write their own psychologies. On the other hand, the psychological apparatus of men experiences sacred pollution or transitional intrusions as threats of self-disintegration. These threats are self-object wounds, and they can lead to rage and to the possibility of aggression and violence. Unlike the idealized mother imago of the narcissistic period, the cultural self-object experience cannot adequately mirror male grandiosity. Consequently, male identification with the now-transformed omnipotent (albeit maternal idealized) self-object remains incomplete. This, I believe, is why men envy and fear women, why they attempt to control and degrade them, and why sacrifice is the male ritual of choice. I am suggesting that male narcissistic self-objects are embodied in the symbols of a culture. I am further suggesting that religious rituals embody and hide these male narcissistic self-objects. And the symbol that ties the male narcissistic need for, resentment of, and envy of the omnipotent maternal self-object (and the women who represent it to men) is the blood sacrifice.

## The Self-Object and the Symbol of Sacrifice

Because the marginality desired and feared by men has a strong connection to narcissism, in a self-psychological understanding, sacrifice (the symbolic act that responds to marginality) is comprised of four interrelated narcissistic self-object functions. Through these self-object functions, sacrifice can express: (1) the grandiose desire for merger with an idealized self-object; (2) the dread of such a merger through the act of separation (de-identification, differentiation, expiation, prophylaxis); (3) the narcissistic rage and violence surrounding the disappointment in the merger with and separation from the self-object; and (4) the symbolic transfer and transformation of omnipotence from the idealized maternal self-object to the grandiose male self.

## Sacrifice as Merger

According to Lévi-Strauss, Douglas, and Turner, sacrifice functions to bring two symbolic orders or domains into the same symbolic proximity. Even if the merger of the two orders only occurs at the instant of the immolation, two orders are joined. This merger of orders in the marginal space has a narcissistic element. A narcissistic merger, identical to a symbolic merger, is one in which differences become more vague. The distinction between the sacred and the profane, like the distinction between the self and the mirroring or merged self-object, is reduced. Classifications break down. Self and object become more connected by becoming less distinct.

When the self-object function of sacrifice occurs in this way, narcissistic merger is not unlike Turner's concept of communitas. Communitas is the experience of unstructured, undifferentiated homogeneity. The significant difference between narcissism and communitas is that Turner understands communitas as the recognition by the participants of equality and human bonds, while the self-objects of narcissism are prestructural, prelinguistic, and thus precognitive. There can be no recognition in a precognitive apparatus. The recognition of communitas is a later development, which contains the energy and form of the earlier, now transformed, narcissistic prestructures. Communitas has to do with understanding sacrifice; narcissism with explaining it. It would be more correct to say that communitas and empathy are equivalent concepts stemming from and containing narcissistic elements expressing the desire to be connected or even merged.

Men sacrifice in order to be connected with their idealized and omnipotent self-objects. The need to merge with the idealized self-object is the most (psychologically) primitive activation of the grandiose self. That activation is, as noted, recognizable in the mirror transference, "in which the child attempts to save the originally all-embracing narcissism by concentrating perfection and power upon the self—here called the grandiose self—and by turning away disdainfully from an outside in which all imperfections have been assigned" (Kohut, 1971, 106). When sacrifice serves to merge the domain of the divine with that of the human (the sacred with the profane, the clean with the polluted), the self-object function is to merge the self with the omnipotent self-object. That is the most archaic form of the sacrifice as merger. Or, if the function is less archaic, the sacrifice attempts to acquire the power of that (maternal) self-object by bringing the two domains into close proximity so that through the victim the power can be transferred from the divine to the human. In this case the men who sacrifice are hoping there is enough similarity (twinship) between the two domains that the transfer is possible.

The least archaic self-object function of the sacrifice as merger is to simply have the omnipotent self-object mirror the power (the need for power) of the men who sacrifice. Under this function would fall the need for power and control in the face of suffering, death, or other unavoidable disappointments. A function such as this led Masud Khan to conclude that "it is precisely this need in the human individual for his or her psychic pain to be witnessed silently and unobtrusively by *the other*, that led to the creation of the omnipresence of God in human lives" (1981, 414).

## Sacrifice as Separation

Periods of marginality, like the potential for narcissistic merger, increase the likelihood of narcissistic anxiety. Psychoanalytically, the self fears its own dedifferentiating fragmentation, its own destruction (which is also the central anxiety in Jung's theory of sacrifice). This fear can be expressed as the fear of the loss of power, control, autonomy, and/or meaning. To merge is to lose the self by becoming nothing again in the original narcissistic state. There is a danger in getting too close to the idealized self-object, because of the potential for the breakup of the self.

Anthropologists argue that the binary classification of social reality is an innate and universal activity. Such an assertion helps us to understand and describe the danger of classification (based on patriliny in the case of sacrifice) breakdowns and margin mergers. As I claimed above, the breakdown of classifications of symbolic structures is felt as a real threat because the created structures of idealized identification are intended to guard against narcissistic fragmentation. Here I am simply adding a self-psychological explanation to Durkheim's theory of the role played by identification, sentiment, and anomie in classificatory systems.

The primal classification, occurring during the narcissistic period of the development of the bipolar self and upon which all subsequent classifications depend (both created and learned), is the classification ultimately threatened by undifferentiated, liminal, and narcissistic merger. I am arguing that anxiety resulting from the breakdown of classifications stems from a prestructural narcissistic stage of development. The cultural relativity of classification systems indicates that the content is not the causative source of anxiety. In other words, anxiety is not simply a learned reaction. The fact that any number of diverse classification breakdowns can give rise to similar states of anxiety suggests that this anxiety is a response to *prestructural* elements, which, through a process of transmuting internalization, creates and fuels the social classificatory structures.

Again, because men have more rigid self boundaries, dedifferentiation or disintegration anxiety leads to a very strong need to differentiate or separate. The sacrifice that serves this self-object function is that of expiation. In this case, the intrusive idealized self-object, which leads to the fragmentation anxiety, is experienced as a dangerous pollution causing the sin, sickness, death, or other change in the classificatory system. The need to maintain separation leads to a split in the social body, as Douglas claims. The sacrifice then functions as a means of splitting off "not-me" parts from idealized reality and placing them outside of the narcissistically fueled classificatory system.

The anxiety (narcissistic dread) surrounding the marginal period is, as I have noted before, fueled by both desire and disgust. In expiation sacrifice, that which evokes disgust (the threat of fragmentation by the intrusive idealized self-object) is classified as 'not-me' and is symbolically embodied in a surrogate or substitute victim, which is killed or scapegoated. Psychologically, the self-object is split into good and bad parts in order to maintain the idealized classifications of reality. Because men presumably classify reality, the split-off parts almost invariably include those experiences having to do with women, sex, and childbirth.

## Sacrifice as Narcissistic Rage and Violence

Hubert and Mauss were amazed by the "remarkable fact that, in a general way, sacrifice could serve two such contradictory aims as that of inducing a state of sanctity and that of dispelling a state of sin" (1964, 58). I believe the two self-objects of the bipolar self help explain how such a contradiction (in Turner's terms, both prophylaxis *and* abandonment) is psychologically possible and how some sacrifices can be either conjunctive or disjunctive or both. Because sacrifice is psychologically an embodiment of self-object functions, the longed-for merger cannot actually take place. Likewise, the separation can never be absolute. Rather, hunger for merger and the desire for rigid ego boundaries reflect the ambivalent tension gradient between the two self-objects. The need to merge is fueled by the longing for the omnipotence of the maternal self-object and for that self-object to mirror the omnipotence of the grandiose self, while the need to remain separate reflects the fear of the intrusive power of the same maternal self-object.

I want to look more closely at the psychology of failed identification/merger and failed idealization/separation. Because male narcissistic identification with the maternal self-object is less likely to receive confirming mirroring from the self-object, the grandiose parts of the self experience the failed identification as a narcissistic injury. Narcissistic injury can lead to narcissistic rage and even aggression. The violence of sacrifice, then, is also a socially transformed expression of the rage resulting from the failed identification with the omnipotence of the idealized self-object. That is part of the answer to the question of the violence of sacrifice. While maternal self-object identification may not receive adequate empathic confirmation, however, later identifications with paternal and other male self-objects are likely to succeed. And what is internalized through male self-objects includes the male self-objects' own internalized experience of failed identification with maternal self-objects.

The internalization of male self-objects also includes other aspects of male identification. Some identifications may reflect psychobiological or cultural vestiges of earlier human evolution. For example, the violent relation between a sacrificial animal and men may have a strong correlation either to the human control over animals that were domesticated and/or to the significance of hunting animals in human evolution. By mentioning this, however, I am not proposing an innate proclivity for male violence. Sacrifice is not simply a cultural way to give men a safe way to kill, although it is that, because of some evolutionary proclivity for violence. I am suggesting that the complex ritual violence performed by men is an ancient way for men to identify with each other as men, and to separate from women. As one anthropologist notes, "In both violent and aggressive action male bonding is the predominant instrument of organization" (Tiger, 1969, 171).

In addition to being a function of violence, male bonding is also a cause of violence. This causal relation results from narcissistic identification within the male bond group and separation from the non-male group (i.e., women children, slaves, captives, and other marginal people, creatures, and self-objects). The split between "me" and "not-me," between group and not-group, reflects the tension between the grandiose self and the threatened fragmentation of the self by the split-off, bad aspects of the idealized self-object (the term *bad* is a judgment that can only rightly be applied after speech is structured; i.e., the original self-objects are pre-structural and therefore neither bad nor good). The group, therefore, is going to perceive outsiders as threats or sources of danger because outsiders affect the narcissistic equilibrium of the group. Outsiders intrude on the boundaries of the group's collective identification (its grandiose self and ideals). Wounds lead to rage and potential violence, as any urban street gang's behavior shows. The sacrificial victim, then is a marginal being on which is focused the 'not-me' (narcissistically split-off) parts, which are then destroyed or violently cut off from the group's culture. This psychological process is identical to Bakan's "idea of sacrifice in which that which is 'me' is made into something "not-me," and in which that 'not-me' is sacrificed in order that 'I' might continue to live" (1968, 79). In the violent response to an intruder, the narcissistic identification with that intruder is apparent because the violence reflects, in Kohut's terms, "the active (almost anticipatory) inflicting on others of those narcissistic injuries which he is most afraid of suffering himself" (1978, 2:638).

## Sacrifice as the Transfer of Omnipotence from the Maternal to the Male

When men bond, they gain self-validation and self-affirmation through a shared, idealized male self-object. The bonding to older men by boys and younger men gives all (young and old) self-respect, confidence, and skills they desire, but it also further separates the men from their maternal self-objects.

This is clearly the case in many secret male societies in which initiation rites often imitate the role of women in childbirth. One social scientist has suggested that these ceremonies "appear to express an envy of the female role. For example, the initiation is often culturally perceived as a rebirth ritual in which men take a child and bring about his birth as a man by magical techniques stolen long ago from women" (D'Andrade, 1958, 196). The role of gender envy has also been discussed by Bruno Bettelheim (1955). Envy indicates that while male bonding attempts to separate the men from the women, the separation conceals a male desire for identification with and acquisition of the power of the maternal self-object. Initiation rites indicate this ambivalence and narcissistic ambiguity. D'Andrade continues: "The need for the initiate to prove his manhood by bearing extreme fatigue and pain [as though in birthing labor and childbirth] appears to indicate some uncertainty in sex identity" (196).

Sacrifice, as Jay (1985) argues, takes away the power and value of descent from the mother and ritually gives it to the father. Male dimorphic dominance, bonding, and the exclusion of women from the center of power are confirmed by sacrifice. The "magical techniques" of women were "stolen" because they were experienced by men as powerful, as dangerous, as intrusive. Men envy the perceived power of women and create ritual actions of blood and rebirth in order to have equivalent power and control over life and death. But Jay's position lacks a male psychology to explain the male perception of women's power. This psychological aspect of sacrifice reflects its twinship self-object function. The transfer of "magical techniques" is the acquisition of skills and talents based on identification and alikeness.

# Conclusion

In this chapter, I have attempted an explanation that does not contradict an anthropological understanding of sacrifice or the self-psychological explanation of narcissism and the male self. I have also fleshed out the psychological part of a theory in which men sacrifice in order to move closer to, gain distance from, or acquire the experience of power and perfection. The ritual reenacts the terror of merger and separation, which men experience as the tension gradient between the grandiose self and the idealized maternal self-object during the early period of narcissism. The idealized reenactment gives men power (from their point of view, the power is made available to them or they receive the effects of it), which was originally located in the experience of the maternal self-object. The cultural function and result of this transfer of power is that women are excluded from exercising cultural power (unless kinship lineage allows one to rule as queen, etc., while the rest are ruled by men—fathers, husbands, and in matrilineal societies, brothers and sons). The need to sacrifice occurs when the male narcissistically invested social structures have their boundaries tested or threatened, that is, whenever self-objects intrude. The psychology of narcissism developed by Heinz Kohut has helped me take several different interpretations and explanations of sacrifice and place them within a context that clarifies, relates, and supports them.

# References

Bakan, D. (1968). *Disease, Pain and Sacrifice: Toward a Psychology of Suffering.* Boston: Beacon Press.

Bettelheim, B. (1955). *Symbolic Wounds: Puberty Rites and the Envious Male.* Glencoe, Ill.: Free Press.

D'Andrade, R. (1958). "Sex Difference and Cultural Institutions." In *Readings in Social Psychology*, edited by Eleanor E. Maccoby, Theodore M. Newcomb, and Eugene L. Hartley, pp. 180–204. New York: Holt Reinhart and Winston.

Douglas, M. (1975). *Implicit Meanings: Essays in Anthropology.* London: Routledge and Kegan Paul.

Geertz, C. (1973). *The Interpretation of Cultures.* New York: Basic Books.

Hubert, H., and M. Mauss (1964). *Sacrifice: Its Nature and Function.* Translated by W. D. Halls. Chicago: University of Chicago Press.

Jay, N. (1985). "Sacrifice as Remedy for Having Been Born of Woman." In *Immaculate and Powerful: The Female in Sacred Image and Social Reality*, edited by Clarissa W. Atkinson, Constance H. Buchanan, and Margaret R. Miles, pp. 283–309. Boston: Beacon Press.

Khan, M. (1981). "From Masochism to Psychic Pain." *International Journal of Psychoanalysis* 60, pp. 413–23.

Kierkegaard, S. (1946). *The Concept of Dread.* Translated by Walter Lowrie. Princeton: Princeton University Press.

Kohut, H. (1971). *The Analysis of Self: A Systematic Approach to the Psychoanalytic Treatment of Narcissistic Personality Disorders.* New York: International Universities Press.

Kohut, H. (1977). *The Restoration of the Self.* Madison, Conn.: International Universities Press.

Kohut, H. (1978). *The Search for the Self: Selected Writings of Heinz Kohut: 1950–1978.* 2 vols. Edited by Paul Ornstein. New York: International Universities Press.

Kohut, H. (1984). *How Does Analysis Cure?* Chicago: University of Chicago Press.

Kohut, H. (1985). *Self Psychology and the Humanities: Reflections on a New Psychoanalytic Approach.* Edited by Charles Strozier. New York: W. W. Norton.

MacCormack, C. (1980). "Nature, Culture and Gender: A Critique." In *Nature, Culture, and Gender*, edited by Carol P. MacCormack and Marilyn Strathern, 1–24. Cambridge: Cambridge University Press.

Philipson, I. (1985). "Gender and Narcissism." *Psychology of Women Quarterly* 9, pp. 213–28.

Tiger, L. (1969). *Men in Groups.* London: Thomas Nelson and Sons.

# 24

# MAURICE BLOCH (b. 1939)

French anthropologist Maurice Bloch was born in Caen, France, attended school in Paris, and received his Bachelors degree from the London School of Economics. He completed his graduate work in Anthropology at Cambridge University, earning a Ph.D. Bloch has taught at a number of institutions in Europe, the United States, Japan, and Scandinavia, including the University of Wales, the University of Paris, the University of California at Berkeley, the University of Stockholm, the National Ethnology Museum of Japan, and the Danish Center for the Humanities in Copenhagen. Since 1990, he has been a professor in the Department of Anthropology at the London School of Economics. He was named a British Academy Fellow in 1990. Bloch has conducted the majority of his field research in Madagascar among the Merina in the north and the Zafimaniry in the south. His scholarly interests focus on issues of ritual, power, and language in culture and society. He has edited several important volumes, including: *Marxist Analyses and Social Anthropology* (1975), *Political Language and Oratory in Traditional Society* (1975), *Death and the Regeneration of Life* (1982), and *Money and the Morality of Exchange* (1989). He has published two volumes of his collected essays: *Ritual, History and Power: Selected Papers in Anthropology* (1989) and *How we Think they Think: Anthropological Approaches to Cognition, Memory and Literacy* (1998). Bloch's three most important monographs are: *Placing the Dead: Tombs, Ancestral Villages and Kinship Organization in Madagascar* (1971), *From Blessing to Violence: History and Ideology in the Circumcision Ritual of the Merina of Madagascar* (1986), and *Prey into Hunter: The Politics of Religious Experience* (1992). Bloch's writing demonstrates an impressive command of ethnographic detail stemming from his own fieldwork and from comparative archival work. Many of his essays and books seek to advance new and challenging theoretical positions as well.

Bloch proposes an understanding of sacrifice based on a theory of ritual he develops in his book *Prey into Hunter*. He begins with an insightful observation. Human beings are living organisms, mortal creatures constantly changing, growing, dying and reproducing, yet they also live as sociopolitical beings, members of what appear to be eternal institutions and permanent cognitive structures. There is a question then of how to solve this intrinsic dilemma of the human condition—the problem of creating stability out of change, structure out of flux, meaning out of impermanence. Bloch suggests this existential fact of being human is so fundamental, it leads to certain "quasi-universal" responses. Simply put, ritual is a mechanism that provides a symbolic means of overcoming this paradox. More significantly however, Bloch goes on to claim ritual processes follow a basic, "minimal structure" that reveals commonalities between many different religious practices, such as initiation, spirit possession, funerals, marriage, and sacrifice. All these (and more) are variations of a fundamental religious drama that has its origin in a basic fact of the human condition.

This "irreducible structure" of ritual Bloch labels "rebounding violence." It consists of two phases, each marked by actual or symbolic violence. Behind this basic ritual drama, Bloch insists, is an understanding of life as being composed of two elements, a "vital side" and a "transcendental aspect." Individual people, and perhaps other beings to varying degrees, embody the very existential dilemma (of being both transformative and permanent) driving the ritual process overall. In ordinary social life, during non-ritual processes, these two sides of life remain in harmony, but in times of transition or of personal or political disruption, this basic dilemma becomes urgent, and the symbolic ritual mechanism of rebounding violence responds. The first phase is a violent expulsion or abandonment of a "native vital element." Akin to the experience of death, this phase, by denying the living and chaotic world of process, momentarily transports ritual participants to the transcendent plane, to a state of life-transcending permanence. The second phase, also exhibiting a violence of sorts, is a process where participants regain vitality, but they obtain it from some non-native, "outside" source (e.g., animals, plants, other peoples, or women). Bloch describes this movement as a "consumption," a "conquest" of an external vitality. Without fully abandoning the transcendental, appropriating this new vitality allows the community and its individual members to reproduce the balance of institutional stability and natural change it requires to exist. This symbolic mechanism of rebounding violence provides society, in its religious rituals, with a means to create the "apparently permanent out of the transformative."

Bloch understands sacrifice as a ritual form adhering to the general symbolic pattern of rebounding violence. Much like ritual initiation (he examines an example from the Orokaiva of Papua New Guinea), sacrificial rituals display two clear phases which correspond to the two broad moments of transformation revolving around "vitality." For sacrifice, these two elements are "self-sacrifice" and "consumption." Earlier theorists have highlighted these elements of sacrifice individually (for example, Evans-Pritchard's "vita pro vita" substitution theory, and Robertson Smith's communion theory), but Bloch interprets them quite differently in terms of his notion of rebounding violence. Here, "self-sacrifice" refers to the identification forged between the sacrificer and the victim, but for Bloch it is only the "vital aspect" of the sacrificer that is removed (killed) with the victim in the ritual. The remaining transcendent aspect is thereby strengthened, as the first phase of Bloch's model specifies. The victim, which is usually a domesticated animal, is particularly well suited to represent both an identification with the sacrificer (it is domestic) and an alien (nonhuman) source of vitality. At the moment of its death, the significance of the animal victim shifts from the former to the latter. The second phase, the "consumption" of a new external vitality, is in this case the communal meal that often accompanies ritual sacrifice, a joyous recovery and restoration. Overall, Bloch argues that sacrifice is a double process of violent expulsion and consumption. It is a common cultural mechanism for addressing the broad problem of "human fluidity" within stable social structures.

Bloch's understanding of sacrifice, what may be called his "violence theory" of sacrifice, is significant because it reveals that violence is an integral part of the human attempt to create and maintain the social order, in particular the sense of transcendence, permanence, and truth such order requires. Different from Girard, however, the point of ritual is not to purge "bad violence" from society. Instead, Bloch sees violence, which may be enacted symbolically, as an inevitable product of social life. Sacrifice for Bloch is just one particularly clear example of this (here explicit) violence, only one form of ritual contributing to this overall human endeavor.

Reprinted here is chapter three from Bloch's *Prey into Hunter: The Politics of Religious Experience*, the chapter devoted to sacrifice. It presents a summary of his approach and two longer ethnographic examples, one from the Dinka of the Sudan, and the other from the Buid of the Philippines.

# From *Prey into Hunter: The Politics of Religious Experience*

CHAPTER 2 began with a discussion of initiation among the Orokaiva. It described how the elders organize a ritual in which the children to be initiated are first associated with pigs, creatures which are seen as very similar to them, and how as pigs the initiates are hunted and symbolically killed by

Maurice Bloch, *Prey into Hunter: The Politics of Religious Experience* (Cambridge: Cambridge University Press, 1992), pp. 24–45. Reprinted with the permission of Cambridge University Press and the author.

masked men representing ancestral spirits or birds. Then, the initiates are isolated in a dark hut in the forest, where it is said that they, like all those who have gone beyond death, have themselves become a kind of spirit. Finally, the children re-emerge and return from the world of the spirits. They re-emerge associated with the spirits which initially killed them, as hunters and consumers of pigs. However, at this stage the pigs which the initiate will hunt are real pigs. From being conquered and consumed as though they were pigs, the initiates have become conquerors and consumers of pigs and of everything which the pigs evoke: vitality, strength, production, wealth, and reproduction.

The initiates' return is accompanied by the whole community, who share in the new-found aggressiveness of the initiates, and all are now predominantly represented as killers of pigs and as eaters of pig meat. As the ritual develops, however, so does the evocation of conquest and soon the killing of pigs is associated with the conquest and killing of people. The pig hunt has come to be a foretaste of warfare and the consumption of enemies.

This matrix of Orokaiva initiation, which is found in many other rituals of initiation, is analogous to the underlying matrix of many of the rituals which have been called sacrifices in anthropological literature. This fundamental connection between sacrifice and initiation has been noted by many commentators. For example Stanner (1960), in a discussion of Australian Aboriginal initiation, shows how the same themes are present there as in biblical sacrifice. Similarly Schwimmer so extends the notion of sacrifice that it includes many aspects of the initiation ritual which was discussed in the previous chapter (1973, 154–9). This continuity will again be argued in this chapter as we compare Orokaiva initiation with a number of rituals which have been called "sacrifice" by the anthropologists who studied them. In the end, however, this comparison will lead to an even wider comparison of ritual forms, taking in such manifestations as funerary rituals, spirit possession and spirit mediumship.

Although this chapter mainly concentrates on two examples of sacrifice, this is not because sacrifice, any more than initiation, is an easily definable term delimiting a distinct type of ritual. To assume this would almost amount to thinking that every case is a variant of a fundamental and original sacrifice. Like a number of recent writers, such as de Heusch (1986), I believe it is right to stress the great variety that exists among the various examples of "sacrifice" as they have been described in the literature. A possible reaction to such a complex state of affairs might be to give a restrictive definition of the term, but this would be to take the very opposite strategy to the one I wish to adopt here. Instead, we need not be too concerned about whether a specific ritual is or is not a sacrifice, since the aim of this book is to include all these phenomena within a wider analytical category, which includes considerably more than even the wide range of rituals which have been labelled as sacrifice. Somewhat similarly, de Heusch concludes his book by saying that trance and sacrifice are part of a more general ritual system than is implied by either term. This is convincingly argued, but the ritual system he suggests goes well beyond phenomena which have been called trance and sacrifice and, indeed, goes beyond even what is commonly referred to as religion.

The anthropological concept of sacrifice should, therefore, be treated like the notion of totemism so effectively discussed by Lévi-Strauss (1962). The phenomena which have been called by names such as totemism or sacrifice are not so varied as to make the words useless as general indicators of linked manifestations. On the other hand these manifestations are so loosely connected that it would be as totally pointless to look for an explanation of sacrifice as such as Lévi-Strauss showed it was useless to look for an explanation of totemism as such. Rather, and again like Lévi-Strauss, we must see what are called sacrifices as a few cases of the very many manifestations of a much wider range of phenomena, some of which may have been labelled sacrifices, some initiations, and so on. It is at this more inclusive level that we must seek explanation.

Two examples of sacrifice have been most prominent in the immense non-anthropological literature on the topic, which proliferated especially at the end of the last century. These are ancient Greek sacrifice and biblical sacrifice. A discussion of these familiar cases can therefore serve as an introduction to the approach to be taken in this chapter.

For the ancient Greeks, as for many of the people who have been studied by anthropologists, all meat eating was a sacrifice. The Greeks never killed domestic animals for food for other purposes than sacrifice (Vernant, 1979, 44). As in the case of the Orokaiva initiation we therefore find an indissoluble link between religion and consumption. Furthermore, the political and military implications of this link are equally present in all these cases. For the Greeks, sacrifices had necessarily to be performed before any legal process could be initiated or before any major act of government could be envisaged. This was because sacrifice gave the sacrificers power and wisdom. Above all, sacrifices were essential before any military enterprise because the performance of the ritual was believed to be strength-giving.

The story of a particularly famous sacrifice has always dominated the traditional nineteenth-century discussions of ancient Greek sacrifice and it can serve to reveal the essential elements of the practice. This is the story of Iphigenia as found in the Greek dramatists, especially the two plays by Euripides, *Iphigenia in Aulis* and *Iphigenia in Tauris*. The Greeks were about to set sail to attack the Trojans when their warlike intentions were weakened by the lack of wind. This problem is normally explained in the Greek sources as a punishment administered by the goddess Artemis for an unspecified offence. A way out of this predicament was, we are told, found in the suggestion made through divination that Agamemnon, the leader of the expedition, should sacrifice his daughter Iphigenia, and thereby launch quite a number of plays and operas.

But, in the Euripides version at least, at the very last moment, just as the knife was about to come down, Iphigenia was replaced by a hind, which was killed instead. No doubt this animal would then have been treated like other Greek sacrificial animals. That is, it would be divided into different parts, some of which would be burnt so that the smell could feed the insubstantial gods, while other parts would be roasted and boiled to be consumed by different groups of humans. For humans, unlike the gods who had escaped the transformative cycles of life and death, need the sustaining and strengthening elements which come from consumed flesh (Vernant, 1979). Thus fortified, the Greeks got their favourable wind and were ultimately able to kill the Trojans, rape the women, and burn the town.

The overall pattern of the story is strong and clear. Agamemnon, the leader and representative of the Greeks, submits to an attack on himself, or something close to himself: his daughter. For the ancient Greeks, children were thought of as the extension of their fathers. In agreeing, however unwillingly, to carry out the sacrifice, Agamemnon was co-operating with an attack from a god directed against him. The first element of the sequence of sacrificial violence evoked by this story is therefore the partly self-inflicted violence intended by the chief protagonist. But then the violence rebounds and, from having been the victim, Agamemnon becomes a violent actor towards others. He eats the strengthening flesh of the sacrificial animal and not only is he restored bodily, but so is the whole situation and so are all the Greeks; the wind returns, the outward movement of the fleet towards their prey begins and ultimately the process reaches its climax as the Trojans and their town are consumed with fire. From having been conquered Agamemnon has thus become a conqueror.

The other story which is always referred to in the discussions of sacrifice, which appeared in such profusion during the last century, is the biblical story of Abraham and Isaac. According to Genesis, God ordered Abraham to offer his son Isaac in sacrifice instead of the usual sheep. In the end Abraham unwillingly agreed to carry out the divine instructions and began to make the necessary preparations. It is difficult to escape the implication that if the sacrifice had been carried out Isaac would have been killed and perhaps eaten. However, again at the last minute, God substituted a ram and Isaac was spared. Furthermore, as a mark of his favour and in return for obedience and self-denial, God promised Abraham to "make descendants as many as the stars of heaven and the grains of the sea shore. Your descendants shall gain possession of the gates of their enemies" (Genesis 22: 18).[1]

The similarities between the story of Iphigenia and that of Isaac are very striking and have often been pointed out. Furthermore, the connection between these two stories of sacrifice and the Orokaiva practice of initiation is clear. In all three cases we find the same elements. Firstly, a terrifying closeness to death on the part of the living is evoked. It is as if there was an element of dare in these stories. In the case of Orokaiva initiation the participants stress how very probable it is that the children will not survive the seclusion period of the ritual. In our two sacrifice stories death is avoided by a hair's breadth. Secondly, those who come close to death in all three cases are children, that is members of society who have life before them and who promise social continuation. In other words, the threatened killing is a killing of human vitality at its most intense and forward-looking. The abandonment of this form of vitality would be the abandonment of life itself for the whole community. Thirdly, in all three cases an animal is, at the last moment, substituted for the child. This means that the actual victim's vitality can be completely abandoned in fulfilment of the original promise to God, the gods or the ancestors, who, because of their non-bodily nature, are simply satisfied with receiving the insubstantial aspect of the animal. Fourthly, in all cases the substantial part of the victim, that is its potential vitality, is obtained in the form of meat by the human participants, who thereby replace and regain the vitality which they had lost in the initial self-denial. Fifthly, this consumption enables the whole community to regain vitality and life to such an extent that they can turn their strength outwards in the form of military aggression against other peoples and their children. The spatial aspect of this final, aggressive outward movement is particularly strongly evoked in both of our cases of sacrifice: by the image of the sea journey towards Troy in the one and the biblical reference to the "gates" of the enemies in the other. Both are images which recall the final military expeditions of Orokaiva initiation.

Several elements of this pattern shared by initiation and sacrifice, especially the movement out of vitality and back again, provided the framework of Hubert and Mauss's "communication" theory of sacrifice (1968 [1899]). This theory of sacrifice was, until recently, the most widely accepted in anthropology and it was the model for the highly influential study of Nuer sacrifice put forward by Evans-Pritchard (Evans-Pritchard, 1956, chapters 8, 9, 10). It was in this form in particular that Hubert and Mauss's theory came largely to supersede an older theory of sacrifice, which goes back to Plato, where the practice is seen as a matter of obligating the gods by means of a gift.

According to Hubert and Mauss, sacrifice is a matter of going towards the divine via the death of the victim and then coming back to the profane. This may be done for two reasons. Communication may be established through sacrifice in order momentarily to enter into contact with the divine so that sins may be forgiven or other benefits obtained. Hubert and Mauss called these cases "rites of sacralisation." Or communication is established with the sacred so that unwanted contact with the supernatural may be brought to an end. These sacrifices were called by the two authors "rites of desacralisation." In both cases sacrifice is above all envisaged as the crossing of the barrier between the sacred and the profane (Hubert and Mauss, 1968 [1899]).

In spite of the clear advance which Hubert and Mauss's theory represents over previous work, it has recently been fundamentally criticized by a number of writers. The main thrust of that criticism is that Hubert and Mauss were unjustifiably influenced by the prominence they gave to Vedic sacrifice and sacrifice as it is understood in the Judaeo-Christian tradition. This led them to assume that what are in reality quite specific models, derived from particular places and periods, could be used to build a universal theory. Clearly this is an ever-present danger in any attempt to generalize on such a vast subject and the criticism seems particularly well founded in their case, since any theory which uses terms such as "sacred" and "profane," terms which cannot be given extracultural referents, cannot form the basis of a general theory of sacrifice or of anything else.[2]

What Hubert and Mauss brought from their reading of ancient Sanskrit texts on sacrifice is the notion that the sacrificer enters the area of the sacred by means of purification of both himself and the victim and can thus communicate with the deity by means of the killing of the victim, which has become a sacred object. For these two authors, sacrifice is a kind of sacrilege which both joins and separates the sacred and the profane. But even if this theory is broadly acceptable for Sanskritic sacrifice—and this will be discussed more fully in the next chapter—it appears that even for ancient India it needs qualification (Biardeau and Malamoud, 1976, 19ff.). Even more significantly it is made perfectly clear by writers such as de Heusch, among others, that the idea of a separation between the sacred and the profane in the terms envisaged by Hubert and Mauss is far from universal, and that, in particular, it does not in any way apply to Africa (de Heusch, 1986, 20–1).

The unfortunate effect of the Judaeo-Christian heritage on the work is partly inherited from previous writers and partly indulged in anew by Hubert and Mauss. This problem is lucidly identified in an article by the French classicist Detienne, which introduces a number of studies on Greek sacrifice (Detienne, 1979). Detienne shows how Hubert and Mauss's work belongs to a long tradition in European history and theology which was already well formulated in the eighteenth century and which reached its apogee in the work of such writers as Cassirer (1972) and Girard (1972). All the writers in this long line implicitly or explicitly sought to make sacrifice the key to the definition of religion and saw Christian ideas of sacrifice as the apogee of lesser forms. As a result they interpreted the phenomena in an evolutionary perspective which saw non-Christian sacrifice as a primitive precursor of the disinterested self-sacrifice of the deity.

Although most of the writers who developed these linked theories were denounced in their time by various orthodox Christians, they were, Detienne convincingly argues, misled by anachronistic or ethnocentric Christian and Jewish concepts. Their work shows, Detienne tells us, "how an all-encompassing Christianity has continued to exercise a secret and surprising hold on the thought of historians and sociologists who were sure that they were inventing a new science" (1979, 35). This comment has been recently further vindicated by de Heusch's severe examination of how much the famous study of Nuer sacrifice by Evans-Pritchard (1956), which largely follows Hubert and Mauss, has been vitiated by the attempt to translate Nuer concepts into Christian theology and vocabulary (de Heusch, 1986, 21–33).

According to Detienne, crypto-Christianity leads to three problems and mis-representations in the way sacrifice has been viewed both in anthropological literature and beyond. Firstly, he rightly argues that the idea of an evolutionary sequence leading to a higher form of sacrifice has made anthropologists ignore the fact that the various phenomena which they have labelled sacrifice are extremely varied and that they demonstrate no essential unity. Secondly, he argues that the majority of authors have underestimated the political importance of sacrificial practices. Again, this is certainly true though a number of anthropologists and Sanskritists to whom he does not refer, such as Middleton (1960), Luc de Heush (1986), Heesterman (1985) and Gibson (1986), should be acquitted of this charge. Thirdly, Detienne argues that classical anthropologists, with the possible exception of Robertson Smith, have failed to see the importance of cooking and eating in sacrifice (Robertson Smith, 1889). To make the point Detienne, together with his co-editor Vernant, called their book *Sacrificial Cooking* (1979). In emphasizing that aspect of sacrifice they have preceded Gibson (1986), who has stressed the importance of eating and to whose work I shall return. Although this sort of stress is very valuable for our understanding of much apparently obscure ethnography, it becomes even more valuable if we expand Detienne's notion of cooking to a much more general concept than the specifically Greek notions he implies. Indeed, Detienne and Vernant run the risk of being accused of doing precisely what they rightly say Hubert and Mauss did when they universalized Sanskritic ideas, since they themselves appear to attempt to foist Greek ideas on the rest of the world. The idea of the centrality of cooking can, however, be retained if we expand it so that cooking is understood as only one stage in the general transformation of animal food which involves consumption and even digestion (Parry, 1985). This process might even be seen to include the escalating chain of consumptions and aggressions, discussed above, which complete rituals of sacrifice and initiation.

I cannot, however, entirely follow Detienne and Vernant when they use their point about cooking as though it negated the significance of the identification of sacrificer and victim and the significance of the self-sacrifice and substitution elements, which so interested Hubert and Mauss, Lienhardt, and Evans-Pritchard and which to them are mere crypto-Christianity. The evidence of some form of self-identification, supplied by the authors on whom I rely for the examples discussed in this chapter, seems inescapable though perhaps the general idea needs reformulating. Perhaps this element is absent in the Greek sacrifices which primarily concern Detienne, but we have already seen that the idea was present and central in one story of sacrifice from the same culture, the story of Iphigenia.

It is possible that the reason why Detienne and Vernant do not recognize the centrality of the element of self-identification with the victim in so many forms of sacrifice goes back to a reading of Hubert and Mauss's where their dismissal of the gift theory of sacrifice was a necessary element of and essential preliminary to their own theory. It is true that Hubert and Mauss's dismissal of the gift theory is, as Detienne and Vernant argue, unsatisfactory. The centrality of gift-giving to deities or ancestors in some form is quite inescapable from most cases of sacrifice in the literature. Even in the case of Vedic sacrifice, where quite specific ideas of cosmogony dominate, Biardeau has no hesitation in saying that, from the point of view of the sacrificer, the essential act is the giving up of something to the deity (Biardeau and Malamoud, 1976, 19). Giving something is the lowest common denominator of rituals which have been called sacrifice, perhaps simply because this is a fundamental meaning of the word in modern European languages. Gift-giving is a central element in the examples discussed by Detienne and Vernant, and ironically it was perhaps their ability to recognize this which led them to reject what Hubert and Mauss have to say so completely, since those authors originally presented their theory as an alternative to gift-theory. This is, however, to pass over much which is of value in Hubert and Mauss's account of sacrifice.

In fact, the importance of gift-giving in sacrifice need not conflict with the idea of self-identification with the victim. We know from Mauss's own work how gifts in very many societies should be seen as part of the giving of the self (1923/4) and Hubert and Mauss again use strikingly similar language to that of the essay on the gift when they stress how inappropriate the contrast between interested and disinterested gift-giving is for the societies to which they are referring (Hubert and Mauss, 1968, 305). This means that the giving of an offering closely associated with the self may also be a form of self-identification with the victim and ultimately the recipient. Interestingly, the same point, as it relates to sacrifice, is made by de Heusch when he points out how no sharp boundary can be drawn between being and having in African symbolism (1986, 310–12). In fact the element of consumption and the element of self-sacrifice are both conjointly present in most cases of sacrifice and it is precisely the combination of these two elements which is so revealing. It is this conjunction which makes it possible to demonstrate the relation of sacrifice to initiation and to argue that the symbolic immolation of the almost-self of the first part of sacrifice and the political, military, and culinary aspects of the second half mutually imply each other.

To illustrate this point further I shall, by way of illustration, give two ethnographic examples which are in many ways complementary. These are, first, the classic study of the Dinka of the southern Sudan by Lienhardt (1961) and secondly Gibson's recent study of the Buid of the Philippines (1986), which appears to support the position of Detienne and Vernant.

Dinka ethnography is deservedly famous in anthropology and so I shall refer to it only very quickly in order to stress those aspects which are particularly relevant to the general argument. Under normal circumstances Dinka sacrifice centrally involves the killing of cattle. It is these people's most important religious rite and the same would be true of many other African peoples. Most commonly, sacrifices are carried out in time of trouble or when people need strengthening. Very often the immediate cause is disease. This leads us to ask the simple but centrally relevant question: why does killing cattle cure people? But before answering this question we need to begin at the beginning of the sequence of events which culminates in sacrifice as a form of curing.

The initial reason for carrying out the sacrifice is when someone, or a group of people, feels penetrated by an outside force, which is believed either to cause or actually to *be* the disease. Disease is used here in a very wide sense of the word to mean almost any kind of trouble. Lienhardt shows how permeable the Dinka feel to such outside forces and how all trouble is explained in terms of such a bodily invasion.

The next stage in the progression towards sacrifice occurs when the person (or persons) who has been attacked tries to find the cause of the trouble. To do this the patient turns to divination or some other diagnostic procedure and in the process of divination the sequence which leads to sacrifice quickens. What follows the diagnostic is the diviner's recommendation for bringing about a cure and this is particularly revealing. Two apparently totally different and opposed ways of curing are common, especially in Africa. These two ways may be tried concurrently, but more usually they appear as two successive stages of the process of finding a cure, since, if the first is not successful, the other will then be tried. The first way of dealing with intrusion is found universally. Once the source of the trouble has been identified, a way is sought to expel the intrusive force. This way of going about things is familiar to us from western medicine. Indeed the Dinka themselves recognize this identity of form and therefore readily welcome western medicine for this sort of practice.

If the first approach fails, however, then the second tack is tried and that is completely different. In this the diviner will suggest that the disease is a powerful supernatural being, a clan divinity or a spirit for example, which cannot, or should not, be resisted and so, instead of expelling the intrusion, the patient should rather submit to the disease and its attack on her body. She should even draw in and identify with the disease against her body, in other words make her body foreign and accept the intrusion against it. This is not expected to occur without a struggle, but the final victory of the intruding force should not be in doubt.

The lives of Christian saints or the story of Job are well-known examples of this pattern and there are many ethnographic cases of this type of turning round of the person against themselves or rather against the bodily aspect of themselves. For example a particularly fine description of this process is given in the book *Human Spirits* by M. Lambek (1981), where this way of dealing with illness by "welcome" is shown to lead naturally to spirit possession. After a struggle when the diseased person is still trying out the first tack of expelling the intrusive spirit she finally agrees to the second tack and instead welcomes the spirit. What this means in this case is that she allows her body to be made a receptacle without will, which can be used by an immortal and external spirit for its temporary incarnation (Lambek, 1981).

In the case discussed by Lambek this second welcoming approach to disease leads to the instituting of a spirit-possession cult, but it could just as easily have been a preliminary to sacrifice. The fact that similar preliminaries can lead to either what we call sacrifice or spirit mediumship shows well how closely these two manifestations are related, a point already made, as we saw, by de Heusch. It also shows once again how misleading the divisions can be within the typology of ritual categories which our academic traditions have imposed. Indeed the close connection between sacrifice and possession can help us understand the Dinka case to which we return.

Here, however, yet another preliminary is necessary before we come to the ritual itself. As was the case for the understanding of Orokaiva initiation, it is necessary to sketch how the Dinka view relations with supernatural beings and with animals, especially cattle. In fact, the main points I want to make on these matters are implicit in the very organization of Lienhardt's book. The book begins with a discussion of the Dinka's association and near-identification with their cattle. It is made clear that this identification is particularly strong in the case of boys and young men. To illustrate this we are shown a picture of Dinka youth dancing in a way that imitates cattle. The book ends, however, with a discussion of the ritual of the death-defying burial alive of a Dinka priest, the master of the fishing spear. The priest should be a very old man who is buried alive in such a way that, after he has disappeared from sight, nothing but his disembodied voice can be heard singing or speaking an invocation. This complementary opposition between cattle and speech, between the bovine strength of youth and the verbal power of the old, which Lienhardt constructs by the very organization of the book, is central to Dinka symbolism.

For the Dinka, cattle and humans are very close and this parallelism, which is evocatively discussed by Lienhardt, is familiar from other parts of Africa. This link between cattle and humans is not unlike that which exists between pigs and humans among the Orokaiva. For the Dinka, cattle represent the beauty of strength, vitality, and sexuality to which humans aspire, but which they possess in varying amounts. In particular, cattle are associated with young men.

But the similarity between the Orokaiva and Dinka cases goes further. This is because, even though Dinka cattle are seen as similar to humans in some respects, in other, equally significant respects, cattle and humans are very different. These aspects are not so stressed by Lienhardt but they emerge from a careful reading of his ethnography.

For the Dinka, a clear difference between humans and cattle lies in humans' ability to speak. Although Lienhardt does not discuss speech in general, he discusses at great length the speech of the Dinka prophets and of the members of the priestly clan, the masters of the fishing spear. This is a kind of ideal speech, cool speech, not often achieved by less sacred mortals. The Dinka believe that prophets and masters of the fishing spear are the permanent mediums of Divinity and of lesser divinities which, in any case, are simply avatars of the supreme God. The speech of the chosen vessels of Divinity is, therefore, particularly powerful, but it is not exclusive to them. It seems that all men, and perhaps some women, can occasionally make their speech reach similar heights, for example when possessed or when acting as diviners. Perhaps the most important aspect of this quintessential speech is that it is always true. This means that when it is used to talk of the future it is prophetic. Ideally it should be declaimed clearly and require few words (Lienhardt, 1961, 139). Everything about this truth-speech contrasts with the associations of cattle. While cattle are youthfully strong but turbulent, mobile, always being exchanged or killed in sacrifice, the true speech of the Dinka is manifested in the old and frail, but is permanent, unchanging, of no particular time and of all times, sober and immortal, beyond process.

This duality of speech and cattle takes many forms. For example the Dinka think of their society as fundamentally divided between warrior clans who are more closely associated with cattle, and priestly clans who bring order, stability, and prophetic speech. This kind of distribution suggests an image of complementarity since it implies that both elements are necessary for life. The Dinka see existence as a combination of a bovine animal vitality and a death-defying order crystallized in the invocations of the masters of the fishing spear.

In stressing this duality in Dinka thought I am not doing what Lienhardt rightly warned us against in a recent article on the concept of the self (Lienhardt, 1985). There, he very properly stressed how it would misrepresent Dinka thought to argue that they have an explicit theory of what makes up the self. Very sensibly the Dinka say that no one can know what a person is like inside. I believe such justified scepticism is found in most cultures, and I have already tried to stress the dangers of such over-explicit exegesis of ideas of the person in the last chapter. What I am talking about when I say that the Dinka envisage the person as part cattle and part speech is, rather, the dramatic sim-plifications which are acted out in rituals. In rituals, unlike ordinary, everyday life, an image of the components of interior states is evoked in a way that is partly iconographic and partly allegorical. These dramatic representations are created in order to bring about a symbolic transformation, but they soon fade after the ritual is done, though they never disappear completely.

After the diviner has told the patient that, rather than resist, she must submit to the external invasion, in most cases he will suggest that this is done by sac-rificing cattle. Why this is a suitable way of co-operating with the external invader becomes evident in the main actions of the rite. First, the victim is associated with the person for whom the sacrifice is being done. Then, in the first part of the sacrifice proper the animal is threatened for long periods with the spear of the sacrificer and it is weakened in a variety of ways but principally by exposure to the sun. Ultimately it is killed. But simultaneously, as this is happening, the other aspect of human society, the cold speech of truth, is strengthened and conquers. Speech is manifest in sacrifice in the invocations and prayers spoken by the master of the fishing spear which dominate the first part of the ritual. The Dinka say that it is the continual speaking of these invocations which weakens and kills the animal and makes its horns, prime symbols of vitality and virile strength, wilt and droop. The very word which the Dinka use as a verb for "to invoke" suggests the violence that is being done to the sacrificial animal as it can also mean "to attack an enemy" (1961, 263). The drama is a tilting of the balance between vitality and unchanging truth, in which vitality is vanquished.

It is, therefore, right to see Dinka sacrifice as involving an identification between sacrificer and victim, as Lienhardt does in the case of the Dinka and as Evans-Pritchard for the Nuer. In spite of de Heusch's objections much of the ethnography confirms their point of view. However, the proposition has to be qualified since it is only *one* aspect of the sacrificer and the community, the vital cattle aspect, which is symbolically weakened and killed in the ritual, but the other aspect, the speech aspect, is strengthened at the very same time as vitality ebbs away. This is why theories of the identification of sacrificer and victim have often been criticized but never overcome. It is not the whole person which is identified with the victim, but only one aspect.

Dinka sacrifice is in its first part a drama of conflict between cattle and speech; as the animal is defeated speech and invocation become triumphant. What the ritual creates by evocation is first a reduction of the complexity of the person and society so that it can appear to consist merely of two opposed elements, the cattle and the invocation, which are represented as visually and auditorily in conflict. Once the image has been established the ritual can reach the next stage as, finally, the speech element conquers.

For the sacrificer and the community the conquest and the killing of the cattle is an external drama which can be experienced as corresponding to the weakening and killing of the cattle element by now evoked in the body. It is in this ritual context, and this context only, that it is right to speak of elements of the person because, in the ritual, different external entities are brought into action to represent and create an internal conflict. What is happening is similar to a morality play where the struggle of good and evil within a protagonist can be represented as objectified by different actors.

But ritual is more complex and more powerful than this simple comparison suggests. Firstly, as will be discussed below, the second half of the ritual breaks away from the theatrical model. Secondly, even in the first part of the ritual discussed above, we are not just dealing with an externalized representation of an internal state, but also with actions which have an experienced internal effect on the body of the participants.

The drama of the victory of speech over cattle occurs out in the open on the ceremonial ground. But the same division and the same tipping of the balance also occurs experientially for both sacrificer and for those less centrally concerned. In order to understand how the killing of the cattle is bringing about a cure it is better to concentrate on this aspect first.

The effect of the ritual on the peripheral participants is revealing in many ways. First, it shows how, in a ritual such as this and in a society such as that of the Dinka, the boundary between the body of an individual and the wider group is weak (Bloch, 1988). Thus, in the Dinka ritual of sacrifice, as in Orokaiva initiation, even though the event might be focused on the central actor (the initiate or the patient), all the others present are not onlookers but co-participants. This continuity manifests itself at the point in the ritual when, as the animal on the ritual ground is weakened and as the speech side is magnified, the onlookers also experience speech overwhelming their internal vitality and they become possessed and speak the words of Divinity. Lienhardt gives a graphic description of the twitching of the flesh of the possessed young men, their cattle side, as it submits to the verbal invasion of Divinity. This twitching of the flesh of the possessed serves well to show how a parallel has been established between the external visible actions of the participants in the ritual and the invisible experiential process which goes on inside their bodies, since the Dinka themselves stress the identity of the twitching of the flesh of the possessed participants with the twitching of the flesh of the animal as it is being slaughtered (Lienhardt, 1961, 137).[3]

The falling into trance of some of the onlookers is illuminating in a number of ways. First, we have once again demonstrated the close affinity of sacrifice and spirit possession. Secondly, because spirit possession is a matter of the triumphant penetration of a transcendental being into the conquered body of a medium, we can see that this is also what sacrifice is all about, that, like spirit possession, it is an appropriate response to the diviner's advice not to resist disease, but rather join the invader entering into your body. In the ritual the sacrificial animal is made to stand for the vitality of the body of the sacrificer while the transcendental speech of the invocations of the master of the fishing spear appropriately represents and is a manifestation of Divinity. By organising the sacrifice the patient is thus completing the attack on his own vitality in order to let the permanent triumph. The weakening and death of the animal is the culmination of this process and publicly represents the victory of transcendental speech. The first part of sacrifice and possession is the completion of the process of joining the invader against one's vital self.

And, of course, all this is exactly what happens in a ritual such as Orokaiva initiation, or rather in the first part of the ritual when the pig element in the children is weakened and killed so that the spiritual element can dominate. But then, with sacrifice as with initiation, there is a reversal. The abandonment of strength and vitality cannot be final. As with initiation, it must be regained. The internal lack of balance in the body, brought about by the victory of the transcendental, must be redressed if life is to go on. And again this poses the problem of how to avoid contradiction so that the second part of sacrifice is not merely a reincorporation of what has so painfully been got rid of.

The Dinka sacrifice solution is very similar to the Orokaiva initiation solution and it revolves around the change in the relation of the sacrificer and victim which occurs at the moment of the actual killing. Lienhardt, like other ethnographers, notes how a dramatic transformation in mood occurs at this point. This is due to the fact that the close association of sacrificer and victim ends at this moment. Up to then there has been a painfully close experiential analogic relation between the two, but once the killing has been done the sacrificer is freed and the dead animal is merely a dead animal on the ground, ready to be cut up and eaten in the second part of the ritual. When that occurs the relation of the victim, on the one hand, and the sacrificer and community, on the other, changes from the analogic to the physical, just as, among the Orokaiva, the pigs of the first part of the initiation were metaphoric pigs while the pigs of the second half are real pigs.

From this point on Lienhardt almost seems to lose interest in the proceedings for reasons which have much to do with his highly intellectual definition of religious experience, which seems to have no place for what is fundamentally a feast. In this point of view he reflects the approach of those writers whom Detienne rightly criticizes for crypto-Christianity and for ignoring the political and consumption aspects of sacrifice in spite of the fact that these aspects are just as present in Christianity. However, if we again agree with Detienne on this, it is not [to] say that what interested Lienhardt is not equally important.

What happens in the second part of the ritual is that the animal is cut up, distributed, and partly eaten there and then amidst a good deal of celebration. By this stage this meat has taken on a quite different meaning from what it had in the first part. No longer does it represent the animal, vital side of the sacrificer; it has become, by the simple fact of killing, the meat of an animal which, because it is an animal, is by nature alien to humans. Its vitality can be consumed without problem by those present in order that, like all meat, it will restrengthen them through its nutritive value.

Unlike Lienhardt, and even more Evans-Pritchard writing of the nearby Nuer, the Dinka attach very great importance to the feast side of sacrifice and to the eating of cattle, in which they revel. Indeed, the Dinka word which Lienhardt translates as "sacrifice" would, according to him, be more straightforwardly translated as "feast," thereby making a nonsense of the refusal to consider the meal as part of the sacrifice (1961, 281). The eating of the meat of the cattle restores vitality which had been analogically lost in the first part of the ritual. Those who had allowed their native vitality to be symbolically vanquished by following the advice of the diviner and performing the sacrifice are now rewarded with the actual vitality of an external being. The meal is that highly pleasurable recovery of this vitality, which has been surrendered in the first part of the proceedings. And here, as with the other consumptions which follow rebounding conquests, this may not be just a restoration of lost vitality. The recovery is triumphalist and outwardly directed. It may indeed lead to a legitimate increase in vitality since the vitality that is now being recovered is conquered and ordered by the transcendental order of the speech of the masters of the fishing spear.

By having allowed one side of themselves to die so that they may become pure speech the Dinka sacrificers can regain the cattle side through the mouth, almost exactly as happened for the Orokaiva initiate. There is a difference in the two cases but it is slight. In the case of the Orokaiva initiation it was the children who were representing pigs in the first part of the proceedings, while in the first part of the Dinka sacrifice it is the cattle which represents the humans, but this difference is of no significance to the general logic of the proceedings.

And the parallel between the two rituals does not end there. For the Orokaiva the consumption of the external pig was also the promise of further more adventurous conquests of a political and military form and, again, the same is true of the Dinka. As in the case of the Orokaiva, Dinka sacrifice takes on a more military idiom as it proceeds. Lienhard tells us that to "make a feast or sacrifice often implies war" (1961, 281), indeed that the rituals often ended either in threatened or real military raids. The expansionist reconquest of vitality is shown once again to lead either to restoration, as in the return of the initiates to the village, or to aggrandisement.

It is because the sacrifice ends in such a feast, which involves not just the legitimate recovery of vitality but, by extension, the recovery of more vitality, as much as one can get, that sacrifice can cure disease in all its forms whether physical or, as is often the case, social and moral. What has happened in the sacrifice is that the specific problem, which was the original cause of the ritual, has been dealt with in a way which is not specifically addressed to it but is, rather, an action which generally reactivates the strength and activity of the social group and which, it is hoped, will overcome the particular difficulty with its general force. This is why the same rituals can be used both to cure specific ills and on a non-specific basis to reactivate the right order of man in society and nature, such as occurs, for example, in annual fertility rituals such as the famous Ncwala of the Swazi (Beidelman, 1966). This point will be discussed further in the next chapter. However, because the culinary, political, and military sides are not developed by Lienhardt, it is best to turn to other ethnographies to understand the second half of sacrifice.

411

The second ethnographic example to be considered in any detail in this chapter is a recent study of the Buid of Mindoro in the Philippines by Gibson (1986). In many ways this ethnography of sacrifice is almost the opposite of that on the Dinka and, as a result, it complements it admirably for the purposes of the present argument. Gibson insists that, while the element of substitution of the sacrificer for the victim is central to the Dinka, it is absent in Buid sacrifice. On the other hand, he argues that the communal and politically significant strength-giving meal in which the animal is eaten is the most important aspect of Buid sacrifice. This approach would certainly delight Detienne. The differences have as much to do with the different approaches of the two authors as they have to do with the differences between Africa and South East Asia. However, in spite of the wide cultural differences, it is to a certain extent possible to reconcile the two studies.

We must start by a consideration of Buid notions of the person as they emerge in ritual. Gibson tells us that the Buid consider that the person is made up of three elements. These three elements he glosses as body, mind, and soul. The body and soul are acquired through the biological processes of birth. They are closely linked. Gibson tells us that the state of the body reflects the state of the soul (1986, 126), but the soul, unlike the body, does not disappear at death but becomes a ghost. Both the soul and the body are driven by asocial, individualistic desires, such as the desire for food and exclusive sexual gratification. These desires are normally controlled by the third element, the mind. The mind develops with adulthood, begins to weaken with the onset of senility and finally disappears at the death of an individual. The manifestation of the mind can be seen in the self-control exercised by the person and by their socially co-operative attitude. The faculty of speech is a sign of the mind and this is especially so in the highest form of speech, the chanting of the spirit mediums. In these concepts the Buid are surprisingly close to the Dinka and this similarity is increased when we take into account Buid ideas about the relation of humans and pigs, ideas which are reminiscent of Dinka ideas about the relation of humans and cattle.

For the Buid, animals share with humans the body and the soul, both of which are driven by desires, but, as might be expected, it is the controlling mind, and therefore speech, which is the element that differentiates humans, especially Buid humans, from animals. The negative side of animality should, however, be balanced with the positive aspect of animality, which is its vitality. Indeed, it appears that, because their bodies and souls are not under the control of mind, the Buid feel that the vitality of animals is somehow stronger than that of humans.[4] From Gibson's book one gets the feeling of a considerable amount of anxiety about the possible lack of differentiation between humans and animals, especially pigs, since pigs are, as he points out, very close to humans because they are domesticated and live directly under the house (1986, 153–5).[5] The Buid seem to be saying that, but for the control of the mind, humans would be like pigs and their society would be as chaotic as that of pigs, as each and every individual would seek to fulfil their selfish desires.

Furthermore, this partial identity with pigs means that, if humans were not under the control of the mind, they would, like pigs who are eaten by humans, become legitimate food for superior beings. How real this worry is becomes clear in the context of funerals, where it is believed that because the dead have lost the protection of their minds and are therefore like pigs, they immediately become potential prey to pig-eating spirits, who treat the corpse as though it were pork. In certain contexts the Buid say that "they are the pigs of the spirits" (1986, 150). One might see this statement as being a shorthand for saying that, but for the protection of the mind, they are as vulnerable to flesh-seeking spirits as pigs are to humans.

The way the mind offers protection from pig-eating spirits is clearest in the rituals of spirit mediumship which are central to Buid religion. Buid spirit mediumship is, like all aspects of Buid society, strikingly democratic, or rather, corporatist. Nearly all households contain a person who, by means of a secret chant, can summon at least one spirit familiar who will make mediumship possible. The summoning of these familiars is so common that Gibson tells us it is very rare for a night to go by in a settlement without some medium being heard chanting. The summoning of familiars by chanting has the purpose of enabling the mind to soar "on the back" of the familiar above the settlement. The reason for such acts of mediumship is, above all, to protect the community from various malevolent spirits who are always seeking to attack the souls of the members as a preliminary to being able to eat their bodies after death.

This almost daily guard-duty is achieved by the process, already much discussed in this book, whereby animal-like vitality is abandoned by the mediums. As a result of chanting, the mind of the medium separates from their soul and body and the freed mind begins to be able to see the medium's familiar approaching. The mind then gets on the back of the familiar and, as it soars, it leaves behind on the ground the merely animal sides of the person, that is the body and the soul.

Again, as in the examples discussed in the earlier parts of this book, this abandonment of vitality is like what happens after death, since the Buid believe that after death the mind returns to a transcendental, undifferentiated community of minds and only the body and the soul remain on earth for a while. The body is then eaten by the evil predatory spirits and the soul becomes for a limited period an egoistical ghost.

The similarity of this example with those from the Dinka or the Orokaiva cases is far from total. In the Buid example the transcendental element, the mind, does not survive the death of the person and is thus different from the Orokaiva spirit aspect which becomes an immortal ancestral spirit. The contrast is further heightened by the fact that the element which *does* survive after death, that is the soul, shares in the animality of the body. These differences are, however, less significant than might at first appear.

This becomes apparent as we return to the subject of Buid mediumship. The almost nightly chanting sessions, which normally involve only one medium, are actually best understood as minor preparations, or practice sessions, for much more elaborate Buid rituals, which Gibson calls seances. These seances are usually occasioned by some major trouble or disease. What makes them different from more common acts of mediumship is the co-operation of a large number of mediums and the presence of the whole community. The point of these large gatherings is that the various mediums can join forces and drive away the powerful evil spirits, who have succeeded in invading the community in spite of the vigilance of the lone medium's nightly patrol. Gibson is at his most evocative when he describes how seances are joint enterprises manifesting the ethos of sharing and solidarity, which the Buid value above all and which is the product of the control exercised by the minds of all the mediums of the community working together.

In such seances the minds of all the important men and some women, helped by their many familiars, are joined together to defeat the intruders. This powerful image of intellectual co-operation enables us to understand better that what Gibson calls the "mind" is not primarily an individual part of the person, but an aspect of a holistic appreciation of the local society. Indeed, such a view of the mind as that which leads to sharing accords well with the general conclusions of Gibson's book. In the seance it is the minds of the community together with their familiars which are once again gathered to fight against the unending intrusions of the spirits. This community of minds and familiars is therefore transcendental to the individual mind of any one person.

By continuing to share the powers of their minds and familiars the Buid act, not as individuals, but as a community. Also, as a community, they are making a bid for survival after individual death. There is, therefore, a sense in which the community of minds and familiars is immortal since, although the minds of individuals come and go, the corporate body of minds remains. This is even clearer in the case of the spirit familiars since these, unlike anything else in Buid society, are inherited by one person from another, thereby implying the familiars' separation from human mortality. This community of minds and spirits is the permanent element of Buid society; it corresponds to the speech of the masters of the fishing spear and the ancestors of the Orokaiva. All these transcendental elements are opposed to individual and unstable elements associated with animals and their vitality, an element which is represented, in the Buid case, by the body and the selfish soul.

If this argument is accepted we are some way towards showing the close parallel which exists between Lienhardt's study of Dinka sacrifice, which stresses the identification of victim and sacrificer, and Gibson's study of Buid sacrifice, which stresses the importance of killing the animal, cooking, and eating it. First, however, we must look more closely at precisely these elements in Buid ethnography.

The important seances of the Buid, when the whole community gets together, not only involve spirit mediumship, but also what Gibson calls sacrifices, that is the ritual killing, cooking, and eating of an animal: a pig or a chicken. These sacrifices are carried out for a number of different reasons. Here, for lack of space, I shall concentrate only on the two most different cases: when the spirits concerned in the sacrifice are beneficial to humans and when the spirits are totally hostile to humans.

Gibson gives an example of a case of the latter type, which was necessitated when a child was believed to be diseased because his house had been invaded by a whole horde of harmful spirits. In order to deal with this trouble a large seance was organized involving many spirits and many mediums. As people began to gather, the spirit mediums called their familiars by chanting, then they began to co-ordinate their various visions into a shared one. It was during this time that what Gibson calls the sacrifice took place. The participants hung a pig upside down from the rafters and then swung it over the child's head. Just as they slaughtered the animal the mediums urged the spirits to leave the child.

Although Gibson would disagree, I think it is inevitable that we must see the killing of the pig as a substitute for the child, which the evil spirits had begun to attack by biting, a form of aggression which the Buid see as a preliminary to aggressive eating. But then, as in Dinka sacrifice, after the moment of the slaughter, everything changes. The insubstantial spirits have been fed the insubstantial soul of the pig and so the humans can indulge as a community in a revivifying meat feast which is specially intended to strengthen the stricken child (Gibson, 1986, 158–9).[6]

When the sacrifice is intended to bring about the intervention of beneficial spirits the ritual is a little different. In the case discussed by Gibson (1986, 172–9) the intent is to bring back the presence of those beneficial spirits who had withdrawn because of an antisocial act by some members of the community. As always, the Buid first try to contact the spirits through the double intermediary of the mediums and their familiars and, as they do this, they invitingly kill the pig on the threshold. They then proceed to the equally important revivifying feast, which, as Gibson convincingly demonstrates, expresses and reinforces the idiom of sharing on which Buid society rests. In the case of the sacrifice to beneficial spirits, and as when evil spirits are addressed, the spirits are invited to come and share in the communal meal. Because of this the spirits are given a little bit of meat to evoke their presence in the human group and enable them to join in.

It is the very great importance which the Buid attach to these feasts, which makes Gibson take a general view of sacrifice which conflicts with that of such writers as Lienhardt and Evans-Pritchard. He argues, as Robertson Smith did, that Buid sacrifice is only focused on the element of a uniting communal meal and that it lacks the element of self-sacrifice and substitution which was central for Hubert and Mauss and Evans-Pritchard. In this conclusion he joined Detienne although, as far as I know, the two authors wrote independently of each other.

The way I see the matter is somewhat different from any of these authors. Gibson's conclusion would follow if one used the label "sacrifice" as though it denoted a discrete analytical category defined by a concern with the ritual killing and consumption of an animal. There is no doubt that this is how the word has been used in the anthropological literature. If one limits the analysis of Buid sacrifice to acts defined in this way, the conclusion reached by Gibson that Buid sacrifice is only a matter of eating the victim is largely convincing, even though the element of substitution is not, even to his own evidence, absent.[7]

But if, like de Heusch, Detienne and myself, we assume that sacrifice cannot be defined cross-culturally and that the word is nothing more than a pointer to a cluser of phenomena which are contained within a wider family of rituals, there is no reason why we should limit our explanatory attempt to the pig killing and eating and ignore other parts of the seance. Indeed, there is a good reason why we should not do so since the Buid themselves make no such distinction. It therefore seems reasonable to analyse the event as a totality, containing both the element of spirit mediumship and the element of pig killing.

If we do this we find that Buid ritual practice becomes much closer in structure to Dinka sacrifice and that it accords with the general pattern of rebounding violence discussed in this book. Buid spirit mediumship is a response to a form of potential trouble, which is imagined as an invasion of hostile invisible forces. The response to such invasion is not to identify with the invading forces, as would be the case in Orokaiva initiation or in Dinka sacrifice, and then turn against one's vitality, but it is something not all that dissimilar. Although the Buid do not join with the invading spirits they transform their society into something of the same order as that of the spirits, a community of insubstantial minds and familiars. In doing this they anticipate individual death since, as will happen after death, they abandon their vital, animal-like element, that is their souls and bodies. But, just as they individually die a little, they are also reconstituted into a wider, non-individual and life-transcending unity, which endures through time as people come and go.

Thus, the part of the seance concerned with spirit mediumship corresponds fairly closely to the first part of Dinka sacrifice with its abandonment of animal vitality in favour of the eternal and unchanging truth of the speech entrusted in the clan of the masters of the fishing spear. In both cases we have an abandonment of practical dialectics which is achieved by a self-inflicted conquest of one side of the self, though in one case this is achieved through the drama of Dinka spirit possession and, in the other, by the extreme control implied in Buid mediumship.

But, as in the other cases we have looked at, this movement to the permanent transcendental cannot be maintained for ever if life is to go on and vitality to be regained, though, as in the other cases, since vitality cannot be regained in the form in which it was lost, it must be regained from an alien source. And so the part of the seance not concerned with mediumship is concerned with what Gibson has called "sacrifice" and eating. Since the mediums cannot remain in their transcendental state and the community cannot be left hanging in mid air they must, like the Dinka in the second part of sacrifice, regain vitality and therefore mortality, which they do through the shared consumption of pig meat.

In the case of a large-scale seance the Buid think of both the departure to the spirit world and the return to vitality as communal matters and it is therefore particularly appropriate that one of the central aspects of the rebounding violence of external vitality among the Buid takes the form of a "communal" meal which incarnates that central Buid value, the idiom of sharing.

Gibson, better than any other ethnographer, shows the significance of the meat eating and how its meaning is to be found just as much in the physiological responses it evokes as in more intellectual associations. This, I am sure, would also have been the case for the Dinka had Lienhardt chosen to include that part of the proceeding in his analysis of sacrifice.

In other words it is the totality of the various types of Buid seances, which all share the same two critical elements—spirit mediumship and meal—which is a close equivalent to the whole of Dinka sacrifice, involving as it does both invocation and feast. It is only Gibson's and Lienhardt's different definition of the event which has led to their appearing to reach such contrasting positions. And, furthermore, both cases are very similar to the Greek and Jewish examples of sacrifice with which this chapter began.

These four cases of sacrifice reveal themselves to be also fundamentally similar to Orokaiva initiation in that all these rituals are based on the same sequence. Firstly, there is a representation of a bifurcation of life between an exaggeratedly chaotic vitality and a transcendental, permanent order which is the basis for institutions. Secondly, there is a representation of the abandonment of chaotic vitality, an abandonment which is caused by an attack on the vital chaotic aspect of the self or of the community. Thirdly, we have a triumphalist recovery of mastered and consumed vitality obtained from an external source.

There is an aspect of the Buid ethnography which, however, seems to go against the assimilation of this case to examples from Dinka or Orokaiva ethnography. One aspect of these ethnographies, emphasized in what has gone before, is how the experience of reproduction becomes the basis for an ideological transformation which I have called rebounding violence and which creates an idiom and a legitimation for aggression and military expansionism. But military expansionism and aggression are, as Gibson clearly shows, values which are totally alien to the Buid, a people who have a horror of all forms of aggression and who will not engage in any kind of domination which would imply the superiority of one person over another. The cause of this lack of aggressiveness is found by Gibson in Buid history. The Buid have for many centuries been in permanent retreat from external aggressors infinitely more powerful than themselves. Their strategy for dealing with this situation has been to withdraw from contact with outsiders and to emphasize egalitarian sharing amongst themselves. The Buid know that any kind of aggression on their part is not possible and, indeed, that it would be counterproductive. So, unlike the Dinka or the Orokaiva, they use the symbolism of rebounding violence to achieve reproduction and that is all. They conquer their pigs like the Orokaiva, but, unlike the Orokaiva, this conquest is not the preliminary for further and different conquests.

That, however, is not to say that the symbolism which underlies Buid religious practice does not contain within itself the possibility of being transformed into an aggressive variant. Indeed, the ethnography of the Philippines offers us proof of this. In two striking books M. and R. Rosaldo unravelled much of the symbolism of the Ilongot peoples of central Luzon (M. Rosaldo, 1980; R. Rosaldo, 1980). Anyone reading their work side by side with Gibson's study cannot but be struck by how similar the basic religious concepts of the Buid and the Ilongot actually are. And yet, in total contrast to the Buid, the Ilongot are a people who value aggression and especially anger, anger which ultimately manifests itself in headhunting directed fairly indiscriminately outside the basic social group.

The similarity and the difference are instructive. The cause of the difference is the different situations in which the Buid and the Ilongot have found themselves during history. Unlike the Buid, the Ilongot were left relatively in peace and had a number of opportunities to attempt to expand. In those conditions the same basic symbolic and religious elements developed in a totally different, aggressive direction.

This comparison can perhaps help us to begin to specify the relation of the idiom of rebounding violence to the reality of military aggression and of actual political forms. The basis of the symbolism is the need for establishing apparently immortal human structures on the necessarily mobile base of human reproduction. This is done by creating an image of an inverted reproduction which ultimately requires the symbolic or actual presence of outsiders, who are there to have their vitality conquered, but who, unlike the main participants, do not then go on to conquer. This construction contains within itself the possibility of a further transformation into an imperialistic form, which appears to flow imperceptibly from the requirements of symbolic reproduction. Whether that potential of the symbolism will be developed and exploited cannot, however, be explained by an analysis of the symbolism itself. This depends on the real circumstances—political, economic, and military circumstances—in which people find themselves. When the actors of the ideology of rebounding conquest are weak and in retreat they will, like the Buid, develop the potential of the structure so that it is only concerned with reproduction. Then the image of consumption of vitality and aggression will stop at the animals. But in different historical circumstances, when expansionist aggression is a real possibility, as it sometimes was for the Ilongot, the symbolism of the reconsumption of vitality is expanded and it becomes a legitimation of outwardly directed aggression.

## Notes

1. All quotations from the Bible in this book are taken from *The Jerusalem Bible*.
2. This criticism of course also applies to the subsequent book by Durkheim: *Les Formes élémentaires de la vie religieuse* (1912), which seems to follow in part from Hubert and Mauss's essay on sacrifice.
3. It is interesting to note in this respect that the clan divinity of the masters of the fishing spear is Flesh. At first sight this might seem contrary to what we might expect until we are told that the flesh associated with this divinity is precisely the twitching flesh which marks the final victory of speech.
4. Gibson makes it clear that pigs have souls and this explains the possibility of their becoming spirits after death, but I am less certain that for the Buid all animals have souls.
5. One manifestation of this is the taboo on laughing at copulating animals, which would somehow endanger this boundary.
6. Gibson rules out the possibility that the pig is given as a substitute on the basis of the fact that none of the meat is given to the spirits. This is unconvincing. In his discussion of other Buid sacrifice Gibson has no problem in saying that the pig is given to the spirits even though they hardly get any meat. Thus in his discussion of sacrifice to the *Afu Daga* he says "it is the life of the pig . . . which is being offered" (1986, p. 175). The reason why no meat at all is given in this case is made clear by Gibson when he points out that in sacrifice to evil spirits, unlike other sacrifices, there is no question of inviting the spirits to share in the human feast-giving. In any case, such reasoning would rule out a similar explanation in very many cases where, as here, no meat is given to the supernatural being, although the fact that the victim is given as a substitute is made quite explicit. An example of this would be ancient Greek sacrifice discussed above. The alternative explanation given by Gibson concerns the nature of animal and spatial symbolism among the Buid. This discussion is to me quite convincing but does not explain why the ritual should drive away the evil spirits.
7. In his enthusiasm to disagree with Evans-Pritchard and Leinhardt he goes so far as to say "the notion that human life and animal life may be regarded as somehow equivalent is at complete variance with Buid ideas concerning the cosmic hierarchy of predator and prey" (p. 179) but his discussion on animal classification implies, as noted above, quite strong ideas of substitutability (pp. 152–8).

# References

Beidelman, T. O. (1966). "Swazi royal ritual." *Africa* 36, pp. 373–405.

Biardeau, M. and C. Malamoud (1976). *Le Sacrifice dans l'Inde ancienne*. Paris: P. U. F.

Bloch, M. (1988). "Death and the Concept of the Person." In S. Cederroth, C. Corlin, and J. Lindstrom (eds.) *On the Meaning of Death*, Uppsala: Acta Universitatis Upsaliensis.

Cassirer, E. (1972). *Philosophies des formes symboliques*. Paris: Gallimard.

Detienne, M. (1979). "Pratiques culinaires et esprit de sacrifice." In J.-P. Vernant and M. Detienne (eds.) *La Cuisine du sacrifice en pays grec*. Paris: Gallimard.

Evans-Pritchard, E. E. (1956). *Nuer Religion*. Oxford: Oxford University Press.

Gibson, T. (1986). *Sacrifice and Sharing in the Philippine Highlands*. London School of Economics Monographs in Social Anthropology n. 57. London: Athlone.

Girard, R. (1972). *La Violence et le sacré*. Paris: Gallimard.

Heesterman, J. C. (1985). *The Inner Conflict of Tradition: Essays in Indian Ritual, Kingship and Society*. Chicago: University of Chicago Press.

Heusch, L. de (1986). *Le Sacrifice dans les religions africaines*. Paris: Gallimard.

Hubert, H. and M. Mauss (1968). "Essai sur la nature et la fonction du sacrifice." In M. Mauss *Oeuvres*, Vol. I. Paris: Editions de Minuit.

Lambek, M. (1981). *Human Spirits: A Cultural Account of Trance in Mayotte*. Cambridge: Cambridge University Press.

Lévi-Strauss, C. (1962). *Le Totémisme aujourd'hui*. Paris: Plon.

Lienhardt, G. (1961). *Divinity and Experience: The Religion of the Dinka*. Oxford: Oxford University Press.

Lienhardt, G. (1985). "Self: Public, Private. Some African representations." In M. Carrithers, S. Collins, and S. Lukes (eds.), *The Category of the Person: Anthropology, Philosophy, History*. Cambridge: Cambridge University Press.

Mauss, M. (1923/4). "Essai sur le don: formes et raisons de l'échange dans les sociétés archaïques." *L'Année sociologique*, 2nd series.

Middleton, J. (1960). *Lugbara Religion: Ritual and Authority among an East African People*. Oxford: Oxford University Press.

Parry, J. (1985). "Death and digestion: the symbolism of food and eating in North Indian mortuary rites." *Man* n.s. 20, pp. 612–30.

Robertson Smith, W. (1889). *Lectures on the Religion of the Semites*. Edinburgh: Black.

Rosaldo, M. (1980). *Knowledge and Passion: Ilongot Notions of Self and Social Life*. Cambridge: Cambridge University Press.

Rosaldo, R. (1980). *Ilongot Headhunting 1883-1974*. Stanford: Stanford University Press.

Schwimmer, E. (1973). *Exchange in the Social Structure of the Orokaiva. Traditional and Emergent Ideologies on the Northern District of Papau*. London: Hurst and Co.

Stanner, W. E. H. (1960). "On Aboriginal religion: II Sacramentalism, rite and myth." *Oceania* 30 no. 4, pp. 245–78.

Vernant, J.-P. (1979). "A la table des hommes." In J.-P. Vernant and M. Detienne (eds.) *La Cuisine du sacrifice en pays grec*. Paris: Gallimard.

# 25

# JON D. LEVENSON (b. 1949)

Jewish Studies scholar Jon Levenson was born, grew up, and attended military school in Wheeling, West Virginia. He received a B.A. in English from Harvard College in 1971, and in 1975 earned his Ph.D. in the Department of Near Eastern Languages and Civilizations at Harvard University. He taught Religion and Biblical Studies for six years at Wellesley College, and then between 1982 and 1988, he taught at the University of Chicago serving as professor of Hebrew Bible in the Divinity School and as a member of the Committee on General Studies in the Humanities in the University. Levenson moved to the Harvard Divinity School in 1988 where he now is the Albert A. List Professor of Jewish Studies. In his work, he examines Biblical texts, literature of Second Temple Judaism, rabbinic midrash, medieval commentaries, and contemporary philosophical and theological writings, to answer questions of literary and theological understanding of the Hebrew Bible. He is also interested in early and modern Jewish-Christian relations, and modern Jewish theology. In addition to releasing more than sixty articles and giving over one hundred and fifty special talks and lectures, Levenson has published nine monographs, including: *Sinai and Zion: An Entry into the Jewish Bible* (1987), *Creation and the Persistence of Evil: The Jewish Drama of Divine Omnipotence* (1988, 1994), and *The Death and Resurrection of the Beloved Son: The Transformation of Child Sacrifice in Judaism and Christianity* (1993). Levenson's work is read far beyond the field of Biblical Studies and is praised for both its solid scholarship, sharp logic, and provocative claims.

In his book *The Death and Resurrection of the Beloved Son*, Levenson examines the "religious idea" of child sacrifice as it appears in the Biblical and extracanonical literature of Judaism and Christianity. He notes that the notion of sacrificing the first-born son to God, despite the horror such an act evokes, was not simply a barbaric act antithetical to the social and religious ethos of ancient Israel. In fact, he argues the opposite—the actual practice of child sacrifice occurred early in the history of Israel. And further, it was "transformed" into various other practices and "sublimated" into various narratives. Early Christian writers adopted the notion as well, and used it to understand Jesus.

Levenson presents a great deal of evidence that not only was child sacrifice performed in the ancient Near East, but that God commands it, deserves it, and responds to it. For example, Phoenician archeological evidence reveals burial urns containing children, in some cases two children of different ages in the same urn (thereby raising doubts they died of natural causes). There is of course the story of Abraham and Isaac in Genesis 22. There is the account of Jepthah's vow to sacrifice his daughter, and Mesha's sacrifice of his son. Most explicitly, a verse in Exodus 22 announces a direct command, "You shall give Me the first-born among your sons." Even the opposition to child sacrifice seen in Jeremiah and Ezekiel, Levenson suggests, indicates that the tradition existed, for certainly these prophets would not argue against a non-existent practice. Taken together, these examples suggest that child sacrifice did occur, but how can it be understood? Why would a father give up his first-born, beloved, son? Levenson's answer is to point to a "theological ideal" at work, one that understands all first-borns (animals, fruits, people) as belonging to God. God has a legal claim on the first-born, and can, perhaps for reasons unknown to human beings, demand that what he has given be returned. Fortunately for all those created by God, this ideal leaves open whether God will actually, in any particular case or at any particular time, make this demand. It was an ideal, a point of law but not a binding code, that allowed a range of implementations. Offering an animal, a sheep for example, could serve as a substitute for a father's first-born child. Levenson is quick to add, however, that this animal substitute is not strictly speaking a replacement for the child, for to deny the value of the child as a sacrifice (to remove him from consideration), suggests the animal substitute is in fact worthless. Substituting an animal for a child was clearly not obligated; it was allowed, with the knowledge that God's claim to the child remained.

Later in the history of Israel, the commandment to sacrifice the first-born became an order to redeem. There were several ritual practices that could lead to redemption of the first-born. Levenson analyzes broad textual evidence and identifies five: the annual Passover celebration reenacting the events in Egypt where the entire Jewish people as first-born of God and literally the first-born sons of Israel were spared, Levitical Temple service of God, monetary ransom in place of service, the institution of the Nazirite, and the practice of circumcision. All of this serves as evidence for Levenson's claim that the theological principles underlying the sacrifice of the first-born did not disappear even as the actual practice, thankfully, did. The general point that all life stems from God and that "the first issue belongs to God," is a fundamental fact within the religion of Israel, and cannot be simply ignored or eradicated.

Unlike most of the other authors represented in this anthology, Levenson does not offer a general theory of sacrifice, one that could explain sacrificial traditions beyond Judaism and Christianity. Still, as he describes the transformations and sublimations of sacrifice in these two traditions, he does reveal aspects of sacrifice. For example, implied here is the notion that the source of life may demand life in return, that what human beings receive is tenuous because God provides all good things, and thus in one sense, all belongs to God. Furthermore, this tradition understands that what human beings give to God in sacrifice, may in the end be returned, resurrected. Something greater may follow. "Generations" will reap a reward after the sacrifice of the few. Sacrifice can, therefore, be understood as a bond between human beings and God. Those who participate (in the Passover rites, or circumcision, for example), gain a special relationship with the divine. In this way, Levenson can be seen to offer, indirectly at least, what could be called an "obligation theory" of sacrifice. People sacrifice, at least those within Jewish and Christian traditions, because they have a sense of duty to do so. This is of course a theological argument, but it is clearly a fine understanding of sacrifice as well.

Reprinted here are two chapters from Levenson's book *The Death and Resurrection of the Beloved Son*: chapter one, "Child Sacrifice in the Hebrew Bible: Deviation or Norm?" and chapter six, "The Sacrifice of the First-Born Son: Eradicated or Transformed?" They do not address Levenson's point about the Christian appropriation of this mythic-ritual complex, but they do present his argument for its significance within Judaism. They also serve as valuable examples of how sacrifice, sacrificial attitudes, and sacrifice-like behaviors survive in later religious traditions.

# From *The Death and Resurrection of the Beloved Son: The Transformation of Child Sacrifice in Judaism and Christianity*

## Child Sacrifice in the Hebrew Bible: Deviation or Norm?

[28]You shall not put off the skimming of the first yield of your vats. You shall give Me the first-born among your sons. [29]You shall do the same with your cattle and your flocks: seven days it shall remain with its mother; on the eighth day you shall give it to Me. (Exod 22:28–29)

Of all the passages in the Bible that have been deemed offensive, none has been deemed so more often than this one, and none has generated greater resistance

Jon D. Levenson, *The Death and Resurrection of the Beloved Son: The Transformation of Child Sacrifice in Judaism and Christianity* (New Haven: Yale University Press, 1993), pp. 3–17, 43–52. Reprinted with the permission of Yale University Press and the author.

to a literal interpretation. That the God of justice and mercy could demand the first-born of herd and flock is a common stumbling-block for moderns. That he should demand the same of human families has been judged an offense much longer, indeed from biblical times themselves.

Among critical scholars of the Bible—that is, scholars who are prepared to interpret the text against their own preferences and traditions, in the interest of intellectual honesty—there is no consensus as to how to understand the second clause of Exod 22:28: "You shall give Me the first-born among your sons." But most would surely accept the reasoning of Roland de Vaux that "it would be absurd to suppose that there could have been in Israel or among any other people, at any moment of their history, a constant general law, compelling the suppression of the first-born, who are the hope of the race."[1] And, indeed, as he states it, de Vaux's position is almost impossible to impugn. Were the norm constant and general, the Bible would surely provide ample testimony, in both law code and narrative, to its existence, and we should not be left guessing. But de Vaux goes further, denying that the biblical writers ever mandate or even accept child sacrifice. Rather, according to de Vaux and the majority of scholars, the gift of the son to YHWH, God of Israel, in Exod 22:28b and similar passages is really not the same as the gift of the first-born male of the cattle and the flocks. The latter are to be sacrificed; the former are to be redeemed, as specified in several passages in the Pentateuchal law codes, for example: "[19]Every first issue of the womb is Mine, from all your livestock that drop a male as firstling, whether cattle or sheep. [20]But the firstling of an ass you shall redeem with a sheep; if you do not redeem it, you must break its neck. And you must redeem every first-born among your sons" (Exod 34:19-20). In sum, that shocking last clause in Exod 22:28 only states the general principle, that the first-born son is to be given to God. The particulars as to how this is to be done appear later, in the separate legal corpus of Exodus 34.[2] It is to be done through redemption, with a sheep perhaps replacing the doomed son.

De Vaux's argument against a literal reading of Exod 22:28–29 would be stronger if those verses were followed by a provision for redemption on the order of Exod 34:20. This is, in fact, the case in Exodus 13, which begins with a demand that every first-born son of man and beast among the Israelites be consecrated to YHWH (v 2) but includes soon thereafter the requirement to "redeem every first-born male among your children" (v 13). Though Exodus 34 and 13 thus show faithful YHWHists how they might—indeed, *must*—evade the sacrifice of their first-born sons, these texts also point up by contrast the *absence* of any such provision in the corpus of law in which Exod 22:28–29 appears.

If it is, in fact, a mistake for us to read the requirement to sacrifice the first-born son in Exod 22:28–29 independently of the provisions for redemption that appear in other textual units, it is a mistake of a sort that numerous Israelites seem to have made. For prophetic literature, at least in the late seventh and early sixth centuries B.C.E., is vehement in its opposition to child sacrifice, which it sees as emblematic of idolatry, for example:

> [5]They have built shrines to Baal, to put their children to the fire as burnt offerings to Baal—which I never commanded, never decreed, and which never came into My mind. [6]Assuredly, a time is coming—declares the LORD—when this place shall no longer be called Topheth or Valley of Benhinnom, but Valley of Slaughter. (Jer 19:5–6)[3]

That YHWH did not command his people to offer sacrifices to his great rival Baal need hardly have been mentioned.[4] The point, rather, seems to be that child sacrifice is something that YHWH finds unacceptable, so that those who indulge in the practice must be worshiping another god. The threefold denial of the origin of the practice in YHWH's will—"which I never commanded, never decreed, and which never came into My mind"—suggests that the prophet doth protest too much. Could it be that Jeremiah's hearers saw themselves not as apostates or syncretists but as faithful YHWHists following the ancient tradition of their religion? If the practitioners of child sacrifice, unlike Jeremiah, thought that YHWH did indeed ordain the rite, then we may have here some indirect evidence that the literal reading of Exod 22:28b ("You shall give Me the first-born among your sons") was not absurd in ancient Israel, as de Vaux and most modern scholars think, and that the practice in question was not always idolatrous, as Jeremiah insisted it was. To be sure, *'ăšer lō'a-ṣiwwîtî* ("which I never commanded") does not necessarily imply that the audience thought the practice in question to have been ordained by YHWH. John Day points to the same expression in Deut 17:3 in connection with an astral cult as evidence that it is better rendered as "which I forbade."[5] If so, then Jeremiah provides no evidence, even obliquely, for an Israelite belief that it was YHWH and not some other deity who instituted child sacrifice in Israel. But the last of the three denials in Jer 19:5 ("which never came into my mind," *wĕlō' 'ālĕtâ 'al-libbî*) would be pointless if the author intended to say only that YHWH forbade the rite in question. It appears, instead, that Jeremiah's attacks on child sacrifice are aimed not only at the practice itself, but also at the tradition that YHWH desires it. Jeremiah wanted child sacrifice to be considered idolatrous in every instance, and, as the majority opinion of scholars shows, history has abundantly granted him his wish.

A passage in Ezekiel can be adduced in further support of our contention that only at a particular stage rather late in the history of Israel was child sacrifice branded as counter to the will of YHWH and thus ipso facto idolatrous:

²⁵I, in turn, gave them laws that were not good and rules by which they could not live: ²⁶When they set aside every first issue of the womb, I defiled them by their very gifts—that I might render them desolate, that they might know that I am the LORD. (Ezek 20:25–26)⁶

At first blush, the meaning of these verses seems clear: the sacrifice of the first-born is indeed an abomination, just as Jeremiah thought. But, whereas Jeremiah vociferously denied the origin of the practice in the will of YHWH, Ezekiel affirmed it: YHWH gave Israel "laws that were not good" in order to desolate them, for only as they were desolated, only as they were brought to humiliation, could they come to recognize YHWH and obey his sovereign will. Here, as often in the Hebrew Bible, God's goodness conflicts with his providential designs: he wills evil in order to accomplish good. The evil that he once willed is the law that requires the sacrifice of the first-born. The good toward which this aims is Israel's ultimate recognition and exaltation of him as their sole God.

That human sin can play a positive role in the larger providential drama is a difficult notion at best. Combining this with the blunt statement that YHWH did indeed ordain child sacrifice, Ezek 20:25–26 has over the centuries had most exegetes running for cover. The simplest way out of the embarrassment is to downplay or explain away the words "I, in turn, gave them laws that were not good" (*wĕgam-'ănî nātattî lāhem ḥuqqîm lō' ṭôbîm*). The trend starts already in antiquity. Targum Jonathan, an Aramaic translation of the prophets, renders Ezek 20:25 as follows:

I, in turn, when they rebelled against My word and refused to accept My prophets, put them far away and handed them over to their enemies. They went after their own foolish inclination and adopted decrees that were not good and laws by which they could not live.

In other words, God did not give them bad laws at all, but only punished them for their rebelliousness by allowing them to follow their own base instincts. With various minor modifications, this interpretation comes as close to being standard as any position in the history of interpretation ever does. Its enduring appeal lies in its shifting of ultimate responsibility for the sacrifice of the first-born from God's decree to Israel's rebellion.

Among modern scholars, the dominant tendency is to associate the disquieting assertion of Ezek 20:25–26 with texts that both condemn a person for his behavior and yet attribute that behavior to God. Most famous among these are those passages in Exodus in which God is said to harden Pharaoh's heart so that Pharaoh will fail to heed the very demand that God bids Moses to make of him.⁷ The theological point here is that God is even behind Pharaoh's resistance to God; nothing is outside divine control. The goal is remarkably close to Ezek 20:25–26: through the succession of plagues that God inflicts upon Pharoah, whose obstinacy he has himself decreed, Pharoah—and the whole world with him—will be brought to a recognition of YHWH: "I have spared you for this purpose: in order to show you My power and in order that My fame may resound throughout the world" (Exod 9:16). As de Vaux puts it, in speaking of Ezek 20:25–26, "all the actions of men, even bad actions, enter into the plans of God, to whom they have a reference as to the first cause."[8] The problem, in short, is solved by resort to a theory of double causality. The ultimate cause is God, whose plans are good; the proximate cause is the human agent, whose deeds are evil. How the two levels of causation can be reconciled is a theological conundrum that exegetes usually do not address.

Though this understanding of Ezek 20:25–26 has much to commend it, there is one aspect of the text to which it does not do justice. The anomaly is nicely stated by one of the most recent proponents of this most common interpretation, Ronald M. Hals:

> Further, it is starkly idiosyncratic that God responded to his people's subsequent disobedience of his commandments by giving them bad laws as a punishment. Where else are God's laws ever seen in such a light? One can only conjecture that the mistakenly and syncretistically literal interpretation of such commands as Exod 34:19, "All that opens the womb is mine" (see also Exod 22:28), which ignored the subsequent clarification, "All the first-born of your sons you shall redeem" (Exod 34:20), was viewed as some kind of divine hardening of Israel's own heart, a shockingly bold affirmation of divine all-causality outdoing even Micaiah ben Imlah (see 1 Kgs 22:19–24) in seeing no problem in a false word from YHWH which aimed at Israel's doom.[9]

*"Where else are God's laws ever seen in such a light?"*—this is exactly the problem. It is also the reason that efforts to assimilate Ezek 20:25–26 to the model of the hardening of the heart are less than convincing. For the assertion in Ezekiel 20 is not that God left a wayward Israel to their own devices, or that he froze them in a posture of defiance like that in which he froze Pharaoh. Rather, the point is that because the people in their rebellion refused to obey YHWH's life-promoting laws (especially those governing the Sabbath [vv 21–24]), he, in turn, saddled them with bad laws that would, nonetheless, ultimately serve his sovereign purpose. The product of his punishment is not a perverted will, as in the case of Pharaoh, or a deceitful oracle, as in the incident about Micaiah to which Hals refers, but rather *the laws themselves*. In a sense, the best way to understand Ezekiel's point is by inverting the theory of double causality; the ultimate cause of the "laws that were not good" was Israel's rebellion; the proximate cause was divine revelation.

Hals misses the key point that the laws referred to in Ezek 20:25 were God's quid pro quo for Israel's apostasy and disobedience. Instead, he constructs a scenario in which God punishes Israel by perverting the Israelites' hermeneutics. As a result, they devise on their own the putative "mistakenly and syncretistically literal interpretation" of the laws of child sacrifice, missing altogether the provisions for redemption of the first-born. But Ezekiel never mentions these provisions, either, and there is no reason to think that he regards the practice of the sacrifice of the first-born as contrary to God's will in the time for which God ordained it. In other passages, in which the target of Ezekiel's preaching is child sacrifice in general, he sees the recipient of the offering as other deities.[10] But here in 20:25–26, where the subject is specifically the offering of the first-born, there is no reason to believe that its recipient was anyone other than the God who gave them the "laws that were not good" in the first place. Those laws are YHWH's retaliation for idolatry, but they are not in themselves idolatrous, only lethal, "rules by which they could not live," "the condign punishment" (in Moshe Greenberg's phrase[11]) for a people that has turned away from the rules "by the pursuit of which man shall live" (v 21).

In Greenberg's judgment, however, Ezek 20:25–26 condemns only those who practiced the popular rather than the normative religion of Israel. Though there is, according to Greenberg, "outside of our passage no evidence" that anyone interpreted laws such as Exod 22:28b as requiring "making over all firstborn males as sacrifices to the deity," still, "at least from the time of the last kings of Judah it was popularly believed that YHWH accepted, perhaps even commanded, it."[12] What is curious in Greenberg's comment is his certainty that popular practice was so radically separate from the normative religion. Why, if there is no evidence in the Bible (outside of Ezek 20:25–26) for the sacrifice of the first-born son to YHWH, did so many Israelites come to adhere to such a practice? And conversely, why, if we know there was a popular belief "that YHWH accepted, perhaps even commanded" such offerings, should we retroject the provision for redemption even onto Exod 22:28b, where it is absent and contradicts the implication of the subsequent verse? The more natural conclusion, it would seem, is that what Greenberg brands as popular religion is simply the continuation of an older normative tradition against which the two great prophets of the late monarchy and early exile, Jeremiah and Ezekiel, turned with passion and vehemence. Because Greenberg follows Jeremiah's view that God never commanded child sacrifice (Jer 19:5), he has no choice but to brand the rite as popular and "pagan" and to rely on the conventional analogy of Pharaoh's divinely hardened heart to explain Ezekiel's opposing opinion. But it is the latter opinion that better fits the biblical data: YHWH once commanded the sacrifice of the first-born but now opposes it. Without recourse to modern historical reasoning, the only explanation for this that preserves the continuity of YHWH's will is the one that Ezekiel, in fact, offers: YHWH's command and Israel's obedience to it were in the way of punishment, a means to bring about the death of those who had turned away from the means to abundant life.

One argument against the literal interpretation of Exod 22:28–29 remains to be addressed. This is the common argument, advanced, for example, by both de Vaux and Greenberg, that there is no evidence for a "constant general law, compelling the suppression of the first-born" (de Vaux) by "making [them] over . . . as sacrifices to the deity" (Greenberg). That this is so should be readily conceded: neither the archaeological nor the textual data suggest any such widespread practice. We need not, however, consign Exod 22:28–29 to some sort of minority tradition, popular or other. There is a third possibility—that Exod 22:28b articulates a theological ideal about the special place of the first-born son, an ideal whose realization could range from literal to non-literal implementation, that is, from sacrifice to redemption, or even to mere intellectual assent without any cultic act whatsoever. If this sounds strange today, it is only because we think of law in terms rather different than those of the ancient Near East. The legal thinking of the latter is nicely highlighted by the oft-remarked lack of evidence in contracts and the like for the implementation of the Old Babylonian legal corpus traditionally known as the Code of Hammurabi (mid-eighteenth century B.C.E.). "The code is not binding," I. Tzvi Abusch observes, "and does not necessarily reflect actual practice; it is, however, a literary and intellectual construct that gives expression to legal thinking and moral values."[13] This is, ironically, how de Vaux himself sees the biblical law of the Jubilee Year (Lev 25:8–17, 23–55). "The Law of the Jubilee," he holds, "appears to set out an ideal of justice and social equality which was never realized . . . it was a Utopian law and it remained a dead letter." In truth, a fertile seed would be a better metaphor than a dead letter, for rabbinic literature indicates that, eventually, such provisions did indeed become matters of practice as opposed to utopian idealism. But that was in a later era. In the Hebrew Bible, there is no evidence for the implementation of the Jubilee.[14]

The ideal character of a provision such as that of the sacrifice of the first-born son in Exod 22:28–29 need not imply the historical accuracy of either Jeremiah's or Ezekiel's negative view of the practice.[15] Indeed, Paul Mosca and others have pointed to a number of texts that can be construed, with varying degrees of plausibility, as describing child sacrifice without pejorative intent. According to Mosca, "the earliest datable reference to the rite" is this difficult and perhaps garbled oracle from Isaiah.[16]

> [30]For the LORD will make His majestic voice heard
> And display the sweep of His arm
> In raging wrath,
> In a devouring blaze of fire,
> In tempest, and rainstorm, and hailstones.
> [31]Truly, Assyria, who beats with the rod,
> Shall be cowed by the voice of the LORD;

> [32]And each time the appointed staff passes by,
> The LORD will bring down [His arm] upon him
> And will do battle with him as he waves it.
> [33]The Topheth has long been ready for him;
> He too is destined for Melech—
> His firepit has been made both wide and deep,
> With plenty of fire and firewood,
> And with the breath of the LORD
> Burning in it like a stream of sulfur. (Isa 30:30–33)

The Tophet(h) (v 33) we have already encountered in Jer 19:6. It was the site in the Valley of the Son of Hinnom (Gehinnom), just south of Jerusalem, at which a cult of child sacrifice was carried on. It would therefore seem natural to associate "Melech" in the same verse in Isaiah with the "Molech" to whom or to which the Torah forbids Israelites to sacrifice their offspring (Lev 18:21; 20:2–5).[17] The identity of Molech—indeed, even the historical accuracy of the o in the first syllable—has long been a matter of sharp controversy and, as we shall see, remains so today. What does not seem controversial is that in these verses from Isaiah 30, it is YHWH rather than some deviant Israelites who utilize the Tophet, consigning Assyria to its firepit. To Mosca, this meant that the Tophet in this period—about a century before Jeremiah—constituted "part of the official YHWHistic cultus" and that "Isaiah himself seems to have had no particular objection to YHWHistic 'passing into the fire,'"[18] though, of course, he would not have tolerated such rites practiced for the benefit of another deity. This may well be the case, and, in combination with the other texts about to be presented, the grisly oracle of Isa 30:30–33 may indicate a place for child sacrifice in YHWHism before Jeremiah's time. The problem, however, is that the oracle in question really does not speak about child sacrifice at all. It talks only of the gruesome death of a hated foe, and it could be argued that the death is more gruesome, and the punishment thus condign, because of its association with an abominated cult-place belonging to the mysterious and abominated Molech. The use of sacrificial terminology to describe YHWH's punishment visited upon an enemy of Israel, by no means unique to this passage,[19] does not suffice to indicate the acceptability of human sacrifice in YHWHism and offers no evidence whatsoever that such practices formed "part of the official YHWHistic cultus."[20] The most that can plausibly be inferred from Isa 30:30–33—and even this is, as I have indicated, not beyond doubt—is that at the time of this oracle, the Molech cult at the Tophet had not yet become emblematic of idolatry.

Mosca makes a stronger case on the basis of an oracle from another eighth-century prophet, Micah:

> [6]With what shall I approach the Lord,
> Do homage to God on high?
> Shall I approach Him with burnt offerings,
> With calves a year old?
>
> [7]Would the LORD be pleased with thousands of rams
> With myriads of streams of oil?
> Shall I give my first-born for my transgression,
> The fruit of my body for my sins?
>
> [8]"He has told you, O Man, what is good,
> And what the LORD requires of you:
> Only to do justice
> And to love goodness,
> And to walk modestly with your God." (Mic 6:6–8)

To de Vaux, the progression of theoretical offerings in vv 6–7 demonstrates the impossibility of the sacrifice of the first-born.[21] "In their disarray," he writes, "the people pass from possible offers to impossible offers, from ordinary holocausts to rams by thousands and torrential libations, and, to continue the progression, the last offer must appear even more impossible—the sacrifice of the first-born." But Mosca reads the progression differently, "from valuable to more valuable to most valuable," and sees the people as repentant, rather than in disarray as de Vaux would have it.[22] Thus, for Mosca, Mic 6:6–8 reinforces the conclusion he drew from Isa 30:30–33, that child sacrifice was at one time part of the official cultus of YHWH. To this George Heider, in turn, objects, pointing out that "what makes this passage so difficult to employ historically is the underlying contrary-to-fact mood established by the context: *none* of the sacrifices is desired by YHWH without the virtues summarized in v 8, so that the prophet has no reason to distinguish otherwise desirable from undesirable offerings."[23] But if Heider has aptly stated the point of the oracle, that sacrifices without the virtues listed in v 8 are bootless, then it would seem strange for Micah to combine an abominated offering with those that YHWH desires. If the sacrifice of the first-born son mentioned in v 7 is offensive to YHWH, then presumably so are all the offerings that lead up to it—the calves, the rams, and the oil. But the language here and elsewhere in Micah (and generally in the Hebrew Bible) does not suggest such a wholesale condemnation of the cultus. More likely, offering of the first-born is grouped with animal sacrifice either because it is on a par with them or, as Mosca argues, it is the most valuable sacrifice and therefore the grand finale of v 7. Evidence from biblical narrative to be analyzed below suggests that Mosca's view is the more probable: the first-born son is the most precious offering.

One other point about Mic 6:6–8 must not go unmentioned. Like Exod

22:28b, Jeremiah, and Ezekiel, Micah knows nothing of a redemption of the first-born son by a sheep or any other means. Micah's language is, in fact, closest to Exod 22:28b, much closer than to those texts that allow or require redemption (such as Exod 34:19–20). "Shall I give my first-born for my transgression?" (*ha'ettēn bĕkôrî piš'î*) is not far from "You shall give Me the first-born among your sons" (*bĕkôr bānêkā titten-lî*). Moreover, mention of the first-born son in each pericope occurs alongside mention of animal sacrifice (Mic 6:7; Exod 22:29). This makes it all the less likely that we are to retroject the provisions of redemption of Exodus 34 and elsewhere into the law of the first-born son in Exodus 22. Rather, what the latter articulates is an ideal of sacrifice, the Israelite father's offering to God of what is most beloved to him, his first-born son, the first fruit of his body presented lovingly to his lord.

There is one text in the Hebrew Bible in which an Israelite father—indeed, the father of all Israel, the Patriarch Abraham—is commanded to offer his son—Isaac, the first-born of Sarah and sole heir to the covenant with YHWH. This text, Gen 22:1–19, will occupy our attention in chapters 11 and 12. Here the point to be made is that whatever the ambiguities of the legal and prophetic materials on child sacrifice, Gen 22:1–19 is frighteningly unequivocal about YHWH's ordering a father to offer up his son as a sacrifice: "And He said, 'Take your son, your favored one, Isaac, whom you love, and go to the land of Moriah, and offer him there as a burnt offering on one of the heights that I will point out to you'" (Gen 22:2). For scholars like Moshe Greenberg, who paraphrases Ezekiel's view of child sacrifice by calling it "at once a murderous pagan practice and an abomination worthy of severest condemnation,"[24] the story of the near-sacrifice of Isaac ought to be a major challenge. For here it is not the wayward people but the faithful God who demands the immolation of the favored son, and not as a punishment in the manner of the hardening of Pharaoh's heart, either, but *as a test of true devotion.* Were the practice of child sacrifice always so alien to YHWH, so "worthy of severest condemnation," would there have survived a text in which it is this act and no other that constitutes YHWH's greatest test of his servant Abraham? If, as Jeremiah puts it, "burn[ing] their sons and daughters in fire" is something which YHWH "never commanded, which never came to [His] mind," then how shall we explain the *aqedah,* the binding of Isaac in Genesis 22?

One solution commands a consensus of extraordinary breadth: that the point of the story is seen not in the initial command to Abraham but in the rescission of it relayed by the angel of YHWH from heaven itself: "Do not raise your hand against the boy, or do anything to him. For now I know that you fear God, since you have not withheld your son, your favored one, from Me" (Gen 22:12). As Shalom Spiegel puts it, "the primary purpose of the Akedah story may have been only this: to attach to a real pillar of the folk and a revered reputation the new norm—abolish human sacrifice, substitute animals instead."[25] Oddly, Mosca, who sees child sacrifice even in Isaiah and

Micah, agrees with Spiegel on the aqedah. "Its original purpose," he writes, "may well have been to explain why YHWH no longer—or never—*demanded* the sacrifice of the first-born son."[26]

As an etiology of the redemption of the first-born son through the death of the sheep, however, the aqedah is, it seems to me, most ineffective. For although Abraham does indeed spot and then sacrifice a ram just after hearing the gruesome command rescinded (Gen 22:13), he is never actually commanded to offer the animal, as he was commanded to sacrifice his only beloved son, Isaac. And, in fact, so far as we know, Israelite tradition never explained the substitution of the sheep for the first-born son by reference to the aqedah; it was the tenth plague upon Egypt that served that role, with the paschal lamb spelling the difference between life and death for the Israelite first-born males (Exodus 12–13). The sacrifice of *that* sheep is commanded emphatically and repeatedly. But more importantly, it is passing strange to condemn child sacrifice through a narrative in which a father is richly rewarded for his willingness to carry out that very practice. If the point of the aqedah is "abolish human sacrifice, substitute animals instead," then Abraham cannot be regarded as having passed the test to which Gen 22:1 tells us God is here subjecting him. For Abraham obeys the command to sacrifice Isaac without cavil and desists—knife in hand, Isaac bound on the altar over the firewood—only when the angel calls to him from heaven. And the burden of the angelic address is not that the slaughter of Isaac is offensive or that the ram is a preferable victim, but that it is Abraham's *willingness to sacrifice his son* that verifies his fear of God. A second angelic address then specifies the reward for having passed the test with flying colors:

> [16]By myself I swear, the LORD declares: Because you have done this and have not withheld your son, your favored one, [17]I will bestow my blessing upon you and make your descendants as numerous as the stars of heaven and the sands on the seashore; and your descendants shall seize the gates of their foes. [18]All the nations of the earth shall bless themselves by your descendants, because you have obeyed My command. (Gen 22:16–18)

No interpretation of the aqedah can be adequate if it fails to reckon with the point made explicit here: Abraham will have his multitudes of descendants only because he was willing to sacrifice the son who is destined to beget them. Any construal of the text that minimizes that willingness misses the point.

The aqedah is often associated with Judg 11:29–40, which tells of the military hero Jephthah's vow to sacrifice, again as a burnt offering,[27] whatever comes out of his door to meet him if he returns in safety from combat with his Ammonite foes. To Jephthah's shock, it is none other than his daughter, like Isaac his "only child,"[28] who greets him, with timbrel and dance no less, upon his return in triumph. Vows being irrevocable, Jephthah carries his out. And so

Jephthah is both like and unlike Abraham. Like the great patriarch, he is willing to sacrifice his "only" child. But whereas Abraham was commanded to do so and then spared, Jephthah was never commanded but actually performed the horrific act.

Among the features of the aqedah unparalleled in the tale of Jephthah's daughter is the lucidity of the former. Many critical features of Judg 11:29–40 remain unclear and therefore subject to continuing scholarly controversy. Some have even doubted that Jephthah sacrifices his daughter there at all, preferring to see in her request to "bewail [her] maidenhood" (v 37) a different form of donation to the deity—consecration as a lifelong celibate priestess.[29] Though it must be conceded that the prominence given the daughter's virginity in vv 37–40 is problematic, it remains true that Jephthah vowed to bring a burnt offering and carried out by means of her just what he vowed.[30] Less clear is the narrator's attitude toward the act in question. Rabbinic tradition sees in Jephthah's sacrifice a punishment for his rashness in making the vow, and not without grounds in the text.[31] We can all wish that the hero had formulated his vow more precisely, taking into account that it might be his own daughter who would come out of his house to greet him, as he was to find out too late. But what is missing in this story is any indication that child sacrifice, painful to father and offspring alike, was inappropriate from *God's* standpoint. Quite the opposite: Jephthah's actions are intelligible only on the assumption that his daughter—he had no son—could legitimately be sacrificed as a burnt offering to YHWH. Had she not been fit to sacrifice, the vow would have been unfulfillable, as he obviously wishes were the case (v 35). The tone of the narrative thus is one of great pathos rather than moralistic judgment. Jephthah and his unnamed daughter are figures reminiscent of the great protagonists of Greek tragedy (Euripides' *Iphigeneia in Aulis* comes to mind immediately). If he has a flaw, it is the rashness and imprecision with which he pronounces his vow, not his willingness to carry it out by sacrificing his daughter to the God who delivered the Ammonites into his hands.

If the tale of Jephthah provides some support for the existence of child sacrifice within the YHWHism that left us the Bible, though less than the aqedah, the story of Mesha is more problematic than either text. King of Moab in the mid-ninth century B.C.E., Mesha finds himself on the losing end of a war with the Kingdom of Israel.

[26]Seeing that the battle was going against him, the king of Moab led an attempt of seven hundred swordsmen to break a way through to the king of Edom; but they failed. [27]So he took his first-born son, who was to succeed him as king, and offered him up on the wall as a burnt offering. A great wrath came upon Israel, so they withdrew from him and went back to their own land. (2 Kgs 3:26–27)[32]

For those who see child sacrifice as "pagan" (to use Greenberg's term), this passage may seem at first to pose no problem: a Moabite king engages there in precisely the sort of rite that, according to prophets like Jeremiah and Ezekiel, typifies idolatry and all that is repugnant to the traditions of Israel. It should not go unnoticed, however, that the terminology of Mesha's sacrifice of his first-born son is almost identical to the language of YHWH's initial command to Abraham in Genesis 22 and to that of Jephthah's vow.[33] At the very least, this argues for more continuity between Israel and its neighbors to the east in the ninth century than the crude dichotomy of Israelite and "pagan" would suggest. More serious is the great "wrath" (*qeṣep*) that falls on Israel in v 27, for there the implication is clear: Mesha's sacrifice worked. By immolating his first-born son and heir apparent, the king of Moab was able to turn the tide of battle and force the Israelites to retreat. Rationalistic commentators conjure up a panic in the camp of the Israelites as the latter learn of this horrid act.[34] But the term *qeṣep* indicates a force external to the people involved. More likely, therefore, is the supposition that the author saw Mesha's sacrifice of his first-born son as having a profound effect upon the deity to whom it was offered, in this case presumably the Moabite national deity Chemosh (whose name is, nonetheless, conspicuously absent from the text).[35] At the least, 2 Kgs 3:26–27 suggests that Israel in the mid-ninth century was not so divorced from the theology of child sacrifice as the great prophets who were to preach two and a half centuries later wanted them to be. At the most, it suggests the full acceptability of this act even to the Israelite author of this narrative.

In their different ways, each of the three texts that we have been examining—the binding of Isaac, the vow of Jephthah, and Mesha's sacrifice—sheds light on the issue of just how we are to take that disturbing last clause in Exod 22:28: "You shall give Me the first-born among your sons." Earlier, I argued that the absence of textual and archaeological evidence for a general practice of child sacrifice in ancient Israel does not require us to interpret "give Me" there as indicating some other form of donation than sacrifice.[36] In the Hebrew Bible, as elsewhere in the cultural world in which it was composed, law often articulates a theological and moral ideal; it does not always stipulate a practice that all can reasonably be expected to undertake. The theology underlying Exod 22:28b is that first-born sons, like the male first-born of animals and the first fruits of the soil, belong to YHWH; they are not the father's, to do with as he sees fit.[37] The clause leaves unclear *whether* YHWH will exercise his proprietary claim on the first son and *how* the father is to honor the claim, should YHWH choose to do so. The aqedah suggests that YHWH might exercise his claim through an oracle, demanding of the father that he make of his son a burnt offering, that is, a sacrifice in which the son is, with the exception of the skin, totally consumed in the fire. The end of the aqedah suggests that God may relent and choose to forgo his option on the son, allowing a sheep to take the place of the human victim. But there is, as I have been at pains to point out, nothing in Genesis 22 to support the idea that

God could not command the sacrifice of the son or that an animal is always to be substituted. Were the latter condition to obtain, the Israelite hearer or reader could rest content that God would never test him as he tested Abraham. But this implies that Abraham's piety was not to be taken as paradigmatic—a most unlikely interpretation.

The story of Jephthah and his daughter suggests, though with less clarity than the aqedah, another way a father might donate his first-born to YHWH: through fulfillment of a vow uttered in extremis. If, with the Talmudic rabbis, we deem Jephthah's vow altogether reckless, then we should not see YHWH as here exercising a claim upon the hero's only child: the whole sorry mess is the father's doing. Whereas the rabbis, however, saw Jephthah's vow as invalid, the Bible seems not to fault him for honoring it once it was uttered. In fact, both he and his daughter are portrayed as devoutly upholding YHWH's law that "if a man makes a vow to the LORD . . . he must carry out all that has crossed his lips" (Num 30:3). "I have uttered a vow to the LORD and I cannot retract," Jephthah, grief-stricken, tells his doomed daughter. "Father," she poignantly replies, "you have uttered a vow to the LORD: do to me as you have vowed, seeing that the LORD has vindicated you against your enemies, the Ammonites" (Judg 11:35–36). This last comment suggests that God may have been exercising his claim upon the first-born in this tale after all. For Jephthah's vow was always conditional upon victory (vv 30–31), and YHWH, in granting the victory, doomed whatever would come out of Jephthah's house to meet him as he returned from battle. The key question is this: is YHWH also behind his daughter's being the first to greet her triumphant father? If not, if this is only a tragic coincidence, then the sacrifice, though evidently totally acceptable to YHWH, was not at his initiative. But if Jephthah's daughter's being the first to meet her father is providential, then it is precisely through this vow that YHWH exercises his claim upon Jephthah's first-born child. In sum, YHWH is indirectly implicated in Jephthah's sacrifice through the sacral norm that vows must be executed at whatever cost and through his awarding Jephthah his victory over Ammon. Whether YHWH is *directly* involved depends upon whether we reckon the role the daughter plays to a hideous coincidence or to the hidden and terrifying hand of providence.

In the case of Mesha, we see a father sacrificing his first-born son, but without any of the strange twists that the stories of Abraham and Jephthah take. It is conceivable that Mesha performed his grisly deed in fulfillment of a vow similar to Jephthah's, with Israel taking the place of Ammon as the enemy whom the deity is begged to consign to defeat. If so, then, as in the case of Jephthah, the vow worked. But whether the sacrifice of Mesha's unnamed son is votive or not, the theology of warfare in the biblical world indicates that at least indirectly, the deity must be seen as lying behind the event. For it was he rather than any earthly figure who determined the outcome of battle, so that when Mesha's sortie failed, he knew that he was not standing in the deity's favor. Given the extremity of the situation, only an extreme act of devotion could turn the tide, and none surpasses a royal father's immolation of "his first-born son, who was to succeed him as king" (2 Kgs 3:27). The failure of the sortie of v 26 was, in Mesha's eyes, the deity's way of telling him that he was at last exercising his claim on the first-born. The sudden Israelite retreat in v 27 is proof that Mesha's theological interpretation of the situation was not in error.

"You shall give Me the first-born among your sons" (Exod 22:28b). Most fathers did not have to carry out this hideous demand. But some did. Abraham knew it was his turn when he heard God in his own voice, ordering the immolation of Isaac. Jephthah knew when it was his only child who met him at home on that day of triumph turned to tragedy. Mesha knew when all earthly strategy failed to break Israel's siege and only the supreme sacrifice could reverse the dire situation.

## The Sacrifice of the First-born Son: Eradicated or Transformed?

Even if it is accepted that there was legitimate child sacrifice in early Israel and that the status of Israel as God's first-born son is a matter of high import in the Hebrew Bible, it could still be argued that the scenario that I have sketched pertains to early Israel but not to Israel after Jeremiah and Ezekiel waged war on child sacrifice about the turn of the sixth century B.C.E. For by the end of that century, the institution seems to have vanished entirely,[38] and yet I have argued for the importance of the myth associated with it, the myth of the death (and often the resurrection as well) of the beloved son, not only to materials that are usually dated in the 500s B.C.E. (such as P, the Priestly Source in the Pentateuch) but even to Christian materials from the late first century C.E. Does this not, my critics may ask, mean a failure on my part to reckon with the eradication of the myth and its attendant practices? Am I not underestimating the effect of the prophetic revolution on the religion of Israel?

The weakness of the question is the assumption that the success of these prophets in combating child sacrifice was as total as their opposition to the practice. The opposition was indeed total. Jeremiah denounces *all* burning of children; he allows for no exception for the first-born son.[39] Ezekiel, as we have seen, goes further: he subsumes the gift of "the first issue of the womb" (*kol-peṭer rāḥam*) under "the laws that were not good" that YHWH gave Israel in the wilderness (Ezek 20:25–26), implying that the gift of the first-born was no better than the presentation of children to Molech (vv 30–31). This uncompromising prophetic opposition is almost certainly related to the position of Deuteronomy, which is usually dated to the end of the seventh century. For Deuteronomy, in exhorting Israel not to serve YHWH in the manner in which the Canaanites serve their gods, points out that those nations "perform for their gods every abhorrent act that the LORD detests; they even offer up their sons and daughters in fire to their gods" (Deut 12:31). The Holiness Code (Leviticus 17–26), usually dated a bit earlier than Deuteronomy, makes essentially the same point, though unlike Deuteronomy, it always names Molech when it condemns the practice (Lev 18:21; 20:2–5).

The case of Deuteronomy is especially revealing because, unlike the Holiness Code, Deuteronomy includes substantial legislation on the disposition of the first-born males of herd and flock:

> [19]You shall consecrate to the LORD your God all male firstlings that are born in your herd and in your flock: you must not work your firstling ox or shear your firstling sheep. [20]You and your household shall eat it annually before the LORD your God in the place that the LORD will choose. [21]But if it has a defect, lameness or blindness, any serious defect, you shall not sacrifice it to the LORD your God. Eat it in your settlements, the unclean among you no less than the clean, just like the gazelle and the deer. [22]Only you must not partake of its blood; you shall pour it out on the ground like water. (Deut 15:19–23)[40]

Compared with the laws of the firstling that we examined earlier (Exod 22:28–29 and 34:19–20), Deuteronomy displays a startling omission: it says nothing whatsoever about the first male issue of the human womb. Whereas Exod 22:28b simply states that the first-born son is to be given to YHWH, without explicit specification of the means, and Exod 34:20 requires the redemption of the first-born son, apparently with a sheep (v 19), Deut 15:19–23 accords no special status at all to the oldest manchild. That this is no insignificant datum is further suggested by the treatment in Deuteronomy of the exodus from Egypt, a theme important to this book. Nowhere does Deuteronomy refer to the deaths of the Egyptian first-borns and the deliverance of their Israelite counterparts through the blood of the paschal lamb.[41] In fact, Deuteronomy allows the Passover sacrifice to be from the herd as well as from the flock and, apparently, to be boiled rather than roasted—both points in evident contravention of the corresponding law in Exodus (Deut 16:2, 7; cf. Exod 12:2–5, 8–9).

The importance of the exodus is a point that Jeremiah and Ezekiel share with Deuteronomy and the Holiness Code. But it has not been noticed that all these documents also share the omission of any reference to the slaying of the Egyptian first-born and the apotropaic effect of the blood of the paschal lamb daubed on the doorposts and lintels of the Israelite houses on the night of the first Passover. What this, in turn, suggests is that the "revolution" in which these sources participated aimed not simply at the *substitution* of animals for the first-born sons, but at the *elimination* of the very idea that God has a special claim upon the first-born son that had to be honored in the cult. The

sources that are most outraged at child sacrifice do not allow for the substitution of a sheep for the doomed son. Their theology seems to have no place for
the substitutionary etiology of the paschal lamb.

That etiology is known principally from Exodus 12–13, a passage that
critical scholars are virtually unanimous in attributing to P, the Priestly Source
of the Pentateuch. About the date of P, however, scholars exhibit no unanimity,
though most still assign the document to the sixth or fifth century B.C.E. If
they are right, and if the substitutionary etiology is ancient, then Exodus 12–13
provides definitive proof of the failure of the sort of reform represented by the
Holiness Code, Deuteronomy, Jeremiah, and Ezekiel: even though the practice
of sacrificing the first-born son was no longer acceptable, the accompanying
myth survived and continued to influence the nature of religious practice. And
even if P is earlier than the sources critical of the substitutionary etiology of the
paschal lamb, the fact that Exodus 12–13 was preserved, included in the
Pentateuch, and taken as normative in some sense in both Judaism and Christianity speaks to the same point: the mythic-ritual complex that I have been
calling "child sacrifice" was never *eradicated*; it was only *transformed*.

From the P account of the rite of the paschal lamb, it is all too clear that
God's lethal claim upon the first-born son has not been eliminated, but only
redirected:

> [21]Moses then summoned all the elders of Israel and said to them, "Go,
> pick out lambs for your families, and slaughter the Passover offering.
> [22]Take a bunch of hyssop, dip it in the blood that is in the basin, and
> apply some of the blood that is in the basin to the lintel and to the two
> doorposts. None of you shall go outside the door of his house until
> morning. [23]For when the LORD goes through to smite the Egyptians, He
> will see the blood on the lintel and the two doorposts, and the LORD will
> pass over the door and not let the Destroyer enter and smite your home."
> (Exod 12:21–23)

The identity of "the Destroyer" (*mašḥît*) who executes the tenth and climactic
plague upon the Egyptians is obscure. Only a few verses earlier, YHWH
identifies *himself* as the one who will "strike the land of Egypt" (v 13). It is
tempting to see v 13 as demythologizing an earlier conception in which
YHWH's control was checked by another being, the mysterious and eerie
Destroyer. A more likely scenario, however, commends itself: the Destroyer
(*mašḥît*) of v 23 is the same figure as "the angel who was destroying"
([*ham*]*mal'āk hammašḥît*) the people of Jerusalem as a result of David's census
(2 Sam 24:16).[42] It often happens in the Hebrew Bible that the line between
God and his angel is so indistinct that the two can be interchanged artlessly
(for example, Gen 16:7–13). If this is the case in Exodus 12, then the Destroyer
is YHWH in his aspect of slayer of the first-born son. This is not an aspect of

the Deity that the biblical tradition is inclined to celebrate, and for obvious reasons. It is, after all, an aspect that recalls Molech and the monster on the Pozo Moro Tower more than the gracious and delivering God of the exodus. And yet the very story of that great act of deliverance, the story of Passover, pays oblique homage to this dark side of the deity. More than that: it specifies a ritual practice that is to ensure that it is the delivering rather than the destroying aspect of God that triumphs. In the P theology, Passover is not only the story of YHWH's victory over Pharaoh. It is also the story of YHWH's victory over himself, and it stands as a continual reminder of just how narrow that victory was: but for the blood of the lamb, the Israelites would have suffered the same catastrophe as the Egyptians.

Though the rites of the paschal lamb constitute the most familiar transformation of the sacrifice of the first-born son, there were, in fact, others, among which the dedication of the Levites is the most developed:

> [16]For they are formally assigned to Me from among the Israelites: I have taken them for Myself in place of all the first issue of the womb, of all the first-born of the Israelites. [17]For every first-born among the Israelites, man as well as beast, is Mine; I have consecrated them to Myself at the time that I smote every first-born in the land of Egypt. [18]Now I take the Levites instead of every first-born of the Israelites; [19]and from among the Israelites I formally assign the Levites to Aaron and his sons, to perform the service for the Israelites in the Tent of Meeting and to make expiation for the Israelites, so that no plague may afflict the Israelites for coming too near the sanctuary. (Num 8:16–19)

Here the underlying assumption is the same as in Exod 22:28b: the first-born son is to be "given" to YHWH.[43] The difference is that in Numbers 8, unlike Exodus 22 but like Exodus 12–13, a substitute is provided. This time the substitute is not the paschal lamb, even though the substitution is again grounded in the tenth plague (Num 8:17), but the male Levites, that is, the caste of minor clerics who, according to P, are to minister to the priesthood of the House of Aaron (the *kōhănîm*). More to the point, the consecration of these Levites into the service of God is conceived as a *sacrifice*: Aaron is to "designate the Levites before the LORD as an elevation offering from the Israelites" (v 11; cf. v 13). Their service exempts the first-born sons of the claim upon their very lives that God acquired when he spared them the fate of their Egyptian counterparts. It bears mention that this substitution of the Levite for the first-born son in attending the priesthood continues in a point of rabbinic law, even though, with the loss of the Temple, the practical importance of both the *kōhănîm* and the Levites has diminished drastically. Today, when there is no Levite available to pour water on the hands of the *kōhēn* (hereditary priest) before he pronounces the Aaronic benediction (see

Num 6:22–27), a man who is his mother's first-born son carries out the honorific task. And if no first-born son is available, the *kōhēn* pours water on his own hands.

According to the census information in Num 3:39–43, the number of first-born males in the wilderness in the time of Moses totaled 273 more than the number of qualified Levites. The solution to the problem came in the form of monetary ransom:

> [46]And as the redemption price of the 273 Israelite first-born over and above the number of the Levites, [47]take five shekels per head—take this by the sanctuary weight, twenty *gerahs* to the shekel—[48]and give the money to Aaron and his sons as the redemption price for those who are in excess. (Num 3:46–48; see also Num 18:15–18)

Thus, Aaron and his sons were given 1,365 shekels as redemption money for the first-born for whom no Levites were available to serve as substitutes (vv 49–51). Here, again, is evidence for the tenacity of the idea that the first-born son belonged to God and must be redeemed if he is to live. And here, again, is the origin of a Jewish practice that endures to this day, the redemption of the first-born (*pidyôn habbēn*). The son who is the first-born of his mother (provided the father is neither a *kōhēn* or a Levite, nor the mother a daughter of either these two classes of Jews) is presented to the *kōhēn*, who then asks the father whether he wishes to donate the child or to redeem him. The father chooses the latter course and presents the *kōhēn* with the redemption money. The *kōhēn*, holding the money over the boy's head, then recites the formula "this instead of that, this in commutation of that (*zeh māḥûl ʿal zeh*)."[44]

Today, the redemption of the first-born is obligatory. In Biblical times, by contrast, there does seem to have been a means for donating the boy for actual cultic service. This happened through the curious institution of the Nazirite (*nāzîr*). Nazirites (who could be either male or female) were specially conse-crated individuals who were subject to restrictions reminiscent of those of the Aaronite priesthood but whose status was independent of lineage (Num 6:1–21).[45] There seem to have been two forms of Nazirite, those who were consecrated for life and those who were consecrated for only a limited time. It is often said that in the Hebrew Bible only two lifelong Nazirites are known by name, Samson (Judg 13:2–7) and Samuel (1 Sam 1:11), who are joined in the New Testament by John the Baptist (Luke 1:15).[46] There may be another, however, in Joseph, who in the series of tribal blessings in Genesis 49 is given the obscure title *nĕzîr ʾeḥāyw* (v 26). This is usually rendered "the elect of his brothers," "the prince among his brothers,"[47] or the like, and may well be only a metaphorical use of the term for Nazirite. But it is surely a remarkable coin-cidence that Joseph, Samson, Samuel, and John are each the first-born sons of a previously barren mother (Gen 30:2, 22–24; Judg 13:2; 1 Sam 1:2; Luke

1:7). In the case of Samuel, the text is explicit that the boy's mother Hannah *donated* him as a cultic officiant as a result of a vow she made at the old Temple in Shiloh:

> And she made this vow: "O LORD of Hosts, if You will look upon the suffering of Your maidservant and will remember me and not forget Your maidservant, and if You will grant Your maidservant a male child, I will dedicate him to the LORD for all the days of his life; and no razor shall ever touch his head." (1 Sam 1:11)

The term rendered "dedicate" here is the telltale verb "to give" (*nātan*). It recalls not only Exod 22:28b ("You shall give Me the first-born among your sons") but also Num 8:16, in which the Levites are said to be "formally assigned" (*nĕtūnîm nĕtūnîm*) to God in place of the first-born son, and, farther afield, Ngaous Stela III, in which Felix and Diodora announce that they have offered (literally, "given back," *reddiderunt*) a lamb as a substitute for their daughter.[48] Having compared the biblical and Punic terminology of donation or dedication, James G. Février concludes that in the case of a first-born male who was vowed as a Nazirite, no substitution was necessary. Like a Levite, the child passed directly into the service of YHWH.[49] (Note that in I Chr 6:1–13 Samuel is actually given a Levitical genealogy.) No claim is here made that the office of lifelong Nazirite was always employed as a means of realizing God's claim upon the first-born, but it does seem on occasion to have functioned in this way and, in so doing, it provides yet another piece of evidence for the continuing vitality of the idea that the first-born son belonged to God. There is no reason to think that the idea lost its vitality after child sacrifice, a practice with which it has strong affinities, met its much-deserved demise.

## Excursus: Was Circumcision a Substitution Ritual?

We have now examined four ritual substitutions for the death of the first-born son—paschal lamb, Levitical service, monetary ransom, and Naziritehood. A fifth is suggested in a comment by a Tanna of the early second century C.E., Rabbi Matia ben Heresh:

> Why did the scripture require the purchase of the paschal lamb to take place four days before its slaughter [Exod 12:3–6]? R. Matia the son of Heresh used to say: Behold it says: "when I passed by you and saw that your time for love had arrived." This means, the time has arrived for the fulfillment of the oath which the Holy One, blessed be He, had sworn unto Abraham to deliver his children. But as yet they had no religious duties to perform by which to merit redemption, as it further says: "your breasts had become firm and your hair had grown, yet you were naked

and bare" [Ezek 16:6–8], which means bare of any religious deeds. Therefore, the Holy One, blessed be He, assigned them two duties, the duty of the paschal sacrifice and the duty of circumcision, which they should perform so as to be worthy of redemption. For thus it is said: "When I passed by you and saw you wallowing in your blood, I said to you 'In your blood live!'" [Ezek 16:6]. And again it is said: "You, for your part, have released / Your prisoners from the dry pit, / For the sake of the blood of your covenant" [Zech 9:11]. For this reason Scripture required that the purchase of the paschal lamb take place four days before its slaughter. For one cannot obtain rewards except for deeds. (*Mekilta de Rabbi Ishmael*, Pisḥa' 5, to Exod 12:6)[50]

What calls forth Rabbi Matia ben Heresh's comment is the Torah's require-ment that the paschal lamb be selected on the tenth day of the month, though it is not to be slaughtered until the fourteenth. His solution to the textual oddity is to point to the responsiveness of God to human action, in this case not transgression but good deeds. To affirm the opposite, to attribute Israel's redemption from Egypt *solely* to divine grace, would be to impute arbitrariness to God and thus subtly to undercut the morality of his will and the appropri-ateness of his actions. But *what* good deeds could Israel have had at the time of the exodus, when the Torah and its hundreds of commandments had not yet been given? The text at hand, Exod 12:3–6, supplies one answer: God redeemed Israel through the blood of the lamb in response to their observance of his instruction to select the appropriate animal four days earlier. A second answer lies in another pre-Sinaitic commandment, circumcision, first enjoined not on Moses, who hears it reiterated on Sinai (Lev 12:3), but on Abraham six generations earlier (Gen 17:9–14). For the task of joining these two command-ments, Ezek 16:6 serves as a heaven-sent prooftext, for the word for "blood" therein is formally plural, *dāmayik*, literally "your bloods," that is, the blood of the lamb and the blood of circumcision. By these two bloods Israel acquired life, meriting deliverance from the House of Bondage.[51]

This emphasis upon the *blood* of circumcision is familiar to anyone versed in rabbinic literature or traditional Jewish practice. Ezek 16:6 is, in fact, still chanted by the *mōhēl* (ritual circumciser) at the ceremony. Circumcision is not, however, the context of that verse, whose addressee is, in any event, female, and blood is absent altogether from the extended account of the revelation of the rite to Abraham in Gen 17:9–14 and from the account of his execution of his new instructions in 17:23–27. But there is one text—among the most obscure and the most disquieting in the Torah—in which blood is indeed a central feature of circumcision:

[21]And the LORD said to Moses, "When you return to Egypt, see that you perform before Pharaoh all the marvels that I have put within your power.

443

I, however, will stiffen his heart so that he will not let the people go. [22]Then you shall say to Pharaoh, 'Thus says the LORD: Israel is My first-born son. [23]I have said to you, "Let My son go, that he may worship Me," yet you refuse to let him go. Now I will slay your first-born son.'"

[24]At a night encampment on the way, the LORD encountered him and sought to kill him. [25]So Zipporah took a flint and cut off her son's foreskin and touched his legs with it, saying, "You are truly a bridegroom of blood to me!" [26]And when He let him alone, she added, "A bridegroom of blood because of the circumcision." (Exod 4:21–26)

This is not the place to explore the compounded obscurities of vv 24–26 and the variety of interpretations that the passage has understandably spawned over the centuries.[52] What is reasonably clear in it is that the blood of circumcision saves Moses from YHWH's sudden attempt to kill him. Since it seems to be Moses and not his son whom the Deity seeks to kill (though even this is hardly beyond dispute), an analogy with Molech or the child-eating monster depicted on the Pozo Moro Tower is not altogether in order. Nonetheless, some association with the death of the first-born son may be present and seems, in fact, to have occurred to whoever placed vv 24–26 after vv 21–23. For the latter text, which we have already had occasion to examine, identifies Israel as God's first-born son, demands the release of this first-born son so that he may render service to his divine father, and threatens the death of Pharaoh's own first-born son if the release does not take place. What ensures that the Israelite first-born males survive the attack of the Destroyer, we shall learn in Exod 12–13, is *blood*, specifically, the blood of the paschal lamb. In short, the blood of circumcision functions within the larger redacted story of Moses and Pharoah as a prototype of the blood of the lamb. It is not the case that the two blood-centered commandments build up a store of good deeds sufficient to invite God's gracious intervention, as Rabbi Matia ben Heresh thought. But that the two texts, Exod 4:24–26 and Exodus 12–13, function remarkably similarly seems clear. And it is made more evident by the placement of the former text after the initial statement of the theme of the first-born son in Exod 4:21–23.

In Exod 4:24–26, it is the blood of the son that saves the father's life: Moses lives because Zipporah has circumcised the boy. Put this way, the incident recalls the story of King Mesha, who survived the Israelite siege because he sacrificed his first-born son and heir apparent (2 Kgs 3:26–27). If circumcision could indeed exhibit something of the character of a substitution ritual for child sacrifice, then it is probably significant that Exod 22:28–29 implies that the first-born son, like the firstlings of herd and flock, is to be given to God on the eighth day of his life.[53] For it is on the eighth day that biblical law requires that circumcision be performed (Gen 17:12; Lev 12:3). Though I know of no indication that circumcision was ever restricted to the first-born son, this circumstantial evidence that the rite may have once functioned as a substitution ritual for child sacrifice, averting the death of the son, should not be ignored. If the evidence has weight, then circumcision must join paschal lamb, Levitical service, monetary ransom, and Naziritehood as a sublimation of child sacrifice in ancient Israelite religious practice. But the obscurity of Exod 4:24–26 and any cultic background that it may have had prevent us in this case from moving beyond conjecture.

Finally, it bears mention that whether or not circumcision had been associated with sacrifice in the Hebrew Bible itself, there is some evidence for exactly this association in rabbinic midrash:

> Rabbi Isaac said: "Man and beast You deliver, O LORD" [Ps 36:7]. The ordinance relating to man and the ordinance relating to beasts are on a par. The ordinance relating to man: "On the eighth day the flesh of his foreskin shall be circumcised" [Lev 12:3]. The ordinance relating to beasts: "and from the eighth day on it shall be acceptable as an offering by fire to the LORD" [Lev 22:27]. (*Lev. Rab.* 27:1)

The homiletical point of Rabbi Isaac's observation is a familiar one in rabbinic literature—to warn against excessive anthropomorphism by stressing God's involvement with animals no less than with human beings. His point would, however, be awkwardly rendered if the only connection between "man and beast" were that something happens to each on the eighth day of life. Rather, it would seem that the connection extends even to the nature of what happens on that fateful occasion, circumcision being itself the way to make the boy an acceptable offering to the LORD. If this is midrash and not plain sense, it is, nonetheless, a midrash that was long waiting to be made.

The survival and elaboration of so many ritual sublimations gives the lie to the charge that the sacrifice of the first-born son was eradicated in Israel. If child sacrifice had been utterly and universally repugnant in ancient Israel, then it would have made no sense to ground these rituals in that very practice. To do so would have been to give them the kiss of death. What these etiologies actually suggest is the opposite, that the impulse to sacrifice the first-born son remained potent long after the literal practice had become odious and fallen into desuetude. The further question can be asked as to whether all the sublimations were of a *ritual* character: were there also *narrative* sublimations of the mythic-ritual complex of the death of the first-born son? Did the same impulse that produced these substitution rituals also contribute to the generation of the several biblical stories of the first-born sons and their narrowly averted deaths?

# Notes

1. Roland de Vaux, *Studies in Old Testament Sacrifice* (Cardiff: University of Wales, 1964) 71.
2. Ibid.
3. See also Jer 7:31 and 32:35.
4. See Paul G. Mosca, "Child Sacrifice in Canaanite and Israelite Religion: A Study in *Mulk* and *mlk*," Ph.D. diss., Harvard University, 1975, 229. But note that the absence of any mention of Baal in Jer 7:31 and of any mention of sacrifice to Baal in Jer 32:35 suggests the expansionistic character of this verse. The absence of *'ōlôt lab-bā'al* in the Septuagint speaks to the same point.
5. John Day, *Molech* (University of Cambridge Oriental Publications 41; Cambridge: Cambridge University Press, 1989) 68.
6. I have departed from the NJPS at the beginning of v 25 because *gam* here intensifies *'ănî* and is not adverbial. Correctly translated, the verse can readily be seen as the condign response to the situation described in v 21.
7. E.g., Exod 4:21 and 7:3.
8. De Vaux, *Studies*, 72.
9. Ronald M. Hals, *Ezekiel* (The Forms of Old Testament Literature 19; Grand Rapids: Eerdmans, 1989) 141.
10. Ezek 16:20–21 and 23:36–39. See George C. Heider, *The Cult of Molek* (JSOT Sup 43; Sheffield, U.K.: JSOT Press, 1985) 365–75.
11. Moshe Greenberg, *Ezekiel 1–20* (AB 22; Garden City, N.Y.: Doubleday, 1983) 368.
12. Ibid., 369.
13. I. Tzvi Abusch, "Hammurabi," *Harper's Bible Dictionary* (ed. Paul J. Achtemeier; San Francisco: Harper and Row, 1985) 371.
14. Roland de Vaux, *Ancient Israel* (New York: McGraw-Hill, 1961) 1.176–7.
15. As we shall soon see, there is ample evidence for the occasional sacrifice of the first-born son in ancient Israel. It is most unlikely that Exod 22:28b is only a secondary expression of an old law about the firstling of animals, as argued by Otto Kaiser, "Den Erstgeborenen deiner Söhne sollst du mir geben," in *Denkender Glaube: Festschrift Carl Heinz Ratschow* (ed. Otto Kaiser; Berlin and New York: de Gruyter, 1976) 24–48.
16. Mosca, "Child Sacrifice," 212. See, more generally, 199–212.
17. But see Heider, *The Cult*, 323, who renders here "for the king it has been established," which seems most unlikely.
18. Mosca, "Child Sacrifice," 212.
19. E.g., cf. Isa 34:5–8.
20. Cf. Heider, *The Cult*, 326.
21. De Vaux, *Studies*, 69.
22. Mosca, "Child Sacrifice," 225.
23. Heider, *The Cult*, 318.
24. Greenberg, *Ezekiel*, 369.
25. Shalom Spiegel, *The Last Trial* (New York: Behrman House, 1967) 64.
26. Mosca, "Child Sacrifice," 85. See also Day, *Molech*, 85: "Gen. 22 is rather to be seen as directed against the offering of human sacrifice to YHWH." Heider (*The Cult*, 273–7) is indecisive on the point.

27. *'ôlâ*, Judg 11:31.
28. *Yĕḥîdâ*, Judg 11:34. Cf. Gen 22:2,12,16, wherein Isaac is characterized as Abraham's *yaḥîd*. On the technical meaning of this term in child sacrifice contexts, see below pp. 26–31.
29. For a balanced discussion, see David Marcus, *Jephthah and his Vow* (Lubbock, Tex.: Texas Tech University Press, 1986), especially the conclusion on 50–5.
30. Judg 11:31, 39.
31. *Gen. Rab.* 60:3. It is interesting that this midrash attributes the sacrifice of the daughter to divine providence.
32. I have removed the brackets around "their own" in v 27 in the NJPS because I endorse the versional readings, *lĕ'arṣām*.
33. *Wayya'ălēhû 'ōlâ* in 2 Kgs 3:27 is to be compared with *wĕha'ălēhû šām lĕ'ōlâ* in Gen 22:2 and *wĕha'ălîtîhû 'ōlâ* in Judg 11:31.
34. For a discussion, see Mordechai Cogan and Hayim Tadmor, *II Kings* (AB 11; Garden City, N.Y.: Doubleday, 1988) 47–8.
35. See John Barclay Burns, "Why Did the Besieging Army Withdraw? (II Reg 3,27)," *ZAW* 102 (1990) 187–94, esp. 191–2.
36. See, e.g., M. Weinfeld, "The Worship of Molech and the Queen of Heaven and Its Background," *UF* 4 (1972) 133–54. Weinfeld is rebutted in Morton Smith, "A Note on Burning Babies," *JAOS* 95 (1975) 477–9, but attempts to answer Smith in "Burning Babies in Ancient Israel," *UF* 10 (1978) 411–13. See also Domenico Plataroti, "Zum Gebrauch des Wortes *mlk* im Alten Testament," *VT* 28 (1978) 286-300.
37. See M. Tsevat, "*BKWR, bekhôr*," *Theological Dictionary of the Old Testament* (eds. Johannes Botterweck and Helmer Ringgren; Grand Rapids: Eerdmans, 1977) 121–7.
38. On this, see George C. Heider, *The Cult of Molek* (JSOT Sup 43; Sheffield, U.K.: JSOT, 1985), 378–82. How long the practice survived among the Jews depends on the dating of Isa 57:5 and 66:3, about which there is no compelling consensus.
39. Jer 7:31; 19:5; 32:35
40. Cf. Deut 12:6, 17; 14:23.
41. For convenience, I use the familiar term "paschal lamb" throughout, though the reader should note that even Exodus 12 allows a kid to be offered (v 5).
42. See Brevard S. Childs, *The Book of Exodus*, OTL (Philadelphia: Westminster, 1974) 183.
43. "Formally assigned" in v 16 is *nĕtūnîm nĕtūnîm*, from the verb *nātan*, "to give."
44. The translation is from Joseph H. Hertz, *The Authorized Daily Prayer Book*, rev. ed. (New York: Bloch, 1948) 1037.
45. See Jacob Milgrom, *Numbers* (Philadelphia and New York: Jewish Publication Society, 5750/1990) 355–8.
46. E.g., ibid., 355. On the Nazirite identity of Samuel, see the text critical notes in P. Kyle McCarter, *I Samuel* (AB 8; Garden City, N.Y.: Doubleday, 1980) 53–4, 56.
47. Thus, the NJPS and the New English Bible (Oxford University and Cambridge University Presses, 1970), respectively.
48. See above pp. 22–3.
49. James G. Février, "Le rite substitution dans les texts de N'gaous," *Journal Asiatique* 250 (1962), esp. p. 8.
50. The translation is from Jacob Z. Lauterbach, *Mekilta de-Rabbi Ishmael*

(Philadelphia: Jewish Publication Society of America, 5694/1933). 1. 33–4, though I have adjusted the biblical quotations to the NJPS, except where so doing would obscure Rabbi Matia ben Heresh's point. On the Tannaitic association of the two bloods, see Lester A. Segal, "R. Mattiah ben Heresh of Rome on Religious Duties and Redemption: Reaction to Sectarian Teaching," *Proceedings of the American Academy for Jewish Research* 58 (1992) 221–41.

51. Note the statement in *Pirque R. El.* 29 that on the night of the original Passover, the Israelites "would take the blood of circumcision and the blood of the paschal lamb and put them on the lintel of their houses," with Ezek 16:6 as the prooftext.

52. On this, see Childs, *The Book of Exodus*, 95–101.

53. On some possible connections of circumcision to sacrifice, see Howard Eilberg-Schwartz, *The Savage in Judaism* (Bloomington and Indianapolis: Indiana University Press, 1990) 175.

# POSTSCRIPT

This anthology has presented twenty-five different approaches to sacrifice, each suggesting sacrifice plays a certain role, or accomplishes a task, expresses a deeper meaning, obscures a more fundamental impulse, provides a needed outlet, offers unique benefits, has a basic meaning, and so forth. Clearly, the notion of sacrifice and sacrifice-like phenomena have generated divergent opinions about their meaning and significance. Understanding sacrifice is controversial, but why? Why has there been such little common understanding when it comes to sacrifice?

Several answers present themselves. First, the sheer complexity of data associated with sacrifice makes it very difficult to organize everything under a common theoretical rubric. From the death of a human being to "giving up" sweets, from killing a pig to pouring out a bit of milk on the ground, the range of human phenomena that could be included in the category of "sacrifice" is vast. Constructing the concept of sacrifice, deciding what to include and what to exclude, is therefore not a simple matter. Where a theorist draws the line between sacrificial and non-sacrificial behaviors, the finite number of criteria used to define that dividing line will greatly affect how he or she understands sacrifice. One explanation for the controversy surrounding sacrifice, then, is that opposing understandings may be beginning with different definitions of what constitutes sacrifice. For example, when Evans-Pritchard claims the communal meal that ordinarily follows the slaughter of an ox is not a part of the sacrificial rite, he can argue more persuasively that Nuer sacrifice does not ordinarily include the notion of communion. Linking the meal with the slaughter would make it more difficult to claim Nuer sacrifice is a matter of "substituting the lives of cattle for the lives of men." In short, stipulating the boundaries of the notion of sacrifice necessarily involves making choices about what is and is not significant. There are many ways to make these choices, and once made vastly different understandings of sacrifice usually result.

A second reason understanding sacrifice is controversial is the fact that different researchers begin with different assumptions about the nature of religion. For many thinkers, sacrifice becomes simply an example of religious ritual, one that may perhaps have certain identifying features like the destruction of a material object, but more importantly one that can be understood just like other aspects of religion. Broader theoretical positions, in this way, can determine a scholar's theory of sacrifice. As examples, consider Frazer's understanding of sacrifice being steeped in magic, Freud's claims linking sacrifice to psychological Oedipal impulses, or van Baal's notion of communication being the essence of sacrifice. Clearly, as opinions about religion diverge, understandings of sacrifice will differ as well. The adequacy of such understandings, whether they arise from interpretations or explanations, can be measured by how well they account for the more specific aspects of sacrificial phenomena, those aspects that can distinguish it from other forms of ritual (e.g., violence, the use of domesticated animals, communal meal, etc.). Choosing to de-emphasize these distinguishing aspects (a common strategy adopted by theorists who feel reluctant to define sacrifice) creates more general understandings of sacrifice, ones which will vary according to how much one or more aspect is stressed or de-emphasized. Here too the theorist makes a choice that ultimately shapes his or her understanding of sacrifice.

A third factor contributing to the diversity of sacrificial theories springs from the widespread notion that religious systems are comprised of symbolic elements, that phenomenological forms gain their force from their "meaning." Despite what cultural agents take as obvious matters of fact, the hermeneutical project maintains cultural elements carry some "added" or "deeper" significance. The aim of this project is to uncover the systems of meaning that drive cultural elements. There is a growing understanding, however, that these systems of meaning are dynamic and plural, that they include contesting versions, and that the situated character of the researcher is implicated in interpreting their content. Different contexts for interpretation, in this way, can lead to differences in understandings of cultural phenomena. For example, many of the essays presented in this anthology have suggested that the sacrificial victim carries very specific but different meanings. A victim may stand for the sacrificer (e.g., as Westermarck insisted), a deity (e.g., as Durkheim argued), both the sacrificer and a deity (e.g., as Valeri asserted), or some concept (e.g., "violence" as Girard claimed). These divergent opinions about the meaning of the sacrificial victim are possible because sacrificial phenomena are taken to be intrinsically symbolic.

Finally, understanding sacrifice is controversial because it is possible to select and emphasize a single aspect of sacrificial phenomena and build from it an interpretation or explanation of sacrifice in its entirety. Different theorists can emphasize different aspects, and different understandings will result. Some (as noted in the previous paragraph) may key upon the character of the sacrificial victim, its symbolic nature or its domesticity, for example. Others may highlight the destruction of the victim (e.g., Burkert, Bloch, and Bataille), while others may focus on the notion of exchange between human and divine beings (e.g., Tylor, Spencer, van der Leeuw, and van Baal). Likewise the character of those sacrificing may be stressed, their social status (Lincoln) or their gender (Jay and Beers), for example. Once defined, at varying levels of generality, these individual elements can be extended to encompass other sacrificial elements as well. Most of the theories of sacrifice collected in this book have employed this strategy.

Common to all of these reasons for controversy in understanding sacrifice is a problem that affects all theoretical projects. There is an unavoidable, though often unrecognized, issue that surrounds all attempts to understand a body of data, phenomena, or experience. It is the question of scale. Faced with something unintelligible, the researcher must settle upon a level of detail from which to begin the question of how that something can be placed in relationship to what is already known. The researcher must generalize from the start, must organize his or her interests, and form concepts. Put differently, the process of understanding is always comprised of a series of choices over how to construct generalities out of diversity. This is the essence of any theory—it is a reasoned attempt to organize multiplicity by accepting a level of generality, by working with concepts that allow *some* differences to be taken as insignificant. Attempts to understand inevitably involve decisions about what should be included and what can be safely ignored. When considering sacrifice, for example, does it matter that the thing sacrificed is valuable, that it is destroyed, that it be alive, that it be domesticated, that it be related to the clan, that it be male or female, that its neck be cut, that it be eaten, that it be a certain color, that it be a willing victim, that it not suffer, that it be a certain age (and so forth to increasingly detailed levels)? Every theory of sacrifice will scale these details and, perhaps unknowingly, set some below the level of interest or significance below which diversity can vary freely without consequence. All of the theories of sacrifice collected in this anthology, indeed like theories of all types, have been subject to this methodological inevitability.

The problem of scale, the issue of how much to generalize, lies at the heart of every theoretical endeavor. The solution, however, is not simply to seek the smallest scale, or achieve the greatest amount of detail. After all, every concept organizes an infinite number of finer and finer distinctions. Instead, every understanding (application of theory) will, by default, have to choose a level of interest, adopt a certain scale for the work of description, interpretation, and explanation. This is perhaps the most fundamental reason why the act of forming an understanding can create controversy—it is because there are different, and equally legitimate, ways to answer the question of scale. How a researcher answers this question, the choices he or she makes regarding which details (differences) can be legitimately generalized (seen as similar), lies at the root of diverging understandings.

In terms of understanding sacrifice, issues of scale affect how precisely the concept of sacrifice is defined, with certain phenomena exhibiting enough features to be identified as "sacrificial," and others not. Placing sacrifice within the broader context of religion also involves questions of scale because, again as the writings in this book have illustrated, the relationship between sacrifice and other aspects of religion (other rituals, notions of divine beings, the religious nature of human beings) can be conceived differently. Scale is an inevitable issue when working with symbols as well. Whenever one thing serves as a "representation," the range of what it represents can differ a great deal. A sacrificial victim could represent the person sacrificing, the community as a whole, or perhaps all human beings. The theorist must specify a level of detail below which there is nothing significant to his or her theory. Likewise, as a theorist emphasizes one aspect of sacrificial phenomena in understanding sacrifice as a whole (the fourth reason discussed above), the nature of that aspect, selecting and defining it from among all other aspects of sacrifice, reveals a choice of scale. It is a different level to highlight the nature of the sacrificial victim as opposed to what is done to the victim, for example.

Why a theorist selects a particular scale from which to work, why he or she chooses one level of generality, may or may not be explicit. Clearly, the choice serves the coherence of the theory. It allows the theorist to account for those details he or she seeks to understand, to organize and relate them in an intelligible way. Beyond this desire for intelligibility, however, it is a different project to explain why a particular researcher puts forward a specific theory, to argue, for example, that some biographical fact (e.g., political affiliation, family history, etc.) explains why he or she has selected a certain scale within which to work. Identifying *why* certain choices are made is different than revealing *that* choices are made in constructing a theory. The former is a secondary level of analysis that follows the methodological consequences of scale.

The points made here about the inherently controversial nature of understanding sacrifice are true for all attempts to understand human phenomena. Scholarly debate, as an argument over the relative adequacy of different descriptions and understandings, is likewise inevitable. Indeed, this sort of controversy is inherent to the production of understanding itself. This anthology, by providing a focused collection of competing theories, illustrates this claim. In this way, it serves as a resource for understanding theory-making in general and should alert students of religion to the kinds of methodological issues that accompany all efforts at understanding.

We end without concluding, without organizing the diverse theories of sacrifice represented here into some grand theoretical position. The aim of this anthology has been to present the range of theoretical positions scholars have put forward in their attempts to understand sacrifice and sacrificial phenomena. Organized chronologically, it has spelled out the development of one controversy that has helped define the study of religion since its earliest days. In the end, much remains of the work of critiquing the old in service of re-constructing the new. The task of settling the controversy surrounding the nature of sacrifice, however difficult (or impossible) that may be, has been left undone. That is something that, while gaining from the material collected in this book, must wait for future inquiry.

# Selected Bibliography on Sacrifice

Amadasi, Maria Giulia, C. Grottanelli, and Nicola Parise. *Sacrificio e Società nel Mondo Antico*. Roma: Laterza, 1988.

Anderson, Gary A. *Sacrifices and Offerings in Ancient Israel: Studies in Their Social and Political Importance*. Atlanta: Scholars Press, 1987.

Arinze, Francis A. *Sacrifice in Ibo Religion*. Ibadan: Ibadan University Press, 1970.

Ashby, Godfrey. *Sacrifice: Its Nature and Purpose*. London: SCM Press, 1988.

Awolalu, J. Omosade. *Yoruba Beliefs and Sacrificial Rites*. London: Longman, 1979.

Baal, J. van. "De Fenomenologie van Offer en Geschenk." *Nederlands Theologisch Tijdschrift* 29 (1975): 1–19.

Baal, J. van. "Offering, Sacrifice, Gift." *Numen* 23 (1976): 161–78.

Baaren, Th. P. van. "Theoretical Speculations on Sacrifice." *Numen*, no. 11 (1964): 1–12.

Barrett, Anthony J. *Sacrifice and Prophecy in Turkana Cosmology*. Nairobi, Kenya: Paulines Publications Africa, 1998.

Bataille, Georges. *The Accursed Share: An Essay on General Economy*. Translated by Robert Hurley. New York: Zone Books, 1991.

Bataille, Georges. *Theory of Religion*. New York: Zone Books, 1989.

Baxter, W. L. *Sanctuary and Sacrifice: A Reply to Wellhausen*. London: Eyre and Spottiswoode, 1895.

Beckwith, Roger T., and Martin J. Selman, eds. *Sacrifice in the Bible*. Grand Rapids: Baker, 1995.

Beers, William. *Women and Sacrifice: Male Narcissism and the Psychology of Religion*. Detroit: Wayne State University Press, 1992.

Beidelman, Tom. "The Ox and Nuer Sacrifice." *Man* 1 (1966): 438–66.

Benson, Elizabeth P., and Anita Gwynn Cook. *Ritual Sacrifice in Ancient Peru*. 1st edn. Austin: University of Texas Press, 2001.

Bergmann, Martin S. *In the Shadow of Moloch: The Sacrifice of Children and Its Impact on Western Religions*. New York: Columbia University Press, 1992.

Bertholet, Alfred. *Der Sinn des kultischen Opfers*. Berlin: W. de Gruyter, 1942.

Biardeau, Madeleine, and Charles Malamoud. *Le Sacrifice dans l'Inde ancienne*. Vol. 79. Paris: Presses Universitaires de France, 1976.

Bloch, Maurice. *Prey into Hunter: The Politics of Religious Experience*. Cambridge: Cambridge University Press, 1992.

Boal, Barbara M. *Human Sacrifice and Religious Change, the Kondhs*. New Delhi, India: Inter-India Publications, 1997.

Bolle, Kees W. "A World of Sacrifice." *History of Religions* 23 (1982): 37–63.

Bonte, Pierre, Anne Marie Brisebarre, and Altan Gokalp. *Sacrifices en Islam: Espaces et temps d'un rituel, cors anthropologie*. Paris: CNRS editions, 1999.

Bourdillon, M. F. C., and Meyer Fortes. *Sacrifice*. New York: Academic Press, 1980.

Bremer, Tom. "Sacrificial Slaughter and Dressing Up: Gender Articulations in Muslim Rituals." *Religious Studies News* 22, no. 3 (1996): 209–13.

Brown, J. R. *Temple and Sacrifice in Rabbinic Judaism*. London, 1938.

Burkert, Walter. *Creation of the Sacred: Tracks of Biology in Early Religions*. Cambridge, Mass.: Harvard University Press, 1996.

Burkert, Walter. *Homo Necans: The Anthropology of Ancient Greek Sacrificial Ritual and Myth*. Translated by Peter Bing. Berkeley: University of California Press, 1983.

Burkert, Walter. "The Problem of Ritual Killing." In *Violent Origins: Ritual Killing and Cultural Formation*. Edited by Robert G. Hamerton-Kelly, 149–76. Stanford, California: Stanford University Press, 1987.

Burkitt, F. C. *The Eucharistic Sacrifice*. Cambridge, 1921.

Cadoux, C. J. "The Religious Value of Sacrifice." *Expository Times* 58 (1947): 43–6.

Carrasco, Davíd. *City of Sacrifice: The Aztec Empire and the Role of Violence in Civilization*. Boston: Beacon Press, 1999.

Cave, Alfred. *The Scriptural Doctrine of Sacrifice and Atonement*. Edinburgh: T. and T. Clark, 1890.

Chilton, Bruce. *The Temple of Jesus: His Sacrificial Program within a Cultural History of Sacrifice*. University Park: Penn State Press, 1992.

Clark, Francis. *Eucharistic Sacrifice and the Reformation*. Oxford: Basil Blackwell, 1967.

Clarus, Ingeborg. *Opfer, Ritus, Wandlung: Eine Wanderung durch Kulturen und Mythen*. 1. Aufl. ed. Dusseldorf: Patmos, 2000.

Clooney, Francis X. "Sacrifice and Its Spiritualization in the Christian and Hindu Traditions." *Harvard Theological Review* 78 (1985): 361–80.

Combes-Schilling, M. E. *Sacred Performances: Islam, Sexuality, and Sacrifice*. New York: Columbia University Press, 1989.

Daly, Robert J. *Christian Sacrifice: The Judaeo-Christian Background before Origen*. Washington, D.C.: The Catholic University of America Press, 1978.

Daly, Robert J. "Is Christianity Sacrificial or Antisacrificial?" *Religion* 27 (1997): 231–43.

Daly, Robert J. *The Origins of the Christian Doctrine of Sacrifice*. Philadelphia: Fortress Press, 1977.

Daly, Robert J. "The Power of Sacrifice in Ancient Judaism and Christianity." *Journal of Ritual Studies* 4 (1990): 181–98.

Das, Veena. "The Language of Sacrifice." *Man* 18 (1983): 445–62.

Davies, Nigel. *Human Sacrifice in History and Today*. London, 1981.

Davison, J. *An Inquiry into the Origin and Intent of Primitive Sacrifice*. London, 1825.

De Vos, G., and M. Suarez-Orozco. "Sacrifice and the Experience of Power." *Journal of Psychoanalytic Anthropology* 10 (1987): 309–40.

Detienne, Marcel. *The Gardens of Adonis: Spices in Greek Mythology*. Translated by Janet Lloyd. Atlantic Highlands, N.J.: Humanities Press, 1977.

Detienne, Marcel, and Jean-Pierre Vernant, eds. *The Cuisine of Sacrifice among the Greeks*. Chicago: University of Chicago Press, 1989.

Dombrowski, Bruno W. W. "Killing in Sacrifice: The Most Profound Experience of God?" *Numen* 23 (1976): 136–44.

Durand, Jean-Louis. *Sacrifice et labour en Grèce ancienne: essai d'anthropologie religieuse, images à l'appui*. Paris and Rome: Découverte, Ecole française de Rome, 1986.

Durkheim, Emile. *The Elementary Forms of the Religious Life*. Translated by Joseph Ward Swain. New York: Free Press, 1965.

Dussaud, René. *Les Origines cananéennes du sacrifice Israélite*. Paris: Ernest Leroux, 1921.

Eilberg-Schwartz, Howard. *The Savage in Judaism: An Anthropology of Israelite Religion and Ancient Judaism*. Bloomington: Indiana University Press, 1990.

Evans-Pritchard, E. E. "The Meaning of Sacrifice among the Nuer." *Journal of the Royal Anthropological Institute* 84 (1954): 21–33.

Evans-Pritchard, E. E. *Nuer Religion*. Oxford: Oxford University Press, 1956.

Evans-Pritchard, E. E. "The Sacrificial Role of Cattle among the Nuer." *Africa* 23 (1953): 181–98.

Evans-Pritchard, E. E. "Some Features and Forms of Nuer Sacrifice." *Africa* 21 (1951): 112–21.

Firth, Raymond. "Offering and Sacrifice: Problems of Organization." *Journal of the Royal Anthropological Institute* 93 (1963): 12–24.

Frazer, James G. *The Golden Bough: A Study in Magic and Religion*. Abridged edn. New York: Collier Books, 1922.

Freud, Sigmund. *Totem and Taboo: Some Points of Agreement between the Mental Lives of Savages and Neurotics*. Translated by James Strachey. New York: W.W. Norton and Company, 1950.

Gayford, S. C. *Sacrifice and Priesthood: Jewish and Christian*. London: Methuen, 1924.

Gibson, T. *Sacrifice and Sharing in the Philippine Highlands*. London School of Economics Monographs in Social Anthropology. London: Athlone, 1986.

Girard, René. "Generative Scapegoating." In *Violent Origins: Ritual Killing and Cultural Formation*, edited by Robert G. Hamerton-Kelly, 73–105. Stanford, Calif.: Stanford University Press, 1987.

Girard, René. *The Scapegoat*. Baltimore: Johns Hopkins University Press, 1986.

Girard, René. *Things Hidden since the Foundation of the World*. Research undertaken in collaboration with Jean-Michel Oughourlian and Guy Lefort. Translated by Stephen Bann and Michael Leigh Metteer. Stanford, Calif.: Stanford University Press, 1987.

Girard, René. *Violence and the Sacred.* Translated by Patrick Gregory. Baltimore: Johns Hopkins University Press, 1977.

Golden, Stephanie. *Slaying the Mermaid: Women and the Culture of Sacrifice.* New York: Harmony Books, 1998.

Gordon, R. L., ed. *Myth, Religion and Society: Structuralist Essays by M. Detienne, L. Gernet, J.-P. Vernant and P. Vidal-Naquet.* Cambridge: Cambridge University Press, 1981.

Gray, George Buchanan. *Sacrifice in the Old Testament: Its Theory and Practice.* Oxford: Clarendon Press, 1925.

Griaule, Marcel. "Remarques sur le mécanisme du sacrifice dogon." *Journal de la Société des Africanistes* 10 (1940): 176–208.

Grottanelli, Cristiano, and N. F. Parise, eds. *Sacrificio e Società nel Mondo Antico.* Rome: Laterza, 1988.

Gusdorf, G. *L'Expérience humaine du sacrifice.* Paris: Presses Universitaires de France, 1948.

Hammoudi, Abdellah. *The Victim and Its Masks: An Essay on Sacrifice and Masquerade in the Maghreb.* Chicago: University of Chicago Press, 1993.

Harner, Michael. "The Ecological Basis for Aztec Sacrifice." *American Ethnologist* 4 (1977): 117–35.

Harner, Michael. "The Enigma of Aztec Sacrifice." *Natural History* 236 (1977): 46–51.

Hecht, Richard D. "Studies on Sacrifice, 1970–1980." *Religious Studies Review* 8, no. 3 (1982): 253–9.

Heesterman, J. C. *The Broken World of Sacrifice: An Essay in Ancient Indian Ritual.* Chicago: University of Chicago Press, 1993.

Heinsohn, Gunnar. "The Rise of Blood Sacrifice and Priest-Kingship in Mesopotamia: A 'Cosmic Decree'?" *Religion* 22 (1992): 109–34.

Henninger, Joseph. "Sacrifice." In *The Encyclopedia of Religion,* edited by Mircea Eliade, 544–57. New York: Macmillan, 1987.

Heusch, Luc de. *Sacrifice in Africa: A Structuralist Approach.* Translated by Linda O'Brien and Alice Morton. Bloomington: Indiana University Press, 1985.

Hicks, F. C. N. *The Fullness of Sacrifice.* 3rd edn. London: Macmillan, 1946.

Hogg, Gary. *Cannibalism and Human Sacrifice.* London: R. Hale, 1958.

Howell, Signe, ed. *For the Sake of Our Future: Sacrificing in Eastern Indonesia.* Leiden, Netherlands: Research School CNWS, 1996.

Hubert, Henri, and Marcel Mauss. "Essai sur la nature et la fonction du sacrifice." *Année Sociologique* 2 (1898): 29-138.

Hubert, Henri, and Marcel Mauss. *Sacrifice: Its Nature and Function.* Translated by W.D. Halls. Chicago: University of Chicago Press, 1964.

Hughes, Dennis D. *Human Sacrifice in Ancient Greece.* London: Routledge, 1991.

James, Edwin O. *Origins of Sacrifice.* London: Murray, 1933.

James, Edwin O. *Sacrifice and Sacrament.* London, 1962.

Jay, Nancy. "Sacrifice as Remedy for Having Been Born of Woman." In *Immaculate and Powerful,* edited by C. W. Atkinson. Boston: Beacon Press, 1985.

Jay, Nancy. "Sacrifice, Descent and the Patriarchs." *Vetus Testamentum* 38 (1988): 52–70.

Jay, Nancy. *Throughout Your Generations Forever: Sacrifice, Religion, and Paternity.* Chicago: University of Chicago Press, 1992.

Jensen, A. *Myth and Cult among Primitive Peoples*. Translated by M. T. Choldin. Chicago: University of Chicago Press, 1963.

Kidner, D. *Sacrifice in the Old Testament*. London: Tyndale Press, 1952.

Kurtz, J. H. *Sacrificial Worship of the Old Testament*. Translated by J. Martin. Edinburgh, 1863.

Leeuw, Gerardus van der. "Die *Do-Ut-Des*-Formel in der Opfertheorie." *Archiv für Religionswissenschaft* 20 (1920–1): 241–53.

Leeuw, Gerardus van der. *Religion in Essence and Manifestation*. Translated by J. E. Turner. Vol. II. New York: Harper and Row, Publishers, 1963.

Levenson, Jon D. *The Death and Resurrection of the Beloved Son: The Transformation of Child Sacrifice in Judaism and Christianity*. New Haven: Yale University Press, 1993.

Lévi, Sylvain. *La Doctrine du sacrifice dans les Brâhmanas*. Paris: E. Leroux, 1898.

Lévi-Strauss, Claude. *The Savage Mind*. Chicago: University of Chicago Press, 1962.

Levine, Baruch A. *In the Presence of the Lord : A Study of Cult and Some Cultic Terms in Ancient Israel*. Leiden: E. J. Brill, 1974.

Lienhardt, Godfrey R. *Divinity and Experience: The Religion of the Dinka*. Oxford: Clarendon Press, 1961.

Lincoln, Bruce. *Death, War, and Sacrifice: Studies in Ideology and Practice*. Chicago: University of Chicago Press, 1991.

Lincoln, Bruce. "Debreasting, Disarming, Beheading: Some Sacrificial Practices of the Scyths and Amazons." In *Death, War, and Sacrifice: Studies in Ideology and Practice*, 198–208. Chicago: University of Chicago Press, 1991.

Linders, Tullia, ed. *Gifts to the Gods: Proceedings of the Uppsala Symposium 1985*. Uppsala: Almquist and Wiksell International, 1987.

Lods, Adolphe. "Examen de quelques hypothèses modernes sur les origines du sacrifice." *Revue d'Histoire et de Philosophie Religieuses* (1921): 483–506.

Loeb, Edwin M. *The Blood Sacrifice Complex*. New York: Kraus Reprint, 1964.

Loisy, Alfred. *Essai historique sur le sacrifice*. Paris: Emile Nourry, 1920.

Maccoby, Hyam. *The Sacred Executioner: Human Sacrifice and the Legacy of Guilt*. London: Thames and Hudson, 1982.

MacLaurin, E. C. B. *The Origin of the Hebrew Sacrificial System*. Sydney: Sydney and Melbourne Pub. Co., 1948.

Maistre, Joseph de. "Eclaircissement sur les sacrifices." In *Oeuvres Complètes*. Lyon: Vitte et Perrussel, 1884.

Malamoud, Charles. *Cooking the World: Ritual and Thought in Ancient India*. English edn., *French Studies in South Asian Culture and Society*. New York: Oxford University Press, 1996.

Mauss, Marcel. *The Gift: Forms and Functions of Exchange in Archaic Societies*. Translated by Ian Cunnison. New York: W. W. Norton and Company, 1967.

McCarthy, D. J. "The Symbolism of Blood and Sacrifice." *Journal of Biblical Literature* 78 (1969): 166–76.

Milgrom, Jacob. *Studies in Cultic Theology and Terminology*. Leiden: E. J. Brill, 1983.

Money-Kyrle, R. *The Meaning of Sacrifice*. London: Hogarth Press, 1930.

Oesterley, W. O. E. *Sacrifices in Ancient Israel: The Origin, Purposes and Development*. London: Hodder and Stoughton, 1937.

Plato. *Symposium*. Translated by Alexander Nehamas and Paul Woodruff. Indianapolis: Hackett Publishing Company, 1989.

Price, S. R. F. "Between Man and God: Sacrifice in the Roman Imperial Cult." *Journal of Roman Studies* 70 (1980): 28–43.

Quaegebeur, J., ed. *Ritual and Sacrifice in the Ancient Near East*. Leuven: Peeters, 1993.

Rachik, Hassan. *Sacre et sacrifice dans le haut Atlas marocain*. Casablanca: Afrique Orient, 1990.

Read, Kay Almere. *Time and Sacrifice in the Aztec Cosmos*. Bloomington: Indiana University Press, 1998.

Ringgren, H. *Sacrifice in the Bible*. London: Lutterworth Press, 1962.

Robbins, Jill. "Sacrifice." In *Critical Terms for Religious Studies*, edited by Mark C. Taylor, 285–97. Chicago: University of Chicago Press, 1998.

Rosolato, Guy. *Le Sacrifice: Repères psychanalytiques. Bibliothèque de psychanalyse*. Paris: Presses universitaires de France, 1987.

Rowley, Harold Henry. *The Meaning of Sacrifice in the Old Testament*. Manchester: The Librarian John Rylands Library, 1950.

Schenk, Richard. *Zur Theorie des Opfers: Ein interdiziplinares Gespräch Richard Schenk (Hrsg.), Collegium Philosophicum; Bd. 1*. Stuttgart: Fromman-Holzboog, 1995.

Siddiqui, Muhammad I. *Animal Sacrifice in Islam*. Lahore: Kazi Publications, 1978.

Smith, Brian K. "Capital Punishment and Human Sacrifice." *Journal of the American Academy of Religion* 68, no. 1 (2000): 3–25.

Smith, Brian K. "Sacrifice and Being: Prajapati's Cosmic Emission and Its Consequences." *Numen* 32, no. 1 (1985): 71–87.

Smith, Brian K., and Wendy Doniger. "Sacrifice and Substitution: Ritual Mystification and Mythical Demystification." *Numen* 36, no. 2 (1989): 189–223.

Smith, Jonathan Z. "The Domestication of Sacrifice." In *Violent Origins: Ritual Killing and Cultural Formation*, edited by Robert G. Hamerton-Kelley, 191–205. Stanford, Calif.: Stanford University Press, 1987.

Smith, William Robertson. *The Religion of the Semites: The Fundamental Institutions*. New York: Schocken Books, 1972.

Smith, William Robertson. "Sacrifice." In *Encyclopaedia Britannica*, 9th Edition, volume XXI, 141–6. Chicago, 1886.

Solie, Pierre. *Le Sacrifice: Fondateur de civilisation et d'individuation, sciences et symboles*. Paris: Albin Michel, 1988.

Spencer, Herbert. *The Principles of Sociology*. Vol. I. New York: D. Appleton and Company, 1882.

Stivers, Richard. "The Festival in Light of the Theory of the Three Milieus: A Critique of Girard's Theory of Ritual Scapegoating." *Journal of the American Academy of Religion* 61, no. 3 (1993): 505–38.

Strenski, Ivan. "Between Theory and Specialty: Sacrifice in the '90s." *Religious Studies Review* 22, no. 1 (1996): 10–20.

Sykes, Arthur Ashley. *An Essay on the Nature, Design and Origin of Sacrifices*. London: Knapton, 1748.

Talbott, Rick F. *Sacred Sacrifice: Ritual Paradigms in Vedic Religion and Early Christianity*. Peter Lang Publishers, 1995.

Tautain, Jules. "Sur quelques textes relatifs à la signification du sacrifice chez les peuples de l'antiquité." *Revue de l'Histoire des Religions* 84 (1921): 109–19.

Thompson, R. J. *Penitence and Sacrifice in Early Israel outside the Levitical Law.* Leiden: E. J. Brill, 1963.

Tierney, Patrick. *The Highest Altar: The Story of Human Sacrifice*, 1989.

Turner, Victor. "Sacrifice as Quintessential Process: Prophylaxis or Abandonment?" *History of Religions* 16, no. 3 (1977): 189–215.

Tylor, Sir Edward B. *Primitive Culture: Researches in the Development of Mythology, Philosophy, Religion, Language, Arts, and Custom.* New York: Brentano's Books, 1871.

Valeri, Valerio. *Kingship and Sacrifice: Ritual and Society in Ancient Hawaii.* Chicago: University of Chicago Press, 1985.

Vaux, Roland de. *Studies in Old Testament Sacrifice.* Cardiff: University of Wales Press, 1964.

Vernant, Jean-Pierre. "Introduction." In *The Gardens of Adonis: Spices in Greek Mythology*, by Marcel Detienne, vii–xli. Princeton: Princeton University Press, 1994.

Vernant, Jean-Pierre. "Le Sacrifice. Le Mythe Grec." In *Dictionnaire des Mythologies*, edited by Yves Bonnefoy. Paris, 1981.

Vernant, Jean-Pierre, Jean Rudhardt, and Olivier Reverdin. *Le Sacrifice dans l'antiquité: Huit exposés suivis de discussions: Vanduvres-Genève, 25–30 août 1980, Entretiens sur l'antiquité classique; T. 27.* Genève: Fondation Hardt, 1981.

Vesci, Uma Marina. *Heat and Sacrifice in the Vedas.* Delhi: Motilal Banarsidass Publishers, 1985.

Westermarck, Edward A. *The Origin and Development of the Moral Ideas.* Vol. I. London: Macmillan and Company, 1912.

Wright, David P. *The Disposal of Impurity: Elimination Rites in the Bible and in Hittite and Mesopotamian Literature.* Atlanta: Scholars Press, 1987.

Yerkes, R. K. *Sacrifice in Greek and Roman Religion and Early Judaism.* New York: Scribner, 1952.

# INDEX